earth
diplomacy

earth diplomacy

INDIGENOUS AMERICAN ART, ECOLOGICAL CRISIS, AND THE COLD WAR

Jessica L. Horton

Duke University Press   *Durham and London* 2024

Printed in the United States of America on
acid-free paper ∞
Project Editor: Bird Williams
Designed by Matt Tauch
Typeset in Untitled Serif, SangBleu Sunrise and SangBleu
Kingdom. by Westchester Publishing Services

Library of Congress Cataloging-in-Publication Data
Names: Horton, Jessica L., author.
Title: Earth diplomacy : Indigenous American art, ecological
    crisis, and the Cold War / Jessica L. Horton.
Description: Durham : Duke University Press, 2024. |
    Includes bibliographical references and index.
Identifiers: LCCN 2023042675 (print)
LCCN 2023042676 (ebook)
ISBN 9781478030492 (paperback)
ISBN 9781478026266 (hardcover)
ISBN 9781478059493 (ebook)
Subjects: LCSH: Arts and diplomacy. | Indian art—United
    States—20th century. | Art, Modern—Political aspects.
    | Cultural diplomacy—United States—History—
    20th century. | Propaganda in art. | Cold War—Social
    aspects—United States. | BISAC: ART / American /
    General | ART / History / General
Classification: LCC NX180.D57 H67 2024 (print)
LCC NX180. D57 (ebook)
DDC 700.89/97073—dc23/eng/20240506
LC record available at https://lccn.loc.gov/2023042675
LC ebook record available at https://lccn.loc.gov/2023042676

Cover art: Oscar Howe, *Acannupapi* (Pipe Ceremony),
1972. Casein on paper, 27.5 × 17.5 in. University of South
Dakota, with permission of the Oscar Howe Family.

Publication of this book has been aided by a grant from
the Wyeth Foundation for American Art Publication Fund
of CAA.

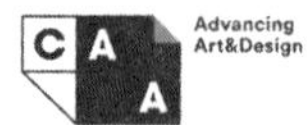

For my father,

Robert Stanley Horton (1946–2022),

a veteran of the Vietnam War

CONTENTS

ACKNOWLEDGMENTS

::::::::::

IN 2013, while finishing my dissertation as a fellow at the Center for Advanced Study in the Visual Arts (CASVA) in Washington, DC, I stumbled on archival evidence of Native American artists' extensive role in Cold War cultural diplomacy. I felt a responsibility to tell this story, not the least because it formed a little-known prelude to the global engagements of contemporary Native artists (the subject of my first book). But I felt clear that the world did not need another study of post-World War II United States cultural hegemony, however critical. I'm grateful to my colleagues at the National Museum of the American Indian (NMAI) and Smithsonian American Art Museum (SAAM) for hosting me as a postdoctoral fellow in 2013–2014, offering me the intellectual space to shape a different narrative. I benefited especially from the generous skepticism of Paul Chaat Smith, my mentor and friend, who was curating *Americans* (2017–2027) for NMAI. *Earth Diplomacy* was born at the intersection of our conversations about the world-shaping power of images of Native Americans and my encounters with the sensuous diplomatic arts on view in another NMAI exhibition, *Nation to Nation: Treaties Between the United States and American Indian Nations* (2014–2025).

This project found a home among the Americanists and material culture advocates at the University of Delaware (UD), where I have worked since 2015. I'm especially grateful to my faculty mentor, Wendy Bellion, and two wonderful department chairs, Larry Nees and Sandy Isenstadt, for supporting my research schemes, including a UD General University Research Grant in 2016. I workshopped related ideas with my coinstructor Ikem Okoye and the students in our graduate seminar, Diplomatic Things: Art and Architecture in Global Contexts, in 2018. I thank members of the Americanist writing group in Philadelphia, Mariola Alvarez, Tiffany Barber, Jason Hill, Leah Modigliani, Erin Pauwels, Gwyndolyn Shaw, and Delia Solomons, for their friendship and keen eyes on nearly all of the chapters. Pascha Bueno-Hansen, visionary leader of the American Indian and Indigenous Relations Committee at UD, helped ground my academic work in Lenape and Nanticoke homelands and relationships. My inspiring friend Sarah Wasserman kept me sane and laughing. I constantly learned from my mentees pursuing new work at the intersection of Indigenous studies, art history, and ecocriticism, including Rachel Allen, Zoë Colón, Christine Garnier, Julia Hamer-Light, Ramey Mize, David Norman, Rachelle Pablo, Kaila Shedeen, Dakota Stevens, Victoria Sunnergren, Marina Tyquiengco, and Zoe Weldon-Yochim.

A two-month-long fellowship at the Georgia O'Keeffe Museum and Research Center in 2018 gave me precious time in Santa Fe–based collections and archives. I'm especially grateful to Ryan Flahive and James McGrath of the Institute of American Indian Arts (IAIA) and Diane Bird and Tony Chavarria of the Laboratory of Anthropology for guiding my dive into the Cold War projects of IAIA and its predecessor, the Santa Fe Indian School. I loved sharing adventures with my friend and host, Carolyn Kastner, on many trips to Santa Fe. In 2019–2020, a Clark Art Institute fellowship and a Warhol Foundation Creative Capital Book Award allowed me a glorious year of research, writing, traveling, and hiking. I was in Chile researching Diné-Mapuche exchanges with the assistance of María Catrileo Chiguailaf when the COVID-19 pandemic erupted. Although I had to give up on a trip to Japan, I'm grateful to Ito Atsunori of the National Museum of Ethnology for sharing his research on Native American art at Expo 70 and scouring Osaka for the whereabouts of the Crow lodge at the center of chapter 4. The extraordinary hospitality of colleagues such as Ana Magalhães, Fernanda Pitta, Ilana Goldstein, and others taught me much about the dynamics of cultural exchange under the vast umbrella of "American" art when I served as a Terra Foundation visiting professor in São Paulo in 2022.

These and other opportunities were supported by letters and advice from my dear mentors Bill Anthes, Wendy Bellion, Janet Berlo, and Terry

Smith. Janet has given more time and love than anyone to my work. I am honored and grateful to be in her luminous orbit.

I received helpful feedback on the ideas in this book during invited lectures at the Courtauld Institute of Art in 2021, Department of History of Art and Architecture at Boston University in 2021, Department of History of Art and Architecture at Harvard University in 2019, and Visual and Media Culture Colloquia Series at the University of California, Santa Cruz, in 2018. I appreciate additional invitations to present this material at symposia and conferences such as Belatedness and Historiographies of North American Art at the Courtauld Institute for Art in 2023, Breaking the Chains: The Legacy of Oscar Howe at the Portland Museum of Art in 2023, Revolutionary Romances: Into the Cold—Alternative Artistic Trajectories into (Post-)Communist Europe at the Staatliche Kunstsammlungen in 2022, Environmental Diplomacy: Exploring Transprofessional Contributions to Global Survival at the Grace School of Applied Diplomacy at DePaul University in 2021, Feminism in American Art History at CASVA in 2020, Boundary Trouble: Self-Taught Artists and American Avant-Gardes at CASVA in 2018, The Buffalo in the Livingroom: Fritz Scholder and Contemporary Native Art at the Plains Art Museum in 2017, Fritz Scholder and the Art World at the Denver Art Museum in 2016, and Shifting Terrain: American Art in a Transnational Context at SAAM in 2015. Early ideas were also shared at conferences of the Native American Art Studies Association, Native American and Indigenous Studies Association, and College Art Association. Too many colleagues to name shared their expertise and hospitality at these events. Bill Anthes, Kathleen Ash-Milby, Julia Tatiana Bailey, Emily Burns, Lynne Cooke, David Peters Corbett, Amelia Goerlitz, John Lukavic, Kathleen Reinhardt, and David Wellman deserve special mention.

My early research and related ideas were published as articles in *American Art*, *The Art Bulletin*, and *Journal of Curatorial Studies*, and as chapters in *Fritz Scholder: Super Indian, 1967–1980* and *Art for a New Understanding: Native Voices, 1950s to Now*. I thank the many reviewers and editors who contributed big-picture ideas and fine-grain edits to help my work shine. Nowhere is this truer than at Duke University Press, where Ken Wissoker's vision has shaped radical new scholarship in Indigenous studies. Editorial associate Ryan Kendall patiently answered all my questions, development editor James Moore assisted with my successful application for a Wyeth Foundation publication grant from the College Art Association, books project editor Bird Williams oversaw the crucial final stages, and two knowledgeable peer reviewers improved the content.

This research would not be possible without the generosity of members of the artists' families, communities, and tribal governments, who shared contacts, protocols, language, stories, archives, meals, and more. I'm grateful to Arthur Amiotte, Renee Bear Medicine, Alita Begay, D. Y. Begay, Timothy Begay, Tamara Billie, Dennis Bird, Diane Bird, Morrison Michael Bird-Romero, Bill Blackman, RaeLynn Butler, Roger Butterfly, Jennifer Denetdale, Ed Kabotie, Doris Kicking Woman, Hattie Kabotie Lomayesva, Inge Dawn Maresh, Rosemary McCombs Maxey, Evelyn Quintana, Howard Rides at the Doore, Lisa Scholder, Ramona Scholder, Rainbow Stevens, and Helen K. Tindel for their contributions. I additionally thank Michael Eugene Harris and Chris Kirkland for allowing me to study and reproduce artworks from their family collections.

I honor my grandma Eula, my cousin Taylor, my dad Robert, and my uncle Joe, who died while I was writing this book. These beloved kin remain a part of me and everything that I do. I leaned on the deep love and support of my strong, creative mother, Ann Horton, and my brilliant, inventive brother, Zach Horton. My family also grew joyfully during the course of this work. My darling husband, Jon Watts, gave me the best gift of listening deeply. I'm thankful that his many sweet people, especially Maggie O'Neill and Al Watts, have welcomed me into their lives.

INTRODUCTION

AT THE AMERICAN LIBRARY in Bucharest in 1972, an oil painting of a larger-than-life Native American man holding a befeathered ceremonial pipe loomed over the heads of two men in dark suits. Standing beside Romanian painter Constantin Piliuta, the library director Robert K. Geis introduced the traveling exhibition, *Two American Painters: Fritz Scholder and T. C. Cannon*, by lauding art's possibilities for "strengthening the friendship between our two peoples"—that is, Americans and Romanians.[1] Yet *Indian and Rhinoceros* (1968) by painter Fritz Scholder (1937–2005), an enrolled member of the La Jolla Band of Luiseño Indians, introduced an unsettling history of Indigenous *earth diplomacy* into the binary logic of Cold War statecraft (plate 1). Before and during the colonization of the Americas, Native leaders foregrounded other-than-human beings and systems—plants, animals, rivers, mountains, weather, and stars—in their negotiations with strangers. They mobilized rituals, regalia, and gifts to forge durable political contracts founded on kinship and reciprocity with all aspects of a living universe. Beginning in the seventeenth century, the smoking of sacred pipes and gifting of peace medals consecrated treaties between Indigenous and colonial nations.[2] *Indian and Rhinoceros* conjures an ensuing practice of painting and photographing Native leaders displaying the material arts of diplomacy during their negotiations with the United States.[3] Initially made

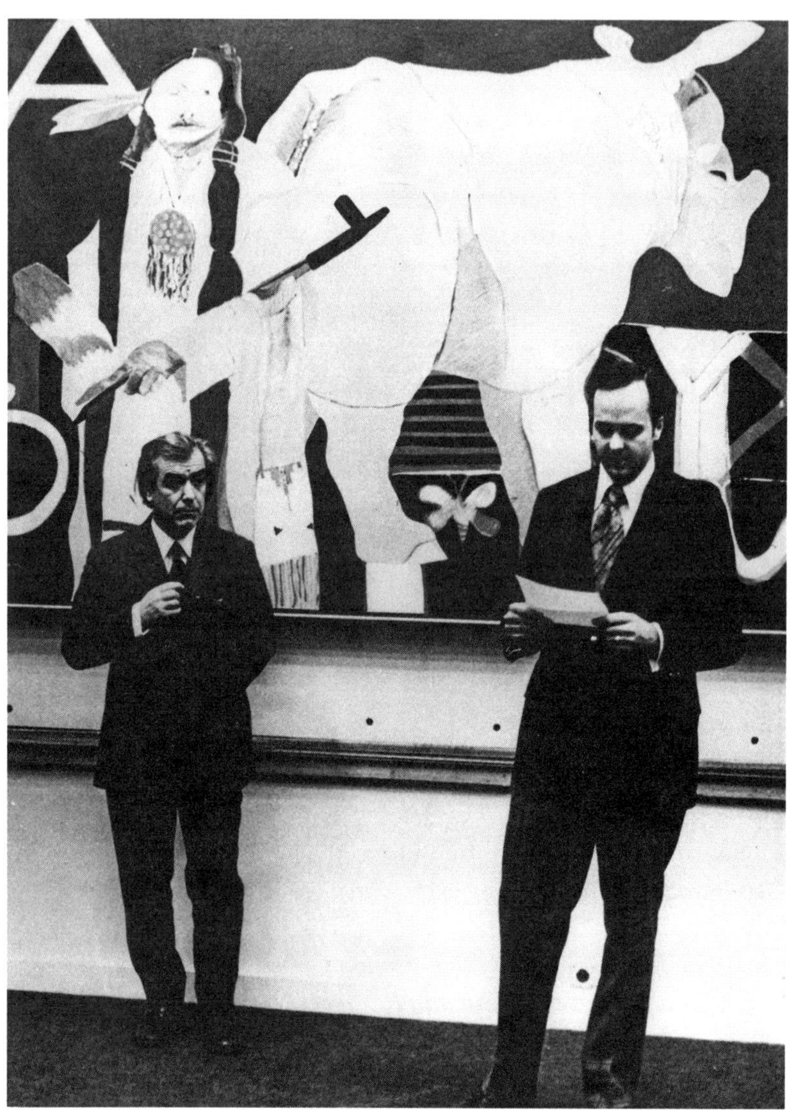

I.1

Painter Constantin Piliuta (*left*) and Robert K. Geis (*right*), director of the American Library, stand before Fritz Scholder's painting, *Indian and Rhinoceros*, at the opening of *Two American Painters: Fritz Scholder and T. C. Cannon* at the American Library in Bucharest, Romania, 1972. Smithsonian Institution Archives, Washington, DC, SIA2015–000190.

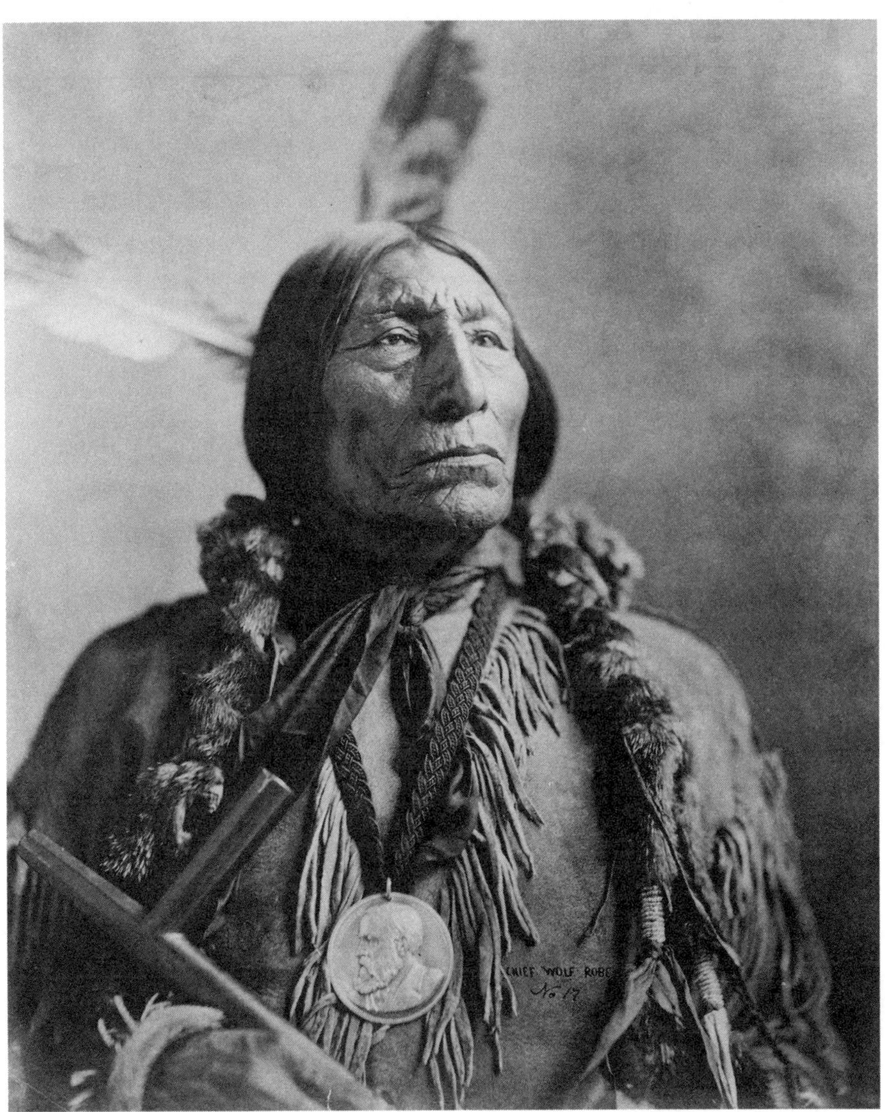

I.2

Southern Cheyenne Chief Wolf Robe with a ceremonial pipe in hand, wearing a silver Benjamin Harrison peace medal, which he received from the federal government in 1890 for assisting the Cherokee Commission in negotiations for the transfer of land, 1904. Silver gelatin print, 42.9 × 35.3 cm. Library of Congress LOT 4863, no. 15. Photograph by Gerthard Sisters.

to commemorate encounters between dignitaries, such portraits circulated as ethnographic curiosities and countercultural icons in American print culture following the federal government's violent campaign to remove Native nations from their ancestral homelands in the nineteenth century.[4]

Scholder painted diplomatic contracts between Indigenous nations and the United States in the wake of a fresh instance of their violation. In 1953, Congress formalized policies known as Indian Termination, which included canceling lingering treaty promises to Native nations, relocating individuals to cities, and opening Indigenous lands to resource development.[5] Bureau of Indian Affairs (BIA) administrators claimed that poor, culturally distinct, and politically autonomous Native communities were "hothouses for communism" and resumed a longstanding process of assimilating them into capitalism.[6] Indian Country was made to host mining operations and nuclear detonations to support the Cold War military-industrial complex, inaugurating toxic forms of "slow violence" that continue to permeate Indigenous bodies and ecologies as I write.[7] The US government's treatment of Native people and land mirrored the top-down modernization policies it promoted in its dealings with foreign governments during the Cold War, marking a sustained effort to advance extractive frontiers around the world. Termination catalyzed a wave of political organizing that culminated in the establishment of the American Indian Movement (AIM) while Scholder was completing *Indian and Rhinoceros*. He arrived with the painting in Romania just as AIM members formed the Trail of Broken Treaties and stormed the BIA headquarters in Washington, DC.[8]

Given the stark politics surrounding it, the painting has been read as a straightforward critique of the BIA, the government agency responsible for decades of Indigenous wreckage. But *Indian and Rhinoceros* works through a more complex condition that is my concern throughout this book: the role of Indigenous diplomats—and the arts that embody their more-than-human relations—within international relations. Scholder ended his tenure as a BIA employee (he worked as a painting instructor at the federally funded Institute of American Indian Arts [IAIA] from 1964 to 1969), only to travel with another government entity, the US Information Agency (USIA).[9] Simultaneous with Indian Termination in 1953, the USIA took charge of a vast overseas propaganda machine and enlisted Indigenous American arts in the ideological battle between capitalism and Communism abroad. For the ensuing two decades, exhibitions and artist tours were commissioned as part of a broad, paternalistic project to manipulate images of Native Americans in the face of mounting condemnation from abroad. The US government was challenged to answer criticism of the colonization of Indigenous people and land, circulated by the Soviet Union and its allies through news media and popular culture as a warning to countries deemed vulnerable to US influence. Equally, the USIA sought to deflect international attention away from Indigenous political organizing that accelerated in response to Termination. While Native activists looked to decolonization movements abroad to bolster their demands for land-based sovereignty and justice, federal agents promulgated narratives of benevolent modernization and multiculturalism overseas.[10] The Indigenous diplomat in this story—the one bearing the pipe *and* the one brandishing a paintbrush—accepts an alternative assignment described by philosopher Bruno Latour: "He sees that the official attachment is not the one to be ready to die for" and sets out to compose an altogether different cosmopolitics.[11]

Earth Diplomacy answers a dearth of scholarship about Native American art at the intersection of Termination and the Cold War. It models an ecocritical art history centered on Indigenous makers in a formative period when modernization mandates, extractive industries, and radical movements were accelerating worldwide.[12] More broadly, this book positions Indigenous diplomatic arts as agents of a necessary project to reimagine our broken system of international relations. I linger on *Indian and Rhinoceros* at the start in order to frame the broader ecopolitical commitments of the project. The painting joins a diverse array of Indigenous creative practices that traveled around the world under the auspices of the USIA and the Department of State (DOS). These arts exceed familiar accounts of American art and diplomacy during the Cold War, which typically center the interests of the US government, its corporate allies, and art world elites. They foreground Indigenous Americans, along with their other-than-human kin, value systems, political priorities, and techniques of persuasion, as creative forces shaping international relations. I propose that Native arts and artists routinely bent Cold War tours toward an alternative project of revitalizing Indigenous diplomatic modalities premised on reciprocal alliances with earth kin.

Indian and Rhinoceros specifically engaged its geopolitical context by way of an intermedial analogy. Painting has been described as a disturbance of Pop art's entanglements with late capitalism because the auratic medium absorbs some effects of popular media while maintaining a reflective distance from others.[13] Scholder exploited the polysemy of that intersection by combining visible brushstrokes with cliched imagery, hard edges, superficial depth, and a cheery palette. He mapped Pop art's famed ambiguity as neither wholly critical nor entirely complicit onto the Indigenous diplomat, an insider-outsider necessarily bound up with the settler colonial institutions that exploit Native land and bodies.[14] *Indian and Rhinoceros* quotes the appropriative gestures by which images of Plains leaders were plucked from the life-worlds of their subjects and endlessly reproduced to serve agendas infused with imperialist nostalgia.[15] The diplomat turns his back on the titular rhino's rear end and an all-caps acronym, "BIA," yet the purple banner on which the letters float takes a sharp bite out of his shoulder. He looks as if he has been pasted into the indeterminate middle layer of a cut-paper collage. At the same time, the man is buttressed by regalia drawn from a Native art history in which the painted image conjoins plant and animal bodies to manifest—to *present*—more-than-human sources of protective power. *Indian and Rhinoceros* thus evinces a "double commitment" to colonial systems of mediation and Indigenous frameworks of immanence.[16] More precisely, the work alerts us to a modern political ecology in which these seemingly incompatible systems cannot be readily disentangled. The painting at once invokes and arrests the Indigenous diplomat's deracination through the chain of mechanical reproduction to make him yet again the agent of an unpredictable relationship.

What about the rhinoceros in the library? I see the looming pachyderm as a third term—and thus an opportunity to establish a new relational pattern—beyond the treacherous binary, *Indian and United States*. The five extant species that once ranged across Africa and South Asia were decimated by trophy hunting in the nineteenth century and illegal poaching in the twentieth.[17] Scholder's variant most closely resembles *Rhinoceros sondaicus*, a single-horned, heavily armored species confined to Ujung Kulon National Park in Indonesia on the brink of extinction as I write. The last-known member in Vietnam roamed a region ravaged by the wartime defoliant herbicide Agent Orange, only to be shot for her horn in 2010.[18] Like Indigenous peoples, rhinoceroses have endured Euro-American colonization, a violence registered by antiwar demonstrators as Scholder painted through the deadliest and costliest year of the Vietnam War.[19] His international hosts may also have thought about Franco-Romanian playwright Eugène Ionesco's popular work *Rhinocéros* (1959), in which the inhabitants of a provincial French town become beasts in a satire of the dual spread of fascism and Communism across Eurasia.[20] By pairing the animal with an iconic chiefly negotiator, Scholder conjured the global, more-than-human scope of Cold War relations, an arena in which long-standing Native "struggles for land and life" intersected warfare, ecocides, and decolonization throughout the majority world.[21]

FRAMING *EARTH DIPLOMACY*

Earth Diplomacy examines an array of Indigenous creative forms—paintings, textiles, adornment, architecture, and artistic demonstrations—that traveled across two decades and five continents under the auspices of the US government's Cold War offensive. These arts were framed by a dominant practice of international relations that furthered the exclusion and exploitation of a vast majority of planetary life. Contemporary artists answered these conditions by engendering new practices of what I call *earth diplomacy*: sensuous material exchanges that invite political alliances inclusive of the land. While Native arts necessarily negotiated the colonial conditions of their making, they were enlivened with affect and spirit in excess of government scripts. They bore a potential to initiate cosmopolitical relationships guided by more-than-human kinship and reciprocity in lieu of extractive modernization projects that were accelerating around the world. I argue that this creative continuum subtly but profoundly deformed the United States' efforts to assimilate the whole earth during the Cold War.[22] At the same time, the aims of *Earth Diplomacy* reach beyond the period and subject matter of my study. Resonating with Indigenous studies scholarship on Traditional Ecological Knowledge, my phrase *earth diplomacy* specifies the transformative potential of Indigenous cosmologies whenever they are activated by Native arts in geopolitical arenas worldwide.[23] This book illuminates arts' capacity to revitalize long-standing Indigenous cultures of reciprocity, toward cultivating a radically different future for international relations.

A few examples of traveling artists and artworks that do not figure prominently in my study serve to indicate the diversity of Indigenous aesthetic preoccupations, political affiliations, and sites of engagement during the Cold War. In 1956, Onondaga-adopted Lenape painter and performer Tom Two Arrows (Tomas Dorsey) shared Haudenosaunee dances, instruments, and stories across Asia while "villagers—Ainus of Japan, Koreans, Formosans—demonstrated their ancient dances for the American visitor."[24] In 1960, members of the All Pakistan Women's

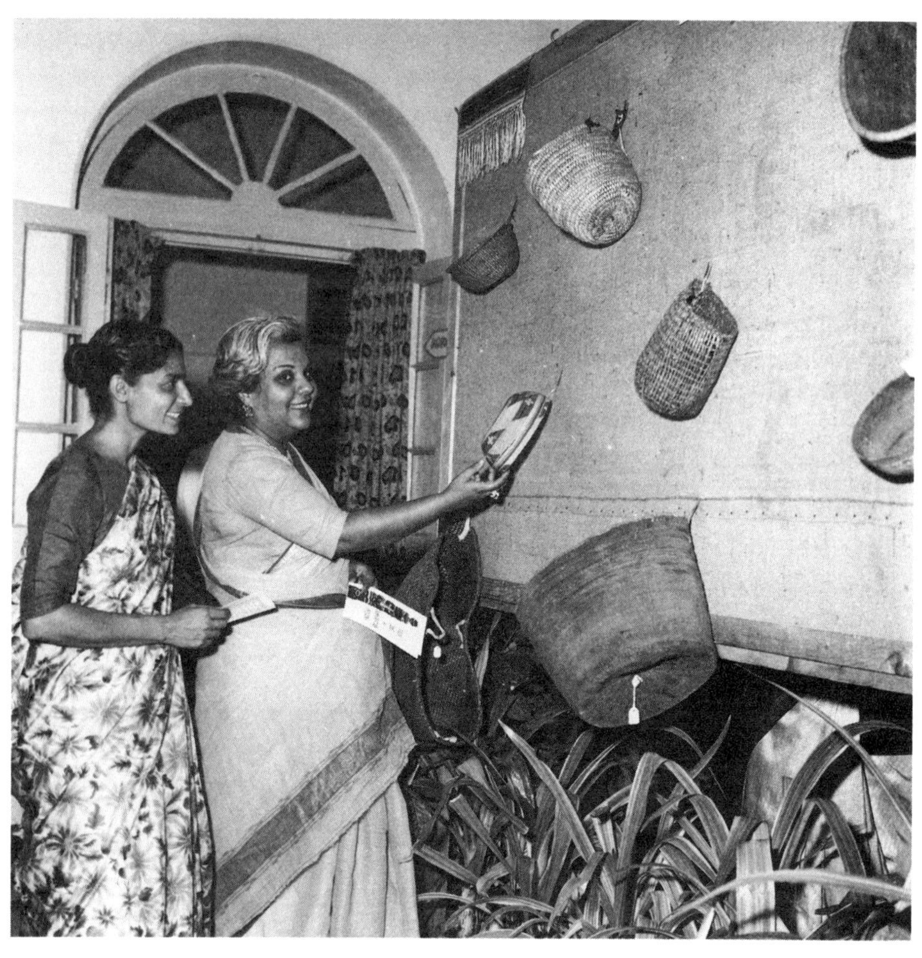

1.3

Begum Tazeen Faridi, secretary general of the All Pakistan Women's Association, and Safia Khan, principal of New Town High School, examine baskets included in *Pacific Northwest Indian Artifacts*, Karachi, Pakistan, 1960. Smithsonian Institution Archives, image #SIA2017–002063.

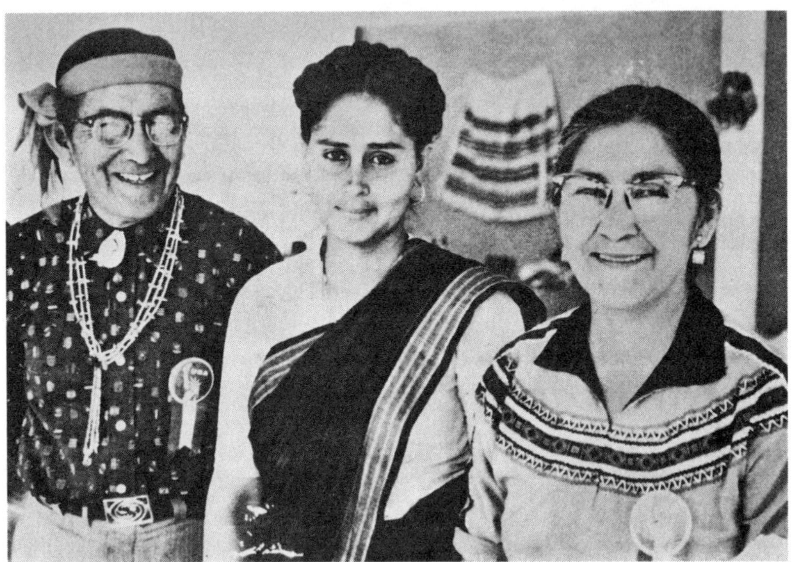

I.4

Fred and Alice Kabotie with "Mrs. Garwell," a local translator at the World Agricultural Fair in New Delhi, 1960. Collection of Hattie Kabotie Lomayesva.

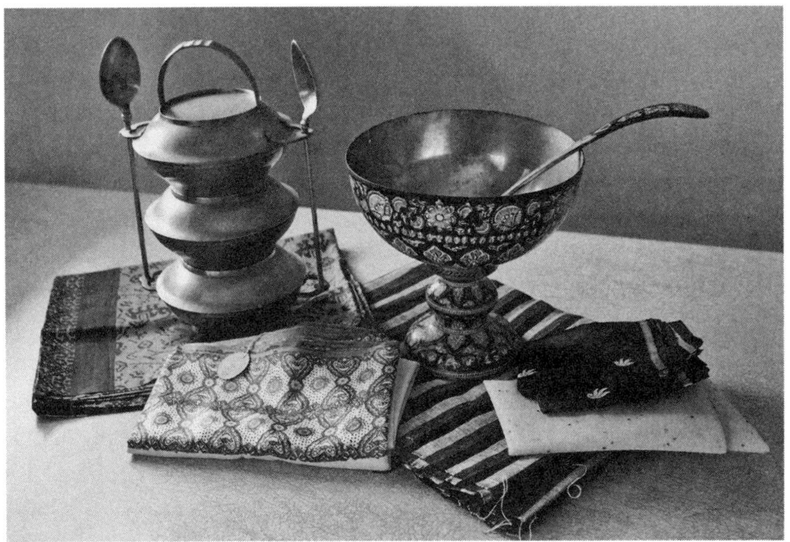

I.5

A lunch box, serving bowl, silks, and other textiles that Alice and Fred Kabotie brought home from their trip to India in 1960. Collection of Hattie Kabotie Lomayesva. Photograph by Jessica L. Horton.

Association handled Yurok and Karuk textiles from the exhibition *Pacific Northwest Indian Artifacts* with apparent delight in Karachi, Pakistan. That same year, a headline proclaimed, "Indians Excited over American 'Indians'!" as Alice and Fred Kabotie created Hopi baskets and silver jewelry at the World Agricultural Fair in New Delhi, India.[25] The couple brought home Indian textiles and metalwork along with a hand-shot film documenting Fred Kabotie's interactions with Brahmins (Hindu priests), hinting at the rich dialogical potential of such journeys.[26] Numerous other celebrated and lesser-known artists, including Harrison Begay, Lorencita Atencio Bird, Darryl Blackman, Helen Hardin, Allan Houser, Oscar Howe, Solomon McCombs, George Morrison, Tonita Peña, Fred Stevens, Bertha Stevens, and Pablita Velarde, nurtured the resilience of Indigenous relational practices in the unlikely shape of Cold War tours.[27] The chapters of *Earth Diplomacy* span the formal and cultural breadth of Native arts that traveled abroad, while providing fine-grain accounts of how earth diplomacy came to inhabit particular constellations of artworks, bodies, and environments.

The arts of *Earth Diplomacy* are united less by a particular material or formal quality than by a common relational ethos, an inheritance from distinct Indigenous systems of knowledge and governance that artists adapted to the challenges of Termination and the Cold War. I regularly refer to these arts as "modernisms" in an effort to capture their shared intervention in period modernization projects while appreciating the heterogeneity of their formal, material, and political affiliations. For the purposes of this book, modernization refers to myriad "processes, systems, and ideologies that beget modernity," such as industrialization, urbanization, assimilation of bodies into labor markets, and intensifying resource extraction necessary to feed a relentless drive for progress.[28] The United States forcefully promoted free-market capitalism as the ideal pathway to modernization in both Native and foreign homelands during the Cold War. This offensive entailed a range of tactics, including Termination policies, coups to install business-friendly governments in the majority world backed by the Central Intelligence Agency (CIA), and soft power demonstrations of the superiority of American culture abroad. Canonical abstract expressionist paintings and Indigenous "crafts" were equally implicated in the US propaganda frontiers.

In its various guises, United States–led modernization was a legacy and continuation of European colonialism that remapped the globe in earlier centuries. Here, it is useful to cite Dené political scientist Glen Coulthard's clear-minded reformulation of Karl Marx's theory of primitive accumulation to address settler colonial processes of dispossession in the latter twentieth and twenty-first centuries. Just as the transition from feudalism to capitalism in Western Europe relied on the conquest of new land and labor to "violently strip—through 'conquest, enslavement, robbery, murder'—noncapitalist producers, communities and societies from their means of production and subsistence," so too did the United States' Cold War offensive seek to transform nonconforming communities into capitalist lifeways by whatever means necessary at home and abroad.[29] Yet my study recognizes the extent to which the Soviet Union and its allies, as well as numerous nonaligned nations, also invested in a race to modernize at the vast expense of human and ecological health, regardless of the ideological banner flown above. The Native modernisms in *Earth Diplomacy* thus constitute critical interventions in a broader system of international relations shaped by competition over *how* (not whether) to modernize. This so-called balance of power has eclipsed alternative cosmopolitics and furthered the exploitation of the earth and its many bodies.

This book approaches Native modernisms as translators of Indigenous relational systems that were incompatible with a capitalist-Communist binary, even as they were entangled in the Cold War modernization battlefield. Admittedly imperfect, *modernisms* is, to my mind, the most critical and capacious term available for the profoundly dialogical arts appearing on these pages. Here, I draw upon a substantial body of scholarship that insists on the capacity of the *s* to decenter a Euro-American modernist canon and contest its underlying spatiotemporal logics in the writing of global art histories.[30] The *s* is not a request for belated inclusion, a formula for yet another multiculturalism that renders radical difference familiar, safe, and sellable within a normative framework of colonial capitalism. Art history can no longer harbor a model in which aesthetic theories and formal innovations emanate from centers in Europe and the United States and arrive in Indigenous and majority world peripheries through the mobility of colonial agents. Nor is it enough to narrate the emergence of a purportedly decentered global contemporary art world after 1989. According to the *Mapping Modernisms: Art, Indigeneity, Colonialism* coeditors, Ruth B. Phillips and Elizabeth Harney, the *s* insists that myriad makers have long shared and shaped uneven global conditions of modernity—the often-devastating circumstances resulting from colonization and modernization—from within their own dynamic times, places, knowledge systems, and traditions of making.[31] Their arts have also traveled the world and affected far-flung people and places. Such dialogical, world-making processes are perhaps most legible-at-a-glance in the work of the Indigenous painters who bookend *Earth Diplomacy*, given that all trained and several taught in art programs that encouraged self-conscious engagement with Indigenous, Euro-American, and majority world art histories (see chapters 1, 5, and the conclusion). But those Indigenous artists whom the USIA categorized as "craftspeople" also reimagined customary arts of sandpainting, weaving, and tipi-making to respond to the damages wrought by modernization in their own communities and around the world (see chapters 2, 3, and 4). In each case, I demonstrate how specific formal and material innovations furthered the translation of Indigenous cosmologies into international relations to inaugurate processes of healing and rebalancing.

Following the transhistorical prompt in Scholder's painting, my approach to artistic modernisms on the global terrain of the Cold War is energized by much older Indigenous material cultures of diplomacy. Native leaders have long relied on affectively rich arts to mediate vast differences and facilitate peaceful cohabitation with other Indigenous nations, European polities, and eventually the United States. Indigenous rituals, regalia, and gifts connected disparate human agents to the potency of other-than-human bodies and systems, engendering familial relations of reciprocity with the earth. Native diplomatic arts did not merely supplement treaties, the written colonial documents of these encounters. They functioned as sensuous contracts in their own right, embodying and extending relational values integral to Indigenous geopolitical frameworks. Native arts navigated global networks and implicated diverse communities in processes of translation, whether or not their makers traveled. They acted as agents of long-term and far-flung encounters intended to transform strangers into kin. These idioms survived and adapted to waves of modern US Indian policy designed to remake autonomous peoples into the dispossessed subjects of capitalism. Indigenous American modernisms' hard-won continuities with historical practices of diplomacy were enhanced by their frequent juxtaposition with customary material culture—Dakota pipes, Tlingit house poles, Diné textiles, Pueblo pottery—in US-sponsored traveling exhibitions. *Earth Diplomacy* draws upon long-standing Indigenous political ecologies and examines their creative redeployment during the Cold War.

From the passage of Termination policy in 1953 to the AIM occupation of Wounded Knee in 1973, this book spans a period of intensifying political radicalism that paralleled the federal government's export of Native American art. While AIM is most often recounted as a series of direct-action spectacles demanding justice from the settler colonial nation, *Earth Diplomacy* recovers an expanded cultural field of diplomacy that intersected, but was not equivalent to such contestation.[32] The United States' longstanding denial of Indigenous nations as political equals fueled diverse forms of Native movement-building, including sustained diplomatic negotiations with those in power, that were overshadowed by the militancy of AIM. As historian Daniel M. Cobb has explored, Indigenous leaders defended their rights to land and sovereignty throughout the period of my study, often borrowing from the language of Cold War international relations and decolonization efforts abroad to make their case.[33] While AIM participants confronted the tyranny of US-Indian relations head-on, few artists discussed on these pages were directly involved in period activism. Some, like Scholder and Oscar Howe, maintained ambivalent relationships with the BIA, the USIA, and the DOS. Others' work was sent abroad without their knowledge, making them unwitting participants in Cold War diplomacy.

An overly simplistic characterization of such differences might read as follows: while activism responds to systemic oppression with resistance, diplomacy invests in the alchemy of kinship. Yet in practice, there is no hard boundary between such seemingly opposite modalities. Indigenous relationalities are not reducible to a binary choice between contestation and accommodation, terms set by colonial nations invested in a violent and competitive international imaginary. As Dakota legal scholar and activist Vine Deloria, Jr., stated, "restoring the old ways" and "a return to the ceremonial uses of the land" informed direct action throughout the 1960s and 1970s.[34] The revitalization of pipe smoking and other rituals knit distinct Native communities together in and beyond the purview of AIM, suggesting that earth diplomacy was an essential ingredient in government-sponsored initiatives and Indigenous activism alike. I argue that Cold War tours of Indigenous American arts helped to carry Native political ecologies through the devastations of Termination and into a new era of diplomatic alliance-building on Indigenous terms, marked by the establishment of the International Indian Treaty Council (IITC) of AIM and the World Council of Indigenous Peoples (WCIP) in 1974.

Ensuring the vitality of Native cultures of diplomacy across the ruptures of Termination was an enormously challenging project that entailed ideological flexibility, political pragmatism, and visionary creativity in the service of a greater holism. This book centers techniques of persuasion in the arts that complement other forms of political engagement, theorizing the sensorial toolkit of artistic modernisms as a powerful means of revitalizing Indigenous ecological and spiritual values. Art invests in earth diplomacy by connecting far-flung people to each other and the land, drawing upon more-than-human sources of power to generate the conditions for collective renewal and rebalancing. My account thus appreciates the fraught nature of artists' positions vis-à-vis the federal government without reinforcing a limited political choice "for" or "against" the settler colonial nation. *Earth Diplomacy* holds that although the United States has exercised a powerful influence, it is by no means an exclusive arbiter of Indigenous modernities. I delimit US hegemony to address what dominant narratives of the Cold War have silenced—namely, Indigenous and other-than-human agents' reshaping of diplomatic milieus through the material exchanges that attached them to others.

The modernisms found on these pages are also not aligned in a one-to-one relationship to Indigenous governments of the period. Historically contingent, circumscribed by colonialism, and often contested by their own citizens, Native leaders were under tremendous pressure to pursue modernization projects in order for their communities to persist as political collectives recognized by the United States. Born from the traumas of Indian Removal, the US government's management of the reservation system entailed efforts to sever leadership from the authority once vested in spiritual knowledge-keepers and institute patriarchy in lieu of kinship- and consensus-based political systems. Federal authorities further fragmented Native communities by diminishing the respected status and creative power of women and two-spirit individuals. (*Two-spirit* is a contemporary, pan-Indigenous term that describes a range of culturally specific nonbinary gender identities.) A defining feature of twentieth-century settler colonialism was the increasing alignment of Indigenous institutions with corporate interests; whether willed or coerced, these partnerships deviated from the diverse earth relationalities that characterized ancestral lifeways.[35]

In light of this painful history of colonial assimilation, Native studies scholars have argued that Indigenous nations must reinvest in customary forms of more-than-human kinship, spirituality, consensus-based governance, and the leadership of women and two-spirit people. Without such radical commitments, Native governments risk perpetuating the heteropatriarchal, ecocidal regimes of colonial nation-states.[36]

Kha-'Po Owingeh (Santa Clara Pueblo) scholar Gregory Cajete writes that "the revitalization of Indigenous knowledge . . . provides the most direct route for Native sovereignty," particularly teachings that support "the natural world as a vital participant and co-creator of community."[37] *Earth Diplomacy* looks beyond formal political institutions and decolonial activism to consider the expansive ecopolitical imagination vested in Native arts. I follow the lead of Jolene Rickard, Heather Igloliorte, and other Native studies scholars in grasping creative praxis as a guarantor of resilient forms of Indigenous geopolitics. Art invests in the vitality of relational systems that are otherwise systematically oppressed in a modern international sphere designed to serve colonial logics of sovereignty.[38] The forms discussed in this book invite a capacious gathering of more-than-human communities across a variety of scales—an earth diplomacy that inhabits and overflows the historically contingent nations and relations that constitute our continuing international (dis)order.

Such expansive relational practices persist in animating both institutional and radical Native politics in the twenty-first century. Consider the United Nations (UN) Declaration on the Rights of Indigenous People in 2007, which culminated decades of lobbying by Native American activists and leaders alike to affirm the "urgent need to respect and promote the inherent rights of indigenous peoples which derive from their political, economic, and social structures and from their cultures, spiritual traditions, histories and philosophies, especially their rights to their lands, territories, and resources."[39] This unprecedented, if nonbinding declaration has its roots Haudenosaunee demands for recognition at the League of Nations in the 1920s and the lobbying of trans-Indigenous alliances such as the aforementioned WCIP and IITC at the United Nations in the 1970s.[40] In those cases, delegates drew upon the power of wampum belts, ceremonial pipes, regalia, singing, and drumming to generate diplomatic assemblages and affect political outcomes.[41] Intertribal coalitions have also worked outside of normative international institutions for the liberation of Native peoples, lands, and waterways from capitalism and colonialism. For example, The Red Nation, established in 2014, builds transnational alliances based on "a politics of caretaking and affirmation . . . being given to us by our other-than-human relatives" that is specifically embodied in *k'é* (Diné kinship).[42] *Earth Diplomacy* recovers a forgotten art history that supported the emergence of global Indigenous justice movements that are flourishing in many forms today.

As I write, diplomacy is thoroughly out of fashion, at once ideologically suspect and practicably disposable. In everyday parlance, the phrase "How diplomatic!" signals an uncritical and disingenuous passivity. Thanks in part to its recent manipulation by Cold War competitors, diplomacy is often confused with propaganda and stripped of its cultural and creative means to engender peaceful cohabitation.

At stake in the diminishment of diplomacy is the survival of life on the planet we share. "As soon as we begin to concern ourselves with the climate, with what belongs to the land . . . we are divided" observes Latour, such that it is impossible to sit down at the negotiating table and come to an agreement for the common good.[43] Philosopher Isabelle Stengers similarly considers the futility of diplomats at the UN Climate Change Conferences as evidence that the global ascendency of capitalism has destroyed "the feeling of interdependence as an operative political affect." Human and more-than-human relationships have been reduced to the predatory interests of wealth accumulation in lieu of affiliations founded in obligation to a collective. Under these conditions, she writes, "we can bid farewell not only to diplomacy but also, I am convinced, to the possibility that humans can, on this earth, safeguard any future worthy of the name." Stengers goes on to map an alternative role for vernacular diplomats as "activators of the imagination," storytellers who diverge from nation-state agendas to renew an atrophied sense of gratitude that humans exist thanks to others.[44] While I share a similar conclusion about artists, her universalizing account of an affective deficit must be tempered with recognition that Indigenous "cultures of gratitude" have persisted alongside and *within* failed modern institutions of diplomacy. Native stories, Potawatomi plant ecologist Robin Wall Kimmerer maintains, are filled with warnings about the dire spiritual and material consequences when humans forget to honor and return the abundant gifts from the earth. "In story, the spring dries up, the corn doesn't grow, the animals do not return, and the legions of offended plants and animals and rivers rise up against the ones who neglected gratitude."[45] Predictive of the damages wrought by colonial capitalism, Indigenous teachings on reciprocity guide the arts of earth diplomacy explored throughout this book.

I maintain that in order to reanimate a beleaguered framework of diplomacy, it is imperative to confront a history in which the knowledges of diverse peoples have been excluded from the realm of political persuasion. It is necessary, in other words, to delimit the process by which modern nation-states have "colonized the spaces of diplomacy," in geographer Jason Dittmer's words.[46] As a growing number of scholars have observed, the apparent bankruptcy of the term reflects a longer history of co-optation by powerful modern nation-states to serve essentialist and exclusionary nationalisms. Consider, for example, the influential phrase *soft power*, coined by international relations scholar Joseph Nye to describe state-led efforts to instrumentalize culture for the purposes of moral persuasion. In Nye's words, soft power names "the ability to get what you want from others . . . with attraction."[47] His case in point is the Cold War, during which the United States and the Soviet Union marshaled culture to expand their spheres of influence abroad, seeking to attract allies and curb each other's authority. As the cultural arm of an arsenal that includes coercive measures such as economic sanctions and military force (hard power), soft power facilitates alliances to serve national self-interest. During the Cold War, soft power functioned as a vehicle for exporting the same forms of extractive capitalism that the United States imposed on Indigenous American nations.

Soft power is inextricable from a broader "balance of power" logic, a venerated Euro-American political theory that has profoundly shaped international relations for more than half a century. Its many scholarly and practical uses share a common definition of power as an anthropocentric capacity to physically or ideologically dominate others. Power is dangerously concentrated in nation-states that are assumed to be self-interested, competitive, accumulative, and expansionist. The hegemonic ambitions of any one player are thus "balanced" by the rise of powerful competitors and the formation of counter-alliances.[48] This cynical, paranoid imaginary achieved a "startling renaissance . . . not only in the pages of learned journals, but in the daily press and in radio" during the Cold War.[49] It was spectacularly materialized in the nuclear arms race as well as the cultural contests between the United States, the Soviet Union, and their shifting allies. The euphemism, "balance," occluded such nations' common policy of exploiting Indigenous people and other-than-human beings in pursuit of extractive dominion.[50] Although increasingly debated after 1989, variations on the theory persist in shaping—and severely limiting—both the study and practice of diplomacy today. This narrow construct has eclipsed the diversity and dynamism of diplomatic relations as they are negotiated "on the ground."[51]

The co-optation of diplomacy during the Cold War perpetuated longstanding patterns of Euro-American colonization that worked to expel a multitude of cosmopolitical traditions from the governance of world affairs. During the early modern period of expansion, European nations increasingly excluded from political negotiations all those who they determined did not possess territorial sovereignty, or statehood. Denial was an active means of disempowering Indigenous peoples.[52] This world-shaping process is evident throughout the Americas, wherein disrespect for Native autonomy and exploitation of land remain profoundly intertwined. When Europeans arrived in the Americas, they encountered myriad culturally and politically distinct Indigenous groups interrelated through conflict, diplomacy, and trade. Following Christopher Columbus's fateful first voyage, the Catholic Church supported the Doctrine of Discovery by divvying up hitherto unknown territories among Spanish and Portuguese competitors based upon their presumed rights of discovery. Following the Treaty of Westphalia in 1648, the papal power of distribution gave way to the pragmatic, albeit often ignored, principle of "effective occupation" of such spaces. However, this concept could not be applied uniformly and unilaterally across their expanding empires, as the Spanish, Portuguese, Dutch, French, and English had to bargain with powerful alliances of Native nations as they vied for dominion in the Americas.[53] Treaties acknowledged that Indigenous people were present in the land before Europeans and—at least in theory—possessed sovereign rights to be respected within the emerging international order. While negotiating power existed on both sides, a goal of such arrangements for Euro-American nations was to accumulate capital through resource dominion. In *Nation to Nation: Treaties Between the United States and American Indian Nations*, historian Robert N. Clinton writes unflinchingly that "treaties with Indian Nations served as a Euro-American legal rationalization and ratification of the colonial dispossession of preexisting civilizations of their aboriginal homelands."[54] In practice, furthermore, Europeans rarely granted treaties with Native nations the status of contractual relationships between equals. Produced amid vast cultural misunderstandings and forms of coercion, treaties set in motion patterns of violability that the United States furthered in the twentieth century.

There were 368 treaties negotiated and signed by US and tribal leaders between 1777 and 1868.[55] Treaties remained a primary vehicle for land cessation, usually through sale. At first, active Native participation was a hallmark of the treaty process, as in other nation-to-nation agreements that the United States formed with sovereign nations outside its own borders.[56] It this context, diplomatic relations were vital to the mediation of cultural and political differences in order to arrive at agreeable means of being-in-common. For Indigenous nations, diplomacy typically did not end with the signing of treaties; rather, it was an ongoing and dynamic process of exchange with the goal of maintaining positive relations. However, the situation shifted significantly after the War of 1812, which mitigated the threat of Native alliances with Britain. Increasingly, the federal government dictated relationships with Native people through preformed policies that were unilaterally—and often duplicitously—enacted. Relegated to the final stage of tribal consent, treaties were stripped of their relational richness and instrumentalized as tools of westward expansion. The violence of Indian Removal, the establishment of a reservation system, and the passage of aggressive assimilation measures were legitimized in part by asymmetrical treaty-making. In 1903, the Supreme Court dealt a final blow, ruling that Congress had plenary power to legislate for Indians, including the right to unilaterally abrogate treaties without tribal consent.[57] While the Indian Reorganization Act of 1934 offered temporary reprieve by reducing federal intervention in Native governance, the path was cleared for the subsequent Termination era.

Products of profound power imbalances, treaties nonetheless speak to the persistence and dynamism of Indigenous cultures of diplomacy amid the ongoing colonization of the Americas. While American Indian political organizations were tremendously diverse upon contact with Europe, historians note that many governed by consensus, with values of cooperation, respect, and reciprocity guiding relationships among human and other-than-human constituents.[58] Power was typically not divinely appointed, hierarchically organized, nor centered exclusively on human individuals and institutions. Rather, as Deloria, Jr. has expressed, aptitude and meaning derived "directly from the world around [Native people], from their relationships with other forms of life."[59] He names extended kinship networks, which include human, animal, plant, and stone relatives beyond the bounds of biological descent, as powerful generators of political efficacy and responsibility. It follows that customary practices of diplomacy did not tend to support the elevation of treaty partners above the earth in binary and hierarchical relationships. Indigenous diplomats worked to position Euro-Americans and their political institutions in a larger network of other-than-human persons with whom it was paramount to maintain good relations.

Rituals, regalia, gifts, and other arts facilitated diplomatic relations through unstable processes of translation and exchange. The practice of

Cherokee carpentry, according to art historian Mark Watson, provided a model for "persuasive, open-ended solicitation of alliances and political commitment" that shaped postcontact dependencies between European and Indigenous nations.[60] "Exchange was a complex symphony, attuned to the nuances of social life," anthropologist and curator Castle McLaughlin writes of carved pipes, quilled and beaded clothing, and other materials that representatives from Eastern Woodlands and Plains nations gifted to the United States. Native delegates put these arts "into motion in order to pledge and affirm alliances, demonstrate status and power, leverage negotiations, secure resources and forgive transgressions."[61] Rickard asserts that the imperatives of Haudenosaunee diplomacy have produced a continuous tradition of "visual sovereignty" in the form of the Two Row Wampum, an abstract representation of peaceable relations between two nations as vessels traveling side-by-side down the same river. Wampum arts embody the values of respect and reciprocity that connect diverse human groups to other beings, land, water, and cosmos—"philosophical principles that transcend the colonial mythology of . . . the modern nation-state construct."[62] Art historian Annette de Stetcher similarly notes that for Huron-Wendat people, "the alliance that each wampum represented was a living one; the 'word,' the terms spoken by each ambassador, had a life by virtue of the ongoing international interaction that it represented" and was kept vital for future generations through oratory arts.[63] Often made from the bodies of earth kin, Indigenous diplomatic arts facilitate the translation of Indigenous political ecologies, the adoption of strangers into more-than-human families, and the instantiation of long-term caretaking responsibilities for all involved.

With apparently unwitting irony, the USIA circulated historical gifts and ritual tools alongside the contemporary Indigenous arts that gave them new life. For example, among Diné textiles and Pueblo pots exhibited in Bogóta, Stockholm, and Munich in 1962 appeared an undated *čʼaŋúpa wakʼá* (sacred pipe). Attributed to the "Sioux" (Očhéthi Šakówiŋ, the seven allied bands of Lakota, Dakota, and Nakota people who compose the Great Sioux Nation), it was made of *iŋyaŋša* (pipestone), a deep red argillite quarried from *čʼaŋnúŋp-okʼé* (known today as Pipestone National Monument in Minnesota).[64] In the text accompanying the display, visitors learned that "the peace pipe was used when Indians met together or when the white men conferred with them over such matters as treaties and the acquisition of land. The area from which the pipestone came was held by the Indians as sacred ground where all

:::::::::

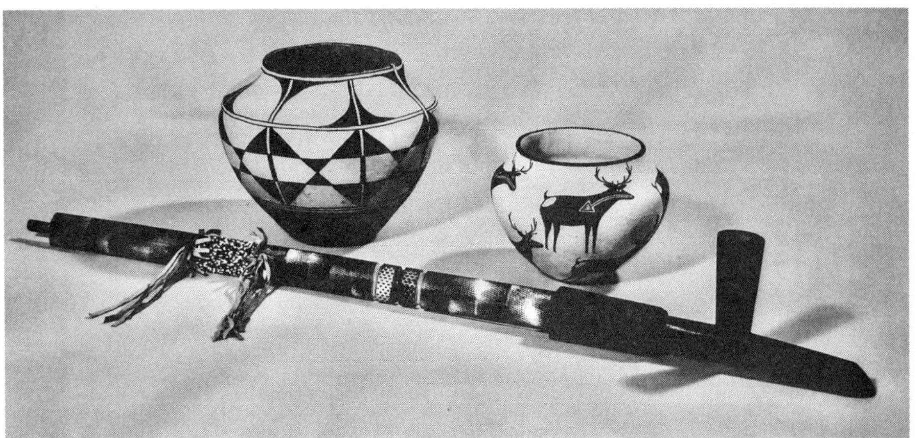

I.6

Sioux Peace Pipe. 37.75 × 5 in. Materials and location unknown. *Back left*: Maria
Tafaya (Santa Clara), pottery bowl. 8.5 × 10 in. diameter. *Back right*: Lucy M. Lewis
(Acoma), pottery bowl. 6 × 8 in. diameter. SIA Project # 64–245, Folder: USIA RU 321,
Office of Program Support, National Museum of American Art, 1956–1981, with
related records from 1947, Box 87, Folder 1: Sandpainting and Handcraft Indian
Exhibition.

Indians met in peace."[65] Unlike the USIA label, Sisseton-Wahpeton Oyate
citizen and feminist scholar Kim TallBear uses the present-tense to describe the ongoing relevance of a Dakota story in which a flood killed
an entire people and pooled their blood in *čhaŋnúŋp-ok'é*; hence, "the
stone is sometimes spoken of as a relative."[66] A prayerful diplomatic tool
carved from pipestone is likewise alive, with the capacity to bond those
who smoke it by connecting them with the whole of the cosmos. By inviting newcomers to pass the pipe, Očhéthi Šakówiŋ dignitaries draw them
into an expansive fold of *mitákuye oyás'iŋ* (all our relations).

The presence of this animate being in a US government–sponsored
art exhibition that traveled abroad at the height of Termination conjured
durable Indigenous diplomatic contracts that surpass interpretations of
treaties as expendable words and alienable rights. An agreement sealed
with smoke is a formalized expression of familial relations that entails
reciprocal responsibilities dynamically enacted over the long term.[67] The
pipe further indicates that Indigenous people have continued to nurture
such bonds through the circulation of art, centuries after the introduction of written treaties and other legal documents. Thus materialized,
Indigenous diplomatic idioms have survived the United States' repeated,

spectacular violation of treaties. *Earth Diplomacy* proposes that Indigenous American arts breathed new life into the political ecologies pictured in *Indian and Rhinoceros* and materialized in "Sioux Peace Pipe." Beyond the survival and redefinition of Indigenous communities as sovereign nations, such creative practices worked to rebalance a disordered universe by activating a capacious network of earth kin.

BEYOND COLD WAR AMERICAN ART

In foregrounding occluded Indigenous and other-than-human agents, *Earth Diplomacy* entails a reassessment of the overdetermined relationship between American art and Cold War politics. My account exits a familiar script in which the United States wielded art as an ideological "weapon" in the binary battle between capitalism and Communism, even as it shares the same troubled historical terrain. In *How New York Stole the Idea of Modern Art: Abstract Expressionism, Freedom, and the Cold War*, art historian Serge Guilbaut provided a methodological blueprint for subsequent studies, focused on the critical exposé of nation-centered ideological manipulations and propaganda coups. Building on studies of abstract expressionists' rise to international prominence in the context of the Cold War by Max Kozloff and Eva Crockoft, he issued a corrective to purely formalist interpretations that foregrounds "the social and political factors that enter into aesthetic production."[68] Guilbaut established that the careers of canonical artists such as Jackson Pollock and Willem de Kooning were propelled by ideologies that simultaneously associated creative freedom with an avant-garde revolt against political instrumentalization (particularly the social realisms promoted first by fascist Germany, then by the Soviet Union) and the universal benevolence of capitalism in the image of the United States. The alleged purity of much postwar abstraction was ideologically malleable, the story goes, precisely because it negated a discernible political stance. Art historian Frances Stoner Saunders subsequently mined this vein of ideological critique by exposing the extent to which the CIA covertly manipulated the work of prominent modernists to serve as propaganda in Western Europe in the 1950s and 1960s.[69] Although the Museum of Modern Art (MoMA) and businessman, politician, and art collector Nelson Rockefeller are key players in the nefarious public-private partnerships she narrates, no mention is made of their patronage of Native modernisms—an element that shaped the abstract expressionist canon (see chapter 2) while introducing profound Indigenous differences into the story of Cold War American art.

As historian Gregory Barnhisel emphasizes, such revisionist accounts tend to a construct a sleek, efficient, univocal propaganda machine in lieu of "a large, diverse, and messy set of official and nongovernmental programs" filled with distinct agendas and ample rivalries.[70] They similarly neglect the multiplicity of artistic practices that were entangled with the Cold War, in which figural traditions endured alongside abstraction and artists pursued their own political commitments and international connections. Historian Michael Krenn has enlarged the topical scope of period studies by mapping an expanse of contested public-private partnerships, highlighting the export of sports, theater, jazz, opera, painting, "folk art," and more (although Native art is again absent). A major player in my own study, the USIA was charged with winning international "hearts and minds" by advocating for the universal adoption of liberal democracy, capitalism, individualism, freedom, and multiculturalism—an ideological project that appeared clear enough on paper, but was perpetually muddied by contingencies and controversies in both domestic and foreign contexts.[71] Notably, the agency struggled to respond to international queries about racism, as numerous scholars have illuminated in relation to African Americans' participation in Cold War programs.[72] Overseas audiences watched civil rights protests unfold while Black athletes, musicians, and painters—"a minority resisting a dominant power through cultural means" in the words of historian Lisa E. Davenport—were paradoxically charged with promoting America.[73] Art historian Alex Taylor reminds us that all such actors were more than mere pawns in a game played on high; they were witting collaborators and canny detractors who altered the course of the cultural Cold War.[74] Conflict emerging from this cacophony led to the near collapse of the international art program in the early 1970s, coinciding with the international prominence of AIM—a confluence that I will explore in the conclusion to *Earth Diplomacy*.[75]

This literature provides a valuable foundation for my study by mapping the ideological frameworks that guided, and at times undermined, alliances between national, corporate, and art world interests. Yet, as is often the case in the historiography of American art, Native makers are a *structuring* absence, an exclusion that shores up the parameters of inquiry and makes certain conceptual possibilities unthinkable. While consistently critical of the United States, much Cold War American art history is marked by an underlying "methodological nationalism" that naturalizes the nation-state as the primary unit of analyses and the ultimate horizon of cultural imagination.[76] The voices of powerful individuals and institutions set the diplomatic agenda; others (marginalized communities, other-than-humans, works of art) are left to respond or defect. Even as many postwar historians of American art have embraced transnationalism, trading US exceptionalism for an emphasis on linkages across cultural categories and geopolitical borders, extractive capitalism is an assumed foundation that delimits how such relationships are imagined. Interpretation of diverse postwar modernisms remains hinged to concepts such as freedom, individualism, multiculturalism, and universalism—Western humanist terms mined by nations and corporations on a path to neoliberal globalization. Indigenous knowledges and practices, particularly those in which humans share power, kinship, and responsibility with other beings and systems, are thereby rendered unimaginable.

Without sustained rethinking, Cold War methodological nationalism continues to curb our ability to imagine a different present and future. In so far as it upholds the binary standoff between Communism and capitalism as an exclusive ideological parameter, this approach quietly underwrites a narrative of post-1989 globalization as the inevitable triumph of the latter. The enduring image of a nuclear standoff between superpowers obscures a more fundamental truth: the Cold War accelerated resource exploitation on all sides, precipitating vast humanitarian and environmental crises that threaten the very future of the earth. We need a methodological toolkit, historical, critical, and creative, that can identify and support the survival of alternative lifeways. It is crucial to reopen Cold War narratives beyond elite political formations to account for the participation of nonconforming collectivities, human and otherwise. Crucially, the familiar language of "race," "nation," and even "human" is inadequate to address the scope of Native diplomatic arts inside and across the borders of the United States. At home and abroad, federal officials failed to suppress the status of Indigenous people and their other-than-human kin as deviant "nations within."[77] My search for scholarship on Indigenous arts implicated in other nations' soft power initiatives suggests that similar dynamics unfolded in US-allied settler nations between World War II and the rise of the IITC and WCIP. Notable examples include the export of exhibitions of Aboriginal art from Australia beginning in the 1940s and Inuit art from Canada in the 1950s and 1960s.[78] More sustained scholarly attention to Indigenous makers who participated in international relations from within their own cosmopolitical traditions is needed to fully historicize diplomacy in the twentieth century and reimagine it in the twenty-first.

It is possible that much vital Indigenous artistic activity has been overlooked *because* it bears the stain of government intervention, in this case hegemonic initiatives overseas. *Earth Diplomacy* wrests a more expansive framework for conceptualizing and practicing diplomacy from the taint of Cold War propaganda. To that end, I do not make a simple case for the inclusion of Native actors within familiar art historical accounts of the period. Instead, I examine how creative practices Indigenized government arts initiatives, transforming them into a surprisingly fertile terrain for the enlargement of Native relational systems around the world. Through diverse artistic forms, a troubling flow of actors—noncompliant Native persons and their other-than-human kin—subtly but insistently deformed a modern international system premised on their externalization and exploitation. At the very moment that federal Indian policy corralled Native people into an oppositional dialectic of assimilation or resistance, Cold War arts initiatives paradoxically stimulated the creative expression of Indigenous diplomatic cultures through unfolding global networks. Put another way, "soft power" became filled with "Red Power," a phrase popularized by Deloria, Jr. to describe a surge in Native political, cultural, and spiritual activity leading up to, and including the occupations of AIM.[79]

NOT THE ECOLOGICAL INDIAN

In arguing for an earth-centered continuum of Indigenous art and politics, *Earth Diplomacy* necessarily confronts an enduring stereotype of the Ecological Indian that was embraced by government, corporate, and environmentalist actors during the period of my study. Deloria, Jr. described the one-dimensional personas that circulated in popular culture: "[Native Americans] were either a villainous warlike group that lurked in the darkness thirsting for the blood of innocent settlers or the calm, wise, dignified elder sitting on the mesa dispensing his wisdom in poetic aphorisms."[80] Non-Indigenous engagements with the latter ranged from manipulations in the service of so-called green capitalism, exemplified by the "crying Indian" who mourned polluted waterways in a famous 1971 Keep America Beautiful ad campaign, to hippies and environmentalists who embraced Native America as a uniform symbol of resistance to capitalism, to genuine, if fleeting, political alliances, for example between AIM and the Black Panthers.[81] While appreciating the complexity of these deployments, I remain particularly skeptical of their origin in a colonial fantasy of premodern holism. As Finis Dunaway has articulated, the Ecological Indian is an anachronism who bears passive witness to the despoilment of wilderness from the sidelines of modernity.[82] Natives and nature are equated, othered, and stripped of their potential for adaptation and response, passively awaiting the advent of extractive capitalism. The stereotype neglects the continuing violence of settler colonialism as well as the hard-won resilience and far-reaching contributions of Indigenous Americans to global modernity. While it may have short-term political utility, the ongoing circulation of this primitivist trope in both popular and academic spaces eclipses the myriad, complex ways in which past and present Indigenous practitioners relate to other-than-human beings and systems under imposed conditions of colonial capitalism. The practices of earth diplomacy assessed on these pages respond to extractive processes through a mixture of negotiation, refusal, and the revitalization of alternative relational systems. In charting the activation of Native political ecologies through the circulation of diverse modernisms, this book aims to replace the one-dimensional figure of the Ecological Indian with a multiplicity of Indigenous earth diplomats: creative translators whose environmental credentials are based on a highly adaptable, always-already political relationship to earthly upheavals.

My corrective draws upon contemporary, interdisciplinary work on political ecology, environmental justice, and decolonization. "Political" has helpfully modified the roots of "ecology" in the natural sciences, a discipline that was bound up with nineteenth-century Euro-American imperialism. German biologist Ernst Haeckel coined the term *ecology* in 1866 to describe the total relationship between organisms and their environments, yet his description of complex relationality stopped short of crediting Indigenous cosmologies and implicating colonial cultures.[83] Subsequent formations of ecology challenged the exceptionalism that Western scientific discourses granted certain human elites; today, scholars are more likely to describe an assemblage of diverse human and non-human agents and processes that are "inextricable from social, political and economic forces."[84] Far from untouched, nature is the site of intensive government and multinational corporate management, privatization, speculation, and extraction, even as it is composed of myriad resistant and resilient beings. While feel-good formulations of ecology-as-interdependency abound, advocates of environmental justice counter by pinpointing global corporate leaders and allied politicians as perpetrators of pollution, deforestation, and other forms of "slow violence" that disproportionately target poor and marginalized communities of color around the world.[85] The logic of extraction, a "withdrawal without depositing," indulges a fantasy of limitless growth for a few while laying waste to an expendable majority.[86] Latin American studies scholar Macarena Gómez-Barris similarly defines *extractivismo* in the Americas as a colonial process of "violently reorganizing social life as well as the land by thieving resources from Indigenous and Afro-descendent territories."[87] It is for this reason that Native Americans frequently experience the impending climate apocalypse as "colonial déjà vu," according to Potawatomi scholar Kyle Powys Whyte.[88] The global map of climate change follows the contours of Euro-American colonial expansion, connecting waves of refugees fleeing uninhabitable territories in the Global South to Indigenous communities displaced from their ancestral lands within affluent northern settler nations.

My phrase *earth diplomacy* builds upon related strands of political ecology dedicated to "sustainable diplomacies" and "earth jurisprudence." Such discourses recognize how thoroughly the modern nation-state system has suppressed the political agency of heterogeneous, ecologically embedded human communities.[89] This structural absence is evident in the spectacular failure of governments around the world to recognize the sovereignty of Indigenous communities or coordinate meaningful action on large-scale catastrophes such as climate change, mass species extinction, and the flight of refugees from increasingly uninhabitable regions. A few international relations scholars have challenged the dominance of statecraft anchored in the self-interest of nation-states and argued for the expansion of diplomatic cultures to encompass other-than-human beings and systems deemed crucial to the survival of all life.[90] At the outset of the essay collection, *Sustainable Diplomacies*, Costas M. Constantinou and James Der Derian write that diplomacy "should not only be concerned with advocacy, policy implementation, and public relations but also—and more crucially—with innovation and creativity, experimentation in finding ways and terms under which rival entities and ways of living can co-exist and flourish (including biodiversity and future generations)."[91] Their articulation draws on the foundational work of political theorist David Joseph Wellman, who has pushed against the secular and anthropocentric rationalization of negotiations in modern international relations. "A new definition of balance of power is in order," he insists, one that incorporates all elements of the biosphere and restores oppressed ecological and spiritual knowledges to the theory and practice of diplomacy.[92] At stake in such inclusions is "a more intimate and profound understanding of the lives, beliefs, and concerns of people 'on the ground.'"[93] Ground is more than a metaphor in his estimation; it points to the "ecological location" of the communities in question, which shapes their sense of connection and responsibility to others with whom they share the earth.[94] The artists of *Earth Diplomacy* similarly work to implicate faraway communities and their environments in sacred homeland ecologies, for example by incorporating sandstone pigments from Diné Bekéyah (the Diné homeland) or portraits of powerful beings that animate the Dakota universe in artworks that retraced the transnational path of capitalism during the Cold War.

In the face of accelerating globalization and its ravages, Native studies scholars and Indigenous leaders have called for a renewed and reconfigured framework of jurisprudence that includes the earth itself. Ecuador and Bolivia led the way by incorporating the rights of Mother Earth into their constitutions, albeit with many challenges to implementation. Artists, curators, and activists are meanwhile reimagining the cultural and legal status of forests, rivers, oceans, and atmosphere, often drawing upon Indigenous frameworks of knowledge.[95] In 2012, artistic codirectors Gerald McMaster of the Siksika First Nation and Dutch curator Catherine de Zegher featured the English translation of *mitákuye oyás'iŋ* (all our relations), an Očhéthi Šakówiŋ prayer, as the title and guiding philosophy of the Sydney Biennale. They mobilized an inspirited diplomatic idiom of kinship among humans, animals, plants, rivers, and mountains to frame a mega-exhibition, a gathering of diverse artistic practices from around the world.[96] In 2016, crowds from New Zealand to Japan took to the streets to speak out against the construction of the Dakota Access Pipeline across sacred Indigenous waterways and burial sites. The Očhéthi Šakówiŋ and their allies chanted "water is life" as ceremonial pipes were passed through camps near the Standing Rock Reservation in South Dakota. The House of Tears Carvers of the Lummi Nation in western Washington arrived bearing a crest pole carved with white buffalo—a sacred being for Očhéthi Šakówiŋ—on a flatbed truck, part of their five-thousand-mile journey to generate solidarity with communities battling the fossil fuels industry in Canada and the United States.[97] A national constitution, a mega-exhibition, and an trans-Indigenous environmental justice movement; in each of these examples, Native political ecologies guided a gathering of more-than-human communities, modeling forms of being-in-common that transcend the borders and logics of modern nation-states.

In such cases and throughout this book, art is mobilized as a sensuous, compelling, and connective tool—an agent of earth diplomacy. It has the potential to distill and mobilize the complex ecologies that bind humans to the earth, returning a vital relationality to the occlusive sphere of the international. My approach puts critical developments in Indigenous studies in dialogue with emergent ecocritical methods in art history, particularly James Nisbet's articulation of the "work of art as an ecological object" during a period of growing environmental consciousness in the United States during the 1960s and 1970s. Ecological processes can challenge habits of discernment and meaning-making because they operate at beyond-human scales: too minute, vast, durational, diffuse, or complex to be readily grasped by the senses and assimilated into existing ideational systems. For Nisbet, artworks are material and theoretical constellations with a unique capacity to condense and render perceptible otherwise elusive environmental conditions.[98]

In my account, art is similarly conceived less as an object than a relational nexus, an affectively charged gathering of materials, bodies, and media. I draw additional inspiration from Dittmer's theory of the diplomatic assemblage, which holds that international relations entail more than the coming together of preformed geopolitical subjects. Their meeting is shaped by a surplus emotional charge from "material circulations—of media, of objects, of bodies and their practices" that can "subtly rework the political cognition of those engaged in foreign policy making."[99] While such insights are often cast as methodologically groundbreaking in relation to a Euro-American canon, they are anticipated by customary Indigenous arts that function as portals between ecological, spiritual, and political systems. Indigenous diplomats have long recognized art's involvement with what philosopher Jacques Rancière has called the "distribution of the sensible," with the potential to shift the boundaries of what is felt, thought, and therefore available to politics.[100] Made of earth and elaborated by human hands, such entities are activated by ritualized exchanges that bind relationships of all kinds. Certain artforms may possess a lifeforce of their own and act on their human interlocutors in unpredictable ways. Energized by long-standing Indigenous material practices, the contemporary arts discussed in this book are similarly imbued with the capacity to illuminate, organize, and affect a thick web of life. Here, my account departs from Dittmer's, which decenters human agencies, because Native artists often wittingly compose assemblages for distinct political purposes. Conceived as persuasive agents in cosmopolitical relationships, Indigenous arts have the potential to recalibrate a modern international system founded on the exploitation of people and land.

Earth Diplomacy names this relational capacity. It references an affective charge generated by the sensuous specificity of artworks and creative practices. Its effects can at times be glimpsed in the colonial archives charged with telling those arts' stories—particularly in historical photographs that index assemblages of artworks, bodies, and environments. But the phrase also points to an interpretive ethics on the part of art historians, such as myself, who assume responsibilities to research Native arts within their historical contexts and contribute to their afterlives in publications and exhibitions. In this context, earth diplomacy entails challenging perceptual habits that too readily support the assimilation of Indigenous arts into the normative representational politics of the United States.[101] It names a commitment to taking seriously the agency of mountains, rivers, plants, and animals—Indigenous relatives and ecological sources of much Native art—within international relations. And it means lifting up arts' ongoing potential to affect political cognition in shifting environments of encounter, including our own.

THE CHAPTERS

My chapters draw upon understudied archives and oral histories to follow select exhibitions, artworks, and makers on their journeys through Indigenous and foreign homelands. Regional biases embedded in the United States' international art program are mirrored in my selections. While the government circulated historical Native arts collections from across North America, contemporaneous artworks and artists' tours—the focus of my study—were most often commissioned from members of Indigenous nations in the Southwest and the Plains. The DOS and USIA inherited these relationships from the BIA's Indian Arts and Crafts Board (1935–present), a New Deal initiative to stimulate a high-end market for Native arts in communities already well-traversed by tourists and anthropologists.[102] The Pueblo, Diné, Blackfeet, and Dakota artists who animate these chapters encountered a morass of stereotypes; as I discuss throughout, Ecological Indian fantasies have most firmly attached to the ceremonial and hunting cultures of the Plains and Southwest. The circulation of such colonial tropes worldwide undoubtedly shaped the US government's selection of artists. My chapters emphasize how

:::::::::

Indigenous makers utilized these fraught conditions to engender diverse practices of earth diplomacy.

Chapter 1, "Contested Kinship: More-than-Human Relations or the Family of Man?," acts as a companion to this introduction by mapping the ideological and geopolitical contours of Cold War Native arts activity in greater detail. I assess the fraught relationship between the US government and Indigenous arts at the crossroads of Indian Termination and USIA propaganda, focusing on the international circulation of a modern painting movement headquartered in New Mexico and Oklahoma. I discuss two well-documented group exhibitions that established the federal government's narrative blueprint for tours of Native modernisms discussed throughout this book. *Contemporary American Indian Paintings* at the National Gallery of Art in Washington, DC, in 1953 and *Contemporary American Indian Paintings from the Margretta S. Dietrich Collection*, which toured the "Near East" from 1964 to 1966, surveyed spare, delicate scenes of Native lifeways that were produced in and around Santa Fe in the first half of the twentieth century. Through these exhibitions, curator Dorothy Dunn, the white founding director of the Studio School (1932–1962) at the Santa Fe Indian School (SFIS), reinvented herself as a cold warrior, exerting an outsized influence on period propaganda concerning Native Americans. In tension with Dunn's narrative, I develop a framework of trans-Indigenous, more-than-human kinship that reconnects the modern Native painting movement to customary practices of Indigenous diplomacy. Functioning as a nonnormative form of geopolitics, Native kinship practices were systematically attacked by the federal government during Termination. They persisted as an unsettling sign of difference in the United States' efforts to expand the frontiers of extractive capitalism throughout the majority world. This contested cosmopolitics can be glimpsed in the Indigenous aphorisms cited throughout the most famous Cold War exhibition, *The Family of Man*, traveled by the USIA to thirty-seven countries from 1955 to 1966.[103] I propose that it was more fully realized through group exhibitions of Native American paintings—and in one case, a painter—that toured in tandem. To develop this argument, I examine the capacious human, plant, and animal families depicted in traveling works by Kha-'Po Owingeh (Santa Clara Pueblo) artist Pablita Velarde, Mvskoke (Muscogee [Creek] Nation) artist Solomon McCombs, and Diné (Navajo Nation) artist Harrison Begay.

Chapters 2 and 3 turn away from painted modernisms to consider the embodied modalities of two Diné earth diplomats who traveled with their work. The *haatali* (singer, healer) Fred Stevens and expert weaver Bertha Stevens demonstrated their respective arts on a three-year-long tour alongside *American Indian Art and Handicraft*, an exhibition of student and faculty artwork from the Institute of American Indian Arts through Eurasia and the Americas from 1966 to 1968. Chapter 2, "Rebalancing Power: Diné Sandpainting and Sand Mining," analyzes Fred Stevens's efforts to safely translate sandpainting, an ephemeral ceremonial art that facilitates cosmic rebalancing, into public demonstrations and durable gifts for the purposes of diplomatic exchange. His altered variants worked against the grain of an established narrative of the secularization and commercialization of Native religious arts after World War II by transferring an ethics of reciprocity from ceremonial to geopolitical agents. They palpably connected Diné efforts to protect sacred homelands from military-industrial incursions to the acceleration of sand mining to feed a global building boom in countries abroad. Stevens grasped sandpaintings' potential to heal an out-of-balance system of international relations when he collaborated with curators to consolidate sand into a lasting gift at the Horniman Museum in London in 1966 and when he stole construction sand in order to demonstrate for the cultural program of the inhospitable Olympic Games in Mexico City amid the global uprisings of 1968.

While her husband's fame occasioned their travels, Bertha Stevens's transformative practice of weaving new places and agents into the vital holism of the Diné homeland, takes center stage in chapter 3, "Earth Mothers: Diné Weaving and Trans-Indigenous Ecofeminism." The 1966–1968 tour occasioned her sharing of a cosmologically derived Diné responsibility to perpetuate all life with disparate women who were similarly negotiating a heteropatriarchal, ecocidal form of international relations. Her exchanges with Scottish, Turkish, and Mapuche weavers prompt me to reassess the Indigenous roots of ecofeminism, a discourse that shaped environmental art, politics, and theory in the final decades of the twentieth century. Its primarily white practitioners sought alternatives to Euro-American patriarchy in majority world women's activism and an essentialized Mother Earth that they borrowed from Native American sources. Like Stevens's textiles, my analysis is modeled on Diné oral stories relating the original transmission of sacred weaving knowledge from Na'ashjéii Asdzáá (Spider Woman) to Asdzáá Náádleehé (Changing Woman) and her human children. Stevens transformed such matricentered knowledge into a practice of earth diplomacy that elevated the customary power of Indigenous women during her visit with Mapuche weavers in Quetrahue, Chile, in 1968.

The remaining two chapters shift attention to artists' creative reconfiguration of Plains diplomatic cultures in the shape of painted lodges and ceremonial pipes, which circulated internationally as icons of environmental holism and countercultural resistance in the 1960s and 1970s. Chapter 4, "Tipis and Domes: Modeling the Blackfeet Cosmos at a World Fair," centers on the Crow lodge, a painted tipi that the USIA commissioned from Blackfeet artist Darryl Blackman for the US Pavilion at Expo 70 in Japan. Garnering a record-breaking sixty-four million visitors, the first Asian exposition was charged with simulating a "city of the future" in an era of whole earth images, dome mega-architecture, and dystopian accounts of Western progress. Drawing on a longer history of exhibiting Native American architectural models in colonial exhibitions, I demonstrate that Cold War World Fairs became stages for Indigenous futurisms in which artists materialized ancient gifts from the earth in order to expand a circle of reciprocity. Chapter 5, "The Truth-Line: Oscar Howe's Sacred Pipe Modernism," charts a shifting history of Indigenous material diplomacy based on the ritual smoking of the *c'aŋúpa wak'á* and its revival during the Cold War. Conjoining diverse Native communities across long distances prior to colonization, this pan-Indigenous practice survived a treacherous history of colonial treaty negotiations to be reimagined by artists and activists in the Termination era. My account centers on the work of prominent modernist painter Oscar Howe, who materialized a theory of Dakota ethics and aesthetics through figurative abstractions that distilled the spiritual and ecological truths he saw embodied in pipe ceremonies. The artist toured as an "American Specialist" to nine countries in Europe, South Asia, and the Middle East in 1971, just as AIM activists were embracing the *c'aŋúpa wak'á* as a potent unifying symbol of Red Power.

In the conclusion, "Artist-Diplomat-Vampire," I return to Scholder's paintings, which conjured the United States' betrayal of its treaty obligations to Native nations before diverse publics abroad at the height of AIM. Disgusted by the federal government's propaganda, the artist defected from a USIA tour in Romania to visit Dracula's castle and paint a little-known *Indian/Vampir* series on canvases that fit in his suitcase. Emblematic of the failure of modern nation-state diplomacy, the small paintings align Native Americans and Transylvanians in a global struggle against dispossession. They foretell the flourishing of alternative cultures of diplomacy beyond the coffin of broken treaties and US propaganda.[104] The narrative of *Earth Diplomacy* draws to a close in 1973, as the AIM occupation of Wounded Knee was broadcast globally and Native art largely fell off the United States' Cold War agenda. Yet IITC and the WCIP would soon fill the void, circumventing federal sponsorship and pursuing diplomatic alliances on Indigenous terms.

Earth Diplomacy delimits the tyranny of US-Native relations in the Termination era. It also foreshadows a dire twenty-first century predicament in which the official disposability of diplomacy collides with the global scale of humanitarian and ecological crises. By illuminating a specific past terrain in which creative and political processes were mutually transformative, I intend this book to hold up a mirror to the present, reflecting the limitations and possibilities that still adhere to our faltering system of international relations. I grasp the top-down application of colonial power as one facet of a larger story centered on creative Indigenous contributions to a modernity that continues to unfold. In a period when the United States was busy consolidating hierarchies and exclusions at home and abroad, the unsettling entanglement of Native art with disparate communities around the world kept the promise of mutual flourishing amid differences alive. The case studies in this book contribute to the pluralized history *and future* of earth diplomacy by taking seriously the imaginative contributions of nonstate actors and the specific lands through which they live and travel. Such practices persist as a vital potential in archives and artforms, regardless of whether the relationships they invite are fully realized in a particular time and place. The arts described on these pages are provocations to reimagine international relations through modalities of kinship and reciprocity beyond the destructive framework of colonial capitalism. The unfinished history of earth diplomacy is embodied in Scholder's pipe-bearing ambassador, who faces outward as if inviting a new relationship to unfold.

1

CONTESTED KINSHIP

MORE-THAN-HUMAN RELATIONS OR
THE FAMILY OF MAN?

THREE OVERLAPPING EVENTS in Washington, DC, in 1953 set the course for Native American artists' journeys into Cold War international relations—and the rest of this book. First, the National Gallery of Art (NGA) debuted *Contemporary American Indian Paintings*, an exhibition that established a narrative blueprint for numerous worldwide tours of Indigenous arts to come. Billed as "the most comprehensive showing of its kind ever to be held in the eastern United States," the 115 spare, delicate watercolors by fifty-nine artists depicted the citizens of diverse Native nations dancing, farming, hunting, weaving, and making pottery, as well as the more-than-human ecologies and cosmologies that sustain such cultural activity.[1] Second, Congress passed House Concurrent Resolution 108 and Public Law 280, which formalized a post–World War II policy of Termination. The latter renounced the government's treaty-based responsibilities to Indigenous nations, compelled individuals to relocate to cities and compete in a wage economy, facilitated the expropriation and extraction of sacred homelands, and granted states unprecedented jurisdiction over the lifeways depicted in the paintings, all in the guise of "granting complete political equality to all Indians in our country."[2] Under Glenn Emmons, commissioner of Indian Affairs from 1953 to 1960, sixty-one Native nations were terminated, impacting 1,362,155 acres of land and 11,466 individuals. President John F.

Kennedy signed the last Termination orders in 1962 amid growing Indigenous demands for sovereignty.[3] Third, newly elected president Dwight D. Eisenhower established the US Information Agency (USIA) to manage a vast propaganda machine around the world in response to "an ominous (and apparently effective) 'cultural offensive' thundering out of the Soviet Union."[4] Alongside sports, music, dance, and radio, the agency greatly expanded the international arts program that evolved from Department of State (DOS) collaborations with public and private entities during the New Deal, making novel demands of Native artists.[5]

The convergence of these events was not coincidental. My analysis of their interrelations locates the Cold War export of Native arts at the center of a retooled US colonization campaign that stretched from resource-rich Indigenous lands, to oil zones in the so-called Near East, to the new frontier of the space race. Functioning as an extended historical introduction to *Earth Diplomacy*, this chapter offers a broad sketch of the ecopolitical dynamics underlying such tours. For approximately two decades following the opening of *Contemporary American Indian Paintings*, Indigenous American arts were deployed internationally to counter Soviet critiques of US colonialism and demonstrate the federal government's benevolence toward Native Americans. The United States promised to lead Indigenous citizens—and by extension global others from regions of economic and military significance to the nation—out of the past and into a modernity defined by the benefits of capitalism. The narrative accommodated cultural differences under the banner of individualism and democratic choice, supporting an image of the United States as a guarantor of peaceful pluralism around the world. At the same time, a diverse group of Cold War participants—from Soviet propagandists to USIA officials to Native activists—understood the United States' contemporaneous relationships to both Indigenous and foreign nations as a continuation of nineteenth-century westward expansion. Indigenous arts were charged with sanitizing a continuing history of conquest and ecocide. Haphazardly deployed and regularly contested, this paradigm appears in various forms throughout the case studies of this book.

While addressing Native peoples' enrollment in period propaganda, I intend this chapter to clear space within an extant scholarship on American art and cultural diplomacy that is narrowly focused on the ideological manipulations of government and other institutional agents. New forms of US imperialism abroad mirrored the ongoing dynamics of settler colonialism during the Cold War. At the same time, the federal government's mobilization of Indigenous arts generated unpredictable, affectively charged zones of interchange around the world—diplomatic assemblages with the potential to transform the multifarious agents involved.[6] To this end, I interrupt my own recounting of top-down narratives that empowered capitalism and nationhood with vignettes of work by Pablita Velarde (Kha-'Po Owingeh [Santa Clara Pueblo], 1918–2006), Solomon McCombs (Mvskoke [Muscogee (Creek) Nation], 1913–1980), and Harrison Begay (Diné [Navajo Nation], 1917–2012), who contributed to the global circulation of an Indigenous painting movement established in New Mexico and Oklahoma during the first half of the twentieth century. Velarde loaned a painting that became a centerpiece of *Contemporary American Indian Paintings* in 1953 and was reproduced for readers around the world on the pages of *National Geographic* in 1955; McCombs traveled with his paintings on a DOS tour to African, Asian, and Middle Eastern countries from 1954 to 1955; and Begay's artwork circulated in a USIA-sponsored exhibition, *Contemporary American Indian Paintings from the Margretta S. Dietrich Collection*, in the "Near East" from 1964 to 1966. Their work introduces a central concern of *Earth Diplomacy*: the varied ways in which Native arts acted as double agents within an unstable global order, exceeding their assigned scripts to work on behalf of abused lands as much as any human polity.

These Indigenous modernisms introduced a horizontal framework of more-than-human kinship and geopolitics into the competitive hierarchies that structured international relations of the period. They conjured traditions of diplomacy that are wholly unfamiliar in the scholarship on Cold War art history—and scarcely recognized in the study of international relations—to date: Indigenous rituals, ceremonies, and gifts designed to knit newcomers into familial networks of reciprocity with the earth. At the same time, Termination marked a renewed commitment to suppressing nonconforming lifeways on an ever-advancing capitalist frontier. This chapter thus introduces *kinship* as the foundation of Indigenous diplomatic cultures and a fundamental arena of Cold War contestation. Native kinship modalities can be glimpsed in the famous photography exhibition traveled by the USIA, *The Family of Man*, which has long been criticized for exporting the heteropatriarchal nuclear family as a universal humanist ideal in international relations. Indigenous cosmopolitics were more fully realized in the USIA's *Contemporary American Indian Paintings from the Margretta S. Dietrich Collection*, as I will explore by focusing on the exhibition's tenure in Iran. While *The Family of Man* has shaped a cynical view of Cold War American art as bound to paternalistic propaganda in the service of expanding an extractive zone, the latter exhibition issued a call for more-than-human kinship as the basis of collective responsibility to sacred lands.[7]

BETWEEN THE "INDIAN NEW DEAL" AND TERMINATION

A photograph of the opening of *Contemporary American Indian Paintings* at the NGA in 1953 foregrounds guest curator Dorothy Dunn, the founding director of the Studio School painting program at the Santa Fe Indian School (SFIS) from 1932 to 1937 and a tireless advocate of the artists trained therein. Dressed in a plain, black-trimmed suit, shoulders drawn and eyebrows raised, Dunn exudes a bemused scholarly authority. Clasped in her hands is a stack of booklets, likely copies of the modest exhibition catalog she authored. As the Studio School's many critics have charged, Dunn presented as the nation's foremost expert on modern Native painting, her voice at turns uplifting and eclipsing the artworks she promoted. To her right stands the exhibition's ultrawealthy sponsor, Mary Benjamin Rogers, in a sparkling cloak and fur stole. An artist, New York socialite, and former wife of the vice-president of Standard Oil Company, Rogers exemplifies Dunn's dependence on a network of elite white patrons to display and circulate the work of SFIS-trained artists. Roger's gloved hand gestures to *The Betrothal* (1953), a painting loaned by Pablita Velarde, the first Indigenous woman to complete the Studio School program in 1936 (plate 2). As I will discuss shortly, the work's articulation of kinship and geopolitics at Kha-'Po Owingeh (Santa Clara Pueblo) introduced a fissure in the assimilative logic that occasioned its display. First, however, it is necessary to grapple with Dunn's outsized role in facilitating Cold War appropriations of Native arts, notably the sedimentation through repetition (with variation) of a multicultural imagination linking Indigenous culture, American art, and the universal benevolence of capitalism and democracy. This legacy persists in framing many discussions of Native American art today.

As the genesis of the Studio School is explored extensively elsewhere, I offer only a brief sketch to contextualize the Cold War engagements of Dunn and former students of the program.[8] Born in Kansas with a degree in education from the Art Institute of Chicago, Dunn taught art to Pueblo and Diné students as part of a broader curriculum at Office of Indian Affairs (BIA) schools in New Mexico from 1928 to 1931.[9] During this time, she witnessed the growth of a transatlantic market for watercolor

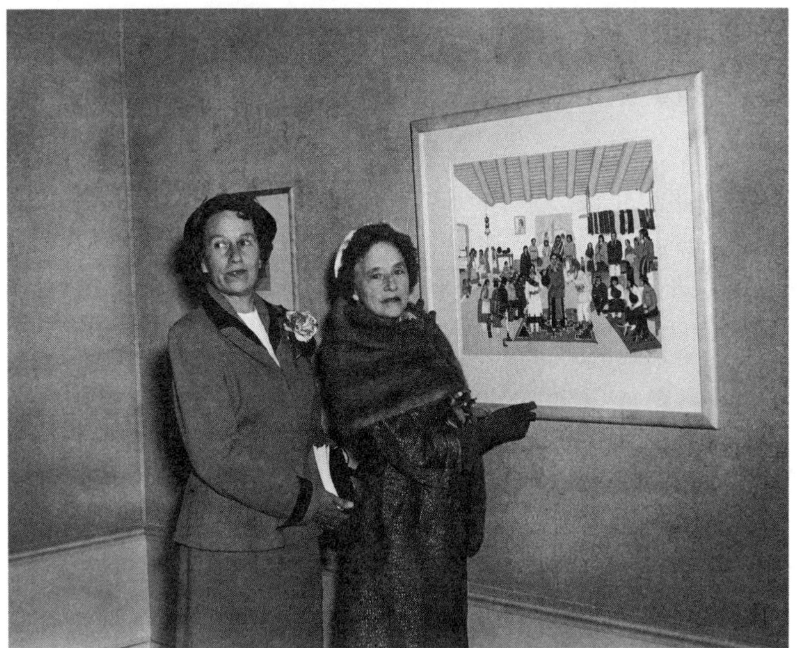

1.1

Dorothy Dunn and Mary Benjamin Rogers at the opening of Contemporary American Indian Paintings at the National Gallery of Art, 1953. RG26B, National Gallery of Art Events Images—Exhibitions and Installations. 26B7_56_001. National Gallery of Art, Washington, DC, Gallery Archives.

....

paintings created by Pueblo artists in New Mexico and Kiowa artists in Oklahoma during the first decades of the twentieth century. Inspired by these precedents, she established the Studio School as a dedicated painting program for training young Native artists at the BIA-run SFIS in 1932.[10]

Dunn's efforts anticipated the Indian Reorganization Act (IRA, often referred to as the "Indian New Deal") of 1934, which temporarily reversed decades of federal policy that aimed to eradicate Indigenous political sovereignty and cultural difference. The IRA was an exception to the modern rule of overturning treaties and betraying diplomatic relations with Indigenous nations, which resumed in full force after World War II. Yet federal support for Native peoples' political, economic, and cultural autonomy was limited by the paternalism of "a powerful nation toward a people living amongst us and dependent on our protection," as President Franklin D. Roosevelt put it.[11] The IRA continued the steady integration of Native people into US nationhood and capitalism, but in a framework of cultural pluralism rather that total assimilation. The development of aesthetic standards, training programs, and an international market for Indigenous art were intended to enhance Native nations' capitalist self-sufficiency through arts production.[12] To this end, the IRA facilitated the creation of an Indian Arts and Crafts Board (IACB, 1935–present) within the BIA, employed Native artists in the Public Works of Art Project, and modestly funded the Studio School.

Dunn was an agent of these reforms in the lives of some two hundred students enrolled in the Studio School program during her five years as director. She urged her pupils to eschew European academic conventions of realism based on linear perspective and perceived color. In place of what Dunn considered to be foreign intrusions or damaging stereotypes, she aimed to cultivate paintings that were rooted in Indigenous values and aesthetics yet recognizably modern. In the tradition of artistic primitivism, she lauded the geometric, color-block patterns and the shallowly inscribed figures found in Indigenous rock art, pottery, textiles, and murals, exemplified in the nearby Pueblo nations and collections of the Museum of New Mexico. Additionally, she urged her students to emulate the style and subject matter of Pueblo and Kiowa artists who had already inaugurated a watercolor painting practice.[13] Finally, she encouraged her pupils to find their "rightful, permanent place" within "world art from early days to modern times."[14] To this end, Dunn introduced them to reproductions of Egyptian frescos Indian and Persian miniatures; Chinese watercolors; ceramics from Rhodes, Crete, and Cyprus; and paintings by Pieter Brueghel, Wassily Kandinsky, and Paul Cézanne from the collections of the Art Institute of Chicago.[15] While their approaches were formally and thematically diverse, the artists generally used pen or pencil to outline discrete figures on otherwise bare paper and fill them in with zones of color using the opaque tempera paints provided. The resulting scenes of Indigenous lifeways and ecologies typically share a shallow depth of field enhanced by the lack of significant modeling and few to no background elements. The spare aesthetic was later dubbed the "Studio style," "traditional Indian painting," and, most pejoratively, the "Bambi" school of painting.[16]

Prominent patrons of the New Mexico—and Oklahoma-based movements felt that they had found an authentic form of modern art with deep roots in US soil, "an artistic treasury not only older but fresher and purer than anything Europe has to offer."[17] Such ideologies shaped early Native paintings' transatlantic forays in the 1920s and 1930s, notable precedents for their worldwide travels during the Cold War.[18] After the Studio School was awarded the Médaille de bronze at the Exposition internationale des arts et des techniques in Paris in 1937, Dunn reported receiving requests for exhibitions on both sides of the Atlantic that exceeded the artistic output of the program.[19] That same year she relinquished responsibility for the students' instruction to Gerónima Cruz Montoya (P'otsúnú, 1915–2015), a former painting student from Ohkay Owingeh (previously San Juan Pueblo). Montoya oversaw the program until the SFIS was replaced by the Institute of American Indian Arts (IAIA) in 1962.[20] Dunn spent the remainder of her professional career curating and publicizing the work of Studio School-trained artists and their Pueblo and Kiowa predecessors. Her efforts relied on support from Margretta Dietrich (1881–1961), the biggest lender—thirty-four works—to the NGA exhibition.[21] A former suffragette from Philadelphia, Dietrich directed the New Mexico Association of Indian Affairs, a major advocacy engine for Native nations, from 1932 to 1953. Dietrich entrusted her collection of 234 paintings to Dunn's far flung curatorial initiatives and, upon her death in 1961, to Dunn's ownership.[22]

Dunn adapted the cultural logics of the IRA for the NGA exhibition, authoring an influential account of Native modernisms that would reverberate through subsequent Cold War tours. She wrote, in the introduction to the 1953 catalog:

> The contemporary artists are not the Indians popularly known through historical account and folklore. Neither are they the Indians of anthropological record. Most of them have been well educated in American schools and colleges. . . . Some artists have chosen to remain on tribal reservations where the native pattern of the immediate environment alters in varying degrees with outer pressures of dominant influences. Others move in the general stream of American life, while retaining a knowledge and appreciation of their distinctive cultural heritage. Although all might produce paintings characteristic of the composite national genre, these artists prefer to offer to American art contributions that are uniquely their own, and which they know would be forever lost if they should not do so.[23]

Dunn pictures a seamless relationship between Indigenous heritage and life in the post–World War II United States. Her brand of Cold War multiculturalism married white desire for Indian authenticity to an integrationist vision of progress.[24]

We are invited to see art as evidence of the compatability of modernity and Indigeneity. Dunn asserts that the paintings are "contemporary in general appearance and individually inventive," yet they derive from "the oldest painting traditions in America."[25] The inclusion of works that thematized intermedial art-making appeared to support her vision of modern art education as a vehicle for the translation of Native cultures into a capitalist marketplace. Montoya's *Pueblo Crafts* (1938) features five industrious Pueblo women making painted pottery, weaving *mantas* (blankets fashioned as capes or dresses) and fitting deerskin moccasins (plate 3a). The scene suggests that craft creation remained embedded in customary lifeways, as the women are wearing versions of the clothing they labor to produce. Yet viewers are invited to admire a tableau of finely wrought wares in the process of being made, a spectacle of artisanal labor common to Santa Fe's booming twentieth-century art market.[26] *Pueblo Crafts* transfers this aura of authenticity from material culture to modern painting, positioning the relatively new medium within a continuity of economically viable Native artistic production.

Dunn cannily harnessed the nationalist sentiments driving support for Native art during the IRA era to an emergent Cold War rhetoric, asserting Native artists' individuality, mobility, freedom, and opportunity. By characterizing Native cultural continuity as a matter of choice, she smoothed over the federal government's energetic renewal of treaty abrogation and coerced assimilation after World War II. At the time of the exhibition, hardline supporters of Termination in the federal government had worked to purge the BIA of former IRA advocates and set the agency to the task of eliminating every "integration barrier" prior to its own planned obsolescence (which never came to pass). The IACB and the Studio School survived the assault as the least offensive institutional remnants of the prior policy era.[27] The composition of *Contemporary American Indian Paintings* largely supported the anachronism of Dunn's account. The vast majority of the works were created prior to World War II; only two painters, Velarde and Andrew Tsihnahjinnie of the Navajo Nation, lent paintings that were contemporaneous with the betrayals formalized by policymakers in the halls of Congress less than three months before the opening and just a few blocks from the NGA.[28] However, the paintings were left undated in the exhibition labels and brochure. These temporal slippages proved efficacious for Dunn's reinvention as a cold warrior, enabling her to export "a New Deal for Native art" as evidence of the government's success in modernizing Indigenous Americans.[29]

::::::::::

Nonetheless, *Contemporary American Indian Paintings* was deeply impacted by the convergence of art and politics in Washington, DC, in 1953. Dunn worked closely with founding director David Finley and long-standing chief curator John Walker, collectors of a Euro-American artistic canon, gatekeepers of aesthetic standards, and administrators of the DOS-funded international art program since 1944. Both men registered their ambivalence concerning the suitability of the paintings for the NGA as well as locations abroad. They temporarily withdrew their initial support for the exhibition when the board of trustees rejected the plan, only to change course and secure the approval of dissenting members when Dunn marshaled international opinion as a gavel. She called on the NGA to affirm "the nation's most native art . . . for reasons obvious to everyone at home and abroad" toward "proving to the nations of the world that the United States highly values the painting of its Indian citizens as a fine art of the primary mode."[30] This strategy revealed her keen grasp of Cold War soft power logics. Finley and Walker similarly raised, then abandoned, a proposal for *Contemporary American Indian Paintings* to circulate in Paris and other European locales. Walker erroneously wrote to Dunn that the paintings were not wanted at the "important French museums." Furthermore, the gallery could not dedicate the necessary staff, whereas the DOS was in the process of forming "a special office for that purpose."[31] This is an about-face, given that for most of the preceding decade, Finley and Walker were reluctant to relinquish the administration of the international art program to federal agents in an effort to protect the nation's great works from the taint of propaganda.[32] Why were these men so eager to hand Native American paintings over to the emergent USIA?

Finley personally collected Studio School paintings and loaned two works to the exhibition, suggesting that aesthetic prejudices were not the root cause of his and Walker's equivocation. I surmise that their commitment to *Contemporary American Indian Paintings* wavered in the face of mounting conflicts surrounding Termination, which erupted in the days leading up to the opening. A telling clue appears in a memorandum that Walker sent to Finley on October 20, 1953. He makes a special point of underscoring the omission of members of Congress and their staff from the list of invitees to the exhibition opening ("We <u>do not</u> plan to invite"), despite adding Eisenhower, his cabinet and staff, the Supreme Court, and a "Diplomatic List."[33] From his experience with the international art program, Walker was keenly aware that the nature and efficacy of art exhibitions in the Cold War cultural offensive abroad was contentious with members of Congress.[34] Bearing the same date in the exhibition archives, a joint newsletter issued by the American Indian Fund (AIF) and the Association on American Indian Affairs, the umbrella organization for which Dietrich worked, expounded on the "crisis in Indian Affairs." AIF chairman Oliver LaFarge wrote unstintingly, "Under the guise of giving Indians 'first-class citizenship' and 'political equality,' both legislative and executive branches are bound they will 'solve the Indian problem' by abruptly revoking the Federal protective relation. . . . The conscience of America must awaken if the worst Indian betrayal in a hundred years is to be averted."[35] LaFarge related that "angry protests and a strong movement for Presidential veto arose quickly among Indians of Oklahoma, New Mexico, Arizona, Washington, Utah, and the Dakotas," implicating nearly all of the communities to which the artists in the exhibition belonged.[36] Meanwhile the National Congress of American Indians and other Native groups condemned Termination as an assault on "our tribal governments as sovereign equals," "a total destruction of all tribes," "a financial invasion by white people," a cynical bid for "uranium land," and a "battle for survival."[37] Given the surge of Indigenous activism, a Congressional majority that was hostile to much art and all Native Americans, and their own longstanding reticence to mix art with politics, Walker and Finley had ample reason to shrink the spotlight on *Contemporary American Indian Paintings*.

Despite the domestic turmoil, Walker's proposed handoff of modern Native paintings from the NGA to the USIA quickly came to pass. Richard Brecker, chief of the exhibits branch of the USIA, requested such work for a Latin American tour following his visit to the NGA, "feeling Indian populations [there] would be particularly interested in seeing the similarity in costumes, customs, tribal legends, and events, shown in the paintings." Reportedly an exhibition of fifty paintings opened in Guatemala City in 1954 and ended in Caracas in 1955.[38] Another exhibition of sixty paintings selected by Harrison Kerr, dean of the College of Fine Arts at the University of Oklahoma, toured the British Isles and mainland Europe from Italy to Finland from 1955 to 1956 and Germany and Austria from 1960 to 1962, featuring translated versions of Dunn's NGA catalogue introduction.[39] Paintings from the Dietrich collection were subsequently paired with Native arts drawn from the Southwest Museum for an American Scandinavian Society–sponsored tour through Northern Europe from 1962 to 1964.[40] Dunn's organization of the "Near East" tour of *Contemporary American Indian Paintings from the*

:::::::::::

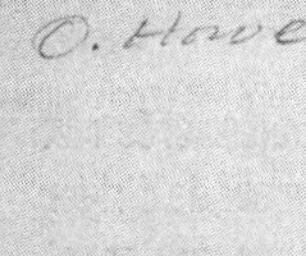
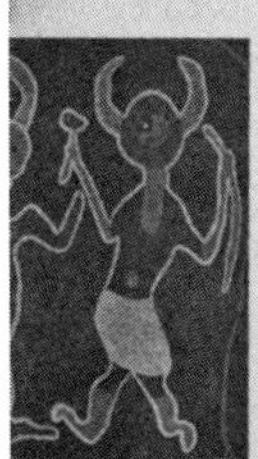
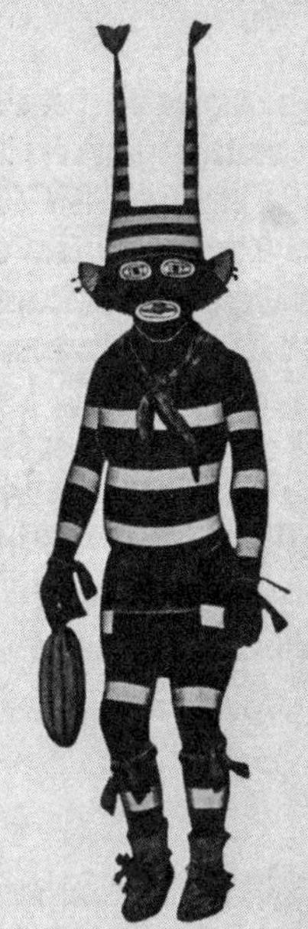

1.2

Artist Oscar Howe's personal copy of the exhibition catalogue, *Contemporary American Indian Paintings*, Royal Museums of Art and History in Brussels, August 16–December 28, 1955. Box 15, Folder 5. Oscar Howe papers, University papers, MS-072. USD Archives and Special Collections, I. D. Weeks Library, University of South Dakota, Vermillion, with permission of the Oscar Howe Family.

Margretta S. Dietrich Collection from 1964 to 1966, including further translations of her long-lived catalog introduction, marked the Studio School's last major involvement in Cold War exhibitions. As I will discuss in chapter 2, the baton was passed to its successor, the IAIA. However, Dunn continued to be an active member of the advisory committee for the Art in Embassies Program, an initiative of the Museum of Modern Art (MoMA) International Council established in 1960, which placed work by Native American and other United States artists in embassies around the world.[41] The NGA exhibition thus launched the Studio School's founder as a liaison for Cold War soft power and a leading author of USIA propaganda.

While Dunn had an outsized influence on government scripts, hers was but one of numerous tangled paths that Native artists traveled into the global Cold War. Her sanitized account of Indigenous modernisms could not hide evidence of the violent forms of colonization that shaped Native lives in tandem with global others. Nor could a framework of benign modernization control Native American arts' affective and interpretive potentials, whether or not the artists traveled by their side. Also included in the NGA archive is a form letter from LaFarge to Rogers urging her to contribute to the urgent fight against "the virtual confiscation of Indian lands and the demoralization of Indian family and community life"—that is, the federal onslaught against the very lifeways pictured in the paintings she patronized.[42] I will now follow the gesture of Roger's gloved hand toward Velarde's *The Betrothal* to more precisely envision the scope of this rhetorical and material battleground.

PABLITA VELARDE'S *THE BETROTHAL*

A centerpiece of the NGA exhibition, *The Betrothal* echoes LaFarge's words in locating kinship at the heart of contemporaneous political contestations. An engagement ritual unique to Kha-'Po Owingeh (Santa Clara Pueblo) is rendered in bright shades of tempera paint with a limited depth of field, little modeling, and sections of paper left bare. The scene draws upon Velarde's cultural upbringing as well as her subsequent training at the Studio School program from 1932 to 1936. A single vertical line meets a wood-beam ceiling, connoting the corner of a whitewashed adobe home. The central image of a domestic union between a youthful woman and man is ostensibly consonant with an enduring ideal of the nuclear family as the foundation of citizenship and private property in the United States. However, Velarde's all-over method grants equal priority to figures located at the edges of the paper. It is a composition suited to a holistic, rather than hierarchical, relational schema, situating the couple "within a wide field of familial feeling" beyond biological descent and heteronormative coupling.[43] For example, the bride-to-be's maternal relatives, who customarily host the betrothal ceremony, are shown with aprons tied over their calico dresses in the corner, as if on break from cooking in the modern kitchen visible through a doorway. They appear intent on a private conversation, an absorbing bond to which Velarde devoted equivalent painterly attention. The artist's even-handed approach to human bodies and material culture mirrors Ohkay Owingeh (formerly San Juan Pueblo) anthropologist Alfonso Ortiz's description of Pueblo ritual and worldview, in which "everything—animate and inanimate—counts and everything has its place in the cosmos."[44] In *The Betrothal*, kinship operates as a more-than-human system of social equivalences, interdependencies, and responsibilities.

Specifically, Velarde pictured a gift economy in motion. Woolen blankets and earthen vessels fill the arms of the relatives who form a loose semicircle around the couple. As Ramón A. Guitérrez has examined, Pueblo engagement rituals followed principles of cosmic harmony and reciprocity to ensure the peoples' peaceful alliances with one another and the earth before and during colonization.[45] Exceeding the couple's bond, gifting perpetuates a vast social mesh necessary to the continuation of all life. The circuit of reciprocities includes humans, plants, animals, and ancestors, including the Corn Mothers, original givers of the seeds of all life.[46] The young woman and man are blessed with eagle feathers by an elderly ceremonial leader who is responsible for conjoining human and divine. They grasp the handle of a double-spouted wedding vase from which those present will drink sacred, life-giving liquids to consecrate the union.[47] The artwork Velarde represented would have been hand-coiled from local clay by skilled women in the groom's family, burnished to a high gloss, painted with a vegetal slip to create the image of a stepped thunderbird in matte, and fired in a low-oxygen environment to produce the "black on black" effect prized within the twentieth-century pottery movement.[48] Made of Nung-quijo ("Clay-old-lady" in Tewa), such vessels present the earth as a maternal relative that shapes both the artform and the impending marriage.[49] In the leftmost corner of the room hangs a carved wooden *katsina*, a figure imbued with the spirit of honored ancestors who become clouds upon death. Such benevolent beings visit the pueblos during the ceremonial

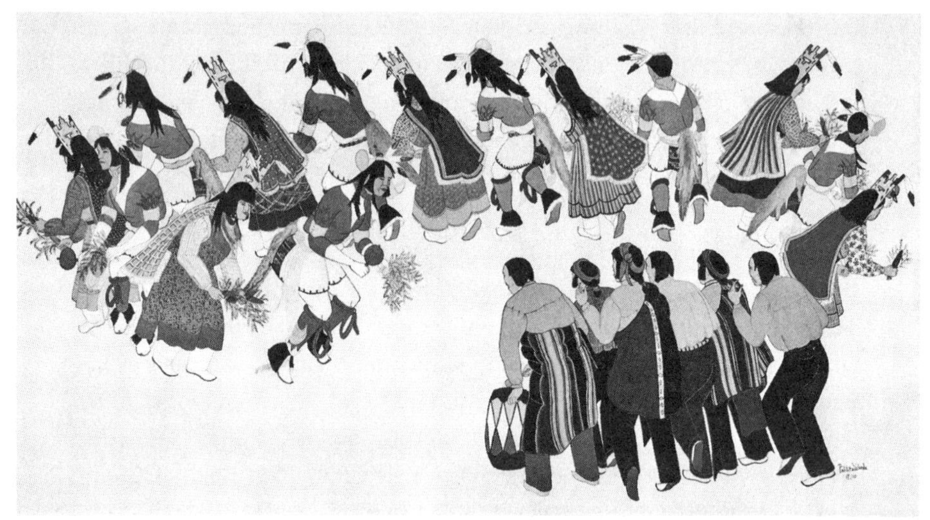

1.3

Pablita Velarde, *Santa Clara Corn Dance*, 1940. Tempera on board, 19.5 × 17.25 in., Margretta Dietrich Collection, Museum of Indian Arts and Culture, 5394/12.

....

season to receive prayers and gifts in exchange for sending precious rain needed to germinate seeds and nourish all life. Elsewhere Velarde joined her Pueblo peers in regularly chronicling the more-than-human dimensions of reciprocity by painting public rituals of gratitude for the annual harvest, exemplified by *Santa Clara Corn Dance* (1940), another of her works exhibited at the NGA.[50]

The activities foregrounded in *The Betrothal*—praying and receiving blessings, feasting, and redistributing material and spiritual wealth through gifting—constitute rituals of adoption that create new kin beyond the bounds of biological descent. More than passive inheritance, Indigenous kinship is "best thought of as a verb . . . that link[s] the People, the land, and the cosmos together in an ongoing and dynamic system of mutually affecting relationships," writes Cherokee literary scholar Daniel Heath Justice.[51] Velarde's detailed tableaus conjoin multiple means of making kin, from betrothing to cooking, coiling, weaving, and dancing, treating each as facets of a more-than-human social continuum. *The Betrothal* furthermore signals a world in which the expansive kinship bonds forged during engagement rituals constitute a resilient form of geopolitics.[52] The boldly patterned Diné textile beneath the couple's feet points to an "intertribal matrix" in which intermarriage, trade,

:::::::::::

feasts, and gifts forge alliances among distinct human polities.[53] Velarde visualizes betrothal as coextensive with enduring Pueblo practices of earth diplomacy.

There are additional hints that *The Betrothal* was composed *for* the arena of conflict described by LaFarge. Here I follow literary scholar Mark Rifkin's proposal that we understand the rhetoric of kinship as "indexing a history of indigenous-settler struggle rather than as merely describing particular arrangements of *home* and *family*."[54] The couple is visibly grounded in—literally standing upon—a modern market system that transformed Diné wearing blankets into "rugs" to suit a particular vision of conjugal domesticity in the decades preceding *The Betrothal* (see chapter 3). Industrial technologies—an oven, gridded windows framed with billowing blue curtains, and what appears to be a black-and-white photographic portrait on the back wall—provide further material evidence of colonial-capitalism that has clashed and intermingled with a Pueblo gift economy and shaped the most intimate spaces of Native life since the arrival of European settlers in the sixteenth century. While an extensive pre–Cold War history of Pueblo marriages is beyond the scope of *Earth Diplomacy*, Guitérrez helpfully summarizes the durability of Indigenous frameworks under Spanish dominion: "Popular custom and canon law were seriously at odds concerning the importance and significance of the betrothal." Friars typically understood the church wedding ceremony to be the binding contract in the eyes of their Christian God. But Pueblo communities continued to prioritize prenuptial rituals centered on forging alliances by gifting and making kin.[55] Betrothals perpetuated systems of more-than-human reciprocity in excess of Christian weddings. They remained vital at Kha-'Po Owingeh following the United States' control of New Mexico in 1848.[56] The inclusion of industrially manufactured objects in Velarde's domestic scene hints at the contemporaneity and transculturalism of Kha-'Po Owingeh betrothals as a hard-won means of political survival.

Seen through the lens of contested kinship, Termination belongs to "a multivalent history of heteronormativity in which alternative configurations of home, family, and political collectivity are represented as endangering the state," writes Rifkin. Kinship structures that assign the powers and responsibilities of leadership to women, treat nonbinary individuals as sacred, and bring strangers, plants, animals, and the earth into the familial-political fold are cast as primitive formations that threaten the rationality and cohesion of the colonial nation.[57] Such practices challenge setter sovereignty precisely because they extend beyond the Euro-American construction of a private domestic sphere to shape Native land tenure, consensus decision-making, and international relations. Indigenous kinship constitutes a practice of diplomacy that is fundamentally at odds with a US expansionist logic of land as white property.[58] These tensions shaped the passage of the Dawes Act (also known as the General Allotment Act) of 1887, a federal project to break up collectively held Indigenous homelands into private plots and appoint a male head of the nuclear family as owner, while opening up the vast remaining territory to white settlement and extraction. The policy ushered in a new era of Native peoples' forced assimilation into the heteronormative legal-political structures of modern capitalism and nationhood.[59] The Dawes Act provided the congressional model for Termination as a "return to the historic principles of much earlier decades" to "treat the Indian of today . . . as a fellow American citizen" as Senator Arthur Watkins of Utah put it in 1957.[60]

A brief glimpse of Velarde's fraught relationship with her home pueblo locates a marriage-property continuum on the frontlines of a renewed federal assimilationist project that touched nearly every aspect of twentieth-century Native life. Born and partially raised at Kha-'Po Owingeh, the artist painted *The Betrothal* in her kitchen studio in Albuquerque, where she lived with her husband, Herbert Hardin, a white police officer, and their two children. In accordance with a 1939 Kha-'Po Owingeh Tribal Council decision, her marriage to an outsider dispossessed her descendants of their tribal membership and rights to inherit their mother's land. In contrast, Kha-'Po Owingeh men who married women outside the pueblo retained their children's privileges. Ostensibly an exercise of self-determination, the 1939 policy was in fact a legacy of the IRA, which empowered the BIA to oversee the formation of the Tribal Council and constitution four years earlier. The resulting separation of religious and secular matters in the pueblo displaced the broad authority of ceremonial leaders such as the elder shown blessing the betrothal in Velarde's painting.[61] It also thoroughly diminished the customary matrilineal structures described by Kha-'Po Owingeh citizen and ethnographer Edward Dozier in 1970: "The women are the most important members of the [household] unit; they own the house, are responsible for the preparation and distribution of food, make all the important decisions, and care for the ritual possessions of the family. . . . Men born into the household and lineage leave the house when they marry."[62] Dozier noted that with the advent of a capitalist wage economy, the situation had changed.[63] In the 1940s, anthropologist W. W. Hill similarly

:::::::::   CHAPTER ONE observed that homes were owned by men and patrilineally inherited.[64] These relationalities, so often naturalized in ethnographic literature, constitute a site of settler-colonial intervention coextensive with the broader arc of federal Indian policy.

Velarde recalled drawing criticism as a "very single girl in the pueblo" who pursued an idiosyncratic vocation as a professional artist. She used proceeds from her paintings to build her own home and studio on land given to her by her father during World War II.[65] "Painting was not considered woman's work in my time. A woman was supposed to be just a woman, like a housewife and a mother and chief cook. Those were things I wasn't interested in," she stated in a 1979 interview.[66] Efforts to straighten the queer shape of Pueblo kinship further framed media attention to Velarde's work as a painter, obscuring the artist's negotiations with the imposition of patriarchy and property at Kha-'Po Owingeh. Dunn led the way in a feature for *National Geographic* in 1955, which included full-page color reproductions of *The Betrothal*, *Corn Dance*, and sixteen other paintings, mostly drawn from the NGA exhibition. In the lengthy accompanying article, "America's First Painters," she detailed artists' modern lives and Indigenous inspirations, concluding that "Indian painting from every standpoint is inherently and uniquely American."[67] Dunn's contribution coincided with a rapid increase in *National Geographic*'s largely white, middle-class subscribers, who may have found comfort in the magazine's race- and class-free narrative of a tumultuous globe.[68] Her article garnered a flood of letters from readers in the United Kingdom, Australia, New Zealand, and elsewhere. Readers requested prints of the paintings and extolled their potential to "obtain a bridge of sympathy between the young people of all the world."[69]

Dunn's description of *The Betrothal* cropped a sanctioned image of conjugal domesticity from the troubling ecosocial mesh depicted: "Despite the wealth of details and interests, this composition is well organized to emphasize the three principal characters—the bride-to-be, wearing a white manta embroidered with fertility symbols; the prospective groom, in festive calico shirt and beaded leggings; and the *cacique*, head of all ceremonials," surrounded by "spotless whitewashed walls."[70] A virginal white dress, a religious officiator, a well-kept home, and a hint of future children—Dunn selectively highlights elements that best rhyme with Christian marital rites and priorities enshrined in the US legal-political system. Her discussion of Velarde's biography follows suit. Upon recounting the painter's growing professional successes, Dunn offered her international readers reassurance that the woman was nonetheless a dutiful wife and mother: "Now Miss Velarde, painting more than ever while managing a home for her husband and two children, is becoming known abroad." Dunn closes with a sentimental story of an English woman who, having done anthropological work at Kha-'Po Owingeh in the past, reportedly mailed Velarde a copy of a photograph taken of her father and mother on their wedding day in 1910.[71]

In the assimilative logic of Dunn's article, Velarde's painting and childbearing are equated in the service of transmitting a dyadic familial norm across generations—a reproduction deemed necessary, Rifkin argues, for Native peoples' deliverance from a prepolitical condition of primitivity into legitimate US citizenship. Journalists repeated the image of Velarde as a white man's wife living in a white man's home, even after her divorce in 1958 and subsequent return to Kha-'Po Owingeh to devote herself full-time to painting.[72] Velarde and her painted stove became Indian accessories to the normative script argued by Richard Nixon during his famous "kitchen debate" with Soviet premier Nikita Khrushchev at the opening of the American National Exhibition in Moscow in 1959 (which notably featured *The Family of Man*). "To us, diversity, the right to choose . . . is the most important thing," declared the president of the United States. "We have many different manufacturers and many different kinds of washing machines so that the housewives have a choice."[73] *The Betrothal* quietly indexes a cosmopolitical relationality in excess of such rhetorical and material assimilations. Tucked under the front edge of a textile in the lower right, the signature reading "PABLITA VELARDE 1953" eschewed the Euro-American convention of assuming one's husband's surname while tangibly connecting the artist's identity to the capacious kinship matrix depicted.

PROPAGANDA FRONTIERS

If distinct arrangements of kinship and cosmopolitics defined Native communities' embattled relationship to the United States following Indian Removal, the Cold War created unprecedented avenues for these conflicts to shape, and be shaped by, international relations. The US government was pressed to respond not only to the growing force of Native resistance movements inside its borders but also, crucially, to the USSR's inflammatory rhetoric. A 1951 article in *Pravda*, the Communist Party of the Soviet Union newspaper, "Answers to Readers' Questions: Tragedy of Indians in the U.S.A.," compared BIA officials to "fascist hangmen." A 1957 article in *Krasnaya Zvezda*, a newspaper issued by the Soviet Ministry of Defense, denigrated the "freedom zealots across the Atlantic" for denying Native nations' rights to self-determination, a situation that the United States was "trying to foist on other countries and peoples."[74] Historian Lucie Kýrová finds that newspaper articles about Native Americans published in former Czechoslovakia and international Communist journals in the 1950s and 1960s presented Native Americans as a once-proud community broken by white greed and racism. Photographs reproduced in such articles often contrasted the visages of nineteenth-century leaders in customary regalia with images of poverty and hard labor on contemporary reservations.[75] In step, the internationally popular mythos of the Wild West was plumbed for political efficacy. During the opening credits for a Soviet-era print of John Ford's *Stagecoach* (1939), intertitles drew viewers' attention to the United States' mistreatment of Native peoples. Meanwhile, "red westerns" filmed on an expanding Soviet frontier in Eastern Europe and South Asia revised the classical Hollywood format by presenting cowboys as violent, greedy capitalists.[76]

Soviet propagandists marshaled the ugly story of Native American genocide and removal in the United States to contrast with the USSR's supposedly enlightened treatment of Indigenous groups in Siberia. During the reign of Joseph Stalin, northward expansion was celebrated for opening up large swaths of land to agriculture and trade. Soviet conquest was posited as uniquely rational and benevolent, "as opposed to the parasitic colonization of the New World by the Anglo-Saxons and Spaniards, who had used for the purpose bands of adventurers, vagabonds and criminals."[77] While European and US colonialism led to cultural stagnation for everyone involved, the Soviet variant supposedly involved progress for Indigenous communities. The USSR promised to extend the same experience to international allies.[78] Although an extensive assessment of such propaganda lies beyond the concerns of this book, I will note that the post-Stalinist regime entailed a wave of Indigenous assimilation and relocation policies similar to those enacted by the United States, clearing the way for unprecedented oil, gas, mineral, timber, and hydroelectric development.[79] Siberia was a dumping ground for nuclear and chemical waste, mirroring the United States' irradiation of the Navajo Nation and other Indigenous territories in the process of developing the Cold War military-industrial complex.[80] This was a propaganda war between settler-colonial superpowers with a shared investment in advancing frontiers of extraction.

The US government and a cadre of unofficial cold warriors responded to Soviet propaganda with a contradictory and ever-shifting stream of images and narratives that recycled key elements from their competitor. Federal spokespeople were forced to acknowledge, and even review, the crimes of the United States, including broken treaties, wars, and displacements of Native people from sacred homelands. However, as the story went, these were atrocities of the nineteenth century. Historian Andrew Denson examines how Voice of America, the USIA's international radio broadcast, framed US Indian policy as "a moral political drama, in which American democracy overcame the nation's history of greed and racial hatred."[81] During a serial program, *American Indian: Past and Present*, in 1965, announcer Wayne Hyde assured international listeners that "the treatment given to Indians by the government a century ago is on the conscience of the white man." However, the United States was "working very hard to make up for lost time [. . .] and to offer the Indian of the future some of the opportunities he was denied many years ago."[82] In 1962, a Native American–themed issue of *Амерuка: America Illustrated*, a Russian-language magazine circulated by the USIA in the Soviet Union, presented the case of Native leaders who wisely chose to "join the twentieth century" by exploiting the oil, uranium, and other mineral wealth "hidden beneath the barren and empty lands of the tribes."[83] A companion essay, "Indian Art Yesterday and Today," featured reproductions of a broad array of Native art, from precolonial stone carvings to the gleaming black-on-black pottery of San Ildefonso artist Maria Martinez. Virginia Olsen presented the work as "samples of that wealth, past and present, which became an inalienable part of America's artistic thought."[84] In an echo of Dunn's rhetoric, the presentation of a seamless aesthetic and cultural continuum from precolonial to present times obscured the cyclic violence of federal Indian policy.

The material consequences of the US-USSR propaganda wars flowed between Indigenous and majority world nations, albeit in uneven and contradictory ways. Supporters of Termination harnessed an intensifying Cold War rhetoric of anti-Communism, individualism, Americanism, and liberation to justify the abrogation of treaties. They variously compared Native American reservations to racialized concentration camps and emasculated Communist collectives—"either an oppressive or dangerously subversive space from which Indians wanted to be freed."[85] The Harry S. Truman administration hired BIA officials to administer a Point Four Program designed to integrate African, Asian, and Latin

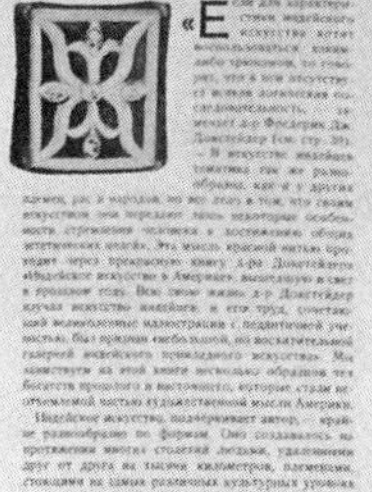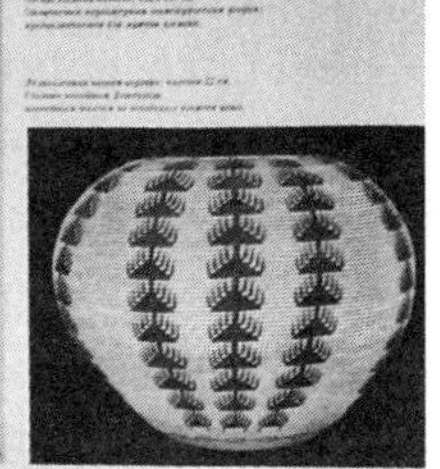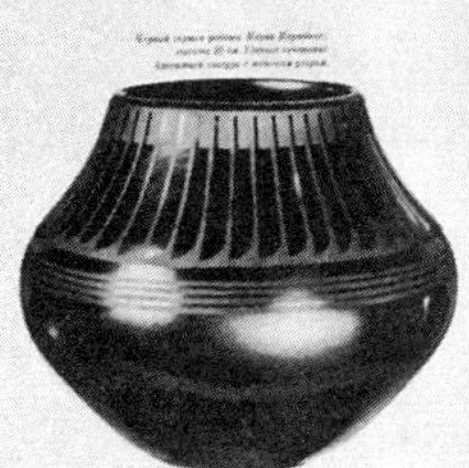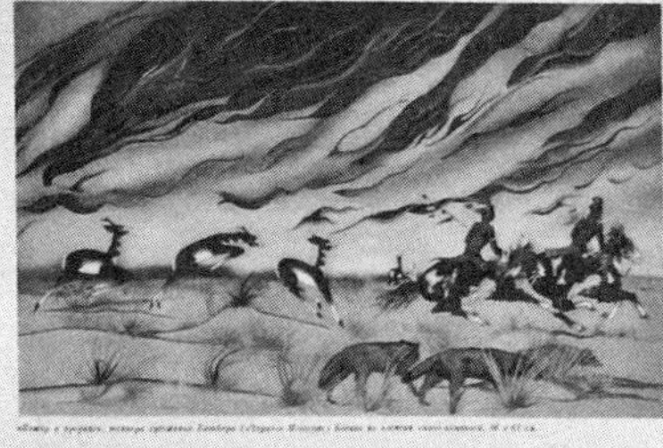

1.4

Virginia Olsen, "Indian Art, Yesterday and Today," *Америка: America Illustrated* (1962), 34–35.

....

American countries into the US model of a free-market economy, based on their experiences offering "special services" to Native nations. The diplomatic benefits of the connection unraveled, however, when Indigenous and international critics attacked the BIA's role in implementing the dissolution of Native American sovereignty.[86] Native leaders wielded international opinion and decolonization movements abroad as a moral cudgel in the face of Termination. Scholars have credited this tactic alongside direct action spectacles for curbing and eventually halting the dispossessive policy in the 1960s.[87] Kýrová and historian György Ferenc Tóth have further noted that narratives emphasizing Native victimhood abroad gradually turned toward a recognition of Indigenous Americans as agents of their own futures. While these authors attribute the transformation to international alliance-building and press coverage during the American Indian Movement (AIM, discussed in chapter 5 and the conclusion of this book), Native artists were already laying a path in the 1950s.[88]

Despite the USIA's efforts to separate the colonial past from the multicultural present, a nineteenth-century frontier mythos was nowhere near exhausted. On the contrary, nostalgia for the Old West was repurposed in political rhetoric and popular culture to legitimize the United States' military and moral leadership of a globe threatened by Soviet enemies. Truman set the tone in a 1951 speech arguing for the necessity of reviving traditional American values "dating back to the frontier days when all members of every family had a task to do in defending their homes and their stockades from marauding savages."[89] The Eisenhower administration's launch of a civil defense program in 1953 similarly presented "nuclear housekeeping" as a patriotic frontier legacy and contemporary moral imperative. The script targeted suburban, middle-class white families as pioneering cold warriors, charged with enacting a heteronormative regime of cleanliness, surveillance, and self-reliance to ensure the nation's survival in case of atomic attack.[90] Hollywood films, TV shows, novels, children's books, and comics further disseminated the story of frontier forebears who "fought to give us our great American Heritage of opportunity, security, and freedom" internationally.[91] Consider the travels of Dell Publishing's famous cowboy-and-Indian duo, the Lone Ranger and Tonto, through Norway, Uruguay, Hong Kong, South Africa, and beyond.[92] Historian Victoria M. Grieve argues that the masked cowboy acted as a symbol of freedom and justice who would "teach Americanism around the world," while his Indian sidekick cast white pioneers' relationships with Indigenous people as a form of benevolent guardianship that the United States was poised to extend to foreign allies.[93] Native Americans' symbolic role in Cold War plotlines thus proved to be malleable. It shifted from dangerous foreign threat to weaker companion in need of protection, modeling the civilizing value of free market capitalism and allyship with the United States.

SOLOMON MCCOMBS'S *CREEK WOMAN'S RIBBON DANCE*

McCombs encountered this propaganda firsthand upon becoming "the first American Indian good will ambassador to be sent abroad" by the DOS in 1954. Born into a prominent Mvskoke Baptist family on a farm in Oklahoma in 1913, McCombs was a citizen of the Muscogee (Creek) Nation in Oklahoma. In 1930, he enrolled in Bacone Indian College, founded by his Scottish granduncle, the Reverend William McCombs. In 1936 he joined the college's modern Native art program (1935–present), established by Acee Blue Eagle, his cousin and lifelong mentor. McCombs worked as a draftsman, designer, and illustrator for the US General

:::::::::

Services Administration from 1950 until 1956 and subsequently for the DOS until his retirement in 1973.[94] He was invited to participate in the DOS International Educational Exchange Service (IEES) tour abroad after a solo exhibition of his paintings at the IACB Gallery in Washington, DC, garnered attention from a DOS official in February of 1954.[95] He would go on to give around thirty public lectures and three radio interviews alongside twenty of his paintings that traveled to Syria, Jordan, Lebanon, Kenya, Uganda, Belgian Congo, Libya, India, and Burma from 1954 to 1955. McCombs's two distinct trip reports, directed to the Creek Indian Council (1956) and the DOS (undated), illuminate Indigenous-majority world relations in a period of upheaval for the Muscogee (Creek) Nation. Unpacking the dialogue between the artist, his Mvskoke kin, and the DOS in words and paint offers a vivid glimpse of the stakes of earth diplomacy for Native nations in the Termination era.

In "My Report to the Creek Nation: Experiences and Observations Abroad," McCombs expressed his hope that news of his tour might "encourage others to develop their talent" and "be of some help" to Mvskoke.[96] The chairman and secretary of the Creek Indian Council responded by declaring the people's pride in claiming an "intelligent, dependable, and loyal diplomat."[97] McCombs was communicating with a relatively new advisory body selected by a principal chief. In 1951, the secretary of the Interior began to appoint chiefs as top authorities within the nation, in tension with the customary leadership of the long-standing de facto National Council of the Muscogee (Creek) Nation. Legal scholars Sarah Deer (Muscogee [Creek] Nation) and Cecelia Knapp have assessed how the National Council adapted the power vested in matrilineal clans and local leaders of *etvlwvs*, agrarian towns that functioned as autonomous, allied polities prior to federal removal of a majority of Mvskoke from the Southeast (present-day Alabama, Georgia, Florida, and South Carolina) to Indian Territory (present-day Oklahoma) in the 1830s.[98] In this system, consensus-based decision-making is circular (not hierarchical) and aims to make "allies of humans and nature. Therefore, the natural propensity of all elements is movement in concert, but this movement implies no direction, linear or otherwise. In this world view, all creatures and events have an *ab initio* right to being, and consequent right to acceptance."[99] This ecopolitical model was aggregated in the Mvskoke Confederacy and formalized by a written Constitution of 1867 in response to colonial incursions. The US government effectively ended recognition of the Mvskoke government during the allotment era leading up to Oklahoma statehood in 1907. Yet, as Deer and Knapp explain, the National Council continued to operate "legitimately in the shadows" by maintaining and adapting core components of Mvskoke cosmology. Self-governance continued in the *etvlwvs* until 1974 when, at the crest of AIM, these local Mvskoke leaders successfully sued the federal government and restored recognition of the 1867 Constitution.[100] McCombs, who retired from the DOS in 1973 and moved to Tulsa, served as second chief of the resurgent nation from 1978 until his death in 1980.[101] "Fluent in the Mvsokoke language, he articulated his vision for continued kinship building," recalls his niece, Reverend Rosemary McCombs Maxey.[102]

Willie C. Jones, a member of the Creek Indian Council and Advisory Board to the Principal Chief, hinted at the challenges facing the nation in a remarkable letter to the artist in October 1955. Jones requested a detailed report on McCombs's tour to present at a future council meeting. He described how Mvskoke were "honored with this diplomatic position," owing "a debt of thanks for the distance you have traveled in the name of justice and welfare of our minority race." Jones gestured toward Termination in stating that the United States wanted to "emancipate our restricted fullblood Indian people within a few short years," and "see all Indians self-supporting as other citizens." Then, in a striking departure, he went on to imagine a scenario in which

> we the Indians take our fight for justice straight to the floor of the General Assembly of the United Nations and let all nations united in this world organization hear our cry and plea, and state that we the Indians had rights under the terms of the Genocide Pact or Convention Treaty approved during the Truman's administration. Now, I would appreciate your views and opinions as to the possibility or chances of Oklahoma Indians sending their own delegates or representatives to this UN soon or later. . . . It is hoped that a national leader like you will some day take a responsible place or seat, in representing our tribes, to let our voice be heard the world over.

This revealing portion of Jones's missive foreshadowed the path of Indigenous earth diplomacy in the 1970s, when the International Indian Treaty Council of AIM and the World Council of Indigenous Peoples would assert the rights of sovereign peoples at the United Nations (see the conclusion of this book). At the same time, Jones held open multiple doors to furthering Indigenous political causes, including federal sponsorship of artistic modernisms. In this spirit, he closed by pledging to

:::::::::   CHAPTER ONE

McCombs, "We the Indians here in Oklahoma will be with you wherever you may be, and *what ever work you may be engaged in for the Indian justice*" (my emphasis).[103] I read "we the Indians" as an admonishment to a relative located near the seat of colonial power to remain loyal to the plight of Mvskoke and American Indians at large.

How did McCombs respond to Jones's call to accountability? Notably, his eighteen-page "My Report to the Creek Nation" differed in focus from the pithy five-page "Report of American Indian Art Exhibit and Lecture Tour" that he evidently delivered to the DOS. While the former offered detailed observations about the cultural, political, and economic conditions of the places he visited, the latter focused almost entirely on artistic developments. In the only section repeated verbatim in both reports, the artist invoked the fraught language of kinship to discuss foreigners' attitudes toward American Indians, which were generally derived from Hollywood films. "Consequently," McCombs wrote, "they do not distinguish between fact and fancy, truth and misrepresentation. I learned that most of the people had developed a strong and sympathetic feeling towards American Indians, probably based on the universal feeling of pity for the underdogs fighting an overwhelming force. They seem to have a feeling of kinship, perhaps from a sense of foreboding that a similar fate may be in store for them. I made every effort to correct false ideas and misunderstandings as I found them."[104] While McCombs found many of his majority world hosts to be uncritical consumers of US popular culture, they nonetheless fit the "romantic, colorful and sometimes pathetic" Indians of Hollywood into a geopolitical imaginary shaped by a profound imbalance of power. Put another way, they stopped short of believing in the Lone Ranger's benevolence. This is the closest McCombs came to criticizing the United States government. Yet he deemed shared victimhood to be an inadequate foundation for establishing common cause with strangers. What other grounds for kinship might he have explored with his international hosts?

Throughout "My Report to the Creek Nation," McCombs was preoccupied less with the fact of shared oppression than the myriad ways that communities abroad adapted to the forces of colonialism and imperialism on the ground. The outcomes he observed cover a spectrum from bare survival to genuine flourishing. Throughout the Middle East, he found people "westernized," but nonetheless maintaining "their old ways of life and habits." He drew parallels between the poverty he encountered in certain Asian, African, and Indigenous American communities, noting for example that "pretty much the same conditions exist in some of the Indian countries of the Southwest." The situation was most dire in Patna, India, where he saw "people swarm up and down the street amidst rickshaws, cars, if any, and sacred cows." He reflected, "The cities of this kind were dusty and it was difficult to breathe at times, but nevertheless, there were all kinds of activity and people went about their business."[105] McCombs repeatedly observed how customary lifeways—including relationships with nonhumans such as "sacred cows"—continued amid poverty and environmental degradation.

Three passages locate McCombs's readers within the expansive legacies of British colonization in Africa and Asia, giving political contours to his emphasis on cultural endurance. In the first instance, the artist noted that his airplane was delayed in landing in Nairobi because of military planes "taking off to do some bombing of the Mau Mau." He described a grim cityscape of schools and homes enclosed in barbed wire, of deserted streets where "British soldiers patrolled . . . night and day."[106] McCombs arrived in the midst of the colonial government's offensive against the Kenya Land and Freedom Army (rebels known as the Mau Mau), who sustained a movement that culminated in Kenya's independence from British rule in 1963. In the second instance, the artist describes a conversation with educators in Bangalore:

> They were surprised to learn that American Indians still retained their traditions, customs, and still practiced some of the ceremonial dances despite the impact of civilization and education. It reminded them of their own people who have absorbed many western customs, but still followed traditional practices. I told them in the remote past the Creeks wore turbans similar to theirs which they still wear. They think that the British introduced the turbans to the Creeks and other Eastern tribes during the early settlement of the British in America, having observed the custom of wearing them during their contacts with the Indians of India.[107]

The violence of the first scene has settled in the second. In this account, both Indians and American Indians maintained and reinvented distinct lifeways under parallel British occupations. Similar headwear conjured their mutual enmeshment in the material-cultural networks of colonial modernity. In these moments, McCombs's report suggests that his tour became an opportunity to locate kinship in shared history—one defined not only by violence and oppression but by sustained creative adaptation. At the same time, the ruptures of decolonization he witnessed in Kenya shadow McCombs's neutral language in this passage, reminding us that the persistence of turbans, sacred cows, and ceremony was hard won.

In a final section, McCombs expressed deep admiration for Burma, where he encountered "brown, cheerful faces," "bright, colorful attire," and "vast expanses of rice fields, rich teak forests." Everywhere was evidence of the long-standing vitality of Buddhism. Once an empire in its own right, Burma shed British and Japanese colonial occupations after World War II to become, in McCombs's view, "one of the most interesting and colorful independent republics in Asia." Neglecting widespread civil unrest and repression of ethnic minorities underway in the 1950s, his ecstatic, touristic descriptions transform the final stop of his lecture tour into the fantasy of a postcolonial promised land. The passage invites the question of what might be possible were Mvskoke to achieve equivalent independence.[108]

Ultimately, McCombs delivered sunny prospects to the Creek Indian Council about the possibilities for overcoming "false ideas and misunderstandings" and establishing common cause through genuine dialogue with artists, teachers, and political actors in the majority world. He was deeply gratified by the "serious and sincere" questions he received about Indigenous Americans. When poor English presented barriers to basic communication, both parties supplemented with body language and "got along very well."[109] The possibilities for cultivating kinship internationally were not bound by the language of the colonizer. Yet McCombs never named a specific political ambition for the search for a shared (nonverbal) language abroad. Certainly he did not place this project in sole service of the United States or the Muscogee (Creek) Nation. Such possibilities were open-ended; they might answer DOS hopes to provide models of Indigenous modernization in the majority world, but equally they might lead to trans-Indigenous alliances at the United Nations.

At the outset of this book, I indicated that Indigenous arts of earth diplomacy are not merely political, but *cosmopolitical* agents; the "one to be ready to die for" is less the historically contingent nation than the vital holism of land and sky, the capacious context for customary Indigenous kinship and geopolitics.[110] It is to artistic modernisms, including McCombs's writing about them, that I now turn for a more complete response to Jones's letter.

In "Report of American Indian Art Exhibit and Lecture Tour," McCombs relates that his hosts were "intelligently interested in learning first hand about American Indian Art. They would spend considerable time studying each painting as though they were trying to make sure they saw and understood every detail. . . . In Africa and in Asia it created great interest because of its similarity to some of the old world art, even down to the details of some of the designs." The generator of these likenesses was not a universal primitivism but the imposition of modernization paradigms that necessitated creative adaptation. McCombs described "a movement to revive their own native art which parallels the movement in this country." He saw new forms of illustration and painting emerging alongside the revitalization of customary forms. These efforts were headquartered in government-run schools for arts and crafts that notably received funding from the Truman administration's Point Four program.[111] This DOS-administered support targeted so-called underdeveloped countries for technical assistance in the fields of agriculture, public health, and education, explicitly mapping policies toward American Indians onto the Cold War offensive abroad.[112] Bolstering his attention to creative agencies in "My Report to the Creek Nation," McCombs ultimately directs his account of artistic modernization toward vivid illustrations of the local creativities stimulated by his visit. At American University of Beirut, an art student experimented with colored earth and plant juices as painting supplies. At Makerere College in Kampala, Uganda, another "decided to try out the American Indian way of staining color on pottery." Inspired by McCombs's demonstrations of Indigenous practices, the students used "the simple materials they had to create beauty."[113] McCombs provides a succinct illustration of the potential for top-down government initiatives—from modern art programs to Cold War tours—to occasion lateral, embodied, sensuous exchanges. These experiments relied on distinct artistic materials sourced from local ecologies, the other-than-human gifts that support earth diplomacy.

How might McCombs's own paintings, which emphasized "the removals, the suffering, the ceremonials and the hunting" of Mvskoke, have contributed to these exchanges? The artist evidently spoke in detail about each of one of the twenty works that traveled. Unfortunately, no list survives in the archives I consulted. Instead, I look to *Creek Woman's Ribbon Dance* (1949), a prize-winning painting from the collection of the Philbrook Art Center (now Philbrook Museum) that toured the United States under the auspices of the Smithsonian Institution's Traveling Exhibition Service in 1954, for clues (plate 3b).[114] It offers a characteristic glimpse of a mobile artistic practice centered on customary Mvskoke lifeways. While McCombs worked for the federal government in Washington, DC, he used his annual vacations to return to the "wide open spaces" of his "real home" (his family farm in Oklahoma) during vacations.[115] According to Maxey, he brought gifts to his many family members, from button-down shirts to used automobiles.[116] During such visits, he attended the Hvsē Opvnkv (Ribbon Dance), the centerpiece of the annual Posketv (Green Corn Ceremony) and the repeated subject of his paintings.[117]

In *Creek Woman's Ribbon Dance*, a spare selection of dancing bodies and stylized plants prioritizes specific, gendered relationships between Mvskoke and their more-than-human kin. The sharply delineated figures occupy a shallow depth of field and an unarticulated cream background. Dancers dressed in long skirts, colorful blouses, patterned shawls, and moccasins form an arc in the middle ground. The frontmost two women carry willow branches "to gather up the prayers of the people" and feed a nearby fire that emits furls of sacred white smoke.[118] A second line of dancers moves in the opposite direction in the background, seeming to exit the frame. The curvilinear formation suggests that the women form a continuous line interrupted only by the edge of the matrix, reflecting the "large, expanding, dynamic counterclockwise spiral" of the live dance.[119] While older women appear to head the dance procession, three small figures—evidently young girls—constitute the tail. Long blue and red ribbons stream from their hair, shoulders, and hands, rippling against the cream background and granting a sense of movement and connection among the otherwise self-contained figures. At the far right, two seated men strike large, round drums. Their open mouths suggest song.

Several stylized, leafy bushes and tufts of grass establish a groundline at the bottom front, while a slender stalk laden with an ear of corn juts horizontally from a gray, moon-like circle positioned in the upper right corner. Sky-born, the corn-and-moon cornice presides over the scene but is not wholly of it; the element signals the cyclical and eternal dimensions of the Green Corn Ceremony. McCombs references the first full moon after the summer harvest, when Posketv was customarily held, prior to the regulation of ceremony by the modern work week in the twentieth century.[120] Lines feather across the surface of the orb and drip down the edge of the support. Watercolor paint turns back into nourishing rain. Or is it sweat? Maxey recalls her uncle's admiration for the dancers who carried on "hour after hour after hour" in the hot July sun.[121]

Like the enduring National Council, Hvsē Opvnkv is an inheritance from McCombs's Mvskoke ancestors who survived the deadly Trail of Tears. Mvskoke geographer Laura Harjo credits the ceremonial dances with maintaining the values and knowledge associated with the corn harvest and *etvlwvs* throughout centuries of colonial assimilation. She describes leaving the contemporary dances with a sense connection between "songs sung in the present and the realization that our Mvskoke relatives sang on the earth before those of us who sing today were materially present, demonstrating and teaching a deep gratitude, singing when *vce* (corn) ripened."[122] McCombs's dance spiral is appropriately organized by matrilineal clans and generations, visually communicating women's customary power as progenitors of children and corn. Participants join a procession that has been ongoing since the beginning of the world, a simultaneity of human ancestors, future generations, and plant relatives. Music, indexed by turtle shells, drums, and open mouths, is the provenance of other-than-human beings and a medium of connection with them. During ceremony, the community is "conversing with, and, in turn, hearing plant speech and song."[123] Entering a liminal state of oneness through sound and movement, the dancers express their "kindred relationality with the reddish-brown soil" and thanksgiving for the cyclical arrival of gifts from the earth.[124]

A GLOBAL NUCLEAR FAMILY?

Native kinship-as-geopolitics persisted as a fault line in government-sponsored art initiatives, forging earth-based alliances beyond the hierarchical and heteronormative international order promoted by the United States. Such instability can be glimpsed in a little-explored Indigenous component of *The Family of Man* (1955), perhaps the most widely seen and discussed exhibition traveled by the USIA. Upon the occasion of its debut at the MoMA in New York, Nelson Rockefeller, then president of the museum's board of trustees, described the cumulative effect of some five hundred photographs depicting the birth-to-death life cycle of individuals and families around the world. He claimed that the exhibition generated "a sense of kinship with all mankind" scaled to the threat of nuclear annihilation.[125] Four versions toured forty-eight countries in parallel to iterations of *Contemporary American Indian Paintings* from 1955 to 1965, reaching an estimated audience of nine million people; in addition, the stand-alone book sold several million copies.[126] Heading each subsection of the exhibition were quotations drawn from the Old Testament, the US Atomic Energy Commission, the Charter of the United Nations, prominent international writers, and,

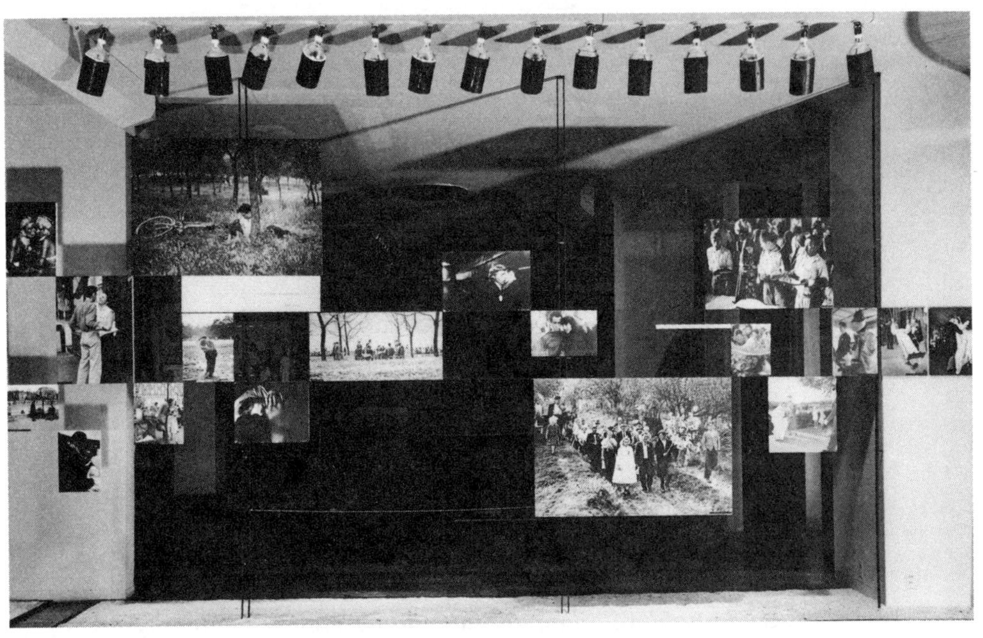

1.5

Installation view of the exhibition, *The Family of Man*. The Museum of Modern Art, New York, NY. January 24–May 8, 1955. IN569.24. Photograph by Ezra Stoller. On the right, the phrase, "We shall be one person" is suspended on a banner above a photograph of a wedding ceremony in Czechoslovakia by Robert Capa, Magnum.

....

most frequently, songs and aphorisms attributed to various Indigenous peoples.[127] Examples of the latter include "We shall be one person" (Pueblo Indian), "With all beings and all things we shall be as relatives" (Sioux Indian), and "The land is a mother that never dies" (Maori). Whether imperfect translations or pure inventions, such phrases invoke more-than-human relationalities at odds with critics' frequent dismissal of *The Family of Man* as a unilateral imposition of the US nuclear family norm in international relations.[128]

What "sense of kinship" is conveyed by the alleged quotations, so decontextualized from the Indigenous agents they credit? At least in part, the words support recent revisionary scholarship emphasizing the exhibition's multivocality in excess of the stated aims of its curator (Edward Steichen), sponsor (Rockefeller), and propagandist (the USIA).[129] Photography theorist Arielle Azoulay writes of the exhibition's archive, "One of the first things to strike my eye is multiplicity; the fact that in spite of the similarity of described situations in different areas of the exhibition, they do not constitute a unified mode of behavior."[130] Yet her reading ultimately positions viewers' encounter with difference inside a humanist frame, understanding the exhibition as a "visual proxy" for the 1948 Universal Declaration of Human Rights.[131] A wider relational web is cast by Kha-'Po Owingeh potter and scholar Rina Swentzell, who writes, "Pueblo people developed a mode of thought that assumes the oneness of human beings with the land, with the earth, and with all other living beings."[132] The concept of *nung*, a Tewa word signifying "people," "clay," and "earth," may have informed the inclusion of "We shall be one person," which was juxtaposed with images of heteronormative coupling and marriage in *The Family of Man*.[133] In a similar spirit, "With all beings and all things we shall be as relatives" is a translation of *mitákuye oyás'iŋ*, an Očhéthi Šakówiŋ prayer of gratitude to the many sacred sources of power—plants, animals, rivers, mountains, weather, stars—that sustain human communities and foster their diplomatic bonds with others (see this book's introduction and chapter 5). To Rockefeller's "mankind," then, we must add Sisseton-Wahpeton Oyate feminist scholar Kim TallBear's observation that "stone is also sometimes spoken of *as a relative*."[134]

Perhaps for some *Family of Man* audiences, these inclusions indulged a long-standing Euro-American stereotype of the Ecological Indian (see this book's introduction and chapter 4).[135] Nonetheless, I read in the phrases an alternative diplomatic mandate, an urging to heed a shared global *political* responsibility to a "mother" earth inclusive of, rather than exclusive to, "Man." For me, they conjure the memory of nineteenth-century negotiations among dignitaries from the United States and Native nations in lieu of the omnipresent Cold War mythos of cowboys and Indians. In such meetings, orators on both sides cast their asymmetrical relationship in explicitly familial terms, such as the "Great Father" (the US president) and his "children" (tribal nations).[136] Such terms functioned as a site of translation between seemingly incommensurate philosophies of kinship and geopolitics: on the one side the heteropatriarchal nuclear family as the moral nexus of citizenship, property and nation; on the other, trans-Indigenous understandings of diplomacy as adoption, a nonmetaphorical ritual for making new kin beyond the bounds of biological descent and the very category of the human. In light of *The Family of Man*'s notable dearth of photographs of Native American subjects, we are further pressed to consider the quotations' relationship to the diverse international subjects who intersected the exhibition as images and audiences.[137] Perhaps there were moments when, as the phrases traveled outside of the United States and underwent translations beyond English, the frameworks they reference felt more familiar (and more familial) than the US nuclear norm.

Bolstering contemporaneous tours of Native American art, this understudied dimension of *The Family of Man* indicates that Cold War cultural propaganda was never a monolith. Government arts initiatives were necessarily multivocal, dependent on the participation of an argumentative "family" of indeterminate shape, and open to the creative deformation of Indigenous cosmopolitics. To crystallize this latter point in relation to the traveling exhibition format, I turn to Dunn's last large-scale international endeavor, *Contemporary American Indian Paintings from the Margretta S. Dietrich Collection* in the "Near East."[138]

HARRISON BEGAY'S *NAVAJO WOMAN WITH SHEEP*

In 1965, fifty-five paintings of Diné sheepherders, Pueblo dancers, and Apache equestrians hung on makeshift walls at the University of Tehran, their story translated into Persian. Reportedly more than ten thousand Iranian students, faculty and other visitors saw *Contemporary American Indian Paintings from the Margretta S. Dietrich Collection* before it traveled to the National Iranian Oil Company's recreation center in Abadan, where it was extended due to popular demand.[139] At the close of the year, an official stationed at the US Embassy reported to Washington, DC, "During my time [in Tehran] there have been two particularly outstanding exhibits: 'American Indian Paintings' and 'Progress in US Space Science.'"[140] More than a decade after their tumultuous debut in Washington, DC, Native paintings were enrolled in an international competition over oil exploitation and the space race, wherein the United States vowed to use its "matchless science and technology to conquer new frontiers for all humankind."[141] Yet the gathering of diverse Indigenous lifeways simultaneously invited newcomers into familial relationships organized "center-to-center-to-center, Indigenous-to-Indigenous-to-Indigenous," a horizontal arrangement that Chickasaw literary scholar Chadwick Allen dubs trans-Indigenous.[142]

I'll enter this discussion through rare photographs from the opening in Tehran, which prompt consideration of the extractive forces that independently shaped and connected Iranian and Indigenous experiences of modernity. One image centers on Ahmad Matin Daftari, former prime minister of Iran (1939–1940), whose gesture directs the gazes

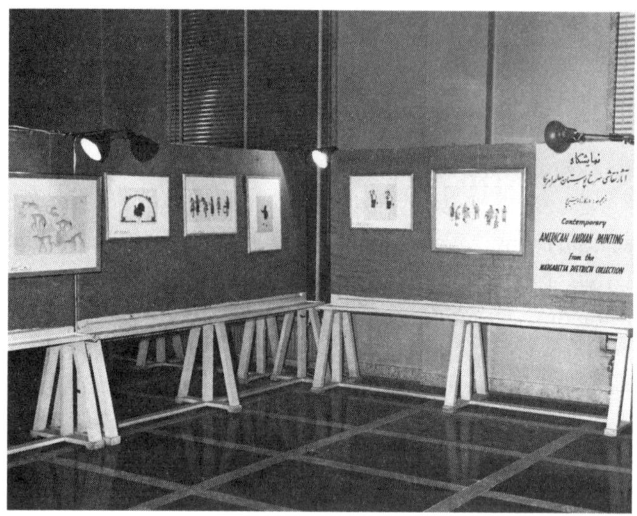

1.6

Contemporary American Indian Paintings from the Margretta S. Dietrich Collection, installation view at the University of Tehran, Iran, in 1965. Provided by Smithsonian Institution Archives, image #SIA2017–002067.

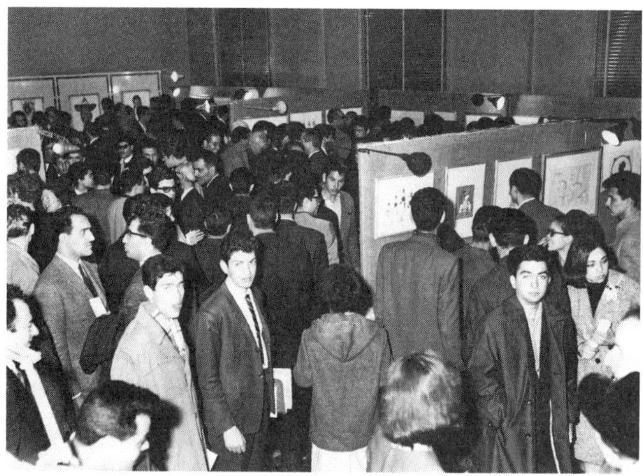

1.7

Contemporary American Indian Paintings from the Margretta S. Dietrich Collection, view of the opening of the exhibition at the University of Tehran, Iran, 1965, with more than one thousand attendees. Provided by Smithsonian Institution Archives, image #SIA2017–002065.

of University of Tehran dean of Fine Arts Houshang Seyhoun and US Public Affairs officer Henry Arnold toward a framed painting on the wall. Holding their attention is a flock of eight sheep surrounding a woman in modern Diné dress carrying a lamb, articulated with delicate lines and gouache paint on an otherwise bare sheet of paper. The figures form a loose semicircle around a magnificent bush with five radial, blooming branches that guide the composition from the bottom center. The leggy animals inspect a sampling of native plants, with the exception of one bold ewe in the corner, who seems to stare back at the suit-wearing authorities. The sheep are simultaneously nourished by diverse desert life and tended by the woman, who has draped the outcome of such labor, a striped wool blanket, around her shoulders. *Navajo Woman with Sheep* (1938) by Diné artist Harrison Begay (1917–2012) condenses the relationship of mutualism among Diné women, animals, and plants needed to bring a new textile into being, offering a visual analog to the Diné phrase, "weaving is *iina'*" ("how life is carried out"; see chapter 3).[143]

Begay painted *Navajo Woman with Sheep* shortly after graduating from the Studio School, while working as a muralist for the Federal Art Project of the Works Progress Administration (1933–1943). The prominence of sheep, plants, women, and weaving in his work intersected a contemporaneous federal program known as Livestock Reduction, a policy with profound implications for customary Diné kinship relations. From 1933 to 1942, BIA officials judged that large herds of sheep and goats exceeded the capacity of Navajo Nation lands and were responsible for desertification, justifying a campaign to exterminate more than half of nearly one million sheep and goats. A less public rationale for the slaughter was the potential barrier that Diné sheepherding presented to the completion of the Hoover Dam, destined to generate hydroelectricity for cities throughout the southwestern United States.[144] Diné women, guardians of land and flocks, were vocal in their opposition to the policy, but their leadership was discounted by the federal agents implementing the program.[145] Sharon Begay recollected, "I remember my grandma crying and she was saying, 'The police just came in here, and I ran out to the corral and told them, 'Don't shoot those animals!' But they shot them anyway. That was like shooting their children.'"[146] Begay's painting does not register the contemporaneous violence done to sheep, so much as the familial bonds that account for Livestock Reduction's lasting trauma. The dynamic symmetry of his composition reflects the foremost Diné aesthetic principle of *hózhǫ́*, encompassing beauty, health, harmony, and balance among the people, their other-than-human kin,

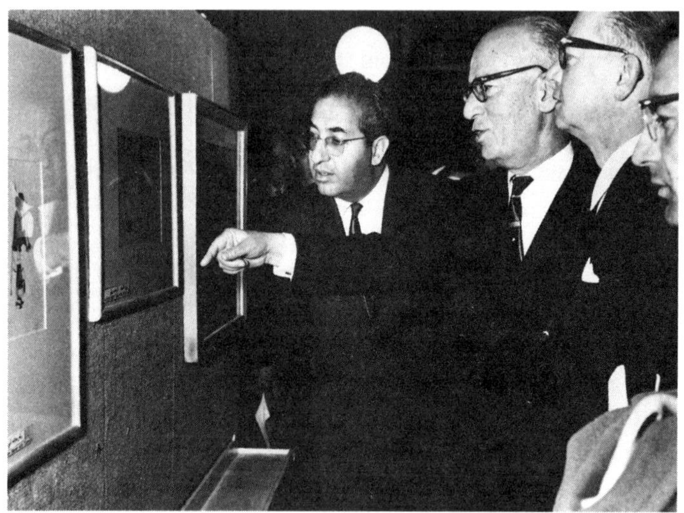

1.8

Contemporary American Indian Paintings from the Margretta S. Dietrich Collection, view of Ahmad Matin Daftari (pointing) discussing Harrison Begay's *Navajo Woman with Sheep* (1938) with Houshang Seyhoun and Henry P. Arnold, University of Tehran, Iran, 1965. Smithsonian Institution Archives, image #SIA2017–002068.

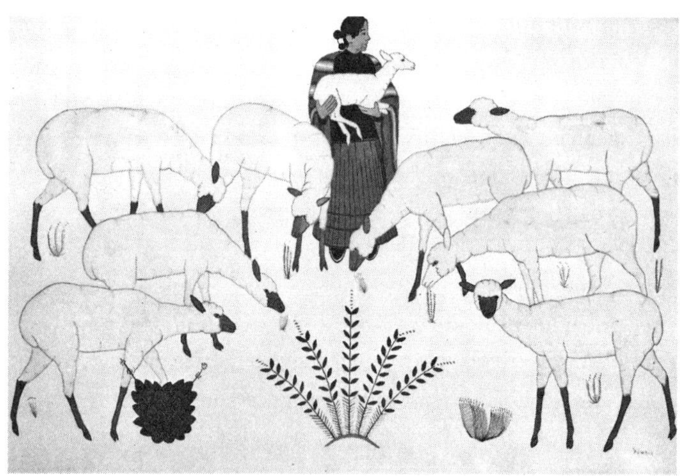

1.9

Harrison Begay, *Navajo Woman with Sheep*, 1938. Location of painting unknown. Photograph provided by Smithsonian Institution Archives, image #SIA2017–002069.

and the animate lands that sustain them. As I discuss at greater length in chapter 3, *hózhǫ́* is a teaching from the beloved Diyin Diné'e (Holy Person), Asdzáá Náádleehé (Changing Woman), whose body formed the land, the sheep, and humans in ancient times. *Navajo Woman with Sheep* connects Diné aesthetics to an ethics of more-than-human kinship and reciprocity, a relationship fundamentally at odds with the capitalist imperatives reshaping Indigenous bodies, ecologies, and arts.

Connecting Begay's pastoral painting to the lasting pain of Livestock Reduction provides a stark contrast to the USIA's selection of the Navajo Nation as the foremost "case history of progress" abroad.[147] The policy translated into dire poverty for many once-wealthy Diné and generated dependence on wages. It created a vacuum for subsequent extractive economies that the US government and private companies pursued throughout the Navajo Nation.[148] Beginning in 1942, more than three thousand Diné were employed in more than twenty-five hundred uranium mines, acting as the lowest paid and least protected labor for the Manhattan Project and the subsequent Atomic Energy Program. Nuclear waste permeated crop soil, sheepherding camps, and countless bodies that continue to suffer radiation poisoning, birth defects, and the slow creep of cancer.[149] In 1949, the secretary of the Interior briefed Congress that the "anti-American foreign press" was using the dire condition of Diné to criticize the federal government's treatment of minorities.[150] Violet Wood's 1962 essay in *Америка: America Illustrated* countered by lauding Navajos' choice to "live the life of the white population surrounding them" and exploit the "richest deposits of oil, uranium, and hard coal" within their homeland.[151] The ecocides underlying this propaganda shape my analysis of Diné sandpainting and weaving in the next two chapters.

We can imagine how Begay's painting accrued an additional, affective charge as it circulated abroad, landing in Tehran at an equally fraught juncture. Federal management of Navajo Nation resources foreshadowed the US government's efforts to control the transnational flow of petrol capital from Iran during the Cold War. The country was strategically important to the project of expanding US economic and military presence throughout the "Near East," a Eurocentric designation for a region that spanned significant oil reserves located between the Soviet Union and Europe. The Central Intelligence Agency backed a coup in the eventful year of 1953 to depose a democratically elected prime minister in favor of concentrating power in the hands of the Shah, Mohammad Reza Pahlavi, an autocrat deemed friendly to Western interests.[152] The following year, US Embassy Public Relations officer C. Edward Wells

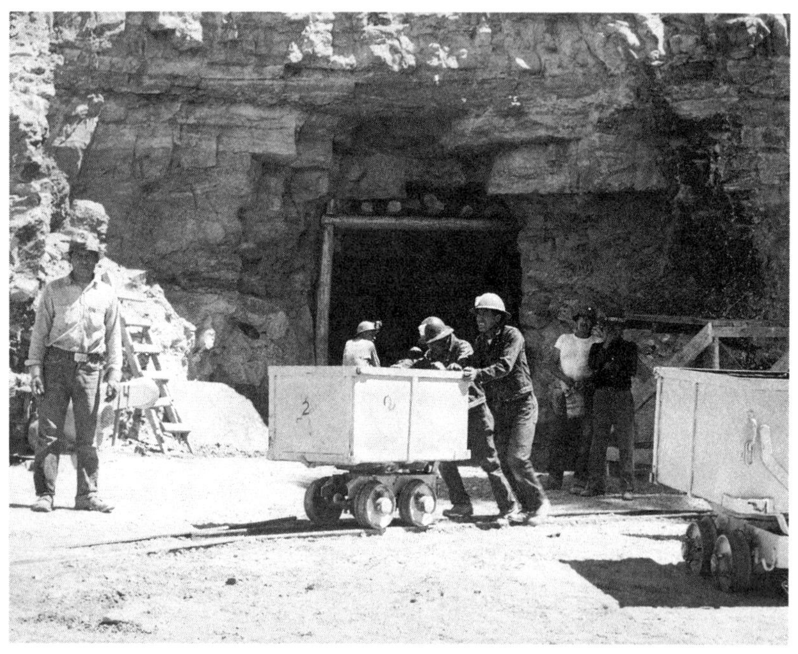

1.10

Diné miners at the Kerr-McGee uranium mine at Cove, Arizona, on the Navajo Nation, 1953. Associated Press file photo.

....

cautioned against sending McCombs to the country alongside African American Olympic track star Malvin Whitfield, "since too much emphasis on our minorities would probably be misconstrued." He noted that Iranians scrutinized the country's "Indian problem" through the lens of Howard Fast's *The Last Frontier* (1941), a sympathetic recounting of Cheyenne struggles against their forced removal from homelands in Wyoming and Montana. The book was translated into Persian "with the backing, it is believed, of an unfriendly power."[153] The alliance between the Iranian and US governments eroded in the 1960s amid deepening Iran-USSR ties and "open and vocal hostility" in the Iranian press toward the United States. When the Lyndon B. Johnson administration authorized a deployment of 150,000 troops to Vietnam in 1965, protests erupted in Iran alongside *Contemporary American Indian Paintings from the Margretta S. Dietrich Collection. Navajo Woman with Sheep* entered a scenario of "arm's length friendship" rather than the seamless "partners in progress" sought by the US government.[154]

:::::::::

The 1964–1966 tour exemplified the USIA's characteristic blend of strategy and contingency when it came to exhibiting art. Government officials bundled the Indigenous painting show with another exhibition, *American Indian Portraits by Winold Reiss*, a choice that undermined Dunn's message of benign modernization by promulgating an older frontier trope of the disappearing Indian. German-born Winold Reiss (1888–1953) created paintings of Blackfeet families from Montana and surrounding regions shortly after he immigrated to the United States in 1913. Framed by the colonial myth of a "fast-passing race" doomed by the advent of modernity, the larger-than-life portraits contradicted the images of peaceful progress that the USIA was anxious to promote.[155] Comments in a visitors' book from the first showing in Thessaloniki in 1964 suggest that the conflicting messages of the neighboring shows enabled, rather than quelled, critiques of the United States. One viewer noted that the "historic and folklore remnants . . . tell us about the life of freedom-loving people fighting nature who were destroyed by the 'civilization' of colonists." Another reviewer evidently missed the recent provenance of the Native-authored paintings, concluding, "If these people would not have been exterminated by fire and iron by the whites they would have made progress in all fields." The US ambassador in Greece wryly concluded, "some people had things other than art on their minds," namely, colonial violence that interrupted the smooth passage of USIA propaganda.[156]

The USIA archives do not clarify why the agency deemed it efficacious to pair the contradictory narratives of imperialist nostalgia and benign modernization. I imagine that the answer lies in the ad hoc nature of USIA exhibition organizing, a process mired in contingencies that compromised ideological clarity and, sometimes, the paintings themselves. While volunteers such as Dunn were responsible for selecting the works and preparing catalogues in English, embassy officials in destination countries decided whether to accept the exhibitions based on spatial and financial resources, political conditions, and assumptions about audiences' interests. Idiosyncracies were introduced at every step.[157] When several paintings were separated from the group and sent to Tunis to accompany a Native American lecture program in 1964, a burst pipe covered them in water and red dye.[158] Restorative treatment of nearly half the paintings in the two exhibitions was needed by the time they reached

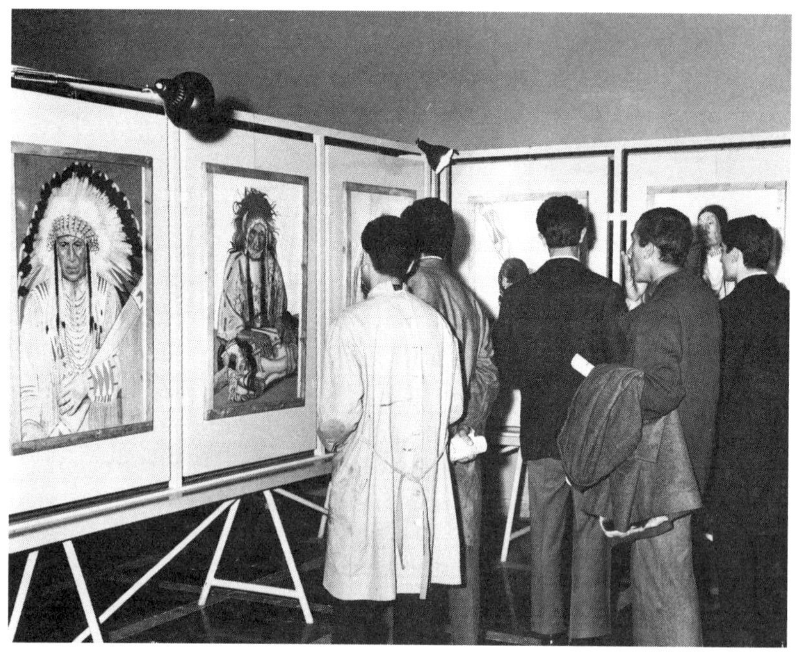

1.11

American Indian Portraits by Winold Reiss, view of the opening at the University of
Tehran, Iran, 1965. Smithsonian Institution Archives, image #SIA2017-002066.
....

Karachi the following July, too late for a scheduled showing; twenty-five
works required "major repair."[159] Dunn later complained that metal foil
pasted onto the backs of many Indigenous-authored works on paper,
apparently added during the refurbishment efforts, became "gritty and
abrasive, endangering the paintings."[160] As the exhibitions languished
in Karachi, planned showings throughout Pakistan and India were canceled due to the eruption of the Indo-Pakistani War.[161] The extempo-
rized nature of the tour hardly bolstered the USIA's message that Native
Americans were flourishing under federal guidance. On the contrary,
the toxic attrition of the paintings abroad forms a potent analogy for the
harms US policymakers visited on the lifeways they depicted.

Such material violence coexisted with the life-sustaining bonds forged
among the paintings and their visitors abroad. Here I acknowledge that
unlike Velarde, McCombs, and the remainder of the artists in this book,
most artists involved in *Contemporary American Indian Paintings from
the Margretta S. Dietrich Collection* were unwittingly contributors to
soft power initiatives. Nonetheless, their paintings extended Indigenous

kinship modalities into Cold War milieus.[162] While a detailed analysis
of each painting in *Contemporary American Indian Paintings from the
Margretta S. Dietrich Collection* is beyond the scope of this chapter, Begay's composition of a more-than-human holism is consonant with the
cosmopolitical themes of many adjoining artworks. For example, the hybrid human-animal figures that advance toward viewers in *Buffalo Dance*
(1939) by Ben Quintana (Cochiti Pueblo, 1923–1944), the overlapping
forms of plant, antelope, horse, and hunter united by abstract lines and
patterns in *Antelope Hunt* (1938) by Ha-So-De (Narcisco Abeyta, Diné,
1918–1998), and the exuberant lateral motion of equestrians welded to
horses with streaming tails in *Apache Warriors* (1939) by Allan Houser
(Chiricahua Apache, 1914–1994), map the familial reciprocities that
bind Indigenous people and other beings during the respective activities
of ceremony, hunting, and warfare. Such artworks transmitted the collective memory of more-than-human relations into new sites of political
struggle and helped to ensure that the global assimilationist project of
the United States remained incomplete.[163]

I afford the group exhibition an additional capacity to further long-
standing, trans-Indigenous practices of earth diplomacy, founded in
familial bonds among diverse human polities and the earth. Three historical sites of exchange inform my reading of the exhibition in this vein.
First, the paintings' mobilization within international relations begs
consideration of the customary role of material culture in forging intertribal relations before and during the colonization of the Americas.
Allen's modifier, "trans," points to a lateral matrix of Native nations,
Indigenous geopolitical alliances forged and maintained by material
circuits. The watercolor paintings join an "old and ongoing story of in-
cised rock and painted hides; of baskets, pottery, and textiles, of fish
hooks, canoes, and projectile points; of carvings, personal adornments,
and sacred objects; of all manner of vessels and tools" that change hands
to consecrate kinships and compel reciprocities.[164] Second, the Studio
School, the art program at Bacone College, new opportunities to recon-
stitute sensuous intertribal exchanges. They regularly borrowed themes
and symbols from their peers' distinct cultural heritages, materializing
trans-Indigenous relations in paint alongside their exposure to global art
histories.[165] Third, we can imagine how the shifting juxtapositions of
artworks on each stop of their international tour invited new, unpredictable relationships with visitors to unfold.[166] Following my theorization of
diplomatic assemblages in the introduction, exhibitions of Indigenous
modernisms had the potential to reshape political cognition by drawing

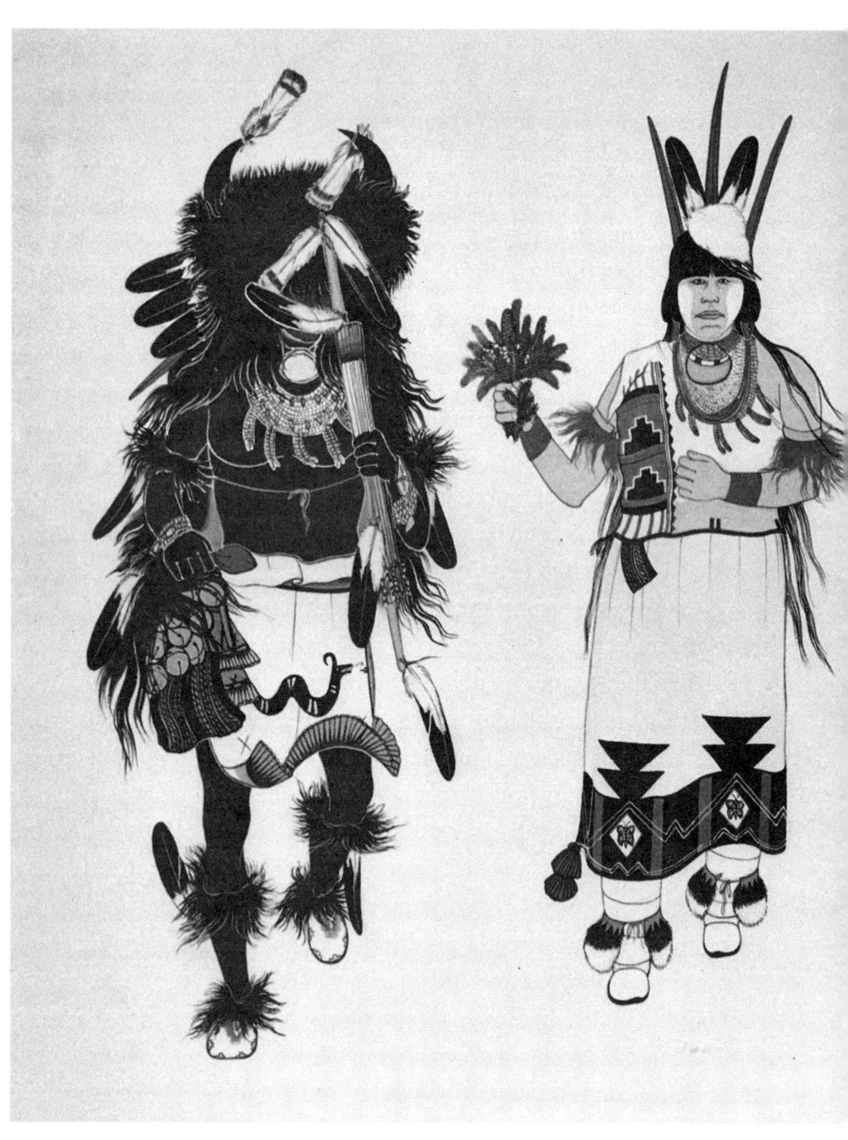

1.12

Ben Quintana, *Buffalo Dancers*, 1940. Tempera on board, 22.75 × 13.75 in.
Museum of Indian Arts and Culture, Margretta Dietrich Collection, 51823/12.
Photograph provided by Smithsonian Institution Archives #011102.

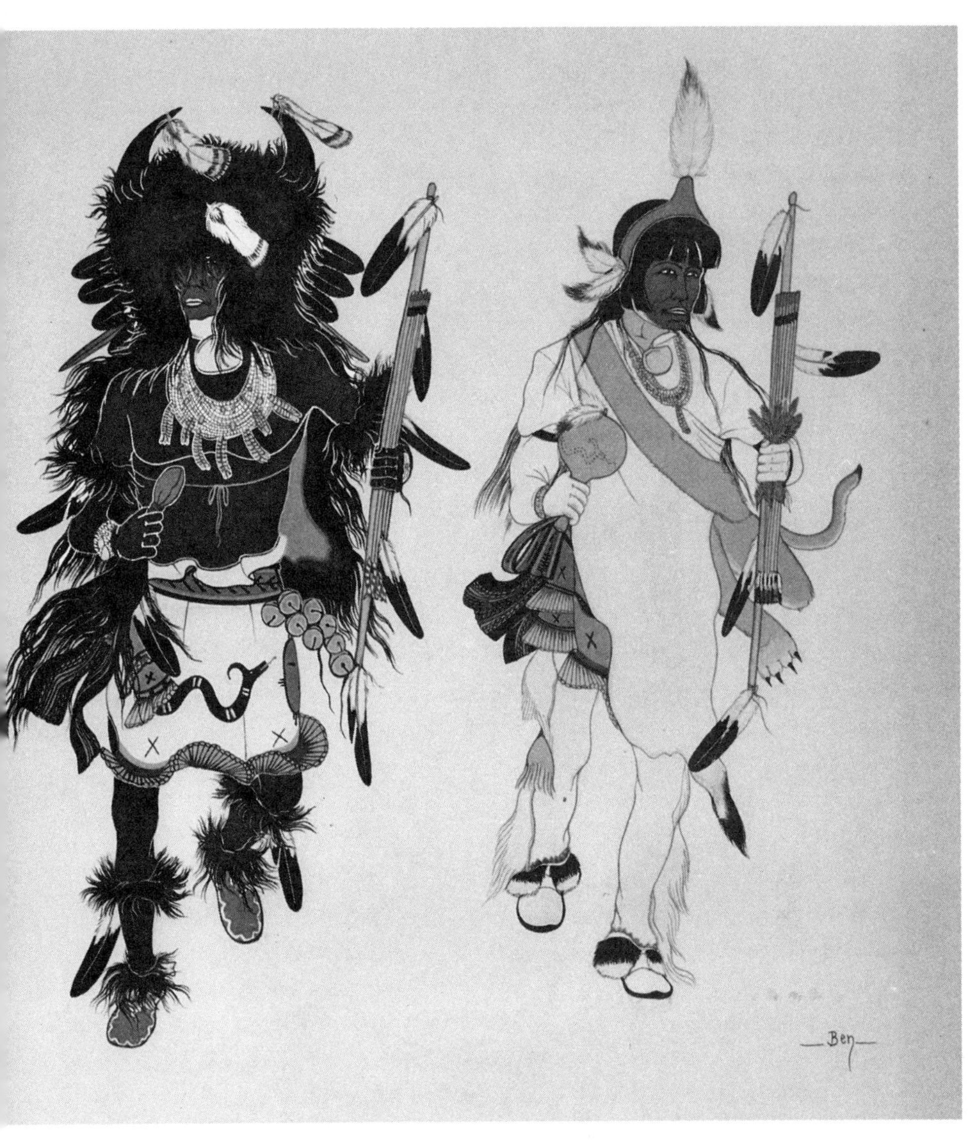

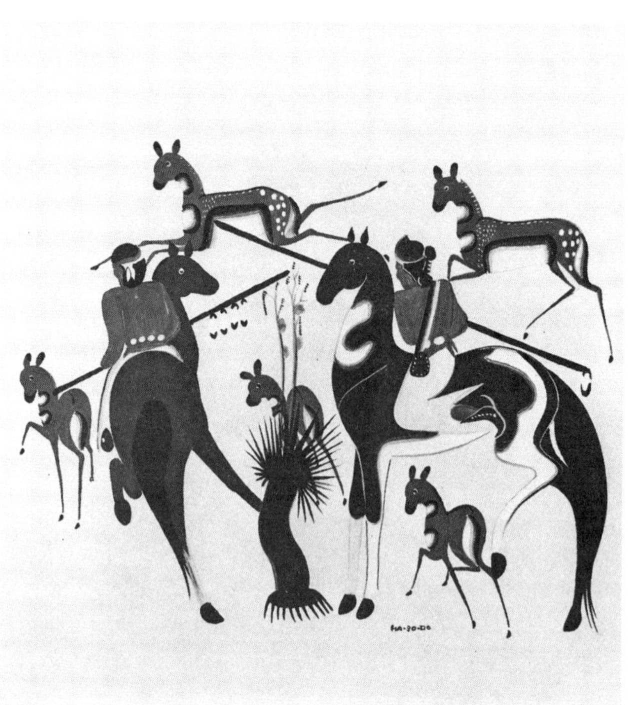

1.13

Ha-So-De, *Antelope Hunt*, 1938. Location unknown. Photograph provided by the Smithsonian Institution Archives #011100.

1.14

Allan Houser, *Apache Warriors*, 1939. Location unknown. Photograph provided by the Smithsonian Institution Archives #011101.

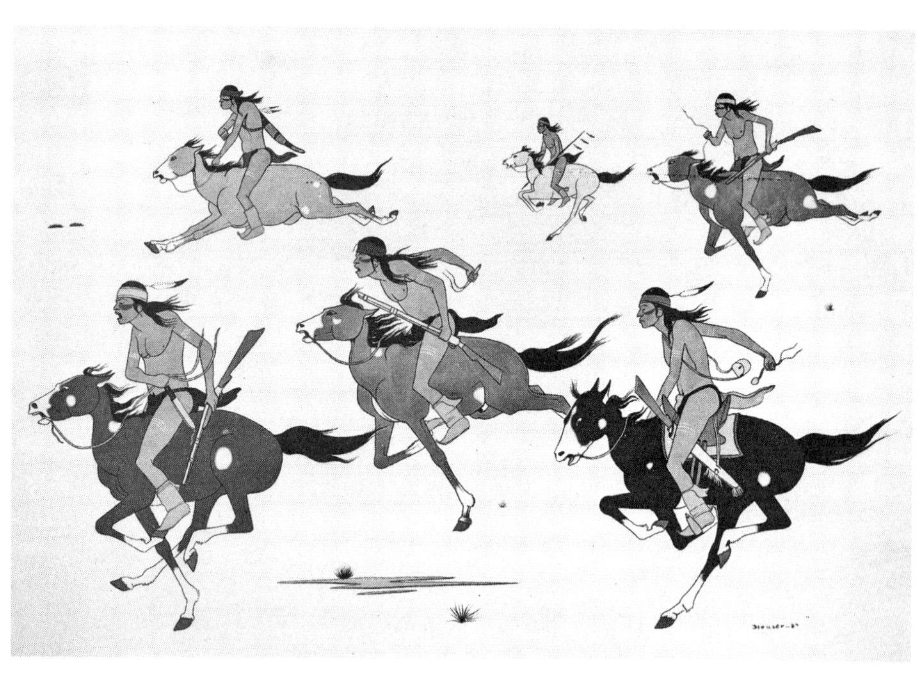

newcomers into affective bonds inclusive of the painted subjects, their environments of display, and other proximate bodies.[167]

To read the exhibition as charged with the horizontal memory of trans-Indigenous diplomacy is to cut across the hierarchies of US-envisioned geopolitics, which position Native nations as racial minorities inside and beneath the settler-colonial nation.[168] Rather, my interpretation reconstructs a capacious family of humans, stones, corn, sheep, buffalo, antelope, and horses, following an Indigenous logic inscribed in *The Family of Man*: "With all beings and all things we shall be as relatives." As I argue throughout this book, such an analytic is needed to recover the pluralism of a modern diplomatic sphere in which Indigenous people and their more-than-human kin have otherwise been systematically discounted. As international relations scholar David Wellman and his followers have argued, dominant practices of diplomacy have only accelerated humanitarian and environmental catastrophes. It is crucial to broaden the sphere of what counts as legitimate participation to a host of nonstate actors who bring distinct cosmopolitical and creative tools to bear on international relations.[169] The Cold War afterlives of the Indigenous works discussed in this chapter translated both life-enhancing and life-threatening forms of connectivity into new and unpredictable diplomatic assemblages abroad. Such arts supported Wellman's vision of a nonnormative geopolitical imagination premised on "an intimate understanding of the relationship a population has with its land, its religious and cultural traditions, its ecological reality, and its neighbours."[170] In and against the destructive logic of a balance of power in international relations, it is to painters, dancers, and weavers we must turn for an alternative account of rebalancing, a framework of reciprocity with more-than-human systems that support the collective flourishing of planetary life. I will look next to the Diné artists Fred and Bertha Stevens, who elaborated on modern painting precedents through their artistic demonstrations of sandpainting and weaving across Eurasia and Latin America from 1966 to 1968.

REBALANCING POWER

DINÉ SANDPAINTING AND SAND MINING

ON SEPTEMBER 10, 1966, the *Scotsman* reported an unusual "Indian Gift to Edinburgh":

> Edinburgh yesterday was presented with a cure for mental illness—a Navajo sandpainting. . . . [I]t will probably be put on display at city schools.
>
> Legend has it that, after a nine-day chant, a person sitting in the picture will be cured. But this will not be possible with the city's painting as it will be sprayed with glue to preserve it.
>
> Lord Provost Herbert A. Brechin received the sandpainting on behalf of Edinburgh at the [English Speaking Union] Gallery.[1]

Sandpainting is a central component of Diné (Navajo) ceremonies that generate healing and protection by rebalancing a disordered universe. *Fringed Mouth with Corn*, created on site for the Edinburgh International Festival by the Diné *hataałii* (healer or ritual specialist) Fred Stevens, was an altered version of a prototype invoked during the Nightway ceremony.[2] How, for whom, and to what ends was a curative art transformed into a diplomatic agent of the Cold War? Was the diagnosis of "mental illness" intended for the city of Edinburgh, or another entity at a different geopolitical scale? Did the application of a fixative cancel

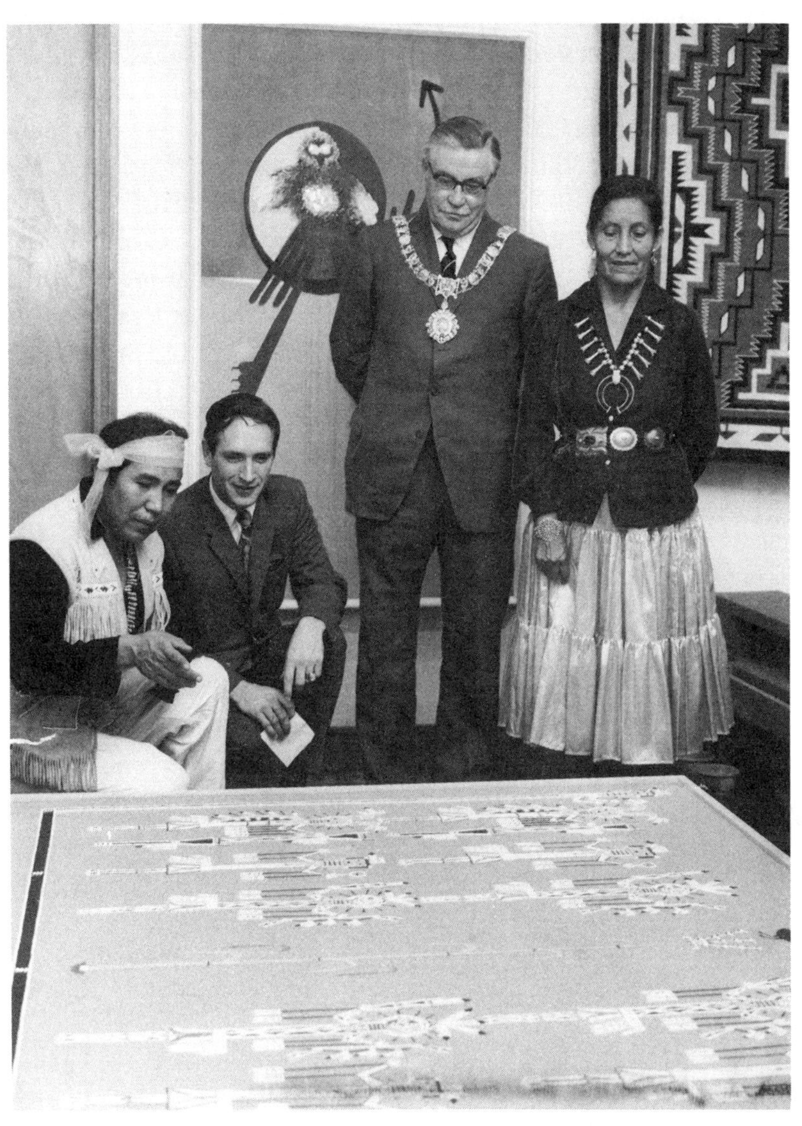

2.1

Left to Right: Fred Stevens, James McGrath, Lord Provost Herbert A. Brechin, and Bertha Stevens with *Fringed Mouth with Corn*, an altered sandpainting by Fred Stevens, at the English Speaking Union Gallery in Edinburgh, 1966. Provided by Rainbow Stevens and Alita Begay.

the cure, or was some more complex alchemy of material, power, and politics at play?

From 1966 to 1968, Fred Stevens (1922–1983) and his wife, Bertha Stevens (1912–1997), an accomplished weaver and the subject of chapter 3, were commissioned by the US Department of State (DOS), the US Information Agency (USIA), and the US Department of the Interior to demonstrate sandpainting and weaving in Scotland, England, Germany, Turkey, the United States, Argentina, Chile, and Mexico (plate 4). They traveled with a sponsor, James McGrath, an artist, poet, and art director of the Institute of American Indian Arts (IAIA), a four-year college that replaced the Santa Fe Indian School in 1962 to provide modern art education to Native American students. In most locations, the Stevenses performed alongside *American Indian Art and Handicraft*, featuring experimental textiles, paintings, and sculptures from the IAIA Honors Collection of faculty and student artwork with Indigenous material culture borrowed from canonical United States and European collections. In this chapter, I focus closely on Fred Stevens's translation of sandpaintings into demonstrations and gifts, illuminating their function as potent devices for assembling people and environments into new relational patterns. Central to this dynamic was the hataałii's reliance on extracted sand, the most mined substance on earth and the literal foundation of the modern cities he visited. Entering a diplomatic arena that excluded the vast majority of planetary life, Stevens was challenged to redress dangerous asymmetries among disparate human communities and a toxifying earth. His sandpainting variants incorporated land and bodies damaged by ecocides into international relations and created a path for collective rebalancing. The artist's work in the United Kingdom is examined at length due to the depth of the archive. However, in closing, I will turn to the contested Olympic Games in Mexico City in 1968 to suggest the relevance of Stevens's practice for Indigenous and majority world justice movements.

The cosmopolitical premise of Stevens's sandpainting translations diverged sharply from the propagandistic interests of the federal government. More so than any other Indigenous community, US officials manipulated the image of the Navajo Nation as an exemplary soft power resource. While I introduced this topic in chapter 1, I will revisit select threads of propaganda here to anchor my discussion of Stevens's work. A special issue of *Америка: America Illustrated*, a Russian-language magazine that the USIA circulated in the Soviet Union, celebrated the alleged benefits of extractive capitalism that guided the government's

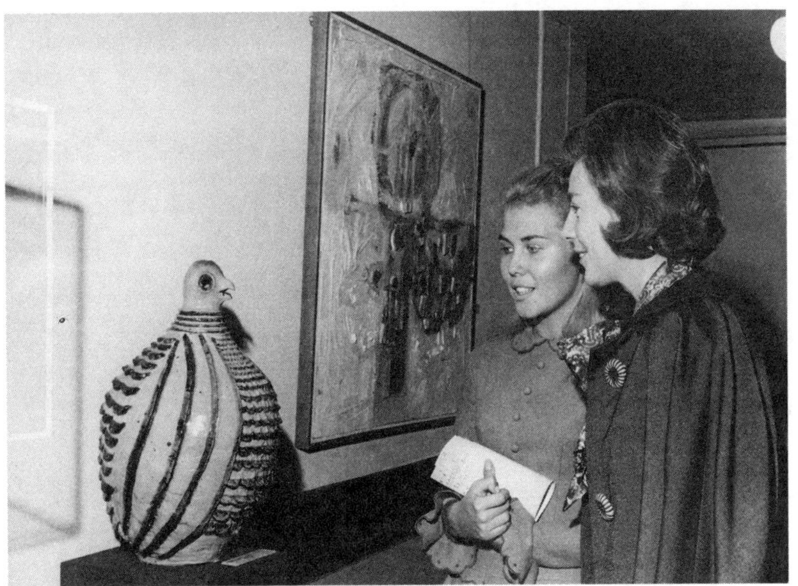

2.2

German visitors viewing *Effigy Jar* by Manuelita Lovato (Santo Domingo Pueblo). *From the Earth and from the Sun*, a painting by Larry Bird (Santo Domingo Pueblo), is visible in the background. *American Indian Art and Handicraft*, Amerika Haus, Berlin, 1966. Image provided by IAIA Archives, Santa Fe, NM RG-1, IAIA Records, SG-6, 1966, Series 7, Exhibits, Box 3, Folder 19.

....

appropriation of Diné art in particular. In "The Navahos—A Case History of Progress" by Violet Wood, the argument went that "the broad tribal lands of the Navaho Indians, where they have grazed their sheep for generations, have yielded a wealth of oil, uranium, and coal. The accruing royalties are being wisely administered by the tribal council for higher education, public works, and health projects that benefit everybody. . . . Thoughtfully, with dignity, and with the dedicated eagerness of a free people, the Navahos have taken the road that leads them into the mainstream of American life."[3] By connecting sheepherding, drilling, and mining in a seamless progression toward becoming American, the narrative obscures the federal government's cyclic violence toward Diné. Citizens of the largest Indigenous nation by population and territory within the borders of the United States, Diné survived scorched earth campaigns and militarized removals in the nineteenth century and forced acculturation, epidemics, and ecocides in the twentieth. An accompanying spread of color photographs displays Diné workers

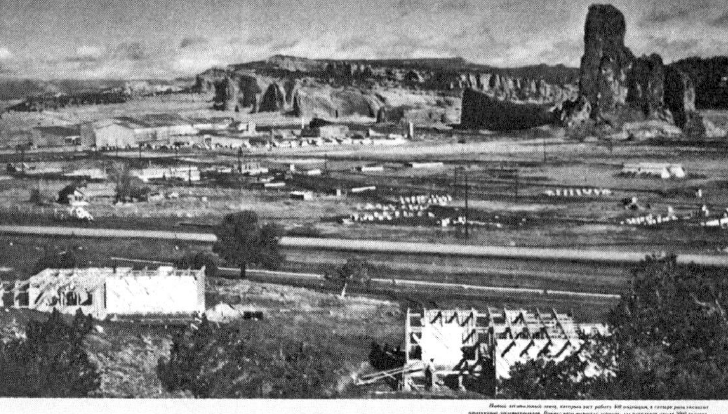

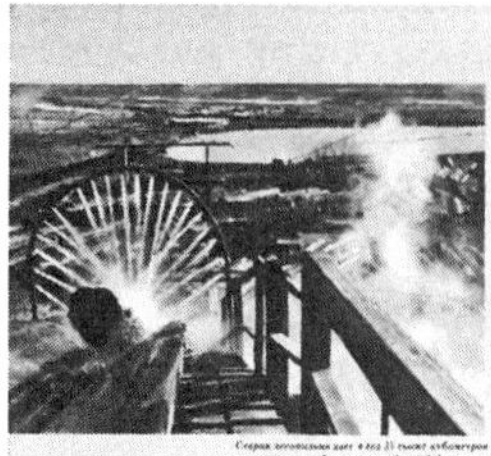

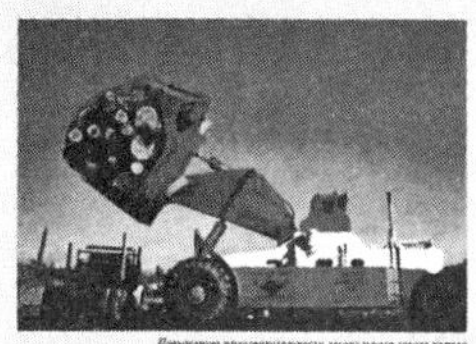

2.3

Violet Wood, spread from "The Navahos—A Case History of Progress," *Америка: America Illustrated* (1962), 30–31.

....

in hard hats and the iconic sandstone mesas of the Navajo Nation dotted with industrial infrastructure in the wake of the Manhattan Project.[4] While the landscape may read as dystopic to contemporary viewers, the images were evidently intended to celebrate the modernization of Diné as beneficiaries of a steady flow of natural resources, industrial technologies, and wages. As I have underscored, freedom and choice were keywords in the USIA lexicon, repeated to persuade foreign audiences that extractive capitalism and liberal democracy were universally beneficial.

These themes were elaborated on the eve of the Stevenses' tour in *The American Indian: Past and Present*, a thirteen-episode program for the USIA's global radio broadcast, Voice of America, in 1965. In the first of two episodes devoted to the Navajo Nation, narrator Wayne Hyde assured listeners that "the Navajo has made much of his painted desert land, and he will make it an even better land in time to come." Yet he cautioned that lingering primitivism presented barriers to capitalist efficiency. "Time means very little to the Navajo. It does not seem to matter too much if something gets done tomorrow, or next week, or next year. . . . He lives in the present." A BIA official working on the reservation further underscored that "it is a problem with which we must deal in attempting to develop industrial operations for the employment of Navajos on and around the reservation."[5] The series crafts the inexorable logic of federal intervention by characterizing Diné land, education, health care, and jobs as "free gifts" from a benevolent government committed to bolstering the self-sufficiency of a backward population. Hyde summarizes with the resignation of a tired parent, "Modernizing the American Indian has been a long, long process and it costs a great deal of money."[6] No mention is made of contemporaneous, devastating federal policy of Termination, let alone the complex forms of negotiation and resistance the policy demanded of Diné.

In reality, the Navajo Nation Tribal Council managed to avoid being terminated by strategically harnessing the BIA's definition of "predominantly Indian." An abject designation on a federal scale measuring progress, the label indicated that Diné were too poor, sick, and uneducated to warrant full integration into the United States.[7] Notably, a report issued by the American Medical Association in 1949 cited the "profound psychological influence" of the hataałii, a highly learned and respected figure among Diné, as an obstacle to the adoption of modern science and medicine on the Navajo Nation.[8] Such definitions of Diné as culturally regressive were double-edged: Navajo Nation leaders were able to negotiate limited forms of political autonomy, so long as they accepted a federal dictate to open sacred lands to corporate leases to facilitate resource extraction.[9] Dire consequences for the health of the people and land continue to unfold as I write. Some Diné environmental activists consider these toxic industries to be "a new class of Alien Monsters," recalling dangerous beings encountered by the First People as they sought to make Diné Bekéyah (the Diné homeland) safe for human habitation in ancient times.[10] The modern beasts were fed by Department of Interior land surveys, alliances between federal agents and industry leaders, and the availability—and expendability—of low-paid Diné miners throughout the twentieth century. It may seem paradoxical under such circumstances that the US government employed Stevens, a renowned hataałii, to demonstrate Diné arts of healing abroad. Yet the events of 1966–1968 are continuous with long-standing dynamics of assimilation, which vacillate between the violent oppression of Indigenous cultures and their appropriation to serve ideological dimensions of US capitalism and nationhood.

The federal government's reliance upon multivocal partners to generate, select, and interpret diverse artistic content nonetheless routinely destabilized this top-down information campaign, a premise on which the alternative narrative of *Earth Diplomacy* is based. The Stevenses' daughter, Rainbow Stevens, emphasized her parents' deviant political attitudes to me, recalling that her father would say about a given federal administration, "Ah, these people are crazy. I don't know what they are fighting for. If they ask me what party I am, I'm a Republicrat!" Breaking with the USIA's pat narrative, she described her father's guiding concern for the survival and safe transmission of sacred truths and her mother's preoccupation with the destitution of the Turkish, Mapuche, and urban Mexican communities encountered during the tour, which Bertha Stevens compared to poverty within the Navajo Nation.[11] When I interviewed McGrath in 2018, he further indicated that the challenge was to "do our own work, try not to have it crumble" under the "heavy imposition" of the DOS. "The one [government] path—which was not the one we were on—didn't see . . . the heart of it." The Stevenses sought to build lasting relationships through "one on one contact with people who are working from their hearts . . . out of their roots and out of their sources." McGrath concluded, "This is what it's about—not about America."[12]

Guiding the Stevenses' international work, as well as my discussion of "the heart of it," are protocols designed to "protect, preserve, and continue Navajo cultural heritage and traditions for future generations."[13] Fred Stevens in particular responded to contemporaneous Diné mandates limiting the circulation of ceremonial imagery by altering and praying over his sandpaintings in an effort to curb their spiritual potency and render them safe for travel. However, guidelines governing the treatment of culturally sensitive materials change according to the community's needs, necessitating consultation with contemporary knowledge-keepers to determine an appropriate course of research.[14] I prepared this chapter with a permit issued by the Navajo Nation Heritage and Historic Preservation Department, including informed consent from the Chinle Chapter Government of the Navajo Nation and the Stevenses' descendants.[15] I recognize a multiplicity of past and present Diné views on whether and how sandpaintings should be reproduced. Given these concerns, I prioritize visual analysis of photographs of the tour and limit my discussion of specific elements of sandpaintings to the descriptions provided by Fred Stevens. I omit images of actual ceremonies, offer only general information about sandpaintings' cultural significance, and foreground Diné perspectives wherever possible.

TRANSLATING CEREMONIES

Through precise coordination of images and materials drawn from the land, sandpaintings seek a nonhierarchical rebalancing of relationships among human and other-than-human beings that populate the universe. All sandpainting variants are intimately connected to Diné Bekéyah, a physical and spiritual homeland that spans Arizona and New Mexico and exceeds the legal boundaries of the Navajo Nation today. Delineated by four sacred mountains, the land is a gateway to the universe. Diné scholar and poet Laura Tohe described how this special place organizes her peoples' "cosmovision of the earth, which includes the sky. As such, the mountains need to be protected because they maintain stability and order throughout the life cycle of all living things, animate and inanimate. . . . In this space Diné would live their lives and establish a reciprocal relationship with Nahasdzáán, Mother Earth."[16] Art historian Janet Catherine Berlo has similarly referred to sandpainting textiles as "cosmoscapes" to highlight the connections they forge between the specific landforms of Diné Bekéyah and the entirety of the universe.[17] I retain the place-based connections indicated in accounts of "cosmovision" and "cosmoscapes" while additionally emphasizing the capacity of sandpainting variants to organize new environments as they traveled beyond the four mountains. These powerful devices mobilize Diné knowledge that is as global in scope as the cosmologies driving the violent expansion of modern nation-states. While the entanglement of these two seemingly incompatible systems is as old as the colonization of Diné Bekéyah, their mutual translation took novel form during the Stevenses' Cold War tour.

The complex of ceremonies that incorporates sandpaintings is specifically concerned with the realization of *hózhǫ́*, imperfectly translated as harmony, order, goodness, health, happiness, and beauty. Hózhǫ́ describes an ideal, ordered universe. Every component—grain of sand, insect, mountain, star—has a rightful place. Persons are in a state of hózhǫ́ when their minds and bodies are in a proper alignment with all else in their physical and spiritual environment. Hózhǫ́ can be disrupted by negative thoughts, malevolent deeds, contact with dangerous things, and excesses of any kind. Mental and physical activity have the power to affect alignments among various elements of the universe and should be controlled and cultivated to positive ends. The aural and visual components of a ceremony facilitate reciprocity between Diné and Diyin Dine'é, or Holy People. Expressed in the humanlike portraits in sandpaintings, the Diyin Dine'é are powerful, mysterious, and potentially dangerous beings present in features of the land. The accompanying chants relate the journeys of Diné ancestors through four lower worlds, at each level disrespecting their local hosts and finding themselves unwelcome. By the time they emerged into the fifth and present world, they learned the value of striving to live in harmony with other beings according to hózhǫ. An efficacious image is a precise replica of one of thousands of unique prototypes that the Diyin Dine'é created in ancient times out of the raw materials of the earth. The first images were painted with rainbows and lightning on sheets of clouds. Diyin Dine'é taught the designs to the First People to assist them in clearing the earth of monsters to make it habitable for humans. Yet humans continue to unleash destructive forces by "following a negative selfish path," wrote Diné educator Ethelou Yazzie.[18] By repeating stories and images from the original encounters with the Diyin Dine'é, the hataałii seeks to rebalance all parts of the cosmos and live a long life in accordance with hózhǫ.[19]

When disharmony occurs, Diné customarily consult a diagnostician, who assesses the source of harm and prescribes the appropriate curative ceremony. Stevens belonged to an elite group of highly trained healers who are commissioned to conduct ceremonies of up to nine days in duration when circumstances require them. Such individuals generally undergo decades of apprenticeship to precisely memorize the chants, images, and other elements involved in their areas of specialization. Ceremonies take place on the floor of a *hogan*, a circular or polygonal dwelling that models the universe, with a doorway facing the sunrise. A sequence of sandpaintings is made by sprinkling crushed, multicolored plant and mineral pigments on a clean bed of sand. The materials are customarily sourced from the surrounding land. Each sandpainting consists of a linear or radial composition featuring portraits of the Diyin Dine'é surrounded by animals, plants, mountains, and other beings of Diné Bekéyah. A hataałii often directs several assistants who painstakingly lay the design over many hours, crafting them to a level of perfection that compels the Diyin Dine'é to enter the hogan and energize the space for healing. The afflicted person sits in the center as the hataałii transfers the colored sands to her body, identifying her with the holy beings. After, the images are erased and the sand is discarded to prevent improper contact with the Diyin Dine'é, as the concentration of power in an efficacious sandpainting can be dangerous in uninitiated hands.[20]

Following colonization by the Spanish in the late sixteenth century, continuous disruptions from warfare, poverty, disease, environmental poisons, and the improper use of Diné words and images by outsiders placed new demands on ceremonies. In 1863, rumors of mineral wealth beneath the ground spurred the US government to forcibly relocate more than nine thousand Diné to destitute conditions at Hwéeldi (Fort Sumner) in New Mexico. In 1868, Diné leaders negotiated a treaty of return and commenced a period of rebuilding their cultural and economic livelihood. The treaty secured Diné sovereignty within the largest Indigenous-governed territory in the United States.[21] It also paved the way for the federal government and private companies to seek relationships with Diné that were "organized around resources," including oil, coal, uranium, sand, cultural belongings, and sacred knowledge.[22] The first known archival recording of ceremonies were sketches made on site by the army physician Washington Matthews in 1884, "much to the horror of the large majority of the assembled multitude."[23] He employed the then-widespread salvage ethnographic argument that Native culture was disappearing to justify the dangerous preservation of sandpainting imagery. In light of this event, it may be tempting to criticize the transcultural journeys of sandpaintings as a form of extraction, in which ceremonial secrets are leached for profit to the dismay of culture-keepers. Yet such colonial-economic determinism oversimplifies the role of the hataałii, who was challenged to translate between incompatible systems of valuing the same land under the immense pressure of assimilation. It also precludes consideration of how nonceremonial sandpaintings affected their increasingly far-flung milieus, which entails looking beyond specific human intentions.

Stevens followed the example of his clan uncle, Hastiin Tł'a (1867–1937), who innovated durable forms of sandpainting amid the cultural devastations of the assimilation era. Tł'a may have been the first to demonstrate the practice publicly, notably participating in the New Mexico Pavilion of the World's Columbian Exposition in Chicago in 1893.[24] As a powerful and respected *nádleehí* (a term referencing several nonbinary Diné genders), Tł'a was adept in healing ceremonies, typically performed by men, and textile arts, usually practiced by women.[25] He befriended Franc Johnson Newcomb, a self-taught ethnographer from Wisconsin, after she moved with her husband, a trader, to Nava, New Mexico in

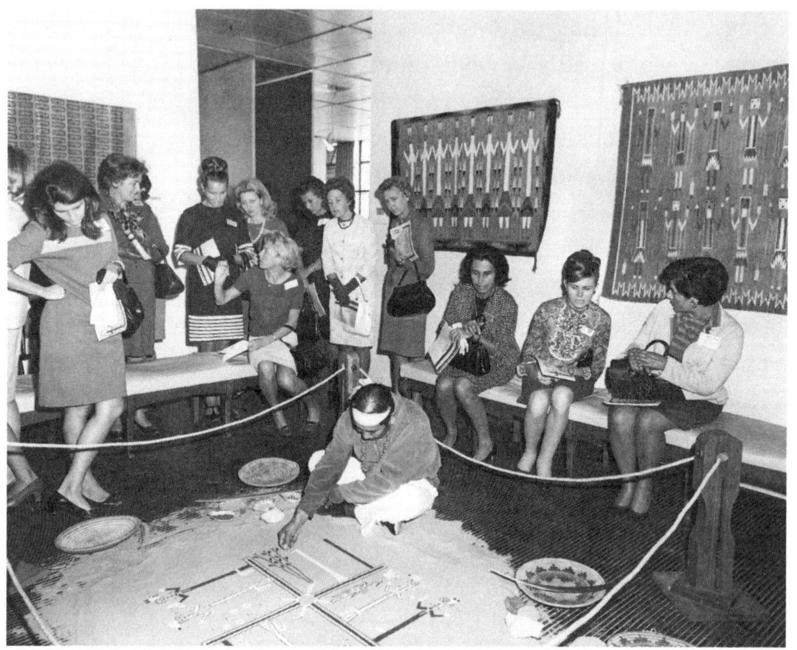

2.4

Fred Stevens creating an altered sandpainting, *Whirling Logs,* at the Museo Belles Artes, Buenos Aires, Argentina, 1968. Provided by Rainbow Stevens and Alita Begay.

....

1915. Working closely together, Tł'a wove full-scale sandpainting replicas while Newcomb recorded over seven hundred sandpainting designs in watercolor. They later urged Mary Cabot Wheelwright, an heiress and patron of Native arts from Boston, to finance a museum of Diné culture. The Museum of Navajo Ceremonial Art (now the Wheelwright Museum of the American Indian) was founded in Santa Fe in 1937 to house the work of Tł'a, Newcomb, and others who set out to archive an ephemeral practice.[26] Tł'a's influence on subsequent weavers is evident in several textiles featuring sandpainting imagery that were included in *American Indian Art and Handicraft*.

Tł'a and Stevens both responded to BIA-managed medical facilities, boarding schools, and economic development projects that systematically disrupted the intergenerational transmission of Indigenous knowledge. Federal efforts to assimilate Diné into a wage economy meant that few individuals could dedicate their early years to learning the intricate ceremonies. Both healers initiated dynamic forms of transmission by forging new relationships among technical, aesthetic, and cosmological elements. Consider, for example, how Tł'a's substitution of yarn for sand fundamentally altered the process of conceptualizing and materializing a design from a prototype etched in memory. In a ceremonial context, a hataałii would typically direct several assistants to lay the design, instructing them to erase and redraw elements until a level of perfection was achieved to call the Diyin Dine'é. Instead of sprinkling removable pigments in successive all-over layers from the sidelines of a horizontal picture plane, weaving on an upright loom required building the design precisely and permanently, row by row, from the bottom up. Now, a single pair of expert hands executed a wholly preplanned design. Tł'a was further challenged to alter select aspects of the compositions in an effort to diminish their spiritual potency and render them safe for circulation.[27] Such images were evidently designed to appeal to certain humans rather than to the Diyin Dine'é.

Stevens followed Tł'a in pursuing dual vocations as a healer and a professional artist. Born in Sheep Springs, New Mexico in 1922, he attended BIA schools and initially earned a livelihood as a baker. Remarkably, he also managed to undergo sixteen years of apprenticeship with his grandfather to memorize complex ceremonial chants and designs, beginning at the age of eight and conducting his first Blessingway ceremony at the age of eighteen. After World War II, he took a job at a hotel restaurant in Lupton, Arizona. The white owner, Leroy Atkinson, ran a private museum in an abandoned movie set behind the establishment, where he employed Native people to demonstrate various crafts to travelers along Route 66. Allegedly, a sandpainting demonstrator became sick, blaming the violation of ceremonial restrictions as the cause of illness. Upon replacing him in the wooden pit inside the museum, Stevens sought to protect against a similar outcome by following Tł'a's technique of altering the compositions and saying prayers at the start and finish of the work.[28] He reportedly alternated between wearing a feather headdress, honorific regalia among Plains nations that was popularized by Wild West shows and print culture, and reading glasses, in order to immerse himself in literature and world affairs during breaks between demonstrations. Eventually, he gained enough confidence to leave the sandpaintings overnight.[29] In 1952, Stevens moved to Tucson with his wife, Bertha Stevens, an expert weaver from Chinle who worked as a housekeeper for the Atkinsons. They helped to establish the Indian Village Trading Post, a popular tourist attraction. The couple achieved acclaim throughout the 1950s and 1960s by dancing in regalia with

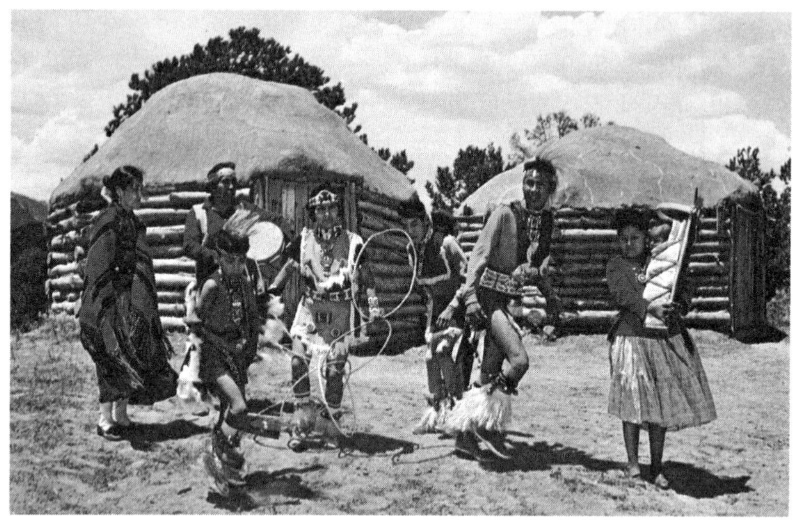

2.5

Postcard featuring the Stevens family performing a Hoop Dance, a powwow dance that originated in Pueblo communities, in Durango, Colorado, date unknown. Photograph by Petley Studios for Dexter Press. Collection of Michael Eugene Harris.

....

their four children and demonstrating their respective arts on a circuit of powwows, rodeos, fairs, and museums. Between 1956 and 1959, Fred Stevens reached an unprecedented audience by creating 113 sandpaintings on national television.[30]

Meanwhile, Stevens privately experimented with techniques to fix shifting sands. His challenge was to produce safe, durable, portable versions of an ephemeral practice, without trading sand for wool or paper. In the early 1950s, he tested a variety of additives and backings alongside a non-Diné friend, Luther A. Douglas (1919–1976), a US Air Force pilot and artist stationed in Tucson. Douglas studied Diné ceremonies following his alleged adoption by a Diné family as a child.[31] Beginning in 1953, he marketed sandpainting variants that incorporated brightly colored crushed glass at the Museum of Contemporary Crafts in New York and other institutions in the United States and Europe. While the two men continued to consult one another, each ultimately developed independent public practices. From 1964 to 1965, Douglas preceded Stevens on a USIA-sponsored tour of an exhibition billed as "Navajo sandpaintings and Indian handicrafts" through northern European countries.[32] According to the accompanying brochure, "the sandpaintings were executed by Navajo medicine men in the actual sand medium, and preserved by Douglas in permanent form with fixative process developed by him." Douglas credited Stevens as an autochthonous ceremonial expert—"a medicine man of high repute"—but said nothing of his friend's technical innovations, perhaps in an effort to preserve a popular, romanticized view of Native religion untouched by modernity.[33]

In 1958, Stevens created what he considered to be his first successful durable sandpainting—a nine-inch-by-five-inch image of a single Fringed Mouth Holy Person, a figure that he multiplied in Edinburgh—using a diluted solution of Duco cement, a common household fixative manufactured by the chemical company DuPont. He eventually settled on a technique of alternating slow-drying, synthetic Elmer's Glue-All with natural pigments to emulate the all-over layering process that was used in the creation of ceremonial variants (plate 5). He tried mass-produced plasterboard, plywood, and particle board as foundations, eventually preferring Masonite, a lightweight yet sturdy engineered wood made from pressure-molded fibers that was used widely in the construction industry.[34] While sand enabled a degree of material and procedural fidelity, Stevens's choice of fixatives and backings slipped damaging Cold War industrial technologies into the very structure of sandpaintings. Such inclusions conjure DuPont's role in nuclear development and other corporate relationships with the Navajo Nation that were poisoning Diné Bekéyah. I consider the significance of such troubling elements in greater depth in the context of the Stevenses' Cold War tour. The artist signed each work on the backside, sometimes leading with his powwow name, "Grey Squirrel (Fred Stevens, Jr.), Navajo Indian Sandpainter and Medicine Man." He also inscribed detailed notes by hand that identified the design's ceremonial origin, materials, and occasionally, instructions for care that underscored their durability: "Douse with running water and stand to drip dry."[35]

In 1962, Stevens taught his siblings what proved to be a lucrative new skill that spread quickly across the Navajo Nation. In *Navajo Sandpainting: From Religious to Commercial Art*, cultural anthropologist Nancy Parezo established his foundational role in the development of a craft industry for durable sandpaintings in the southwestern United States in the 1960s. Drawing upon interviews with Stevens, she emphasized his desire to economically assist his family. She continued, "Stevens decided to make sandpaintings in a permanent medium because he believed it was his duty to preserve Navajo culture, especially the rapidly disappearing ceremonies, for future generations of Navajos and Anglo-Americans."[36]

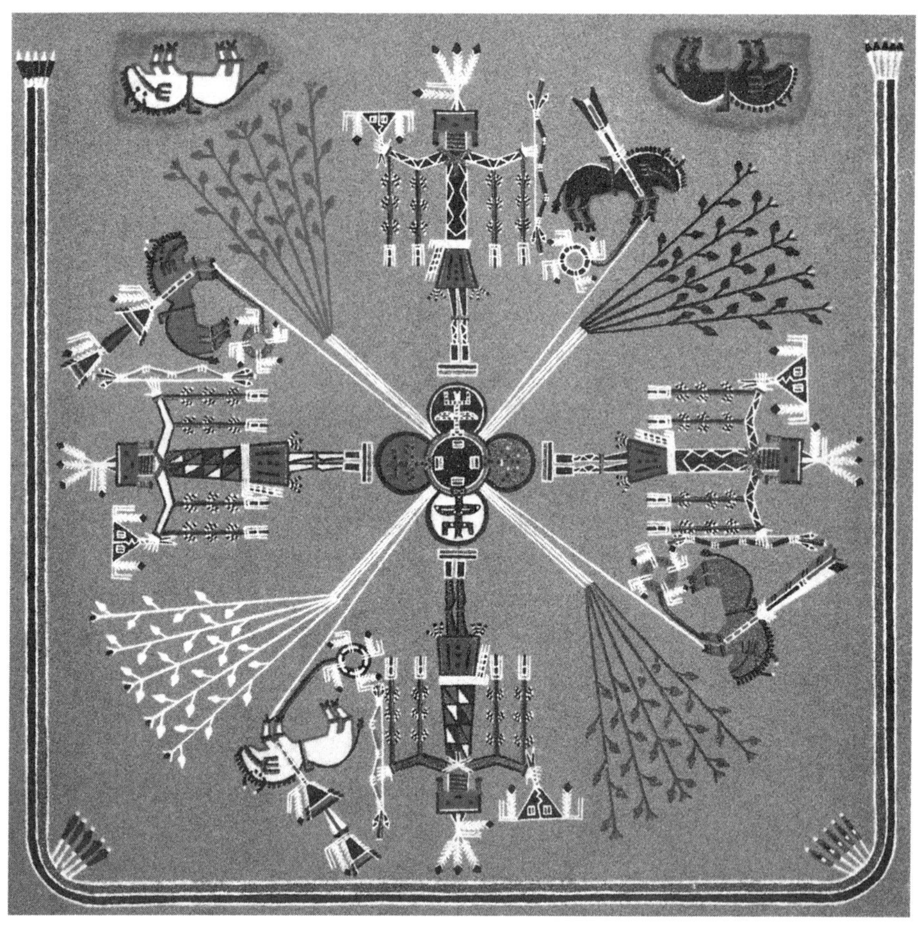

2.6

Fred Stevens, *Buffalo Who Never Dies*, Male Shooting Way Chant, date unknown.
An altered sandpainting made of pulverized sandstone, silicon, and mineral rock on
Masonite, 24 in. × 24 in. Collection of Michael Eugene Harris.

Stevens's daughter similarly underscored his lifelong commitment to the transmission of sacred knowledge, a rationale supported by his difficulty, like Tł'a's before him, in identifying and training apprentices. Rainbow Stevens related that because her father learned at a young age, "his brain was fresh and open and he gathered all these things." In contrast, his aspiring students were often past the age of twenty. "He would laugh and say, 'They can't do it. They don't have it up here'" (she pointed to her head).[37] The concern was registered by the Navajo Nation Tribal Council in 1954, which approved a proposal to publish a detailed account of the Blessingway as a teaching guide for young Diné by a vote of fifty to eighteen. The decision was characteristically controversial, notably facing opposition from council member Bizahalani Bekis, a hataałii, who stated, "I want to hold on to the old traditions and not be too liberal with it." According to historian Wade Davies, all those who spoke at the meeting agreed on the necessity of continuing the ceremonies, but the precise relationship between protocol and the means of perpetuation caused consternation then, as it does now.[38]

The proposal passed at an especially precarious moment for Diné physical and spiritual health. BIA-administered medical care was grossly underfunded and understaffed in the face of widespread tuberculosis and trachoma, even as new epidemics of cancer and alcoholism indexed the shifting economy of extraction. While many Diné continued to turn to ceremonies while attempting to access inadequate BIA services, physicians regularly dismissed the hataałii as a charlatan or a superstitious impediment to scientific progress.[39] In the early 1950s, some Diné healers succeeded in brokering agreements with BIA providers to cooperate on holistic approaches to health, foregrounding a principle of different yet complementary powers.[40] Almost immediately, Termination interrupted the fragile truce. In 1955, US government transferred the administration of medical care on the Navajo Nation to the US Public Health Service (PHS) on a path toward the dissolution of federal trust responsibilities to Native nations.[41] The move did not ultimately lead to a withdraw of federal support, so much as occasion "a flurry of Navajo efforts to shape and broaden their healing options" toward greater medical self-determination in the 1960s.[42] Put another way, the transfer enhanced the need for a localized practice of earth diplomacy to ensure that the flood of PHS newcomers who lacked knowledge of Diné culture would come to value the power of the hataałii alongside that of Western doctors. The transition provides some context for Stevens's choice to pursue public-facing demonstrations and artistic experiments while continuing to perform, teach, and advocate for ceremonies among Diné peers. It specifically foreshadows his efforts in 1978 to charter *Diné Be'ezéé' Ííł'íní Yee Da'ahótą'ígíí*, an association of healers who developed standards for ceremonies, trained a younger generation, and promoted respect for Diné medicine among physicians.[43]

But a regionalist, preservationist framework cannot fully account for the cosmopolitical implications of Stevens's multifaceted practice.[44] His apparent concern with perpetuating vital knowledge must be distinguished from a static notion of preservation that easily shades into nostalgia. The latter reduces him to an accomplice of capitalist assimilation, indicating that he hardened ephemeral practices into "permanent" and "secular" objects to be marketed, collected, and displayed.[45] I characterize Stevens's altered sandpaintings as nonceremonial because they lacked crucial elements needed to attract the Diyin Dine'é. However, Diné cosmology does not support their definition as permanent or secular. Diné commentators emphasize that there is no limit to the sacred in a universe animated by *niłch'i*, imperfectly translated as "the holy wind," which endows beings with life, breath, thought, speech, and motion and connects them to the entirety of the world.[46] Tohe writes that the concept of the sacred "can be linked with almost everything—'sacred water,' 'sacred buffalo,' or 'the four sacred mountains,' while in the Western world this term has lost much of its consecrated meaning, except within the context of religion."[47] While Stevens sought to curb the ceremonial efficacy of his traveling sandpaintings, he still treated them as unpredictable agents, praying over them and occasionally crediting them for unexpected problems that emerged during the couple's travels. Rainbow Stevens related that on her parents' way to Santiago in 1968, the airplane engine caught fire, forcing an emergency landing "at a small airport somewhere in Brazil or someplace. They got off the plane. An old man went up to the plane, saw the burned-out engine. He fell over in a heart attack. My father being a medicine man, he always made prayers before they went anywhere. My dad said, 'If I didn't pray, we wouldn't have made it.'"[48]

I maintain that Stevens's experiments in durability were but one stop on a longer journey dedicated to rebalancing a world riven by Termination and the Cold War. The significance of travel to the Stevenses' lives and art is suggested by their descendants' ludic practice of pointing to an airplane passing overhead and exclaiming, "There go grandma and grandpa!"[49] James McGrath was attracted to the couple's anomalous work when he traveled across the Navajo Nation in 1965 in search of sandpainters with cosmopolitan credentials to accompany his USIA tour the following year.[50] The US Department of Commerce had already selected the Stevenses to demonstrate their arts at the Paris International Trade Fair in March of 1966, and they would return to London to perform at Buckingham Palace in 1971.[51] I propose that during the couple's worldwide travels, Fred Stevens set out to disempower sandpaintings, only to invest them with new and different kinds of potency. His variants worked to translate a Diné ethics of reciprocity from ceremonial to geopolitical agents.

MINING

I begin substantiating this claim with a simple observation: Stevens's sandpaintings were quite literally composed of their changing locales. While the artist ground his pigments by hand from the plants and rocks of Diné Bekéyah, it was not practical to haul large quantities of local sand to Edinburgh, Ankara, or Santiago. Rather, McGrath wrote letters to foreign hosts in advance requesting their assistance in securing a source of approximately "one square yard of clean, natural or buff colored sand (not white)"—enough to provide "a 3" base on the platform."[52] Ian Gilmour, the director of the English Speaking Union Gallery, replied confidently, "I feel sure we must have plenty around Edinburgh."[53] Such communications point to the corporate traffic in mined materials that connected regional geologies to global industries during the Cold War. How, precisely, did Stevens interact with the conditions of mineral extraction that upended the sacred foundations of sandpainting—and the very ground of his tour?

McGrath's unvarying appeal for a purified form of sand in countries as geologically disparate as Scotland and Mexico was not unreasonable. Aggregates collectively categorized as "sand" in English are found to varying degrees in soils around the world, in dynamic interplay with other elements of an ecosystem. Environmental scientists assert that "sand particles play an important role in the velocity of flow of geological agents like wind and water, thereby protecting the biological richness and diversity."[54] Sand is also a key ingredient in cement, glass, paint, and other industrial materials used widely for construction. According to architectural historian Adrian Forty, sand-dense, reinforced concrete "became a formidable weapon in the arsenal of the Cold War," as Eastern and Western blocs tried to outperform one another in leading a building boom.[55] This activity caused a global spike in sand mining. The sharp aggregates needed

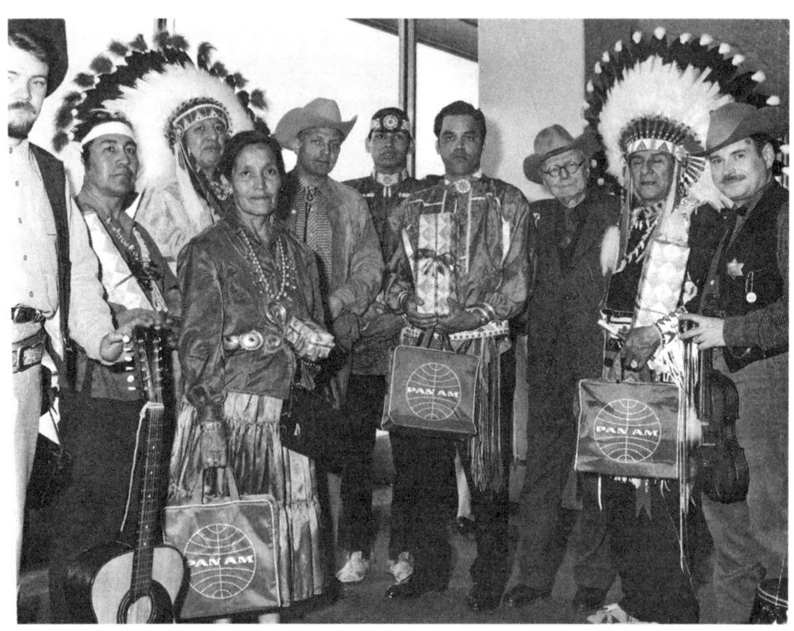

2.7

Bertha Stevens (*foreground*) and Fred Stevens (*left*) with other Native American performers and government officials associated with the Paris International Trade Fair at Orly Airport in Paris, March 25, 1966. Photograph by Serge Holtz. Provided by Wilmerine Stevens and Alita Begay.

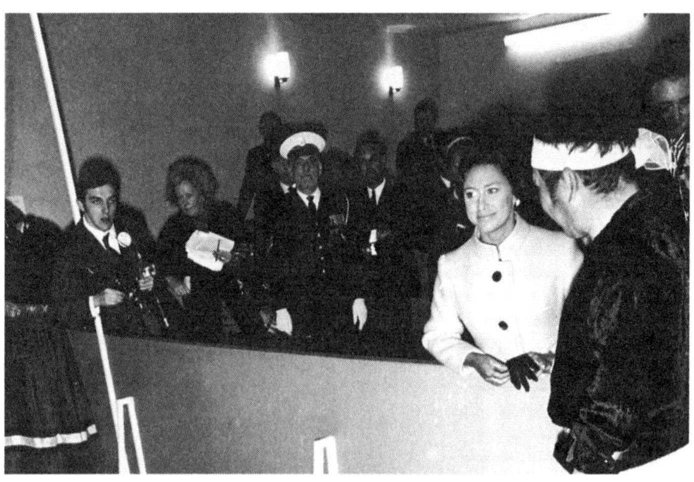

2.8

Fred Stevens meets Princess Margaret in London in 1971. Collection of Michael Eugene Harris.

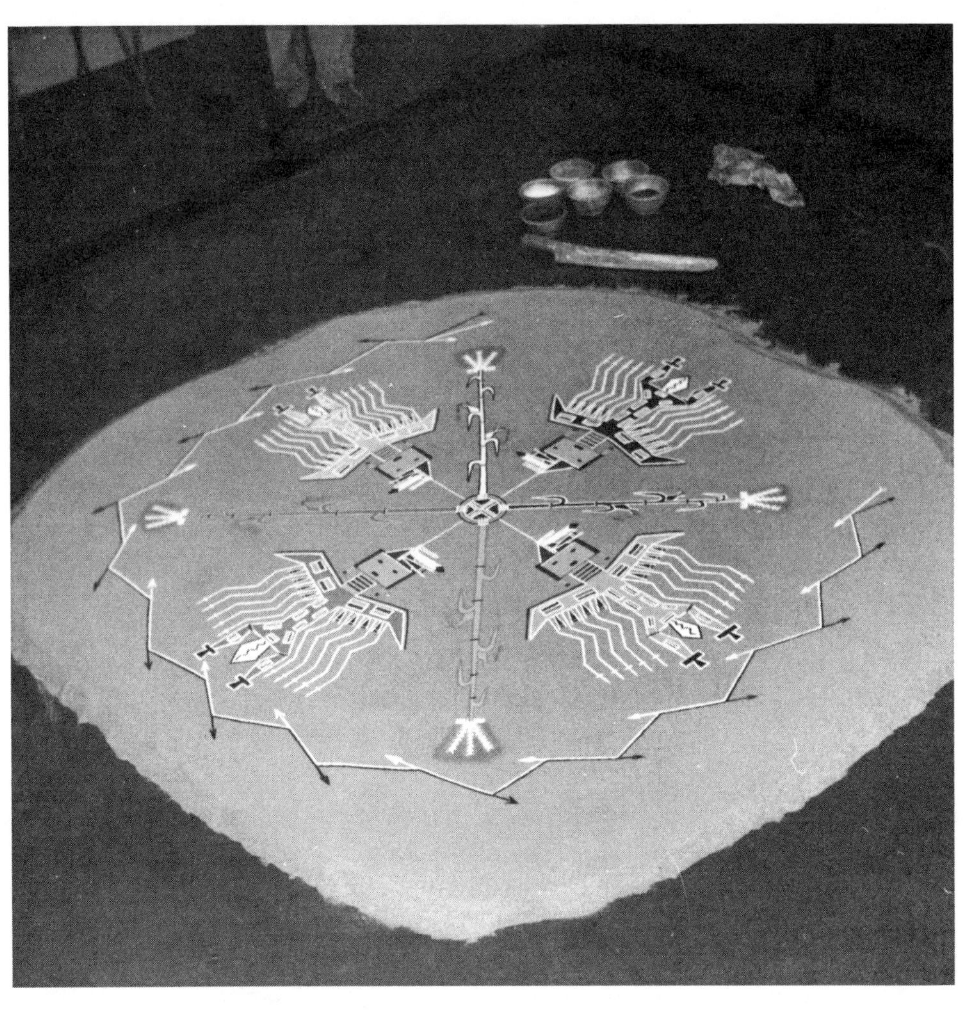

2.9

Fred Stevens, *The Four Thunders*, an altered sandpainting at Amerika Haus, Berlin, 1966. Provided by IAIA Archives, Santa Fe, NM. MS03, Box 24, F.9, I.6.

for strong and cohesive concrete were extracted in increasingly large quantities from the shorelines of rivers, lakes, and oceans, revalued as a discrete resource, and reformed into buildings and infrastructure.[56] A nation's capacity to "modernize"—a highly contested theme in Cold War international relations—could be quietly measured in grains of sand. Here, the warning issued by the hour glass in seventeenth-century *vanitas* was prescient. While the Stevenses traveled, the accelerated mining of sand worldwide was causing proportionate environmental degradation. Mineral extraction irreversibly altered the composition and mass of the earth's surface by stripping nutrient-rich soils. It precipitated the collapse of landforms, rerouted waterways, and rapidly outpaced the renewal of the particulate through geological processes.[57] Cold War modernization set in motion what some journalists are now calling a "deadly global sand war," as the overmining of the essential substance led to critical worldwide shortages after 1989.[58] The transnational production of sandpainting similarly depended on the fraught conditions of sand's deracination.

At the same time, the specificity of McGrath's request for "clean, natural or buff colored sand (not white)" indicates that Diné Bekéyah, the literal and cosmological foundation of sandpainting arts, remained Stevens's privileged referent. Throughout the ecologically diverse canyons, plains, and mountains, all the necessary materials could be gathered rather than mined. Yet, as the concrete infrastructure pictured in *Америка: America Illustrated* hints, industrial demand for sand profoundly affected Diné Bekéyah. Sand may appear benign compared to uranium, a well-studied carcinogen that was extracted in large quantities by Diné laborers to feed Cold War nuclear development (see chapter 1). Yet when these slumbering elements are awakened in mines, they are admixed by wind and water and dispersed in volatile combinations throughout the land. More broadly, sand and uranium meet inside a transnational system of finance, extraction, and cheap labor premised on "withdrawal without depositing . . . from poor and communities of color."[59] Both substances linked the reshaping of Diné minds, bodies, and land to the "slow violence" of modernization paradigms that US was aggressively promoting in its transactions with foreign governments during the Cold War.[60] McGrath's report that "sand was most difficult in Mexico" further hints that sandpainting registered the volatility of geopolitical as well as geological agents, a topic to which I will return in the conclusion to this chapter.

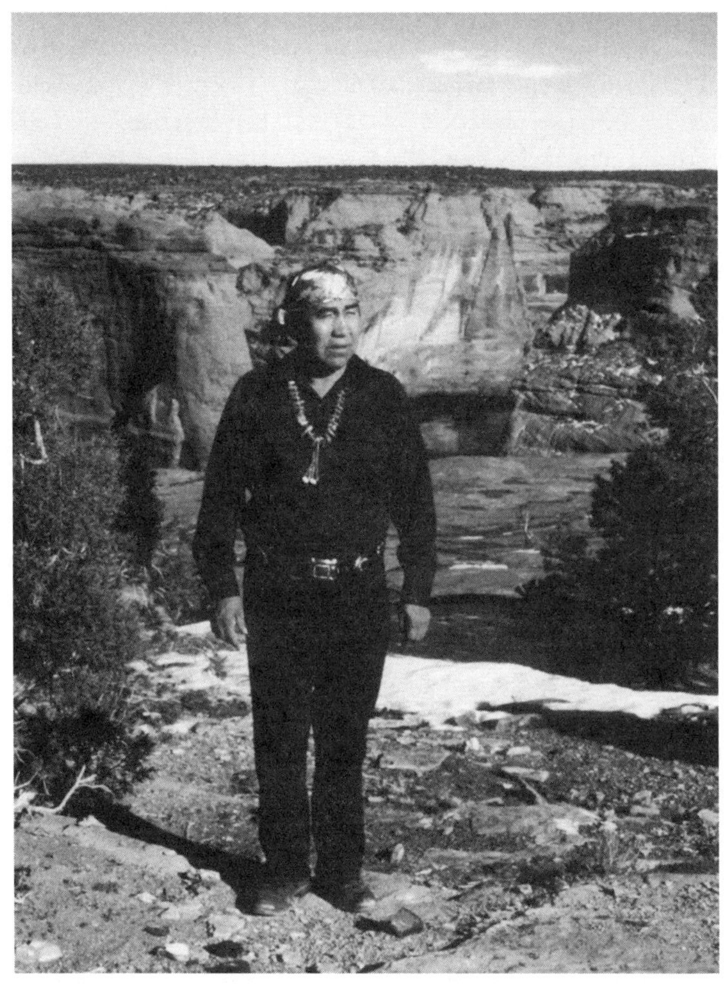

2.10

Fred Stevens standing on the edge of Tséyi' (Canyon de Chelly)
in Chinle, Navajo Nation, Arizona, date unknown. Collection of
Michael Eugene Harris.

A traveler alongside McGrath and Stevens, sand points to the "more-than-rational, and indeed the more-than-human, nature" of international relations. Here, I again cite Jason Dittmer's theory of the diplomatic assemblage, which highlights the capacity of nonhuman materials and systems to produce nebulous *affects* as well as quantifiable effects upon their political milieus (discussed in the introduction to this book). Mined sand is a prime example of the charged "material circulations—of media, of objects, of bodies and their practices" that shaped the scene of diplomacy beyond any single national agenda.[61] Following Diné accounts of cosmology, I recognize sand as an emissary of vital, agentive lands. It is thus a diplomatic actor in its own right. Its role in Stevens's international work was more than haphazard. By folding extracted earth into the very substrate of sandpainting, he adapted Diné healing arts to answer accelerating ecocides that were otherwise sanctioned in Cold War international relations. Sand was violently torn from its rightful place in the universe, only to be reterritorialized within the holistic framework of hózhǫ́. Stevens literally and figuratively worked against the grain by reversing the extractivist logic of "withdrawal without depositing." As he sprinkled precise lines of pigments brought from the canyons of Diné Bekéyah upon an unstable foreign ground, he realigned sand in a reliquary of his beloved homeland. By extension, disordered relations were reassembled into an orderly cosmoscape. If Diné Bekéyah was in dire need of rebalancing, Stevens's treatment of mined sand implicitly acknowledged that such a project could not be realized in isolation. How might this material practice have affected his international hosts and visitors?

DEMONSTRATING

In the form of live demonstrations, the Stevenses' work touched a wide variety of political actors, from Members of the Greater London Council to Mapuche women (see chapter 3). The final USIA report for *American Indian Art and Handicraft* recounted more than 30,000 visitors in Scotland, England, Germany, and Turkey, and more than 125,000 in Argentina, Chile, and Mexico.[62] A good number of these guests must have encountered the Stevenses in the process of creating a sandpainting or a textile, as the couple labored in public view for at least six hours a day.[63] News stories, magazine features, radio interviews, and television shows further disseminated their work as "a first rate attraction" to those who could not attend in person.[64] I turn now to consider the particular appeal of Fred Stevens's demonstrations for a diverse array of recipients. Focusing on an affective potential lodged in archival photographs of Stevens at work, my account diverges from scholarship emphasizing the colonial gaze as a means of primitivizing and possessing Indigenous artistic labor.

Visitors at all tour locales were provided basic information about sandpainting ceremonies. Stevens evidently authorized McGrath to offer commentary and answer questions during his demonstrations in English-speaking contexts, thereby freeing the hataałii to concentrate on laying designs and reciting chants.[65] In "Art in the Sand," an essay included in an exhibition brochure and reproduced in the language of each host country, Diné artist Alfred Clah, a former IAIA student, wrote that "the spirits are 'compelled' to attend this ceremony sung in their honor."[66] Yet we know that Stevens used multiple strategies to disengage the Diyin Dine'é from Cold War encounters, an approach that I propose shifted, rather than cancelled, sandpaintings' powers of attraction. Crucially, the afflicted individual who sits at the center of a ceremonial painting was absent from the scene of demonstration. A photograph from the first tour stop reveals a woman and four children—among some five thousand visitors reported in Edinburgh—sitting on a tiered wooden platform that raised them above Stevens.[67] Barricades kept bodies at bay, excepting the wayward limbs of restless children. Stevens worked on a platform that framed and elevated the bed of sand, a presentation that varied ad hoc in other locales. In Ankara and Buenos Aires, for example, an unframed pile of sand was placed directly on the floor while large standing or seated crowds peered over ropes. Yet the basic formula of a group of onlookers that is purposefully elevated and distanced by physical infrastructure was consistent. The photographer typically completed a circle of downward gazes centered on the sandpainting and its maker.

The conventions I describe locate Stevens in a genealogy of influential sandpainting demonstrations in urban centers. A brief survey includes Tł'a's efforts at the World Columbian Exposition in Chicago in 1893, a prominent presentation by Charlie Turquoise and assistants at the opening of *Indian Art of the United States* at the Museum of Modern Art (MoMA) in 1941, and the inclusion of Ben Junior's work in *Magiciens de la terre* in Paris in 1989 (an event that is dubiously billed as the first truly "global" art exhibition).[68] An iconic photograph of the MoMA event features seven well-dressed visitors peering down over a metal

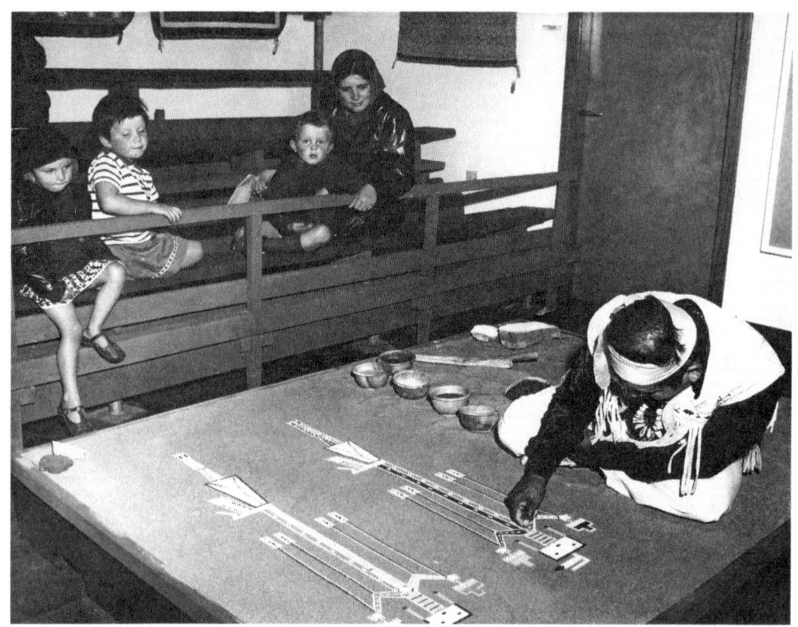

2.11

Fred Stevens creating an altered sandpainting, *Fringed Mouth with Corn*, at the English Speaking Union in Edinburgh, 1966. Provided by Rainbow Stevens and Alita Begay.

....

barricade at the seated Diné men at work, recalling the hierarchical spatial dynamics of "human zoos" at colonial expositions.[69] The ripples of the MoMA demonstrations can be traced through the work of the Indian Space Painters and the abstract expressionists in New York City, notably Jackson Pollock's early efforts to "paint" with sand on a horizontal surface at his feet. W. Jackson Rushing has critically assessed Pollock's belief that "he was authorized to appropriate the art forms, myths, and rituals of Native America" as "the transcultural psychic property of Everyman."[70] Scholars have understood such Euro-American projections of "distance and difference" onto Indigenous bodies as a hallmark of modernist primitivism.[71]

While critiques of the colonial gaze and associated dispossessions are often warranted, on their own they risk relegating Native arts to the role of mute muse in a developmental story of Euro-American art. Indigenous makers are thereby cast as naive or cynical performers in Pollock's primal scene. Photographs can overdetermine such readings by transforming the dynamic and interactive features of demonstrations

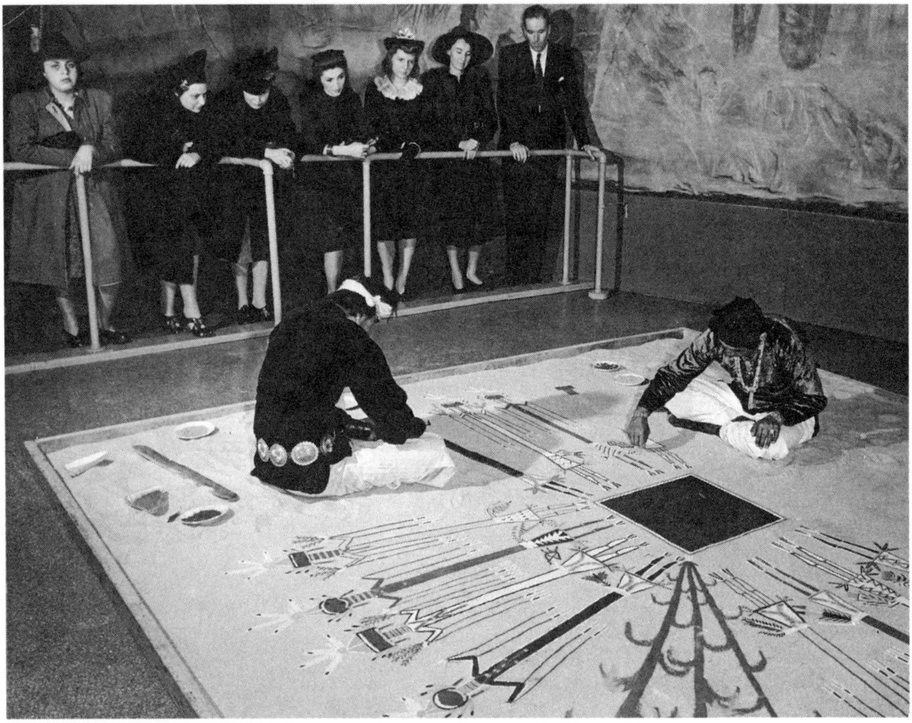

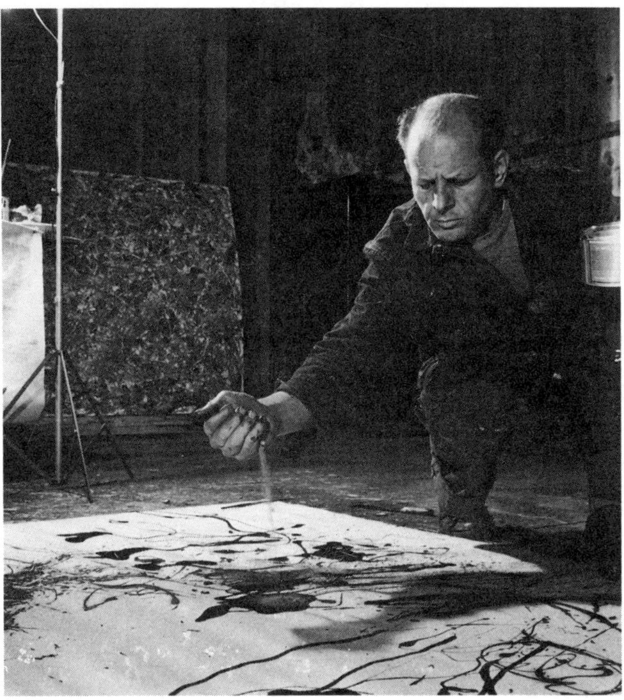

2.12

Sandpainting demonstration during *Indian Art of the United States* at the Museum of Modern Art, New York, March 26, 1941. Photographic Archive. Museum of Modern Art Archives, New York. IN123.52. Photograph by Eliot Elisofon.

2.13

Artist Jackson Pollock *Dribbling Sand on Painting While Working* in his Studio, 1949. Martha Holmes/The LIFE Picture Collection/Shutterstock.

into frozen sightlines that privilege non-Indigenous perspectives. Just as the analytic of modernist primitivism too readily accepts the objectification of both hataałii and sandpainting, soft power assumes their co-optation. Both frameworks need reexamining in light of Stevens's canny demonstrations. As international reviews indicate, the hataałii regularly alerted his visitors that he was in full command of the scene. One journalist confirmed that "Mr. Stevens was not out of place" at the English Speaking Union Gallery, having "displayed a rare sense of humor" among other signs of cultural ease.[72] Another asked Stevens how long it normally took him to finish one of his sandpainting designs. He allegedly shrugged and replied, "Regularly nine hours. But with all these tea breaks, who knows?"[73] A member of the press in London noted that "visitors were surprised that Fred and Bertha speak very good American"—better, the joke hints, than the reporter.[74]

It is equally crucial to consider that visitors watched a sandpainting in the midst of *being made,* a dynamic process that presented obstacles to objectification. Stevens invited them to observe his precise movements, listen to his recitation of accompanying chants, and track minuscule changes in the sandpainting composition for a timespan of minutes to days.[75] Two Diné premises are worth underscoring here. First, human subjects are not the center of the world; they are but one component of a complex web of relations that constitute animate lands. As Berlo summarizes, sandpaintings invoke "a multidimensional universe in which there is no viewer per se, only participants." Accordingly, "a fixed, one-point Albertian relationship to landscape . . . makes no sense, and was never sought."[76] While this effectively accounts for the embedded position of a patient in the middle of a ceremonial variant, it also has implications for Stevens's demonstrations. Consider, for example, photographs of restless crowds milling around the perimeter of his working space in Buenos Aires. Perhaps they were searching in vain for an ideal angle to view the sandpainting-in-progress, but the image unfurled in four directions on grains of sand that spilled near their feet, confounding any attempt to establish a clear "distance and difference" between subject and object. Stevens's dynamic demonstrations, I maintain, had the potential to knit disparate agents together into a process of mutual transformation. Here verbs such as *making* and *becoming* are more relevant than the fixed identities assigned to elements of still photographs.

As they rotated necks and bodies, the guests mirrored the implied movement of the figures inside the sandpaintings. This brings me to a second point: Diné language and art emphasize a world in perpetual motion. This is expressed in a prevalence of verbs that emphasize "to go" rather than "to be" in the chants that Stevens recited in *Diné Bizaad* (Diné language) while he worked. It was also available to nonspeakers as a function of the designs he employed to visualize cosmological relationships. The travels of the First People through Diné Bekéyah and their encounters with other sacred beings are reconstituted in the repetition and dynamic variation of lines, shapes, and colors—the dance of patterns in a sandpainting. Stevens's variants exhibit what anthropologist Alfred Gell theorizes an "inherent agency in decorative forms." He describes "forms which do not simply refer to (represent) agency in the external world, but which produce agency in the physical body of the index itself, so that it becomes a 'living thing.'"[77] Such material webs function as mind-traps for visitors, inducing attachments not only to physical things, but to the social projects they entail.[78] Here, we can begin to recover from the photographic archive a sense of the compelling nature of sandpaintings—their ability to call and hold the attention of new kinds of agents—within Cold War milieus. Stevens worked methodically to captivate his guests in the orderly yet vibrant universe mapped by multicolored sands. I propose that he set out to transform visitors into participants in a shifting assemblage that connected international sites of demonstration to Diné Bekéyah.

Interactive and open-ended, sandpainting demonstrations warrant reconsideration within emergent ecocritical art histories beyond the familiar framework of modernist primitivism. Since their first appearance at world fairs, Diné demonstrators anticipated Euro-American artists' growing preoccupation with ecological systems in the 1960s. As the MoMA example underscores, Diné arts were highly visible to members of a postwar avant-garde commonly credited with originating what was then loosely termed "process art." Hence, art critic Robert M. Coates pondered in the *New Yorker* in 1967, "aren't the ceremonial sand paintings of the Navajos—made painstakingly, only to be danced on once and then immediately swept away—to be considered an 'instant' art far antedating our efforts in that direction?"[79] In art historian James Nisbet's assessment, process marked a "turn away from a strictly subject-oriented understanding of action" to highlight the perpetual becomingness of human subjects and their more-than-human milieus in tandem. He identifies a "holistic, interrelational grasp of creation" that cut across the genres of environmental, postminimalist, conceptual, and performance art. Nisbet's prime example, Robert Morris's *Continuous Project Altered Daily*, 1969, notably included a square bed of earth

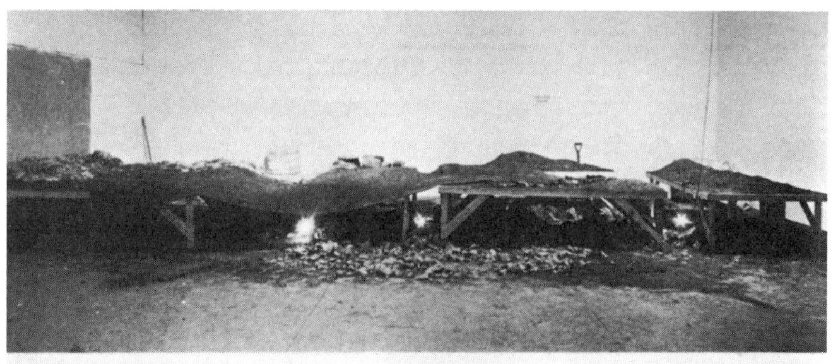
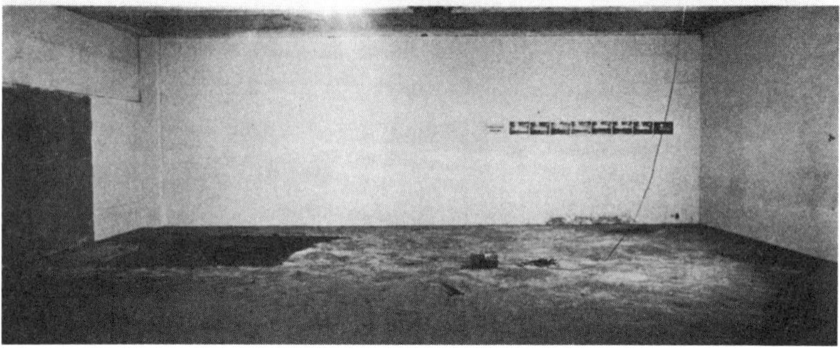

2.14

Robert Morris, *Continuous Project Altered Daily*, 1969. Earth, water, grease, plastic, felt, wood, thread, light, photographs, sound. Estate of Robert Morris.

. . . .

placed directly on the floor of the Leo Castelli Warehouse in New York, surrounded by industrial waste. The artist rearranged and serially photographed the materials over the course of the exhibition. The result was "a kind of ecological composition" in which artistic actions, environmental situations, and the distinct properties of plastic and decomposing matter engaged in a "mutual energy exchange."[80] In Stevens's demonstrations, crushed minerals from Diné Bekéyah, regionally mined sand, and diverse participants similarly met and mingled for a duration of minutes to days.

Morris himself traced the "recovery of process" to Pollock, recognizing in the webs of industrial paint more than an index of the artist's hand. Rather, he saw a "sympathy with matter . . . [that] acknowledges the inherent tendencies and properties of that matter."[81] His materialist account differs from dominant interpretations of abstract expressionism in the vein of heroic individualism and mythic universalism, which primed the movement as a soft power export.[82] Although Morris omitted Indigenous makers, his protoecological lineage implicitly connects members of the New York avant-garde to the Diné demonstrators they admired. Rather than treat Pollock as inventor, I recognize that he shared Indigenous teachers with Stevens, a fellow Cold War traveler. Whether Pollock gleaned the "right" lessons is irrelevant in the context of this book, as a new interpretation of the postwar avant-garde is not my aim. Rather, I want to highlight the need for an expanded genealogy of art and ecology centered on Native makers while recognizing that their "mutual energy exchange" with others. Writing such a history furthermore entails looking beyond the narrow purview of "American" art to consider how mounting environmental catastrophes connected Indigenous agents to international relations.

We can glean much about Stevens's engagement with ecological processes by looking closely at *Whirling Logs*, a uniquely well-documented sandpainting that he first demonstrated, then gifted to the Horniman Museum in London on his second tour stop. Like the *Fringed Mouth with Corn* sandpainting in Edinburgh, it is part of the Nightway ceremony. The paintings and oral recitations relate episodes in the journeys undertaken by one of the First People, a hero with visionary powers.[83] He encountered dangers throughout Diné Bekéyah and was assisted by the Diyin Dine'é, who invited him into their homes and gifted him the practical and ceremonial knowledge necessary for his people to live according to hózhǫ.[84] In the Horniman archives, a rare typed document by Fred Stevens relates the hero's emergence at a sacred lake "in the South-Western corner of the State of Colorado in La Plata Mountains." Stevens continues:

> The great circle in the center of the painting represents the lake. The four black bars extending outwards represent the black logs that floated to the shore to the four directions. . . . On the logs the black figures sitting at the end represent the male deities and the female Navajo deities represented by a white figure with a square mask over the face . . . to the East the white corn plant, to the South the great bean plant, to the West the yellow pumpkin plant and to the North the tobacco plant. . . . The four figures guarding the Whirling Log are the deities that gave the Navajo their chants and the songs and the painting; They carry the Universe on their back with dots of stars. . . . The rainbow goddess surrounds the painting acting as the house . . . for the figures.[85]

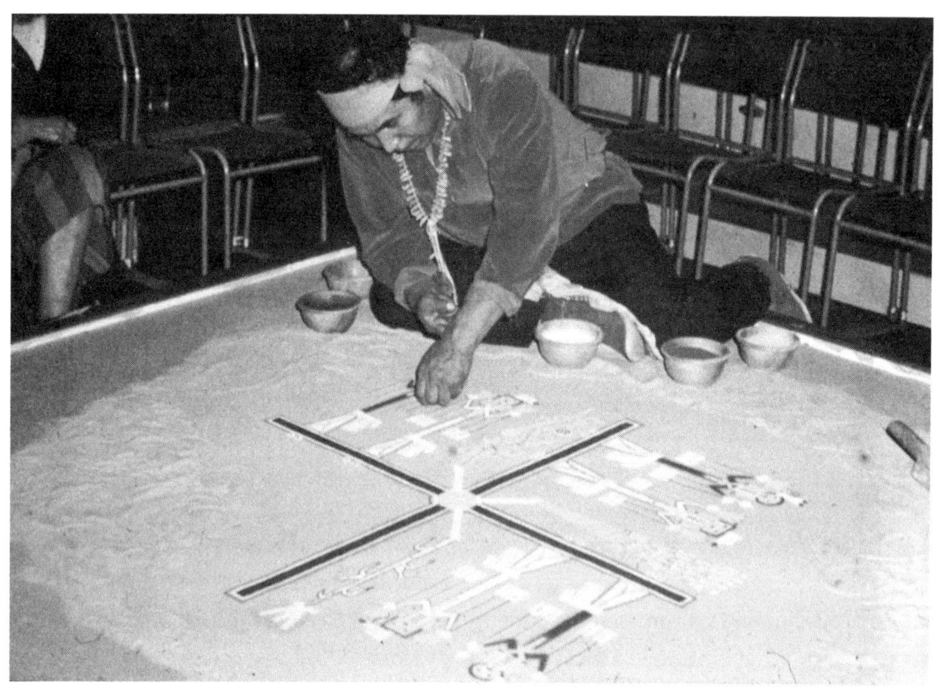

Fred Stevens creating an altered sandpainting, *Whirling Logs*, at the Horniman Museum in London, 1966. Provided by the Horniman Museum and Gardens, London.

. . . .

Whirling Logs is divided evenly into four quadrants that are anchored and connected by the bold black arms of the cross. Within this stable order, movement is conveyed by the varied orientations of the sacred figures who ride the logs, creating a sense that they are spinning in a circular motion around the whirlpool of the lake. Contained within the geometry of the composition, their movement appears measured, coordinated, and purposeful.[86] Like the circular dwelling of a hogan, the rainbow guardian frames an opening to the east to greet the rising sun. Justice Raymond D. Austin, a Diné legal scholar, writes that "the Holy Beings use the rainbow as a mode of travel between the spiritual realm and the human world, to shrink distances between points, and to bridge chasms."[87] After visiting the house of the Diyin Dine'é, the hero is sent home to his people on the back of a rainbow, carrying with him the ceremonial knowledge needed to establish hózhǫ́.[88] *Whirling Logs* invited the Stevenses' Horniman Museum hosts and visitors to follow the arc of the rainbow guardian from feet to head. In doing so, they retraced an ancient journey during which the hero established responsible and nurturing relationships among humans and land.

The travel narratives of the Nightway establish a deep historical context for the Stevenses' own forays abroad, as they, too, were received in the "houses" of powerful strangers. By composing the very substance of Diné Bekéyah on British soil, Stevens framed the arrival of Earth Surface People abroad as the renewal of a long-standing commitment to rebalance the world. I further propose that he harnessed sandpaintings' power of attraction to extend a Diné ethics of reciprocity from the sacred ecologies of his homeland to his specific hosts and visitors at the Horniman Museum. Stevens continued in the Horniman text: "This sand painting must seem completed but it isn't at all." He listed the omission of subtle but crucial aspects, from the leaves of bean stalks to the bars of rainbows to the zigzag of lightening.[89] These choices helped to safeguard foreign visitors, as an unfinished design is less likely to call the Diyin Dine'é. The altered image still had to be irresistible in order to be efficacious, but Stevens carefully shifted the appeal from the Holy People to human geopolitical agents. I suggest that he did so in order to safely welcome his British hosts and visitors into the hogan of Diné Bekéyah, implicating them in the lively yet balanced universe that sandpaintings engender. A guest of the Horniman Museum, he returned the hospitality.

While I suggest with some confidence that this invitation was issued, it is more difficult to assess whether and how it was answered. Photographs of the tour, like the ropes and platforms they picture, contain the demonstrations. Visitors' participation in an open-ended and potentially transformative process—a mutual becomingness of subjects and objects—must be recomposed in our imaginations. Still, I see hints of attraction in bodies that strain toward the hataałii and his work, spilling past railings and ropes. Consider the hundreds of local school children who, as one reporter for the *South London Press* put it, "swarmed" to watch Stevens demonstrate at the Horniman Museum.[90] Equally suggestive are members of the Greater London Council, the city's administrative body, who take advantage of the privileges of hosting to lean in and over the unfolding image. Approached as a collection of mediated fragments rather than an arbiter of all interpretive possibilities, the tour archive is full of reminders that visitors encountered sandpainting in media res. They bent, stretched, and craned not to look at a finished object, but to follow the colored particles that fell from Stevens's pinched fingers and whirled around a lake. Perhaps they also felt the rhythm of chants

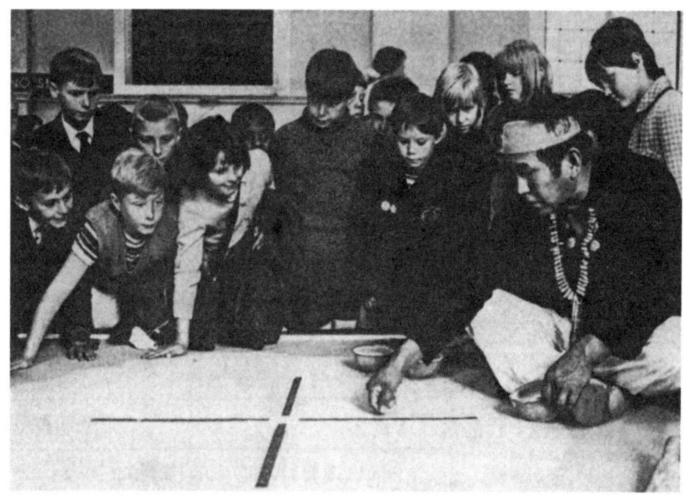

2.16

Newspaper clipping featuring Fred Stevens creating an altered sand-painting, *Whirling Logs*, for an audience of schoolchildren at the Horniman Museum in London. *The Times*, September 19, 1966. Provided by IAIA Archives, Santa Fe, New Mexico. RG03, Box 20, Folder 6, I.2.

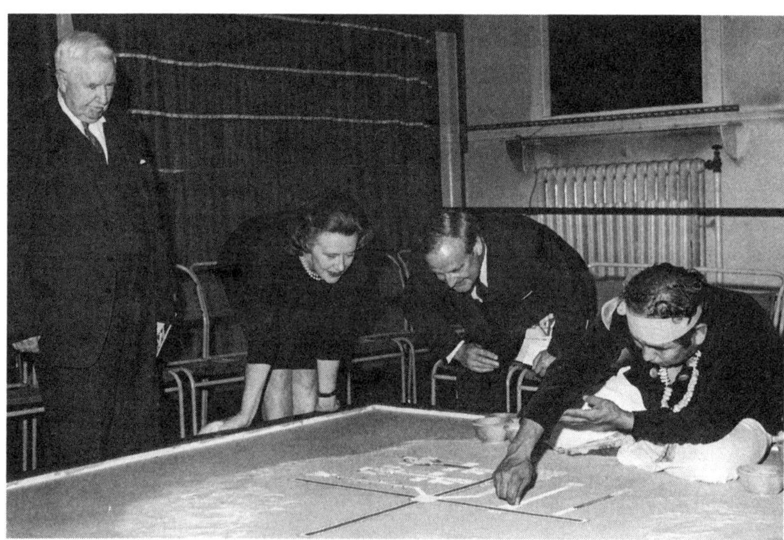

2.17

Nancy Kefauver, director of the Art in Embassies Program of the US Department of State with two members of the Greater London Council, watching Fred Stevens create *Whirling Logs* at the Horniman Museum in London, 1966. Provided by IAIA Archives, Santa Fe, New Mexico. RG03, Box 6, Folder 5, I.5.

recited in a language they could not decipher. By definition in process, demonstrations ensured that sandpainting remained a verb: in motion, coming-into-being, eluding objectification and possession.[91] The archive of these events holds open the possibility that it was Stevens's hosts and visitors who were rehoused and realigned.

GIFTING

Demonstration was only one stage in the long life of *Whirling Logs*. "We have to do this if we want to *preserve* this painting" (emphasis mine) wrote Stevens of the elements he omitted.[92] The tour inflected his experiments in durability with unprecedented material, social, and political dimensions. Here, I propose that preservation was neither an archival nor a commercial endeavor, as Parezo has indicated. Rather, Stevens collaborated with select international hosts to turn sandpaintings into gifts. Within the long history of Indigenous earth diplomacy, gifts have functioned to draw strangers into relationships of kinship and reciprocity with all living beings. "We inhabit a landscape of gifts peopled by non-human relatives, the sovereign beings who sustain us," writes Potawatomi plant biologist Robin Wall Kimmerer.[93] Indexing this abundance, gifts implicate receivers in a circuit of reciprocities that extends from the human givers to the generosity of the earth. In contrast to the violable contracts that the US government has negotiated with Indigenous and foreign nations, gifts are designed to transform fleeting political encounters into long-term relationships replete with mutual responsibilities. A closer look at the transformation of *Whirling Logs* helps to lay bare the stakes of Indigenous gifting as a dynamic component of earth diplomacy.

A report authored by three Horniman curators indicate that the challenges involved in securing *Whirling Logs* were distinct from Stevens's earlier efforts. They wrote, "The sand painter agreed in advance that an attempt could be made to preserve his design, provided that it remained incomplete. . . . He made available samples of pulverized sandstone and charcoal for experiments in consolidation."[94] Evidently, Stevens did not publicly demonstrate his well-honed technique of layering sand and glue, instead offering his support for the museum staff's behind-the-scenes efforts. While the curators do not mention Stevens's leadership again, knowledge gleaned from his decades of experimentation with various products and techniques must have been integral to the process that unfolded. Here it is worth recalling the *Scotsman*'s report that *Fringed Mouth with Corn* was "sprayed with glue to preserve it." Rather than instigating a wholly new experiment, the Horniman staff repeated, and perhaps refined, nearly two decades of Stevens's technical innovations.

Like Stevens's experiments in the United States, this process relied upon postwar developments in chemistry, engineering, and manufacturing. The curators reported on the building of a shallow, rigid, seven-by-seven-foot wooden tray reinforced with Handy Angle, a patented system of steel frames and bolts developed in the UK, to permanently house the painting (plate 6).[95] Just as the sand was locally sourced, they replaced American glue with diluted Casco Extra-Bond, a readily available equivalent of Nordic manufacture. An initial coat was painted onto the bottom of the tray to bond the first layer of base sand; the remainder was applied after Stevens completed his public demonstrations. At this point, the staff built a ten-foot cubicle of heavy-duty polythene sheeting reinforced with Handy Angle to protect the sandpainting from dust and damage. The cage doubled as staging for photographs of *Whirling Logs* taken from directly overhead. The staff proceeded to apply a fine mist of the bonding agent evenly across the surface in several coats to stabilize the topmost granules, using "an aerosol spray-gun (made by Shandon Scientific Company)."[96] Next, thicker layers were added with the help of a "weedol applicator" attached to a watering can. Staff occasionally probed the painting with a needle to assess whether the spray had effectively permeated and solidified the one-inch-thick bed of sand. In a final step, electric heat fans were placed around the sides and suspended above the painting to cure it. The curators proudly reported on the end goal of their month-long intervention: "Now it was possible to take [the sandpainting] through the exit doors of the Lecture Hall, tilting it again to 45 degrees, and round the outside of the Museum, in through the main doors and to its final place [of exhibition] in the South Hall."[97]

Mined sand, synthetic glues, herbicide applicators, steel braces, electric fans, bean stalks, and pumpkin vines—*Whirling Logs* was remade as a hybrid of postwar industrial technologies and the earth they upended. The hardening of the sandpaintings cemented it more firmly into the extractive economies reshaping the Stevenses' tour locale. New relationships were consolidated with the layers. Diné Bekéyah continued to unite disparate agents and materials under a shimmering, arched roof. But now, the hero traversed a plastic rainbow, an amalgam of sandstone and synthetics that fused La Plata Mountains to London and beyond. At the same time, *Whirling Logs* condensed and reassembled elements

::::::::::

that were already connected. A former colonizer of Indigenous American homelands, Great Britain worked alongside the United States to advance extractive industries worldwide during the Cold War. The sandpainting changed hands while citizens of the Navajo Nation and the United Kingdom differently navigated a burgeoning transnational landscape of sand mines and oil wells, concrete towers and nuclear arsenals.

While *Whirling Logs* materially embedded industrial products and processes, the work should not be seen as condoning their damaging effects. On the contrary, such inclusions better positioned the sandpainting to carry out the urgent project of rebalancing a world riven by the twin monsters of extraction and toxicity. *Whirling Logs* reprised the Holy People's original gifts to humans, cloud painting prototypes that enabled the survival of Diné in ancient times and compelled their descendants to redress new forms of evil. As a gift made from damaged elements of land, the sandpainting specifically implicated the Stevenses' British hosts and visitors in this collective responsibility. The work offered an international path to redress ecocidal paradigms by restoring reciprocity with the earth—the cosmic balance necessary for Diné and British bodies to thrive in connection with others around the world.

On behalf of whom or what did Stevens gift this extraordinary device? Unable to ask the maker, I turn to *Whirling Logs* for additional clues. As a cosmological map of a homeland that Diné have long defended against military and corporate incursions, the sandpainting is not reducible to the representational logic of the United States. While the USIA aimed convince foreign audiences that Diné traveled a unilateral path into US capitalism and nationhood, the rainbow delineates an alternate route, inviting visitors to follow the hero into the protective fold of Diné Bekéyah.[98] Nor can *Whirling Logs* be explained solely as an emissary of a worldly political institution, the Navajo Nation. In 1923, the BIA implemented the first tribal council with the primary aim of approving oil and other mineral leases. While the establishment of the Navajo Tribal Code in 1962 expanded the council's jurisdiction according to customary Diné values, its activities were circumscribed by US investments in extractive industries at the time of the tour.[99] Contemporary Diné commentators nonetheless highlight the perseverance of hózhǫ́ in art, ceremony, and natural law, an ideal guiding intergenerational efforts to restore the spiritual and ecological health of Diné Bekéyah. Notably, a protective rainbow came to decorate the Navajo Nation's Great Seal in 1952 and flag in 1968, symbolically enfolding the historically contingent nation in a capacious framework of universe as hogan.[100] Austin writes, "Ask a Navajo person, 'What is Navajo sovereignty?' and expect the response to be '*Nááts 'íílid nihinazt'íí*' (It's the sacred rainbow that surrounds us)."[101] The rainbow bridges worldly authority with cosmological truth. It signals the capacity for Diné knowledge and art to support more-than-human flourishing within a compromised geopolitical order. Perhaps it is safest to say, then, that Stevens gifted on behalf of Diné Bekéyah, for the good all members of an indivisible earth. By reassembling damaged relationships among people and the earth, *Whirling Logs* promoted the restoration of cosmic balance necessary for Diné bodies and ecologies to thrive in connection with others around the world. Stevens's sandpainting responded to the limited political imaginary of the colonial nations that framed Diné Bekéyah and the tour, pointedly working to transmit the healing promise of reciprocity into a broken system.

As a demonstration, *Whirling Logs* invited strangers into a temporary assemblage composed of bodies, postwar technologies, and land. As a gift, the sandpainting propelled mutual obligations to maintain hózhǫ́ into a precarious future. The only extant sandpainting from the Stevenses' tour, *Whirling Logs* persists at the Horniman Museum today. It was conserved in 2004 and reinstalled in the entryway to the museum in 2018, where it welcomes visitors to the World Gallery with "a shared indigenous American understanding of generosity and respect as the basis for all social relations."[102] The sandpainting's expansive ethics contrasts with a global surge of violent nationalisms and catastrophic climate changes as I write. Colonial nations that drew the map of modern geopolitics continue to turn their backs on displaced humans and the ravaged land, seeming to indefinitely suspend any promise of earth diplomacy. An emissary of Diné cosmology that has endured and adapted to colonial violence, *Whirling Logs* presses us to imagine forms of collective life that will outlast a failing international system. More than an act of preservation, consolidation enabled a temporal extension of the relational principles at the heart of Diné Bekéyah. The sandpainting is a tangible reminder that hózhǫ́ is renewable, pressing new visitors to rebalance relationships with the earth, the ultimate host.

A NORTH-SOUTH AXIS OF TURMOIL

The Stevenses' travels through Latin America amid global political uprisings in 1968 point to another vital context for earth diplomacy, one in which material practices of reciprocity nurture anticapitalist, decolonial, and trans-Indigenous solidarities beyond a Euro-American axis. While I treat this subject more extensively in the chapters that follow, I conclude this one with a glimpse of sandpaintings' entanglements with the tumult surrounding the Olympic Games in Mexico City, the last stop of the Stevenses' tour. The 1968 event was made famous by two instances of resistance: the raised fists of African American athletes Tommie Smith and John Carlos during the US national anthem, indicating solidarity with Black Power and labor movements unfolding around the world, and the student uprising in Mexico City, which targeted the Olympics as an emblem of the dispossessive dominion of capital and nation. Amid the cacophony, sand resurfaced to quietly bridge the sensuous appeal of earth diplomacy and the oppositional fervor of activism.

The Diné couple performed at the International Exhibition of Popular Art, a cultural program with forty participating countries that accompanied the sporting event. Their DOS invitation was intended as a cultural complement to the Alliance for Progress, a program initiated by the Kennedy administration in 1961 that used corporate investment as a tool of diplomacy across Latin America.[103] In a parallel agenda, the reigning Partido Revolucionario Institucional (PRI) used the Olympics as a platform to champion the so-called Mexican miracle of postwar growth before the eyes of international guests.[104] Art historian George F. Flaherty has explored how the PRI's hospitality, while seemingly magnanimous, was a means of asserting the authority and property of the state, while obscuring "inhospitable social, political, and economic structures, such as the displacement and dispossession characteristic of Mexico's capitalist modernization."[105] The International Exhibition of Popular Art revealed commonalities in how the Mexican and United States governments approached Indigenous arts and crafts, namely treating them vehicles for assimilating Native peoples while claiming them as evidence of unique national identities on a global stage.[106] Such Olympic exercises of soft power were undermined when the student movement erupted across the city. Demonstrators contested the PRI's top-down vision of seamless progress, chanting, "¡No queremos Olimpiadas, queremos revolución!" ("We don't want Olympics, we want revolution!")[107]

In 2018, McGrath told me a story that did not make its way into official reports. In the days leading up to the games, he and the Stevenses were startled by "all of a sudden hearing rifle shots" near their hotel. "The government cracked down on student protests right outside our window," he concluded.[108] McGrath referred to the Tlatelolco massacre that unfolded on the night of October 2, concurrent with the Stevenses' arrival. The deadly attack by Mexican paramilitary forces on peaceful demonstrators took place at the Plaza de las Tres Culturas, where the foreign ministry headquarters was built atop Aztec ruins. It was part of a broad government suppression of labor unions, farmers, students, and Indigenous groups who were committed to exposing the gross inequities of modernization.[109] The events helped to catalyze the founding of the Ejército Zapatista de Liberación Nacional (EZLN) the following year, marking a sustained challenge to the exploitation of Indigenous land and labor that mirrored the growth of AIM to the north.[110] The escalating violence in Mexico City meanwhile precipitated a breakdown in the choreographed gentility of nation-state soft power. "People were on their toes all the time," said McGrath. "We got [the] lowest support of any place."[111] His journal of the tour notably recorded the groups' repeated, failed entreaties to the Mexican Olympic Committee and the US Embassy alike to secure usable sand.[112]

On the night before the opening, McGrath and Stevens took matters into their own hands. They located a building site near their hotel and "snuck out [with sacks] and got some sand."[113] Construction zones were materially and symbolically critical to Mexican nation-building during the Cold War, even as they relied upon the penetrative force of transnational capital on the model of the Alliance for Progress. The pair's late-night journey thus marked a quiet rupture in the corporate-national-diplomatic contracts driving modern international relations. Transformed from honored guests to thieves in the night, their illicit movements inadvertently paralleled the spatial tactics of the student-led uprising, which demonstrated that "the city was itself a medium capable of being harnessed to challenge the PRI's illegitimate sovereignty," in Flaherty's estimation.[114] Stolen sand, a byproduct of contested modernization, smuggled the volatility of 1968 into the very foundation of sandpainting.

Stevens went to work as usual the next day, sprinkling the substance on the floor of a designated space inside the International Exhibition of Popular Art. He wrested sand from the inhospitable agendas of competing nations, only to employ it in an alternative construction of home, reintegrating the contested substance within the holistic framework of hózhǫ. I see his methodical chants and gestures as a crucial companion to the raucous uprising on the streets outside and around the world. Stevens's sandpainting translations exemplify earth diplomacy by drawing upon more-than-human sources of power to generate collective renewal and rebalancing in the direst of circumstances. As the affective and

::::::::::

inspirited "glue" that binds durable relationships, such sensuous modalities are a necessary complement to direct action in the creation of resilient justice movements. Indeed, Stevens's sandpainting translations anticipated the crucial role that diplomacy would play in EZLN, AIM, and other radical Indigenous organizations that took root as the Diné couple's journey drew to a close, as I will discuss in subsequent chapters. I turn now to Bertha Stevens's matricentered textile arts, highlighting the empowerment of Indigenous women in an expanding "extractive zone" that targets those agents most responsible for perpetuating life.

EARTH MOTHERS

DINÉ WEAVING AND TRANS-INDIGENOUS ECOFEMINISM

:::::::::::

IN 1968, as political activism roiled around the world, the Diné (Navajo) artist Bertha Stevens (1912–1997) sat quietly weaving at the Biblioteca Nacional in Santiago, Chile. A photograph from her two-part, three-year diplomatic tour through Eurasia and the Americas reveals the artist seated before a customary upright wooden loom, using a shed rod to part the curtain of fine wool threads that form the warp of her weaving. While the photograph is rich in detail, its apparent centerpiece, the textile, is a plain field of white. Only with careful study can we discern a few rows of the weft, the striped bottom border of a project just begun. Contextualized within a modernist market that has concentrated value in the formal qualities and regional stylistic classifications of Diné textiles, the photograph is defined by blankness: the art is not there, at least not yet.

But as our attention is freed to wander, we encounter glimmers of an ecorelational aesthetics that does not reside solely in the object. In the fore- and middle ground, baskets are filled with raw and carded wool of various shades, pointing to the raising and shearing of sheep in Diné Bekéyah, the physical and spiritual homeland of Diné in southwestern North America. Variegated flocks, as well as the desert plants that nourish them and stain their wool, are integral to women's wealth, kinship networks, social responsibilities, and creative process. Wool fibers also bind

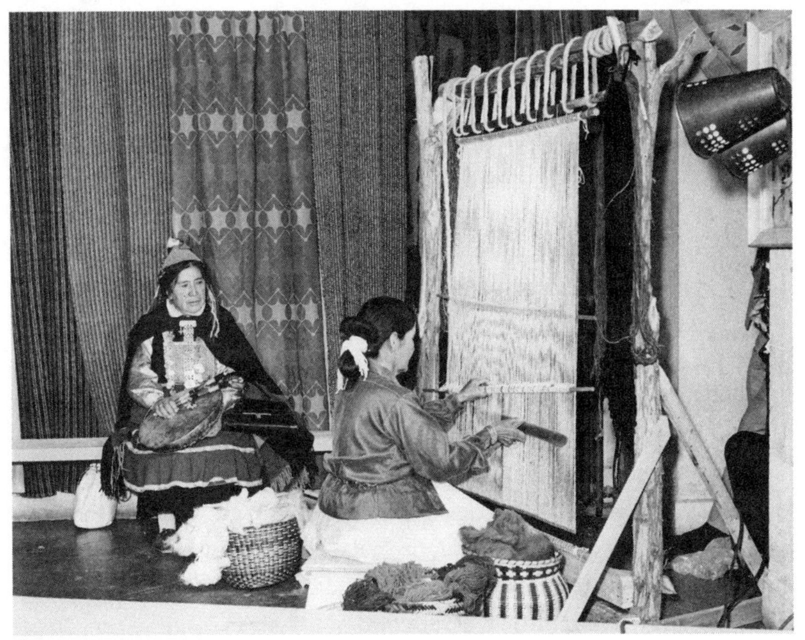

3.1

Juana María Castillo watches Bertha Stevens weave at the Biblioteca Nacional, Santiago, Chile, 1968. Provided by Rainbow Stevens and Alita Begay.

....

Bertha Stevens's long black hair into a *tsiiyéél*, a distinctive hourglass-shaped bun, communicating the orderly nature of her thoughts to discerning viewers. Disciplined thinking—patience and tenacity—brings order to the chaos inherent in one's mind, on one's loom, and in the world; it is necessary for *sa'ah naagháii bik' eh hózhǫ́*, the foremost Diné principle, translated as a long life lived in beauty, harmony, happiness, and reciprocity with all beings in the universe (often shortened to *hózhǫ́*; see chapter 2).[1] Contemporary Diné artist D. Y. Begay elaborates that weaving is *iina'*, "an extraordinary Navajo word that describes how you live, how life is carried out, and how life is respected in the Navajo world."[2] It is a core teaching of the beloved Diyin Dine'é (Holy Person), Asdzáá Náádleehé (Changing Woman), whose body formed the land, the sheep, and the people. Having acquired knowledge of weaving by watching Na'ashjéii Asdzáá (Spider Woman) at work, Changing Woman transmitted the responsibility to learn by observing and teach by showing to her human daughters, a pedagogical precedent for Stevens's demonstrations abroad.[3]

While Diné are customarily matrilineal and matrilocal—that is, they trace kinship and inheritance through their mothers' side of the family—I use the more capacious term, matricentered, to emphasize the cosmologically derived responsibility of women and *nádleehí* (a term referencing nonbinary Diné genders) to perpetuate all life. Beyond biological reproduction, their roles might include raising adopted children, nurturing crops and sheep, building consensus on decisions that impact the land and community, or growing a textile, conceived as bringing a new person into being.[4] Commanding distinct forms of creativity and power, women are paramount to protecting the vitality of Diné Bekéyah from what Latin American studies scholar Macarena Gómez-Barris calls the "extractive zone," an expanding resource frontier that the United States pursued intensively in relation to the Navajo Nation, Chile, and other Latin American countries during the Cold War.[5] Gómez-Barris assesses, "Colonial capitalism's territorial expansion in the Américas has historically operated through the appendages of state violence, especially through a biopolitical strategy that converts original territories into extractive zones."[6] Mirroring the United States' pursuit of Termination and aided by its administration of the Alliance for Progress to spur corporate development across Latin America, Chile's genocidal policies forcibly displaced Indigenous inhabitants, transferred their homelands into state and commercial property, enrolled them as labor in agroforestry and mining industries, and reduced their conditions of livability to bare life.[7] "Weaving is iina'" assumes a new urgency amid such devastations. Returning to the expanse of white threads, we may begin to see how the unfinished textile is replete with cosmopolitical knowledge embedded in a North-South axis of crisis.

The interweaving of minds and bodies at work in this Department of State photograph extends to the seated woman wearing silver jewelry and other fine regalia who watches Stevens work. While a formal caption describes her generically as "a Chilean Mapuche of the South," her name is Juana María Castillo. Resting squarely in her lap is a *kultrün*, a round, shallow drum made of stretched goat skin that is conceived by Mapuche as a womb that bears the universe.[8] Teetering on the edge of her thigh is another container for the world, a shiny, rectangular handbag with a manufactured metal clasp and a strap wedged in the crook of her arm. The luggage accompanied Castillo and Luisa Morales, president of the Mapuche organization *Centro de Madres* (Center for Mothers), on a four-hundred-mile journey from the community of Quetrahue to greet Bertha Stevens and her husband, the *hataałii* (ceremonial healer or singer) Fred Stevens, with song. Two lights jutting into the upper right corner of the photograph mark the staged nature of the meeting. While US and Chilean officials sought to script the scene as an authentic ethnographic performance, it is evident that the women activated other dynamics, notably connecting the Indigenous cosmologies manifested in the textile and drum to the colonial-capitalist expansion signaled by the punctum of the purse.[9]

The photograph answers additional, gendered silences in a vast literature about Cold War international relations. Bertha Stevens joins only a handful of Indigenous American women as artist-travelers in United States archives. Often accompanied by more famous husbands who occasioned the invitations and commanded the interviews, they have yet to receive more than a sentence or two of acknowledgment in published histories of the era.[10] In media reports on the couple's tour, Fred Stevens's humorous commentary and spectacular sandpainting demonstrations overshadow Bertha Stevens's quiet persistence. Tour director James McGrath's initial letters to foreign hosts privilege "our Sandpainter, to be assisted by Mrs. Bertha Stevens, his wife, who is also a weaver (and if we have space, she will set up a loom in the exhibition area)."[11] Building on my previous discussion of Fred Stevens's altered sandpaintings, this chapter devotes equivalent attention to Bertha Stevens's demonstration that weaving is iina', focusing on the reciprocal exchange of creative knowledge among disparately located women who negotiated the ecocidal policies of the nation-states that framed them.

My aim in placing Bertha Stevens's encounter with Mapuche at the very center of *Earth Diplomacy* is not merely additive, as in an effort to include Indigenous women's neglected stories to enhance the diversity of Cold War narratives. Their exchange is definitional, requiring theorization of the gendered dimensions of earth diplomacy and its oppression within the patriarchal order of relations among modern nations. Stevens's global travels prompt me to revisit the entanglement of Native women's art and diplomacy with *ecofeminism*, a discourse that shaped scholarship and activism in the final three decades of the twentieth century, before falling out of favor. Her woven exchanges unsettle dominant assumptions about cultural difference circulated by mainly white practitioners, which were focused on Indigenous and Asian women, united by a generic "Mother Earth," and charged with primitivism and essentialism. Following a handful of other scholars, I see the alleged failings of ecofeminism not as grounds for dismissal, but rather as a prompt to establish an alternative, trans-Indigenous genealogy in the overlooked context of cultural diplomacy.

ECOFEMINIST ANCESTORS

In customary Diné and numerous other Indigenous societies, women are responsible for the creative continuation of more-than-human relations of kinship and mutualism, a vital component of earth diplomacy. But from the first moments of contact, European colonizers undermined Native leadership structures by insisting on negotiating with the "chiefs," real or fictive. Of European invention, the term "tends to homogenize a remarkably diverse group of men and women who received their leadership positions in many ways," including family lineage, healing power, battle prowess, prodigious gifting, oratory skill, and creative vision.[12] As Quo Li Driskill, Mark Rifkin, and others have illuminated, colonialism can be usefully narrated as an unfinished project of straightening the queer shape of Indigenous peoples' relationships to land and each other.[13] In such accounts, United States hegemony over Native people and territory entails the fragmentation of earth-based collectives and their coerced assimilation to the norm of the male-headed, nuclear, property-owning family, a fundamental unit of extractive capitalism and an ideological mainstay of the Cold War (underscored in my discussion of the touring photography exhibition, *The Family of Man*, in chapter 1). The installation and regulation of heteropatriarchy as a function of European colonization around the world has had dire consequences for the earth, understood by some matricentered Indigenous communities to be a sacred, powerful female progenitor. Nonetheless, against the odds, more-than-human bonds of kinship and reciprocity remained vital during the Cold War. Indigenous agents ignored the gendered scripts provided by the United States, Chilean, and other governments to honor women's creative roles in the dissemination of earth diplomacy.

The role of feminism in my analysis of these dynamics is at once crucial and fraught. Recent, well-meaning critiques of gender in international relations have presumed the universality of a patriarchal order, inadvertently dismissing Indigenous frameworks of land, power, and politics. At the outset of the volume, *Gender and Diplomacy*, editors Jennifer A. Cassidy and Sara Althari confidently assert that "men have functioned as the primary authors and facilitators of the geopolitical order since the beginnings of human history." They continue,

"Indeed, the culture and structure of diplomacy has been defined and constructed by the chronicles of men. Whilst modernity continues to challenge archaic patriarchal infrastructures, the practice of diplomacy remains adherent to conventional notions of gender. As a result, diplomacy continues as a sphere rife with power dynamics, which serve to reinforce gender inequality and perpetuate the historical 'otherization' of women."[14] In assuming that gender subordination is consistent across time, space, and cultures, their critique overlooks colonialism as a historically contingent yet world-shaping force connecting patriarchy to modernity. In a contemporaneous edited volume, *Gendering Diplomacy and International Negotiation*, Karin Aggestam and Ann E. Towns similarly note the underrepresentation of women in current international relations and ponder "to what extent diplomatic culture contains gendered scripts and may pose structural barriers for female diplomats and negotiators."[15] While their emphasis on the performativity of gender creates possibilities for subversion and alternative scriptwriting, they again limit the investigation to a classical European lineage by tracing the origins of modern diplomacy "back to ancient Greece."[16] Relegated to an assessment of good and bad universalism, such analyses neither displace Eurocentrism nor recover pluralism in the diplomatic sphere.

To date, little effort has been made to discuss the gendered dynamics of diplomacy in relation to ecofeminism, a discourse in which Native women's power emerged as a central yet contested theme in the final decades of the twentieth century. I treat the convergence of these discourses as a useful step toward theorizing and historicizing Indigenous women artists' roles as earth diplomats. While the term "ecofeminism" stands in for a diversity of positions, it is anchored in a by-now-familiar critique of the anthropocentric dualism of nature and culture. Ecofeminists have in turn mapped that binary construction onto the exploitation of earth-associated women and the ascendency of history-making men in a framework of heteronormativity. Karen Warren goes so far as to state that "what *all* ecofeminists agree about . . . is the way in which *the logic of domination* has functioned historically within patriarchy to sustain and justify the twin dominations of women and nature."[17] Art historian Jane Blocker usefully expresses the problem as a fundamental, gendered binary of earth and nation. Each "stands at the top of a lengthy list of related concepts. The earth is prehistorical, female, primitive, of the body; the nation is historical, male, colonial, of the mind."[18] Although some ecofeminists approached this dichotomy as though it was timeless and universal, more often its worldwide appearance was attributed to Western colonialism and imperialism, giving rise to a modern nation-state system that privileges male leaders, embraces resource extraction, and persecutes alternative relationships among gender, nature, and culture. This discourse generated much creative theorizing about more-than-human entanglements, as well as damaging cultural fictions that sank the mothership by the end of the twentieth century.

The term "ecofeminism" is typically attributed to French scholar Françoise d'Eaubonne in an essay published in 1974.[19] However, amid the multiculturalism of the 1980s and 1990s, it became popular for predominantly white practitioners based in the United States and Western Europe to assert that ecofeminism sprang up spontaneously around the world in the form of grassroots, women-led environmental activism.[20] An equally prevalent touchpoint for ecofeminists was the apparently common truth among Indigenous and Asian Indian peoples that the earth is a beloved mother and all beings are related, giving rise to an ethics of land care coeval with the equality, complementarity, and fluidity of gender roles. Finally, pagan origins, the "white Indians of an imagined (and researched!) European past," in the words of Women's studies scholar Noël Sturgeon, offered apparent ancient evidence of earth-based goddess worship as yet another path into ecofeminism.[21] It may seem less problematic for white ecofeminists to look to their own ancestors, instead of appropriating others'—and in fact, some Indigenous critics and advocates of antiracism urged such a direction. However, as Sturgeon assessed, pre-Christian European, Native American, and Asian Indian women were often conflated into a timeless, idealized Indigeneity and elevated as the desirable ecological "other" to industrial societies.[22] From such a vantage point, ecofeminism's patron saint, "Mother Earth," is a wholly generic deity presiding over the search for ancient and contemporary alternatives to ecocidal patriarchy. Herein lies the most serious charge of essentialism: the primitivist fantasy of an outside, mapped onto time, geography, or culture, is an ideological mainstay of colonialism. This in turn is the violent global terrain in which difference (human and otherwise) fights for its life. In light of such sustained critiques, the term ecofeminism was "effectively discarded" by the end of the century.[23]

Even as ecofeminism fell out of scholarly favor, many of its proponents' core insights were uprooted and repurposed under the banners of ecocriticism and new materialism in the 2000s. Education scholars Annette Gough and Hilary Whitehouse write of the "amnesia" by which "new materialist thinkers have tended to ignore the genealogical connections with ecofeminism."[24] Similarly, some Native studies scholars, myself included, have taken contemporary thinkers to task for claiming the novelty of intellectual paradigms centered on ecological enmeshment and other-than-human agency.[25] Indigenous peoples have long articulated such truths, but their contributions are rarely credited as compelling insights about a shared modernity. In the course of this research, I have come to recognize that even a cursory genealogy of recent ecocritical thought points back to ecofeminism, where matricentered Native American and majority world communities, both real and imagined, were front and center. I conclude that by throwing out the discourse, a key portal for Indigenous cosmopolitics was inadvertently slammed shut, severing theory from its lived foundations and making way for new appropriations. This chapter pursues another course. I aim to rethink the plural origins and diplomatic potential of "Mother Earth" beyond the projection of primitivism, specifically foregrounding the contributions of Native artists, scholars, activists, and diplomats.

MOTHER EARTH UNDER SIEGE

It is important to recognize that ecofeminism, too, has an Indigenous prehistory. In 1986, Pueblo author and ecofeminist contributor Paula Gunn Allen argued that the "Native American roots of white feminism reach back beyond Sacagawea."[26] Following her prompt, historian Sally Roesch Wagner has established that nineteenth-century leaders of the National Woman Suffrage Association Matilda Joslyn Gage, Elizabeth Cady Stanton, and Susan B. Anthony were informed by their experiences in Haudenosaunee territory in upstate New York, where they identified the customary political and spiritual authority of Native women as a form of "matriarchate" or "mother rule."[27] Gage publicly advocated for suffragists to follow the lead of the Haudenosaunee, arguing that the "division of power between the sexes in this Indian republic was nearly equal," while clan structures "demonstrated woman's superiority in power."[28] In the first decades of the twentieth century, encounters with Diné and Pueblo understandings of gender and land-centered governance inspired additional white feminist theorizing about matricentered utopias.[29] Dina Gilio-Whitaker of the Colville Confederated Tribes posits Indigenous women organizers as core contributors to Native rights, feminism, and environmental justice, highlighting the leadership of Laura Cornelius Kellogg (Oneida), a founding member of the

Society of American Indians in 1911, and Zitkála-Šá (Gertrude Simmons Bonnin, Lakota), president of the National Council of American Indians from 1926 to 1938.[30] Formed in 1974, the Women of All Red Nations continued this legacy by addressing sexism and the marginalization of women's customary power in and beyond the American Indian Movement (AIM).[31] Hence, while some Native women have looked sidelong at ecofeminism as yet another flavor of New Age spiritual appropriation, others have contributed to the discourse by foregrounding its tangible Indigenous debts.

My analysis is likewise inspired by debates surrounding Cuban-born artist Ana Mendieta's earthworks following her arrival in the United States as a refugee in 1961. Mendieta's exploration of her body in relation to Indigenous rituals and land has been criticized alongside ecofeminism for its "constant repetition of an unquestioned, generic (gyneric) Great Mother," as artist and critic Mira Schor put it.[32] Blocker counters, "To whose traditions are we referring? Is the problem that Mendieta could not produce dialogue, conflict, or complexity in her image of woman or, rather, that we presume too quickly a familiarity with that image? Whom do we picture in our minds when we think of Woman? For what earth, what nature, does that Woman stand?"[33] Implicit in Blocker's questions is a suggestion that critiques of essentialism may invent the very uniformity they set out to deconstruct. Similarly, opponents of Mother Earth may find themselves in the awkward position of telling Native people that their varied assertions of matrilineal kinship with the land veer into perilous colonial fictions. Indigenous studies scholar Vanessa Watts articulates the problem with unusual clarity. Her own Anishinaabe and Haudenosaunee oral histories inform a lived theory of "Indigenous Place-Thought," centered on the insight that the female land is "alive and thinking and that humans and non-humans derive agency through the extensions of these thoughts."[34] Turning to Sturgeon's critique of an ecofeminist Mother Earth, Watts argues that "essentializing categories of Indigenous cosmologies should not be measured against the products of Euro-Western mistakes. . . . To disengage with essentialism means we run the risk of disengaging from the land."[35] Watts effectively identifies the danger, but in my estimation, it is not necessary to concede Mother Earth as an essentialized representation to make this argument. The earth of Mendieta's performances is dynamic and elusive; it cannot be apprehended as an object. On the contrary, the artist's famous *Silueta Series* (1973–1980) generates sensorial excess as the human body encounters earthly elements. Art historian Amanda Boetzkes has proposed that the series invites an ethical orientation to the nonhuman world by foregrounding the earth's boundlessness and refusal of Western representational systems.[36] Similarly, Watts's assessment of the earth as the living, breathing locus of all agency decenters a colonial subject-object binary as the foundation for essentialist identities of all kinds. She foregrounds material dependencies and ethical reciprocities in lieu of static representations.

A related case from the recent historiography of Indigenous studies illuminates the political stakes of these debates, although it unfolded outside of the framework of ecofeminism. Sam Gill, a non-Native scholar of Native North American religions, drew ire from Indigenous commentators when he set out to debunk the antiquity of Mother Earth as a Native icon in his 1987 book, *Mother Earth: An American Story*. Gill argues that she has "come into existence in America largely during the last hundred years" and "cannot be adequately understood and appreciated apart from the complex history of the encounter between Native Americans and Americans of European ancestry."[37] A generous reading suggests that Gill's aim was not to delegitimize Native truths so much as problematize their corralling into a universal icon purified of colonialism. *Mother Earth* explores how Euro-Americans have manipulated the equation of Indigenous land with an archetypal Native woman's body to serve US nation-building, exemplified in the invention of a sexually inviting Pocahontas to symbolize the so-called New World as a "mother of us all."[38] Still, a critical review by Vine Deloria, Jr., of Gill's book is instructive for my purposes. The esteemed Dakota scholar argues that Gill's reliance on ethnographic citations misses the political contexts in which Native people selectively translated their cosmologies for outsiders. Mother Earth is found in "minutes of councils and treaty negotiations. . . . Indians were not sitting around seminar rooms articulating a nature philosophy for the benefit of non-Indian students after all. They were trying to save their lands from exploitation and expropriation."[39] Deloria, Jr. does *not* argue that Mother Earth is mere political pageantry, a form of strategic essentialism in which colonized people instrumentalize stereotypes that originate in Euro-American contexts. Rather, he indicates that Native people have mobilized their own diverse cosmologies in the dominant language to contest the dispossessive policies of the settler state.

Several lessons for ecofeminism can be distilled from the varied accounts I've cited. First, any search for a culturally pure or singular alternative to ecocidal patriarchy in Native communities is bound to fail before the lived complexity of Indigenous negotiations with colonial modernity. Second, dismissing "Mother Earth" because she is implicated in primitivist fantasies does violence to the plurality of Indigenous truths that bind human minds and bodies to animate lands. What if instead we consider this English abstraction to be a function of translation, undertaken by Indigenous negotiators when their communities and homelands are under siege? It follows that Mother Earth is not an object available for abstraction (or extraction); like Bertha Steven's textile, she points to a process of weaving distinct Indigenous peoples, places, and polities into a network of kin to withstand colonial deracination. She "implies a relation of mutuality and enacts a shared being-in-common," as art historian Jonathan Flatley has articulated on behalf of a queer affective politics.[40] To offer my own terms, the pluralized and politicized Earth Mothers of Deloria, Jr.'s account are invoked as diplomatic agents. By harnessing their rhetorical and material power, Native leaders have worked to ensure that all their relations—human, plant, animal, river, and mountain—are present and participating in nation-to-nation negotiations.

CHANGING WOMAN AND WOVEN CONTRACTS

Yet to fully account for the diplomatic roles of Indigenous daughters, it is imperative to widen our view beyond the "hard power" politics of modern international relations (see chapter 2). If, as I have established, the Euro-American authors of a dominant geopolitical order "colonized the spaces of diplomacy" by denying the legitimacy of Native women's land-based leadership, attention to the efficacy of their arts can help to recover their contributions.[41] Documentation of Diné textiles in the possession of Pueblo, Kiowa, Cheyenne, Lakota, Blackfeet, and other Native nations indicates that weavers facilitated trans-Indigenous diplomacy and trade throughout the nineteenth century. German painter Karl Bodmer painted a Blackfeet man wearing a Diné striped blanket and a Pueblo silver pendant on an expedition in 1832–1834.[42] Brulé Dakota artist Wa-po-cta-xi (Battiste Good) characterized 1858–1859 as "Many-Navajo-blankets winter" in his reproduction of a Winter Count, a pictographic historical record documenting each year with a single event of significance.[43] While Diné called their prestigious striped wearing blankets *hanoolchaadi*, referencing women's process of preparing the wool, their commercial rebranding as "chief's blankets" likely reflects their

:::::::::

omnipresence on the plains, even as the label imposes a colonial gender hierarchy on a matricentered artform.[44] Euro-American commentators have most often attributed the travels of Diné textiles to intertribal commerce. However, such exchanges were also embedded in diplomatic relations, as suggested by a Lakota delegation's reciprocal gift of a ceremonial pipe to Diné to help secure a military alliance against United States invaders around 1875.[45] Both weavers and wearers incorporated Plains, Pueblo, European, and Mexican materials and design elements prior to their inclusion of United States symbols during treaty negotiations.[46] The United States flag resonated with the striped format and coloration common to Diné textiles, such that "the Indian agent from New Mexico, in a full suit of buckskin, presented Mrs. Lincoln with a red, white, and blue Navajo blanket" in 1862.[47]

Diné historian Jennifer Nez Denetdale's account of her female ancestors' creativity following their militarized removal from Diné Bekéyah in 1864 provides a model for my own study of Bertha Stevens's tour. It was Denetdale's maternal great-great-grandfather, Hastiin Ch'il Hajin (Manuelito), who formally signed the treaty of 1868, ending the peoples' traumatic internment at Hwééldi (Fort Sumner) in New Mexico and enabling their return to the shrunken boundaries of their homeland. But it was her great-great-grandmother, Asdzáá Tł'ogi, (Juanita), translated as "Lady Weaver," who exerted a powerful influence on the negotiations and oversaw the reestablishment of hózhǫ́ in the reservation era that followed. Given that Diné women "convey the kinship ties essential to tribal existence," her leadership ensured the resilience of her people amid intensifying colonization.[48] In 1874, Asdzáá Tł'ogi was the only woman to join her husband's delegation to meet with President Ulysses S. Grant in Washington, DC. While federal agents were redefining Native nations as wards of the state in an effort to strip them of political autonomy, Denetdale explains that her ancestors believed that "talking directly to the President was one of their rights" in their ongoing efforts to protect Diné Bekéyah.[49] The delegation indicates that Native leaders continued to understand themselves as diplomatic equals, including the lone woman in their ranks. Denetdale's interviews with other descendants suggest additional rationales for Asdzáá Tł'ogi's participation. According to Faye Yazzie, "She spoke well and maybe she could persuade the President to let the Navajos keep their lands. Manuelito said the President's back was 'stiff' and perhaps Juanita's words could 'soften' him."[50] The inclusion of an esteemed orator and weaver was likely deemed a diplomatic advantage at a time when federal agents were keen to support a market for Diné textiles. Having curtailed customary means of subsistence, the government issued aniline-dyed yarn as annuity goods and licensed reservation trading posts as capitalist hubs, where Diné weavers experimented with an influx of new materials and designs.[51]

Asdzáá Tł'ogi's remarkable, unfinished textile, acquired by Indian agent William F. M. Arny during her trip to Washington, DC, cathected these transformations into an eloquent agent of diplomacy (plate 7). Still attached to a loom, it takes the form of an elongated American flag interrupted by a burst of vertical, serrated zigzags in vivid hues such as green and orange. In the blue canton on the upper left, the artist substituted a field of white crosses for the five-point stars that symbolically unify the colonies on the paradigmatic flag of the period. Four such figures drift into the red and white stripes at right, including a singular and striking blue variant. The artist's creative interpretation of the flag motif likely reflects her encounters at Hwééldi. There, new materials, such as Germantown yarns in vibrant, synthetic colors, commingled with novel design elements, such as vertical zigzags and sawtooth edges common to Spanish colonial weaving in northern Mexico, giving rise to a new genre of energized textiles popularly known as "eye dazzlers." Weavers readily associated variants of the cross motif with Spider Woman, who first taught Changing Woman, mother of the Diné, sheep, and textiles, how to weave.[52] Diné representations of stars typically have four, not five, points, associated with Changing Woman's power, cosmic directionality, and the sacred balance of hózhǫ́, as well as the protection and vivification of celestial light, feathers, shells, and pollen.[53]

How should we read the relationship between the foremost expression of US patriotism and Asdzáá Tł'ogi's unorthodox interpretation—and by extension, the relationship between Indigenous women and a colonial-patriarchal government bent on extracting resources from the land they are charged with protecting? Hwééldi culminated a period of military clashes across Diné Bekéyah that made Diné acutely aware of the power vested in the United States flag.[54] Following Asdzáá Tł'ogi's innovation, the icon became a mainstay of textile design, endlessly adapted in dialogue with Diné aesthetic principles.[55] I foreground her remarkable textile to indicate an alternative way in which Native women were present at the negotiating table, even when they were barred from participating in the flesh. Whereas the invited "chiefs" invoked the power of their female ancestors through the common rhetoric of Mother Earth, Diné women sensuously manifested their cosmopolitical kin in the form of diplomatic arts.

Denetdale interprets her great-great-grandmother's story in light of Changing Woman's legacy of creativity and power.[56] Diné poet and scholar Laura Tohe similarly points to Changing Woman's teachings to assert that "Diné women continue to possess the qualities of leadership and strength and continue to endure and ultimately to pass on those qualities to their daughters, even though there is no word for feminism in the Diné language."[57] Such an interpretation prompts me to briefly revisit the oral histories discussed in the previous chapter, this time foregrounding the activities of the most benevolent and beloved of the original Diné teachers. Daughter of darkness and dawn, Changing Woman was raised on pollen from the sun, clouds, and plants. Through her union with the Sun, she gave birth to Naayéé'neizghání (Monster Slayer) and Tóbájíshchíní (Born for Water), who set out to rid the fifth world of Monsters in order to make it safe for humans.[58] She generated the matrilineal clans from the skin of her back, breasts, and arms. Diné know that they are made of white (male) and yellow (female) corn, which, like the earth itself, is associated with Changing Woman's body.[59] Some accounts relate that Changing Woman similarly created the gift of sheep, horses, and goats from parts of her body, giving rise to the kinship expression, "with our sheep, we were created."[60] Others tell that as her twin sons witnessed sheep grazing across Diné Bekéyah in each of the four directions, they changed into the sagebrush, saltbush, and other plants that nurture life.[61] Regularly described by contemporary Diné commentators as the personification of *Nahasdzáán* (Mother Earth), Changing Woman models "good and proper behavior towards the earth, animals, and other human beings" who are understood to be fundamentally interrelated.[62]

In 1975, Diné educator Ethelou Yazzie narrated the origins of weaving during the hero twins' journeys through Diné Bekéyah. They came upon a hole in the ground with "spider webs all over the walls. In the webs were feathers from all kinds of birds. (Collecting feathers was Spider Woman's hobby.)"[63] A weaver, she taught the brothers chants and prayers needed to ask for holy assistance to succeed in their mission. Upon hearing of her talents, Changing Woman paid Spider Woman a visit in order to learn the art of weaving and teach the Diné how to use it to survive and thrive. Yazzie continues, "Spider Woman was one of the greatest women of all time. Today she would be a scientific or engineering genius. She could foresee events, know plans, understand the laws of nature. Spider woman was able to interpret natural law, and put it to use for the Navajo people."[64] Stories of the original exchanges between Spider Woman and Changing Woman underscore the gendered, relational origin of Diné art, kinship, jurisprudence, and visionary power. By raising sheep and weaving textiles, Diné maintain a reciprocal relationship with sacred women ancestors while carrying forward their inherited responsibility to achieve complementarity, balance, and fluidity through the continuous creation of hózhǫ́.

Asdzáá Tł'ogi translated the teachings of holy women into the recognizable form of the flag, or what her Očhéthi Šakówiŋ (Lakota, Dakota, and Nakota) neighbors referred to as *Tunkasila yapi*, "the one they call Grandfather."[65] More than exhibiting patriotism toward the paternalistic United States, she joined Indigenous women artists from other nations who wove, beaded, and quilled idiosyncratic variants of the banner to serve their own priorities.[66] Describing the impetus behind this efflorescence among Plains Native nations, Aaninin scholar and curator George Horse Capture stated, "I personally believe that our devotion and patriotic spirit is not for 'mom's apple pie,' but for 'grandmother's dry meat.' We are dedicated to our 'country'—the physical land, not the country as most other groups think of it. This is our country. It makes no difference whose name is on the deed."[67] Asdzáá Tł'ogi similarly transformed an icon of devotion to the "Great Father" into a sensuous medium for "Mother Earth," the cosmopolitical foundation of Diné claims to land and sovereignty under siege.[68] On the conventional flag, the rectilinear boundaries of the blue canton fully contain the star-colonies, promising the unification, completion, and closure of the United States. This totalizing figure is designed to assimilate Diné Bekéyah, such that the signed and dated treaty of 1868 was, for all its apparent finality, violable. However, if "a symbol that stands for a power is the power," as anthropologist Gladys Amanda Reichard once observed of Diné arts, then Spider Woman's wandering crosses counterbalance such worldly and specifically patriarchal authority. They channel matricentered sources of vitality such as shimmering light, feathers, and corn pollen.[69] Customary Diné teachings surely guided this choice, as weavers select specific colors and other design elements to harmonize male and female principles[70] From this perspective, art functioned as a diplomatic vehicle for Native women to redress the dual "logic of domination" by invoking powerful female progenitors.

The pointedly unfinished nature of the textile echoes Denetdale's discussion of the 1868 treaty as an opportunity for Diné to "develop a cultural dimension of Navajo sovereignty" that incorporates their relationship to Diné Bekéyah.[71] The prominent gap in the weft marks a transition between stripes and zigzags, exposing a rainbow-hued warp that otherwise invisibly supports the iconic red and white geometry of the flag. This visual-material contact zone can be read as an analog for the relationship between the Diné and the United States as a work-in-progress, an affiliation that is simultaneously interdependent and open-ended. Diné artists learn to incorporate imperfections to ensure room for improvement, as growth is "what makes life worth living" according to Diné knowledge-keeper Harry Walters.[72] Maintaining a positive mindset and following proper procedures for nurturing a textile "like a person" are valued over the appearance of the final product, as visual markers of beauty alone may prove deceptive—without substance.[73] Such a process includes "songs and rituals that involve the sheep" and "extend to the land—to Mother Earth. Weaving is nothing without all these other elements."[74] Asdzáá Tł'ogi's woven flag highlights the need for a processual, reciprocal nation-to-nation relationship that incorporates whole of the environment that supports life. This approach challenges the violability of one-time treaties from the perspective of federal agents by offering growth-oriented weaving as a model for durable political relations. Translating holy women's vital teachings and sensuous power, her textile proposes an earth diplomacy guided by mutual, long-term commitments to cultivating hózhǫ́.

STEVENS'S TEACHERS

These connections were reprised during the Cold War as another "lady weaver," Bertha Stevens, traveled and translated Changing Woman's legacy. I propose that like Asdzáá Tł'ogi's "flag," Stevens's experimental artistic practice was modeled on the original exchange between holy women. However, Stevens's activation of the relational potential of weaving necessitated her negotiation with a market-centered textile taxonomy that came to dominate the reception of Diné women's art in the United States in the twentieth century. In this section, I examine the artist's known educational landscape and oeuvre in order to contextualize her demonstrations abroad as the intensification of a lifelong practice of interweaving new places and agents into the dynamic holism of Diné Bekéyah.

Born in Chinle, Arizona, in 1912, on the edge of Tséyi' (Canyon de Chelly) in the heart of Diné Bekéyah, Stevens first learned to weave from her grandmother. This immersion in customary Diné values survived her reeducation at Albuquerque and Fort Apache Indian boarding schools at the height of federal assimilation policies. According to her daughter, Rainbow Stevens, Bertha Stevens didn't talk a lot about her experiences, except that "she wore a uniform and didn't have much to eat."[75] These are clues to the traumatic impact of a government-managed system designed to absorb Native children into the mainstream of white capitalist society using military training techniques. Christian gender roles were enforced; girls were taught to "cook, clean, keep a home sanitary, and care for a family," following a Euro-American logic that "a civilized home needed a civilized woman at its center." As historian John R. Gram has assessed, "the education of Indian girls was a microcosm of the reeducation of Native Americans as a whole."[76] It is possible that Bertha Stevens participated in the Albuquerque Indian School's "outing system," which placed some Native children as domestic labor in white households during the summer.[77] While working as a housekeeper for Leroy Atkinson's hotel and restaurant in Lupton, Arizona, in the 1940s, she married Fred Stevens, who worked as a pastry chef, kitchen helper, and sandpainting demonstrator in the associated Native craft museum. As I discussed in chapter 2, the couple traveled a widening circuit of powwows, rodeos, fairs, and museums to perform dances and demonstrate their respective arts in the 1950s and 1960s.

These mobile years for the Stevenses paced rapid changes in weaving praxis across the Navajo Nation. From 1878 to 1917, the famed trader John Lorenzo Hubbell operated a trading post in Chinle. Weavers were encouraged to incorporate bold patterns and vivid aniline-dyed red commercial yarns along with natural shades of wool associated with Ganado, the location of his most famous post. After trader Leon H. "Cozy" McSparron purchased the post in 1917, he collaborated with Mary Cabot Wheelwright, an heiress, patron of Diné arts, and owner of a Native craft shop in Boston (see chapter 2), in a sustained effort to spur a shift in the style, materiality, and finesse of regional textiles. Wheelwright was part of a broader contingent of white women involved in the Eastern Association of Indian Affairs (EAIA) who campaigned to revive older styles of weaving because they determined that "most modern Navajo rugs have degenerated to such an extent in design, color and weave that it is difficult to believe that they are made by the same people who wove the beautiful textiles collected a few decades ago, and now to be found in museums and private collections all over the country."[78] Wheelwright in particular objected to the introduction of "harsh aniline colors and oriental rug designs."[79] "Oriental" referenced the popularization of multiple borders, a central medallion, and hooked motifs among Diné weavers.

Such features were introduced by traders in the form of Anatolian textiles and published paper patterns.[80] In contrast, the "Chinle style" she admired featured repeating patterns on horizontal bands that continued to the edges of the textile. Wheelwright sought a middle ground between the vivid colors of commercial yarns and the spare palette of undyed wool, emphasizing warm browns and yellows along with pastel shades such as lavender, pink, and green. The EAIA program entailed introducing hand-colored photographs of desirable older textiles to the weavers for inspiration, with the expectation that they would return the photographs for recirculation. Wheelwright's biographer notes that the "weavers proved reluctant to give them back," a telling detail that hints at how thoroughly communities were dispossessed of their intergenerational textile wealth by the combined effects of reservation poverty, Euro-American market demand, and traders' low compensation for their work.[81]

The EAIA's push for weavers to return to nineteenth-century precedents was decidedly nonlinear. Wheelwright's cousin and fellow EAIA member, Lucy Cabot, went so far as to partner with Dupont, a chemical company involved in nuclear development in the Southwest (see chapter 2), in an effort to manufacture powdered dyes in shades of reds and blues that mimicked the softness of native plant dyes. In 1931, she worked with Diné students at the Santa Fe and Fort Wingate Indian Schools and offered workshops at trading posts on the laborious process of preparing the dyes.[82] However, the addition of acetic acid caused burns and the chrome colors yellowed in the sunlight. Weavers ultimately rejected the toxic intrusion, even as they readily experimented with plant dye recipes and reconfigured design traditions, such that the EAIA-Dupont collaboration was retired in 1934.[83]

A textile that Stevens wove for a demonstration at the Stark Art Museum in Texas in 1981—one of only two extant completed works that I have located—features the vegetal-dyed colors associated with the Chinle revival, notably a warm brown made from walnut husks and a vivid yellow made from sumac.[84] Given that she departed Chinle shortly after McSparron assumed the post, it is likely that her early textile education combined her grandmother's embodied memory of nineteenth-century sheepherding, sheering, carding, spinning, plant gathering, and dyeing, as much as the painted and photographed examples introduced by Wheelwright.[85] As I indicated at the outset of this chapter, weaving is a complex, ecorelational process that exceeds the visual-aesthetic register of objects. Although white patrons are most often credited for

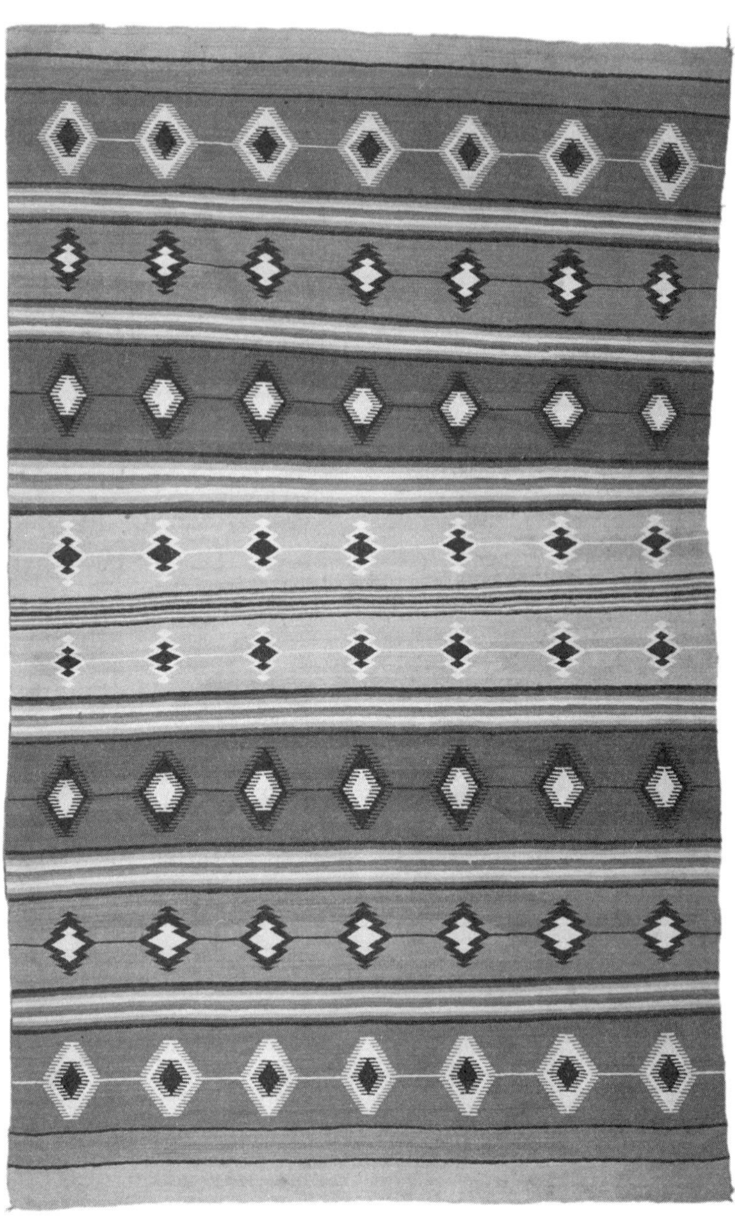

3.2

Artist unknown, Diné textile in the revival style from Chinle area. Museum of Northern Arizona, Flagstaff, E4292. This textile won first prize at the Gallup Ceremonial in 1935 or 1936. Mary Cabot Wheelwright created the prize in 1930 "to encourage the use of vegetable dyes."

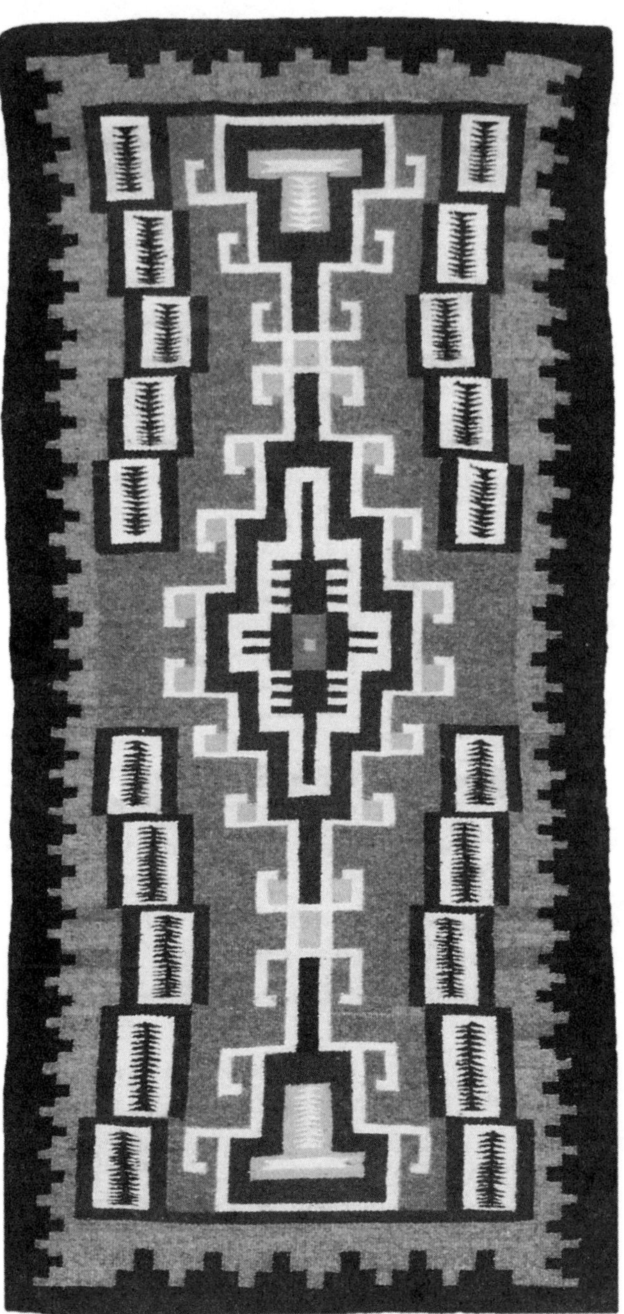

3.3

Bertha Stevens, textile, 1981. Natural handspun wool and vegetable dyes, 50½ × 25 in. Stark Museum of Art, Orange, Texas, 82.6.1.

inducing stylistic and material shifts, the revivalists relied heavily upon older weavers' recollections of praxis. Stevens's visits to Chinle and permanent return in 1966 to live in her matrilineally inherited hogan provided opportunities to continue her local weaving education. Yet she chose to pair "Chinle colors" with a centered medallion composition, rather than a banded pattern, for the Stark Art Museum. The stepped diamond features hooked appendages reminiscent of Anatolian figures, indicating that she absorbed new knowledge into a dynamic weaving practice that mirrored her lifelong mobility.

Specifically, Stevens's 1981 work reflects her education in the exceedingly fine style known as Two Grey Hills (so named for nearby land features), gleaned from her husband's paternal female relatives in Toadlena, just north of Lupton.[86] Charles Herring, then-owner of the Toadlena Trading Post, claimed that there were twelve particularly excellent weavers active in the area from 1942 to 1956, a period that likely spans Stevens's initial visits. Herring was the son-in-law of George Bloomfield, one of two white traders who established trading posts in the region around 1912. Bloomfield was known to instruct Diné women in matters of quality, color, and design, notably introducing examples of Anatolian textiles that were disapproved of by Wheelwright. Among the second-generation innovators was Daisy Taugelchee, then touted as "the most famous Navajo weaver living today."[87] She and other weavers in the area perfected the creation of virtuosic "gauze-weight tapestries [that] are translucent when held to the light" using only a soft palette of sheep's wool selectively augmented with native plant dyes. The intricate, symmetrical designs often feature single or double stacked diamonds that radiate from the center, contained by concentric rectilinear borders. The famed finesse of Two Grey Hills weaving located Stevens at the epicenter of a modernist art market that elevated their muted elegance to world renown.

Stevens's textile education in Toadlena reintroduced elements that white patrons worked to expel from her childhood home. Her incorporation of a central, stepped diamond with hooked borders in 1981 reflects her grasp of Two Grey Hills design fundamentals, only articulated in Chinle colors. Her decision to visibly relate the lessons of disparate teachers contradicted the contemporaneous hardening of a Euro-American classificatory system that divided Diné textiles according to regional aesthetic criteria. Studies such as Charles Avery Amsden's *Navajo Weaving: It's Technic and History* (1934) and Harry P. Mera's *Navajo Textile Arts* (1948) categorized modern weaving based

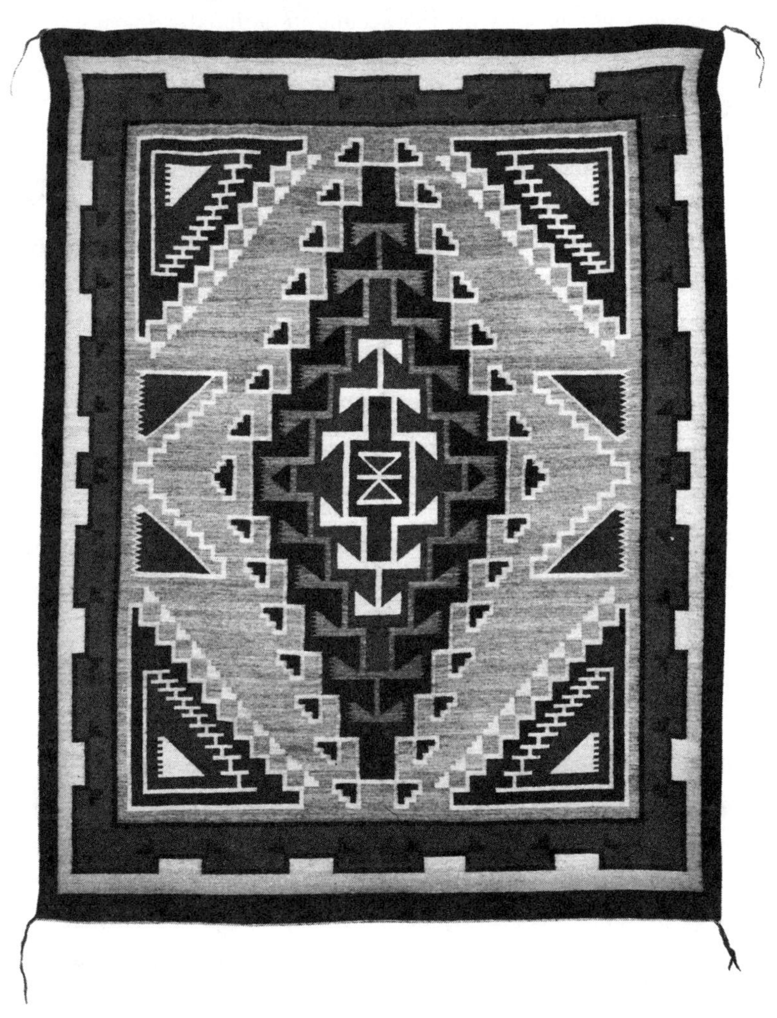

Daisy Taugelchee, textile, *Two Grey Hills*, Toadlena, New Mexico. Natural wood, vegetal-dyed, hand-spun yarn, 47.5 × 37 in. Private Collection.

on an evolution of styles associated with particular trading posts.[88] Predominantly white men, traders were credited with schooling weavers in matters of form and design, establishing a transnational market, and rescuing the artform from cultural demise. Anthropologists and curators further relegated weaving to a secular, functional, domestic sphere opposite the sacred domain of sandpainting arts.[89] As Wheelwright's story indicates, white women also significantly shaped the textile market art as patrons, dealers, buyers, anthropologists, and social reformers.[90] Art historian Jennifer McLerran notes that displays of Diné textiles in Victorian homes were popularly thought to demonstrate "the enlightened consciousness of the consumer" and the "presumed universality of such properly 'feminine' domestic pursuits."[91] Such gendered ideologies created opportunities for white feminists to pursue vocations beyond the home, at times inspired by the autonomy they observed among Pueblo and Diné women. Just as often, their exercise of relative freedom relied on reproducing the managerial relationship their male counterparts pursued with Indigenous women artists. In sum, the popular diminishment of Diné weaving through its association with domestic labor and secular markets remained relatively constant in the twentieth century.[92]

By the time they debuted at the Museum of Modern Art in New York in *Indian Art of the United States* in 1941, Diné "wearing blankets" were thoroughly redefined as "rugs" ideally suited for modernist home décor. Curators Frederic H. Douglas of the Denver Art Museum and Rene D'Harnoncourt, then head of the Department of Interior's Indian Arts and Crafts Board, explained in the catalog that "fine Navajo rugs . . . are among the most durable floor coverings that can be found."[93] They exhibit a "careful balance of design and color" that "blend with any surroundings that are truly of the twentieth century."[94] The primitivist construction of an affinity between avant-garde modernism and Native art "done without interference from Whites" would go unchallenged for much of Stevens's lifetime.[95] So, too, would the seemingly opposite assumption, reiterated by Frederic Dockstader, former director of the Museum of the American Indian, Heye Foundation, in 1987, of a white "economic base upon which all of the weaving efforts are based," without which "it seems quite probable that the weaver's world would have unraveled long ago, leaving only a faded fragment."[96] This regime severed textiles from the interconnected web of land, people, and cosmos and revalued them as secular commodities ideally suited to domestic display. The imposition of Euro-American gender hierarchies further pacified the cosmopolitical charge of textiles and makers, readying the lessons of

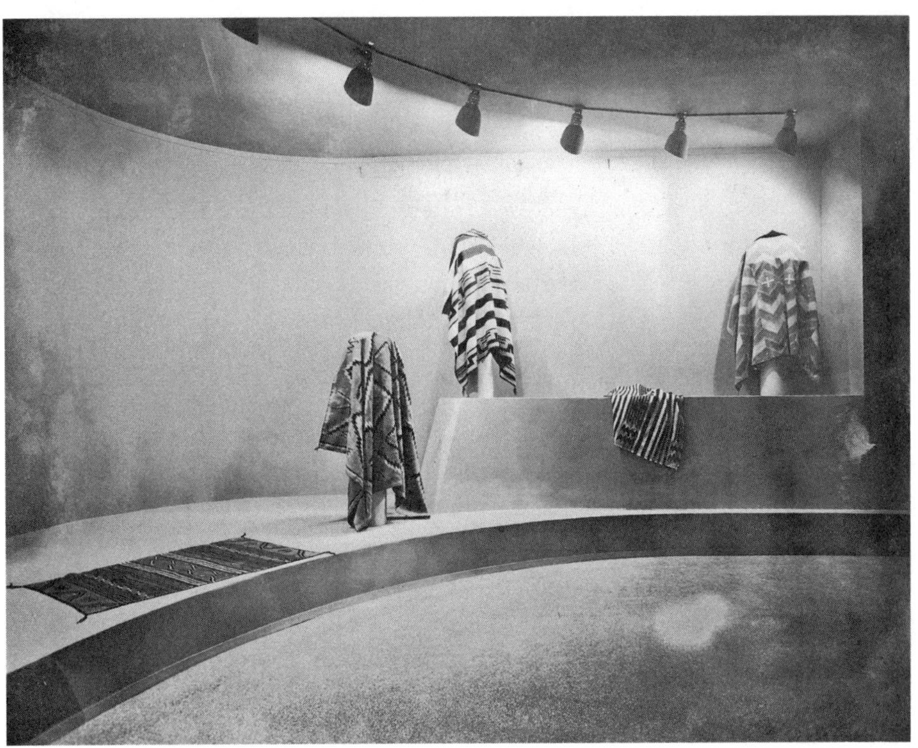

3.5

Installation view of Diné textiles in the exhibition *Indian Art of the United States*, January 22–April 27, 1941. Museum of Modern Art, New York. Photographic Archive. Digital Image ©Museum of Modern Art/Licensed by SCALA/Art Resource, NY.

....

grandmothers for capitalist assimilation. In Stevens's case, the classificatory system threatened to sever the teachings of her Chinle kin from those of her new relatives in Toadlena—and by extension, the foundational exchange between Spider Woman and Changing Woman, through which experimentation was encouraged. Following traders' dictates runs counter to the Diné principle, *aashi bi'bohlii*, imperfectly translated as "it's up to you," which emphasizes personal creativity in weaving.[97]

As anthropologist Kathy M'Closkey has reassessed, the dominant assumption of a commercial rationale for weavers scarcely masks the widespread poverty on the Navajo Nation. For a majority, the market proved dispossessive. Drawing on interviews with makers active at the turn of the twenty-first century, she argues that Diné women persist in weaving despite insufficient economic returns because it manifests relationships to land and people and is vital to the reproduction of life itself.[98] One of her unnamed consultants stated, "All of it begins at creation with Spider Woman. The rug is sacred—enfolded. . . . There is wealth in it. . . . Our hearts are in it."[99] Another elaborated, "Life grows out of the land, woman grows out of the earth. . . . Women change the world. [They] rear sheep, shear sheep, and weave all the movements and tensions into a rug."[100] Yet some of M'Closkey's interviewees expressed their reluctance to share specific weaving knowledge with outsiders because "they take it away from you" and "traders don't care about sacred songs."[101] Anthropologist and curator Jill Yohe underscores that weavers' selective silences point to the inalienability of certain kinds of weaving knowledge, even as a temporary manifestation, the textile, may be gifted or sold.[102] From this perspective, outsiders' misidentification of the artform as "secular" and "domestic" may index Diné resistance to the extraction of holy teachings, on par with the sandpainting translations discussed in chapter 2. I conclude that the topological—a Diné approach to weaving as a matricentered, relational, growth-oriented process that perpetuates the vitality of land and community amid colonization—is never wholly subsumed by the typological—a Euro-American classificatory regime that isolates, aestheticizes, commodifies, and domesticates the finished textile.[103]

These recent, scholarly reassessments of the sacred, gendered significances of weaving and its silences resonate with Rainbow Stevens's description of her mother's quietly powerful labor. Bertha Stevens "never talked about feminism" but "she owned sheep and spun her own wool. She did her own dyeing . . . [with] different herbs . . . She made money." Although "lots of people bought her rugs," Rainbow Stevens emphasized that her mother was "careful with her weaving. It was spiritual to her. She wouldn't let her yarn lie around anywhere."[104] Beyond Bertha Stevens's routine textile sales, she regularly demonstrated and taught weaving techniques, notably holding workshops for the Idyllwild School of Music and Arts (now Idyllwild Arts) at the institute's campus in the San Jacinto Mountains of California and at home in Chinle from 1976 to 1992.[105] Rainbow further stressed that although her mother was "a well-known traveler" among her Navajo Nation peers, she "never bragged about going overseas." Her favorite foreign word was an expression of generosity, *bitte schön* ("here you go" or "you're welcome" in German). Rainbow continued, "She was a gentle person, a very quiet one. She loved to help people. She was very honest and truthful. . . . When she really meant business she would look at me and say 'Wilmerine' and I would say 'uh oh.' But she was a very good person."[106] Hard work, honesty, patience, gratitude, and humility—modeled by Changing Woman, such customary qualities manifested in textiles as a material extension of their makers' state of mind.

The archive of the Stevenses' worldwide travels adds significantly to our knowledge of Bertha Stevens's artistic practice. Several color photographs reveal that the artist had already honed a tendency to merge and elaborate on regional design repertoires, as seen in the Stark Art Museum commission. A photograph of her demonstration at Amerika Haus in Berlin, the third stop of her Eurasian tour in 1966, shows the artist similarly deploying colors, patterns, and motifs in idiosyncratic combinations (plate 8). Our partial view of the work-in-progress reveals a pair of terraced diamonds side by side, flanked at top and bottom by pairs of white, hexagonal forms rimmed with black. The bold shapes recall the curvilinear, hooked figures seen in Anatolian textiles that Bloomfield used as models, which Stevens would soon have the opportunity to contextualize during her next stop in Ankara. Yet she again replaced the swaths of beige and grey associated with Two Grey Hills with fields of Chinle reddish-brown. She further departed from her Toadlena peers, who often mirrored their medallions solely on a horizontal axis, by mirroring hers across a vertical axis. A color photograph of Stevens spinning wool in Mexico City in 1968 reveals the opposite approach: the textile-in-progress visible on the loom behind the artist features borderless, horizontal banded patterns associated with the Chinle, articulated in the greys, whites, beiges, and blacks associated with her Toadlena relatives (plate 9). Each textile was evidently a new permutation, an opportunity for Stevens to relate teachings from her grandmother to those of her newer kin and innovate upon this interwoven foundation.

Stevens's combinatory and creative approach is in full evidence in the second of two extant works I have located, a small textile likely advanced during a demonstration at the Hudson River Museum in 1972 (plate 10). The topological is cannily wed to the typological, opening up the black border of the textile to values that exceed the object. The visual field is filled with nested triangle and diamond motifs with alternating serrated and terraced edges, symbolically associating the textile with mountains and clouds.[107] Stevens's use of handspun wool in a muted, natural palette of white, grey, beige, and black identifies her with Two Grey Hills, as does her choice of a dominant diamond pattern. Here, she has repeated the medallion across both horizontal and vertical axes, such that four diamonds occupy the main field. Four is a sacred number across all Diné arts, conjuring the procreative power of Changing Woman, seasonal cycles, cosmic directionality, and Diné Bekéyah's protective mountains. The associated ideal of dynamic balance supersedes an isomorphic register to integrate the woven pattern with the vast tapestry of land and cosmos.[108] At the bottom left, a slim brownish grey line cuts across the black border to the edge of the textile, as if to point the way. The inclusion of a *tjontii* (translated by contemporary weaver D. Y. Begay as "the way out," popularly referred to as a "spirit line"), expresses the core principle of growth guiding every aspect of textile production. So long as this one remained imperfect—incomplete—Stevens was freed to carry on the process of creation by bringing another into being.[109] White, four-armed crosses are included three times along the vertical axis. The memory of Spider Woman's pedagogy, which transmitted the very means of establishing hózhǫ́ to Changing Woman and her human children, is centrally present in Stevens's homage to the ongoing exchange of weaving knowledge. I propose that by citing and exceeding an overdetermined stylistic scheme, Stevens labored to communicate the processual and relational dimensions of textile arts.

AFFECTIVE EXCHANGES IN SCOTLAND AND TURKEY

In Ankara in 1966, Bertha Stevens reportedly showed her Turkish visitors the work that she "started in Washington, continued in Paris, Edinburgh, and London, and completed in Berlin" (see plate 8). The journalist's observation hinted at weavings' capacity to model geopolitical interactions, a role that vastly exceeds assignations of regional styles.[110] In order to better conceive of the artform as a means of forging relationships—familial, ecological, cosmological, and diplomatic—I turn now to Stevens's exchange of weaving techniques with culturally disparate women during her travels. This process activated and extended the embodied knowledges imparted by her many Diné teachers. The archive of her journey further illuminates that the relational dynamics attending her movement between colonial metropoles and extractive zones were shaped by normative scripts as well as affective dimensions in excess of cultural habit.

Letters sent by Elizabeth Mackay, secretary of the Edinburgh Weavers' Guild, to McGrath and others at the Institute of American Indian Arts (IAIA), offer a glimpse of Stevens's uneven interactions with Scottish weavers during her initial tour stop at the English Speaking

Union Gallery in Edinburgh. Mackay noted that in addition to members of her own amateur guild, weavers from all over Scotland attended.[111] Among the renowned artists who reportedly "enjoyed [the experience] immensely" was Kath Whyte, head of the embroidery and weaving program at the Glasgow School of Art from 1948 to 1974.[112] While the extent of Stevens's impact on Scottish weavers is difficult to assess, the immediate popularity of her work in Edinburgh evidently changed McGrath's view that her primary value lay in assisting her husband. Greeted with enthusiasm by Scottish women who wove, she was subsequently presented as an artist and demonstrator in her own right.

Following the group's departure, Mackay wrote to McGrath requesting supplemental materials on Diné weaving history and technique in order to prepare an article for publication in the UK-based Association of Guilds of Weavers, Spinners and Dyers *Quarterly Journal*.[113] McGrath apparently provided her with notes prepared by a volunteer from the Museum of Navajo Ceremonial Arts in Santa Fe (now the Wheelwright Museum of the American Indian), which the eponymous patron established in 1935. The document outlines the progressive, classificatory system that Wheelwright helped to develop.[114] However, Mackay's finished article largely ignored the narrative in favor of her own first-hand observations of Stevens's tools and techniques:

> She spun her wool on a wooden spindle and carded with identical hand carders to those used in this country. The wool she had spun for her warp was much thicker than the wool she wove the rug with. She inserted her wool as a tapestry weaver would but merely with her fingers (no shuttles were used). Her beating she did with polished wood comb with long handle with a slight point at the end. If Mrs. Stevens wished to make a very small shed of two or three threads she merely inserted the pointed end of her wooden comb to give her the necessary opening. The design is carried entirely in her head, she uses no charts of any description.[115]

The secretary's fine-grain sketch addresses a specialist audience, a community of weaver-insiders who share a common vocabulary. The approach is comparative, calling attention to Stevens's command of elements that were variously familiar and foreign to the association's readership. At the same time, Mackay's matter-of-fact delivery approached that of a technical manual, canceling ethnographic fascination, a romance with the exotic. Unlike some British journalists, who preferred to call

Stevens Morning Star (a name she acquired on the powwow circuit), Mackay evidently found her Anglophone surname sufficient.[116] The passage furthers the potential of Stevens's demonstrations to facilitate the corporeal transmission of weaving practice among women by rendering the scene with enough precision for an interested reader to mimic the techniques. A note of admiration finally enters when the secretary underscores Bertha Stevens's mental prowess. Mackay registers the principle of disciplined thinking necessary for Stevens to cultivate hózhǫ́ on the loom.

Mackay's description of her peer's skilled presentation makes the author's subsequent turn to ethnographic generalities jarring. She writes, "All traditional weaving and basketry woven by the squaw has a distinct imperfection or break, having been done deliberately in this manner to let the spirits out."[117] Whereas Stevens's technical abilities warranted her treatment as an equal, her cosmological commitments evidently triggered Mackay's projection of primitivism. The secretary collapses the individuated, respectable "Mrs. Stevens" into the generic, derogatory "squaw," a polysemous term that first traveled from a trans-Indigenous lexicon into English-speaking colonial contexts in the seventeenth century.[118] Three centuries later, it had come to "encode difference, twisting indigeneity and femininity to . . . convey inferiority, inversion, weakness, simplicity, impoverishment, mysticism, opposition, and irrelevance."[119] Having enthusiastically extended Stevens's invitation to transcultural skill-sharing, Mackay erodes the bond by resurrecting a boundary of absolute difference common to the transatlantic history of ethnographic performance (see chapter 2). A more violent variant of primitivism appears in a *South London Press* article covering the couple's subsequent stop at the Horniman Museum in London. Titled "Children Flock to Watch Red Indian Fred and His 'Squaw,'" the unnamed writer simultaneously infantilizes the couple and renders their marital relationship as a gendered and racialized form of property ownership.[120] As early as the seventeenth century, "squaw" conjured an image of downtrodden and exploitable Indigenous wives among Europeans. "Indian squaws were beasts of burden, unquestionably obeying 'braves' who beat them for any insubordination," inviting their further abuse by white men.[121] The relational potential of Bertha Stevens's demonstrations was in tension with the continued circulation of patriarchal, primitivizing stereotypes in the United Kingdom.

Although Mackay does not comment on Stevens's dress, "squaw" further bears on the Diné weaver's self-presentation as an agentive component of her demonstrations. On her Eurasian tour, Stevens paired a long, gathered, metallic gold skirt with a loose-fitting red blouse and elaborate silver and turquoise accessories that matched her husband's. The style was widely embraced by Diné women following their encounter with commercial cloth at Hwééldi, generating what Nancy J. Parezo and Angelina R. Jones describe as "an elegant statement of cultural revitalization, high self-esteem, and ethnic identity."[122] More than a visual spectacle, Stevens's donning of shimmering cloth and metal conjures Diné reverence for reflective substances as a conduit to more-than-human sources of vivification and protection. Diné educator Ruth Roessel notes that the full skirt of a woman sitting down connotes a hill, further connecting Stevens to land and home when she was seated at her traveling loom.[123]

Embodying matricentered Diné values, Stevens's sartorial choices put pressure on the nationalistic fervor surrounding the "squaw dress," a fashion sensation among white women in the United States during 1950s. The style paired relatively form-fitting bodices with variations on the colorful, three-tiered skirts and concha belts worn by Diné matriarchs. Designers and consumers appropriated Indigenous women's embodied expression of spiritual values as raw material for performances of national belonging.[124] The dress was a component of a so-called American Look that was actively manipulated as a soft power resource abroad, communicating that US citizens were "a free people, a happy people, a prosperous people. It is a wordless yet unmistakable announcement of the difference between Communist rule and democratic government," Lord and Taylor president Dorothy Shaver declared in 1952.[125] In the same instant, the dress's connotations of exceptionalism were resignified by Native artists, notably in collaborations led by Scottsdale-based Cherokee designer Lloyd Kiva New to create a distinctive clothing line that replaced the designations "squaw" and "American" with the names of well-known Native nations: Cherokee Dress, Seminole Skirt, and Navajo Ponies Shirt.[126] Cofounder of the IAIA and president from 1967 to 1978, New was connected to the Stevenses through his orchestration of *American Indian Art and Handicraft*, the traveling exhibition that occasioned their demonstrations abroad (see chapter 1). Bertha Stevens re-Indigenized the "squaw dress" on her own terms by rejecting the fashionably tight, tucked bodice and asserting the skirt's origins in Diné survivance through a glittering articulation of hózhǫ́ on tour.[127] I see her dress and her weaving as dynamic elements of a diplomatic assemblage that exceeded the stultifying and at times violent projection

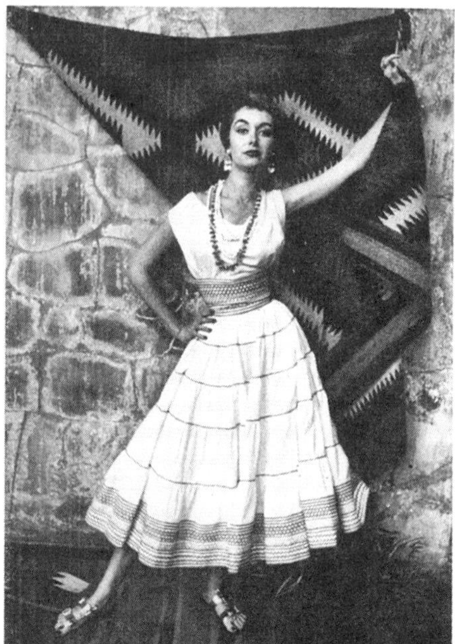

BRAIDED HEM copies Indian basket design, is 10 yards around. Dress is by Betty Johnson ($49.95), is worn with jeweled thong sandals (Bernardo, $13).

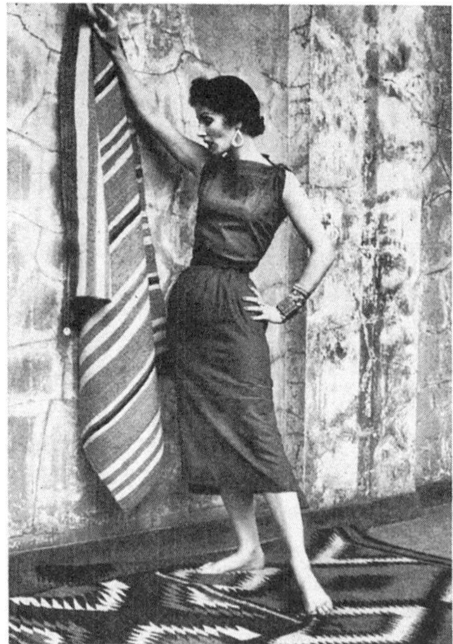

NAVAHO DESIGN is appliquéd on hem and bodice of tasseled two-piece sheath ($65) by Lloyd Kiva of Scottsdale, Ariz., who is half Cherokee himself.

3.6

Life Magazine, July 6, 1953.

of stereotypes across the Atlantic. In this view, the inconsistencies in Mackay's article point to the affective charge of an encounter that intersects, but is not reducible to, colonial ideologies.

While the documentation of Stevens's time in Turkey is comparatively sparse, there are hints of an extended encounter that enabled her to recontextualize knowledge of Anatolian textiles that had long shaped Diné art histories through the dictates of white traders. Following her demonstration of weaving and carding wool at the Turkish-American Association in Ankara, McGrath notes that "Bertha Stevens traveled to the Goerme Balley in Cappadocia to visit local weavers, taking her spindle and wools. The Turkish women welcomed her, invited her to their loom, and exchanged spindle techniques."[128] A lengthy article in *Christian Science Monitor* further emphasizes the synchrony of Stevens's practice with local technologies and aesthetics, noting that Stevens visited "some of Turkey's rug-weaving centers" and "managed to find a special needle on the local market, though at home she must have her needles made to order."[129] On the surface, the suggestion that Stevens fit in with the unnamed weavers in Turkey served soft power narratives that were focused on transforming transcultural sympathy into political goodwill toward the United States. Such a framing also resonates with the long-standing Orientalization of the western United States through Euro-American agents' importation of stereotypes about colonized lands and peoples from Asia and the Middle East.[130] Yet such encounters simultaneously enabled Diné and Turkish women to redirect the transmission of creative knowledges away from universalizing primitivism and toward alternative relational schemas.

While the tour archive is silent on whether and how the weavers utilized this opportunity, Rainbow Stevens indicated to me that her mother became keenly aware of the sociopolitical injustices affecting her exchange with Turkish women. Although government officials sought to "only show them the good things," Bertha Stevens was struck by the poverty she encountered in the countryside, noting flies, illness, water scarcity, and huts made with bricks of cow manure. She drew parallels with home, telling her daughter, "Navajos, we're poor, but we're rich compared to some people." The local textile she brought home to Chinle was later stolen from her family's hogan, conjuring the dispossessive commodity flows connecting the Navajo Nation to Turkey.[131] However, a shared condition of oppression is only one of the relational strands that Indigenous artists activated on tour, as I have emphasized throughout this book. Returning to the Stevenses' better-documented visit with Mapuche in 1968, I conclude with a vivid demonstration of how the trans-Indigenous exchange of textile knowledge and associated cosmologies may strengthen the protective power of Earth Mothers in and beyond the extractive zone.

DINÉ-MAPUCHE WEAVING

The Stevenses' visit with Mapuche entailed a dense relay of embodied interactions centered on weaving, sandpainting, singing, dancing, storytelling, cooking, dining, and gifting—activities variously imbued with anticolonial resistance and more-than-human power. I emphasize in particular how Castillo, Morales, and Bertha Stevens pursued the formation of affectively charged cosmopolitial bonds that superseded Chile-US relations. Deepening my discussion of trans-Indigenous kinship from chapter 1, I consider how Diné and Mapuche women artists may have forged relationships of care and solidarity with one another more readily than with the ambassadors of colonial states. Both groups engaged in mimesis to translate Indigenous values across language barriers and geographical distances, connecting sa'ah naagháii bik' eh hózhǫ́ to *kümefelen* ("the good life"), an analogous Mapuche imperative "to maintain an order in the spiritual and biological world."[132]

In Santiago, Bertha Stevens demonstrated her technique for spinning wool and sipped *muday*, a potent Mapuche "liquid of life" made of fermented corn or wheat, with Castillo and Morales.[133] The Mapuche women studied her tools closely, reportedly commenting, "The instruments that you use for weaving are very similar to ours."[134] The Diné couple retraced their hosts' route southward to Temuco, a small city located in the center of Indigenous ancestral territory. They demonstrated their respective arts at the Chilean North American Institute of Culture, where newspapers reported that "the Mapuches arrived in groups, evidently interested in learning something that could be in parallel to their own traditions," noting in particular that Bertha Stevens "worked on a loom similar to that of Mapuche women."[135] In the nearby village of Quetrahue, Castillo and Morales invited the Stevenses to dine, sing, dance, share stories, and learn about local weaving practices. The visit began with a breakfast of *mate* (a loose-leaf tea sipped from gourd cups) and *tortillas de rescoldo*, followed by cultural activities in the courtyard of the village. There, "Fred Stevens made some demonstrations of his art with spiritual roots" and "sang a song from his land, sweet and emotive," accompanied by the kultrün and a *trutruca*, a trumpet made from a coiled expanse of native forest bamboo.[136] By merging his voice and language with Mapuche instrumentation, Stevens intersected his hosts' responsibility to "induce altered states of consciousness through rhythmical drumming, dance, and the use of rattles," a practice of cosmic rebalancing that must have resonated with the hataałii's own rituals.[137] Rainbow Stevens related her mother's experience of dancing with Mapuche women and helping them cook lunch in a large cauldron over an open fire. "She noticed the chickens were missing. . . . The chickens that were running around were in the pot! When they went to eat, she only took a couple of bites but my dad really went for it!"[138] Embedded in the humor of this intergenerational memory is the Stevenses' introduction to *yafü tuwün*, a matricentered Mapuche ethics of care that includes "valuing the diet as a source of spiritual energy, motivation, and strength."[139]

During a speech in the courtyard, Mapuche hosts presented the Diné couple with a gift of two customary belts woven by local women from colorful, dyed wool. The pair in the Stevenses' family collection likely included *trariwe* (an elaborate design worn by women) and possibly *trarichiripa* (a simpler design worn by men). (The family's trariwe were misplaced at the time of writing, so I'm including a roughly contemporaneous example of trariwe from the well-studied collection of the Museo Regional de La Araucanía in Temuco.) The elaborate geometrical symbols express women's identity and power, embedded within a broader social, territorial, and cosmological order that was established with the creation of the Mapuche world. The colors red (blood), black (knowledge), and white (peace) predominate, signifying the sacredness and wisdom of the wearer. Such garments are intended to protect and strengthen wearers' wombs throughout pregnancy and demanding household, farming, and parenting tasks.[140] Belts were an appropriate gift for Fred Stevens as well as Bertha Stevens, as they are worn by *machis*, healers who transcend colonial gender binaries to act as "the spiritual center of Mapuche society" in a role similar to that of the hataałii.[141]

Their combination of regalia, speech acts, use of the kultrün, and offerings of muday and trariwe (and possibly trarichiripa) may identify Castillo and Morales as machis. Usually practiced by women or gender-ambiguous individuals, machis counterbalance the political authority of patrilineal Mapuche leaders on reservations imposed by the Chilean state in 1884, by channeling power from the holy realm of ancestors.[142] María Soledad Falabella Luco has further characterized Mapuche gender

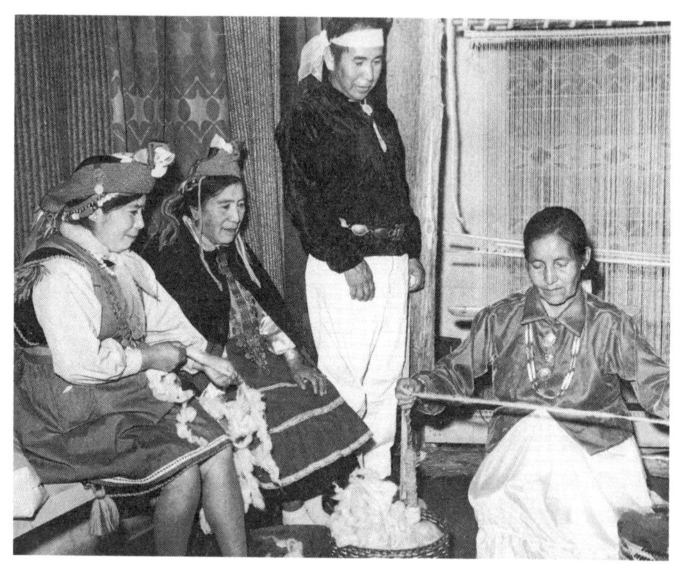

3.7

Juana María Castillo and Luisa Morales with Bertha and Fred Stevens, Biblioteca Nacional, Santiago, Chile, 1968. Provided by Institute for American Indian Arts, RG03_01_09_0036_001.

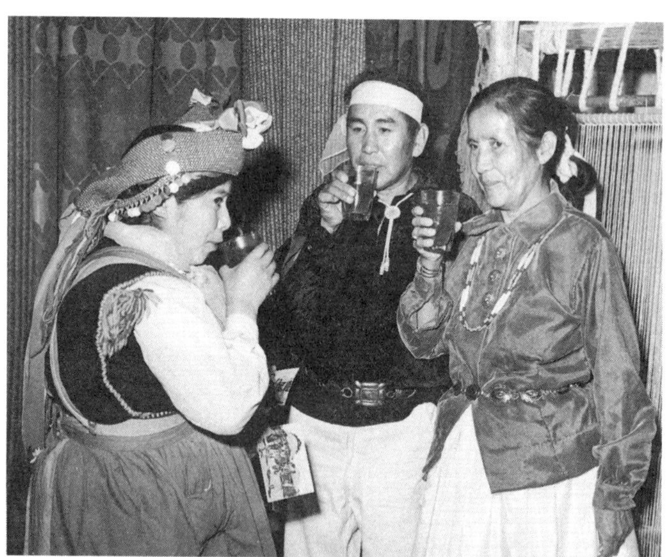

3.8

Luisa Morales drinking *muday* with Bertha and Fred Stevens, Biblioteca Nacional, Santiago, Chile, 1968. Provided by Institute of American Indian Arts, RG03_01_09_0036_002.

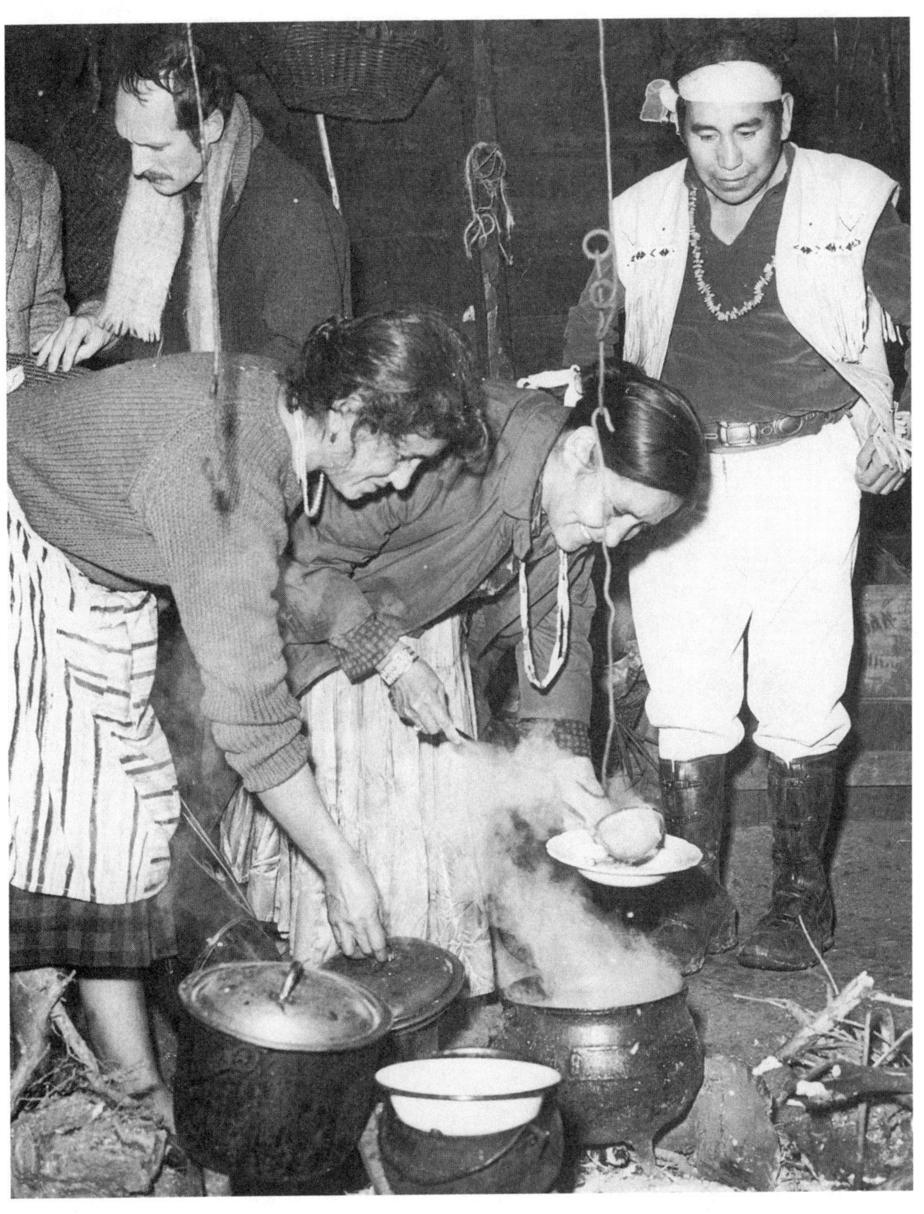

3.9

Bertha Stevens assists Mapuche hosts in preparing lunch in Quetrahue, Cautín Province, Chile, 1968. Provided by Rainbow Stevens and Alita Begay.

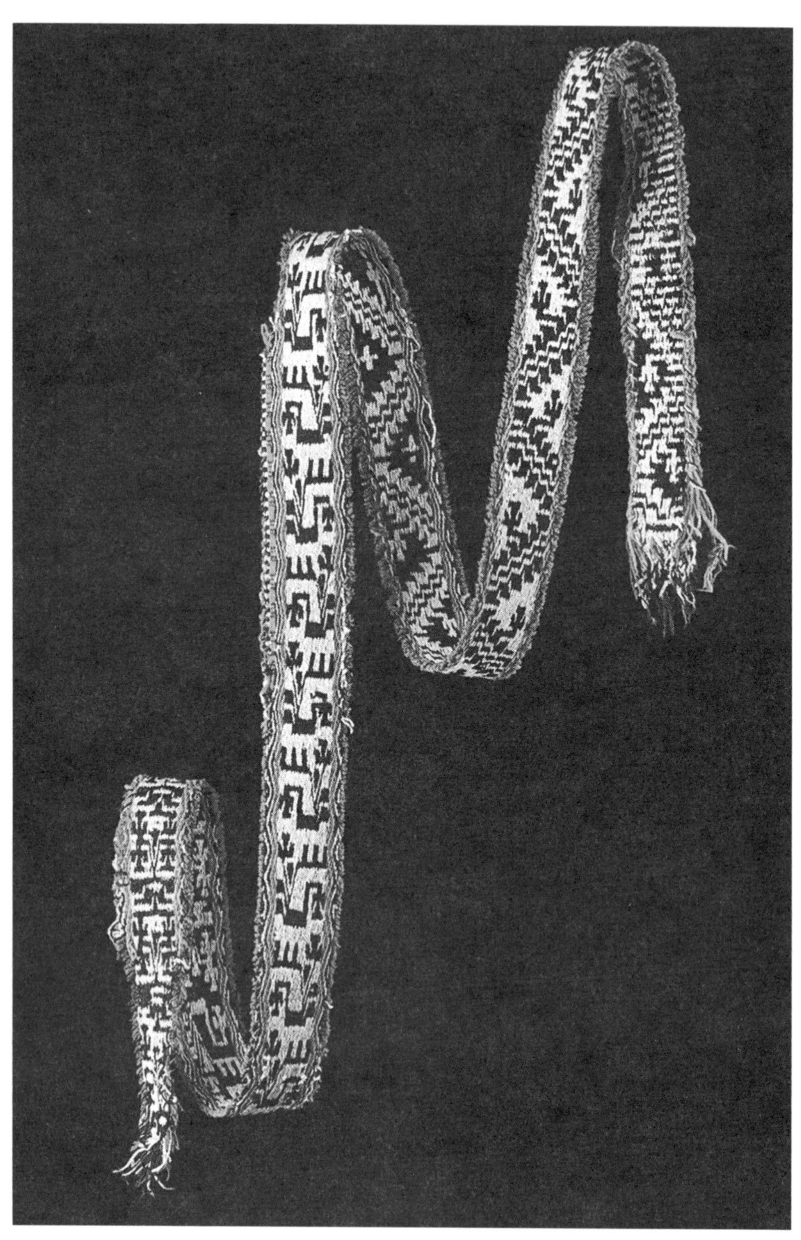

3.10

Mapuche *trariwe* (woman's woven belt) belonging to a machi (spiritual healer).
Wenteche territory. 234 × 6.2 cm. Collection of Fajas Textiles Mapuches, Museo
Regional de la Araucanía, Temuco, inv. 2267. Photograph: Juan Pablo Turén.

construction as "a contested field in which traditional Chilean dichotomous heteronormativity is resisted by a 'set of complimentary and mutually respectful confluences that seek the balance of *küme felen*, the good life.'"[143] Resonating with the Diné principle of sa'ah naagháii bik' eh hózhǫ́, küme felen emphasizes that individual mental, physical, and spiritual health derives from the equilibrium without fragmentation of all beings born from *mapu*, the earth, the ultimate womb.[144] Scholars have established the growing significance of Mapuche women as machis with the moral authority to perpetuate küme felen during colonization. Channeling more-than-human kinship and power, they bear a "potential of 'queering' Chilean national discourse" in a society that has otherwise been forced to accommodate European patriarchy.[145] Gómez-Barris underscores that "Mapuche agency can be articulated against statecraft, whether through the sound of the sacred drum, the invocation of the ancestral realm, or the spiritual figure of the machi."[146] Exemplified by Morales in her capacity as the Stevenses' host, machis furthermore act as intercultural negotiators who gain power from their contact with foreign agents and materials.[147] They may invite guests into the home to sit down, drink muday, and share news, stories, and gifts, thereby establishing the "communal ties of belonging."[148] Put another way, machis are earth diplomats, harnessing the cosmopolitical legitimacy, cultural openness, and sensuous tools needed to weave strangers into kin.

In March of 2020, I met María Catrileo Chiguailaf, a prize-winning Mapuche linguist and anthropologist, in the shady courtyard of the Museo Regional de La Araucanía in Temuco, to discuss gendered Mapuche practices of diplomacy.[149] Her gift to me, an English-Spanish-Mapundungun (Mapuche language) dictionary that she authored, sat on the bench between us.[150] Fifty-two years earlier, she hosted the Stevenses in Temuco in her capacity as president of the Mapuche Institute of Culture, a nongovernmental organization dedicated to perpetuating Indigenous culture and language. When I asked Chiguailaf how the Stevenses may have been folded into local hosting protocols, she reflected, "When outsiders go to visit with the Mapuche people, they're not invited to enter the home immediately. First [the Mapuche] go outside, see the outsiders . . . ask questions about their dealings, their interests, ideas and *then* they could be invited to enter the house, but it's not common." She paused. "There is a difference, though. If a Mapuche comes to a house . . . he's treated as friendly, but if a *wingka* [non-Mapuche] comes, he stays a little bit outside." She laughed.[151] Additional insights into Mapuche

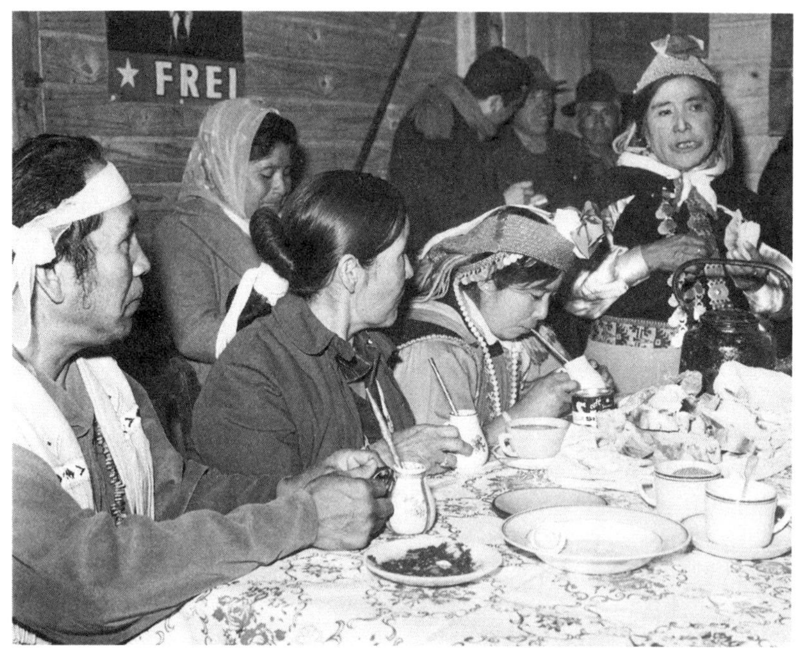

3.11

Juana María Castillo (*far right*) and Luisa Morales hosting the Stevenses for breakfast in Quetrahue, Cautín Province, Chile, 1968. Provided by Rainbow Stevens and Alita Begay.

....

hospitality can be gleaned from a Department of State photograph of the Stevenses' breakfast in Quetrahue. The photographer arrested Castillo in the act of speaking at the apex of a diagonal row of diners (Fred Stevens, Bertha Stevens, and Morales), her raised hand grasping a tortilla and exposing the intricate design of the trariwe tied around her waist. Four other Mapuche appear in soft focus along the wooden wall behind her, their recessed position and plainclothes underscoring her splendor and prominence. She commands our attention along with the Stevenses. By inviting her guests indoors to drink tea and eat a nutritious meal, Castillo perhaps exercised her communally derived authority to receive certain strangers in the manner of relatives. A journalist reported on the intimate setting: "The Navajo couple . . . took notice of the trust and ease with which the inhabitants of Quetrahue interacted with them. It was as if they were celebrating family members that had not visited for a long time."[152]

Chiguailaf's words further hint that unlike Mapuche encounters with Euro-American difference, which are marked by violence and necessitate caution, their Diné guests readily joined in a mutual production of *likeness* that may have in turn facilitated the creation of kinship bonds. Likeness is not sameness, as one reporter registered by detailing Fred Stevens's observations of visible variances among Diné and Mapuche ecologies, housing styles, and weaving technologies.[153] Rather, in Flatley's formulation, likeness is a politically efficacious "third term aside the same-different binary," one specifically negated by the oppositional dichotomies—Communism versus capitalism, woman versus man, primitive versus modern, Native versus white—that hardened into battlelines during the Cold War.[154] More than passively apprehended as a matter of essence, similarities are actively generated through bodily imitation. This is a fundamental tenet of Diné artistic transmission that the Stevens exercised abundantly during their visit with Mapuche. When the couple demonstrated their respective arts and answered invitations to imbibe tea through silver drinking straws, play the kultrün, dance, cook, and weave in the style of their hosts, they engaged Diné pedagogical principles of teaching by showing and learning by doing that aligned them more closely with existing Mapuche practices. As Flatley insists, the mimetic facility is in turn "the condition of possibility for affective affiliation," a queer form of being-in-common that machis are uniquely positioned to initiate.[155] Beyond an effective exchange of creative knowledges, Mapuche hosts' and Diné guests' willing participation in the production of likeness may have predisposed them to forge familial bonds of the sort registered by members of the press.

At stake in the encounter between heterogeneous diplomats is the formation of trans-Indigenous kinship, a framework introduced in chapter 1. As theorized by Chickasaw literary scholar Chadwick Allen, trans-Indigenous names the formation of lateral, nonhierarchical relationships among Native peoples that precede—and persistently exceed—European colonization.[156] While the popular discourse of transnationalism may leave the vertical hierarchy of settler-Indigenous in place, trans-Indigenous relationships are often organized horizontally, as a decentered practice of cooperation among people and the lands they hold sacred.[157] For Allen, Indigenous arts (or "signs" as he calls them) are especially potent agents of trans-Indigenous kinship because, in the process of changing hands, they simultaneously adapt and fuse the diverse cultural-political worlds of their makers.[158] When the Stevenses received trariwe as gifts, they were invited to encircle their bodies with matricentered signs of Mapuche kinship, enveloping them in the more-than-human holism of küme felen. In that instant, the cosmopolitical charge of the textile was drawn into proximity—and potential synthesis—with Bertha Steven's open warp, a nascent manifestation of the dynamic holism necessary for sa'ah naagháii bik' eh hózhǫ . Conjoining distinct imperatives to seek complementarity, balance, growth, and reciprocity with all life on earth, Diné-Mapuche weaving "enacts a shared being-in-common," a queer Indigenous relationality subject to more than a century of oppression by Chilean and US governments.

As foregrounded in the breakfast scene, Indigenous women translated ancestral teachings to strengthen a trans-Indigenous bond amid the ongoing dispossessive acts of the patriarchal governments that framed their meeting. Behind the diners, the name "FREI" is legible, emblazoned in white letters beneath a portrait of the contemporaneous president of Chile, Eduardo Nicanor Frei Montalva. When I showed her the photograph, Chiguailaf found the overt political imagery to be highly unusual for a Mapuche home at that time. Given the United States' significant military and financial support of Frei as a centrist counter to the rise of radical left alliances in Chile, she speculated that it may have been added by a US or Chilean official in the service of soft power.[159] Severed at the neck by the upper border of the photographic print, the leader's (perhaps inadvertent) visual decapitation cancels his symbolic authority over the gathering and makes way for Castillo's speech act at the head of the table. His formal suit and tie fade before the flash of her trariwe and silver jewelry, worn to convey an "ecstatic feeling" that mirrored Bertha Stevens's own predilection for luster.[160] Chiguailaf similarly cropped the Chilean state from view when talking to reporters at the conclusion of the Stevenses' visit when she proclaimed the exchange "a real vehicle for mutual knowledge" and urged that "people from Temuco, located at the [Mapuche] hearth, should organize a response to our visitors of Santa Fe and the Navajo tribe."[161] In keeping with a Mapuche ethics of reciprocity (*mañum*), her proposal privileges the trans-Indigenous, rather than international, character of a continued exchange.

While the linguist pursued relationships with Diné just a few years later during a Fulbright professorship in the United States, immediate plans for a Mapuche delegation to Diné Bekéyah were interrupted by intensifying political unrest. Chile was caught between radical social movements and pressure from the US-dominated Alliance for Progress concerning foreign investments in the nation's lucrative copper mines.

The Frei government's suppression of miners' rights and top-down modernization of agriculture deepened the long-standing disenfranchisement of Mapuche. Shortly after the Stevenses' visit, the region around Temuco became a "hotbed of uprising" as radicalized groups seized landed estates claimed by ancestral right.[162] Sustained Mapuche resistance to multinational corporations and the Chilean state remained urgent at the time of my visit there in 2020. As I indicated at the outset of this chapter, historiographers have emphasized ecofeminism's dual origins in an ancient Indigenous Mother Earth and the spontaneous eruption of majority world activism. But they have missed the shared ground of diplomacy, where disparate women dined, danced, and wove together. We must follow Earth Mothers through their many sites of translation, as the ecocidal patriarchy driving dominant international relations necessitates the counterweaving of a cosmopolitical commons.

4

TIPIS AND DOMES

MODELING THE BLACKFEET
COSMOS AT A WORLD FAIR

A "HUGE CONE-SHAPED TENT 4 meters in diameter, 6 meters in height" greeted visitors to the US Pavilion at Expo 70 in Osaka, Japan. The tipi was but one physical manifestation of Maistoikokaup ("Crow lodge" in Siksiká, the language of the Blackfoot Confederacy), an Indigenous artistic and spiritual praxis named for its avian designs and origins.[1] The semicircular canvas, boldly painted with zoomorphic and geometrical figures, was formed into a tipi with the support of eighteen wooden poles. The US Information Agency (USIA) commissioned the lodge from Ampskapi Pikuni (Blackfeet Nation) artist Darryl Blackman (1941–1971) during the summer of 1969. From March to August of 1970, it loomed over displays of Pomo baskets, Pueblo ceramics, Diné textiles, and other Indigenous arts in the Native American section of the Folk Art Exhibition inside the US Pavilion. After the exposition closed, the USIA gifted the lodge to the city of Osaka.[2]

The tipi's bouquet of wooden support poles stretched toward the pavilion's vast clear span elliptical roof, evoking a relationship to the dome as the dominant architectural paradigm in hippie communes and world fairs alike in the 1960s and 1970s. Amid the rise of the first National Aeronautics and Space Administration (NASA) satellite images of the whole earth, Plains tipis circulated internationally alongside domes as icons of environmental holism and countercultural resistance. Yet comparatively little attention has been paid to tipis as a dynamic ecopolitical architecture in their own right—one that significantly contributed to a Termination-era groundswell of Indigenous activism and earth diplomacy. A sustained analysis of this distinctive structure has arguably been stymied by romantic stereotypes about the environmental credentials of Plains cultures, which accelerated during the period of my study. This chapter holds that while tipis were steeped in the popular mythos of the Ecological Indian, painted variants were harnessed by Blackman and other artists to support complex articulations of Indigenous geopolitics, mirroring the multivocal ecofeminism discussed in chapter 3. Considering the divergent cosmologies of tipis and domes side by side exposes fault lines in a period discourse that celebrated spherical holism as an antidote to ecological despoilation.[3] I will specifically examine how the Crow lodge in Osaka modeled a tripart Niitsítapi ("The Real People," the modern Blackfoot Confederacy) universe shaped by more-than-human alliances. This vast referent governed the tangible and intangible dimensions of customary tipi praxes and shaped novel adaptations in the era of Indian Termination and the Cold War. As was the case for Fred Stevens's sandpaintings, Blackman's creation of painted tipi variants on commission for far-flung receivers entailed a significant reconfiguration of Indigenous protocols. Such negotiations continue to generate controversy within the Blackfoot Confederacy. Accordingly, conversations with the Blackfeet Nation Tribal Historic Preservation Office, Blackman's relatives, and elders who recall his ceremonial activities guided my research for this chapter.[4]

Expo 70 is an apt occasion for reassessing the Crow tipi as an agent of earth diplomacy. The events opened under the official banner of "Progress and Harmony for Mankind," a universalizing rhetoric long familiar to world fairs in Europe and North America. Garnering a record-breaking sixty-four million visitors, the first Asian exposition was charged with simulating a "city of the future" amid increasingly dystopian accounts of Western progress. Supersized space-age architecture and immersive multimedia environments disseminated a techno-utopic vision premised on bodily and environmental controls. The expo's official theme, "Progress and Harmony for Mankind," was met with widespread critiques of nuclear violence, imperialism, rampant industrial pollution, and the Vietnam War—conditions that shaped the postwar relationship between the United States and Japan.[5] For this reason, historians have pointed to the massive undertaking as simultaneously the apotheosis and death of world fairs.[6] As the story goes, widespread

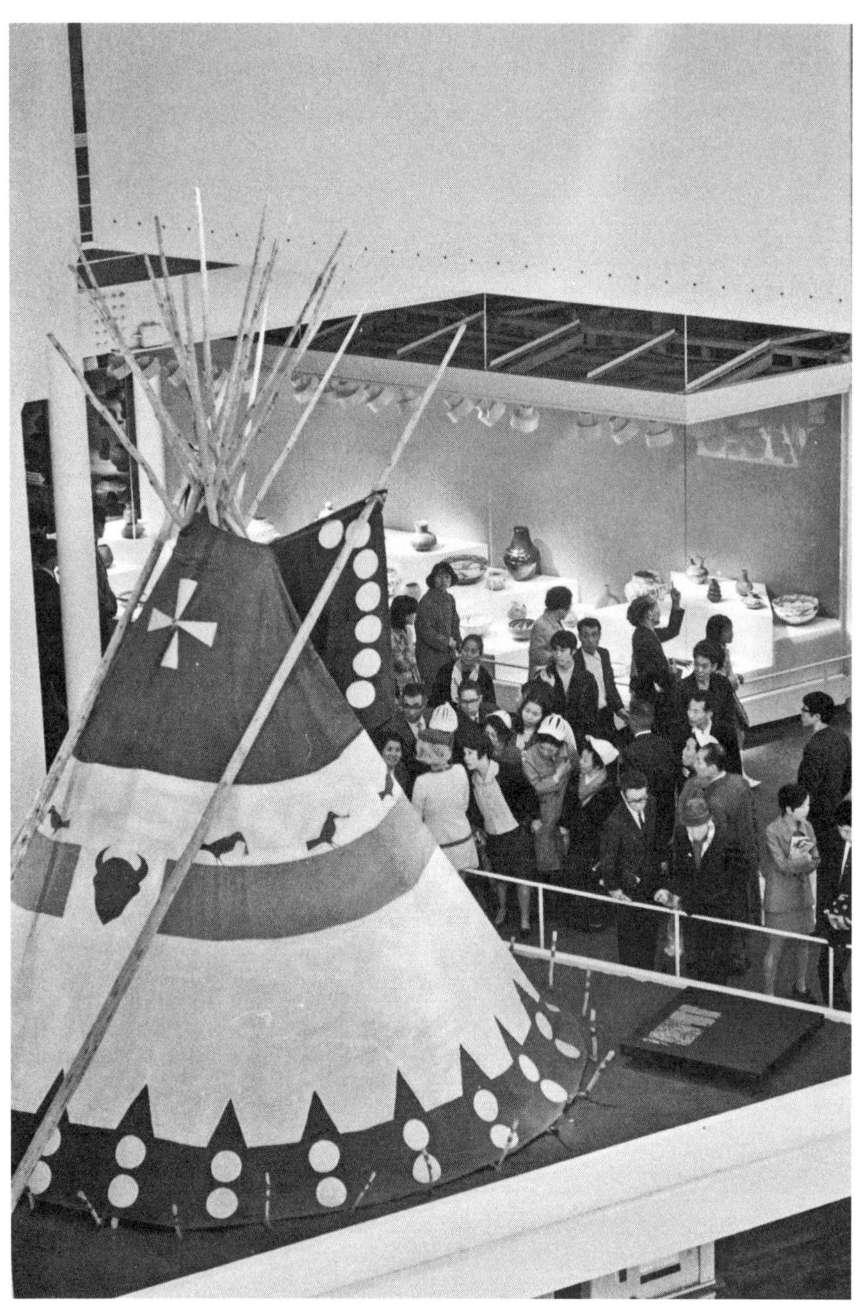

4.1

Darryl Blackman, Crow lodge, with Pueblo pots displayed in the background in the
United States Pavilion at Osaka 70 in Osaka, Japan, 1970. NACP Still Photographs,
306-exn-3315–11.

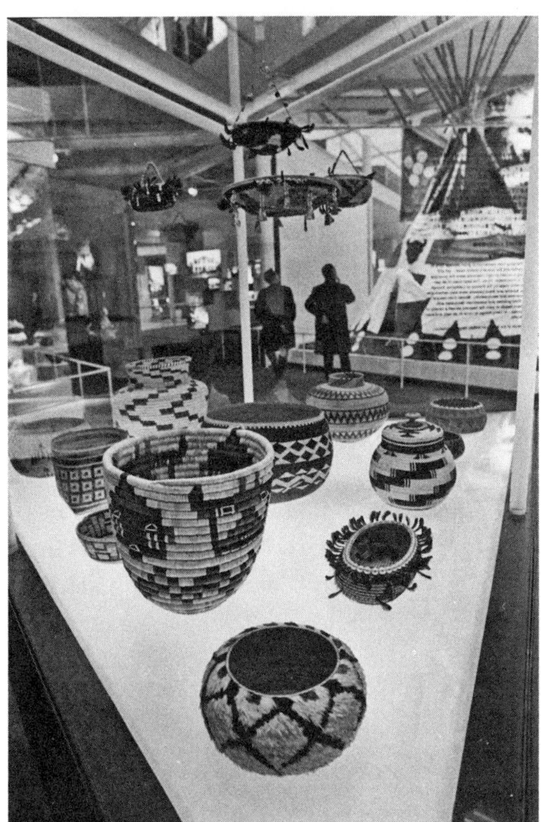

4.2

Pomo, Yurok, and other California Indigenous baskets with Darryl Blackman's Crow lodge displayed in the background in the United States Pavilion at Expo 70 in Osaka, Japan, 1970. NACP Still Photographs, 306-exn-17–9.

4.3

Diné textiles and silverwork with Darryl Blackman's Crow lodge displayed in the background in the United States Pavilion at Expo 70 in Osaka, Japan, 1970. NACP Still Photographs, 306-exn-3398–27.

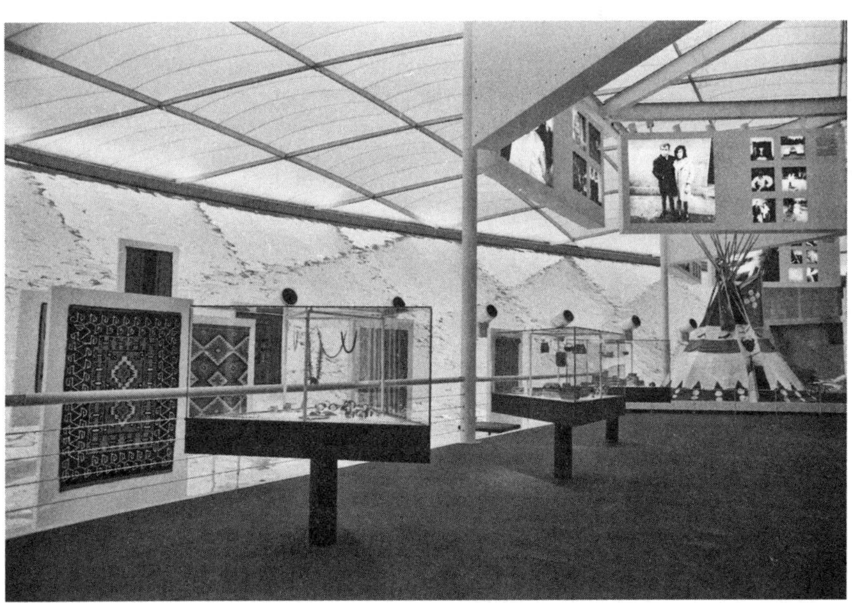

public disillusionment with a triumphant narrative of Western progress ideologically gutted mega-expositions, rendering them as ruins. But dismissing the whole enterprise as a failed bid for hegemony misses the distinct contributions made by Indigenous art and architecture, standard inclusions in world fairs from their efflorescence in Europe and North America in the nineteenth century to their global spread during the Cold War. Expo 70 provided the stage for an alternative Indigenous futurism, one in which ancient gifts from earth beings are materialized by human artists to expand a cosmic circle of reciprocity.

"A MULTILAYERED BLACKFEET REALITY"

The tipi can be glimpsed in whole or part in numerous archival photographs of the pavilion. While most of the extant documentation is in grayscale, a lone color photograph of the newly completed lodge erected on the lawn of the Museum of the Plains Indian in Browning, Montana, reveals a bold red-black-and-white scheme punctuated by swaths of unarticulated cream cloth (plate 11a). In the description that follows, I've inferred likely colors for parts of the tipi that are not visible in this view. Thick bands of black paint frame the top and bottom of the cone. A pale cross (probably white or unpainted canvas) made of four elongated triangles appears high in the dark field on the back of the lodge. The topmost band extends into a pair of flared ventilation flaps at front. The tips of the flaps are pulled open by two long poles that stretch diagonally to the floor behind the lodge. The triangular flaps and dark serrated band at the base of the structure are filled with painted white circles evoking constellations and meteors. The tipi is bisected at center by a thick red band, which breaks at the front and back to make way for the frontal silhouettes of two large black buffalo heads. Black birds in profile appear to perch on the top edge of the band, forming a frieze; each is articulated with a pale dot of an eye and holds a small red triangle in its beak. The remaining sixteen poles function as an internal frame for the canvas. They exit and cross at the top of the cover, reaching skyward, an inverted miniature of the hidden conical frame below.

The idea to commission this striking lodge for display in Japan originated with Myles Libhart (1931–1989), an artist, scholar of Plains art, and director of Museums, Exhibitions, and Publications for the Indian Arts and Crafts Board (IACB) of the Department of the Interior. Libhart approached Blackman to negotiate the contribution in August of 1969

::::::::::

during a visit to the IACB's Museum of the Plains Indian in Browning, Montana. Phyllis Montgomery, the exhibition coordinator for Expo 70, who was based in Washington, DC, reported on the outcome of their encounter in a letter to Jack Masey, the prominent exhibition designer for the US Pavilion, on August 21. She introduced Blackman as "a Blackfoot Indian . . . whose tipi work is very highly regarded" and elaborated on the commanding presence of the yet-to-be-realized artwork. "Myles recommends that . . . we allow Mr. Blackman to paint the tipi in his own clan design, which combines such motifs as stars, landscapes, buffaloes and crows. (Myles is trying to obtain a photograph for us of Mr. Blackman's own 30′ high tipi bearing the same design. In any case, he assures us that the final product is bold and very handsome). . . . We hope funds are available for this tipi, as we are convinced it would be a striking addition to our folk art area."[7] Montgomery's identification of the painted motifs as a "clan design" is misleading; as I will discuss, the rights to such images could be transferred between (and beyond) Niitsítapi family groups. She goes on to emphasize Blackman's enormous personal tipi as a reassuring prototype for the commission. Montgomery's claims seem designed to reassure the pavilion organizers that the proposed commission would meet benchmarks of cultural authenticity and aesthetic excellence. At the same time, her letter cast Blackman as contractor and the tipi as commissioned art in a capitalist system. She made no mention of the work's eventual transfer as a diplomatic gift from the USIA to the city of Osaka. While the precise origins of that decision remain obscure, it seems to have been reached near the end of Expo 70, and thus beyond the timeframe of the lodge's creation.

Numerous features of the commission destabilized the tipi's status as a commodity from the start. Montgomery noted that Blackman would "donate his tipi poles to the project since poles are characteristically obtained in the spring—too late for our deadline."[8] While her statement rationalizes Blackman's offer as a function of material scarcity, it also hints at the persistence of a Niitsítapi gift economy entangled with colonial capitalism. Lodgepole pine trees used for tipi supports are harvested seasonally from the foothills of the Rocky Mountains. The scarcity of timber in a grassland environment meant that many other Plains nations historically relied on a network of trade and diplomacy to acquire such prized necessities; "a set of well-seasoned poles is looked upon as a valuable asset and is not to be parted with for trifles," ethnographer Clyde Wissler observed in his detailed study of Blackfeet material culture in 1910.[9] Niitsítapi are unique among their neighbors for their

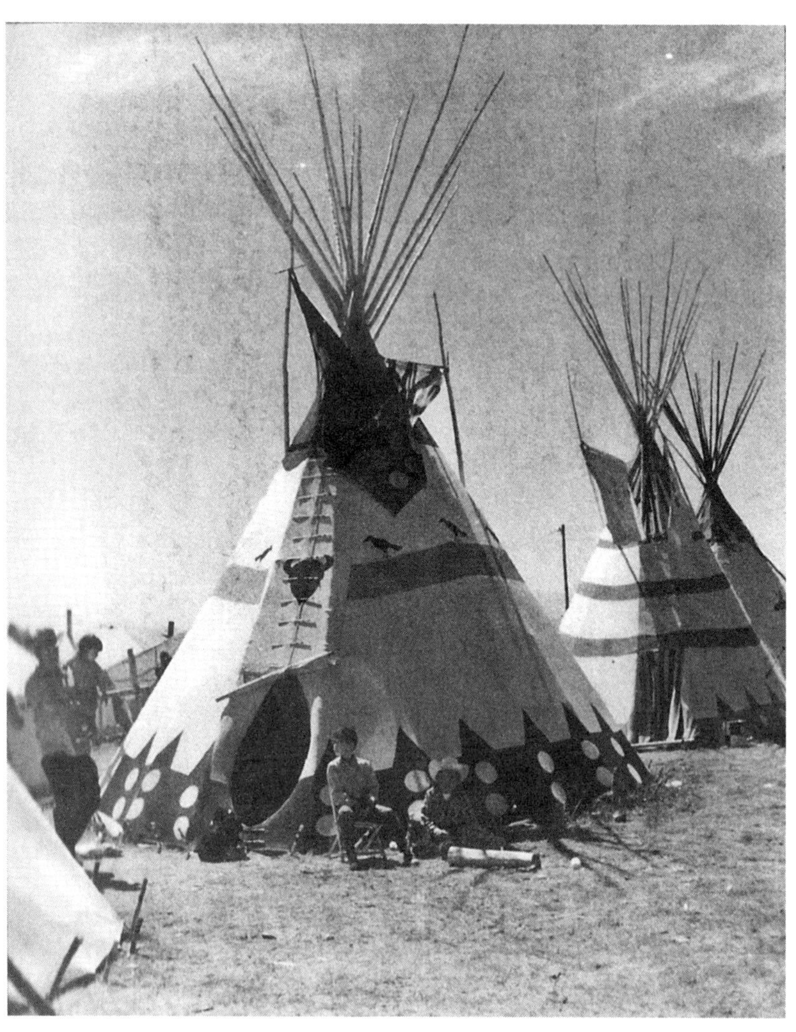

4·4

Darryl Blackman's Crow lodge erected at the North American Indian Days, a powwow, in Browning, Montana, 1970. Don Schmidt Photo, Glacier Studio.

access to abundant stands of pines for trading and "erecting their own magnificent tipis."[10] Blackman's generosity imparted gifts from forest and prairie ecologies abroad, pointing to an ethics of more-than-human reciprocity that guides all aspects of tipi arts.

To frame this argument, it is necessary to unpack the changing role of architecture in Niitsítapi political ecology before and during colonization. I begin with what is obfuscated in Montgomery's account: the sacred emergence of the Crow Tipi and other *niitóyis* (tipis) as gifts from supernatural guardians, inaugurating a circuit of more-than-human reciprocities that persisted through Blackman's lifetime and into the present.[11] The spiritually potent gift included precise guidelines for painting the tipi and assembling an associated medicine bundle, along with a corpus of songs, prayers, and protocols governing reproduction and transmission. A sacred being, the medicine bundle would typically hang inside or on a tripod outside the lodge. These various elements constitute what anthropologist Brian Noble calls a "tipi praxis that is a dense articulation of tangible and intangible, human and nonhuman elements, and of specific social means for continually extending the complex."[12] Throughout this chapter, I capitalize "Crow Tipi" in order to refer to the entire constellation of material and immaterial elements constituting the praxis, inclusive of Crows, the more-than-human beings who first gifted it. I use the lower-case "tipi" or "lodge" to refer only to an architectural manifestation of the praxis. The Crow Tipi joins other painted lodge praxes that function to renew and enlarge a vast circle of alliances with more-than-human beings.

Blackman belonged to the Ampskapi Pikuni (sometimes referred to as Pikuni or South Piegan), citizens of the modern Blackfeet Nation in northwest Montana. Established by treaty in 1855, their lands at present span 1.5 million acres on the eastern edge of the Rocky Mountains.[13] Ampskapi Pikuni is the southernmost of four distinct Indigenous polities, including the Kainai (Blood), Siksiká, and Apatosi Pikuni (North Piegan) in Canada, that compose the Niitsítapi, the modern Blackfoot Confederacy.[14] The confederacy's vast ancestral territory encompasses the western grasslands and forested foothills of the Rocky Mountains from present-day Alberta and Saskatchewan to Montana, including much of Glacier National Park. Oral histories demarcate numerous sacred sites throughout this land, meeting places where more-than-human beings gifted Blackman's ancestors the knowledge and material abundance necessary to thrive.[15] Today, many members of the alliance view the US-Canada border as "an artificial barrier that separates families."[16]

In the winters preceding the reservation era, the Ampskapi Pikuni set up villages in the protective shield of densely forested valleys. In the summers, the dispersed nations of the Niitsítapi gathered for the Okan, a variant of the annual Sun Dance ceremonies practiced by numerous Plains nations (see chapter 5). Mirroring the shape of an unraised tipi cover, participants arranged their pale, gleaming lodges into an enormous open semicircle on the plains.[17] European and United States commentators dubbed these encampments "white cities," a phenomenon that circulated widely in prints based on a scene painted by Swiss artist Karl Bodmer, who accompanied a German expedition to the headwaters of the Missouri River in 1839. Four decades later, white trader James Willard Schultz wrote evocatively, "White were the four hundred new, buffalo-leather lodge-skins of the Pikuni camp; those of the Sun priests, medicine men, painted in vivid colors with symbols of their sky gods, sun, moon, and the stars, and the birds and animals of their visions, their dreams."[18] Only a select subset of tipis in the innermost row of the camp bore such vivid imagery. The symbols and narratives painted on tipi covers marked the dwelling places of extraordinary families and the meeting places of revered warrior societies.[19]

Like Fred Stevens's sandpaintings, Blackman's tipis cannot be divorced from the sacred ecologies that locate the Niitsítapi within a relational cosmos. The painted features of the lodge manifest what contemporary Ampskapi Pikuni historian Rosalyn LaPier describes as a "multilayered reality where the extraordinary experiences of the Blackfeet with the supernatural were interwoven with the natural."[20] She articulates the tripart division of the Niitsítapi cosmos: the Above world, home of Spomitapi, the sky beings, such as Thunder, Sun, Moon, and Morning Star; the Below world, home to Ksahkomitapi, the earth beings, including plants, animals and rocks; and the Water world, where Soyiitapi, underwater beings, live.[21] "All this is laid out on painted tipis," stated the late Apatosi Pikuni ceremonial specialist Allan Pard.[22] The Above world is a dark zone smattered with bright, starry orbs in the shape of storied constellations; the equal-arm cross at back is Lip-isówaahs, Morning Star, child of Sun and Moon, indicating the sacred origins of the design in a dream. The light (often unpainted) Below world hosts zoomorphic figures, the supernatural beings who gifted the tipi praxis to humans. The Water world typically appears at the base of the tipi, demarcated by serrated mountain peaks or rounded hills. It is filled with rows of pale circles—meteors or puffball mushrooms, children of

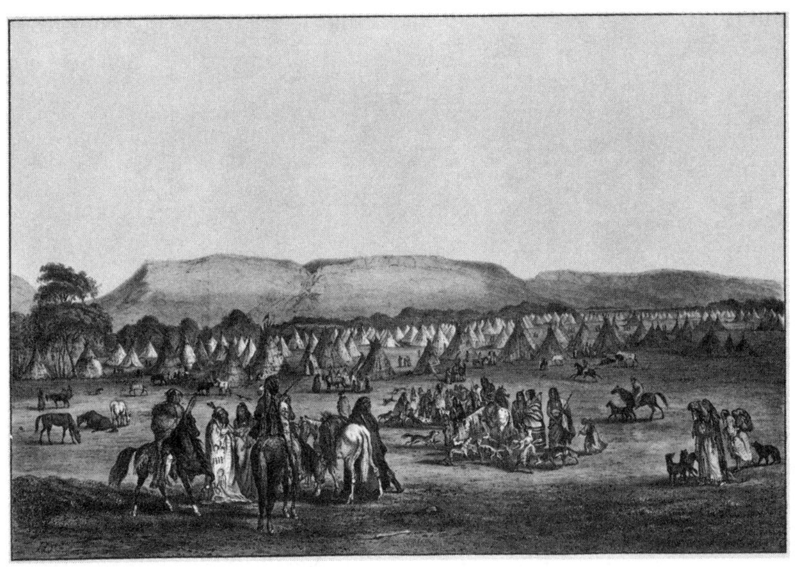

4.5

Karl Bodmer, *Encampment of the Piekkan Indians,* 1842. Hand-colored lithograph on paper. 51 × 36 cm. National Portrait Gallery, Smithsonian Institution; gift of Betty A. and Lloyd G. Schermer. NPG.99.169.1.

....

the stars who "fell to earth."[23] When the flap door of the tipi is properly oriented to the east, so too do the figures on it greet the rising sun, the source of Ihtsipaitapiyopa, the vital lifeforce that animates all things (sometimes referred to as the Creator in a Christian rhetoric).[24]

The Niitsítapi have continuously adapted these conventions to their changing ecological and political conditions, locating Blackman within a "tradition of architectural experimentation" that spanned the advent of colonization.[25] Tipis were in wide use when Spanish conquistadors arrived in the sixteenth century. The covers doubled as suitcases for belongings that were pulled by dogs on wooden platforms lashed to tipi poles. As Niitsítapi acquired Spanish horses, they reorganized a semisedentary society into hunting bands that followed the annual migrations of buffalo.[26] A quintessential portable architecture, lodges are designed to regulate the temperature extremes of baking summer heat and winter ice storms, withstand tornadoes, and quickly collapse to facilitate efficient movement. Rainwater is naturally directed to the ground along the long, smooth surface of the poles. Frequently, an interior liner provides an additional barrier to drafts and water condensation. The flaps on either side of the smoke hole at top can be opened for ventilation when fires are burned inside. With the extra hauling power of horses, tipis grew larger, their surface areas expanding to enfold families in a spiritual force-field manifested by the designs.[27]

As lodge covers wear out quickly from weather and use, making new forms is key to the realization of their inherent power. Into the twentieth century this was a gendered communal practice; men generally held the rights to reproduce and transfer the designs while the creation and care of their material foundations, tipi poles and covers, were typically the provenance of women. Until the orchestrated demise of the buffalo in the 1880s, guilds of highly skilled women painstakingly crafted the tents from buffalo cow hides. Artists scraped, tanned, cut, and stitched between eight and twenty hides, each weighing ten to twelve pounds, to create small hunting lodges and large group dwellings that could house as many as eight families.[28] Following the traumatic loss of sacred buffalo herds, women and men began to produce covers from canvas obtained from white traders. In a characteristic embrace of the new, they achieved new heights of technical virtuosity with the lighter and more flexible material. They refined the smoke flaps and created a tight, smoother fit over the support poles. They replaced bone and sinew tools with steel needles and manufactured thread, enabling the addition of hems and straps for tipi stakes at the bottom of the covers.[29] The Plains tipi of the twentieth century—the iconic form that Libhart desired for Expo 70—was canvas, not hide.

Like other tipi designs gifted during dreams, the images associated with the Crow Tipi record their origin in a transformative encounter between an exceptional human and a spiritual guardian. Oral histories specify that the lodge originated among members of the Buffalo Chip band while they were camped in the Porcupine Hills of present-day southern Alberta in a time before horses. In 1950, Ampskapi Pikuni spiritual leader Yellow Kidney recounted how a hunter left a cache of meat in a corral overnight following a successful buffalo drive. When he returned the next morning, he found a lodge painted with the figures of fourteen crows. Two supernatural Crow People appeared and offered the lodge to the man in exchange for the gift of meat to feed their children.[30] The narrative underscores that sharing one's material abundance has significant rewards. Such tangible generosity garners spiritual gifts—in this case, an invitation to dwell in the house of an avian protector and call upon that relationship in times of need.

In turn, the inheritance of the Crow Tipi is governed by community-sanctioned rights and protocols. The keeper of a design bears an exclusive right to reproduce it, as well as the responsibility to relinquish the rights by transferring custodianship to another through ceremony. More generally, one is obligated to honor and repay the generosity of animal protectors to benefit the community.[31] Yet one-time keepers are not alienated from these sacred obligations upon the transfer of tipi praxes; rather, such exchanges extend genealogies, with former custodians ceremonially adopting the new caretakers as children.[32] Many accounts of this relational complex prioritize terms such as "intellectual property" and "owner," language that is embedded in capitalist valuation and ripe for cultural misunderstanding. I follow the urging of some contemporary Niitsítapi scholars and ceremonial specialists in preferring terms such as "keeper," "custodian," and "caretaker."[33] Like all English translations, these terms are imprecise, but they better conjure a relationship of reciprocity, the foremost value governing the Niitsítapi cosmos.

When correctly realized, tipi designs transcend mere representation. The images are charged with the power of sacred ecologies that are simultaneously depicted (as symbols) and manifested (as paints and other material adornments). To realize crow and buffalo designs that originated as earth gifts is to ceremonially manifest their vitality in a new time and space. Customarily, a spectrum of vivid hues is sourced and prepared from particular plants, animals, and sacred places. Like the designs they manifest, paints are governed by strict rituals and responsibilities, such as singing special songs and making offerings at their gathering sites.[34] Next, a skilled artist—often a ceremonial practitioner, who may or may not be the keeper of the design—oversees the outlining of prototypical forms. The custodian's friends or family might be enlisted to help complete the painting. Pard elaborates, "When we paint symbols . . . all of the holy things . . . will recognize the person calling to them for protection or help . . . [and] put that power on that thing or person."[35] When decorated with sacred paints, tipis arts can call forth the abundance, protection, and authority bestowed by more-than-human guardians. This principle of material activation persisted with the introduction of manufactured brushes and paints in the twentieth century, which Blackman used at least some of the time.[36]

Yellow Kidney's telling of the Crow Tipi history specifies that the whole community benefits from the "wonderful gift from the crows." When the recipient of the Crow Tipi consulted with spiritual leaders from the Buffalo Chip band about his vision, they determined, "We'll use it as protection for our people and also to insure good fortune in securing bison. The lodge will be used to draw the bison to us." Importantly, the praxis binds crows, humans, and even horses together as family, resonating with the kinship modalities I have discussed throughout this book. Yellow Kidney continued, "The owner was told that all the crows were his children. That some of them were his horses."[37] His account reinscribes the horse, a Spanish colonial introduction, into a network of kinships bound together by rituals and gifts.[38] The animals "liked the Crow Lodge, and gather about it. . . . Horses were so fond of the lodge that the bottom was made ragged by their chewing." Niitsítapi citizens found that their herds increased through custodianship and transfer of this powerful praxis.[39]

Tipi transfers anchor a customary Niitsítapi political system centered on character, consensus, and distributed authority. Ampskapi Pikuni historians Joseph Scott Gladstone and Donald D. Pepion recount how prior to interference from the United States and Canada, affiliation within the bands that compose the nations of the confederacy was self-selecting and fluid. Leadership required community consensus on one's "outstanding personal characteristics" including demonstrated skill in hunting, warfare, ceremony, and diplomacy. Echoing the tenets of the Crow Tipi history, Gladstone and Pepion emphasize generosity as a cornerstone of customary Niitsítapi leadership: "As good hunters, recognized leaders would share wealth with the needy and invite others to feast at his tipi lodge."[40] The stewardship of painted lodges was customarily limited by an expectation that an individual would transfer lodge bundles to new custodians within four years, thereby decentering power and extending the web of alliances.[41] By regifting the rights and responsibilities, tipi caretakers maintain harmonious relationships across the three layers of the Blackfeet universe, ensuring what Blackfeet scholar Betty Bastien calls the "balance that is necessary for health, prosperity, and long life."[42]

Put another way, tipis are vehicles of earth diplomacy—what scholars have called "ceremonial treaty making" or "treaty ecologies"—among Niitsítapi nations and the many other beings with whom they share mountains, grasslands, waterways, biosphere, and celestial realm.[43] To sit and smoke in council is to inhabit concentric rings of reciprocity connecting the conical tent, the encampment, and the cosmos. Tangible and intangible goods are exchanged between parties to signify that they are bound together as relatives, with mutual vows of cooperation and goodwill. They must avoid conflict and help one another in times of hardship.

Such ritualized generosity is expected among members of the various bands and nations of the Blackfoot Confederacy, relatives such as crows, buffalo, and horses, and the other nations with whom the Niitsítapi nations have negotiated territory and sustenance, including Britain, Canada, and the United States.[44] One's responsible caretaking of the circuit of alliances through ongoing transfers guarantees the return of tangible and spiritual goods to the individual, family, community, and cosmos.[45] One must tend the eternal flame of reciprocity. These protocols survived, adapted, and bolstered Blackfeet resistance to settler colonial dominance in the twentieth and twenty-first centuries. Tipi praxes helped to transmit elements of customary governance through intensive colonization to inform a broken system of international relations.

CABINS AND CATTLE

Tipi praxes withstood particularly dramatic changes to Ampskapi Pikuni lifeways following the nation's settlement on the Blackfeet Reservation in the wake of the Lame Bull Treaty of 1855. Treaty commissioner Isaac Stevens, governor of Washington Territory, sought an economical route for the transcontinental railroad west of the Mississippi River and an assimilationist mandate that the Blackfeet would survive on cattle and crops.[46] Alongside buffalo, tipis were targeted in intensive federal efforts to assimilate Plains nations to a sedentary life of farming and livestock. Wissler recounted in 1933, "From the first every effort was made to induce the Indians to construct and occupy a log cabin. It seems to be that if the Indian could be induced to give up the tipi he must necessarily abandon his roaming habits." All this in spite of the fact that "it is obvious that the tipi was more sanitary and better ventilated" amid the deadly sweep of European epidemics.[47] At stake in the dramatic transition to reservation life was, as Bastien articulates, "living in the circle, . . . living in the consciousness that everything is connected and has consequences. Government and business had made every effort to seduce Niitsítapi to forfeit this principle. Such efforts continue this day."[48] Painted lodges are much more than passive mirrors to this struggle. Blackman in particular contributed to a reconfigured tipi praxis in negotiation with the onset—the onslaught—of colonial capitalism.

Blackman's short life spanned the Termination era, "when genocide was going full force," as respected Ampskapi Pikuni elder Doris Kicking Woman (b. 1949), told me.[49] Blackman was among a minority of young Ampskapi Pikuni men who stayed on the reservation instead of moving to city slums under devastating relocation policies from the Bureau of Indian Affairs (BIA).[50] By then, oil, more so than cattle, had become the desacralized "second buffalo." The Blackfeet Tribal Business Council (BTBC), which replaced sacred structures of governance with an economic purview under BIA oversight in 1922, negotiated oil leases and distributions of revenue to citizens. Some Ampskapi Pikuni leaders fought to re-invest this capitalist institution with a sovereign agenda, notably preventing a federal campaign to terminate the nation.[51] Nonetheless, for many who lived on the reservation, dire poverty, disease, and a vast, untreated epidemic of alcoholism took their toll. Kicking Woman notes that "all of the people who knew the songs and how to do the ceremonies were dying. . . . A lot of that was lost and the kids were raised with no respect for anyone or anything." She recalls that traditional cultural ways were not important to most young people.[52]

Blackman's activities scarcely register in scholarship to date. Yet new archival research and conversations with his contemporaries have convinced me that he was "really instrumental" to the transmission of Niitsítapi arts during this time of duress.[53] He specialized in making a wide array of customary forms, including pipes, medicine bundles, regalia, tipis, and lodges associated with the Okan.[54] Blackman learned customary paint-gathering, tipi-making, and related protocols from his grandmother, Sippi (Mary Fred Blackman, who was Cree and a skilled herbalist), who raised him in a traditional household with numerous half-siblings and cousins. Bill Blackman, Darryl's nephew who later grew up in the same home, showed me the treadle that Darryl, Darryl's mother Cecile, and Sippi used to sew the canvas covers.[55] Blackman was meanwhile trained in ceremonial practice from his great-uncle-in-law, Fish Wolf Robe, a respected community leader who recognized and cultivated the boy's talents from a young age. It was Fish Wolf Robe who transferred the Crow Tipi to his talented nephew.[56]

Blackman's best friend and fellow artist, Howard Rides at the Doore, noted that Darryl was respected in the community for his artistic and spiritual knowledge. The artist's repertoire spanned a customary, gendered division of the arts, from sewing covers and his grandmother's dresses (typically done by women) to painting tipis and singing ceremonial songs (typically done by men).[57] Roger Butterfly (b. 1950) remembers Blackman, his half-brother, as an intercultural translator. Blackman could talk about ceremonial matters with elders in fluent Siksiká and just as easily "use big words" in conversation with white interlocutors. Butterfly remembers helping his brother paint covers after Blackman returned from undergraduate studies at the University of Montana. When the younger man marveled at how quickly and accurately Blackman could cut the canvas, Blackman joked, "You just have to know algebra and geometry!"[58] Although Blackman and Doore were known for their drinking and other shenanigans, they also stood out for their unusual commitment to customary lifeways. Kicking Woman told me, "We went to ceremony after ceremony." For this exceptional group of young people, the feeling was, "I'm going to go to that because I feel good about it, it makes me happy, and I'm going to do what I can to make that continue."[59] Blackman's friends and relatives lament the loss of critical knowledge when he died prematurely from alcoholism in 1971.

In 1964, Blackman participated in the international return of a medicine bundle associated with the Beaver Tipi, an event which may have influenced his approach to the Osaka commission five years later. The tipi rights, medicine bundle, and custom-made regalia were ceremonially gifted in 1943 to a wealthy Swedish couple, Estelle and Folke Bernadotte, by Yellow Kidney, three-times caretaker of the Crow Tipi, and his wife, Insimaki. Following customary tipi praxes, gifts were exchanged and the Bernadottes were adopted as daughter and son to Insimaki and Yellow Kidney, obligating the Swedish couple to act as responsible kin and caretakers.[60] Following her husband's death, Estelle Bernadotte traveled in person to the Museum of the Plains Indian in 1964 to regift the bundle to the Ampskapi Pikuni. The being was received by Earl Old Person, chairman of the BTBC (1964–2008) and honorary lifetime chief (1978–2021), in full regalia. "Behind him came Darryl Blackman, likewise dressed in all the magnificence that only the Blackfeet can portray."[61] The artist, who was probably wearing buckskin clothing of his own making, presided over the rare ceremonial return of a sacred being—a full-circle homecoming.[62] Some elders in the nation reportedly advised that the repatriated bundle should be entrusted to the museum for safekeeping.[63] Such counsel reflects the preciousness and precarity of such items during Blackman's lifetime. Few bundles remained in the community, having been sold by community members or seized by outsiders during bouts of starvation, disease, and social upheaval in the late nineteenth and early twentieth centuries.[64]

Friends and family told me that as his alcoholism progressed near the end of his life, Blackman made cultural items for sale to white collectors, who may have believed that they were heirlooms. He notably sold his work to the well-known sculptor and collector Bob Scriver, who owned a taxidermy museum in Browning.[65] Whether Blackman explicitly misled such recipients or let them think what they wished about the items is unclear. There is no evidence that he willfully obscured the provenance of items made for Ampskapi Pikuni, hinting that he might have made ethical distinctions between those inside and outside of the community. Such bifurcation is suggested by memories shared by Kicking Woman and Doore of the transfer of a tipi and medicine bundle to Scriver and his wife, the writer Mary Scriver, in 1969. The two young men mixed clowning into the procedures, a memory that Kicking Woman and Doore still laugh about to this day.[66] Doore explained to me that "we were doing that because we instructed it but didn't *approve* it" (emphasis his). He and Blackman shared the opinion that Scriver was exploitative, using the Ampskapi Pikuni "for his own ends."[67] Their irreverence contradicted the "solemn and ancient religious ceremony" described by Mary Scriver in the *Glacier Reporter*.[68]

Blackman participated in novel forms of creation and transmission that likewise reshaped tipi praxes during this period.[69] In 1973, Libhart and Southern Plains Indian Museum curator Rosemary Ellison noted that contemporary lodge makers were challenged to develop "creative new works" that could interface with museums and a growing market. The curators credited "increasing interest in Indian identification" and the occupations of the American Indian Movement (AIM) for popularizing Plains tipis.[70] However, as employees of the IACB, both were unacknowledged agents of the accelerating demand. All three of the IACB's museums operated shops dedicated to furthering an international market for Plains Native arts and crafts.[71] Indigenous-owned businesses also sprang up to answer commercial demand in this period, such as Blackfeet-run Heart Butte Industries, which specialized in both plain and painted tipi covers.[72] As the market for Plains tipis grew beyond the production capacity of Native artists, white-owned enterprises gladly filled the void. One manufacturing company in Wyoming reproduced "patterns provided by their Indian customers [including Crow, Cheyenne, and Blackfeet from Canada] in the production of an authentic line of tipis."[73] Oregon-based Nomadics Tipi Makers, in continuous operation since 1970, has documented the global spread of their products, including several tipi campgrounds in Japan.[74]

In a prominent series of books about Niitsítapi culture and history published in the early 2000s, Adolf Hungry-Wolf, a white ceremonial practitioner who married into the Blackfoot Confederacy, lamented that painted tipis were beset by "confusion and duplication, especially with a lack of knowledgeable elders on this subject. Sometimes there are several examples of a well-known design, with no one being certain who actually owns the proper rights. Another recent custom has seen some descendants of former painted-lodge owners to copy ancient designs on their own lodges, claiming rights owned by grandparents or other ancestors, even though this changes the original meaning and power. . . . Yet another recent custom is for some painted-lodge owners to make duplicates for sale, without ceremony, to museums or art collectors."[75] Blackman was a leading innovator of the latter practice. Alongside the Crow tipi, he created numerous variants of painted tipis as commissioned art, possibly paying their caretakers for the use of the designs. Doore recollects helping him to produce an estimated fifty painted tipis for the Museum of the Plains Indian, the Smithsonian Institution, and the Heard Museum. *Glacier Reporter* noted that following Expo 70, the USIA commissioned a second tipi—an Otter lodge—from Blackman for an exhibition that opened in Lebanon and toured the Middle East.[76] Rather than view Blackman's multifaceted activities as evidence of "confusion," I see witting adaptations attuned to the variable circumstances of tipis' widening circulation; the artist was far from ignorant or dismissive of communal norms.

Doore notes that at the height of their production, he and Blackman still consulted with elders to ensure the correctness of the designs, smudged and prayed over the finished lodges, and folded the covers in a customary manner before taking them to the post office.[77] At one point, the duo switched from earth paints to water-based commercial paints, which enabled them to decorate as many as two covers per day, depending on the complexity of the design.[78] A similar blend of customary and novel techniques can be seen in a series of photographs from the archives of the Museum of the Plains Indian. In one, the artist is seen tracing the forelegs of a Yellow Horse tipi on the lawn of the museum with the assistance of Sippi and other relatives and friends. Members of the collective hold commercial brushes and cups of paint poured from metal cans visible in the background of a second photograph in the series. The group's collaborative approach and embrace of new materials perpetuated a dynamic history of tipi-making on the Plains. These details indicated that like Fred Stevens, Blackman cared for the cultural transmission of tipi praxes within the Blackfeet Nation, even as he innovated new forms for external agents.

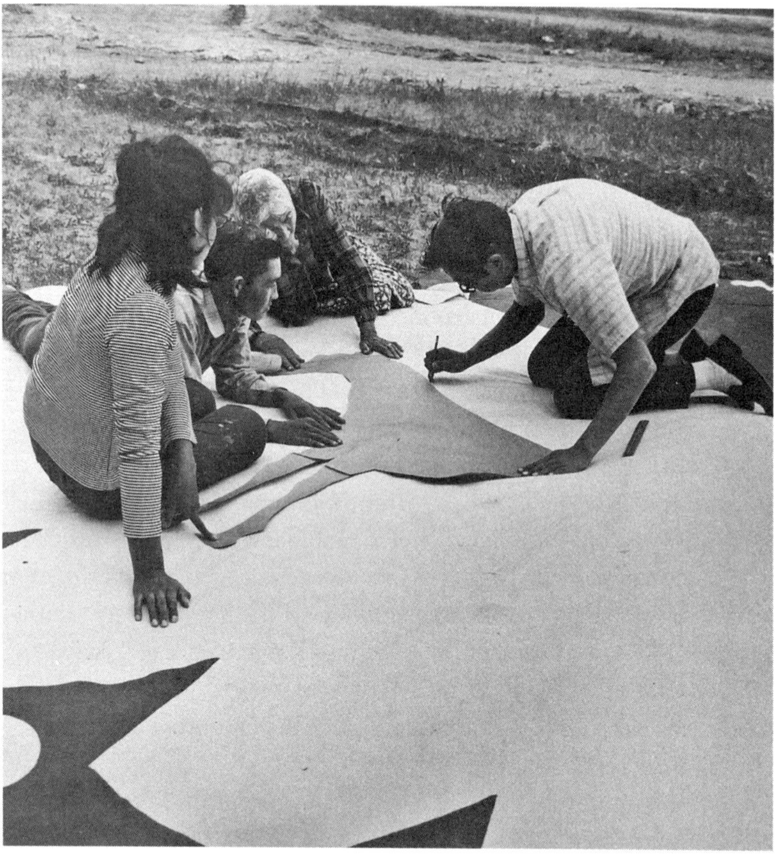

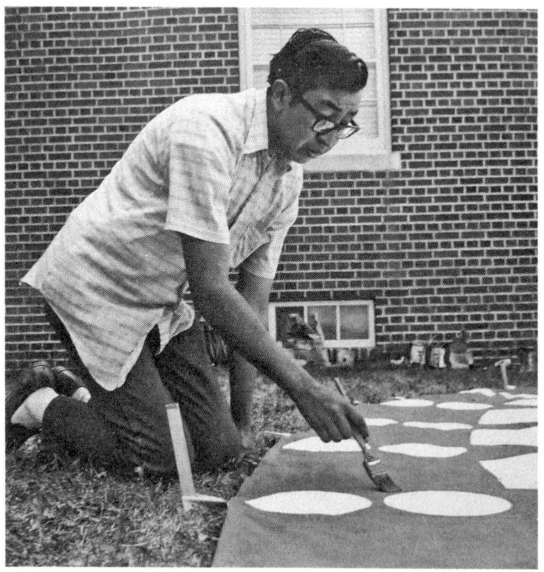

4.6

Darryl Blackman with his grandmother, Sippi, and other relatives and friends, working on a Yellow Horse lodge at the Museum of the Plains Indian in 1969. Provided by the Museum of the Plains Indian, North Browning, Montana.

4.7

Darryl Blackman paints a Yellow Horse lodge at the Museum of the Plains Indian in 1969. Provided by the Museum of the Plains Indian, North Browning, Montana.

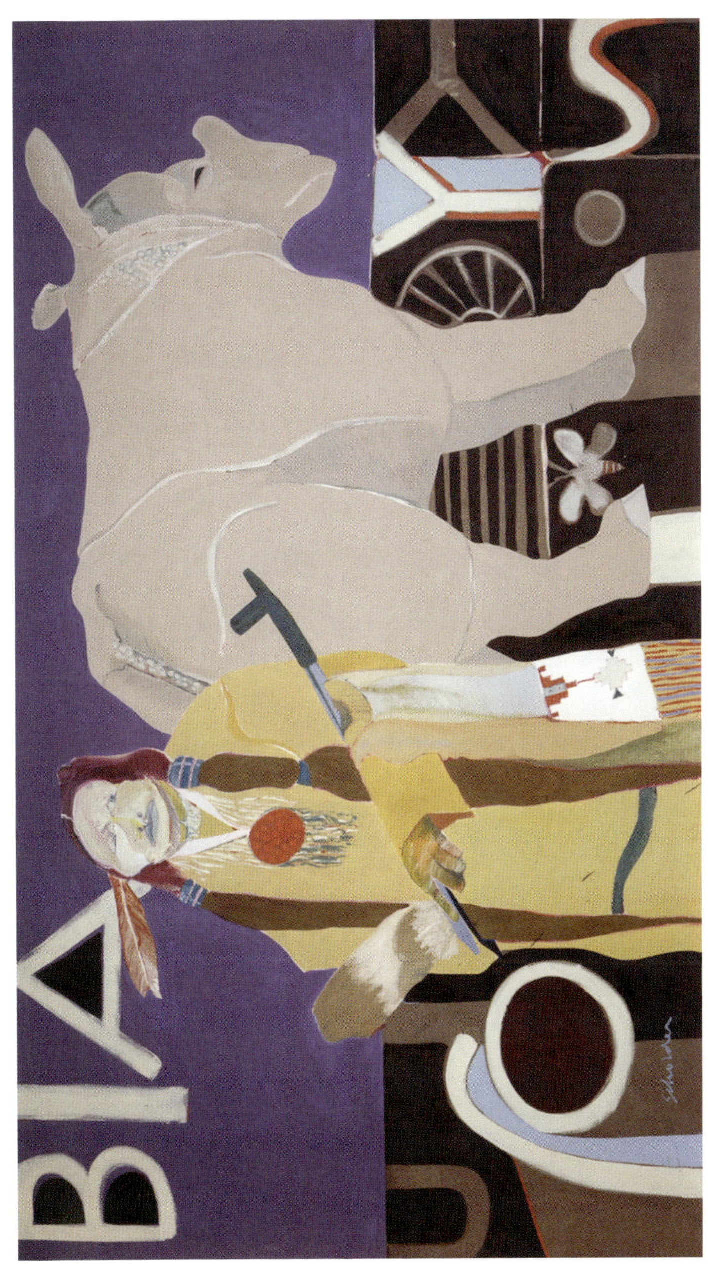

P.1

Fritz Scholder, *Indian and Rhinoceros*, 1968. Oil paint on canvas, 304.8 × 172.72 cm. National Museum of the American Indian, Smithsonian Institution, Washington, DC, 26/8066.

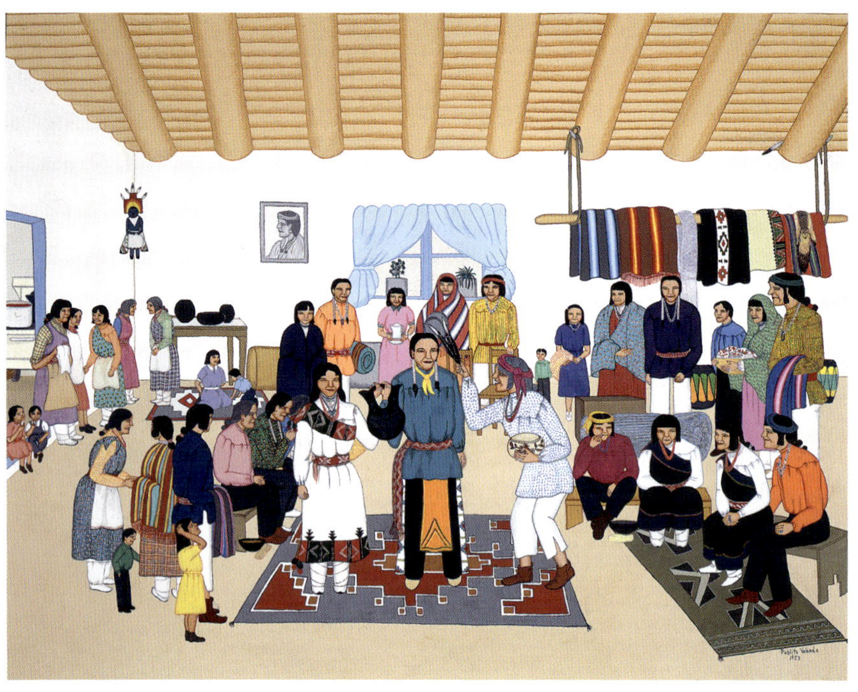

P.2

Pablita Velarde, *The Betrothal*, 1953. Tempera on canvas board, 55.5 × 71 cm. Heard Museum Collection, Phoenix, Arizona, gift of James T. Bialac, with permission of Helen Tindel.

P.3a

Gerónima Cruz Montoya (P'otsúnú), *Pueblo Crafts*, 1938. Tempera on board, 29.25 × 128.125 in. Margretta Dietrich Collection, Museum of Indian Arts and Culture, Santa Fe, NM, 54002/13.

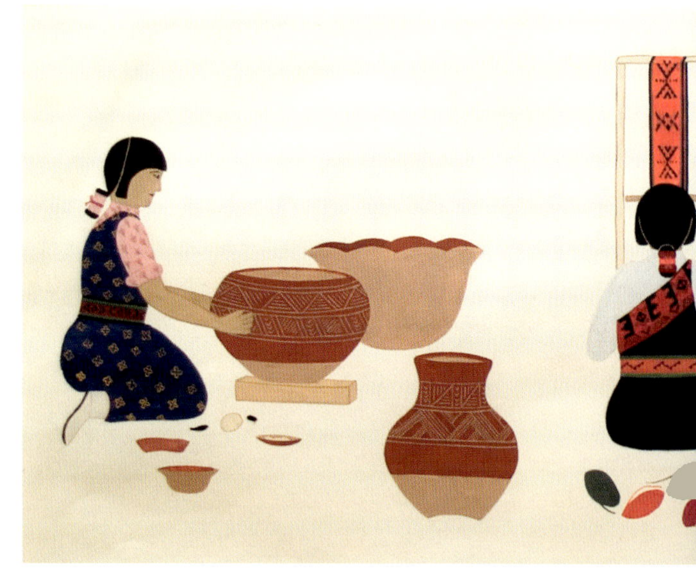

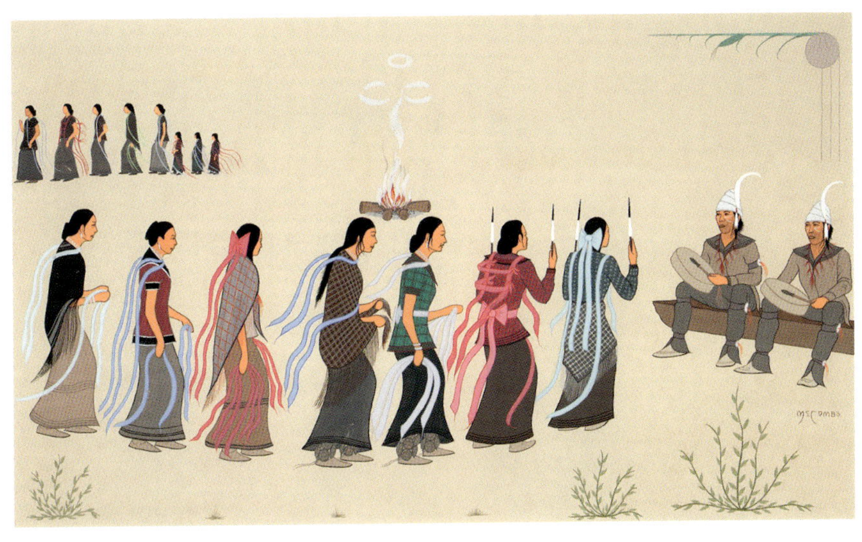

P.3b

Solomon McCombs, *Creek Women's Ribbon Dance*, 1949. Watercolor on board, 22.25 × 32.25 in. Philbrook Museum of Art, Tulsa, Oklahoma, 1949.15.

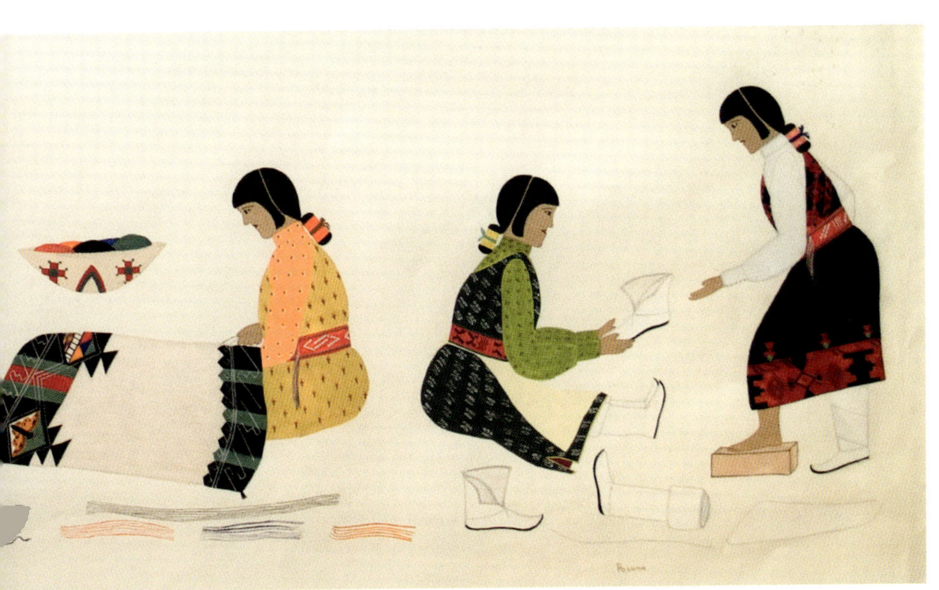

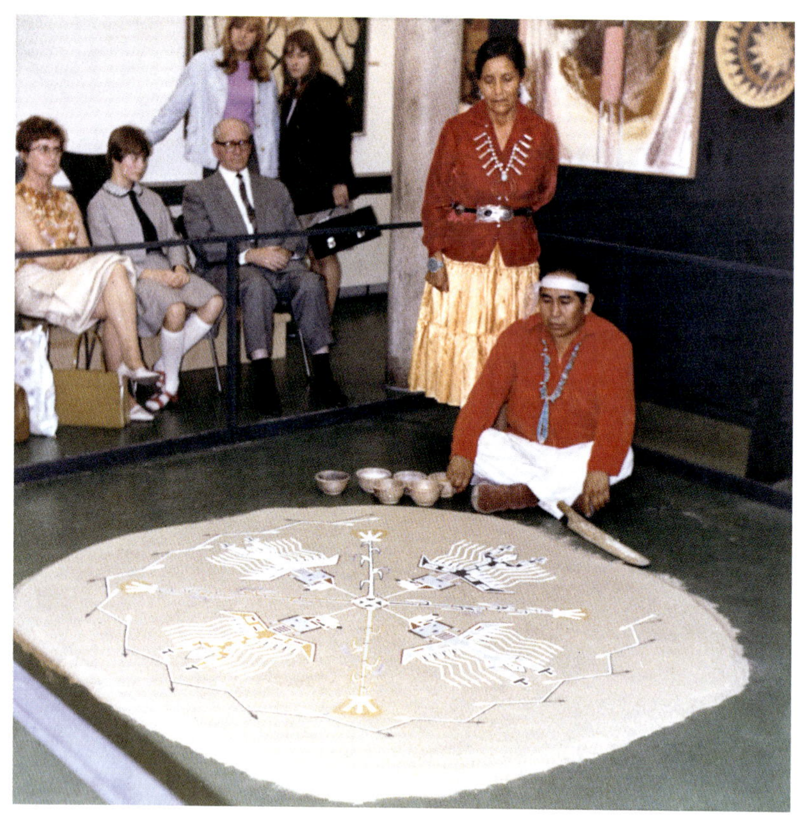

P.4

Bertha Stevens and Fred Stevens with *The Four Thunders*, an altered sandpainting by Fred Stevens, at Amerika Haus, Berlin, 1966. Image provided by IAIA Archives, Santa Fe, New Mexico. MS03, Box 24, F.9, I.5.

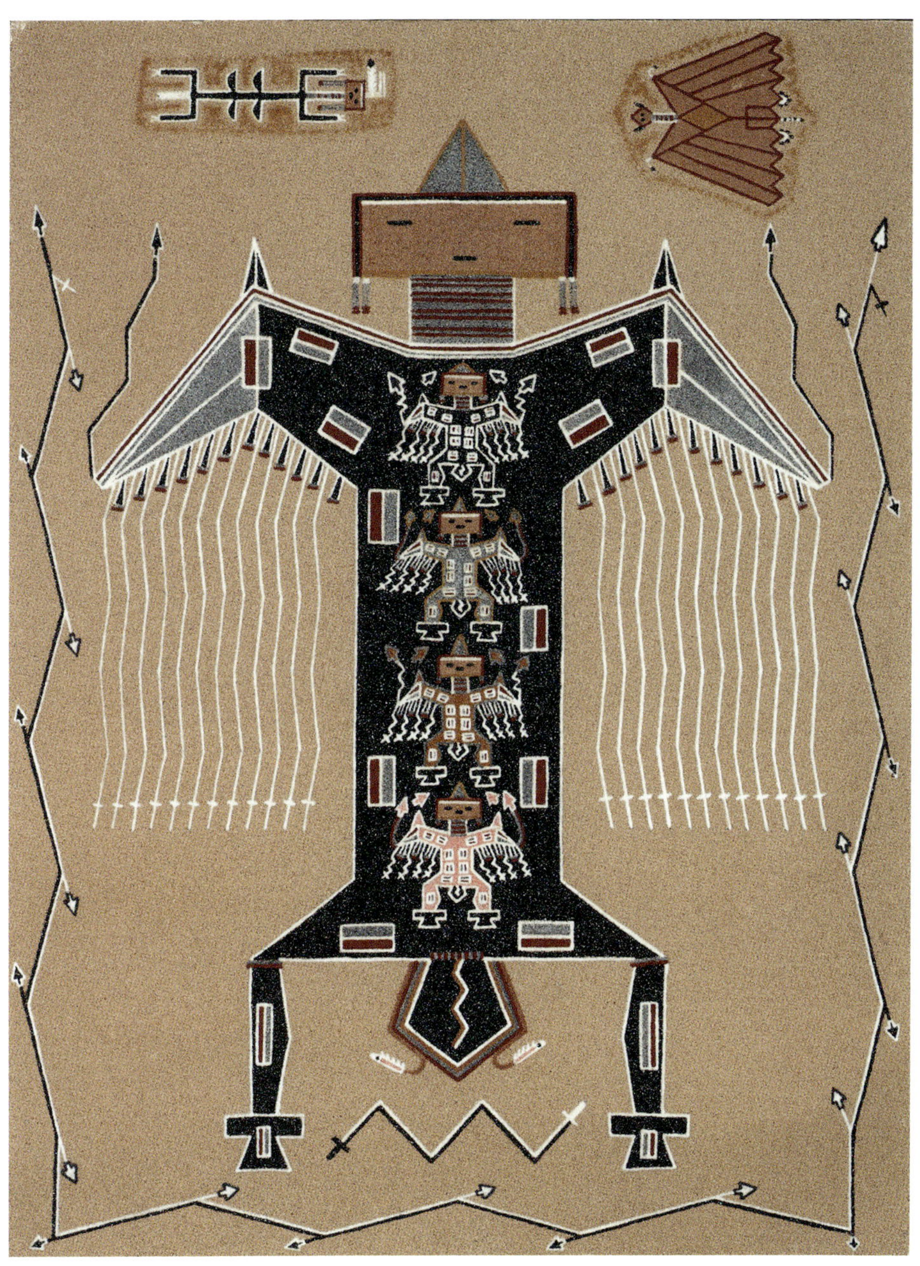

P.5

Fred Stevens, *Big Thunder*, Male Shooting Way Chant, date unknown. An altered sandpainting made of pulverized sandstone, silicon, and mineral rock on Masonite, 36 × 24 in. Collection of Michael Eugene Harris.

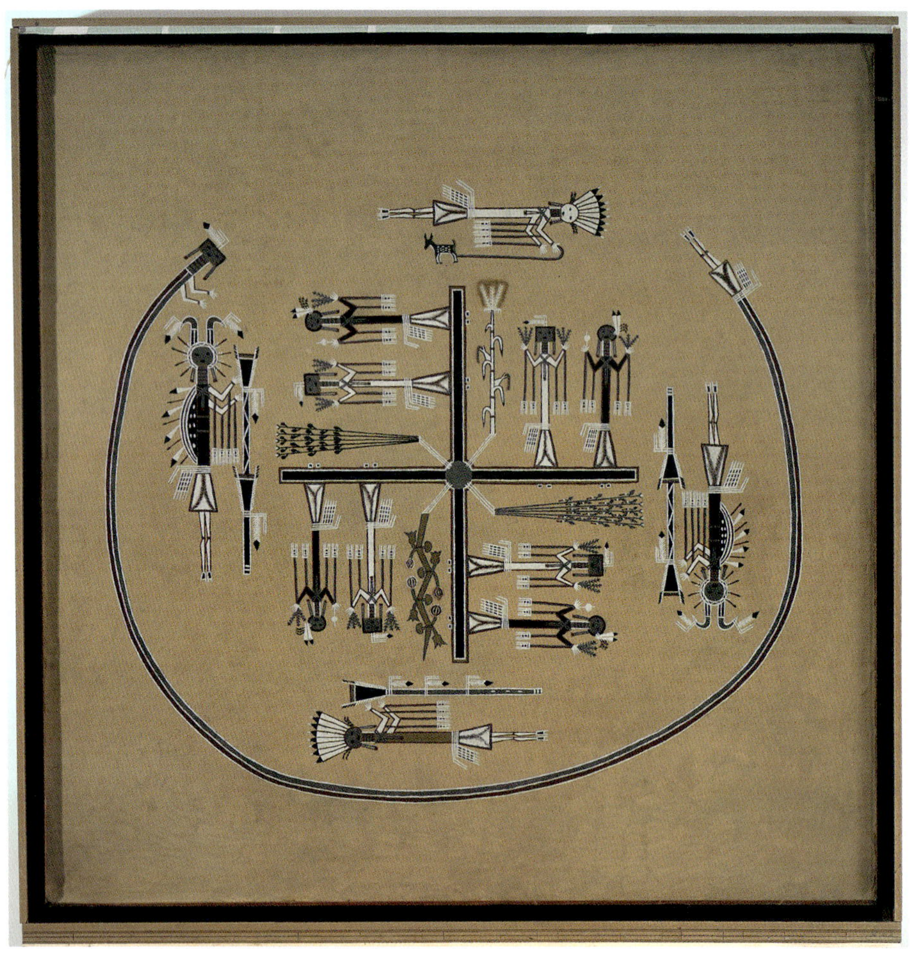

P.6

Fred Stevens, *Whirling Logs*, 1966. An altered sandpainting made
of pulverized sandstone, synthetic glue, and mineral rock, 7 × 7 ft.
Horniman Museum and Gardens, London.

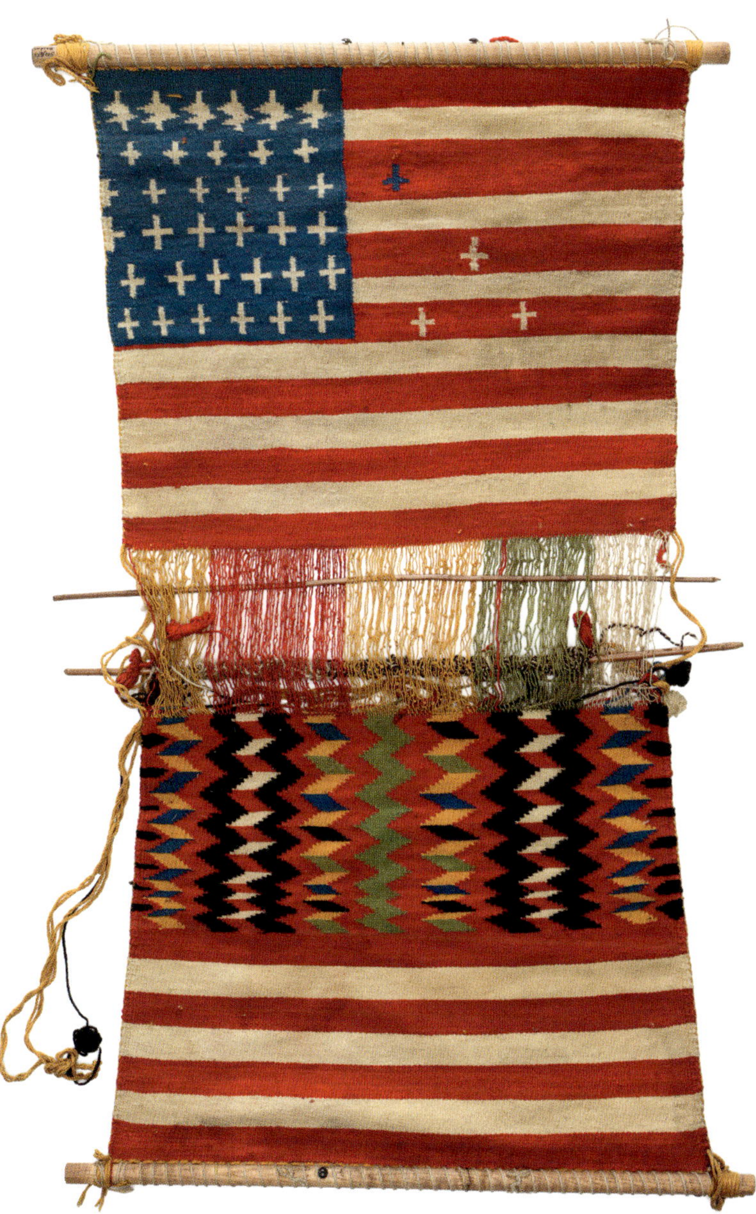

P.7

Weaving on a loom by Asdzáá Tłogi (Juanita) that was acquired by William F. M. Arny, 1874. E16494, Department of Anthropology, the Smithsonian Institution, Washington, DC. Photo by Donald E. Hurlbert, Smithsonian Institution.

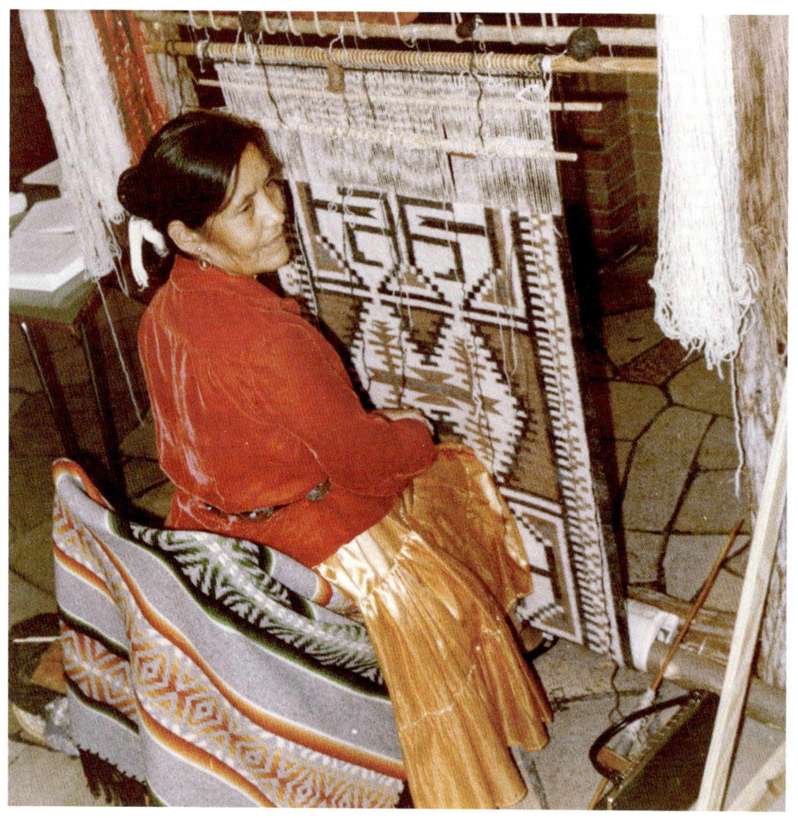

P.8

Bertha Stevens weaving at Amerika Haus, Berlin, 1966. Provided by the Institute for American Indian Arts, MS03_06_0153.

P.9

Bertha Stevens spins wool with a textile-in-progress at the Olympic Games in Mexico City, 1968. Provided by Rainbow Stevens and Alita Begay.

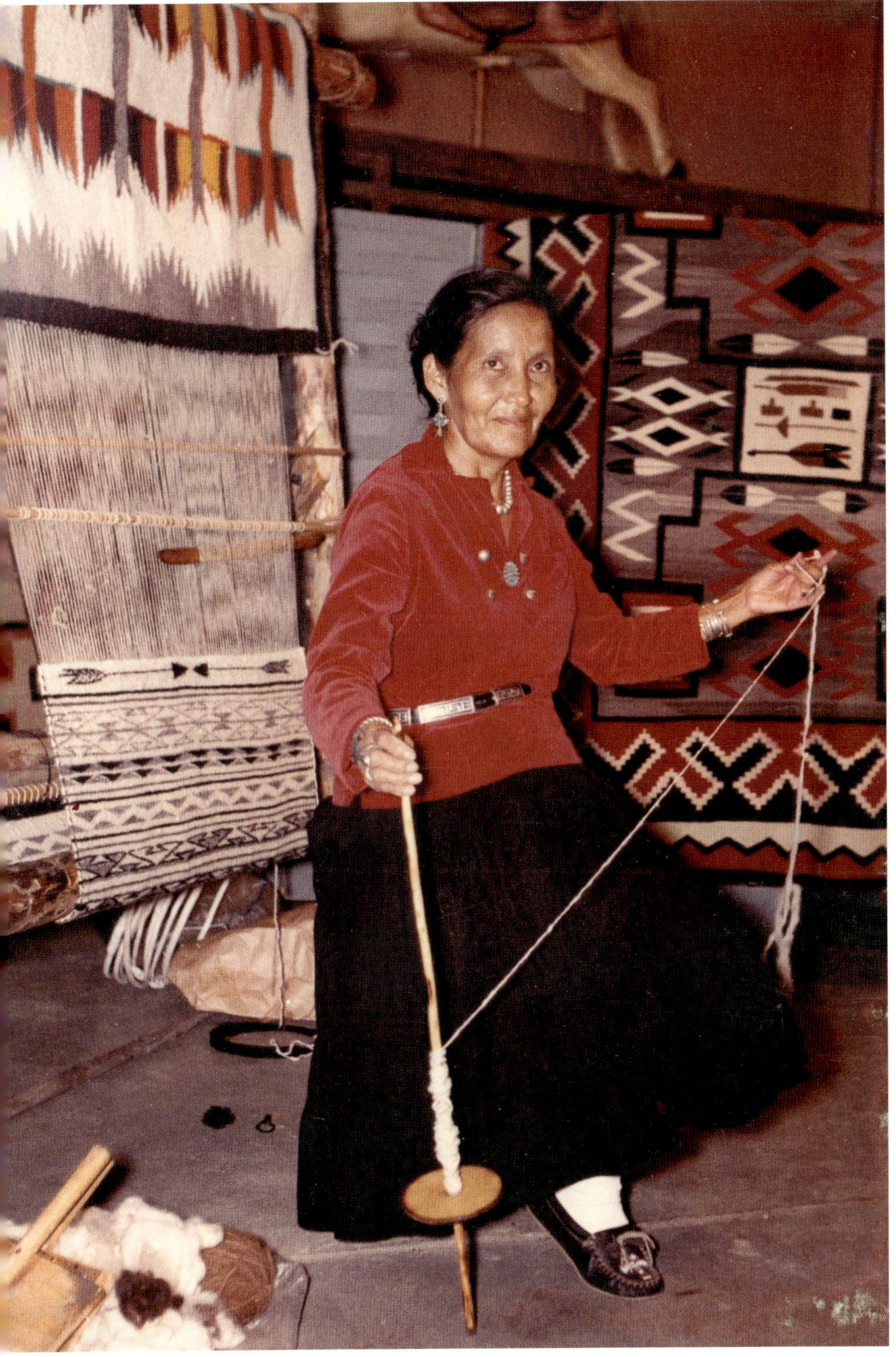

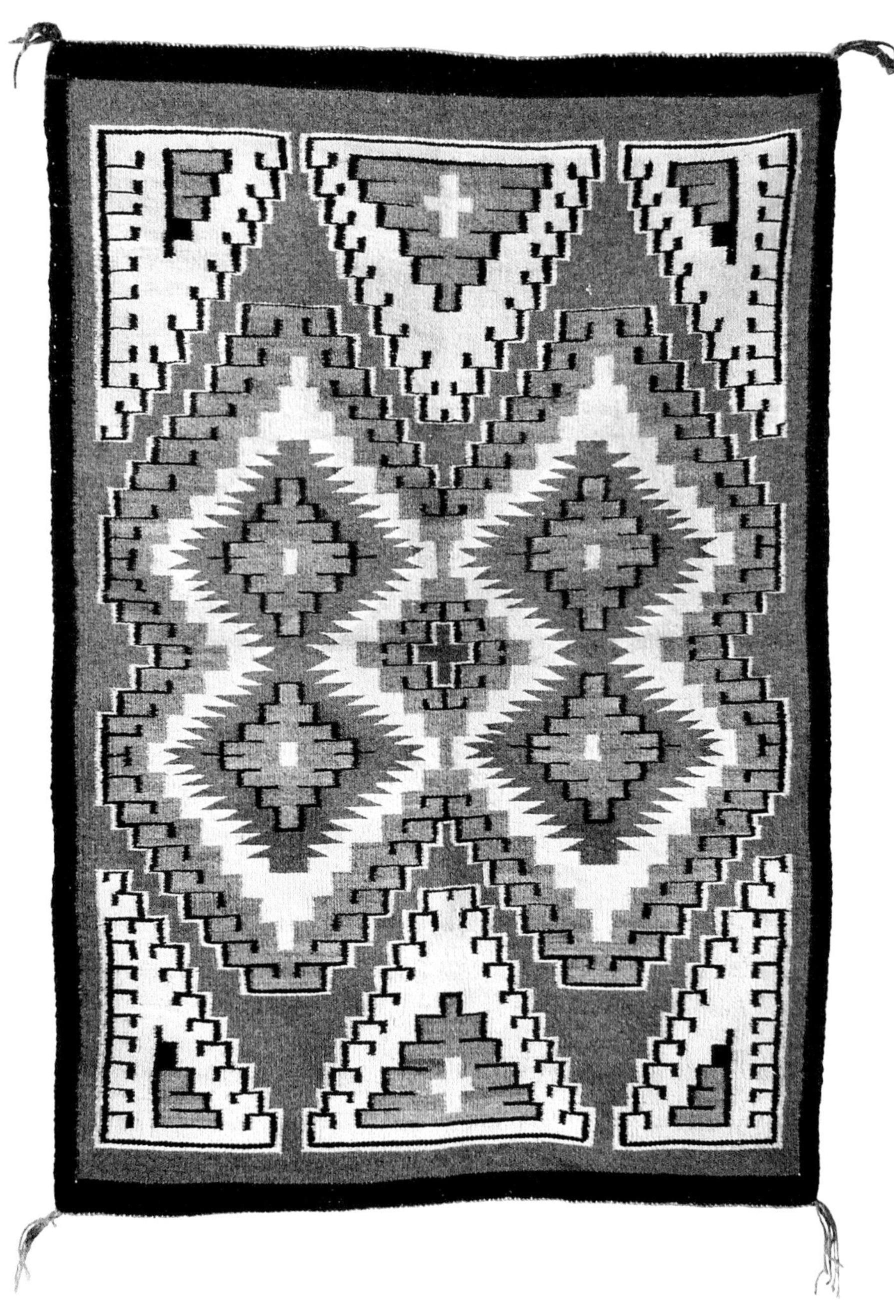

P.10

Bertha Stevens, textile, 1972. Hand-spun wool woven in natural colors, 48.5 × 33.5 in. Private collection. Photograph by Jessica L. Horton.

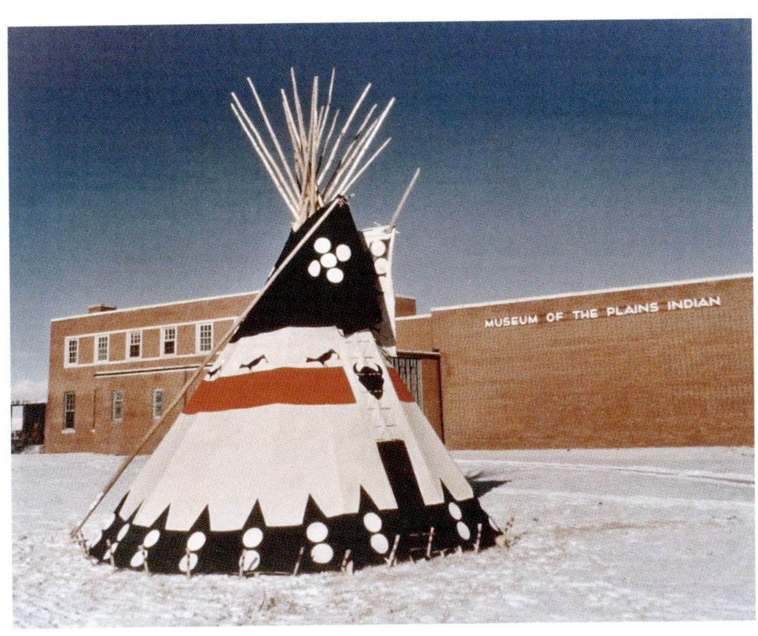

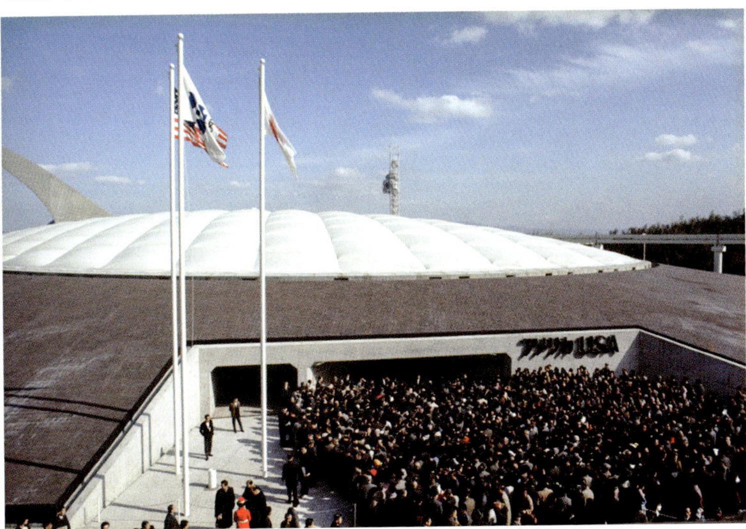

P.11a

Darryl Blackman, Crow lodge, 1969. Painted canvas, buckskin, and lodgepole pine. Erected in front of the Museum of the Plains Indian, North Browning, Montana, 1969. Photograph provided by the Department of the Interior.

P.11b

United States Pavilion at Expo 70 in Osaka, Japan, 1970. Provided by Chermayeff and Geismar, and Haviv.

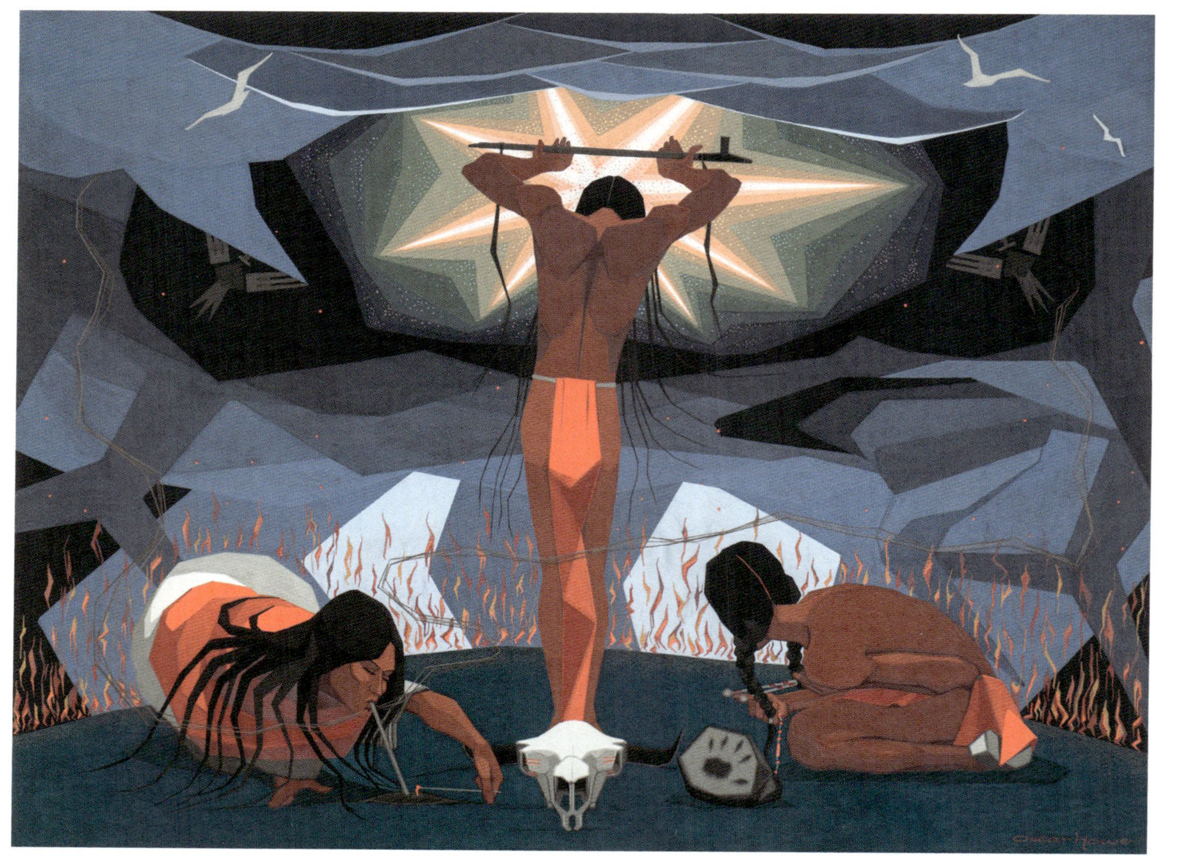

P.12

Oscar Howe, *Calling on Wakan Tanka*, 1962. Casein on paper, 25.75 × 33.5 in. University of South Dakota, Vermillion, with permission of the Oscar Howe Family.

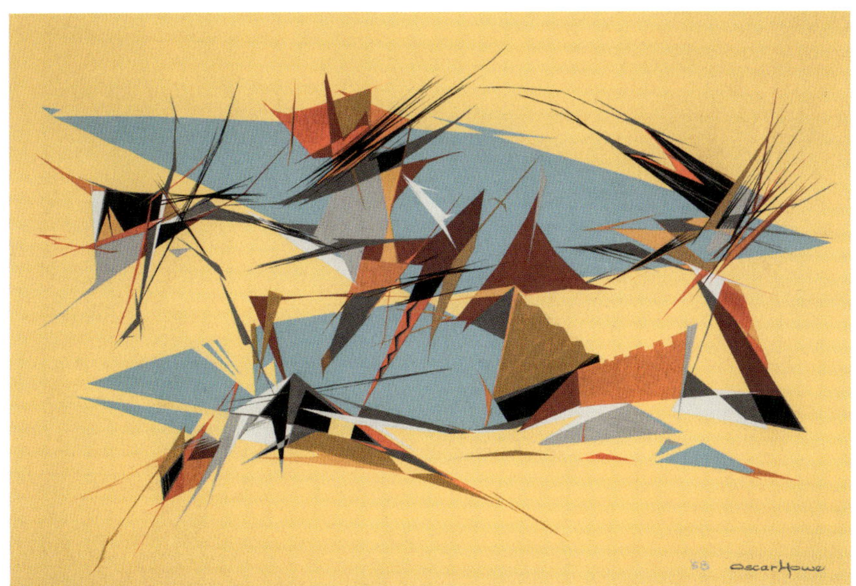

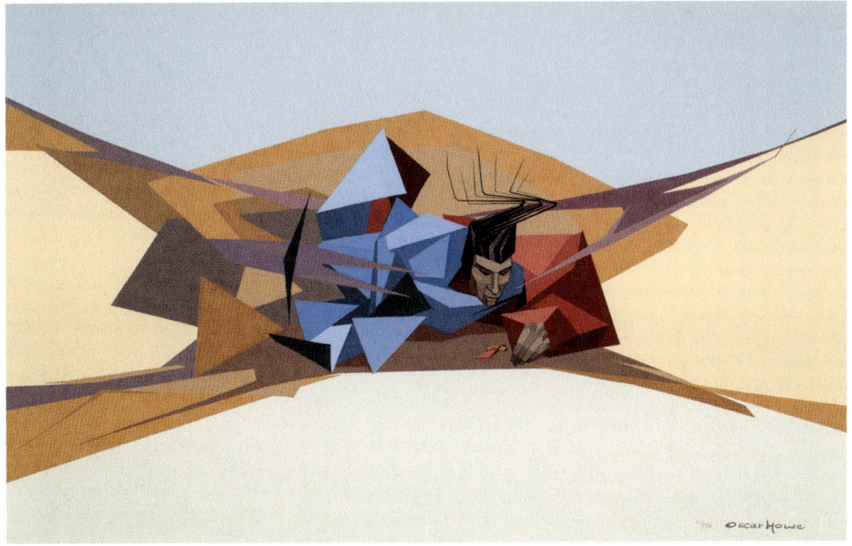

P.13a

Oscar Howe, *Rider*, 1968. Casein on paper, 17.375 × 26 in. University of
South Dakota, Vermillion, with permission of the Oscar Howe Family.

P13b

Oscar Howe, *War and Peace Dancer*, 1971. Casein on paper, 16 × 25.375 in.
University of South Dakota, Vermillion, with permission of the Oscar Howe
Family.

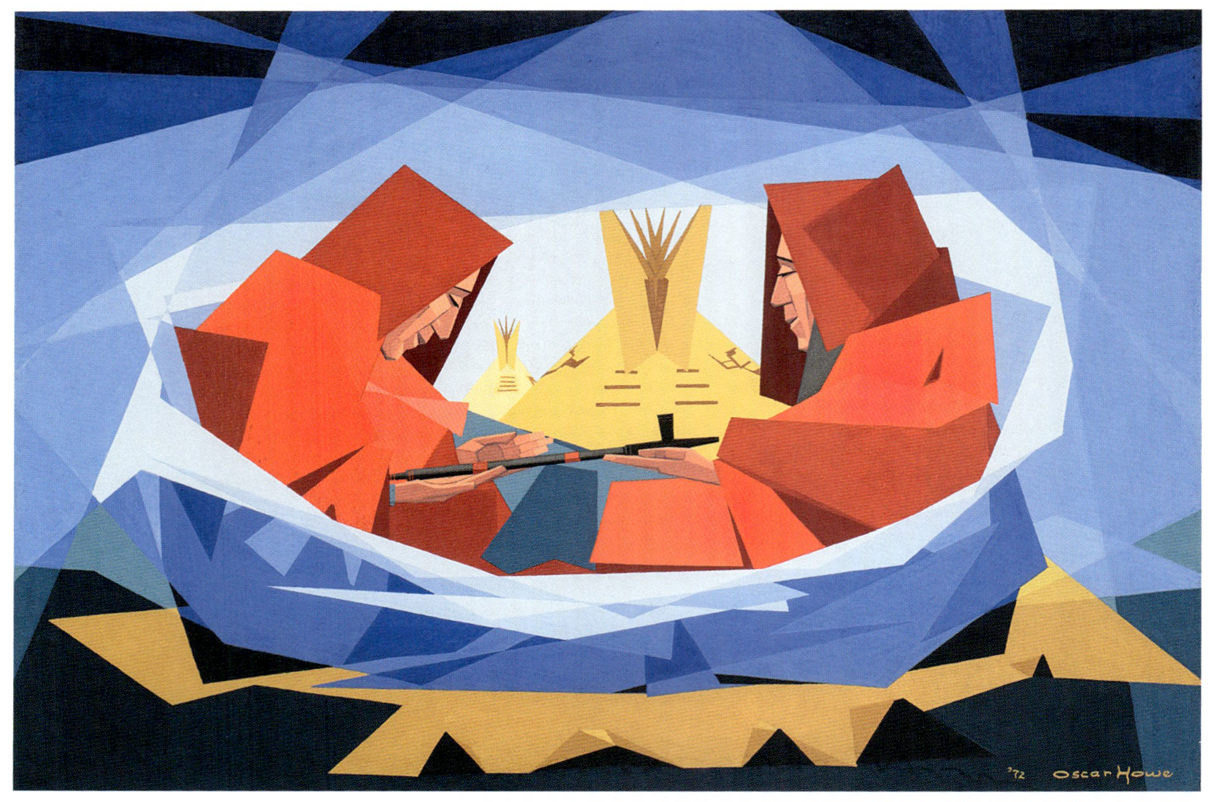

P.14

Oscar Howe, *Acannu-papi* (Pipe Ceremony). 1972. Casein on paper, 27.5 × 17.5 in. University of South Dakota, Vermillion, with permission of the Oscar Howe Family.

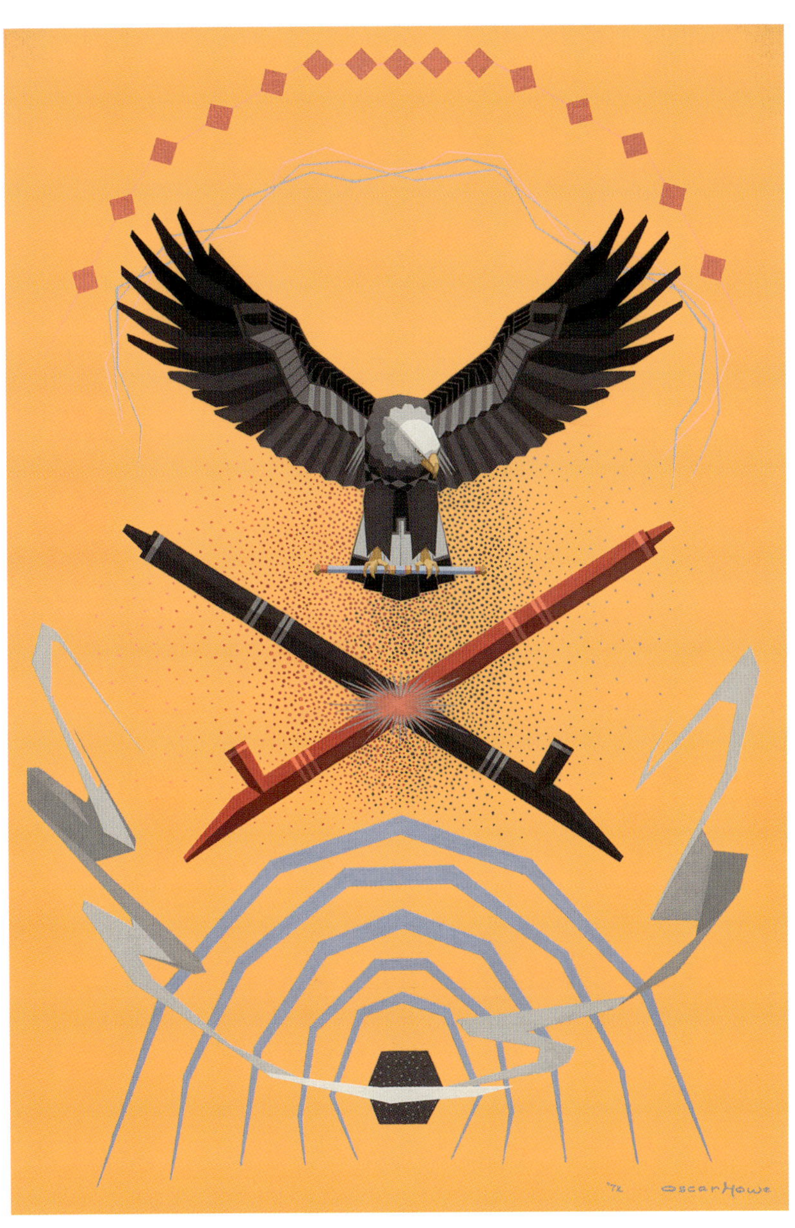

P.15

Oscar Howe, *Marpeya Wopazo (A Sign in the Sky)*, 1972. Casein on paper, 26.75 × 18.3125 in. University of South Dakota, Vermillion, with permission of the Oscar Howe Family.

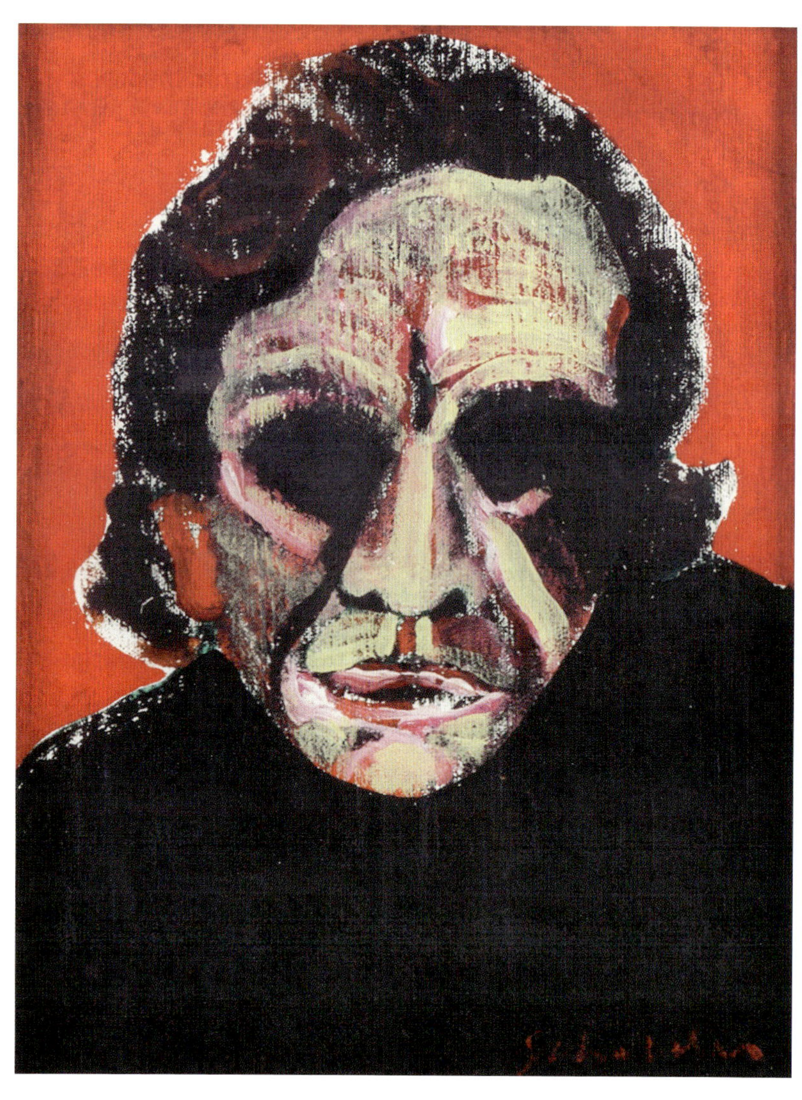

P.16

Fritz Scholder, Self Portrait as a Vampire *Self Portrait as Vampire*, 1972. Acrylic on canvas, 31.5 × 24.5 cm. Collection of the Estate of Fritz Scholder.

During his visit to Japan at the close of the events, Libhart claimed that the Crow tipi was the first variant from the Crow Tipi created for use outside the "Blackfeet tribal circle."[79] Certainly, it was unique among the many commissions Blackman negotiated, as it was drawn from the praxis in his own care. Following the lead of Insimaki and Yellow Kidney, he made careful choices while negotiating the commission that anticipated the lodge's displacement from Niitsítapi land and culture. Unlike the older couple, however, Blackman chose to retain custodianship of the Crow Tipi, rather than ceremonially transfer the praxis abroad. Whether an associated medicine bundle was in his possession at the time is unclear, but he is recorded as the keeper of the Crow Tipi until just before his death in 1971, when he sold the rights to the Mad Plume family.[80] Blackman clearly differentiated the commissioned variant from the reproductive rights, instructions, songs, and prayers associated with the praxis. Still, as I will argue, the Crow tipi was not wholly severed from the Crow Tipi in Osaka.

As I indicated at the outset of this chapter, Blackman negotiated the commission with pavilion organizers who narrowly prized authenticity and aesthetics over the relational values governing the praxis. They erected the finished tipi on an elevated platform abutting partition walls on the third floor beneath the elliptical dome room of the pavilion, positioning it so that visitors could face the front entrance. This decision maximized the tipi's visual impact, likely at the expense of protocols stipulating that the door should be oriented to the east to greet the rising sun.[81] By conceptualizing the commission as merely an object, these designers inadvertently dislodged the tipi and its presumed referent (Blackman's personal tipi) from the nexus of immaterial values guiding both.

This objectification of the Crow tipi continued a long tradition of displaying Indigenous architecture at colonial world fairs in Europe and the North America. Dating to at least to the nineteenth century, such exhibitions ranged from full-scale, lived-in villages to diminutive dioramas that could be "apprehended at a glance."[82] As art historian Alexander Marr has assessed, nineteenth-century anthropologists made, collected, and commissioned model tipis and other Indigenous architecture to fit an evolutionary scheme, using these forms to assess Native peoples' location on a scale from primitive to civilized. Visitors were invited to "peek into a world that was supposedly pre-contact: a pure, mythic place devoid of non-Native contaminations." For some white classifiers, Indigenous arts contained clues to the origins of Euro-American society, a search that denied Native people their rights to coeval, creative practices of dwelling in contested homelands.[83] This proclivity accords with architectural historian Annabel Jane Wharton's assertion that models, while forming a polysemous genre, share a common status as "epistemic operators" that "work to make the world in some way or another more accessible."[84] We might conclude that in the context of world fairs, all Native architectural models are assimilative, assisting in a colonial process of molding Indigenous arts into the linear and universalizing shape of progress. Recalling the colonial politics of the cabin, deracinating Indigenous architecture for distant display was another step in ongoing efforts to empty and claim Indigenous homelands.

Yet the Crow tipi was no mere accessory to a "cartoon world picture" that exoticized, trivialized, and assimilated colonized others at Expo 70.[85] Historians of Native art have observed how Indigenous makers (who were also among the visitors to exhibitions) vested worlds of meaning in architectural models, employing them in pedagogy, ceremony, and novel forms of cultural renewal in the reservation era.[86] Notably, Blackfeet and other Plains artists who worked for colonial markets and museums could draw upon their own traditions of model-making, in which children learned to erect and care for small-scale tipis in preparation for the responsibilities of adulthood.[87] Doore told me that he and Blackman played "cowboy and Indian" in miniature tipis in Sippi's household as children. Later, they used small-scale forms to practice painting designs.[88] At the same time, colonial markets necessitated new, experimental arrangements between models and their referents, as the former were pressed to address receivers who were unfamiliar with—or potentially biased toward—the latter. Here, Wharton's definition needs significant modification, for in such contexts, Indigenous-made models could strive to render *their* worlds adaptable and communicable, rather than render "the world" (which I read as singular, universal, and thus Euro-American) accessible. Put another way, at least some Native models were cannily designed to withstand geographical and cosmological displacement from their culturally embedded referents. It follows that it is impossible to ascribe a "consistent mode of power to the house diorama" in the reservation era.[89] The effects—and the *affects*—of such architectures are relational, necessarily negotiated among makers, forms, receivers, and new environments.

How might we understand the status of the Crow lodge that resulted from these dialogues, poised somewhere between the sacred relationalities governing a tripart Niitsítapi universe and the colonial-capitalist nationalisms that continued to dominate Cold War world fairs? Although Blackman avoided ceremonial transfer, I insist that the Crow tipi was not fully objectified at Expo 70, nor was it entirely divorced from cosmic circuits of reciprocity. Rather, I propose that the lodge selectively translated fundamental premises of the Niitsítapi cosmos for international hosts and visitors in Osaka. Underlying this argument is the notion that "model" names a particular kind of agentive representation, as slippage between the noun and verb forms suggests. Literary scholar Martin Brückner and art historian Sandy Isenstadt posit that however tangible their forms, models do not leave behind the conceptual worlds of their makers. Rather, they function as "records of the processes by which seemingly immaterial ideas are made manifest." Thus, models do much more than passively mirror an existing object, as terms such as "duplicate," "copy," and "replica" suggest. They "amalgamate knowledge . . . and practice," collecting and organizing relationships among elements that can be both tangible and intangible, material and imagined.[90] Specifically, I consider that the referent modeled by the Crow tipi was not merely another Crow tipi (as in Blackman's personal lodge) but the Crow Tipi, the metapraxis informing all material iterations.

The artist reoriented this cosmopolitical referent toward a hypothetical assemblage of the future in Osaka. With the exception of Libhart, the receivers of the Crow tipi were by and large unknown to Blackman—various United States and Japanese officials and Expo 70's far-flung visitors. The lodge answered a double challenge to gather select material and immaterial knowledges into a compact form and adapt those knowledges to the concrete and imagined demands of a distant time, place, and people. To transmit distinct features of a Niitsítapi world across such a vast gap required specific material innovations. Inevitably, the process, the *modelwork*, altered the praxis. As Brückner and Isenstadt attest, in "guiding how something is represented, [models] also modify what is represented. That is to say, the model's materiality—its physical presence, its sensible materials, the volume it occupies—affects how we understand its referent." Within the variable history of models, the Crow tipi was more "prospective task" than "mimetic craft."[91] Framed by a relentless drive for progress, the lodge was specifically challenged to hold the integrity of past and place to the future, in keeping with the organization of such concepts into a perpetual, indissociable circuit of exchange within a Niitsítapi cosmos.

What is the material evidence of this process? Preceding the lodge itself is a booklet of notated diagrams that staff from the Museum of the Plains Indian mailed to the USIA in Osaka.[92] The twenty-five page instructional manual was produced by museum personnel with Blackman's collaboration and final approval.[93] In order to teach novices how to erect a tipi at a distance, the notes and images translated protocols for correctly raising a functional dwelling into portable, readable form. They prepared these fundamentals, normally transmitted through live observation and bodily mimicry, to bridge significant gaps in time, space, and cultural fluency on paper. Specifically, the instructions anticipated the material strangeness of the exhibition site and offered guidelines to ensure the integrity of the structure in this alien environment. For example, one diagram predicted a floor of "wood or concrete," rather than soil, and specified the creation of wooden "shoes" that could be nailed to the flooring to prevent the poles from sliding on such a hard surface. The manual also provisioned for nails, rather than customary wood pegs, to be driven into the floor through the loops at the base of the cover. One revealing note instructs the users to "determine [the] direction tipi will face," indicating the authors' awareness that an orientation toward the rising sun would likely not be prioritized for the purposes of exhibition. However, the manual also exerts the preferences of its makers. The instructions for the ear flap poles specify that the flaps, a dynamic element regulating air circulation, should remain fully open. This position not only maximized the visual impact of the starry constellations painted on the flaps, but also ensured the movement of Ihtsipaitapiyopa's animating force through the interior of the tipi. These details suggest that one conceptual aim of the manual was to retain the potential for a lived cosmology to manifest within novel conditions of display.

Another function of the diagrams was to invite the lodge's foreign hosts to an embodied form of learning that exceeded the ocular register of the exhibition. In order to succeed in the difficult task of raising the Crow tipi for the first time, novices had to reanimate the static diagrams and notes in three dimensions. For example, to ensure that the bottom edge of the cover was elevated precisely two inches from the floor, users were instructed to adjust the poles by employing a "twisting, lifting action." Such exertion demanded an intimate relationship to the material properties of the lodge. While the number of participants was not specified in the manual, achieving a smooth, tight-fitting, conical form

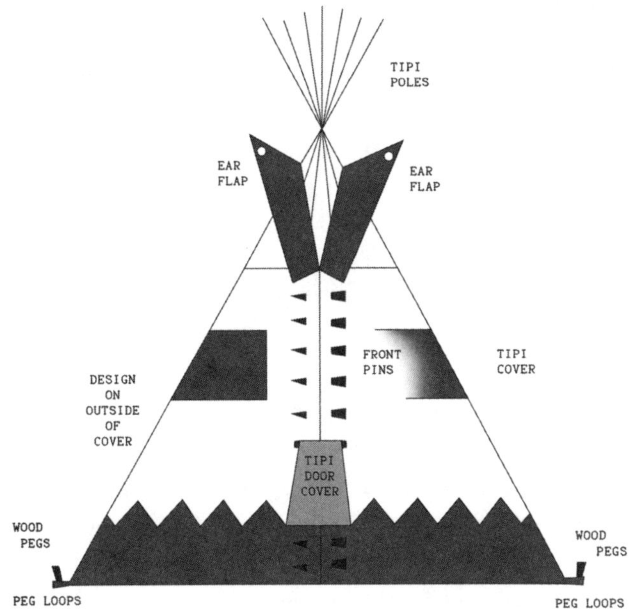

4.8
"Identification of Parts—A," produced by the Museum of the Plains Indian, North Browning, Montana, with Darryl Blackman, 1970. Recreated diagram based on a photocopy in the archives of the Museum of the Plains Indian by Gunjan and Ashish.

TIPI POLE SHOE - A

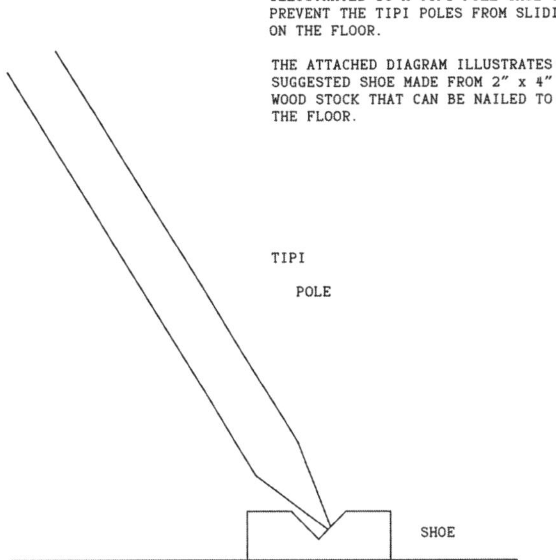

4.9
"Tipi Pole Shoe—A," produced by the Museum of the Plains Indian with Darryl Blackman, 1970. Recreated diagram based on a photocopy in the archives of the Museum of the Plains Indian, North Browning, Montana, by Gunjan and Ashish.

without prior experience required a team of people. They would need to first conceptualize, then coordinate their actions to grapple with the enormous weight of the canvas, the length of the poles, and the precise tension and balance among elements. In short, erecting the tipi was a challenging and humbling physical task for the uninitiated. Success demanded intellectual and bodily commitment from a collective; it could not be mastered in a glance. I'll return to this theme in the conclusion, when addressing the raising of the tipi as a gift to the City of Osaka.

Considering the Crow tipi in relation to hosts' bodies turns me to the critical issue of scale. Montgomery sent detailed instructions for a smaller version of Blackman's personal lodge in 1969—"the diameter of the tipi base is to be 13′, and the height, including tipi poles, is not to exceed 19′"—approximately two-thirds the size of the artist's own lodge. The measurements were predetermined by the elevated platform in Osaka as "the layout for the Indian area of the Folk Art exhibit became more refined."[94] Perhaps the logistics of shipping a large, heavy item internationally were also on the organizers' minds. In the end, the custom layered plywood crate packed with the cover and poles and reinforced with steel straps consumed forty-five hours of construction labor and weighed approximately a thousand pounds.[95] As these details illuminate, the rescaling of the lodge stopped short of miniaturization, a process that scholars have equated with conceptual trivialization and visual possession.[96] Instead, the tipi retained its status as architecture, falling on the small end of Niitsítapi lodges designed for dwelling.

The photographic archive of Expo 70 suggests that the erect tent continued to elicit intimate, sensorial interactions scaled to the human body. USIA photographs show numerous visitors touching the flaps of the open door, bending to peer inside, and craning their necks at close range to follow the poles skyward. The concentration of these activities at the entrance pointed to the potential for congress inside, while the open door implied a welcome. Although the invitation was never, to my knowledge, answered, the Crow tipi still presented itself to visitors as habitable—and, by extension, hospitable. These aspects of the commission resonated with customary forms of earth diplomacy wherein, as I've discussed, visiting parties were invited to sit and smoke in a nonhierarchical formation determined by the base of the tent.

Scale thus enabled the translation of a key Niitsítapi concept into Expo 70: the architectural emplacement of newcomers within a circle of reciprocity governing a tripart cosmos. More precisely, the Crow tipi's modest-but-not-miniature scale positioned the lodge to mediate between

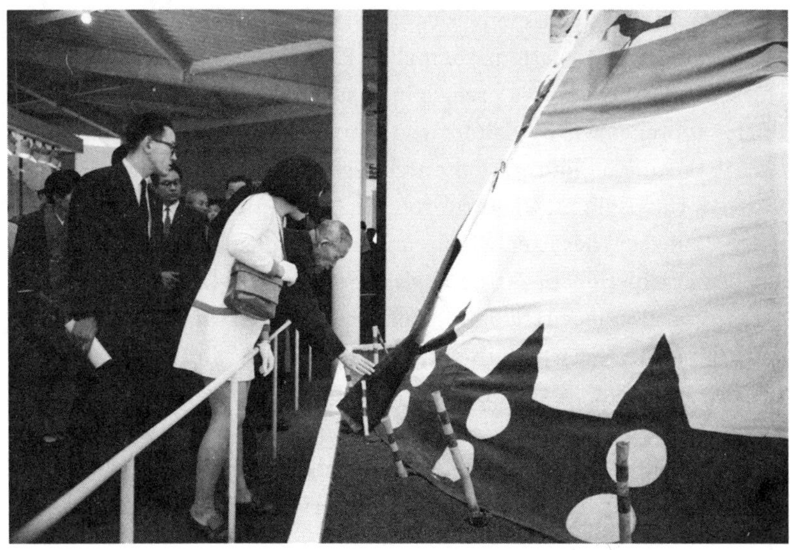

4.10

Visitors touch the canvas and peer through the open door of the Crow lodge by Darryl Blackman in the United States Pavilion at Expo 70 in Osaka, Japan, 1970. NACP Still Photographs, 306-exn-3199–9.

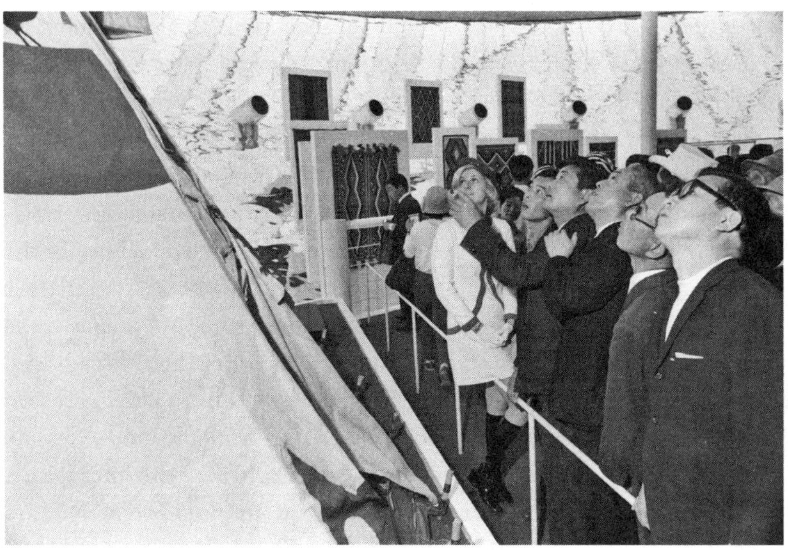

4.11

Visitors gaze upward at the Crow lodge by Darryl Blackman during a tour of the United States Pavilion at Expo 70 in Osaka, Japan, 1970. NACP Still Photographs, 306-exn-3326–9.

the seemingly opposite modalities of dwelling and display. Consider how Montgomery's instructions compelled Blackman to "fit" Niitsítapi architectural concepts to a preordained stage. This meant readying the tipi for apprehension by visitors who were bound to orient their bodies at once to the unique address of the architecture and the exhibitionary protocols of the pavilion. Visitors' potential range of responses to the tipi was curtailed by the latter, which emphasized efficient, linear movement and ocular experience—"10,000 visitors an hour"—with the support of extensive surveillance technologies.[97] Those photographed subjects who paused in collective wonderment, activating haptic and reflective experiences, acted against the rationalization of visitor flows. The tipi invited such adverse behavior. It refused to relinquish its potential as a portal connecting humans to one another, animal guardians, and the whole of the cosmos, even as it conceded to singularization as one aestheticized object among many.

Then there is the matter of the painted figures, conduits for specific, more-than-human bestowals of power and protection. Representations of Crow tipis across the twentieth century show variability in the designs; for example, they may utilize a very thin or extremely thick red line at the middle, and a narrow or wide serrated black band containing a single or double line of orbs at the base. Some lodges omit the black base altogether. The Osaka variant exhibits the most replete compendium that I have seen to date.[98] It bears a thick, bright red middle band and two rows of fallen star children filling the unusually high, jagged peaks of the wide black base band. Such extremes, while adhering to a customary repertoire, suggest a will to embolden and beautify the allowance.

This tendency is also evident in Blackman's personal lodge. However, the Osaka tipi includes a striking, apparently novel addition: the crows carry small, triangular pendants of red-painted buckskin in their beaks.[99] Critically, this element visually and materially translates the idea of meat sharing from the oral history. Its significance is captured in Yellow Kidney's description of the first Crow tipi: "There were two rows of crows painted upon the cover, each row standing upon a red line representing the blood of the bison. In the rear where the lines join, a buffalo skull is drawn. That represents the fat on the side of a buffalo's head, which is the favorite food of the crow."[100] In the customary tipi described, the treasured gift of caloric meat must be inferred by those familiar with the history. Knowledgeable insiders would recognize the abstract red bands as buffalo blood. They would note the doubled relational capacity of the lines to support crow bodies and point to the sides of the

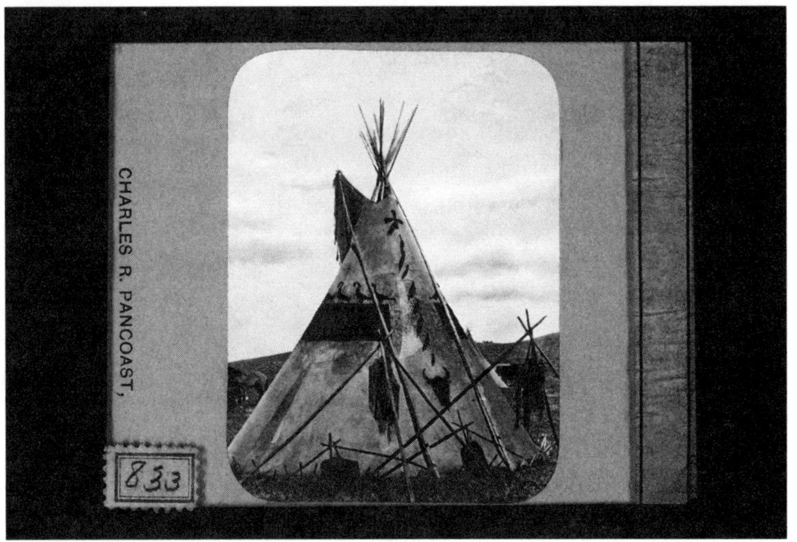

4.12

Walter McClintock, *Crow tipi*, undated. Hand-colored lantern slide, 8 × 10 cm. Yale Collection of Western Americana, Beinecke Rare Book and Manuscript Library, New Haven, Connecticut.

....

buffalo head, the source of the preferred meal. Such a viewer might further relate the buffalo and crows to the human hunter in the story, a critical but unseen link in the meat exchange. There is evidence that some reservation-era artists before Blackman chose to translate this episode from the oral story into pictorial form by painting small circles or triangles of red meat in the mouths of the crows. The morsels may have functioned didactically, spanning potential gaps in the transmission of oral knowledge in an era of intensifying colonial assimilation. Visualizing the offering would have helped to guarantee that a core significance of the praxis—the Crow Tipi's origin in a more-than-human circuit of gifts—was communicable to uninitiated viewers. Following Pard, we must also consider that the painted medallions would have been charged with the sacred power and protection of the animal guardians they depicted. An interpretation informed by Niitsítapi cosmology holds that all designs are portals through which ancient gifts from the earth arrive in a novel time and place.

Perhaps anticipating the tipi's deracination at Expo 70, Blackman further literalized the treasured head meat. As Kicking Woman observed, attaching painted buckskin medallions mirrored the historical practice of hanging skins and other sacred found materials such as feathers on the exterior of lodges in order to count coup, represent a good deed, or honor the spiritual endowment of a more-than-human gift.[101] Similar offerings are made to the sun in the Okan medicine lodge. In Osaka, buckskin necessarily stood in for absent buffalo bodies in the wake of their decimation at the hands of colonial agents. Nonetheless, the fleshy triangles viscerally realize the myriad transfers connecting animal and human bodies in a Niitsítapi cosmos. Blackman may have withheld the Crow Tipi, but he nonetheless manifested the intangible principle most in danger of being lost in (capitalist) translation—that of more-than-human reciprocity. As a physical addition that was technically extraneous to the terms of the commission, the pendants furthermore acted as a gift: a new link in the unending chain of generosity that the praxis underwrites. A reading of the pendants as materialized reciprocity is further bolstered by the aforementioned gift of Blackman's personal poles. Like buffalo meat, deerskin and tree are offerings from the earth whose value exceeds the logic of capital. Blackman's inclusion of these elements positioned the Crow tipi to activate, rather than merely picture, new nodes in the circuit of exchange. Read within the framework of earth diplomacy, the lodge was endowed with the potential to compel still further acts of generosity, making demands of old and new allies alike.

THE ECOLOGICAL INDIAN AND THE HOBBYIST TIPI

Situating the Crow tipi relationally among Niitsítapi, United States, and Japanese agents entails a deeper consideration of Plains tipis' transnational travels through ecoarchitectural discourses of the 1960s and 1970s. The lodge acted as a Niitsítapi ambassador in Osaka amid the dramatic growth of environmental consciousness worldwide. Rachel Carson's *Silent Spring* (1962) and Miyamoto Ken'ichi and Shōji Hikaru's *Osorubeki Kōgai* (Fearsome Pollution, 1964) spurred public concern with the toxic toll of industrial pollution in the United States and Japan respectively.[102] A few years later, the first satellite images of the whole earth galvanized popular discourses of planetary holism. As I explored in the previous chapter, Indigenous people were cast as model caretakers of a precolonial planet due to their purported belief that the earth is a mother and all living things are her children. While the transnational visibility of tipis harkened at least to the traveling Wild West shows of the nineteenth century, their image was buoyed by this postwar surge in environmental attention.[103]

During the 1960s and 1970s, the US government's long-standing betrayal of Native Americans resonated with diverse communities' growing sense of disenfranchisement from US political and economic systems. Simplistic slogans about holistic Indian values inspired countercultural efforts to drop out of urban capitalist society and return to the land.[104] Outside of the ecofeminist circles discussed in the previous chapter, the stereotype of the Ecological Indian was most often expressed as a proud and tragic Plains warrior-chief with his triad of material culture: the feather headdress, the pipe, and the tipi. The figure neatly combined spiritual reverence for the virgin expanse of precolonial wilderness, embodied in the extinguished buffalo, with fierce resistance to the incursions of white modernity, be it the US cavalry or the bulldozer.[105] *Life Magazine* touted the "Rediscovery of the Redman" by white countercultural agents, who viewed "the dispossessed Indian as America's original dropout," in 1967. The non-Native builders of the commune of New Buffalo near the pueblo of Taos in New Mexico, determined to honor "the sacred part of nature that nurtures us all," erected their own "white city" of tipis that same year. Activists in Berkeley posted the image of the nineteenth-century leader of the Apache resistance, Geronimo, as the moral face of the communal garden they wished to protect in 1968. And soft drink companies sponsored the famous tear that rolled down the cheek of Iron Eyes Cody, an Italian-American actor in Plains garb who paddled across trash-filled waterways in Keep America Beautiful television advertisements beginning in 1971.[106]

As these examples suggest, the Ecological Indian was ripe for appropriation to serve a range of non-Native political projects. Accordingly, scholars have criticized the stereotype as a primitivist fantasy that denies Native people a coeval claim to modernity. Finis Dunaway describes Cody as a silent ghost, an anachronistic witness to a perverse present unfolding without him. "The Crying Indian appears completely powerless, unable to challenge white domination."[107] As historian Paul Rosier articulates, a conviction that Indigenous belief in an inspired earth puts inherent constraints on consumption locks desirable Native Americans in a precolonial past and underwrites a narrative of cultural decline for modern communities living with colonial-capitalist toxicity.[108] Put another way, the Ecological Indian encourages the judgment of good (pure) and bad (polluted) Native Americans based on a Euro-American wilderness ideal. When concepts such as holism and sustainability are fixed in advance of white encounters with Native people, it becomes all the harder to differentiate Indigenous intellectual and creative production from the all-encompassing stereotype. The Ecological Indian thus sidesteps the challenging work of translating Indigenous cosmologies and threatens to eclipse politics altogether.

Often, the transcultural travels of the tipi in the 1960s and 1970s followed this white environmentalist script. In 1957, *The Indian Tipi: Its History, Construction, and Use*, written by a pair of non-Native hobbyists, helped to launch Plains architecture into the counterculture of subsequent decades. Authors Gladys and Reginald Laubin enumerated the practical and aesthetic benefits of tipis:

> Other tents are hard to pitch, hot in summer, cold in winter, badly lighted, unventilated, easily blown down, and ugly to boot. The conical tent of the Plains Indians has none of these faults. It can be pitched, if necessary, by a single person. It is roomy, well ventilated at all times, cool in summer, well lighted, proof against high winds and heavy downpours, and, with its cheerful inside fire, snug in the severest winter weather. . . . Moreover, its tilted cone, trim smoke flaps, and crown of branching poles, presenting a different silhouette from every angle, forms a shapely, stately dwelling even without decoration. Properly made, pitched and furnished in the true Indian way, it offers all the requirements of a good home, safety, comfort, privacy—even luxury. In short, other tents are made to sell. The tipi is made to live in.[109]

Ethnographers had previously circulated equivalent laudatory accounts of tipis; the Laubins's innovation was to combine a simplistic cultural history of the form with a practical guide to "make, use, and enjoy" one's very own lodge. Emphasizing the tipi's suitability for holistic living, they promised to free their readers from reliance on capitalist exchange, the system underwriting the popular outdoor recreational activities such as camping in a conventional tent. At the same time, they cast themselves—and, by extension, their readers—as the white saviors of an Indigenous architectural practice endangered by the adoption of rectilinear housing in the reservation era. They declared, "For many summers we have been the only persons actually living in a tipi on the Standing Rock Sioux reservation. . . . The Indians tell us they have not seen a lodge like ours, furnished and arranged as in buffalo days, in more than seventy years."[110] As Blackman's story indicates, the couple overstated the success of federal assimilation policies that discouraged tipi-making in the twentieth century. Their argument stoked Ecological Indian fantasies and lent moral legitimacy to the majority white users of their instructional guide. This potent combination perfectly anticipated appropriations of the tipi in the decades to come. Still, as Blackman's tipi commission suggests, the stereotype of the Ecological Indian both obscured *and* enabled Indigenous peoples' capacity to adapt to modern ecocides.

COLONIZING CUBES AND SHELTERING SPHERES

The Laubins' treatise helped to position the tipi alongside the dome, appealing to a do-it-yourself ethos that connected older forms of Indian hobbyism to the emerging counterculture.[111] Despite their marked differences in origin and appearance, both architectures came to signal a radical departure from the political establishment in the United States. Countercultural theorists mapped this perceived deviance onto a more elemental distinction between squares and circles, cubes and spheres. These arguments were prominently rehearsed on the pages of the countercultural bible, *Whole Earth Catalog*, first published by Stewart Brand in 1968. Famous as a proponent of cybernetics and holistic thinking, Brand dated his interest in Native Americans to a 1963 visit to the Wasco and Paiute Confederated Tribes of the Warm Springs Reservation in Oregon. He joined the Native American Church and began to spend his summers among Paiute, Diné, Hopi, Niitsítapi, Očhéthi Šakówiŋ, and other Native groups, an immersion that he deemed a "revelation."[112] Brand extracted a simplistic lesson for the *Whole Earth Catalog*: a recognition attributed to Indigenous peoples the world over that all things—food, shelter, life—came from the earth. It followed that reciprocity was the seed of collective survival: "Take care of nature, and it will take care of you."[113]

In the definitive final edition of the catalog from 1971, an excerpt from *The Indian Tipi* was reproduced in a twenty-six-page section titled "Shelter."[114] It was sandwiched among the words of pragmatists and philosophers invested in reinvigorating the discipline of architecture with global vernacular forms. A prominent excerpt from anthropologist Paul Oliver's introduction to *Shelter and Society* (1969) criticized the colonial impulse of Western modernists to rehabilitate diverse peoples around the world "in buildings often alien to the way of life and in totally inappropriate structures for the climate and environment."[115] In cities, the "granite face" of such structures confront communities who "struggle to preserve their humanity and identity" while breathing its "fume-laden air."[116] Throughout *Shelter and Society*, Native American architecture joined forces with the "new geodesic vernacular" to resist a hegemonic rectilinearity.[117]

In a telling real-world juxtaposition, the most famous artists' commune of the period, Drop City, established near Trinidad, Colorado, in 1965, hosted a forgotten white canvas tipi alongside their architectural innovation, the *zome*.[118] Drop City builders loosely translated the work of architect Buckminster Fuller, who first patented the geodesic dome in 1954.[119] Their haphazard patchwork of structures made from plywood, stucco, tar, chicken wire, and scavenged automobile parts inspired architect Steve Baer's how-to manual, *Dome Cookbook*, in 1968. Baer voiced a collective ethos obsessed with breaking out of the orthogonal confines of the architecture discipline. He questioned whether the cube was officially dead or "another type of life form that with its characteristic rectilinear grid is slowly taking over the planet like some kind of galactic impetigo?"[120] Here and elsewhere, the cube is characterized as an alien colonizer. In a chapter for *Shelter and Society*, Drop City resident Bill Voyd similarly hinged the critique of cubic imprisonment to spheric solutions. "Houses in our society are walls, blocking man from man, man from the universe, man from himself." In contrast, he explained, "To live in a dome is—psychologically—to be in closer harmony with natural structure. Macrocosm and microcosm are recreated, both the celestial sphere and molecular and crystalline forms."[121] Underlying the iconicity of both tipis and domes was an ecstatic commitment to the elemental form of the sphere.

Omnipresent in countercultural treatises on spheres were the first satellite images of the whole earth (1967). These NASA-generated photographs pictured the planet as a singular and fragile biosphere, a superorganism demanding reverence and protection. Emblazoned on the cover of *Whole Earth Catalog* was the archetypal sphere hovering in space: a complete, self-regulating superorganism, beautiful, solitary, and vulnerable. The image underwrote the architectural turn toward circles and spheres as more consonant with organic processes, the cyclical patterns of life at both elemental and cosmic scales. Brand and his colleagues assumed that whole earth images had an immediate and universal affective power, inspiring viewers to strive to live more sustainably on this one precious planet.[122] Contemporary criticism has, however, rendered the beloved figure of the planet newly questionable. As art historian James Nisbet points out, the image replaced human sensory embeddedness in ecosystems with the disembodied image of the earth as a superorganism separate from living, breathing bodies.[123] Fuller believed that a combination of innovations in science and technology with government management could liberate individuals from everyday environmental responsibilities so that they could be selfish in harmony with others—a vision of human alienation from communal and ecological systems in the guise of sustainability.[124] To see the earth as an aesthetic object furthermore relied on government-sponsored technologies embedded in the Cold War space race. Satellite images offered the earth itself as ripe for control and assimilation, furthering the global ambitions of the United States. By issuing an invitation to further corporate-governmental management for the "good of the species," this artificial holism effaces the unfinished histories of colonialism and imperialism.[125] Whole earth images emerged from and fuel the competitive, capitalist internationalism that this book equates with a broken diplomatic imaginary. They are indissociable from a remarkably antireciprocal impulse.

It is here that the dome and the tipi definitively part ways. For the dome ultimately modeled a universe poised for military-industrial control. Fuller built one of his first geodesics prototypes for the Pentagon garden, and by the time he patented the dome in 1954, the US military was using it as housing for radar installations of the Distant Early Warning Line in order to spot Soviet bombers in the Arctic.[126] This tradition extended to Cold War world fairs and persisted as an uncomfortable precedent for the countercultural conviction that spheric holism was an antidote to capitalist alienation. Exemplified in pavilions in Kabul, Afghanistan in 1956, Poznan, Poland in 1957, and Moscow, Russia in 1959, the USIA had for some time seized on the geodesic dome as the preferred mega-architecture for international expositions.[127] Consider the two-hundred-foot-tall US Pavilion at Expo 67 in Montreal, perhaps the most famous of Fuller's offspring. Overseen by Masey for the USIA—a role repeated at Expo 70—the pavilion and its exhibitions at once "foretold the first moonwalk" and "successfully marginalized critics of the US government on race and on Vietnam."[128] The "one world" of the dome and the United States' ambitions to assimilate the whole earth were allies in a shifting Cold War world order.

A growing uneasiness with the dome's technocratic origins is registered in the preface to Lloyd Kahn's *Domebook 2* (1971), another

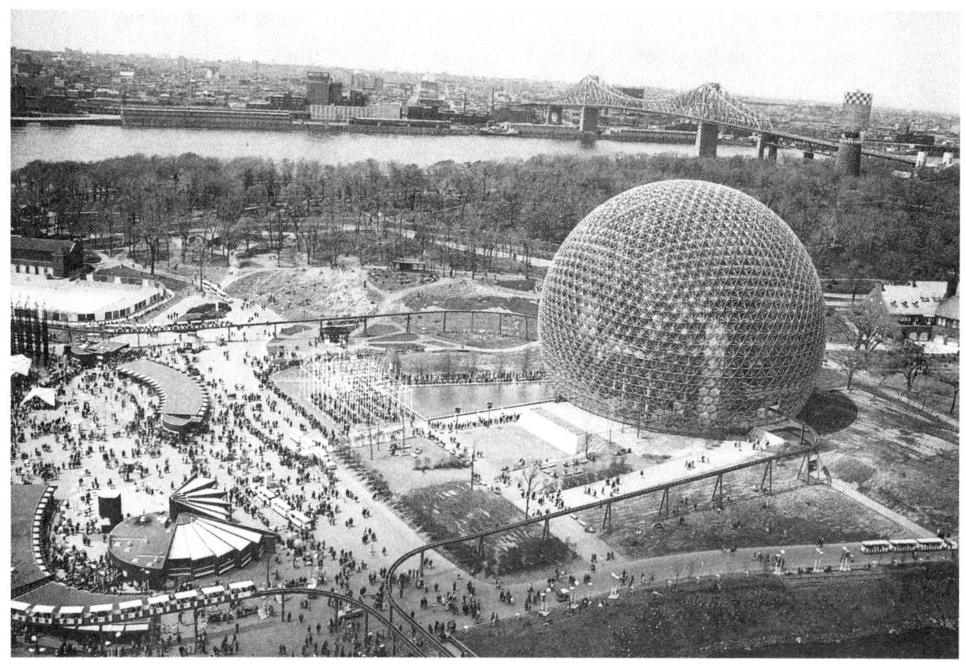

4.13

The United States Pavilion at Expo 67 in Montreal, 1967. NACP Still Photographs, 306-exn-48.

....

prominent countercultural sourcebook that was excerpted in "Shelter." The manual opens with a quote from the *Black Elk Speaks: Being the Life Story of a Holy Man of the Oglala Sioux*, a 1932 book by American writer John G. Neihardt that was partially based on the narrative of Oglala Lakota elder Black Elk. Widely embraced by hippies and activists after it was reprinted in 1961, *Black Elk Speaks* was subsequently criticized by scholars and Lakota ceremonial specialists for embellishing Indigenous lifeways to please white audiences. Crucially, the excerpt establishes Plains cosmology, and the tipi in particular, as an alternative origin for contemporaneous spherical architecture. Black Elk allegedly connected the elemental form of the circle with the planet and the tipi: "You have noticed that everything an Indian does is in a circle, and that is because the Power of the World always works in circles, and everything tries to be round. . . . The sky is round, and I have heard that the earth is round like a ball, and so are all the stars. . . . Our tepees were round like the nests of birds, and these were always set in a circle, the nation's hoop, a nest of many nests, where the Great Spirit meant for us to hatch our children." [129] Hoop, stars, planet, nest, tipi—the preface effectively linked dome-building to the moral righteousness and spiritual order of Plains Indigenous cultures and through them, the very nature of the cosmos. At the same time, the selection deactivates the potential threat of this alternative architectural origin story by locating Indigenous power wholly in a time before white men. Black Elk reportedly continues, "But the Wasichus (whitemen) have put us in these square boxes. Our power is gone and we are dying." The passage ends suggestively, with an invitation to the imagination: "We are prisoners of war while we are waiting here. But there is another world."[130] While the subsequent pages of *Domebook 2* sketched the contours of "another world," the tipi disappeared from it. Like the Crying Indian, the tent is a marker of the past with no claim on the future. Rather, it was replaced by "a new indigenous architecture in the deserts, valleys, and mountains of America."[131] "Another world" was relegated to the "one world" of the dome.

Native Americans make another brief appearance in *Domebook 2* in what may be an oblique reference to the pole structure of a tipi in an oft-cited interview with Fuller. The architect is asked about the future of the dome in the wake of its global travels, from Drop City to the Expos. He responded that he had arrived at a system in which it was possible to go into the forest and "take those short little saplings and produce a beautiful geodesic truss dome of various sizes. And I saw then that this was something an individual going back to the art of the Indian and doing things very neatly [could do]." Yet Fuller did not cast the homology as grounds for indebtedness to Indigenous architecture; rather, his findings occasioned a colonial pedagogy. The crucial gap "between the naked illiterate native and what I could with my head and my hands" was basic spherical trigonometry, he concluded. As he traveled the world bearing the gift of mathematical knowledge, he was able to "infect the natives with great enthusiasm for [geodesics]." This discovery was useful and pleasant to the locals because they could "get into quite large space controls, absolutely free clear span space control," and ultimately, "have a higher advantage over nature."[132] Here, Fuller places the dome in a tradition of colonial architecture designed to extend territory and school the Natives on the advantages of controlling their environment.[133] In a genealogy premised on expansion and assimilation, the settler cabin is a more appropriate ancestor than the tipi.

In the same instant, Indigenous activists were reclaiming the tipi for their own brand of public dissent. During the occupation of Alcatraz Island in San Francisco Bay in 1969, an unpainted lodge reportedly belonging to white actor and anarchist Peter Coyote stood high on the bluffs facing the Golden Gate Bridge.[134] It prominently signaled the reclamation of the rocky site, home to a decommissioned maximum-security prison abandoned by the US government six years earlier, as "Indian land." Led by the urban activist group Indian of All Tribes and their non-Native allies, the occupation was widely considered to be the first public event of the AIM, in spirit if not in name. For eighteen months, the group used the unprecedented attention from Hollywood stars, journalists, and countercultural activists to lambaste a nation that "has systematically stolen our lands, destroyed a once-beautiful and natural landscape, killed off the creatures of nature, polluted air and water, ripped open the very bowels of our earth in senseless greed." Among their various visions for repurposing the prison was a center for "ecological studies based on an Indian view of nature—that man should live with the land and not simply *on* it."[135] Wearing stereotypical Plains garb, the activists alternately lampooned and indulged the counterculture's equation of Indigenous Americans with unadulterated nature.

The juxtaposition of the tipi with the abandoned prison presented a more destabilizing temporality. In a black and white photograph of the island evidently taken from the air, the plain conical tent gleams, surrounded by dark coastal vegetation on a natural promontory above the rocky cliffs. It's curvilinear symmetry contrasts with the gridded facade of the enormous penitentiary farther up the hill, echoing contemporaneous critiques of the cube as a figure of incarceration and alienation. Replacing a nineteenth-century military prison that housed Confederate sympathizers and resistant Native Americans, the six-hundred-cell structure was completed with inmate labor in 1912.[136] The activists pointedly reinforced a relationship between reservation and prison.[137] Both zones are subjected to a racialized logic of "bare life" in which the rights of the nation's undesirables are suspended and their bodies made vulnerable to the direct application of state power. Such locations are a structuring norm rather than exception to national life; the Indian reservation and contemporary detention center form a continuity across geography and history.[138] By juxtaposing the tipi and the prison, Indians of All Tribes set out to expose the hidden matrices of Indigenous dispossession on which the modern myth of the democratic capitalist nation—and, by extension, the United States' ambitions as a global superpower—rested.

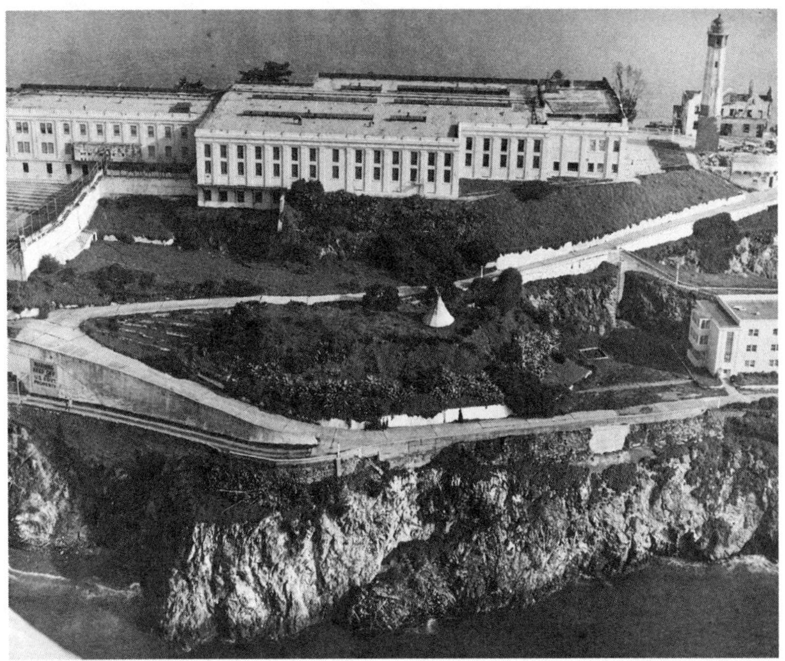

4.14

An unpainted lodge reportedly belonging to white actor and anarchist Peter Coyote, erected during the occupation of Alcatraz Island. Aerial view, January 24, 1971. NARA-Pacific Region (SF), RG269, Records Relating to the Disposal of Alcatraz Island, 1961–1973, Box 9, Folder 6.

....

As this example suggests, the conical white tent was a flexible medium for political articulation in the 1960s. In the best of cases, the architecture was wrested from dominant forms of primitivism and used to communicate a conjoined project of Indigenous and environmental justice. Anything but passive mourners, AIM activists would continue to erect tipis to signal the "liberation" and reclamation of colonized spaces, including the BIA headquarters in Washington, DC, in 1972 and Wounded Knee, South Dakota, in 1973.[139] Their lodges countered the broken hoop of precolonial holism with the promise of a white city to come. Yet the unpainted tipi never quite transcended its own conditions of iconicity, legible at a glance thanks to its mass reproduction across space and time. In the 1960s and 1970s, both Native and non-Native peoples treated tipis as blank canvases—sometimes quite literally—on which various affective and activist projects could be projected. As Doore put it, "a white tipi is just a white tipi." A painted tipi, on the other hand, is a "tabernacle."[140] As unadorned lodges traveled between New Buffalo and Wounded Knee, they further exposed the superficiality of alliances between the white counterculture, environmentalists, and Indigenous radicals. Frustrated AIM activists would complain that a longstanding white romance with authentic Indians and purified wilderness impeded any deep investment in contemporary Indigenous justice and renewal.[141] This chapter illuminates how traveling tipis activated a different ecopolitics; one that remained attached to specific histories and cosmologies due to the transformative addition of painted designs.

THE "JAPANESE APACHE" AND TOXIC FUTURISM

While fantasies of precolonial Natives and nature permeated postwar US discourses of holism, oppression and justice were threaded through Japanese ecological discourses in this same period.[142] Beginning in the late 1950s, journalists and science fiction writers developed an alternative image of the Ecological Indian as the harbinger of an impure future. In this tradition, survival depended on creative adaptation to conditions of colonization and rampant toxicity. This difference was fueled by the United States' implementation of widespread military, political, economic, and social policy during the occupation of Japan from 1945 to 1952 and Okinawa until 1972, a relationship that has been described as colonial.[143] The occupation accelerated corporate growth and with it, the unregulated contamination of environments and bodies. Pollution narratives also contained critiques of Japan's own history of imperialism and settler colonialism in relation to other Pacific nations and Ainu, peoples indigenous to the islands.[144] This dystopian tradition anticipated the countercultural backlash against Expo 70 and conditioned the diplomatic reception of Indigenous arts exhibited there.

During these same postwar decades, Japan was targeted with particular intensity as a new market for Hollywood's "cowboys and Indians." It was a genre that some Japanese critics harnessed to scrutinize the colonization of humans and land alike. Osaka, a center of military-industrial production, was key to this redefinition. Literary scholar Takayuki Tatsumi has documented how the Western genre become "so widely naturalized and domesticated" in Japan in the 1950s that a band of scrap thieves surviving in the "junkyard" of Osaka earned the nickname "Japanese Apache."[145] Here "junkyard" references the site of the former Osaka Army factory, the largest munitions plant in Asia, destroyed by B29 fighters on August 14, 1945. The US military removed all weapons and materials deemed usable, leaving some three thousand weapons partially buried in the ground. After the Japanese government seized the site as national property in 1952, it became the center of an illicit trade in iron and other valuable metals. The miners of the so-called Japanese Gold Rush were nearby shantytown dwellers, who smuggled scraps by boat through the contaminated Nekoma River at night.[146]

Those who raided the decommissioned plant included poor Japanese citizens of the mainland, Okinawans, and a majority of Korean immigrants from a series of colonial occupations that brought Japan and the United States into close alignment. Japan launched a massive offensive to wipe out local culture, language, and history in Korea after the Japanese imperial government annexed the neighboring state in 1910, in what was dubbed the Japan Korean War (1910–1945). This occupation ended after Japan was attacked with nuclear bombs in the final throes of World War II and the United States took control of national policy (1945–1952). The United States also occupied South Korea and eventually faced off with the Soviet Union, which controlled North Korea, during the Korean War (1950–1953). Finally, the US military persisted in occupying the Japanese island of Okinawa (1945–1972). The transnational flow of valuable weapons and steel resulting from these conflicts supported Japan's US-dominated postwar modernization efforts. "The destruction of war and the construction of the city go hand in hand," writes Takayuki of this period. Populations dispossessed by colonial-capitalist nations and toxic pollution consumed scraps in the shadow of such shiny symbols of industrial progress.

Reporters first dubbed the scrap thieves "Japanese Apache" during an eight-month-long struggle between the smugglers and the police in 1957–1958.[147] The moniker drew on the popularity of John Ford's *Fort Apache* (1948) and *Fort Rio Grande* (1950) and Robert Aldrich's *Apache* (1958). Set during the genocidal period of Indian Removal in the United States, these films heroized the Apache leader Geronimo. As the name "Apache" traveled through Hollywood and into Japanese reportage, it lost its ethnic-historical particularity and merged all Plains chiefs and warriors into a flexible icon of resistance.[148] A bit of journalistic flair further migrated into a radical literary imagination with the publication of the popular science fiction novel *Nippon Apattchi-zoku* (*The Japanese Apache*) by journalist Komatsu Sakyō in 1964. The eponymous cyborgs of the novel subsist on a diet of iron and other metallic scraps thanks to their superevolutionary mutations. References to the analogous survival tactics of Indigenous Americans are sprinkled throughout. For example, the name of Komatsu's fictional hero, Jiro Niké, bears a phonetic relationship to Geronimo, and the "bizarre" diet of the scrappers is compared to the "taste of cigarettes and chewing gum that American Indians had taught us."[149]

As Komatsu suggests, Native Americans were a tangible presence in Japan through their military service during World War II, the postwar US occupation, and the Korean War. Members of more than thirty Native communities, including Comanche, Lakota, Apache, Anishinaabe, Oneida, Diné, and Hopi, mobilized their bilingual skills as code talkers and translators. Their mediations rested on transcultural fluency, upending colonial stereotypes about authenticity.[150] Likewise, the trope of the Plains chief emerges from Komatsu's sci-fi adventure as the scrappy leader of dystopian futurity, rather than the proud warrior of frontier nostalgia. Impure "Indians," real and imagined, carved out a precarious, creative form of survival amid the ruins of war in Osaka. In 1994, former scrap thief and novelist Yang Sok Il took up these themes as an explicit site of intersectionality between displaced Koreans and Native Americans, writing of the Japanese Apache, "Our fathers came down to Japan, 'cause they had their lands stolen by the colonialists. Whether Indians or Koreans, the repressed people have shared many things."[151] Yang foregrounds a common thread of colonization, a shared Korean-Apache experience of violence and dispossession via Japan and the United States.

Indigenous Americans emerge more thoroughly as agents of this common history in Anishinaabe author Gerald Vizenor's 2004 novel, *Hiroshima Bugi: Atomu 57*. Indebted to the author's own US military service in Japan during the 1950s, the protagonist, Ronin, is the son of an Anishinaabe translator for General Douglas McArthur, who oversaw the postwar occupation of Japan, and a Japanese bugi (boogie) dancer. Like Kim, Ronin subsists illegally among ruins—in this case, in the preserved skeletal dome of the Peace Memorial Park in Hiroshima, the city's former commercial exhibitions hall and one of the few buildings to survive the nuclear decimation of 1945. His trickster-like performances contest nationalist narratives of racial purity, victimhood, and peace embedded in Japan's relationship to the United States and the balance-of-power logic of Cold War nuclear determent.[152] Vizenor's character may have been influenced by the USIA's Atoms for Peace exhibits, which traveled throughout Japan in the 1950s as part of a soft power initiative to rebrand nuclear power as a benevolent technological revolution with "unlimited possibilities for mankind."[153] As he writes elsewhere, "Mythic peace is not a balance, but the cause of . . . dominance."[154] In *Hiroshima Bugi*, the memorial dome emerges as the foremost symbol of "fake peace," belying the body count of imperialism and colonialism in both countries.[155] Ronin's ludic performances are allied with the illicit activity of the scrappers, as both treat the ruins of a violent modernity as a stage for impure forms of survival and resurgence.

IN THE RUINS OF EXPO 70

In 1964, the same year that Komatsu published *Nippon Apattchi-zoku*, he joined Thinking the Expo, an independent study group of Japanese intellectuals and artists who influenced the planning for the 1970 event. The novel's postapocalyptic imaginary anticipated the futurist debates surrounding Expo 70, giving credence to cultural historian William O. Gardner's characterization of the fair as "a multivalent, multi-authored 'science fiction.'"[156] For the Osaka officials in charge, it was an opportunity to showcase Japan's postwar recovery and rise to become the third largest economy in the world. The event promised to project their city and nation upon a global stage as leaders of a techno-utopic civilization.[157] It also provided stimulus for development of the region, including high speed transportation, mass housing, and natural resource management deemed fitting for a model "city of the future." Importantly, the opening of the expo coincided with the controversial ten-year automatic renewal of the US-Japan Security Treaty that supported US military and economic activity in Japan, including the unpopular combat base and nuclear storage on Okinawa.[158] Japan was the linchpin of the US efforts to cement influence and keep Communism at bay in the Pacific amid ongoing international protests against the Vietnam War. However, sustained challenges to the top-down vision of progress came from Thinking the Expo members as well as a dynamic popular protest movement that accompanied the planning, realization, and aftermath of the event.[159] Elaborating on Gardner's evocative description, I conclude with the unsettling presence of Indigenous American art within the contested landscape of the US Pavilion and the expo as a whole.

Under intensive public scrutiny, the US Pavilion logged the most visitors of any pavilion at the expo; the Soviet Union ranked second. The officials in charge of the design pursued a familiar strategy of limited accommodation in the face of trenchant critique. Ultimately, they laid plans to further the linear, developmental ethos of progress that had long defined world fair architecture, a continuity that demanded novel engagements with multimedia environments and whole earth discourses during the Cold War. Given that Masey had already worked closely with Fuller to erect a spectacular (and very leaky) geodesic sphere at Expo 67, the chief designer and his team sought something closely related yet new for Expo 70.[160] The winner of the commission was a New York–based firm who based the building on a concept first developed by the NASA in 1967. The pavilion was distinguished by a translucent roof made of vinyl-coated fiberglass, supported by steel cables and held aloft by blown air (plate 11b). The enormous elliptical cover protected 100,000 square feet of floor space, an area equivalent to "two football fields." The press release bragged that it was the largest and lightest clear span, air-supported roof ever built, capable of withstanding "all natural forces," including earthquakes and 125 mph typhoon winds. It was deemed applicable to "stadiums, shopping centers, warehouses, factories, sports arenas, crops, and even cities"—that is, "wherever a controlled environment is desired."[161] Promising large human populations the capacity to weather the forces of geology and climate in the Pacific and on the moon, the US Pavilion provided a universalist answer to the Osaka officials' charge to simulate a futurist civilization.

Masey and his fellow USIA officials were challenged to advance such avant-garde claims while avoiding the impression of hard power (military might). The low-lying elliptical form contrasted with the imposing rocket-like facade of its foremost competitor, the Soviet Pavilion. The building followed a formula that Masey successfully employed at Expo 67 in Montreal, mixing "earlier world's fair grand designs with a new minimalist modernity." In the mix was a dose of camp that promised to mask the deadly seriousness of the United States' imperial aims in the Pacific with self-deprecating humor.[162] The structure was variously teased and lauded in the press as a "Band-Aid," a "giant pincushion," and an "extraordinary wafer."[163] As a reporter for *ABC News* summarized, "It has been described as a floating waffle and a structure that carries the Nixon low-profile foreign policy too far down. On the contrary, architects have been lyrical about its revolutionary concept."[164] Masquerading simultaneously as diminutive (garnering playful, affectionate nicknames) and cutting edge (garnering design awards and admiration from critics), the pavilion was a canny soft power response to heightened public scrutiny in Japan.

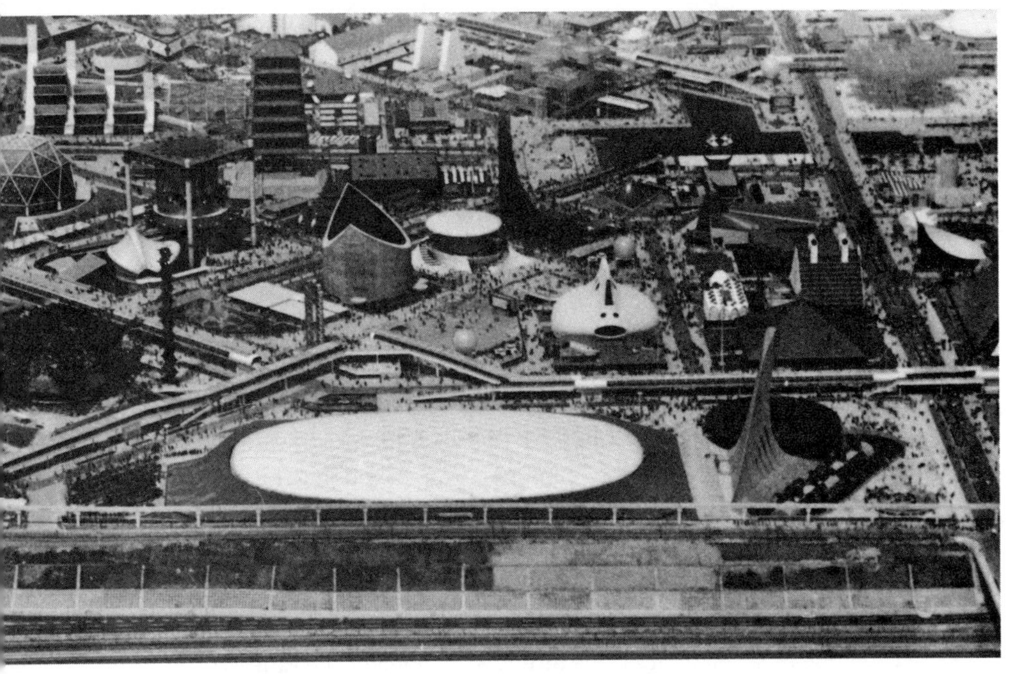

4.15

United States Pavilion at Expo 70 in Osaka, Japan, 1970. NACP Still Photographs, 306-mex-65–2-20.

....

Yet in fundamental ways, the elliptical dome continued Fuller's technocratic vision of the future in dialogue with the surveillance mechanisms of various national and private actors at Expo 70. Like a space ship, the US Pavilion promised to land in new and potentially hostile locales and enable the flourishing of human civilizations through exerting intensive bodily and ecological controls. While Fuller's values informed the design, geodesics were invoked directly in the pavilions of Germany and France and in the Pepsi Pavilion, a collaboration between Pepsi Corporation and the Experiments in Art and Technology that provided additional, informal representation for the United States. The latter structure has since functioned as a case study in the late-twentieth century convergence of avant-garde claims about the liberatory potential of immersive multimedia environments and the manipulation of spectacle to serve corporate capitalism.[165] These various dome architectures open onto a broader, technology-enabled "laboratory of governance" at Expo 70. Throughout, flashing multimedia displays doubled as channels to feed information about visitors' movements into monitoring rooms from which security personnel could be dispatched on demand. Dispersed networks also fed data to the Expo 70's Operations Control Center, a $350 million security hub based on a model that originated with NASA's Mission Control Room and was successfully applied to a world fair for the first time at Expo 67. The center anticipated protest and other unruly crowd behavior with strategies such as the aptly named Baffarō sakusen (Operation Buffalo), designed to quell a stampede. As the mythos of the Great Plains circulated in Japan, the nation's Self-Defense Forces took the side of the US Cavalry in preparing to subdue a bestial crowd. Space-age architecture, cybernetic information flows, and surveillance centers worked in tandem to further a long-standing "colonial desire to secure and extend the habitation . . . of the nation" common to Japan and the United States.[166]

Despite the gesture toward humility represented by its low elevation, the US Pavilion functioned as a stage for the country's Cold War ambitions to "penetrate outer space." The architecture pointedly rhymed with the largest and most popular of the interior exhibitions, *Space Exploration*, one of seven exhibitions intended to depict "the tapestry" of the country, including sports, folk arts, painting, photography, architecture, and new media arts.[167] Devoted to celebrating the Apollo 11 moon landing of 1969, the exhibition at one point hosted a major media spectacle, a visit from the astronauts. Nixon's White House determined that sending these popular heroes to Japan would be "a very effective antidote to current criticism of the US."[168] On the contrary, as Teasel Muir-Harmony has explored, this exercise of soft power prompted intensive Japanese scrutiny of US priorities. For example, the most popular display, a moon rock, recalled the government's geological surveys of Indigenous homelands in the Indian Removal era and elicited comparison with the country's contemporary neglect of earthly forms of exploitation. Here were the specters of colonialism and imperialism that the pavilion was otherwise charged with banishing.[169]

How are we to understand the inclusion of Indigenous American arts within the contested dynamics of lunar colonization and "Operation Buffalo"? Indigenous handmade objects formed a special section of the Folk Arts Exhibition, which included wooden weathervanes, gravestone carvings, and Shaker furniture. With the exception of the Crow tipi commission, Pueblo pottery, Diné textiles, California Indigenous baskets, and Northwest Coast crest poles were loaned from multiple institutions in the United States and abroad. The grouping was touted as "the most diversified single collection of American folk art objects ever to be shown in Asia" and "of particular interests to the Japanese because of the rich tradition these arts enjoy in Japan."[170] If space-age dome architecture was positioned on the avant-garde edge of the United States, Native art was meant to anchor a home-spun American past in dialogue with Japanese craft histories. Frederick Dockstader, director of the Museum of the American Indian (MAI), who assisted in assembling the Indigenous arts section and later visited Expo 70, offered an additional rationale. In an essay for an Expo-themed issue of *Art in America*, he wrote, "Starting, logically, with the American Indian, our aboriginal heritage is manifested in pottery, basketry, weaving and masks, which have been selected for this exhibition to accentuate the use of earth, animal and plant life. This was the forte of the Indian, and few have equaled his ability to create harmony with nature."[171] Mirroring the *Black Elk Speaks* excerpt that opened *Domebook 2*, the arts of the Ecological Indian were positioned as an aesthetic forebear to the cutting-edge environmental design of the US Pavilion.

However, Native art's equation with preindustrial holism was not uniformly applied, as Masey's previous collaboration with the IACB at Expo 67 in Montreal suggests. During the earlier event, Lakota headdresses, Diné silverwork, Yurok regalia, and a Haida crest pole met in a special section of the geodesic dome dedicated to Indigenous adornment. Two extraordinary Native arts commissions were detached from customary bodily relationships and given "a bold new application as contemporary architectural decoration" for Fuller's pavilion. Working with the Tipi Shop, Inc., of the IACB's Sioux Indian Museum, Lakota artists Sophie and Joseph New Holy created twelve extraordinary beaded headdresses with long feather trailers. The regalia was mounted on faceless black spheres and hung high in the arc—a spectacular, ghostly procession unmoored from Očhéthi Šakówiŋ histories. The display effectively captured the drift of Plains icons through global popular culture. Below, a cascade of more than five hundred unique beaded medallions covered a low-lying exterior wall enclosing the adornment display. The discs were created for the occasion by members of the Oklahoma Indian Arts and Crafts Cooperative.[172] Functioning like contemporary art installations, these commissions displayed a collective creative charge that canceled any equation with primitivism and the past. The organizers intended these experimental forms to serve the image of an "American Spirit" of ingenuity that included guitars, weathervanes, mouse traps, quilts, and geodesic domes.[173]

Some Expo 67 visitors saw nothing but "Indians, cowboys, Raggedy Ann dolls and Hollywood" inside the pavilion.[174] Others may have

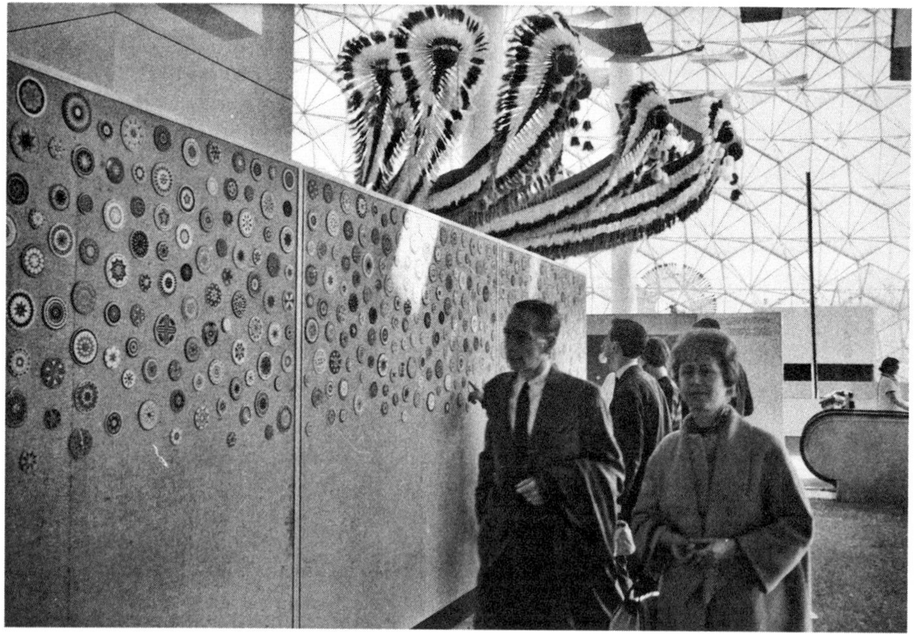

4.16

Headdresses by Lakota artists Sophie and Joseph New Holy and beaded medallions by the Oklahoma Indian Arts and Crafts Cooperative in the United States Pavilion of Expo 67. NACP Still Photographs, 306-mex-12–1-28_2.

....

connected the headdress parade and beaded constellation to the more destabilizing diplomatic assemblage issued by the nearby Indians of Canada Pavilion. In that better-known case, Canadian officials similarly planned to envelop Indigenous people and art into a linear and totalizing vision of the settler nation to celebrate the one hundredth anniversary of Canadian Confederation. Yet scholars attribute the pavilion's popularity to precisely the opposite impulse: Indigenous invitees who took part in the planning process demanded a separate space as part of the growing movement for sovereignty that spanned the United States–Canada border. In-house architect J. W. Francis based the steel and wood building on "a dwelling that would be uppermost in the public's mind": the Plains tipi, translated into an awkward planar spire akin to roadside kitsch.[175] Despite the stereotyped structure they inhabited, Indigenous participants mounted what art historian Ruth B. Phillips deems "a radical critique of the standard progressivist representations of Aboriginal history."[176] The narrative was augmented by major

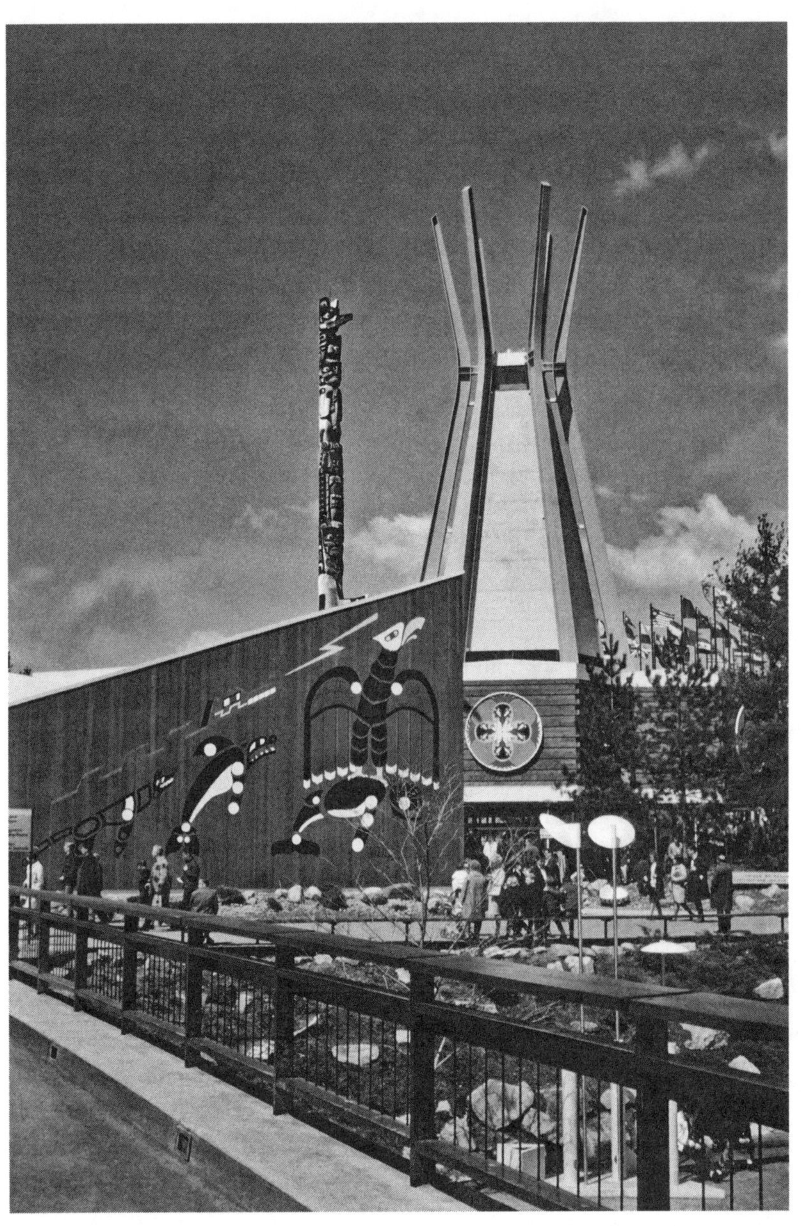

4.17

The Indians of Canada Pavilion, Expo 67 in Montreal, Canada. Alamy Stock Photo.

commissions of murals and sculptures by contemporary artists such as Norval Morrisseau (Bingwi Neyasshi Anishinaabek First Nation), Alex Janvier (Cold Lake First Nations), and Gerald Tailfeathers (Blood Reserve, 1925–1975), a Kainai member of the Blackfoot Confederacy who had previously trained in figurative painting in the Blackfeet Nation in Montana. Tailfeathers contributed *Blackfoot Design*, one of a series of painted medallions based on women's beadwork and quillwork that re-Indigenized the exterior of the tipi-like pavilion.[177] The pendants called out to the headdresses and medallions adorning the architecture of the US Pavilion, echoing forms of material diplomacy that long connected Plains nations across the imposed border between settler nations.

Similar trans-Indigenous relays crossed the grounds of Expo 70. Inuit artists were integral to the Canadian Pavilion, a massive pyramid of mirror-sheathed walls intended to conjure a wilderness imaginary—tall mountains, the glitter of Artic ice, and the big skies of the plains.[178] This time, a delegation of four sculptors and printmakers, John Pangnark—who was replaced by James Pootoogook after his early departure—Syollie Amituk, Eliyah Pootoogook, and Paul Toolooktook, demonstrated their arts during six-hour shifts in view of some twelve thousand visitors each day. They created carvings from stone and plaster while seated beneath a monumental plaster bas-relief mural depicting customary Inuit lifeways crafted by graphic artists Kenojuak Ashevak and Johnniebo Ashevak for Expo 67. The mural was allegedly gifted to Japan for display in the associated Museum of Fine Arts, while smaller carvings created on site "became important as gifts to the many heads of state and royalty who toured the building."[179]

Customary Native American arts were furthermore collected and presented as the centerpiece of Japan's own presentation. In 1969, Hiroaki Okada (1932–2004), a Japanese cultural anthropologist, visited museums, galleries, and private collections across the United States to assemble 133 customary Indigenous artworks, including Hopi katsinas, a Kwakwaka'wakw house pole, a Papago basket, and a beaded Amskapi Pikuni bonnet adorned with eagle feathers, for Expo display. The collection of these items evinced the transnationalism of Cold War ethnography, including relationships that Hiroaki formed while holding a Fulbright award at the University of Wisconsin and organizing the eighth International Union of Anthropological and Ethnological Sciences Conference in Tokyo and Kyoto, 1968–1969. In advance of his trip, Hiroaki worked with the Robert H. Lowie Museum of Anthropology (now the Phoebe A. Hearst Museum of Anthropology) at the University of California, Berkeley, to facilitate a transfer of Northwest Coast and Alaskan items in exchange for Ainu material culture from Japan. The Indigenous American arts were destined for the museum inside the Tower of the Sun, a seventy-meter-tall structure designed by Thinking the Expo member and artist Okamoto Tarō as the centerpiece of the Expo 70 Theme Pavilion.[180] These items were positioned alongside other Indigenous arts from around the world to serve the fantasy of "Progress and Harmony for Mankind," as visitors physically climbed and symbolically ascended from primitivistic to futuristic civilization inside the tower.

The developmental tropes in evidence throughout the Expo were disrupted when the tower was targeted as a stage for antiprogressive countermemories at the hands of Japanese critics. In April, a young antiwar agitator, Satō Hideo, climbed into its shining gold face, a glittering panopticon that poked its head above the fray. At the literal highpoint of the event, he agitated a crowd of several thousand to "crush the Expo."[181] In essence, Satō pictured the lofty "city of the future" leveled by a bomb. Likewise, conceptual photographer Tōmatsu Shōmei published a photo essay pointedly titled "That Bastard of an Expo" in the countercultural Japanese periodical *Ken* in 1970. Mirroring Ronan's ludic performances before the atomic peace dome in Hiroshima, Tōmatsu superimposed images of A-bomb victims from Nagasaki over the Expo's pavilions, countering the amnesia of progress with the lingering atrocities of World War II. In another of the twenty-four collages, the image of the Pepsi Pavilion hovered like a space ship over a US B-52 bomber flying over Okinawa.[182] Japanese artists and critics created an alternative image economy in which nationalistic assertions of folk and primitive pasts, mega-architecture, and futuristic space exploration were reconnected to modern atrocities. Military ghosts haunted triumphant progress at Expo 70, ensuring that any vision of the future had to grapple with unfinished histories of violence.

Such instances reinforce architectural historian Felicity Scott's claim that architectural modernism (without the *s*) reached a breaking point around 1970. No longer viable was the dubious promise of "megastructures, domes, and 'environmental design'" to provide overarching solutions to the trenchant social and ecological damages wrought by capitalist modernity.[183] Embodied in the corporate and national pavilions at Cold War world fairs, such utopic fantasies were a "grand old vehicle . . . sputtering its way to the junkyard," in the words of critic Reyner Banham.[184] Shortly after Expo 70 closed, Komatsu published an embittered review of the Expo's repressions and omissions titled

"Turning from Expo to Pollution: The New Stage of Future Studies."
He gave a prescient account of anthropogenic climate change as the end
game of the paradigm touted as "Progress and Harmony for Mankind."

> If the "accumulation of heat and carbon gas" in the air and water
> resulting from the enormous energy consumption of our giant
> industrial society reaches a certain level, then the "thermal bal-
> ance" of the atmosphere and oceans will naturally collapse. If this
> happens, the polar ice might melt and cause a great advance of
> the oceans, or cloud cover might increase, causing a "man-made
> ice age." This is not simply a science fiction fantasy. . . . I have my
> doubts, however, about whether our hypertrophied "industrial
> civilization" can learn to "behave modestly" before it is visited
> with destruction.[185]

Komatsu skewered the pretend humility of the US Pavilion, which delivered yet another one (super-)size-fits-all solution to collective futures
that left the mighty excesses of extractive capitalism intact. The author
had already voiced his doubts about the reform potential of industrial
giants in *Nippon Apattchi-zoku*. In both cases, he attributed environmental ruination to the long reign of colonial capitalism, rather than an
apocalypse to come.

The first Asian exposition, for all its record attendance, proffered a
totalizing vision of planetary holism that was already in ruins. Its critics
rightly connected the fantasy of universal progress to the violence destruction of human and other-than-human life unfolding in Osaka and
everywhere in the world. Might Komatsu have also have recognized in
the Crow tipi and other Indigenous North American items lived evidence
of the impure, creative survival strategies attributed to the "Apache"
cyborgs in his novel? Native arts rivaled spacecrafts and moonrocks in
proffering a vision for the future—one that did not attempt to corral the
global diversity of ecologies and histories into an artificial holism subject
to governmental and corporate control.

A NIITSÍTAPI FUTURISM

Informed by Niitsítapi teachings that adapted to ecocidal colonialism, the Crow tipi stood intact within the ideological junkyard of the
fair. As the sole commission in the US Pavilion, the lodge was a witting

contribution to the multivocal science fiction of Expo 70. Amid Japanese critiques of human and environmental destruction, the architecture issued a counterproposal for a Niitsítapi futurism modeled on the concentric circles of the tipi, camp, and cosmos. A growing scholarship on Indigenous futurisms holds that Native peoples have already suffered an apocalypse of immense proportions in the form of colonization. In the face of continued rather than novel threats to the fundamentals of life, endurance is a long game. It is as much the purview of ancestors as avant-gardes, and it must be situated within the multiplicity of Indigenous temporalities beyond the violent colonial logic of progress.[186] Futurist practices draw from nonlinear narratives based on spiraled shape of Native temporalities, prophecies issued in original stories, and Traditional Ecological Knowledge based on close observation of the changing environment.[187] Indigenous futurisms are described by Mvskoke geographer Laura Harjo as the imagination of "other possible worlds to live in that refuse elimination at the hands of settler colonialism"—the endgame of progress, to be sure.[188] The Crow tipi rejected both the nostalgic premodernity of the Ecological Indian and the avant-garde futurism proffered by Cold War world fairs. Formally and conceptually, it circled back around, activating ancestral knowledges to withstand the violence perpetuated by Cold War international relations and dream a future beyond colonial capitalism's claims to inevitability. The lodge modeled a more-than-human circle of alliances—an earth diplomacy governed by reciprocity, the core tenet of Niitsítapi treaty ecologies.

The Crow tipi's futurist potential was ironically galvanized by the USIA when it was reconceived as a gift destined for the city of Osaka. Libhart traveled to Japan to oversee this politically loaded material transfer, ostensibly as a representative of the US government. On October 12, 1970, the tipi was raised in Osaka's city hall. A photograph published in several Montana newspapers shows one individual working to position the slack cover over the frame of support poles, with several other potential helpers positioned at intervals around the base.[189] The activity reportedly took two hours in unschooled hands, presumably with the help of the instructional manual. However halting, the process "amazed" visitors.[190] A ceremony followed in which Libhart gave a detailed speech about the lodge's origins. His talking points were recorded on stationary from the Mitako Hotel in Kyoto. While at one point he patronized the Crow Tipi history as a "simple but colorful legend," elsewhere he expressed admiration for this capable and creative architecture. Lodges are uniquely adapted to permit flourishing in the

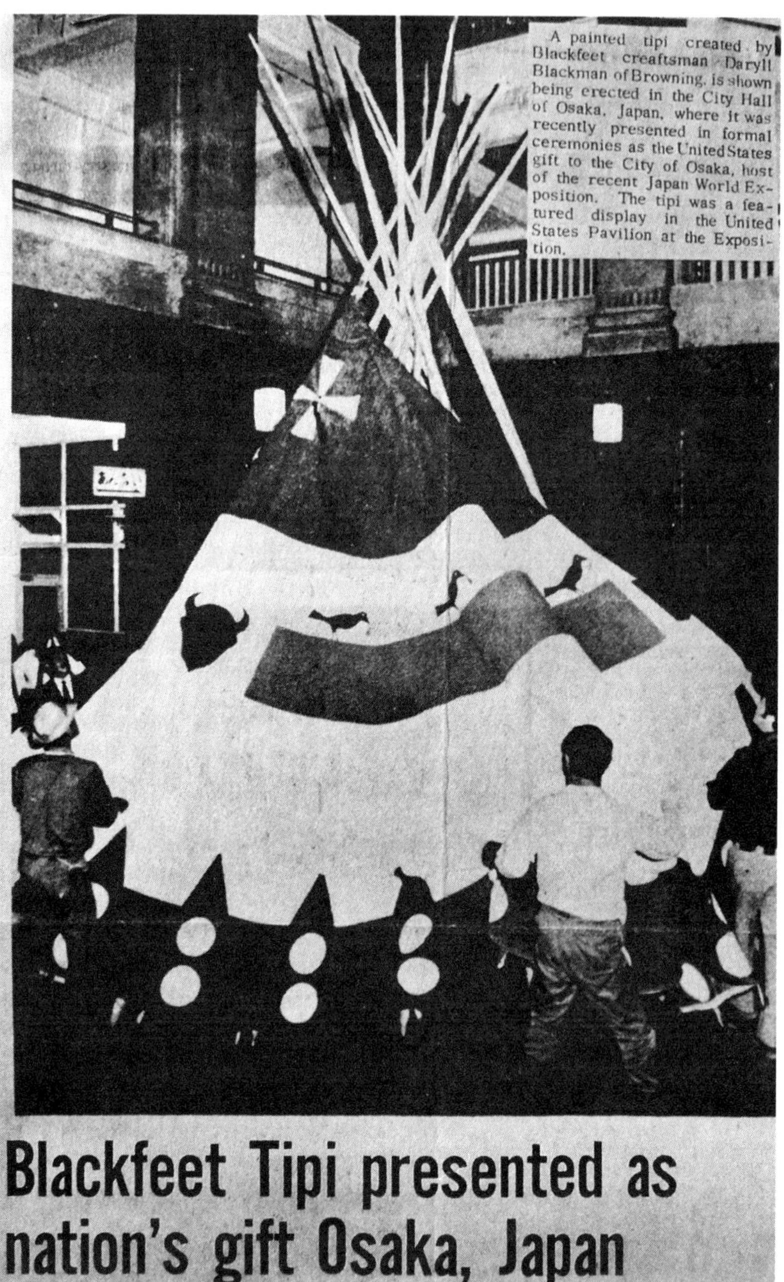

4.18

"Blackfeet Tipi presented as nation's gift Osaka, Japan." *Cut Bank Pioneer*, December 24, 1970. Newspaper clipping provided by the Museum of the Plains Indian.

"severe Plains climate," he noted, which prompts comparison with the environmental extremes driving expo mega-architecture and Komatsu's critique. Unlike the US Pavilion's drive to control alien ecologies, however, the tipi exemplified Blackfeet "religious regard and reverence for the forces of nature. . . . An animal or plant, a rock or the wind, or any of the celestial bodies, could become a special helper to an individual." Libhart went on to detail the praxis, underscoring that it was a spiritually powerful bird who "gave the warrior-hunter various songs & dances and instructed him in the creation of the Crow tipi design" in exchange for gifts of food and protection.[191] He effectively outlined an architecture of more-than-human reciprocity.

Libhart's notes are equally striking in their omissions. There is no soft power rhetoric, no explicit language claiming the lodge as an ambassador of the United States. The Crow tipi was presented as a gift to Osaka to enhance "studies of the U.S.A," as a reporter for the *Mainichi Shimbun* put it; but who exactly was it from and for?[192] Those who witnessed the ceremony were left to search the lodge—its avian and celestial figures, its small triangles of skin-meat, its pine bouquet, its open door—and make connections to the story of original reciprocity among crow, buffalo, and hunter. The tipi simultaneously begged a relationship to the Japanese tradition of environmental critique I have discussed, in which "Apache" came to replace a purified Ecological Indian with the image of scrappy survivors amid the polluted ruins of modernity. There were ample clues, in other words, for a reception in Osaka that canceled the gift's tidy alignment with the dominant powers of city and nation.

As I have argued throughout this book, Cold War international relations perpetuated long-standing colonial dynamics of expansion, extraction, and assimilation—patterns that found space-age expression in dome mega-architecture at world fairs. The Crow tipi stood in fundamental tension with a past and future of "Progress and Harmony for Mankind," a drive to exploit the planet that devastated both the Blackfeet Nation and Osaka. I propose in closing the lodge could only be a dual gift from Indigenous agents and the earth, delivered by US intermediaries to other survivors of violent modernization abroad. Like the other practices of earth diplomacy elaborated throughout this book, the tipi modeled a distinctive vision for the interwoven past, present and future of international relations based on a widening circle of reciprocity. This was a holism apart from that of the US Pavilion and the modern genealogy of domes, for it in no way sought to manage and ultimately usurp human and ecological differences. Rather, the architecture called for a consensual harmonization of disparate polities' common responsibilities to nurture and share gifts from the earth. This is the customary foundation of Niitsítapi tipi praxes and more broadly, treaty ecologies that create a ritualized path to the peaceful cohabitation of mountains and grasslands in North America. More-than-human alliances among human, crow, buffalo, horse, and deer remained the cosmopolitical referent for a model of Indigenous futurism in Osaka.

The Crow tipi was further pressed to rescale Niitsítapi precepts to an era of whole earth images beyond the one-dimensional stereotype of the Ecological Indian. The lodge answered new forms of technocratic expansion and control that extended from the planet's biosphere to outer space. Shaped by ancestral knowledges and the myriad crises of colonial capitalism, it proposed an ecopolitical alternative to a simulated city of the future that belied Osaka's own legacies of war and pollution. Though diminutive compared to the surrounding mega-architecture, the Crow tipi answered Expo 70's exhausted claims with a promise to enfold visitors in a "multi-layered Blackfeet reality," a tripart cosmos connected by reciprocity.

THE TRUTH-LINE

OSCAR HOWE'S SACRED PIPE MODERNISM

IN HIS UNDATED, hand-written "A Partial Explanation of Dakota Art," Oscar Howe (1915–1983) noted that the "peace pipe & smoking have a significant feel of being straight." The painter regularly associated the quality of straightness with movement, direction, righteousness, and truth, exemplified by "flights of birds, animals . . . charging in a straight line, line of defense among warriors, lightening, a blow (wind or hand slap), people try to grow tall and straight, arrow or spear in space, to look straight ahead."[1] Linking ethical human behavior to that of animals and weather, his commentary opens onto an ecological theory of Dakota aesthetics that connected his painterly and political entanglements in the 1960s and 1970s. The artist's Cold War international tour in 1971 offers an especially vivid entry point for my examination of his long-standing artistic engagement with Indigenous diplomatic idioms in this chapter. Howe spent nine weeks traveling through nine countries in South Asia and the Middle East (what the United States then referred to as the "Near East") as an "American Specialist" with the Department of State (DOS), lecturing about his paintings and teaching immersive seminars on artistic methods. I will examine how, amid the stuttering relationships between self-interested nations, notably the state-sanctioned violence that defined the United States' involvement in Pakistan and India, Howe's pedagogical exchanges stimulated a translation of local customary arts into diverse modernisms while disseminating a Dakota diplomatic ideal of long-term reciprocity with an expanding circle of kin.

I argue that Howe's tour was an extension of his sacred pipe modernism, my shorthand for a lifelong artistic practice that supported the revitalization of trans-Indigenous practices of diplomacy centered on smoking the *c'aŋúpa wak'á* (sacred pipe). His Dakota ancestors created pipes made from stones and animal bodies as tools of prayerful communication with Wak'á T'áka (often spelled Wakan Tanka and translated as "the Great Spirit" or "the Great Mysterious"), a powerful, energetic force uniting all parts of the Dakota universe. The pipe was further enrolled as an intermediary between the Očhéthi Šakówiŋ (the Seven Council Fires, or seven allied bands of Lakota, Dakota, and Nakota people who comprise the Great Sioux Nation) and their desired political allies, including other Indigenous groups, the United States government, and foreign states in the modern international system.[2] Howe was specifically related to Yanktonai chiefs and orators who "earned the respect of prominent Americans that in turn helped to leverage Sioux diplomacy through the complexities of the nineteenth century."[3] His ancestors offered the pipe to fold strangers into the circle of *mitákuye oyás'iŋ* ("all our relations"), a network of kin that included bison, eagles, rivers, and mountains.[4] Smoking meant assuming a responsibility for what Dakota anthropologist Ella Deloria once described as the guiding principle of Dakota life: "Obey kinship rules; one must be a good relative."[5] Howe frequently represented this powerful device in his painting and writing. Beyond its appearance as an object, I will articulate how the rich history and sensibility of pipe ceremonies—aesthetic, spiritual, ecological, and diplomatic—engender a rethinking of the straight line as a foundation for both modernist abstraction and political relations. Howe's translations of customary Dakota diplomacy brought painterly formalism, an institutionalized discourse about Indigenous modernisms, and Cold War politics into a mutually transformative relationship. This work subtly shifted the conditions of possibility not only for Native artists but for a worldly practice of international relations that continues to exploit and exclude both Indigenous and ecological agents.

My discussion of Howe's earth diplomacy entails a reassessment of the artist's polemics concerning Indigenous modernism, which have attained a mythic status in the discourse about twentieth-century Native American art. Born on the Crow Creek Reservation in South Dakota in

1915, Howe survived the violent, assimilationist federal Indian boarding school system. He went on to study under Dorothy Dunn and Gerónima Montoya at the Studio School at Santa Fe Indian School (1934–1938) and earn a master of fine arts at the University of Oklahoma (1952–1954), programs credited with formalizing and professionalizing a modern Native American painting movement (see chapter 1).[6] From 1957 until his death in 1983, Howe traveled widely for exhibitions, commissions, and lectures while employed as a professor of art at the University of South Dakota.[7] Today, the artist is most often remembered for writing "the first manifesto of Indian modernism and artistic autonomy" in the form of a public letter to Jeanne Snodgrass, curator of Native American art at the Philbrook Art Center (now the Philbrook Museum of Art) in Tulsa, Oklahoma, upon the rejection of his painting, *Umine Wacipi: War and Peace Dance* (1958) from consideration for a prize in the thirteenth Indian Art Annual competition in 1958.[8] Responding to Howe's abstract idiom, the jurors infamously considered it "a fine painting—but not Indian."[9] Howe's letter called out the paternalism of Native and non-Native institutional gatekeepers who prescribed a rigid definition of authenticity in Native American art.[10] While this incident has secured Howe's reputation as a renegade in a classic avant-garde posture, it has overshadowed the reciprocal relationships that the artist enjoyed with powerful institutions that defined Native art and shaped American Indian policy, including universities, museums, and government agencies.[11] Neither refusal nor complicity adequately characterize the artist's role in this network. He recognized and vocalized its colonizing work, yet consistently chose to work within it, engaging in forms of translation and negotiation. In other words, there was continuity between the diplomatic sensibility of Howe's paintings and the relationships he pursued around them; both entailed a creative extension of Dakota principles beyond the trail of broken treaties with the United States that shaped modernity for many Indigenous peoples.

Howe's creative practice of diplomacy charted a course apart from the two dominant images of Native Americans that circulated globally in the same moment, shaping public perception of Indigenous politics. The first is the Ecological Indian, famously appropriated by corporations and environmentalists as in the 1971 Keep America Beautiful ad campaign. The second is the resistant warrior, expressed through the dominant use of Plains imagery in the American Indian Movement (AIM), which was garnering unprecedented media attention during Howe's tour. As

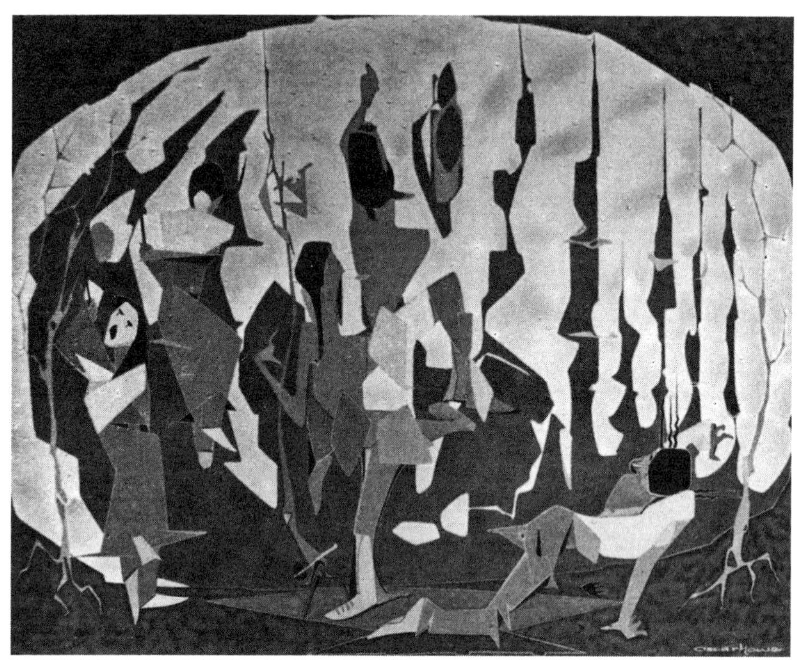

5.1

Oscar Howe, *Umine Wacipi (War and Peace Dance)*, 1958. Location unknown.
Casein on paper. With permission of the Oscar Howe Family.

....

I indicated in the introduction, AIM responded to the systemic failure
of US–Native diplomatic relations with direct action. The spectacular
cancellation of US treaty obligations during the Termination era—and
more broadly, denial of Indigenous nations as equal partners in political
negotiations—fueled a turn to armed occupation. Like the majority of
artists in this book, however, Howe was not involved in overt activism.
He maintained close ties to South Dakota senators, the Bureau of Indian
Affairs (BIA), and the DOS while AIM participants were confronting the
US government head-on. At the same time, the revitalization of the pipe
as a ceremonial agent and a pan-Indigenous symbol of unity during AIM
points to a variegated field of earth diplomacy, one that connected Indigenous activism to Cold War tours of Native art beyond a binary political
choice of friend or foe. Using the subtle sensorial toolkit of visual and
oratory arts, Howe's tour marked an imaginative extension and retool-
ing of Dakota diplomacy.

In 1971, *Panorama*, a monthly magazine published by the United States Information Service (USIS) to "promote understanding and friendship between the people of Pakistan and the people of the United States of America," reported on Oscar Howe's tour of South Asia.[12] "Hundreds of Pakistanis viewed a collection of Howe's Indian paintings—on color transparencies—and heard the imminent American Indian artist's discussion of them when he toured Pakistan early this year. Howe . . . met with artists, art students and laymen alike in American centers in the country's major cities."[13] Nested within the Bureau of Educational and Cultural Affairs inside the DOS, the American Specialist program recruited United States citizens of distinguished ability in the fields of science, literature, and the arts.[14] Following a briefing on the country destinations in Washington, DC, Howe embarked in January, 1971, on a sixty-five-day trip to more than twenty cities in nine countries: Turkey, Greece, East and West Pakistan (now Bangladesh and Pakistan, respectively), India, Ceylon (now Sri Lanka), Iran, Israel, Cyprus, and Lebanon. Loosely designated the "Near East," this volatile region was valued by the US government as a gateway to oil resources as well as a military and ideological base in the effort to limit the spread of Communism (see chapter 1). Unusually, Howe spent three weeks in Pakistan, where he taught two week-long intensive seminars based on his distinctive Dakota theory of painting and built durable relationships guided by reciprocity with students and instructors. As scholar Eddie Welch has previously detailed, Howe developed a particularly impactful lifelong friendship with one of his hosts, Rashid Ahmad Arshed, a painter, historian, and principal of the Central Institute of Arts and Crafts in Karachi, Pakistan.[15]

DOS concerns about safety and expenses prevented Howe from bringing actual paintings on tour. Instead he delivered slide lectures that incorporated forty transparencies of his artworks to audiences that included artists, students, diplomats, and journalists.[16] Although the specific content of these presentations went unrecorded, *Panorama* published color reproductions of painted Dakota historical and ceremonial subjects representing more than three decades of Howe's output and noted that he explained "significant features of his paintings."[17] *Calling on Wakan Tanka* (1962), occupying a half page at the center of the article and almost certainly included in Howe's slide lecture, is key to the relational map I draw in this chapter (plate 12). The painting establishes a

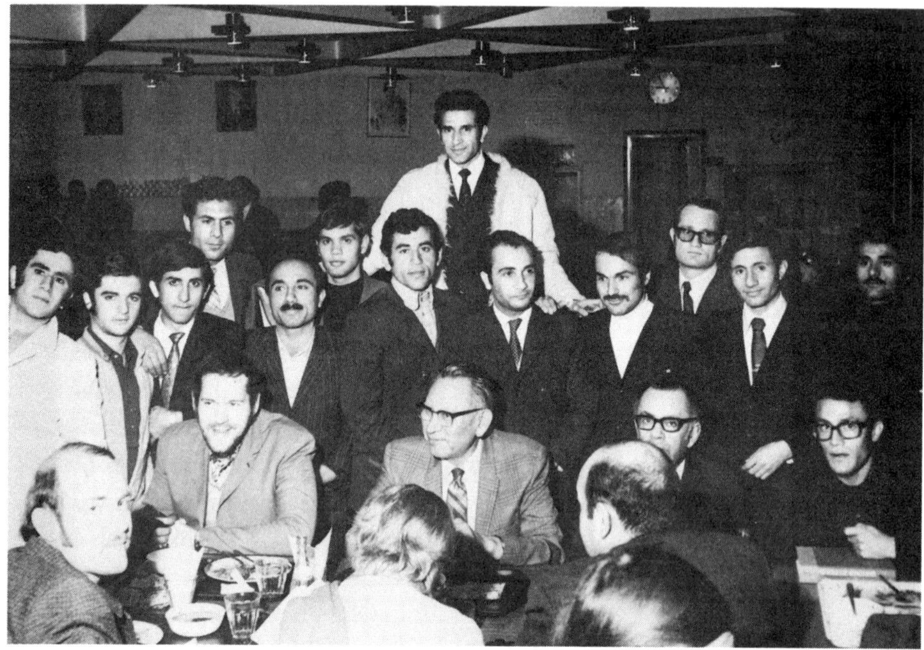

5.2

Oscar Howe (*seated at center*) at a formal reception in his honor in Tehran, Iran, 1971. United States State Department, American Specialist Tour [731], 1971, Box 1, Folder 50. Oscar Howe Papers, Photographic Materials, MS-072. USD Archives and Special Collections, I. D. Weeks Library, University of South Dakota, Vermillion, with permission of the Oscar Howe Family.

....

genealogical bond between pipe ceremonialism, a foundation of Dakota spiritual, ecological, and political systems, and the artist's idiosyncratic practice of modernism. By unpacking its connection to Indigenous ceremony and history, I will begin to map the deviation of Howe's diplomatic values from those exercised by the United States government in relation to both Native Americans and potential "Near East" allies.

Howe's expository statement about the painting for a later publication gives us clues about what Pakistanis might have heard:

A Sioux Indian family . . . at prayer before a returning storm. They are in the act of appealing to the Great Spirit to stop the storm from reversing or returning. There are dark wide streaks of rain falling and a tornado in the distance. . . . The moment at the end of the prayer, a flash of light bursts through the storm clouds, with rays streaming focally all colors of the rainbow. . . . [It] is an unusual star burst of a "peaceful lightning," so called by the Sioux—thus a good sign from the Great Spirit who can control the elements in answer to their prayers. . . . The ceremony was done to complete the cycle of nature (earth, life, sky, and the four cardinal points). The inhaling of burned plant life from the earth symbolizes the life from the earth to sky and the cosmic or spiritual meaning of life in relation to nature and Wakan Tanka.[18]

Howe's didacticism indicates a pedagogical function for *Calling on Wakan Tanka*, as it provides a mediated window into pipe smoking and its underlying philosophical premises for audiences uninitiated in Dakota idioms. Apparently motivating this artistic project was Howe's conviction, expressed in a private letter in 1959, that "we owe it to our forefathers to tell all there is about Indian Culture and continue, what had been so cruelly interrupted by the white man."[19]

In Howe's triangular composition, the three praying figures belong equally to the green plane of earth and the vast sky. The central figure bisects the page, seeming to rise out of the buffalo skull at his feet, head bent in supplication as he holds a pipe aloft. Fire, lightening, mythological thunderbirds, and naturalistic avian figures invoke *mitákuye oyás'in*, the prayer of gratitude for the kinship that unites all beings in a *wak'ą* (sacred) universe. Howe's use of interlocking plane shapes (shapes made with straight lines) in variegated colors further unify the elements of his composition. The *T* shape of the silhouetted pipe bowl, the starred lightening, the triangles of textile draped on angular bodies, and the zigzag of smoke that curls around them and rises into a planar sky appear as shifting facets of a single cloth that we can imagine extending far beyond the edges of the page. Howe's onetime student, Oglala Lakota artist Arthur Amiotte (b. 1942) offers a compelling description of such an endlessly folded world: "Life is like a huge design. Each part of the design is made up of the happenings, acts, and interactions of people with each other and the world. You must know that this design is completed by the intervention of Wakan Tanka. People and this world and all that is in it are only a part of Wakan Tanka, the lesser part when you consider the limitlessness of eternity and the universe, and the limits and relative insignificance of matter as we know ourselves and this world to be."[20] Amiotte credits Howe with introducing him to Očhéthi Šakówiŋ aesthetic principles during the Oscar Howe Summer Institute, a training program for young Native American artists at the University of South Dakota, in

1961.[21] Shortly after, Howe represented the intercession of Wakʿą Tʿąka in the "huge design" of painting and world with a bright flash of "peaceful lightening" that radiates from the upper center of the composition. A starburst in warm tones of white, yellow, and orange surrounds the man's bent head and outstretched arms. The pipe is sharply silhouetted in this centrifugal forcefield.

Calling on Wakan Tanka cites and diverges from a European tradition of crucifixion scenes. In this respect, the painting forms a visual precedent for the foundational book by Dakota legal scholar and philosopher Vine Deloria, Jr., *God Is Red: A Native View of Religion*, first published in 1972. Artist and author shared an ecological stance toward spiritual immanence in which humans are embedded in relations of continuity and dependency with land and other beings. Both contrasted this "Native view" with dominant interpretations of Christianity that emphasized (white) human supremacy over mute, objectified matter and ascendancy to a heavenly realm beyond earth. Deloria, Jr. compared monotheistic traditions based on "the pretense that the earth simply does not matter, that human affairs alone are important" with Indigenous spiritual practices "taken directly from the world around them, from their relationships with other forms of life."[22] In *Calling on Wakan Tanka*, a triad of human bodies anchors the composition, but the central figure's historical identity is emptied out; Howe's depicted him from behind in angular, interlocking shapes that are stylistically continuous with the surrounding environment. The flanking figures at the base engage in separate acts of prayer to the holism of Wakʿą Tʿąka rather than devotion to a Christlike intercessor. Crucially, the diagonal of the pipe has replaced the horizontal bar of the ultimate Christian symbol of ascendance, the cross.

Howe's substitution invokes the inspired nature of all components of the earth. Throughout the painting, he references customary Dakota understandings that an inner spirit is more fundamental to identity than physical form. This vital force is separable from the body, although it may temporarily animate humans, animals, trees, rivers, and mountains, and other persons in a continuous sacred-ecological plane of existence. The concept of a shared interiority that cuts across formal differences anchors Dakota recognition of humans as humble dependents in an "overarching interspecies collective" made up of more-than-human relatives.[23] Yet in discussing the painting, Howe noted that "a small spirit resides in an unusual thing," indicating that not all forms of vitality share equal status. For example, the rock bearing a hand print communicates a heightened numinosity, a potent portal to Wakʻą́ Tʻą́ka. Although the artist's translation of the latter concept as the "Great Spirit" infers a god-like status, numerous accounts by Lakota, Dakota, and Nakota people indicate that Wakʻą́ Tʻą́ka does not refer to a single entity; rather it names the totality of the energetic charge that enables movement and life. Amiotte wrote, "Wakan Tanka is all that is wondrous, awesome, powerful, and infinite. . . . Perhaps this is why we call him Great Mystery."[24] He indicates that Wakʻą́ Tʻą́ka cannot be fully known by humans, although aspects may be revealed through dreams, vision quests, and ceremony. Smoke from tobacco or sweetgrass is a particularly potent means of prayerful communication with this holism. It transcends the boundaries of bodies and languages to connect the intention of the smoker to all that is wakʻą́. In Howe's painting, hairline strands of smoke in shades of gray create a subtle, secondary frame for the scene, interweaving body, earth, and sky. By smoking and offering the pipe, Howe's family reinforces bonds of kinship and dependency among humans and other-than-human communities, uniting them in the great design of the world. As the work hints, only by regularly engaging in reciprocity with this expansive network of relatives will good things—power, knowledge, medicine, direction (or salvation from a fiery storm)—come to the individual or group.

Howe elsewhere painted the story of Ptesáwi, White Buffalo Woman, a sacred being who temporarily adopted the form of a beautiful woman to deliver an archetypal object, the Buffalo Calf Pipe, to the Očhéthi Šakówiŋ. Amiotte wrote, of Ptesáwi's legacy, "We were given ceremonies in which we pray with the pipe, ways that we may stand before Wakan Tanka so that he will instruct us about our place in his design."[25] Her gift is remembered and activated during the annual renewal ceremony, the Sun Dance, which historically united Indigenous communities across the plains at the time of the summer solstice (see chapter 4). This intertribal gathering is of vital spiritual, economic, and political significance, serving to redistribute resources and cohere peaceful relations among disparate peoples. By returning to this sacred center, individuals realize their responsibilities to all beings by "assisting in the ongoing process of creation."[26] Ptesáwi's gift is presented along with a Sun Dance scene in a ten-panel mural cycle that Howe completed for the Works Progress Administration in the Mobridge City Auditorium in South Dakota in 1942.[27] Ptesáwi wears a fringed buckskin dress and an eagle feather in her black hair, facing directly out of the painting as if to offer visitors the pipe in her hands. Howe's 1946 painting *Calf Woman and Pipe* diverges from such typical depictions of Ptesáwi as

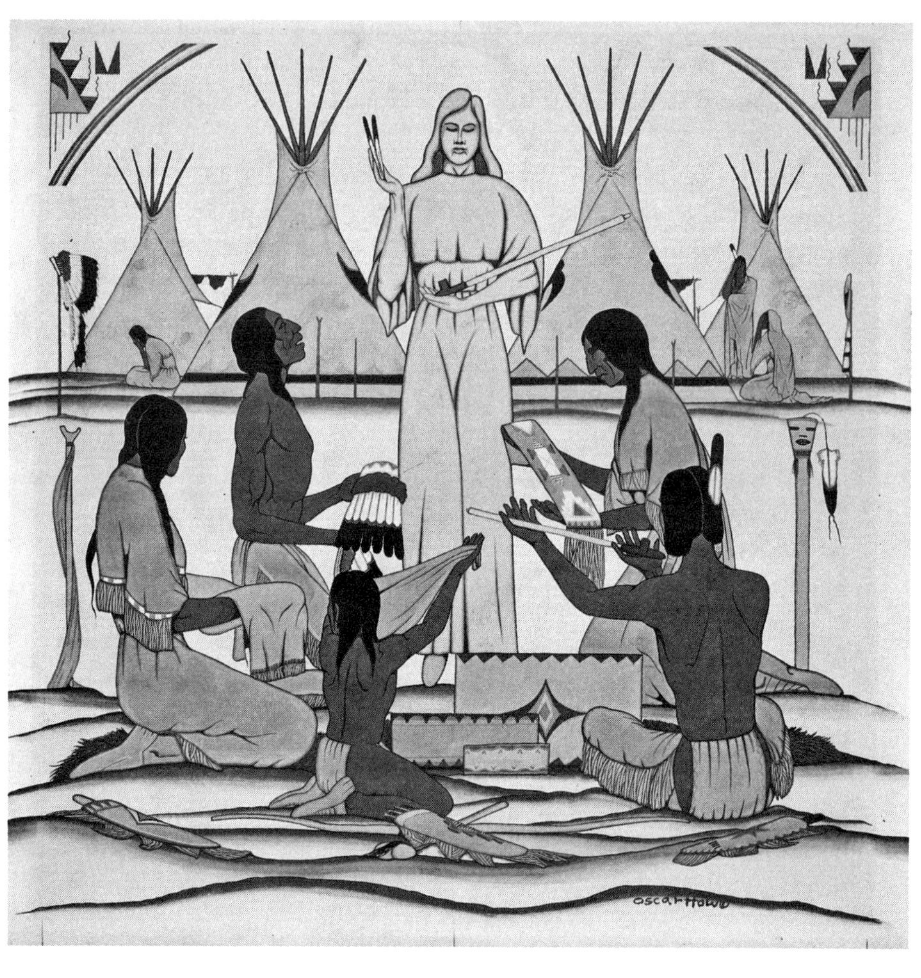

5.3

Oscar Howe, *Calf Woman and Pipe*, 1946. Gouache on paper, 13.625 × 13.125 in.
University of South Dakota, Vermillion, with permission of the Oscar Howe Family.

phenotypically Native. The figure's blonde hair and fair skin rework the role of whiteness in the story, which is typically reserved for the sacred buffalo calf into which she transforms. His substitution is allusive of the pipe's role in brokering Dakota alliances with Euro-Americans through adoptive rituals, which mobilized Ptesáwi's legacy to make "outsiders into 'natural relatives' through kinship terminology."[28] Howe specifically conjured Indigenous practices of instantiating nonbiological kinship in the midst of a pervasive logic of racial othering in postwar United States.

By invoking the sacred origins of peaceable diplomacy with white settlers, Howe followed the example of his ancestors, Yanktonai orators who occupied Mnísota Makhóče (land where the waters reflect the clouds), a prairie homeland between the Minnestota and Missouri rivers.[29] They were members of the Očhéthi Šakówiŋ who negotiated with the United States during the final, traumatic years of Indian Removal. A portrait of Howe's maternal grandfather, Mato Wakokipe-sni (Not Afraid of the Bear), followed nineteenth-century portraiture conventions concerning the depiction of Native chiefs as friends of the state. Standing in full feathered regalia, the leader holds a pipe and a fringed leather tobacco bag, each intricately woven with European trade beads in star and diamond patterns. When invoked in nation-to-nation negotiations, smoking ceremonies transform strangers into family and compel relationships of reciprocity within the broader circle of mitákuye oyás'iŋ. "The spirit in the smoke will soothe the spirits of all who thus smoke together and all will be as friends and all think alike," stated the Oglala Lakota healer George Sword in the late nineteenth century.[30] Often paired with oratory, gifting, and dancing, pipe smoking is a powerful diplomatic vehicle for persuasion and unification.

This potential was not lost on Euro-Americans who at least initially embraced the pipe as a means of securing Indigenous nations as allies. When Captain Merriweather Lewis and William Clark led the Corps of Discovery Expedition to claim western lands as part of the United States, they determined that the pipe was "greatest mark of friendship and attention" not only among the Očhéthi Šakówiŋ, but among countless Native groups who smoked it to consecrate intertribal familial-political bonds.[31] But this initial encounter with the United States, like so many to come, was studded with misunderstanding and coercion as much as thinking alike. Through the westward expansion of the United States, Native peoples were steadily reduced from diplomatic partners to supplicants—or enemies—of the state.

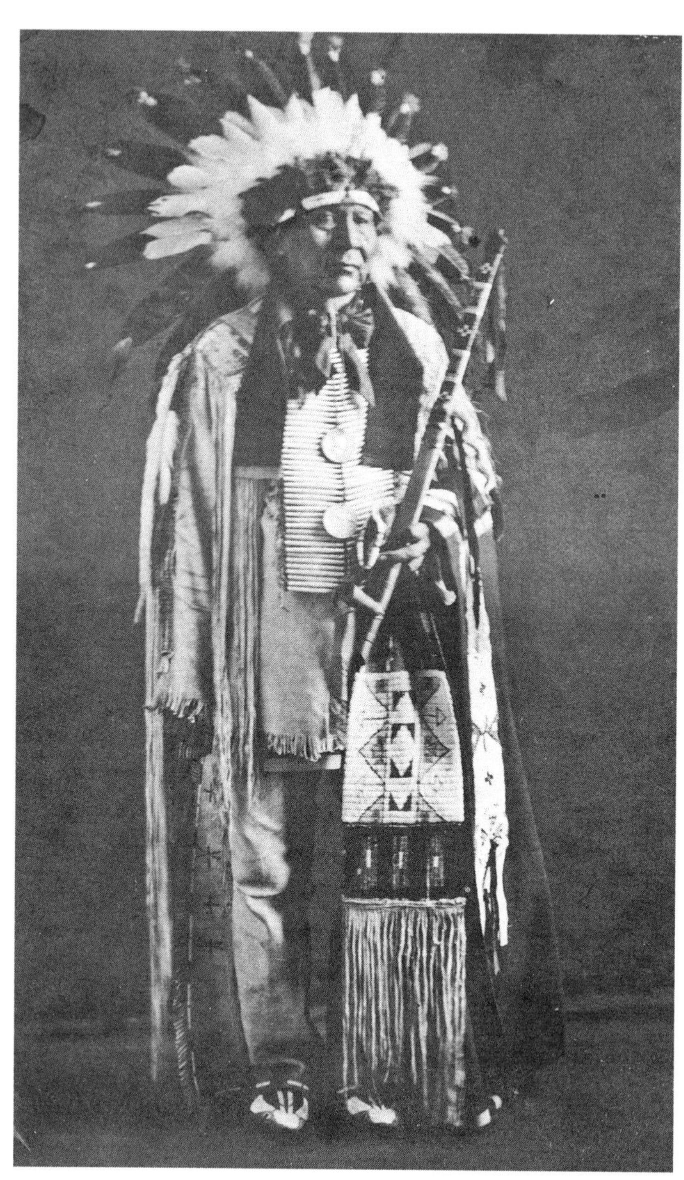

5.4

Oscar Howe's maternal grandfather Mato Wakokipe-sni (Not Afraid of the Bear) [2973], undated. Box 1, Folder 32. Oscar Howe Papers, Photographic materials, MS072. USD Archives and Special Collections, I. D. Weeks Library, University of South Dakota, Vermillion, with permission of the Oscar Howe Family.

Howe's ancestors oversaw the devastating loss of Dakota lands through the violation of treaties and ensuing resistance. After the establishment of Minnesota as a state in 1858, the United States annexed Dakota treaty lands, cut off access to *čhaŋnúŋp-ok'é*, the sacred site for quarrying red *iŋyaŋša* (pipestone), and grossly mismanaged annuity payments, resulting in mass starvation.[32] In 1862, some Dakota retaliated by attacking settlers, leading President Abraham Lincoln to order the public hanging of thirty-eight Dakota men in the largest mass execution in US history.[33] Howe related that his maternal great-grandfather Matoska (White Bear) was awarded a government medal for trying to prevent the uprising on the grounds that the "killings of white people was a wrong thing for understanding and for good relationship." The artist traced his Dakota name, Mazuha Hokshina, often translated as Trader Boy, to his great-grandfather's diplomatic efforts to "correct the wrong."[34] Following an intertribal Sun Dance in 1866, Howe's paternal great-grandfather, Ho-hoo-non-pee (Bone Necklace), a head chief of the Lower Yanktonais, invoked the moral conscience of the Northwestern Indian Commission on the upper Missouri concerning the impacts of white encroachment on subsistence hunting:

> My tongue is not forked. I speak the truth, and offer you clean hands. . . . Every year the Great Father's white children come out to us with good words for my people; but that is all. . . . My Great Father is sending his white soldiers all over our country, and is driving the wild game from my children's mouths. . . . My fair land is all turned over as by a whirlwind. No more can our warriors plant and fish in safety by the wooded brook-side, nor my young men hunt the buffalo on the plains. . . . I look out on the face of my native rivers and plains, and I love them well. I also love the whites, and do not want to fight them; but I cannot hold my young men from going to war when they see the game driven from their country.[35]

Ho-hoo-non-pee's oratory conjured the ethics of familial bonds and peace medals, diplomatic gifts from the US government, to underscore the violation of promises made during nation-to-nation treaties.

Ho-hoo-non-pee's warning of warfare was prophetic, as conflicts escalated following General George Armstrong Custer's discovery of gold in Pahá Sápa (the Black Hills), an Očhéthi Šakówiŋ sacred center in 1874.[36] After the government again withheld annuities and drove communities to the brink of starvation, select leaders, including Mato Wakokipe-sni, signed the Agreement of 1877. Contested to this day, the maneuver over-turned the land protections of the Fort Laramie Treaty of 1868, confined the Great Sioux Nation to diminished islands of land, and initiated the era of assimilation.[37] In 1883, the US Code of Indian Offenses rendered the intertribal Sun Dance illegal and forced it underground. It was targeted alongside other Indigenous ceremonies in a campaign to stamp out cultural practices that redistributed wealth, reinforced Indigenous cultural and political sovereignty, and challenged the ascendancy of the capitalist state.[38] By the time of Wakokipe-sni's portrait, likely taken around the turn of the twentieth century, aggressive assimilation policies and programs ensured that the survival of Dakota ceremonial knowledge was covert and circuitous. Stripped of its political efficacy vis-à-vis the United States, the ubiquitous "peace pipe" came to signal a generic and timeless Indianness in a colonial image economy. Wakokipe-sni's self-fashioning kept the memory of the pipe as a sacred diplomatic interme-diary alive, even as it was trivialized as an ethnographic curiosity.[39]

During Howe's years as a professor at the University of South Dakota, he took his family on regular trips to čhaŋnúŋp-ok'é, which has been managed by the National Park Service as Pipestone National Monument since 1937. Describing her father's lifelong engagement with the sacred sites and rituals associated with the cʼaŋúpa wakʼá, Inge Dawn Maresh told me that "he was trying to communicate peacefully to another cul-ture."[40] *Calling on Wakan Tanka* likewise worked to convey the spiri-tual and political significances of the pipe in the wake of its desecration and appropriation by the United States. By connecting this familiar fig-ure to "the original way of smoke prayer," Howe reminds us that Dakota history is dynamically transmitted and altered by Indigenous agents through ceremony, oral storytelling, hide painting, sensuous practices of diplomacy, and the artist's own work. Neither Mato Wakokipe-sni's portrait nor Howe's painting accept the federal government as the exclu-sive arbiter of Native modernity. The stakes of connecting the modernist line to ceremony were high.

PEDAGOGY IN PAKISTAN

The paternalism that defined the United States' treatment of Indigenous nations constituted a deep relational pattern that was extended and re-molded to the exigencies of international diplomacy during the Cold War. As I discuss at the outset of this book, the US Information Agency

(USIA) was established in the same instant as the Indian Termination policy for the purposes of disseminating capitalism; both perpetuated a logic of assimilation that was part and parcel of the ever-expanding borders of the United States. Howe first explicitly engaged this context in 1966, when he agreed to send a painting on an extended tour with the Art in Embassies Program (AIEP), established in 1964 to "tell America's story through the thoughtful international presentation of American artistic achievements." The AIEP displayed artworks that were gifted or loaned by individuals, galleries, corporations, foundations, and museums to the DOS for a minimum of two years in US consular and embassy residences and offices worldwide.[41] Howe's selection of a just-completed work, *Sacro-Wi-Dance* (Sun Dance, 1966), suggests a canny appreciation for the continuities between the United States' policy concerning Indigenous Americans and exercise of soft power abroad.[42] Articulated through a series of interlinked ovoids in a fiery palette, his dancers melt into the central disc of the sun, the source of Wakʿ ą́ Tʿ ą́ka. Only a black swirl of hair remains to demarcate a third figure in the lower right, expressing unification "with the holy rhythm of that which causes all life to move."[43] While the Sun Dance was undergoing a widespread revival on the plains in the 1960s, the full ceremony remained illegal in the United States until the passage of the American Indian Religious Freedom Act in 1978.[44] Embassies in Singapore, Brazil, Hungary, and the Republic of Dahomey (now the Republic of Benin) thus hosted an illicit image of "all our relations" that was irreducible to the national exercise of soft power that set it in motion.[45] *Sacro-Wi-Dance* widened the circle of mitákuye oyás'iŋ to include dependency and reciprocity with the earth amid the severely constricted relationality attending Cold War capitalism.

A photograph taken at the opening reception of a USIA circulating exhibition, *Pacific Northwest American Indian Artefacts* in 1960, suggests that a similar challenge awaited Howe upon his arrival in Karachi. It pictures Pakistani school children "playing Indian" with the son of the US Ambassador to Karachi. In this ludic exercise of soft power, Pakistanis symbolically become wards of the United States by inhabiting the country's emptied archetypal image, a Plains Indian in a befeathered headdress.[46] The photograph recalls my discussion of the USIA's mixed messages in chapter 1. The agency at times muddied its argument that a benign process of Indigenous modernization was underway by indulging a long-standing international romance with noble savages. The image further indicates the colonial self-interest underlying the United States' uneven treatment of Pakistan as the nation's "most allied ally" due to

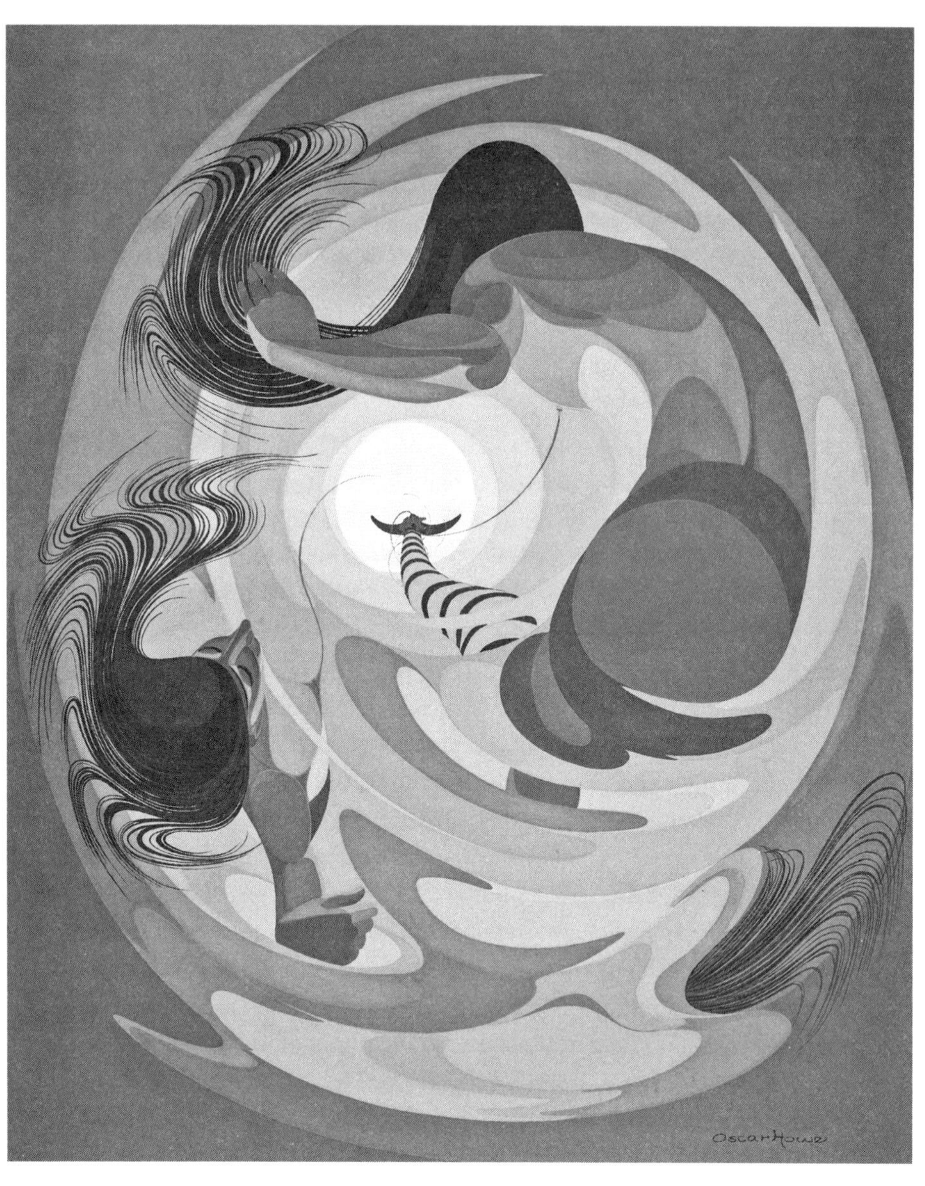

5.5

Oscar Howe, *Sacro-Wi Dance* (Sun Dance), 1965. Casein on paper, 28 × 22 1/2 in.
University of South Dakota, Vermillion, with permission of the Oscar Howe Family.

Pakistan's strategic position within a global chain of alliances encircling the Soviet Union.[47] Pakistan was born as an independent Muslim state in 1947 out of the partition with India, a lengthy process that ended formal British colonial rule. Almost immediately, a military coup overturned the new democratic government, resulting in a series of dictatorships centered in West Pakistan. The US government sent the first of many ambassadors in 1948 to embrace the strongmen and establish a secret military intelligence base that enabled spying on Soviet and Chinese competitors. Parallel soft power initiatives soon reshaped the landscape for modern art education in Pakistan. Howe's host, Arshed, has detailed the United States' involvement in the National College of Arts in Lahore, his alma mater and the oldest leading art institution in the country. The school was established in 1875 as the Mayo School of Industrial Arts by the British Crown in India and transferred to the Department of Industries, West Pakistan, following partition. From 1958 to 1961 it became a "laissez-faire environment" under the appointment of Principal Mark Ritter Sponenburgh, previously the dean of the arts at the University of Oregon. Arshed wrote, "With financial help from the Asia Foundation, Ford Foundation, and other sources, within three months of his arrival he had recruited new faculty from Pakistan, the UK, the USA, Canada, and Japan."[48] From military outpost to arts education, the United States approached Pakistan as a frontier in its expanding Cold War empire.

By the mid-1960s, Pakistan was riven by ongoing military conflict with India over the Kashmir region in the north and internal conflict between the ruling elite in the west and the underrepresented Bengali majority in the east. Consumed with the Vietnam war, President Lyndon B. Johnson avoided diplomatic engagement and downsized military involvement. Moscow and China readily filled the void. Howe's trip planning and travels landed in the midst of renewed diplomatic ties between the Richard Nixon administration and a dictatorship under former army general Yahya Khan. In what was known as Operation Searchlight, Nixon secretly turned to Pakistan to initiate a thaw in the United States' two-decade-long standoff with China. In December of 1970, on the eve of his trip, a relatively free election shifted power from West Pakistan to East Pakistan; in response, Khan ordered a brutal crackdown on Bengali separatists. On March 26, 1971, scarcely a month after Howe's visit, a newly independent state of Bangladesh (formerly East Pakistan) charged the Pakistani Army with the genocide of three million people, carried out with the help of United States-made armored military carriers.[49] In April, American diplomats in Pakistan sent a cable protesting the United

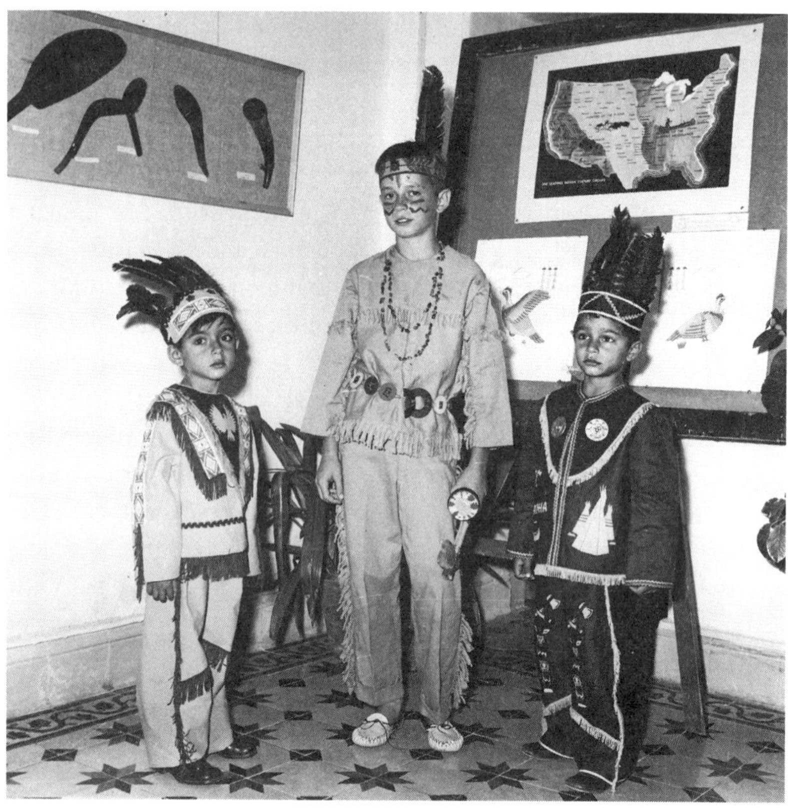

5.6

The son of an ambassador to the US Embassy in Karachi teaches Pakistani children how to "play Indian." USIA exhibition *Pacific Northwest Indian Artifacts*, University of Karachi, 1960. Smithsonian Institution Archives, image #SIA2017–002064.

....

States' complicity: "Our government has failed to denounce the suppression of democracy. Our government has failed to denounce atrocities. . . . Our government has evidenced what many will consider moral bankruptcy."[50] Arshed offered a parallel vision of diplomacy in ruins in his discussion of the fate of the US Embassy in Karachi. Richard Neutra's "elegant masterpiece" of 1956 became "a fortress with paramilitary forces posted at the gate" and eventually an "abandoned building, covered with dirt and barbed wire . . . a ghostly and disturbing picture."[51]

Howe thus traveled in the midst of a political rupture that echoed the United States' abrogation of diplomacy and ensuing violence on the nineteenth-century plains. Although Operation Searchlight was classified, the artist was certainly aware of the escalating conflict that marked his tour and its aftermath. During his briefing in Washington, DC, he was given country notes that outline the extent of British colonial rule and the turbulent partition with India. Howe must have read that the constitution was suspended when Khan took power in 1969, that "East Pakistan maintains that it has been under-represented in the central Government and denied its share of central Government resources," and that "the process of achieving a political consensus acceptable to the martial law authorities and politicians may take some time to evolve."[52] While the notes are filled with predictable platitudes concerning the military dictatorship, Howe had the opportunity to develop a more nuanced perspective on Pakistanis' precarity and grievances through firsthand encounters with local communities. The only surviving reference to these issues, Howe's trip notes document "near trouble: avoided riot area in Rawalpindi [West Pakistan] on way to lecture at Islamabad and changed lecture place (Am. Univ. Center) to USIS center in Calcutta, because of rioting in front of Am. Univ. Center."[53] Howe concluded that the worst living conditions he encountered on the tour were in Dacca, East Pakistan, and Calcutta, India.[54] The local situations invited comparison to the ravages of colonialism on Native American reservations, where the artist described his "own two brothers and their families . . . in shacks, looking forward only to die, no hope, no belief, nothing but emptiness."[55]

While Howe is typically described as mild-mannered and reserved, there is evidence that his vocal concern for the urgency of Indigenous American cultural survival made DOS officials uneasy. Arshed later recalled that George Naifeh, the Cultural Affairs officer at the US consulate in Karachi, privately warned him, "Professor Howe was a highly sensitive and emotional person, and I should be very careful in how I handled him. This warning might have been the result of the US State Department's briefing on Mr. Howe's sensitivity on matters of American Indian history."[56] Naifeh's apparent characterization of Howe as "emotional" discounts the authority he wielded as a credentialed professor and cultural historian of his people. In contrast, Arshed was careful to note that Howe's status as a teacher and his passionate engagement with the "loss of American Indian Culture and Civilization" commanded "love and respect" from Pakistanis.[57] He recounted that toward the end of Howe's lecture in Karachi, the older artist's "voice became louder than normal and his lips quivered" as he spoke about the importance of perpetuating Očhéthi Šakówiŋ cultural forms, inspiring a standing ovation from the crowd.[58]

Howe's role as a pedagogue enabled a more subtle and sustained translation of Dakota idioms into the overlapping spheres of artistic modernisms and international relations. An account of his week in Turkey in the newspaper *Yeni Asir* utilized an ironic reversal of the stereotype perpetuated by the "playing Indian" episode a decade before: "A member of one of the most warlike Indian tribes, the Sioux, came to Izmir. Do not immediately think of an Indian with an axe in his hand, arrows on his back, on an unsaddled horse, building fires for signaling. This person is Professor Oscar Howe, who has done research on his ancestors' history and has depicted them in his pictures, who is on a journey introducing the Sioux people to countries all over the world."[59] Echoing the tenor of the article, Arshed recalled, "It was for the first time that I was looking at an American Indian in person, interestingly in a suit and tie, as opposed to what one is accustomed to seeing in Hollywood movies; wearing scant clothes, painted faces, and fancy headdresses made of feathers. . . . In a few hours, we were like good friends who had known each other for years."[60] These descriptions of the self-possessed scholar located Howe at a remove from "his ancestors' history," making him the subject, rather than the object, of a gaze upon "the Sioux." In them, he related to the Indigenous past as a professor and painter, a distance that his public (composed of those who engaged with his lectures and classes, as well as those who read newspaper and magazine accounts) was likewise invited to inhabit. Howe's suit and credentials opened a space in which he could redraw the relationship between Indigenous past and present apart from the stereotypes that circulated in his stead.

Howe's lesson plans for two week-long intensive seminars taught at the Central Institute of Arts and Crafts in Karachi and the Institute of Fine Arts in Lahore, West Pakistan, are revealing in this regard. Characteristically, he did not lead the seminars with Dakota cultural foundations, choosing rather to embed those insights in a general and accessible program of study based in his distinct method of painterly abstraction. During an introductory session, he urged the students to "maintain flexibility to absorb 'complexities' of art," rather than subscribe to a given "ism," and follow their intuition to create unique compositions.[61] A photograph reproduced in *Panorama*, mislabeled as an "illustrated lecture," reveals Howe's profile in a plaid suit, button-down shirt, and tie in the midst of what appears to be a classroom demonstration. I surmise that it offers a glimpse of his instruction at the Central Institute of Arts and Crafts, where he took over five sessions of a three-hour-long life drawing class normally taught by Arshed.[62] The principal recollected an

::::::::::

impactful lesson that could very well be the one pictured: "[Howe] emphasized the importance of fast moving lines in figure drawing. . . . He then demonstrated the point he was driving at by drawing a figure in action in a few seconds."[63] This description corresponds with Howe's notes for the second day's lesson on what he called nonobjective composition, defined by a "conscious effort to avoid recognizable objects."[64] In the photograph, Howe is seen shading in a line drawing on a large sheet of paper affixed to an easel, several zones of which are already densely inscribed. Seated students are clustered around him in a semicircle, their heads turned toward Howe, clasping large sheets of paper readied for the lesson. In the lower right corner, a cropped hand grips a drawing utensil fixed on the page, apparently mimicking Howe's movements. Perhaps this student is realizing Howe's intent to "train by kinesthetic means to concentrate as a discipline."[65] Arshed elaborated that the students anticipated that the visiting professor would "introduce some special techniques and tips on life drawing." Instead, they were encouraged "to ignore the model and draw instead randomly; flowing circular shapes without preconceived notions."[66] In this program, Howe's overturning of Indian stereotypes was matched by his authoritative upending of academic drawing conventions.

It was not until the fourth day that Howe offered an explanation of the "Sioux Indian. <u>lines emphasis</u>" (underlined three times in a demonstration of priority). He followed with an exercise in which the students followed his own method to "intuit points, dots, marks (connect them)."[67] As I will explore at length in the next section, Howe developed this technique to reprise the "painting of the truth" ceremony of his ancestors, in which skilled artists recorded important events in the community on paper following the verbal cues of an oral historian. Howe's recommendation that the DOS develop programs that "encourage the native artists and art students to find involvement in their own native art forms" helps to further clarify the aim of these exercises.[68] He offered a hands-on model for how the students could draw on their past to articulate diverse modernisms. Dakota ceremonial arts were fully present in his seminars, but transformed from an ethnographic designation into a flexible, open-ended generator of shared practices of abstraction.

Arshed claimed that Howe's demonstration of the Dakota point-to-point technique "left the students in awe." By the end of the week "all barriers between the teacher and the students were broken," which was "fruitful in academic terms and in terms of personal relationship and

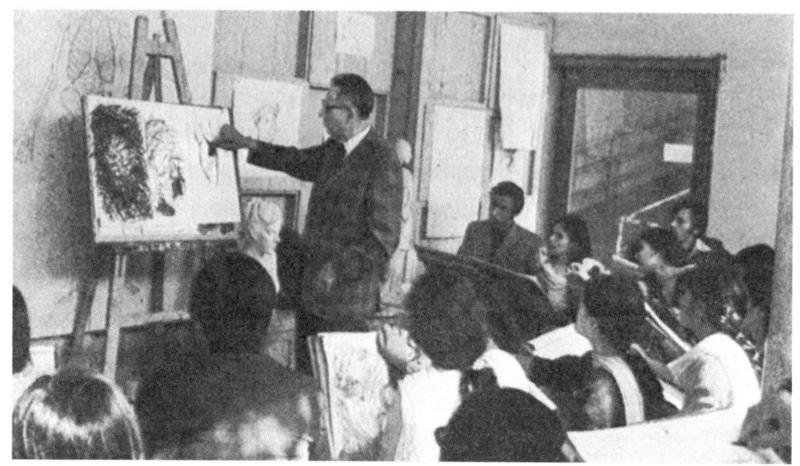

5.7

Oscar Howe probably teaching a seminar at the Central Institute of Arts and Crafts in Karachi, 1971. Photograph published in "Preserving Sioux Art," *Panorama*, 1971, Box 59, Folder 7. Oscar Howe Papers, Family Papers, MS-072. USD Archives and Special Collections, I. D. Weeks Library, University of South Dakota, Vermillion, with permission of the Oscar Howe Family.

....

friendship on both sides."[69] Howe likewise saw his engagement with Pakistani students as a highlight of the trip, noting, "It was very touching to me how appreciative the students in Pakistan were. I had more time with them and got to know and like them better."[70] These relationships engendered material forms of reciprocity, as evinced by a senior student's gift of a painting to Howe at his farewell party and Howe's many letters to support Arshed's pursuit of opportunities to teach and study in the United States, a topic to which I will return at the conclusion of this chapter.[71] Despite his brief tenure in most tour locations, Howe maintained warm, long-term correspondences with numerous other artists and scholars who shared his investment in the aesthetic revitalization of customary artforms through a malleable language of modernism.[72] Such values, shared and exchanged through art and friendship, chart a course apart from the "moral bankruptcy" of the United States' contemporaneous Pakistan policy.[73] As *Calling on Wakan Tanka* suggests, Howe's tour occasioned a specific translation of Dakota idioms that was nonetheless continuous with the artist's long-standing practice of relational modernism—an earth diplomacy born equally from ancestral customs and the ruptures of Indian Removal.

Unlike Fred Stevens (see chapter 2), Howe was neither a ceremonial expert nor a regular participant; he primarily contributed to the resilience of ancestral practices through painting and pedagogy.[74] His works were necessarily translations of elders' songs and stories and research into customary Dakota art and religion in academic and museum contexts. Howe was immersed in Dakota language at birth, but illness and poverty, more than customary practices, dominated his early years. His biographer relates that, at the age of six, Howe's mother Ella Fearless Bear took him to a dance that included a "donation ceremony," where he was presented with a pony and the name Ksapa, "the intelligent, understanding one."[75] The story indicates the survival of Dakota practices of bestowing names and redistributing wealth persisted despite federal censorship.[76] One year later, Howe was sent to Pierre Indian School, a boarding school run by the BIA. Language suppression, beatings, malnutrition, skin and eye diseases, and depression plagued his first three years of formal education. Howe related that when he became suicidal, school officials determined that the boy was hopeless and sent him back to the reservation.[77] There, his maternal grandmother, Shell Face, took over his education in Dakota spirituality and history. Howe wrote:

> Most of my background knowledge of the Dakota Sioux culture, though some of it was still practiced or carried on during my early boyhood . . . came from my grandmother, who lived to be one hundred years old. . . . I heard the stories and every detail of the Sioux culture, the attitudes, the feelings, the expressions, and meanings of the Sioux people of their day. She would not only tell these stories, but she would sing with the feeling of words in songs connected to the stories. . . . The beauty and truth of these people had inspired me in my work to try to equal the meaning and feeling in beauty of the verbal part with the visual form.[78]

According to the artist's biographer, Shell Face drew the symbols she recollected in the dirt, translating words and sounds into images.[79] The intimate relationship between aural and visual expression that characterized Dakota ritual would persist as a major theoretical preoccupation throughout the artist's career.

Howe's foregrounding of Dakota ceremonial and diplomatic idioms found support in his later art education. As I discussed in chapter 1, the

Studio School's founding director, Dorothy Dunn, encouraged Native students to base their tempera paintings on tribal customs, in keeping with the temporary reversal of federal assimilation policies during the New Deal. Upon enrolling in 1933, Howe was exposed to Plains hide paintings, Persian miniatures, and German expressionism.[80] Working in close dialogue with Pueblo and Diné peers, his early work contributed to what would later become codified as the "Studio style"—representational images of Indigenous ceremonial and everyday subjects, rendered in flat, opaque blocks of color without an articulated background. A hand-painted, signed poster from 1935, currently held in the Musée de l'Homme archives in Paris and briefly discussed in chapter 1, hints that the transatlantic purview of the Studio School may have elicited Howe's engagement with diplomatic idioms from the beginning of his long career as a painter. A woman stands in profile, lifting her arms diagonally; one hand grips a feathered pipe while the other gestures skyward with an open palm. She wears a yellow dress decorated with tassels and geometric patterns that suggest quilled, painted, or beaded buckskin. The buffalo skull that emerges from her skirt reinforces that this is Ptesáwi.

Howe and his classmates spent their Easter holiday weekend painting images on two-hundred machine-lettered posters, which were rushed to Paris to advertise an exhibition of student paintings that opened at the Musée de l'Homme a few weeks later. The event was organized by Paul Coze, a French artist who supported Native performers abroad and directed an Indian hobbyist club based on extensive collections of Plains material culture that he assembled from several tours of North America. Howe likely met Coze during the man's visit to the Studio School the previous spring; perhaps he learned of the Frenchman's interest in pipe ceremonialism, which entailed "playing Indian" in fancifully crafted tipis in Paris.[81] White Buffalo Woman conspicuously directs the straight line of her pipe at Coze's name, as if to issue an invitation. While Coze welcomed the students' creative contributions to his circle of artists, hobbyists, and ethnographers in Paris, Howe summoned Coze to join the relational web of Dakota kinship and political power—a circle that had recently expanded to include the "élèves de l'école indienne de Santa Fe," Howe's new artistic community. Already in 1935, he wed the ceremonial and diplomatic significances of the pipe to engender a symbolic exchange between members of distinct collectivities in what Dunn characterized as an "act of international goodwill."[82] Here, and in many subsequent

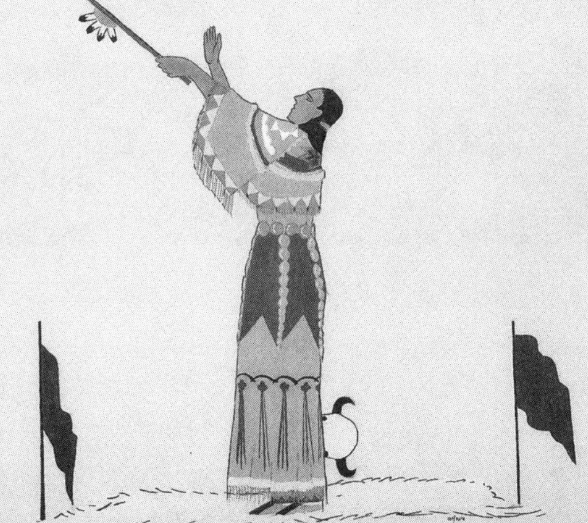

5.8

Oscar Howe, poster announcing *Art Peau-Rouge d'aujourd'hui*, 1935. Tempera on paper, 20 × 13 in. Muséum national d'Histoire naturelle, Santa Fe, New Mexico, with permission of the Oscar Howe Family.

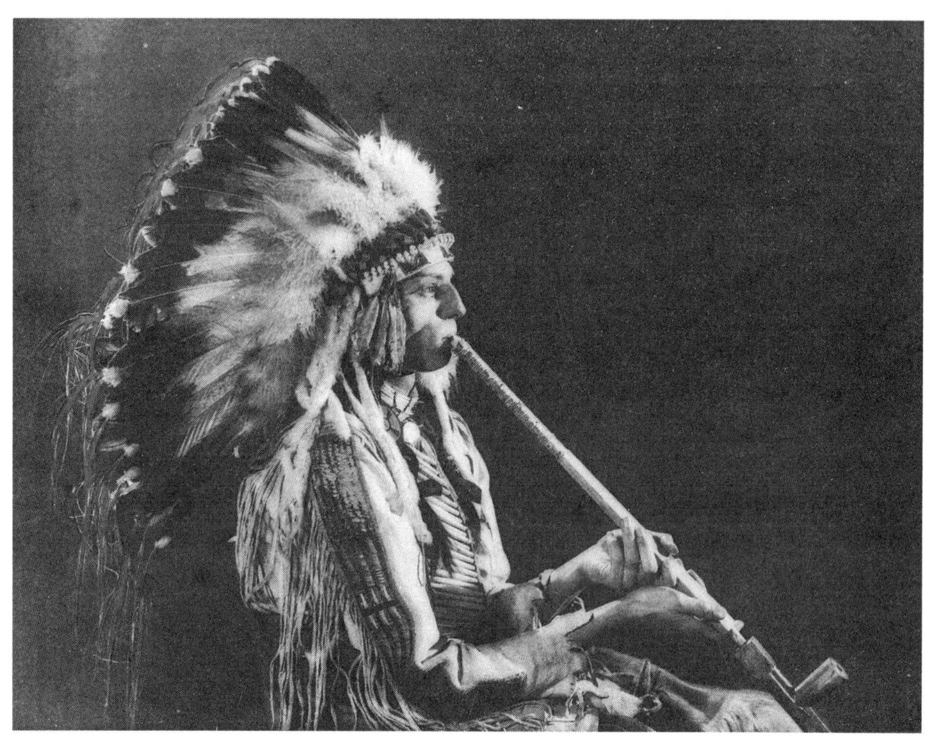

5.9

Hand-colored photographic portrait of Paul Coze, ca. 1928. Provided by
Patrick Bertrand.

....

Studio School exhibitions, the artwork traveled in the artist's stead, acting simultaneously as a translator and ambassador.

After working as a muralist for the Works Progress Administration
and serving in World War II, Howe resumed his research into Dakota art
at the University of Oklahoma in 1952. That year marked the retirement
of the Swedish American painting instructor Oscar Jacobson, who since
1926 had supported Native artists in translating Plains artistic traditions
into modern media on a path parallel to that of the Studio School. Jacobson began collecting Howe's work for the university museum (now
the Fred T. Jones Museum) in the 1930s and commissioned the younger
artist to illustrate *North American Indian Costumes, 1564–1950* (1952),
a limited edition portfolio of pochoir prints published by C. Szedwicki
in Nice, France.[83] Howe's MFA thesis established a theory of Indigenous
modernism that diverged from Jacobson's construal of Native artists
working intuitively in relation to nature, a stereotype that evacuated

::::::::::

the cultural complexity and creative agency of Indigenous makers.[84] In the text accompanying an exhibition of his paintings, Howe emphasized original "intellectual insight" and "conception over perception," tenets that led him toward abstraction.[85] His rhythmic and orderly patterns and colors were a formal means of expressing "the Indian's poetic and religious concepts of nature . . . philosophically the Indian is within the environment of nature."[86] Howe's thesis further aligned his straight and broken lines with Dakota belief in "unrelenting truth or righteousness," an ethics derived from nature and embodied in customary geometric arts.[87] Painting the earth was presented as a matter of profound ethical and aesthetic inquiry.

As a professor of art at the University of South Dakota, Howe refined these ideas by correlating his artistic process with the historical practice of recording important Dakota events by painting images on hide. He described a "painting of the truth" ceremony comprised of a speaker who relates the event, an artist who renders it visually, and selected witnesses who verify the artist's interpretation. The painter would plan the entire design in his mind beforehand as a series of "aesthetic points." He would then execute it by connecting the points with straight lines during the ceremony, engaging in "kinesthetic movement" that matched the rhythm of the oral recitation. What Howe called "truth" was embedded in his first language, Dakota, in so far as it came "from nature, closely aligned with nature, [and] describes natural happenings with much beauty." His position contrasted with much twentieth-century linguistic theory that posited an unbridgeable gap between symbol and referent, language and world. For Howe, the material-spiritual world generated and manifested in speech and song; he stated, "When an Indian speaks his formal language it is like nature speaking—maybe the sounds in the language came from the sounds of nature and the elements."[88] Composing a painting was conceived as a form of writing wherein the challenge was to equal the beauty and meaning of spoken words.

Echoing the ethical subtext of his great-grandfather Ho-hoo-non-pee's 1866 speech, Howe further stressed that verbal ("straight tongue") and visual ("straight line") communications were truthful and righteous in so far as they were aligned with the particular shape of Dakota land.[89] His ancestors derived an ethical-aesthetic principle of straightness from the open grasslands and ascendant sky of the plains region. Myriad sights and sounds exhibited "straight smooth movements," such as rainfall, lightning, sunbeams, and bird flight. Howe concluded, "The old Dakota proved a point in art that line does come from nature, and he made use of the truth-line to chronicle his environmental happenings."[90] Here again, Howe's thinking closely echoes that of Deloria, Jr., who argued that for American Indians, truths were not assumed to be universally valid in all times and places, but rather emerged "directly from the world around them, from their relationships with other forms of life. Context is therefore all-important for both practice and the understanding of reality."[91] As their words suggest, humans are not exclusive in their capacity for revelation; rather, truth is embedded and cocreated in interactions with other-than-human agents and processes. Anything but static, straight lines expressed the motion and vitality of a world animated by Wak'ą́ T'ą́ka. Linear geometric painting was conceived as a visual index of ecological relations.

Howe maintained that a privileged figure attesting to the "natural" origin of the truth-line is the *tahokmu*, or spiderweb, conventionalized in patterns of oblong diamonds such as those decorating Not Afraid of Bear's tobacco pouch. He related a story of a young man who tried to join a war party to go into battle only to find that he could not kill or steal. That night he had a dream in which he learned the meaning of all colors and designs. At the center of them all was a diamond, a geometrical nucleus from which other lines emanated. "When he awoke, he found he actually was looking through a dewdrop on a spider's web."[92] Howe accordingly claimed that "all Sioux painting used this design, its development, or parts taken from it."[93] Relating a version of the story that Howe told him in 1961, Amiotte elaborated that the young man saw a "multicolored prism-like display of light" from the dawning sun, illuminating the lines of the web and offering a vision of the "fundamental structures" uniting Dakota art and life.[94] A web consists of radial filaments connected by concentric lines; with its potential for indefinite extension, this form recalls the "huge design" of the world, the infinite mystery of Wak'ą́ T'ą́ka, and the interconnectedness of all beings.

Following Dakota understanding that power is bestowed on individuals through dreams and visions, Howe's story presents the capacity to paint as both a spiritual endowment and an ethical obligation. The young man's new knowledge was honored by the community, earning him the status of a "brave."[95] He was transformed from prospective warrior, charged with killing, to artist, tasked with the peaceful propagation of life. Sisseton Wahpeton Oyate scholar Kim TallBear similarly invokes the phrase "a relational web" as a spatial metaphor that "requires us to pay attention to our [more-than-human] relations and obligations here and now." She counterposes the ethics of the web to an American dream

:::::::::

that justifies violence toward Indigenous humans and other life-forms in pursuit of a futurist fantasy of plenty.[96] As a gift from Wakʿą́ Tʿą́ka, the tahokmu compels reciprocal acts of creativity. We can see how this principle undergirds the "peaceful lightning" in *Calling on Wakan Tanka*. According to the internal narrative of the painting, spiritual intercession is a response to ritual smoking. Yet the presence of the archetypal tahokmu is doubly emblematic of the artist's responsibility to perpetuate the dynamic web of being. Like the spider, he weaves a design that must be habitable and nurturing—one in which he is entangled from the start. Akin to the pipe bearer, he is an embedded participant in ongoing creation, a ceremonial agent. Painting *is* praying, an offering to Wakʿą́ Tʿą́ka. It fulfills the obligation of the original tohokmu gift and compels favor in turn, moving along the chain of reciprocity that binds "all our relations."

RELATIONAL MODERNISM AND THE SPIDERWEB

Howe claimed a wholly Indigenous origin for the tahokmu. Yet in practice the capacious design principle mediated his engagement with artistic modernisms that had long excluded Native makers while encouraging the appropriation of Indigenous forms. In his foundational account of postwar cultural politics, *Native Moderns: American Indian Painting, 1940–1960*, Bill Anthes positions Howe and his Indigenous peers as negotiators of a long-standing, fantastical colonial binary: to be Native was to be primitive, traditional, communal, bound to place and past; to be modern was to be individual, inventive, universal, belonging to a (placeless) present and future. Here the salvage ethnographic paradigm of the nineteenth century persisted, suppressing or devaluing transcultural forms as evidence of atrophy. Anthes clarifies that a persistent myth of "two worlds"—one Native, one modern—meant that "Native modernism engages—whether by design or circumstance—the politics of modern identity."[97] By conjoining the signs of "Native" and "modern" and their seemingly apposite meanings, Howe's painting practice refused the exclusivity of these terms.

Building on this framework, I propose that Howe's art and theory were generative of still another set of terms for thinking through Indigenous people's role in modernity. As I have underscored, customary Dakota culture was never a monad; leaders practiced sensuous modalities of persuasion, including the incorporation of foreign materials and motifs into diplomatic arts, to negotiate their alliances with other collectivities before and during colonization. Howe's insistence on the ongoing dynamism and relevance of such relational idioms included, but also exceeded, questions of human identity and difference. I read his merging of aesthetic traditions as an analogous practice of diplomatic weaving, a means of forging relationships of kinship among disparate human group and the more-than-human agencies at stake in the ceremonial arts that he so vehemently defended. Beyond the "and" of hybridity, his work superseded the anthropocentrism of the Native-modern binary as the ground for what was realizable in both politics and art. The tahokmu effectively concentrates this ethic-aesthetic. It embedded, rather than centered, human relations in a wider sphere of ecological reciprocities. I propose that Howe deployed it to widen modernism's relational web, treating art as an alternative arena for a sensuous practice of diplomacy that was routinely suppressed in formal political contexts.

Here, the differences between Howe's translations of Dakota aesthetics and dominant discourses and practices of modernism are significant. A long-standing art historical method of comparison remains useful for grasping this relationship, so long as the focus remains on the entanglement, rather than autonomy, of the things compared. Beyond the stylistic commitments of his paintings, Howe utilized comparative methods in his role as professor of art at the University of South Dakota by lecturing on famous episodes in Euro-American modernism alongside underrepresented Native American artistic traditions. Given that press coverage of Howe's mature work regularly deemed it "cubist" and assumed a direct line of influence, a consideration of his relationship to the long life of that early twentieth-century movement is particularly revealing. Whether they celebrated, decried, or denied Howe's purported cubist influences, such accounts tended to map the artist's style neatly onto the Native-modern binary during his lifetime. For example, Will Robinson, director of the South Dakota State Historical Society from 1946 to 1968, used the comparison to disparage Howe's nonrepresentational leanings, writing that "his art is too modern and does too much offense to nature to appeal to me. . . . If you like unnatural semi-cubist art, Oscar is a good one."[98] In contrast, Frederick Dockstader, onetime director of the Museum of the American Indian, Heye Foundation, rejected the characterization of Howe's art as "Indian Cubism," citing unsupportable claims that the artist was ignorant of European precedents.[99]

The Philbrook Art Center episode is telling in this regard. Scholar and curator Mark White has recounted that "the abstract style of the painting [*Umine Wacipi: War and Peace Dance*], thought by many to emulate analytical cubism, surprised those people familiar with the works Howe had entered in previous annuals, inevitably leading the Philbrook's jury to perceive Howe's new style as a derivation of European modernism."[100] But there was nothing inevitable about the conclusion that Howe's painting was "not Indian." Although reproductions of the now lost painting are poor, we can discern that the five humanlike figures in shades of pink, lavender, and blue are composed of triangular and rectilinear building blocks similar to those that appeared in his later tahokmu paintings. Instead of a central diamond, however, these and other inchoate, shadowlike forms appear stretched across the surface of an uneven yellow oval that intersects the edges of the paper, interrupting the traditional right-angled frame. Anya Montiel has written evocatively that "it seems as if the picture plane is distorted and is viewed through a fisheye lens where everything is convex, being stretched and rounded on the edges."[101] However, the oval lacks the machinic precision of a photographic apparatus. In place of a technological metaphor, I propose an organic one drawn from Howe's theories: it is as though we are watching the dance reflected and distorted on the surface of a shimmering dew drop. While the fragmentation of forms in analytical cubism has been likened to a shattered mirror in which "the violence of our era has metaphorically split the human image asunder," the convex lens of the dew drop assembles an ecological holism.[102] The artist's experiment in abstraction translated design principles that he emphatically located in Indigenous ceremonial arts and oral traditions, a position signaled by his use of both Dakota and English language in the title.

Scholars have repeatedly read the jurors' rejection as a defense of what had come to be seen as "traditional Indian style," the codified and kitsch products of Dunn's classroom where Howe got his start (discussed in chapter 1). Howe's response is in turn treated as an unambiguous critique of the Studio School: "Who ever said, that my paintings are not in the traditional Indian style, has poor knowledge of Indian Art indeed. There is much more to Indian Art, than pretty, stylized pictures. There was also power and strength and individualism (emotional and intellectual insight) in the old Indian paintings. Every bit in my painting is a true studied fact of Indian paintings. Are we to be held back forever with one phase of Indian painting, that is the most common way?"[103] The standard interpretation is less convincing when read alongside the gratitude that Howe elsewhere expressed for his tenure at the Studio School, where he felt challenged to "figure out one's own way of doing drawings."[104] One year after the Philbrook episode, Howe wrote another impassioned letter protesting comments made by Robert M. Quinn, a professor of art at the University of Arizona, at the Directions in Indian Art Conference (funded by the Rockefeller Foundation) in 1959. There, a plan for the Institute of American Indian Arts was born to replace the Studio School as ground zero for modern Native art. Quinn disparaged Dunn's teaching methods as a "fraud," stating that Persian rather than American Indian art was taught at the Studio School.[105] Howe responded, "We did a lot of research into tribal symbolism and relied on material handed down to us direct from our forefathers. I believe I can safely state, had it not been for the training at the Santa Fe Indian School under Miss Dorothy Dunn, you would have had no need to hold any conference on Indian Art (Painting) to day, because there just simply would not be any to speak about."[106] Howe's intimate, lifelong correspondence with Dunn reveals that the two shared ideas about the strength of customary Native arts as a foundation for modern painting and bemoaned the impoverished state of the market-driven discourse on Indigenous art, which Dunn felt was perpetuated by the newly formed institute.[107] Given this context, I surmise that the phrase "pretty, stylized pictures" was intended to address to the postwar calcification of the Studio School legacy, specifically Howe's contemporaries who made formulaic work to please patrons invested in salvage ethnographic paradigms, rather than condemn Dunn or the institution.

To my mind, the more radical passage in the letter offers a fundamental redefinition of customary Indigenous art as a generator of modernism. Howe's statement that there was "power and strength and individualism (emotional and intellectual insight)" in the historical arts that he studied is notable, given how ideologically charged the concept of "individualism" had become in Cold War aesthetic debates. It was a tenet of the United States' assimilation of Native people into a capitalist economy, designed to break bonds among communities engaged in collective landholdings, redistribution of wealth through gifting ceremonies, and inheritance by way of nonnormative kinship systems. As I explored in the introduction, reservations were cast as homegrown "hothouses for communism" in need of dissolution.[108] Here, the individual signaled an atomized wage earner or property owner deemed the proper unit of capitalism. Scholars have likewise articulated how the value of individualism was keyed to late modernism, specifically abstract expressionism, a favorite government export during the Cold War. As the story goes, American avant-gardes "remade the individual subject as transcendent and universal" by minimizing referentiality, a potentially dangerous signifier of the particularity and contingency of identity and tradition.[109] In each of these domains, Cold War agents equated individualism with capitalist subjectivity. Howe's pithy statement reclaimed the term as a customary Dakota value synonymous with "emotional and intellectual insight"—that is, with the special status granted artists as visionary participants in the ongoing creation of the world.

It is striking, in this context, that commentators regularly associated Howe's work with the older tradition of cubism rather than the contemporaneous avant-garde. While such anachronistic comparisons underscored Howe's unoriginality and derivation, I suggest that he embraced the intersection as an opportunity to expand his circle of legitimate art historical kin. In the decades after World War II, scholarship on cubism abounded, serving to anchor understandings of the evolution of formalist abstraction on both sides of the Atlantic. Clement Greenberg set the tone in his 1940 essay, "Towards a Newer *Laocoön*," arguing that "the destruction of realistic pictorial space, and with it, that of the object, was accomplished by means of the travesty that was cubism."[110] Readings of the paintings and collages of Pablo Picasso and Georges Braque as instantiating a radical turn away from European traditions of referentiality to articulate "the flatness of the surface" became de rigueur in subsequent decades. Such approaches located the cubist avant-gardes as the formalist forefathers of the abstract expressionists in a linear evolution of modernism. By the early 1970s, these interpretive frameworks came under scrutiny for their eschewing of sociopolitical significance, reflecting the upheavals of the civil rights era and burgeoning feminist and postcolonial methodologies.[111]

Howe anticipated the latter turn in his class lectures at the University of South Dakota by offering an idiosyncratic reading of cubism alongside historical Native arts. In several recorded sessions in 1960, he characterized the cubism of Pablo Picasso and Georges Braque as a "sophisticated game" in which "figures in the world are turned inside out and upside down" to "create a confusion or loss of identity."[112] At the same time, these new compositions reflected Picasso's education in "old primitive, African art, Indian art, World art, he studied it all and he also read a lot."[113] In a different lecture Howe noted that the cubists' ambition to achieve internal consistency through a build-up of uniform parts was "comparable to such works of primitive art as the American totem pole."[114] Rather than setting up a hierarchy between European modernism and its others, either by criticizing cubism's appropriation of "primitive" art or by celebrating the movement as an exclusive origin for subsequent modernisms, Howe opted for a neutral mode of comparison between equally valid artistic traditions. Here, cubism was like customary Dakota painting in that both addressed a community initiated in a particular aesthetic language. Howe's analysis of a culturally specific cubist collective challenged the primacy of the individual artist-genius as well as the universalizing assumptions of formalist art history that dominated scholarship on cubism and its legacies.

Yet the aim of the exercise was not to deconstruct the avant-garde. Rather, Howe established a foundation for mutual legibility and exchange across different but equal creative traditions. To instill comparable familiarity with Native American and Euro-American art histories in a new generation of practicing artists in 1960 marked a radical departure from mainstream art historical pedagogy centered on a highly exclusive canon. Now, Howe could situate his own practice in relation to cubism without assumptions of derivation and anachronism. In 1963 he told his students, "Looking at my paintings you'll notice that from the first one, it's gone into more cubistic, perhaps more geometric, at least more lines and more straighter lines. This comes also from the Sioux Indian pictograph writing which says that a straight line is righteous and it is the truth."[115] Holding firmly to Dakota foundations, he could comfortably draw associations with a classical genealogy of modernism to invite a relationship without hierarchy. His statement further suggests that superficial formal similarities had profound epistemological and ethical stakes, namely concerning the nature of truth.

Among his most abstract mature works, *Rider*, completed in 1968, is a strong candidate for exploring these themes (plate 13a). The title sends us searching for a figure on a horse, a project that is stymied as we become caught in the dense web of a double tahokmu. Two irregular blue diamonds float in a sea of yellow. They at first glance appear as layers sandwiched between the colored ground and the cacophony of linear geometric shapes in shades of brown, purple, black, and white, suggesting shallow spatial recession. This possibility is overturned as we focus attention on the lower left and right quadrants, where the orange plane has sliced wedges into the diamond. On the left, a triangle and square of the same shade impede the cohesion of other shapes. Parts retreat, only to surface again, in a situation of entanglement. Thin spears and whispy hairlines cluster in energy zones that expand toward the edge of the page. As our eyes move, the composition seems to pulse and radiate.

::::::::::

To align *Rider* with the increasingly contested formalisms that drove
the contemporaneous study of modernism entails reading its geometric
shapes as the building blocks of an autonomous world, elevated from
the continuum of mute matter by the inventive subjectivity of the artist. Period analyses of cubism held that its radical contribution lay in
the embrace of signs severed from worldly referents; now "the plastic
arts were freed from the slavery inherent in illusionistic styles."[116] For
formalists such as Clement Greenberg, the end goal was the embrace of
flatness as a fundamental condition of painting, while for advocates invested in semiotics such as Rosalind Krauss and Yve-Alain Bois, the key
insight was that art could function as a language of arbitrary signs un-
hinged from their worldly referents.[117] In either case, art is locked with
the artist inside an anthropocentric universe that is severed from the
earth.[118] This position contrasts with Howe's assertion to his students
in 1960 that "there's no sharp division between human and animal art."
He continued, "In the arithmetic design of a spider's web, utility and
beauty are inseparable. . . . Here nature shows man the way to develop
the geometric ornament of his own after her models. . . . The art of man
is part of nature's total creation."[119] Rather than liberating art from the
"slavery" of imitation, Howe saw the material products of human hands
as fundamentally embedded in earthly patterns. While he stipulated that
some humans are unique in making nonutilitarian art "for purposes of
self glorification," the products remained ontologically akin to those of
animal manufacture, just as all life-forms are related without hierarchy
in a wak'ą world.[120]

Howe's use of the tahokmu formalized a set of possibilities for
imagining the intimate relationship between image and world. To recall
his story of its origins, the web is contained and miniaturized through
the lens of a dew drop. Here the "frame" for the image is not a severing device, a window onto an artificial view that has replaced earthly
referents. Instead, the dew drop circulates with the spider through
a shared milieu. It is caught in the web, as much as the web is caught
in it. Dew is a mutable element in cyclical processes of environmental
exchange, just as the lens of the human eye is continuous with the liquid, porous, sensing body. The lesson of the dew drop is to call attention to the ecologically integrated and relational nature of makers and
made things. We might consider that a painting, like a dew drop, is less
a window, an architectural device that partitions human and land, and
more an ecological lens, an embedded device that concentrates a link in
a mesh of material relationships. A tahokmu composition is at the same

time an organized microcosm of the replete design of the world. The orb condenses and miniaturizes interdependencies that are otherwise too durational, diffuse, or complex to be sensible to human beings.[121] The spider/artist weaves/paints a web/composition while inhabiting it. The dew-painting cradles the image while caught in it. Neither painter nor painting can be divorced from the earth.

A spiderweb is a particularly potent figure for conceiving of ecological embeddedness. Its efficacy as a home effectively captures the etymological root of ecology in the Greek term *oikos*, or "household." Ecology was first coined by German zoologist Ernst Haeckel in 1866 to conceive of the irreducible relationship between organisms and their environments.[122] As the spider constructs a web-home, it joins heterogeneous elements of the material world together to form a unique relationship characterized by interchanges and dependencies. The web remains transparent to its surroundings, often hiding in plain sight. It is vulnerable to its milieu, continuously broken and rebuilt. As environmental philosopher Tim Ingold has theorized, its meshwork is "a tangle of threads and pathways. . . . It is because organisms are immersed in such force fields that they are alive. To cut the spider from its web would be like cutting the bird from the air or the fish from water: removed from these currents they would be dead."[123] Importantly, the web's radiating lines do not connect organism and world by way of terminations and enclosures; the points of contact are multiple and open-ended. As Howe repeatedly emphasized, straight lines should not be conceived as static delineations of objects nor fixed relationships between them, but rather as trajectories of movement and growth. The loose threads at the periphery of the web suggest the provisional nature of stopping points; the web-home is the nucleus of many journeys. Howe's title, *Rider*, conjures the Indigenous equestrian-warrior-hunters who followed herds of animals on seasonal migrations following the European introduction of horses on the plains. For customary Dakota, land was not strictly bounded and "home" was not propertied. Like the spider who carries and creates a household by unspooling radial, connective lines, the equestrian moves and lives within an ever-expanding web of mitákuye oyás'iŋ.

In *Rider*, Howe has furthermore doubled the design, entangling two sticky webs, two households. In the context of the colonial Native-modern dualism, *Rider* poses a relationship between *oikos* that is neither binary (differences reinforced) nor hybrid (differences overcome), so much as interdependent, constituted by social and material exchanges. There are hints of referents for this consideration. The predominant blue and yellow conjure the expansive prairies and skies of Mnísota Makhóčhe, while certain shapes seem architectural; a rhomboid with a scalloped top allusive of a walled fort appears opposite a split triangle suggestive of a tipi. Yet nothing here is organized as in a traditional landscape. There is no horizon, no clear orientation, no figure-ground relationship, no measure of distance between subject and object, nor viewer and picture. *Rider*'s abstract composition could be described as ecological. Elements invoking landforms and human-built structures are reorganized outside of the conventions of naturalism to emphasize the dynamic filaments, the material flows that connect and reshape them. Put another way, the painting activates perception without perspective. It reminds us that we sense in so far as we are embodied, breathing inside cycles of air, water, and soil that cross the thresholds we construct. We are riders of growth lines that link our "house" to myriad others'.

This ecologically enmeshed painting recalls not only the animal teachers of Dakota design, but the material foundations of customary paintings in plant and mineral pigments on tanned deer or buffalo skins. The latter announce their vegetal and animal materiality at a glance, as the uneven planes and contours of stitched buffalo hides index bodies and shape the images inscribed on their surfaces. Yet the materials that Howe employed in his mature paintings are no less richly earthen. He insisted that industrially produced Fabriano paper and casein paint were qualitatively close to the skin paintings of his ancestors. Here, we may recall philosopher Timothy Morton's assertion: "Art is ecological insofar as it is made from materials and exists in the world. It exists, for instance, as a poem on a page made of paper from trees."[124] Howe worked with a skin-like page that was furthermore bound up with the colonization of the Americas; the prosperous Italian town of Fabriano, founded in the Middle Ages, milled fine papers variously made from pulped hemp, cotton, or linen rags, felted wool, and animal gelatin as early as the thirteenth century. Relying on imperial expansion to source large quantities of cloth, Fabriano became one of the first places in Europe to manufacture high-quality paper on an industrial scale. This served to establish the region of Umbria as an important printing center during the crucial early years of conquest in the Americas.[125] Italian paper hosted some of the earliest European-made images of Indigenous Americans, a process of "engraving the savage" that profoundly impacted those communities' reception and treatment in colonial metropoles.[126] Perhaps inadvertently, Howe's preferences placed him in a visual-material lineage linking industrial paper production, intensive consumption of water, plant, and animal resources, and the global circulation of images amid colonial expansion.

Howe meanwhile valued opaque, water-based casein paints derived from animal milk protein because they "keep the edges of the lines straight" and "the colors have their own surface movement," qualities he associated with the spare forms drawn by his ancestors.[127] Of ancient pedigree, such paints underwent a commercial revival during World War II, when the American company Sherwin Williams developed Kem-Tone, a variant that incorporated synthetic rubber and styrene to produce a fast-drying emulsion that did not spoil.[128] Howe probably encountered the recipe during his military service in North Africa, when he painted camouflage on army vehicles. Casein was valued by the United States government because it lacked reflective gloss and could not be detected by the new technology of infrared photography.[129] Howe's ancestors had mixed mineral and plant pigments with tree resin and boiled buffalo hoof jelly to create durable dyes.[130] His choice of manufactured casein paints relied instead on domesticated animals raised on industrial farms and chemicals produced in laboratories and factories. The artist stipulated adding water until the paint reached "dairy cream consistency," conjuring cattle ranches and farms that dotted the plains in the wake of the orchestrated destruction of buffalo herds.[131] Like the mined sand in Fred Stevens's sandpaintings discussed in chapter 2, Howe's materials indexed the colonial transformation of Indigenous land and bodies. They suggest a powerful need for an earth diplomacy that could reckon with the toxicity of colonial modernity. Such material malleability should not be read as a diminishment of the Dakota world, so much as a dynamic extension of the foundational principle of mitákuye oyás'iŋ. Howe's Yanktonai artist-ancestors readily incorporated glass beads of Italian manufacture, paper from ledger books, and other Euro-American products sourced through trade and diplomacy at military forts on the plains. Dakota beadwork, paintings, and drawings circulated back through colonial economies in a sensuous process of exchange, interweaving foreign materials and symbols into indissociable new wholes that expressed the potential for contact to generate kinship.

Rider's diplomatic sensibility is prefigured in a famous crayon and graphite drawing on paper by a Kiowa man named Wohaw, completed during his captivity at the US Army prison in Fort Marion, Florida, in 1877. A man stands with two pipes in his hands, offering them to a buffalo on the left and a cow on the right. Beside his left foot is a miniature semicircular tipi camp, while his right foot intersects a rectilinear grid suggestive of

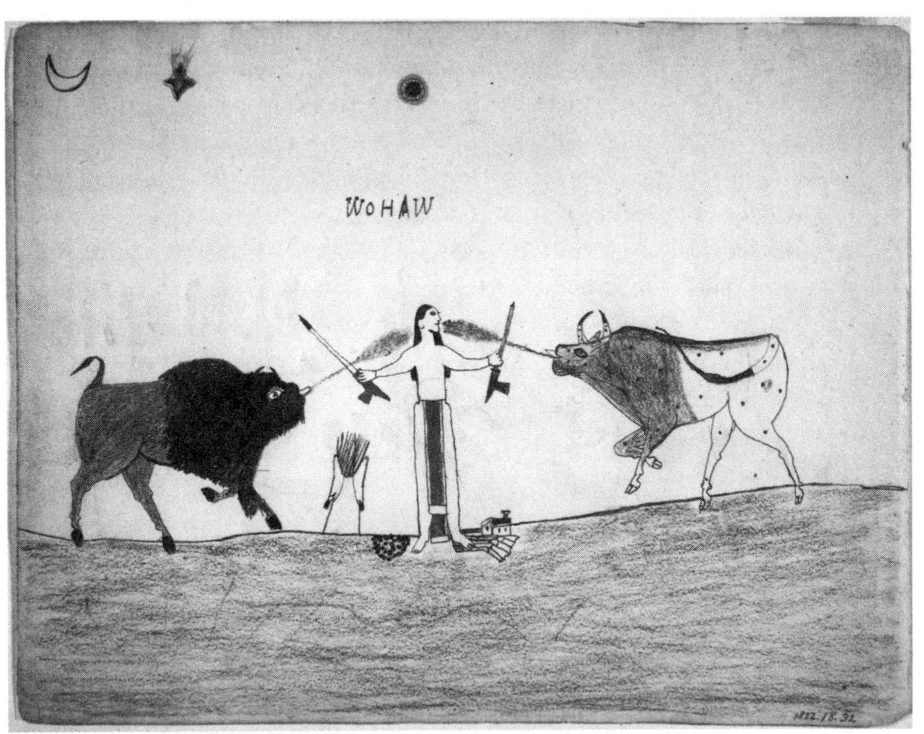

5.10

Wohaw, drawing, 1877. Graphite and crayon on paper, 8.25 × 11.75 in. Missouri History Museum, Saint Louis (1882 018 0032).

....

a tilled field and a wood framed house with a chimney.[132] The man faces right, as if to make peace with the white settler modernity represented by the cow, crops, and farmhouse. Yet, like Howe's, his negotiation of a transformed earth is infused with memories of the tipi circle and buffalo kin, indicated by the simultaneity of his pipe offerings and the reciprocal gift of animal breath that greets him from both sides. Against the assimilationist "two worlds" myth that was violently expressed in Fort Marion's mantra, "Kill the Indian, and save the man," Wohaw's relational circle expanded.[133]

Customary Dakota diplomacy produced a thorough interweaving of colonial and Native worlds with a larger cosmos. The doubled tahokmu of *Rider* likewise expresses an earth diplomacy coextensive with the changing earth and sky. The painting recalls that the rectangular enclosure of the fort and open circle of the tipi, architectures of distinct yet interconnected modernities, hosted rituals of alliance and adoption that transformed both societies before and during the brutal expansion of the United States. *Rider* does not meditate on this past in any overt way. Rather, I propose that its achievement is to transfer a historically grounded Dakota diplomatic sensibility into a communicable language of modernist abstraction. If, in Howe's estimation, cubism spoke to a particular community of aesthetic initiates, his deployment of an Indigenous ecological design principle widened the circle considerably. Just as Howe's forebears incorporated European materials and aesthetics into their diplomatic exchanges with colonial nations, the tahokmu effected translation without a loss of Indigenous meaning. Artist and artwork practiced a relational modernism, migrating Dakota idioms from the nation-to-nation contexts that were violently suppressed by Indian Removal and Termination.

WAR AND PEACE

Howe's story relating the origins of the tahokmu posited the artist as a peacekeeper, a diplomatic agent. Yet the artist's worldly and painterly commitments were routinely tested by the imposition of state-sanctioned violence, signifying violation of diplomatic contracts and rupture in the chain of reciprocity. Completed just prior to his Cold War tour, Howe's *War and Peace Dancer* (1970) explicitly engaged this dilemma, linking the tahokmu to pipe ceremonialism as well as the artist's long-standing preoccupation with the theme of war and peace (plate 13b). A single oblong, irregular diamond in a shade of deep ochre centers the composition. Triangles and quadrilaterals in warm browns, purples, blues, reds, and black disassemble from its core. Long spears of purple and brown shoot diagonally to the edges of the page, suggesting forceful movement outward. The tahokmu divides the page into quadrants of rich cream and blues, suggestive but never designative of prairie lands and vast skies. The clear articulation of a head and hand emerging from the rightmost facet of the diamond sends us searching for a body; the blue, red, and black triangles become like arms, shoulders, and folded robes. A small red and brown object in the shape of a cross lies next to the hand. Here, as in the face and fingers, Howe has precisely shaded the planar geometry to create dimensionality, producing an image that shifts between patterned abstraction and narrative representation. Embedded in the ecological web of tahokmu, the human figure "gazes at a broken peace-pipe hatchet, knowing the symbolic meaning," in Howe's words.[134]

Manufactured in both Europe and the Americas, pipe tomahawks typically featured an iron axe blade fused to a wooden pipe stem, thereby combining colonial and Indigenous technologies, materials, and meanings. As Scott Manning Stevens has analyzed, by the eighteenth century, tomahawks were associated with a sweeping stereotype of warlike Indians. They reified "a false dichotomy imposed by Euro-Americans of the difference between savagery and civilization."[135] At the same time, colonial representatives commissioned pipe tomahawks as diplomatic gifts to Native leaders during treaty negotiations to signal an increasingly disingenuous choice between war and peace. In *War and Peace Dancer*, only the axe head remains, conjuring the failure of diplomatic negotiations—on what grounds, we do not know. Yet war is not the opposite of peace, nor is it inevitable. Other aspects of the painting establish the ambiguity and uncertainty necessary for ethical deliberation and choice. Howe described a dance in which each participant is dressed in red or blue to represent war or peace, respectively; the leader, shown in the painting, represents simultaneously "the ugliness of war and the beautiful serenity of peace" as he travels from tipi to tipi throughout the camp.[136] Howe's dancer merges the artist-peacemaker and warrior into one. Purples and browns further muddy the clarity of the political binary mapped onto the pipe tomahawk and primary colors.

War and Peace Dancer provides a contact point between Howe's theories of customary Dakota arts and the roiling political present he negotiated as artist-turned-diplomat. It was completed during ongoing domestic and worldwide opposition to the United States' role in Vietnam, the acceleration of AIM, and Howe's own preparations to assume the uncomfortable mantle of "American Specialist" on a nine-country tour abroad. The dancer faces an emblem of failed diplomacy, conjuring the tragic fate of Dakota negotiations with the US government from Indian Removal to Termination. Confronting the toll of broken treaties and stolen lands, AIM turned to modalities of (re)occupation and resistance, eventually taking up arms. What hope remained for customary techniques of political persuasion amid the colonial-capitalist lockdown of US-Indian relations? The Cold War broadened the frame for this question: Was diplomacy mere dissembling, variously a cover and a vehicle for the United States' ongoing imperial activities at home and abroad? As Jonathan Flatley has discussed in relation to Andy Warhol's work in the 1960s, the battlefields against domestic social justice movements and international Communism narrowed "the space we share with others" to the absolute poles of sameness (peace as assimilation) and difference (war as opposition).[137]

In withholding such binary choices, *War and Peace Dancer* mirrored Howe's lifelong enmeshment with government agents and institutions who played myriad roles in shaping Indigenous modernity. From the trauma of a military-style boarding school to the sympathetic revival of Native art and culture at the Santa Fe Indian School, he was intimately subject to the BIA's contradictory policies regarding assimilation. His stint as a muralist for the Works Progress Administration continued that theme, only to be curtailed by World War II. Howe negotiated his role in the war with a characteristic will to compromise: "I certainly didn't like the idea, the war ideas, but I thought of doing my duty the best way I can. I was asked to go to officers' training school five times. I refused."[138] Howe's artistic talents were redirected toward drawing technical maps for his battalion as well as painting camouflage on army vehicles.[139] The government continued to shape his postwar institutional path: the GI Bill paid for Howe's bachelor degree at Dakota Wesleyan University, where he began his teaching career, and he worked for the BIA as the director of arts at the then-reformed Pierre Indian School before accepting a long-term position as a professor at the University of South Dakota in 1957.[140] His work was subsequently collected by the Indian Arts and Crafts Board and featured regularly in the annual Invitational Exhibition of American Indian Paintings in a dedicated Department of Interior gallery in Washington, DC.[141]

As he gained a reputation as a talented artist and educator in South Dakota, Howe developed personal relationships with politicians of divergent sympathies. He enjoyed a particularly intimate friendship with George McGovern (1922–2012), a Democrat who represented South Dakota in the US House of Representatives in 1956 and in the Senate from 1962 to 1974. The fellow veterans met as students at Dakota Wesleyan University, where they shared an interest in regional history. McGovern had opposed Termination and the US offensive in Vietnam, introducing unsuccessful legislation to curb both in the Senate.[142] In 1957, he wrote to Howe asking for a loan of paintings to fill his bare office walls: "We have so many visitors that I am anxious for them to see the best products of SD art."[143] Inge Dawn Maresh recalls watching the funeral of John F. Kennedy on television in McGovern's Senate office in 1963 while on a family trip associated with Howe's solo exhibition at the Indian

Art Gallery in the Department of the Interior.[144] Subsequently McGovern and his wife, Eleanor, purchased a painting by Howe titled *Dancing Deer*, initially for the dining room of their home.[145] In 1973, the senator wrote to Howe, "You would be delighted to see how beautiful it is in our new office here in the New Senate Office Building."[146] Although they were not close friends, Howe also received support from Karl E. Mundt, a Republican South Dakota senator (1948–1973) who advocated for Termination while serving on the Indian Affairs Commission. The support of both senators was instrumental throughout the multiyear process of securing and realizing his invitation to tour with the DOS in 1971.[147] Mundt wrote to the program director, Virginia Cooper, "He is an Indian, an artist, a man who can explain his own paintings, and one who can contribute to the cultural life of his own nation and of others. . . . I endorse his application without any reservation whatsoever, and I urge you to try to find some spot for him in your program."[148]

Howe also befriended Benjamin Reifel, a Republican from South Dakota, the first Očhéthi Šakówiŋ politician elected to the House of Representatives (1961–1971) and an advocate for Native American artists. A former field agent for the BIA, Reifel continued to work with non-Native allies to promote the policies of President Franklin D. Roosevelt's "Indian New Deal," while acknowledging that "Indians cannot depend on the Interior Department to uphold its moral trust obligation" to protect Indigenous lands and sovereignty. Reifel's answer to this dilemma was strategic pragmatism rather than militant resistance to Termination. He urged his fellow Native Americans, "We are less than 1 million out of 220 million people. That means we have to cite the factual content of treaties instead of giving diatribes against the government. And we have to make an effort to find our friends."[149] While Howe similarly chose to build relationships with ideologically disparate subjects and forego direct action, he departed from Reifel's disparagement of activism. Howe wrote in a letter to Dunn in 1959, "Fortunately there are finally some young leaders coming up, there is quite a bit of protest now, still not enough yet." He described his support for Indigenous student organizing at the University of South Dakota, while indicating that his own worldly work lay in the vitalization of Native modernisms.[150] Howe's practice of aesthetic shapeshifting mitigated the polarizing politics of Termination and the Cold War while holding out the possibility of relational transformation.

In 1960, Reifel helped to arrange Howe's invited appearance on the popular television show, *This is Your Life*, where he was interviewed by Vincent Price, an actor, art collector, and chairman of the Indian Arts

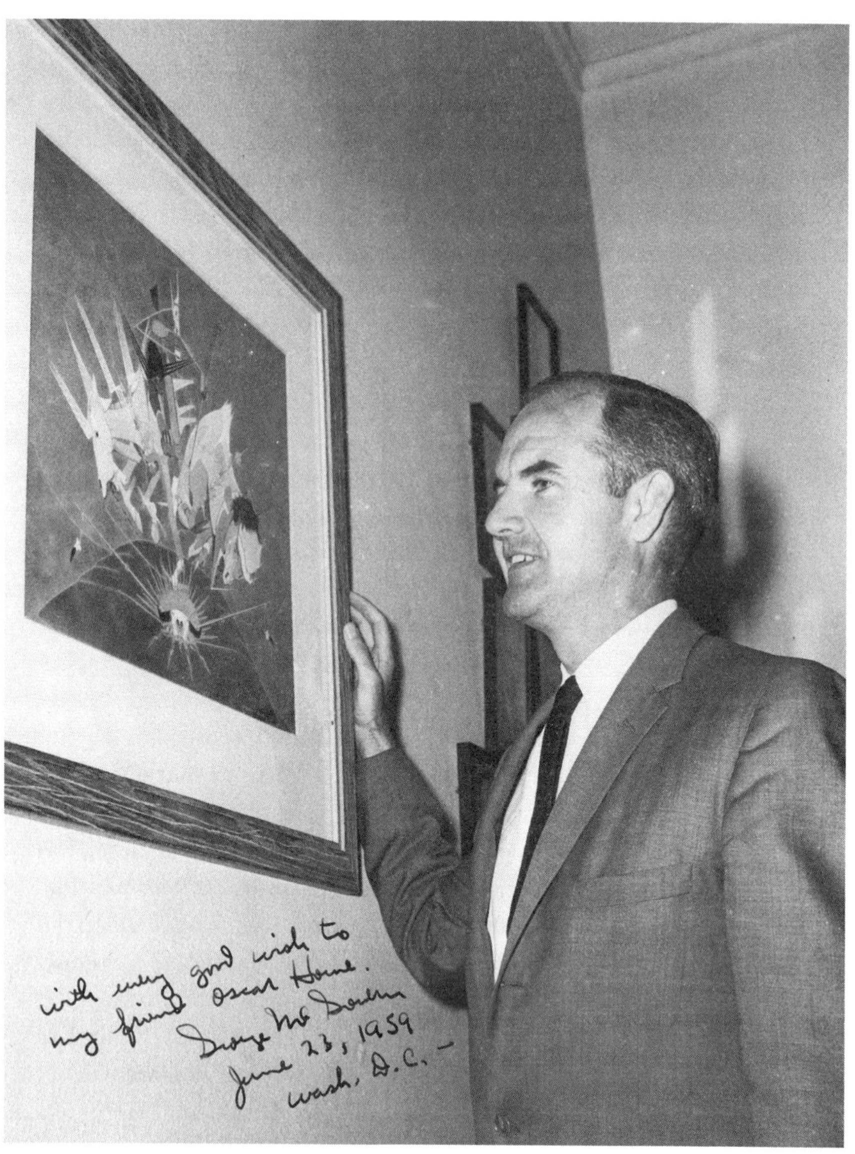

5.11

South Dakota Congressman George McGovern in his United States House of Representatives office with Oscar Howe's *Last Buffalo Hunt*, 1959 [584]. McGovern signed and dated the photograph with the note, "with every good wish to my friend Oscar Howe," on June 23, 1959. Box 1, Folder 2. Oscar Howe Papers, Photographic materials, MS-072. USD Archives and Special Collections, I. D. Weeks Library, University of South Dakota, Vermillion, with permission of the Oscar Howe Family.

and Crafts Board from 1967 to 1972.[151] The program included a close-up shot of controversial painting that Howe had just completed, *Massacre at Wounded Knee*. In his words, it was a "semi-objective" depiction of the infamous 1890 event, revealing US Cavalry troops firing upon a group of Lakota men, women, and children huddled in a pit that is rapidly becoming a mass grave. In the background at far left, a cavalryman waves the American flag while aiming a smoking canon at a group of standing women, whose arms are raised in surrender, dead bodies strewn at their feet. In 1959, Howe commented in a letter to Dunn about the in-progress painting: "Wounded Knee drove home the impossibility of escape from white subjugation. This massacre has remained in the minds of the Sioux as a symbol of injustice and abuse at the hands of the white man."[152] Following the work's reproduction in the *Mitchell Daily Republic* and the *Minneapolis Tribune* in February of that year, Will Robinson, director of the South Dakota State Historical Society for 1946 to 1968, immediately decried it as a "historical distortion," declaring that "there is not one iota of evidence to sustain the belief that there was any ordered or organized brutality."[153] Perhaps fueled by the crowd-generating aura of scandal, *This Is Your Life* host Ralph Edwards announced to the show's national audience that his production company had purchased the painting, "a masterpiece by an American Indian," to give to Dwight E. Eisenhower, president of the United States from 1953 to 1961. It remains in the collection of his Presidential Library in Abilene, Kansas.[154] What the Republican president thought of the painting remains a mystery, but certainly its unambiguous condemnation of orchestrated slaughter flew in the face of an administration that oversaw Termination as "another step in granting complete political equality to all Indians in our nation" and the "logical culmination and fulfillment of more than a hundred years activity by the Federal Government among the Indian people."[155]

Beyond its commentary on government injustices, *Massacre at Wounded Knee* nods to an art historical binary, a "frozen opposition between idealist formalism and socialist realism" that was mapped onto Cold War politics with increasing fervor.[156] The strong realist bent of *Massacre at Wounded Knee* is a stylistic anomaly in the artist's mature work. As Welch noted, the painting reveals "an explicit intent to place the victims and aggressors in clear divisions."[157] It is an opposition maintained by the ironic reversal of the primary color scheme, as "peaceful" blue soldiers attack "violent" red Indians. Offering an unambiguous countermemory of what many consider to be the culminating event of

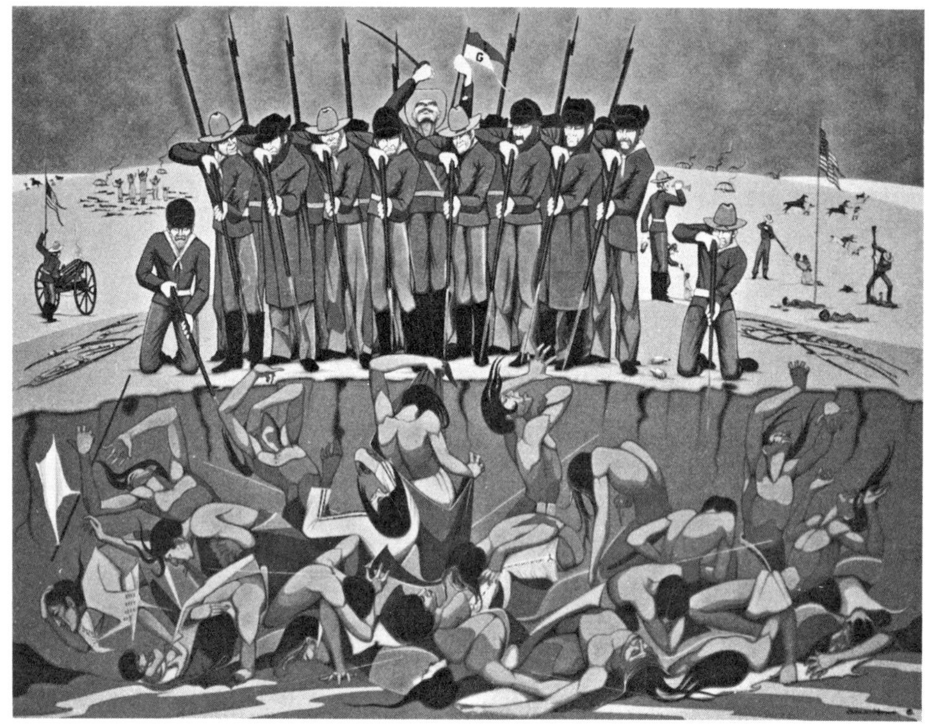

5.12

Oscar Howe, *Wounded Knee Massacre*, 1959–1960. Gouache on paper, 22 × 28 in.
Dwight D. Eisenhower Presidential Library. National Archives and Records Administration, Abilene, Kansas, acc. no. 60.618.

....

Indian Removal, the painting foreshadowed AIM activists' armed standoff against federal agents at the burial site in South Dakota in 1973. Yet elsewhere Howe took care to distinguish his painting practice from confrontational politics, insisting, for example, in his letter to the Philbrook that he would not be pegged as a "social protest painter."[158] Such a statement suggests that he was keenly aware of broader aesthetic debates that villainized social realism as propagandistic illustration in the service of Communist authoritarianism—an association that *Umine Wacipi: War and Peace Dance* visually rejected. Two years later, *Massacre at Wounded Knee* similarly served to cancel the image of Howe as a unilateral champion of abstraction-freedom-individualism, a cluster readied for appropriation on behalf of Cold War capitalism. Seen together, the paintings clarify the artist's refusal to be pinned to one side of an aesthetic-political binary.

Howe did not sustain such extreme stylistic swings; his subsequent work characteristically wed geometric abstraction and representational elements into seamless wholes. This aesthetic elasticity opened onto a degree of political flexibility, ultimately serving a capacious project of building and maintaining good relations amid the widespread hostilities of the 1960s and 1970s. I suggest that this process entailed neither capitulation for selfish gain, nor strategy in the service of a defined political goal. Rather, I take seriously the Dakota diplomatic underpinnings of Howe's paintings and the noninstrumental relationships he formed around them. Here the artist's penchant for purple conjures yet another association for the web of tahokmu: Iktómi (Spider), a Očhéthi Šakówiŋ trickster who invented language, stories, and games. Iktómi is a morally ambivalent character, "neither good nor evil," capable of morphing between animal and human form and conversing with nonhuman relatives who cannot speak.[159] As Pekka Hämäläinen articulates in a sweeping reassessment of Lakota history, Iktómi offered guidance for Očhéthi Šakówiŋ to navigate the splintering effects of colonial warfare and displacement.[160] Hämäläinen writes, "By the mid-eighteenth century, the Očhéthi Šakówiŋ was expanding, contracting, and loosening at its seams all at once, coming on the verge of disintegration, only to find cohesion in its collective traditions, shared history, and age-old commitment to the idea of a single kindred community. It survived because of, not in spite of, its startling malleability."[161] Under such dire conditions, diplomacy upheld the possibility of transforming strangers and enemies— Indigenous, European, and their mixed offspring—into allies and even family. Even in the guise of warrior, Iktómi the entangler upheld the ever-present promise of relational change through "the alchemy of kinship."[162] This possibility is kept alive by Howe's painted dancers, fellow shapeshifters who maintain an open path when confronted with a broken pipe tomahawk.

SPIRITUAL REVIVALISM

In 1972, Howe completed two strikingly confident paintings centered on the cʼaŋúpa wakʼáŋ. They were produced on the heels of his Cold War tour and on the eve of the armed occupation of Wounded Knee, the most spectacular public event of AIM in 1973. These works suggest an expansive spiritual and worldly role for the contemporaneous revival of pipe ceremonies, one that pointedly circumvents the United States as the dominant agent of Indigenous politics. *Acannupapi* (*Pipe Ceremony*) depicts an ostensibly diplomatic gathering (plate 14). Two angular figures enfolded in garments of warlike red emerge from the center of a prism comprised of interlocking shards of peaceful blue. They face each other, their gazes focused downward on the pipe that they are passing between them. Unlike the solitary figure confronting a broken pipe tomahawk in *War and Peace Dancer*, their mutual, tactile connection to an integral tool of ceremony suggests the successful establishment of kinship and aversion of violence. A pair of golden tipis rise from the background of the vignette, indicating a possible context: an intertribal gathering, a meeting of oikos of the sort that defined life on the plains before and during colonization.

While Howe was painting *Acannupapi*, Vine Deloria, Jr., forecast that intertribal activism based exclusively on political outrage was bound to fail. He wrote in 1971, "For by returning to Indian religions, by adopting the traditional customs by which tribal members related to one another, by forming useful and efficient alliances with forces in contemporary society, by these means alone could the red men ensure their survival."[163] Deloria, Jr. described a political relationality born of ceremony, that is, an inspirited articulation of Indigenous power emanating from the land, rather than a purely oppositional force. His account was descriptive as well as prescriptive. Contemporaneous grassroots organizing among Indigenous spiritual leaders across the United States and Canada, including the establishment of the first Indian Ecumenical Conference in 1970, cultivated religious self-determination and cooperation across diverse spiritual persuasions in tandem with political justice.[164] Meanwhile the reprinting of *Black Elk Speaks: Being the Life Story of a Holy Man of the Oglala Sioux* in 1961 and publication of *The Sacred Pipe: Black Elk's Account of the Seven Rites of the Oglala Sioux* in 1967 helped to catalyze young, urban Indigenous activists, many of whom were removed from ancestral practices, to adopt a trans-Indigenous interpretation of Očhéthi Šakówiŋ spirituality. Amid an explosion of publications concerning Native traditions, the books formed "a kind of sacred national Indian religious canon" that bridged popular culture with academic study in emergent Native studies programs across the United States.[165] Smoke meanwhile connected the culturally and ideologically disparate constituents of AIM. A number of Očhéthi Šakówiŋ spiritual leaders applied the relational ethos of mitákuye oyás'iŋ to the challenges of coalition-building across factions that spanned reservation and urban Indigenous communities.[166] For example, Sicangu Lakota medicine man Leonard Crow Dog presided over a Sun Dance and other ceremonies "calling on

:::::::::::

the spirits for help, health, and strength" during the AIM occupation of Wounded Knee.[167] Ceremonial revivalism grounded AIM in a sense of collective origins, provided an internal mechanism for the negotiation of political grievances and goals, and facilitated cultural autonomy, regardless of whether US officials passed the pipe.

Yet the spiritual dimension of pan-Indigenous organizing was overshadowed by the "militant rhetoric and flamboyant style" of AIM's loudest leaders, which provoked the enduring stereotype of the Plains warrior in the dominant media coverage.[168] This tension was evident in the most public AIM event of 1972, the Trail of Broken Treaties, which coincided with the completion of Howe's sacred pipe paintings. Three car caravans departed from Los Angeles, San Francisco, and Seattle, stopped in communities with a high density of Native Americans to assemble participants, converged in Minneapolis (where AIM was headquartered), and continued on to Washington, DC. Their aim was to demand a meeting with BIA officials to present the Twenty Points Paper, a detailed path to Indigenous justice centered on the restoration of land, cultural autonomy, and equal standing as sovereign nations in relation to the United States. Notably, article 18 stipulated, "The Congress shall proclaim its insistence that the religious freedom and cultural integrity of Indian people shall be respected and protected throughout the United States, and provide that Indian religion and culture, even in regenerating or renaissance or developing stages, or when manifested in the personal character and treatment of one's own body, shall not be interfered with, disrespected, or denied."[169] Behind the paper's ostensibly unified demands lay a process of ceremonial revivalism that worked to knit disparate Native communities across the United States into new networks of kinship and alliance. Caravan leaders attempted to draw attention to trans-Indigenous diplomacy by declaring the BIA headquarters "the American Indian embassy," even as their bid for a hearing with the US government quickly broke down. In contrast, media coverage reiterated a narrative of militant opposition by highlighting the destruction of BIA files and desecration of the building during the subsequent occupation. This stereotype was cemented in the popular imagination when violence erupted during the armed occupation of Wounded Knee just a few months later. Picturing the intertribal "embassy" of the tipi circle, *Acannupapi* belies the predominant association of AIM—and by extension, all Native people—with an armed, antigovernment force.

A second sacred pipe painting, *Marpeya Wopazo* (*A Sign in the Sky*), entered this turbulent scene with a more far-ranging proposition for an earth diplomacy (plate 15). The highly schematic image foregrounds a pair of interlocking pipes as a means of engendering relations of reciprocity among not only disparate Native constituents, but all elements of the vibrating universe. The red and grey-tone instruments form a diagonal cross fused at center by a starburst—a burning mass of tobacco or a perhaps a supernova. Below, concentric ribbons of pale blue form a starry hexagon, tapering near the bottom of the page in the suggestion of a broken half-spiderweb, an airy, unfinished home that is open to new attachments. Angular tendrils of grey smoke emanate from the pipe bowls to arc across the web, while a mirrored set of coils encircles the bald eagle above, drawing the domains of raptor and spider into an open circle. As in *Calling on Wakan Tanka*, *Marpeya Wopazo* emphasizes "a sign in the sky," only now the means of prayer and responsive spiritual intercession are merged into a single, pulsing constellation.

Howe's ecorelational vision quietly contests the appropriation of the eagle on the United States coat of arms in 1782 to express the unity, sovereignty, and might of the new formed nation. In the latter representation, the eagle is emblazoned with an escutcheon in the colors of the national flag and clutches a bundle of arrows and an olive branch, mirroring the war and peace symbolism of the pipe hatchet. Turned in the direction of peace, the raptor's beak holds a banner inscribed with the phrase "Out of many, one," in Latin. Howe's majestic bird, a sacred messenger of Wakʿą́ Tʿą́ka in the spiritual economy of the Očhéthi Šakówiŋ, flies directly toward the viewer, wings outstretched in perfect symmetry, holding a ceremonial wand. His variant counters the implied absorption of the Očhéthi Šakówiŋ into the aspirational political totality of the United States, yet the circle remains pointedly open. Subtending Deloria, Jr.'s words, the painting quietly delimits the competitive nationalism modeled by the colonial state to locate Indigenous philosophical truth and political power in an earth diplomacy. The painting proposes an alternative path to peace through the nonassimilative relationality expressed by the web of mitákuye oyás'iŋ.

As much as *Acannupapi* and *Marpeya Wopazo* speak to the immediate tumult of Indigenous justice movements, they also conjure a quieter lineage for the revitalization of ceremony and diplomacy: artistic modernisms which had for decades engendered the translation of ancestral knowledge into vibrant new forms. The relational charge of *Acannupapi* and *Marpeya Wopazo* is doubled: both paintings simultaneously represent the entangling function of pipe smoking and embody the enmeshing of oikos through Howe's distinctive deployment of the point-to-point technique. Here, *Acannupapi* and *Marpeya Wopazo* occasion my final reflection on the efficacy of the artist's 1971 tour, particularly his seminars in Lahore and Karachi. Howe's pedagogy in Pakistan indicates just how far the connective potential of geometric abstraction could extend beyond the page, becoming a potent tool on an expansive path to "find our friends." Although his students did not hold a pipe, they nonetheless experienced something akin to its "significant feeling of being straight" when they mimicked Howe's gesture of connecting disparate points on the page before them. Like the angular smoke tendrils that connect bodies, land, and sky in the artist's mature paintings, the coordinated practice of drawing linear figures by "kinesthetic means" had the potential to create tactile, material bonds among participants. Howe's exercises paired embodied, intuitive experiences with an intellectual mandate; practicing ancestral Dakota design principles was meant to encourage students to find parallel inspiration in their own cultural idioms, such as the Persian miniature tradition that was taught alongside international modernist trends at the Central Institute of Arts and Crafts in Karachi, long familiar to Howe through Dunn's instruction at the SFIS.[170] As I have already discussed, Howe's pedagogy avoided the totalizing tendencies that some commentators have associated with modernist abstraction, particularly those that served the assimilative exercise of soft power during the Cold War. I have characterized his approach to form as relational rather than universalizing—that is, he encouraged the mutual translation of diverse aesthetic languages as a means of making kin.

The diplomatic potential of artistic modernisms is finally registered in the epistolary friendship that Howe continued with Arshed until his death. The first four years of this exchange reveal Howe's extensive efforts to reciprocate Arshed's hospitality by securing a position for the younger man to study and teach in the United States. The Dakota artist's efforts were pointedly stymied by the United States' ongoing involvement in the rupture between East and West as well as the unresolved conflict between Pakistan and India. In February of 1971, while Howe was still traveling, Arshed requested that his new friend serve as a recommender for his application to the Cranbrook Academy Scholarship for advanced studies in fine art.[171] Although the application was ultimately unsuccessful, Howe continued to petition McGovern for advice and assistance, writing, "My personal contact with Mr. Arshed has proven very favorable and most rewarding as a friend, teacher and artist. He is young, articulate . . . academically proficient in the field of teaching and has much individual art accomplishments. I regard him highly in his profession and as a person of much integrity."[172] McGovern responded regretfully in September of 1971 that "the present internal problems of the Pakistan Government have created serious problems with the on-going programs for this purpose."[173] The artists' interpersonal friendship thus operated according to values that were starkly absent from nation-to-nation diplomacy, where reciprocity was forever in ruins. Upon his eventual migration to the United States in 1975, Arshed wrote to Howe, "I shall always remember the part you played in making my dream true."[174] Today, the artist is internationally recognized as a leader of Pakistani modernism for his translation of customary Arabic calligraphic arts into precisely measured curvilinear and planar abstractions, an "expression of peace, serenity, and spiritualism" in the artist's words.[175] The two men's artistic trajectories, like their lives in general, relate in a manner akin to the crossing of pipes in *Marpeya Wopazo*.[176] Each line stretches simultaneous toward distinct ancestors, while "a flash of peaceful lightening" connects them in the larger design of the universe.

A crossroads in the map of Howe's own far-ranging artistic journey, *Marpeya Wopazo* also acts as a legend; it gathers key elements of his other paintings, clarifying their identities and interrelationships. Rendered in the artist's characteristic color-block geometries, the meeting of spider and bird realms connects the ecological foundations of Dakota diplomacy to his expansive practice of relational modernism. Like his contemporaries who were engaged in spiritual revivalism, Howe reprised ceremonial idioms for a shapeshifting aesthetic that answered to, but also transcended, the colonial-capitalist mandates driving the frontiers of Termination and the Cold War. *Marpeya Wopazo* contextualizes Howe's moment within the adaptive toolkit of his Dakota ancestors, who had long translated Indigenous relational values into their exchanges with diverse peoples and ensured the flourishing of earth diplomacy amid the devastations of Indian Removal. Howe's sacred pipe modernism provides a vital link in a relational imagination that has yet to be realized in the constricted sphere of international relations.

CONCLUSION

ARTIST-DIPLOMAT-VAMPIRE

::::::::::

IN 1972, during the first leg of his United States Information Agency (USIA) tour through Eastern and Western European capitals alongside the exhibition, *Two American Painters: Fritz Scholder and T. C. Cannon*, Fritz Scholder defected. The artist skipped out on his remaining engagements in Bucharest and convinced his local guide to take him to Transylvania. He climbed the stairs of "Dracula's Castle" with his then wife, Ramona Scholder, at sunset, telling her stories drawn from the vampire-themed books in his library.[1] Upon resuming his official tour in West Berlin, Scholder created at least eleven small paintings on portable canvases that he carried in his suitcase. He titled the series of chiefs and warriors with hungry, hollowed eye sockets *Indian/Vampir*. One of the works features the artist's own shadowed visage floating in a vivid red pool (plate 16). Seemingly painted in haste, the flow of crimson cuts a sharp line around the artist's black hair and torso, but it also spills inward. Blood-red demarcates an earlobe, outlines a deep furrow between two black caverns that swallow the eyes, and flecks the sickly yellow-and-pink skin. Scholder carried a self-portrait of the artist-diplomat-as-vampire home from his Cold War tour.

Indian/Vampir exploited numerous meanings attributed to the immortals as they traveled through Western European and North American popular culture. Bram Stoker's popular and long-lived 1897 novel inaugurated fascination with vampires throughout the English-speaking world. Along with casting multiethnic Transylvania as a "frightening region on the edge of Europe," Count Dracula and subsequent versions of the villain embodied the threat of reverse colonization—the resurgence of an arcane, racialized force that threatened the rational progress of empire.[2] In US horror films during the Cold War, the vampire slid from colonized to Communist threat. *The Return of Dracula* (1958), *Curse of the Undead* (1959), and *First Man into Space* (1959) featured repulsive immigrants and aliens infiltrating and infecting the nation.[3] Such plotlines converged around "the New World capitalist . . . [who must] hunt down and destroy the vampiric threat to emergent bourgeois dominance," as postcolonial critic Jean Fisher wrote. Her revaluation of the vampire as a model for creative acts that resist assimilation into normative knowledge regimes is equally relevant to Scholder's series.[4] The artist belonged to still another community of vampire-seeker, those who approached Transylvania not as a source of dangerous criminality and illness but a "magical realm that held the possibility of 'enchantment'" amid global modernization regimes that sought to banish alternative cosmologies.[5] Upon visiting, he declared it "a beautiful place."[6]

While undoubtedly canny about the vampire's shapeshifting in Euro-American contexts, Scholder was also intimate with the fate of the figure in Romania. In the 1960s, Western tourists began to flock to Bran's ("Dracula's") Castle near the city of Brașov in search of an experience to anchor the fiction. The mansion bore only a tenuous connection to Vlad III, a tyrannical fifteenth-century regional ruler who became dubiously associated with Stoker's novel in Cold War–era vampire literature. After socialist authorities restored and reopened the castle as a medievalist museum in 1957, the spectacle of spires and turrets jutting from a mountain of stone became an alluring destination for outsiders' vampire hunts. Romanian leadership meanwhile resisted the association between Transylvania and a blood-thirsty Dracula. Under the Communist dictatorship of Nicolae Ceaușescu from 1965 to 1989, Vlad III and other medieval authoritarians were lauded as heroes who defended the nation against foreign threats. Promoting a character of animalistic alterity contradicted Ceaușescu's attempts to rationalize, modernize, and unify the country, including polities targeting Hungarian and other ethnic minorities for assimilation in the Transylvania borderlands. In 1972, New York-based General Tours stepped in, working with Pan-Am Airline to launch the first Dracula-themed tour in Romania.[7] Visitors were advised to stock up on garlic to ward off evil.[8]

Scholder avoided the New York tour and its premier destination, Bran's Castle, scoffing at the "number of in quotations, 'official' castles of the historical Vlad the Impaler." Claiming to have done his homework, he climbed to an unmarked ruin on top of a mountain.[9] Scholder's tenure at Institute of American Indian Arts (IAIA) in northern New Mexico had brought him into close contact with hordes of "ugly tourists" in search of a different supernatural spectacle: Pueblo ceremonies.[10] The artist would likely have agreed with Cree folksinger Buffy Sainte-Marie's determination that white Westerners were the truest vampires, adept in cultivating primitivist desire and extracting value from Indigenous and majority world cosmologies. In 1967, Sainte-Marie described countercultural fascination with Indians as "the weirdest vampire idea," declaring, "The white people never seem to realize that they cannot suck the soul out of a race."[11] General Tours' establishment in a remote, contested corner of a socialist nation testified to the extraordinary reach and assimilative power of American capitalism in the late Cold War.[12]

Yet Scholder knew very well that he could not claim a position outside of this circuit of desire, a reality he had spent several years exploring in paint. Like many of the artists in this book, he willingly fraternized with the USIA, an agency that both fed on and fueled the hunger of which Sainte-Marie spoke. In a later interview, Scholder recalled being "naive" about the United States' Cold War soft power machine until his arrival in Bucharest. The artist found a picture of himself with students at the IAIA, reproduced in a beautiful color publication titled *America* that was sitting on the coffee table of an ambassador's palatial home. The text made no mention of his resignation from the school due to BIA mismanagement in 1969. Scholder concluded, "I realized that this was propaganda."[13] Building on his earlier exploration of delegation portraiture in *Indian and Rhinoceros* (see the introduction and plate 1), *Self Portrait as a Vampire* characteristically acknowledged the Indigenous artist-diplomat's dependency on the lifeblood of the very nation that oppressed him. It is a portrait of impurity more than alterity. It registers the ambivalence of intimacy, a liminal condition of being with—but not wholly of—settler colonial power.

At the conclusion of his Romanian leg, USIA officials pronounced Scholder a "definite program asset." They made a familiar claim that his works "evidenced the vitality and freedom of expression that characterize creative life in America."[14] Contrast this with the ravaged, skull-like visage in Scholder's *Indian with Beer Can* (1969), which Comanche curator Paul Chaat Smith characterized as "the visual equivalent of storming the Bureau of Indian Affairs in Washington, D.C., or occupying Wounded Knee on the Pine Ridge Reservation in South Dakota, only darker and scarier."[15] While the tour excluded this most famous and controversial of Scholder's paintings, Romanian reviewers nonetheless noted something deeply amiss with the artist's figuration. Scholder similarly bent the visual languages of Pop and expressionism toward themes of liminality and violence in touring works such as *Dog and Dead Indian (Warrior)* (1971). One reviewer noted the "unsettling . . . psychological and social content" and concluded that "to be an Indian is to be unfairly treated by history, throwing the lasso around the neck of the locomotive which *is* history and its laws."[16] The reference to cowboys and railroads hints at the influence of "red westerns" throughout Eastern Europe, which often challenged imperial discourses of progress through narrative reversals favoring Indigenous protagonists.[17] Another writer determined that "[Scholder's] figuration . . . places the Indian human in the background of panic and loneliness. The artist . . . displays a type of humor which threatens to become sarcasm when his direct expression employs phantasms of his tradition."[18] The author cited *Indian and Rhinoceros* as evidence of the artist's cynicism, suggesting that the significance of the unused "peace pipe" as an emblem of diplomatic betrayal was not lost on her (see the introduction). While comments in the visitors' book kept by USIA officials were generally laudatory, a less sympathetic entry determined that "the American embassy which supervises the ways by which the USA is made known, should detect what is useful and what isn't. . . . The impression upon the youth is unfavorable."[19] For two decades, the USIA had counted on Native American art to assure international visitors that the United States offered diverse communities safe harbor—provided they were wage-earning, freedom-loving capitalists. With AIM occupations and Vietnam War atrocities in the international news, Scholder's paintings tested the limits of the USIA's spurious multiculturalism.

Earth diplomacy and the federal government parted ways around this time. Native artist tours notably fell off the USIA agenda in the wake of AIM's most visible actions, including the aforementioned Trail of Broken Treaties to Washington, DC, in 1972 and the armed occupation of Wounded Knee in South Dakota in 1973 (see chapter 5). As the global press covered this surge, tours of Native art became a diplomatic liability for the United States.[20] Reflecting on IAIA's Cold War activities, James McGrath recalled that the "tide turned with little or no political support" after secretary of the Interior Stewart Udall and his wife Lee

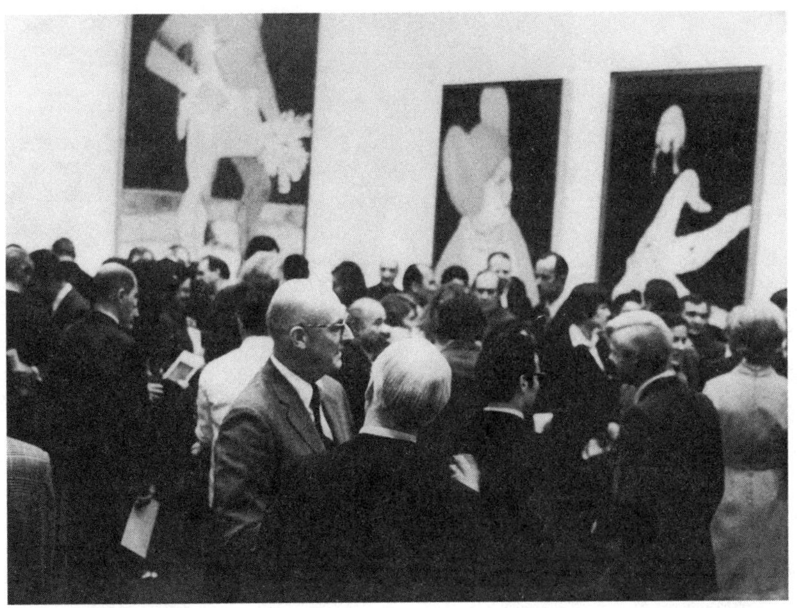

C.1

Opening of *Two American Painters* at the American Library in Bucharest, Romania, 1972. American ambassador Leonard C. Meeker is seen at center in front of the Fritz Scholder paintings *Super Indian No. 1* (*left*), and *Dog and Dead Indian (Warrior)* (*right*). The painting at center does not appear in the catalogue and remains unidentified. Smithsonian Institution Archives, Washington, DC, SIA 2015–000189.

....

Udall, who were major supporters of Native art, left Washington, DC, in 1969.[21] Other categories of creative practice also proved to be politically unruly. By the early 1970s the Cold War art offensive as a whole was faltering because, as historian Michael Krenn has argued, art could not be held apart from the cacophony over Vietnam and other signs of US imperialism—it was "terribly imprecise" as a weapon.[22] Culminating two decades of fertile yet fraught creative activity mediated by the US government, Scholder's tour brings this book to a close.

But *Earth Diplomacy* does not open with a ceremonial pipe, only to end with the nowhere of diplomatic failure. As my introductory reading of Scholder's *Indian and Rhinoceros* established, Indigenous American artists were pressed to triangulate their relationships to the majority world with settler colonial governments during the Termination era— and indeed, throughout much of the postcontact history of North America. Scholder's creation of *Indian/Vampir* signaled mounting skepticism

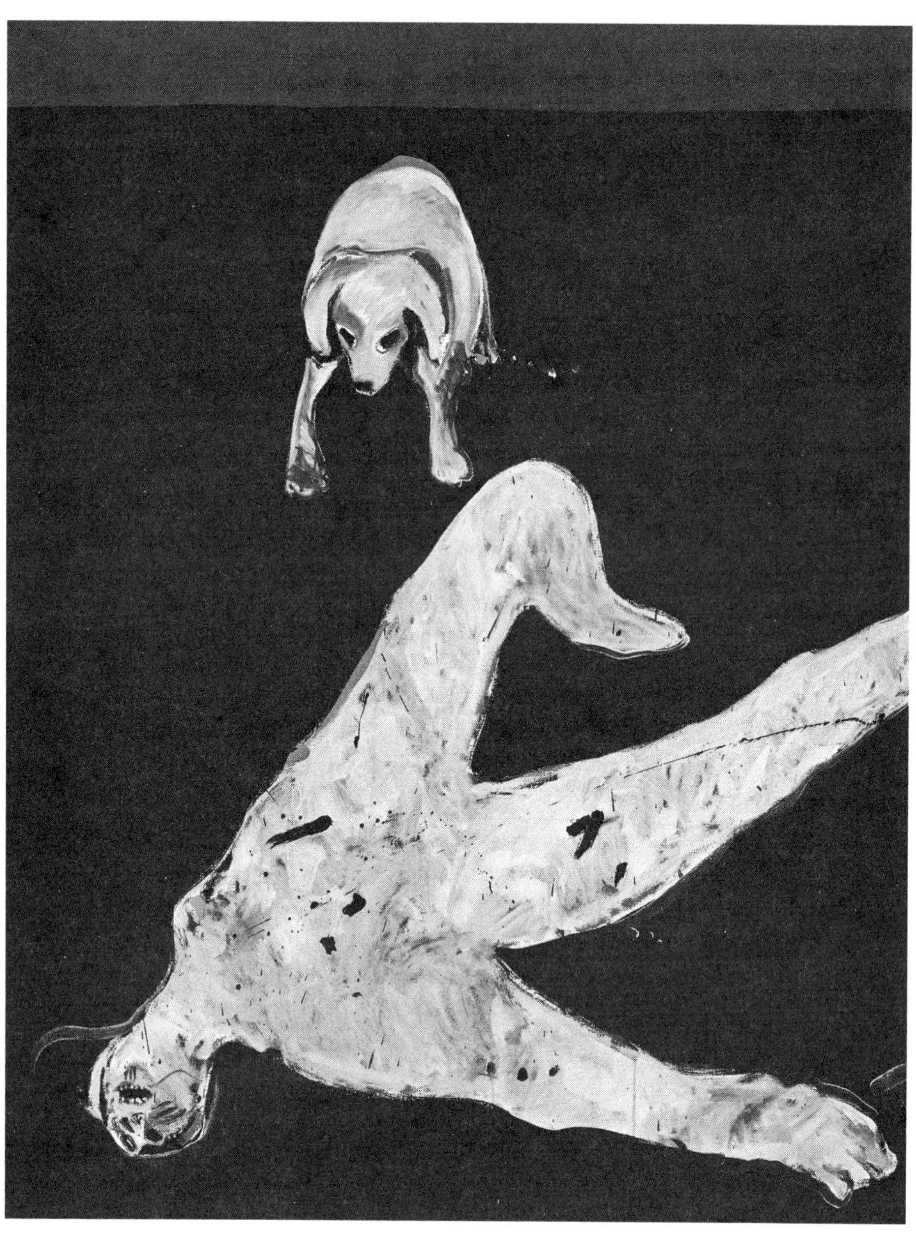

C.2

Fritz Scholder, *Dog and Dead Indian (Warrior)*, 1971. Acrylic paint on canvas, 72 × 54 in. Promised gift from Vicki and Kent Logan to the collection of the Denver Art Museum.

toward Indigenous relationalities that overly relied on the friendship and goodwill of colonial agents. Yet turning one's back on diplomatic negotiations with the United States did not foreclose the abundant possibilities for relating to others. Consider, for example, that under Ceaușescu, multiethnic minorities were subject to Romanianization, an aggressive policy of assimilation that mirrored Indian Termination.[23] Scholder's tryst with Transylvanians, like his pipe-bearing chief, explored the grounds for alliances with dispossessed communities around the globe—a possibility engaged by all of the creative agents in this book.

Interpreted through the lens of earth diplomacy, vampires also have the potential to activate more-than-human kinship, reciprocity, and regeneration. Human merges with bat, connected by a material conduit of blood-food necessary for survival. Their confluence concentrates spiritual power, conveying immortality beyond the finality of death (the endgame of Western progress the world over). Persisting through upheavals across ages, vampires contradict colonialism's will toward extinction. Theirs is the spiraled temporality of renewal, of simultaneity with ancestors, future generations, and other-than-human beings, common to Indigenous ceremonies.[24]

Indian/Vampir foreshadowed new possibilities for earth diplomacy that were then gathering force beyond a long-standing Euro-American colonial axis. As I have indicated throughout this book, Native American political organizing, galvanized by Termination and inspired by decolonization in the majority world, accelerated throughout the Cold War and informed the rise of Red Power. In 1972, Indigenous delegations from the United States and Canada attended the United Nations (UN) Conference on the Human Environment in Sweden but were not yet organized in solidarity. During the occupation of Wounded Knee the following year, AIM representatives pressed the UN office in New York to recognize the United States' abrogation of treaties as a violation of human rights.[25] A more sustained campaign for international support was launched with the establishment of AIM's International Indian Treaty Council (IITC) in the United States in 1974 and the World Council of Indigenous Peoples (WCIP) in Canada in 1975. Formed during a meeting of some five thousand representatives of more than ninety Native nations on the Standing Rock Sioux Tribe's land, IITC forged relationships with radical political movements around the world and sought recognition for Indigenous sovereignty, culture, and land at the UN. In October of 1975, Indigenous delegates from nineteen nations and four continents traveled to Tseshaht territory on Vancouver Island in British Columbia and established the

WCIP, building on connections forged by the National Indian Brotherhood (now the Assembly of First Nations) of Canada throughout Europe, Africa, and the Pacific.[26] As Cold War tours of Native art diminished, the IITC and the WCIP carried the earth diplomacy pipe, circumventing federal sponsorship to pursue transnational alliances on Indigenous terms.

At the formative UN International Non-Governmental Organizations Conference on Discrimination against Indigenous Populations in the Americas in Geneva in 1977, the IITC asserted the rights of Indigenous peoples under international law and laid a path for the UN Declaration on the Rights of Indigenous People in 2007.[27] The UN's framework of human rights was not an adequate container for Indigenous political sovereignty, nor did it account for the well-being of plant, animal, river, and mountain kin as a core component of Native cosmopolitics. Yet subtending these definitional limits were ongoing practices of earth diplomacy that ushered more-than-human reciprocity back into the halls of international relations. The opening events featured a march to the UN Conference Center at the Palais des Nations that was filled with prayer, song, oratory, and a sacred pipe ceremony. "The work of the whole place had been halted," observed José Barreiro (Ismaelillo), a member of the Taino Nation of the Antilles and then editor of the Mohawk Nation newspaper *Akwesasne Notes*, as he gazed up at the many faces watching the procession from the palace windows. "The sight of many Native delegates wearing regalia signaling their tribal belonging, carrying sacred objects such as pipes and fans, and hearing their singing and drumming echo off the walls" must have been affectively and politically compelling for those members of the United Nations drawn into the multisensory assemblage.[28]

These sensuous practices were followed by speeches calling for a framework of earth jurisprudence that transcends the anthropocentrism of modern international relations to extend legal rights to nonhuman beings and systems.[29] The words of leaders from across the Americas converged on sacred land and sky as the foundation of all meaningful life. Representing Haudenosaunee, Chief Oren Lyons addressed "the duty of all human beings to respect not only 'human rights,' but the rights of all the beings of the Creation." Leaders also spoke of the vast destruction of Indigenous lands and bodies under settler colonial governments from Chile to Canada, giving special attention to the United States as "the monster, the base and control of overwhelming exploitation—the force, economic and military, behind this process."

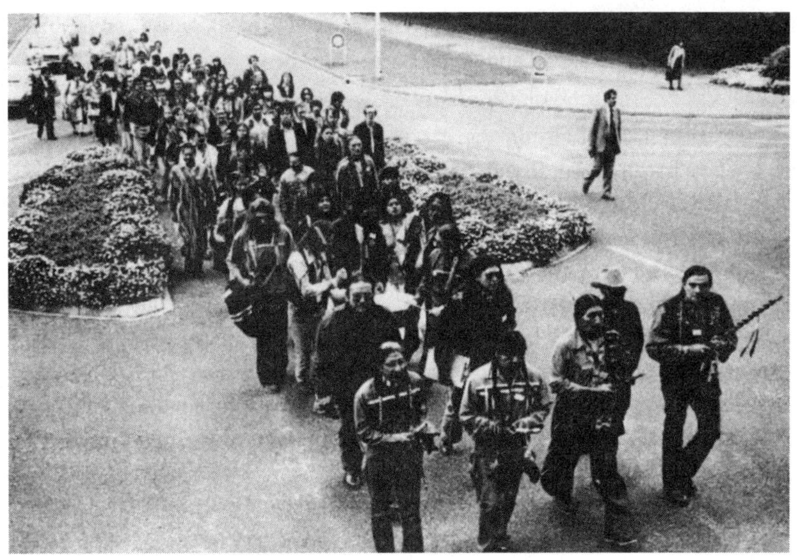

C.3

Sacred pipes lead a procession of Native American delegates to the Palais des Nations in Geneva, 1977. *Akwesasne Notes* 2005 [1978], 66.

. . . .

As Barreiro put it, while each leader outlined the distinct experiences of their own peoples, their words "seemed to fold together like the cloth that wraps the Sacred Pipe." The Lakota activist Larry Red Shirt initiated a pipe ceremony by discussing its many manifestations during AIM, describing how, "over and over, the mind of men changed by the power of that prayer and what the smoke represented."[30] Here, as in many past and future sites of earth diplomacy, Indigenous arts and rituals called a more-than-human gathering into being. This capacious UN delegation envisioned—and temporarily realized—a practice of international relations that was capable of affirming life.

Presaging such developments, the arts of this book provided a crucial link in adapting Indigenous cosmologies to the volatility of geopolitics in the latter twentieth century. Artworks, demonstrations, and gifts withstood the devastations of Termination and addressed a dangerous imbalance of power in Cold War international relations. As exemplars of earth diplomacy, they worked to restore reciprocity to a modern nation-state system premised on the extraction of value from labor and land. Art is the unrecognized catalyst of what Anishinaabe

political scientist Sheryl Lightfoot calls a "transformational norm vec-
tor" in international relations, "pointing the way toward some alternative ways of doing global politics and new imaginings of political order."[31]
An accumulation of similar creative acts has guaranteed the perseverance of earth diplomacy to inform still other global Indigenous justice
movements that are flourishing today.

NOTES

1   "Scholder-Cannon Exhibit," USIA report materials from American Embassy in Bucharest, December 12, 1972. SIA 000315, Box 14.

2   For example, see, Depkat, "Peace Medal Diplomacy in Indian-White"; Harjo, "Introduction"; McLaughlin, *Arts of Diplomacy*.

3   Among the earliest examples, the portraits of four Iroquois leaders painted by John Verelst upon their diplomatic visit to London in 1710 combined ethnographic curiosity with political utility. See Muller, "From Palace to Longhouse." For other illuminating studies that foreground Native leaders' agency in the creation of their portraits, see Hutchinson, "Dress of His Nation"; de Stetcher, "Of Chiefs and Kings"; Zamir, *Gift of the Face*.

4   For an account of the changing status of photographed Native leaders from dignitaries to icons, see Goodyear, *Red Cloud*.

5   The notion of art as a "weapon" was first articulated in Crockoft, "Abstract Expressionism."

6   Cobb, *Native Activism in Cold War America*. See also Burt, *Tribalism in Crisis*.

7   See Voyles, *Wastelanding*; Masco, *Nuclear Borderlands*; Nixon: *Slow Violence and the Environmentalism of the Poor*.

8   Horton, "Painter, Traveler, Diplomat."

9   Winona Garmhausen, interview with Fritz Scholder, July 1975, IAIA-MS-07, Garmhausen Papers, Box 4, Folder 7.

10   Cobb, "Talking the Language of the Larger World," 162; Denson, "Native Americans in Cold War Public Diplomacy"; Kýrová, "Right to Think for Themselves," 76–77; Slezkine, *Arctic Mirrors*, 306. See also Rosier, "They Are Ancestral Homelands."

11   Latour in conversation with Davis, "Diplomacy in the Face of Gaia," 51. Here, Latour adapts Isabelle Stengers's point that diplomats, as translators, face an inherent risk of becoming betrayers. See Stengers, *Cosmopolitics II*, 376–77.

12   I'm building on a handful of foundational studies of postwar Native American art history that address Indian Termination and the Cold War, notably Anthes, *Native Moderns*; and Gritton, *Institute of American Indian Arts*. Other single artist monographs, essays, and exhibition catalogues are cited throughout this book.

13   Foster, *First Pop Age*, 6.

14   Foster, *First Pop Age*, 7.

15   Ronato Rosaldo writes that "the agents of colonialism long for the very forms of life they intentionally altered or destroyed." "Imperialist Nostalgia," 108.

16   Foster, *First Pop Age*, 62.

17   This history is recounted in Orenstein, *Ivory, Horn, and Blood*.

18   Chris Baraniujk, "We Know Exactly How the Vietnamese Javan Rhino Went Extinct," *BBC News*, September 21, 2016, http://www.bbc.com/earth/story/20160920-we-know-exactly-how-the-vietnamese-javan-rhino-went-extinct; Orenstein, *Ivory, Horn, and Blood*, 29, 119–20.

19   Hall, *Vietnam War*, 89.

20   See Caute, *Dancer Defects*, 339–40; Quinney, "Excess and Identity," 39–40.

21   I borrow the phrase from Anishanaabeg environmental activist Winona LaDuke, who articulates the conjunction of Native sovereignty and environmental justice concerns in *All Our Relations*.

22   The concept of the "whole earth" references the first satellite images of the planet that circulated widely in popular culture after 1967, notably on the cover of the green lifestyle magazine, *The Whole Earth Catalog*, first published in 1968. See Maniaque-Benton, *Whole Earth Field Guide*.

23   Nelson and Shilling, eds., *Traditional Ecological Knowledge*.

24   *New York Herald Tribune*, December 30, 1956, quoted in Prevots, *Dance for Export*, 112.

25   "Indians Excited over American 'Indians,'" *Wallace Farmer*, February 6, 1960: 24–25; "Histórico Encuentro de Navajos y Mapuches," *El Diario Austral*, Temuco, July 24, 1968. IAIA RG-1 Exhibit Buenos Aires Argentina, SG-8, 1968, Series 7 Exhibits, Box 5, Folder 5.

26   Hattie Kabotie Lomayesva, in conversation with the author, Riverside, CA, 2015.

27   Solomon McCombs Papers, 1941–1974, National Anthropological Archives, Smithsonian Institution, https://sova.si.edu/record/NAA.1974.0401?s=470&n=10&t=C&q=African+American+photographers&i=471.

28   Harney and Phillips, "Introduction," 5.

29   Coulthard, *Red Skin, White Masks*, 7–8.

30   While this literature is large and growing, I have found the critical overviews in the following texts especially useful for Indigenous North American art histories: Anthes, *Native Moderns*; Doyle and Winkiel, *Geomodernisms*; Friedman, "Periodizing Modernism"; Harney and Phillips, "Introduction"; Mercer, *Cosmopolitan Modernisms*; Phillips, "Aesthetic Primitivism Revisited"; Thomas, *Possessions*. Beyond the modernisms discourse, scholars have offered compelling accounts of Indigenous North American travelers and mobile cultural forms as agents of modernity, for example: Burns, *Transnational Frontiers*; Deloria, *Indians in Unexpected Places*; Feest, *Indians and Europe*; Thrush, *Indigenous London*; Weaver, *Red Atlantic*.

31   Harney and Phillips, "Introduction," 7–10. *Mapping Modernisms* is the first publication to result from the Multiple Modernisms Project, which was inaugurated by a workshop at the Clark Art Institute in 2010.

32   The definitive account is Smith and Warrior, *Like a Hurricane*.

33   Cobb, "Talking the Language of the Larger World"; see also Rosier, "They Are Ancestral Homelands."

34   Deloria, Jr., *God Is Red*, 10.

35   Gilio-Whitaker, *As Long as Grass Grows*, 70–71.

36   This literature is vast. See discussions in Driskill et al., ed., *Queer Indigenous Studies*; Justice, Rifkin, and Schneider, "Sexuality, Nationality, Indigeneity"; Suzack et al., eds., *Indigenous Women and Feminism*; Moreton-Robinson, *Sovereign Subjects*; Teves, Smith, and Raheja, eds., *Native Studies Keywords*.

37   Cajete, "Native Science and Sustaining Indigenous Communities," 19.

38   Igloliorte, "Arctic Culture/Global Indigeneity"; Rickard, "Visualizing Sovereignty in the Time of Biometric Sensors."

39   "United Nations Declaration on the Rights of Indigenous Peoples," 3; Lee, "Navajo Nation," 170–86. For more on this history, see Henderson, *Indigenous Diplomacy and the Rights of Peoples*; Lightfoot, *Global Indigenous Politics*.

40   Akwesasne Notes, ed., "Deskaheh"; International Indian Treaty Council, "For the Continuing Independence of Native Nations";

Geneva Declaration, "For Human Rights and Fundamental Freedoms," in Cobb, *Say We Are Nations*, 167–71, 172–75; Crossen, "Another Wave of Anti-Colonialism," 542–48.

41 Tóth, *From Wounded Knee to Checkpoint Charlie*, 143–44, 158. Tóth reports that Deskaheh carried a wampum belt from the Museum of the American Indian to demonstrate the Haudenosaunee sovereignty at the League of Nations in 1922 (144).

42 Melanie K. Yazzie, quoted in Banerjee, "From the Red Nation to the Red Deal," 439, 446; "About," Red Nation, accessed November 6, 2023, https://therednation.org/about/.

43 Latour, *Facing Gaia*, 243. Latour sketches an imaginary path toward a renewed diplomacy in which Euro-Americans (those he calls the "Moderns") negotiate with the value systems of global others who are finally treated as equals in the face of the climate change. Latour, *Inquiry into Modes of Existence*, especially 12–23.

44 Stengers, "We Are Divided." A discussion of the diplomat as an analogy for the public, political negotiations required of climate researchers appears in Stengers, *Cosmopolitics II*, 376–92.

45 Kimmerer, "*Mishkos Kenomagwen*, the Lessons of Grass," 31.

46 Dittmer, *Diplomatic Material*, 12.

47 "Joseph Nye on Soft Power," *Foreign Policy Association*, February 22, 2016, https://www.youtube.com/watch?v=_58v19OtIIg. Nye's classic account is *Soft Power*. He has continued to extend his analysis in relation to current events, including the rise of China and climate change.

48 I address assumptions common to balance of power discourses rather than parse differences within this large and diverse literature, drawing especially from David Joseph Wellman's critique of Hans J. Morgenthau's paradigmatic *Politics Among Nations*. See Wellman, *Sustainable Diplomacy*, 14–18. For other recent overviews, see Sheehan, *Balance of Power*; Vasquez and Elman, *Realism and the Balance of Power*; Zartman, *Imbalance of Power*.

49 Haas, "Balance of Power," 442. Haas's influential assessment of the theory was contemporaneous with the formation of the USIA.

50 Gómez-Barris, *Extractive Zone*, xviii. During the 1950s and 1960s, the Soviet Union pursued the removal and assimilation of Indigenous peoples and intensified resource extraction, mirroring United States policy. Bartels and Bartels, "Indigenous Peoples of the Russian North and Cold War Ideology," 268.

51 Wellman, *Sustainable Diplomacy*, 4.

52 Conastantinou and Der Derian, "Introduction," 9.

53 Savelle, *Origins of American Diplomacy*, 200.

54 Clinton, "Treaties with Native Nations," 15.

55 Harjo, "Introduction," xi.

56   Clinton, "Treaties with Native Nations," 23.

57   Clinton, "Treaties with Native Nations," 30.

58   Clinton, "Treaties with Native Nations," 19.

59   Deloria, Jr., *God Is Red*, 67.

60   Watson, "Jimmie Durham's *Building a Nation*," 1004. See also Watson, "Diplomatic Aesthetics."

61   McLaughlin, *Arts of Diplomacy*, 36.

62   Rickard, "Visualizing Sovereignty in the Time of Biometric Sensors," 469.

63   de Stecher, "Integrated Practices," 56.

64   The items were borrowed from the collection of the Indian Arts and Crafts Board (IACB), an agency within the Department of the Interior that was established in 1935 to promote Native nations' economic development by growing a modern market for Native arts. While the Pueblo pots in the photograph were transferred from the IACB collection to the National Museum of the American Indian in 1999, Conor McMahon, chief curator of the IACB, was unable to find information on the provenance or whereabouts of the pipe. Email to the author, July 12, 2021.

65   In 1964 the exhibition traveled to Stockholm, Helsinki, Oslo, Copenhagen, Berlin, Belgrade, and Munich for month-long showings. USIA Circular "Confirming Itinerary for Project 64–245," Washington, DC, to Belgrade, Berlin, Copenhagen, Helskinki, Oslo, Stockholm, April 2, 1964. SIA Project # 64–245, Folder: USIA RU 321, Office of Program Support, National Museum of American Art, 1956–1981, with related records from 1947, Box 87, Folder 1: Sandpainting and Handcraft Indian Exhibit.

66   TallBear, "Indigenous Reflection on Working Beyond the Human/ Not Human," 233. For an art historical treatment of Dakhóta pipestone, including the colonial circumstances under which *iŋyaŋša* was dubbed "catlinite," see Johnson, "George Catlin, Artistic Prospecting, and Dakhóta Agency in the Archive."

67   Clinton, "Treaties with Native Nations," 19–20.

68   Guilbaut, *How New York Stole the Idea of Modern Art*, 7. See also Crockoft, "Abstract Expressionism"; Kozloff, "American Painting During the Cold War."

69   Saunders, *Cultural Cold War*.

70   Barnhisel, *Cold War Modernists*, 8.

71   Krenn, *Fall-Out Shelters for the Human Spirit*, 1.

72   Allied studies of African Americans as Cold War cultural diplomats include Blake, "Cold War Diplomacy and Civil Rights Activism"; Davenport, *Jazz Diplomacy*; Dudziak, *Cold War Civil Rights*; Krenn, *Diplomacy*; Thomas, *Globetrotting*; Von Eschen, *Satchmo Blows up the World*.

73 Davenport, *Jazz Diplomacy*, 16.

74 Taylor, "Transnational Transactions," 93.

75 Krenn, *Fall-Out Shelters for the Human Spirit*, 5.

76 Wimmer and Schiller, "Methodological Nationalism."

77 Deloria, Jr. and Lytle, *Nations Within*.

78 See Bleiker and Butler, "Radical Dreaming"; Vorano, "Inuit Art."

79 Initial uses of the phrase are credited to members of the pan-Indigenous activist organization, the National Indian Youth Congress, at the American Indian Capital Conference on Poverty in 1964 and to Deloria, Jr., at the convention of the National Congress of American Indians in 1966. Josephy, Nagel, and Johnson, "Introduction," 13. Bradley G. Shreve argues that the phrase should be exclusively associated with militancy in *Red Power Rising*, 6–8; 159. I uphold Deloria, Jr.'s more expansive definition of the revitalization of Indigenous spiritual and land-based power that underlay overt political activity during this period, discussed in *God Is Red*, 10.

80 Deloria, Jr., *God Is Red*, 25.

81 See Dunaway, *Seeing Green*; Rosier, "Modern America Desperately Needs to Listen"; Siddons, "Red Power in the Black Panther"; Smith, *Hippies, Indians, and the Fight for Red Power*; Sturgeon, *Environmentalism in Popular Culture*, especially chapter 2, "Frontiers of Nature: The Ecological Indian in U.S. Film," 53–79; Gilio-Whitaker, *As Long as Grass Grows*, especially chapter 5, "(Not So) Strange Bedfellows: Indian Country's Ambivalent Relationship with the Environmental Movement," 91–110.

82 Dunaway, *Seeing Green*, 89.

83 Haeckel, *Generelle Morphologie der Organismen*, 286. By comparison, scientist Alexander Von Humboldt's nascent theory of global ecological interconnectivity, which influenced Haeckel, drew upon Indigenous cosmologies and criticized the environmental impacts of Spanish colonialism and slavery. See Humboldt, *Personal Narrative of a Journey*; Sachs, "Ultimate 'Other.'"

84 Demos, *Decolonizing Nature*, 7.

85 Nixon, *Slow Violence and the Environmentalism of the Poor*.

86 Vargas, "On Extraction," 113; Voyles, *Wastelanding*.

87 Gómez-Barris, *Extractive Zone*, xvii.

88 Whyte, "Indigenous Science (Fiction) for the Anthropocene," 227.

89 Dittmer, *Diplomatic Material*, 12.

90 See Conastantinou and Der Derian, "Introduction"; Wellman, *Sustainable Diplomacy*.

91 Conastantinou and Der Derian, "Introduction," 2.

92 Wellman, *Sustainable Diplomacy*, 30.

93   Wellman, *Sustainable Diplomacy*, 4.

94   Wellman, "Promise of Sustainable Diplomacy," 25. Wellman's use of "ecological location" in turn draws on Spencer, *Gay and Gaia*.

95   See Demos, "Rights of Nature"; Lightfoot, *Global Indigenous Politics*, 3.

96   A version of the prayer was published in de Zegher, "Arc Are Ark Arm Art . . . Act!," 104. See also LaDuke, *All Our Relations*.

97   "About the Journey," *Totem Pole Journey*, October 25, 2016, https://totempolejourney.com/about-the-journey/. See Horton, "Indigenous Artists Against the Anthropocene," 67–69.

98   Nisbet, *Ecologies, Environments, and Energy Systems*, 3.

99   Dittmer, *Diplomatic Material*, 3.

100   Rancière, *Politics of Aesthetics*, 12–13. Rancière's insights are usefully mobilized to assess the Australian government's diplomatic deployment of Aboriginal art in Bleiker and Butler, "Radical Dreaming."

101   Robinson, *Hungry Listening*, 13.

102   McLerran, *New Deal for Native Art*, 93–101.

103   Turner, "*Family of Man* and the Politics of Attention in Cold War America," 55–56.

104   Krenn, *Fall-Out Shelters for the Human Spirit*, 5.

CHAPTER 1. CONTESTED KINSHIP

An earlier version of the final section of this chapter was previously published as "Plural Diplomacies between Indian Termination and the Cold War: Contemporary American Indian Paintings in the 'Near East,' 1964–1966," *Journal of Curatorial Studies* 5, no. 3 (October 2016): 340–66.

1   "'Contemporary American Indian Painting' Exhibition to Open November 8 at the National Gallery of Art," press release, National Gallery of Art, November 8, 1953, 1. NGA Archives, Microfilm 7A7, Exhibition Files, 1942–1970, Contemporary American Indian Painting: November 8–December 6, 1953.

2   Dwight Eisenhower, "Statement by the President," August 15, 1953, quoted in Rosier, *Serving Their Country*, 163. I capitalize "Termination" to refer to the overarching policy, realized through numerous discrete presidential and congressional actions from the mid-1940s until the mid-1960s.

3   Gritton, *Institute of American Indian Arts*, 71.

4   Krenn, *Fall-Out Shelters for the Human Spirit*, 89.

5   In 1938, the DOS established the Division of Cultural Relations with the primary aim of facilitating cultural and scientific exchanges with Latin American countries; in 1941 it provided

policy guidelines for a traveling exhibition of American painting funded by millionaire and art collector Nelson Rockefeller, head of the Office of the Coordinator of Inter-American Affairs (OIAA); in 1944 the NGA took over administration of an Inter-American Office, modestly funded by the DOS. Krenn, *Fall-Out Shelters for the Human Spirit*, 17–18.

6   Dittmer, *Diplomatic Material*, 3. See also the introduction to this book.

7   See Gómez-Barris, *Extractive Zone*. See also the introduction to this book.

8   See Eldridge, "Dorothy Dunn and the Art Education of Native Americans"; McGeough, *Through Their Eyes*.

9   The Office of Indian Affairs was renamed the Bureau of Indian Affairs (BIA) in 1949. Following common scholarly practice, I use "BIA" anachronistically to signal the agency's continuity.

10   Bernstein and Rushing, *Modern by Tradition*, 5–14. The Santa Fe Indian School opened in 1890 as a federal boarding school designed to assimilate Native American children in the wake of the Dawes Act of 1887 (discussed in this chapter). See Hyer, *One House, One Voice, One Heart*, 4–5.

11   Quoted in Champagne, "From Full Citizenship to Self-Determination, 1930–1975," 154.

12   For an analysis of these programs, see McLerran, *New Deal for Native Art*.

13   For overviews of Pueblo and Kiowa painting precedents, see Brody, *Pueblo Indian Painting*; Fur, *Painting Culture, Painting Nature*; McGeough, *Through Their Eyes*; Wyckoff, "Collective History of Native American Painting."

14   Dunn, *American Indian Paintings of the Southwest and Plains Areas*, 288, 287.

15   Dunn, *American Indian Paintings of the Southwest and Plains Areas*, 287.

16   Charles A. Daily, "Major Influences on the Development of Twentieth-Century American Indian Art," 149. On the eroding reputation of the Studio School from the mid-1950s and after, see Anthes, *Native Moderns*, xv, 159.

17   Christian Brinton, "My Idea of American Indian Art," radio address, WOR, New York, December 15, 1931, transcription, Martha and Amelia Elizabeth White Papers, SAR, AC18.337.

18   Anthes, "'Why Injun Artist Me'"; Berlo, "Szwedzicki Portfolios of American Indian Art"; Horton, "Cloudburst in Venice"; Horton, "Performing Paint, Claiming Space."

19   Dunn, *American Indian Paintings of the Southwest and Plains Areas*, 313.

20   Bernstein and Rushing, *Modern by Tradition*, 12.

21   Margretta S. Dietrich, letter to NGA chief curator John Walker, August 31, 1953. NGA Archives, Microfilm 7A7, Exhibition Files, 1942–1970, Contemporary American Indian Painting: November 8–December 6, 1953.

22   Vina Windes, "USIA Sends Santa Fe Art Abroad," *New Mexican*, June 20, 1965, 2. International Art Program, National Collection of Fine Arts, Smithsonian Institution, Laboratory of Anthropology Archives, 93DDK.041.2. The collection is currently held at the Museum of Indian Arts and Culture in Santa Fe, New Mexico. Unfortunately, many of the paintings appear to be misplaced or lost.

23   Dunn, *Contemporary American Indian Paintings*, n.p.

24   Deloria, *Playing Indian*, 150.

25   Dunn, *Contemporary American Indian Paintings*, n.p.

26   Roediger, *Ceremonial Costumes of the Pueblo Indians*, 114–15, 127–31. See Dilworth, *Imagining Indians in the Southwest*, especially "The Spectacle of Indian Artisanal Labor," 125–75.

27   Rosier, *Serving Their Country*, 143.

28   None of the literature accompanying the exhibition provided dates for the paintings. However, Velarde dated her loan, *The Betrothal* (1953), and Dunn indicated that Tsihnahjinnie created "new work" for the exhibition in a letter to John Walker, April 27, 1953. NGA Archives, Microfilm 7A7, Exhibition Files, 1942–1970, Contemporary American Indian Painting: November 8–December 6, 1953.

29   McLerran, *New Deal for Native Art*.

30   Dorothy Dunn, letter to David E. Finley and John Walker, January 8, 1953; David E. Finley, letter to Dorothy Dunn, January 18, 1953. NGA Archives, Microfilm 7A7, Exhibition Files, 1942–1970, Contemporary American Indian Painting: November 8–December 6, 1953.

31   David E. Finley, letter to Yvon Bizardel, June 25, 1953; John Walker, letter to Dorothy Dunn, February 25, 1953, p. 2; John Walker, letter to David Finley, May 13, 1953. NGA Archives, Microfilm 7A7, Exhibition Files, 1942–1970, Contemporary American Indian Painting: November 8–December 6, 1953.

32   Krenn, *Fall-Out Shelters for the Human Spirit*, 22.

33   John Walker, memorandum to David E. Finley, October 20, 1953. NGA Archives, Microfilm 7A7, Exhibition Files, 1942–1970, Contemporary American Indian Painting: November 8–December 6, 1953.

34   Krenn, *Fall-Out Shelters for the Human Spirit*, 22–23.

35   Oliver LaFarge, *Indian Affairs* no. 7, newsletter of the American Indian Fund and the Association of American Indian Affairs,

Inc., October 20, 1953, 1. NGA Archives, Microfilm 7A7, Exhibition Files, 1942–1970, Contemporary American Indian Painting: November 8–December 6, 1953.

36 LaFarge, *Indian Affairs* no. 7, 2.

37 NCAI Declaration of Indian Rights, quoted in Champagne, "From Full Citizenship to Self-Determination, 1930–1975," 165; "Statement of Zuni Indian Veterans of World War II and the Korean Conflict," February 17, 1954, and "Resume of the Emergency Conference of American Indians on Legislation," February 26, 1954, quoted in Rosier, *Serving Their Country*, 172–73.

38 "Home Again," *Tulsa World*, December 18, 1955. NGA, Scrapbooks, Vol. 46: Press Clippings, 51.

39 Dunn, *American Indian Paintings*, 332; exhibition catalogue, *Peinture indienne américaine contemporaine*, August 16–December 28 (Brussels: Musées Royaux d'art et d'histoire, 1955), SIA: RU 321, Office of Program Support, National Museum of American Art, 1956–1981, with related records from 1947, Box 54, Folder: Contemporary American Indian Paintings, 1955. Although it was independently organized, Dunn emphasized the exhibition's continuity with the NGA showing. In 1956, she described it as "an exhibition now in its third year," and in 1968, she recalled that it was requested by the USIA immediately after the NGA closing. LAB Anthropology, Dorothy Dunn, letter to Frederick J. Dockstader, September 1, 1956; Dunn, *American Indian Painting of the Southwest and Plains Area*, 332.

40 Dunn, *American Indian Painting*, 332–33.

41 "The Art in Embassies Program," brochure, Department of State, n.d. OHP, Subgroup 2: Family Papers, 1903–2011, Series VI: American Specialist, 1971, Correspondence, 1966–1987, Box 48, Folder 16.

42 Oliver LaFarge, letter to Rogers, November 19, 1953. NGA Archives, Microfilm 7A7, Exhibition Files, 1942–1970, Contemporary American Indian Painting: November 8–December 6, 1953.

43 Freeman, *Wedding Complex*, 98. Freeman's argument that wedding rituals enact forms of intimacy beyond conjugal partnership is discussed in Rifkin, *When Did Indians Become Straight?*, 100.

44 Ortiz, "Ritual Drama and Pueblo World View," 143.

45 Guitérrez, *When Jesus Came, the Corn Mothers Went Away*, 23, 10.

46 Ortiz, *Tewa World*, 13.

47 The role of the vase in Kha-'Po Owingeh marital rituals is discussed by potter Teresita Naranja in LeFree, *Santa Clara Pottery Today*, 77–78.

48 See LeFree, *Santa Clara Pottery Today*; Schaafsma, *Kachinas in the Pueblo World*.

49 Naranjo, "Cultural Changes," 187–89.

50 Pueblo Corn Dances (a colonial label given to the ritual) are discussed in Lange, "Tablita, or Corn Dances of the Rio Grande Pueblo Indians."

51 Justice, "'Go Away Water!,'" 150–51.

52 Rifkin, *When Did Indians Become Straight?*, 7–8.

53 Rifkin, *When Did Indians Become Straight?*, 133.

54 Rifkin, *When Did Indians Become Straight?*, 11.

55 Guitérrez, *When Jesus Came, the Corn Mothers Went Away*, 263.

56 Descriptions of the betrothal ceremony followed by an optional church wedding appear in LeFree, *Santa Clara Pottery Today*, 77–78; and Hill, *Ethnography of Santa Clara Pueblo, New Mexico*, 159–161.

57 Rifkin, *When Did Indians Become Straight?*, 5.

58 Rifkin, *When Did Indians Become Straight?*, 39.

59 Foreshadowing the Public Law 280, the US government began restricting certain benefits to Native women who legalized their customary marriages according to states' jurisprudence during World War II. Euro-American ideals concerning gendered labor, childrearing, and conjugal domesticity further shaped BIA and other welfare programs in Indigenous communities such as Aid to Families with Dependent Children in the postwar era. Anderson, *Changing Woman*, 74–76.

60 Watkins, "Termination of Federal Supervision," 48.

61 Dozier, "Factionalism at Santa Clara Pueblo," 182.

62 Dozier, *Pueblo Indians of North America*, 137.

63 Dozier, *Pueblo Indians of North America*, 138.

64 Hill, *Ethnography of Santa Clara Pueblo, New Mexico*, 20–21.

65 Reed, *Woman's Place*, 248.

66 Velarde spoke these words in a 1979 interview quoted in Reed, *Woman's Place*, 241. The gendered dynamics of Pueblo painting are explored at length in relation to the pathbreaking work of Velarde's mentor, Tonita Peña (Quah Ah, 1893–1949), which was included in the NGA exhibition and traveling USIA-sponsored off-shoots. Hawley, "Tonita Peña and the Politics of Pueblo Art." See also Fowler, "Gender, Modern Art, and Native Women Painters in the First Half of the Twentieth Century"; Jantzer-White, "Tonita Peña (Quah Ah), Pueblo Painter."

67 Dunn, "America's First Painters," 377.

68 Lutz and Collins, *Reading National Geographic*, 38–39.

69 Trevor Barnes, Derbyshire, England, letter to Dorothy Dunn, September 3, 1955, D. Franklin Hudson, South Australia, letter to

Dorothy Dunn, October 3, 1955; Bernardino del Boca de Villaregia, Novara, Italy, letter to Dorothy Dunn, April 13, 1955; Laboratory of Anthropology Archives, 93DDK.014

70 Dunn, "America's First Painters," 361.

71 Dunn, "America's First Painters," 361–63.

72 Reed, "Mixed Messages," 112.

73 Quoted in May, *Homeward Bound*, 17.

74 Quoted in Rosier, *Serving Their Country*, 183.

75 Kýrová, "Native Americans, Socialist Propaganda," 1–2.

76 Bohlinger, "East Is a Delicate Matter," 390; Lavrentyev, "Red Westerns–A Short History."

77 Slezkine, *Arctic Mirrors*, 306.

78 Slezkine, *Arctic Mirrors*, 307, 319.

79 Bartels and Bartels, "Indigenous Peoples of the Russian North and Cold War Ideology," 268; Slezkine, *Arctic Mirrors*, 337.

80 Brightman, Grotti, and Ulturgasheva, "Introduction," 5; Voyles, *Wastelanding*.

81 Denson, "Native Americans in Cold War Public Diplomacy," 4.

82 *The American Indian: Past and Present*, "Indian of the Future," August 14, 1965. International Broadcasting Bureau, Voice of America. NA, RG 306: USIA, 1900–2003, 128756.

83 Wood, "Navahos," 28.

84 Olsen, "Indian Art," 36, 34.

85 Rosier, *Serving Their Country*, 112.

86 Rosier, *Serving Their Country*, 141–42.

87 See Cobb, *Native Activism in Cold War America*; Denson, "Native Americans in Cold War Public Diplomacy"; Rosier, *Serving Their Country*.

88 Kýrová, "Right to Think for Themselves," 102–16. György Ferenc Tóth argues that AIM activists intervened in transatlantic histories of "playing Indian" and manipulated the stereotypes to "make political claims." Tóth, *From Wounded Knee to Checkpoint Charlie*, 3.

89 Harry S. Truman, quoted in Oakes, *Imaginary War*, 131.

90 Oakes, *Imaginary War*, 113.

91 George Trendle, the creator of *The Lone Ranger*, quoted in Grieve, *Little Cold Warriors*, 30.

92 Grieve, *Little Cold Warriors*, 28.

93 Frank Meurer, quoted in Grieve, *Little Cold Warriors*, 30.

94 "Solomon McCombs," 10.

95 Nested within the DOS, the IEES was kept apart from the USIA. Like the latter agency, the program was charged with conveying "the human side" of foreign policy, focusing on the face-to-face sharing of educated and well-to-do Americans' ideas, values,

knowledge, and skills. Bu, "Educational Exchange and Cultural Diplomacy," 396–97.

96   Solomon McCombs, "My Report to the Creeks: Experiences and Observations Abroad," 1–4. AAA SMP, Box 5: Miscellany, Folder: Lectures, Unpublished Writings, Subject Files.

97   A. R. Thomas, Secretary, and Turn Bear, Chairman, Creek Indian Council, letter to McCombs, December 10, 1955. AAA SMP, Box 1: Correspondence, 1941–1954, Folder: Correspondence, 1955–1957.

98   Deer and Knapp, "Muscogee Constitutional Jurisprudence," 163, 129. Other nations descending from the Mvskoke include the federally recognized Poarch Band of Creek Indians in Alabama, Seminole Nation of Oklahoma, Seminole Nation of Florida, and Miccosukee Tribe of Florida, and numerous other nations operating without federal recognition (125).

99   Wickman, *Tree that Bends*, 16–17.

100   Deer and Knapp, "Muscogee Constitutional Jurisprudence," 123–25, 135–36, 164.

101   "Solomon McCombs," 10.

102   Rosemary McCombs Maxey, letter to the author, Tuesday, May 30, 2023.

103   Willie C. Jones, letter to Solomon McCombs, October 28, 1955. AAA SMP, Box 1: Correspondence, 1941–1954, Folder: Correspondence, 1955–1957.

104   McCombs, "My Report to the Creeks," 5; Solomon McCombs, "Report of American Indian Art Exhibit and Lecture Tour," 2. AAA Acee Blue Eagle Papers, Series 2: Collections; Box 12: Native American Miscellany, Folder: McCombs, Solomon, Report of American Indian Art Exhibit and Lecture Tour.

105   McCombs, "My Report to the Creek Nation," 10, 8, 15.

106   McCombs, "My Report to the Creek Nation," 11.

107   McCombs, "My Report to the Creek Nation," 16–17.

108   McCombs, "My Report to the Creek Nation," 18–19.

109   McCombs, "My Report to the Creek Nation," 5.

110   Latour, *Facing Gaia*, 243. This quotation is also discussed in the introduction.

111   McCombs, "Report of American Indian Art Exhibit and Lecture Tour," 3–4.

112   Rosier, *Serving Their Country*, 138–43.

113   McCombs, "Report of American Indian Art Exhibit and Lecture Tour," 4.

114   Jean Nordling, Curator for Exhibitions, Philbrook Art Center, letter to McCombs, March 5, 1954. NAA SMP, Box 1: Correspondence, 1941–1954, Folder: Correspondence, 1954.

The SI's Travel Exhibition Service "got into the overseas art exhibit business" in 1951; in 1965, the USIA initiated a transfer of the responsibility to organize art exhibits to the SI, while the USIS would continue in the work of circulating them abroad. Krenn, *Fall-Out Shelters for the Human Spirit*, 86, 209–14.

115 Solomon McCombs, draft letter to Claude J. Legrand, c. 1956, AAA SMP, Box 1: Correspondence, 1941–1954, Folder: Correspondence, 1956–1957; Solomon McCombs, 1963, quoted in Wyckoff, *Visions and Voices*, 179.

116 Rosemary McCombs Maxey, in conversation with the author, telephone, May 10, 2023.

117 See, for example, *Preparation for the Ribbon Dance* (1978), gifted by the artist to the Gilcrease Museum in Tulsa. "Preparation for the Ribbon Dance / Solomon McCombs," Gilcrease Museum, accessed November 13, 2023, https://collections.gilcrease.org/object /021674.

118 Paper, *Dancing for Life*; 103.

119 Harjo, *Spiral to the Stars*, 120.

120 Paper, *Dancing for Life*; 102.

121 Maxey, in conversation with the author.

122 Harjo, *Spiral to the Stars*, 5–8, 122.

123 Koons, "Dancing Breath," iii, 132.

124 Harjo, *Spiral to the Stars*, 123; Paper, *Dancing for Life*; 103.

125 "Nelson Rockefeller Speaks at Preview of Family of Man Exhibition," press release, Museum of Modern Art, New York, NY, January 24, 1955, 1.

126 Zamir and Hurm, "Introduction," 1.

127 "Each section of the exhibition is headed by a quotation from world literature, many from the distant past. Research for these options was done by Dorothy Norman." *Family of Man*, press release, January 26, 1955, Museum of Modern Art Archives. https://assets.moma.org/documents/moma_press-release_325965 .pdf?_ga=2.107571594.946036151.1629834442–966563191 .1629834442.

128 Steichen, *Family of Man*, 15, 55, 63. For a paradigmatic critique, subsequent scholars typically look to Barthes, "Great Family of Man." The position I describe is best articulated in Sekula, "Traffic in Photographs"; and Philipps, "Judgment Seat of Photography."

129 Shamoon Zamir and Gerd Hurm highlight public and scholarly responses focused on the exhibition's capacity to "sustain a mutually supportive dialectic of difference and sameness and not on the erasure of difference." Zamir and Hurm, "Introduction," 4.

130   Azoulay, "Family of Man," 20–21.

131   Azoulay, "Family of Man," 20.

132   Swentzell, "Feminine World," 221.

133   Naranjo, "Cultural Changes," 190; Swentzell, "Feminine World," 226; Trimble, *Talking with the Clay*, 6. Tewa is the language spoken at Kha-'Po Owingeh.

134   TallBear writes of the red stone that Dakota people have long utilized to carve ceremonial pipes, quarried from a sacred site now managed by the US National Park Service as Pipestone National Monument in Minnesota, in *Cryopolitics*, 196.

135   Deloria, *God Is Red*, 25.

136   Trafzer, "Introduction," 14.

137   To my knowledge, Native Americans living in the United States were not pictured in the exhibition or book, nor were Maori of Aotearoa (New Zealand). Two photographs taken by German-born Canadian photographer Richard Harrington of Inuit communities in the Arctic and the purported quotations sufficed to represent Native North America. Steichen, *Family of Man*, 21, 153.

138   McCombs, "My Report to the Creeks."

139   Henry P. Arnold, "American Indian Painting Exhibit," USIS Tehran, March 11, 1965; Betty J. Abel, letter to Dorothy Dunn, October 5, 1967. International Art Program, National Collection of Fine Arts, Smithsonian Institution, Laboratory of Anthropology Archives, 93DDK041.

140   Henry L. Davis, USIS Tehran, Program Report, 1965. NA, RG 306, USIA, 1900–2003, Iran, Folder 2/2, 1960–1967.

141   Spiller, *Frontiers for the American Century*, 1.

142   Allen, "Trans*national* Native American Studies?," 7.

143   Contemporary Diné artist D. Y. Begay elaborates that *iina'* is "an extraordinary Navajo word that describes how you live, how life is carried out, and how life is respected in the Navajo world." Begay, "Weaving Is Life," 48.

144   Voyles, *Wastelanding*, xiii, 39–47.

145   Weisiger, "Gendered Injustice," 438–43. See also Weisiger, *Dreaming of Sheep in Navajo Country*.

146   Quoted in Spragg-Braude, *To Walk in Beauty*, 26.

147   Wood, "Navahos."

148   Voyles, *Wastelanding*, 59; Chamberlain, *Under Sacred Ground*, 81. See also Benally, "Diné Binahat'á,' Navajo Government," especially chapter 4 (138–73).

149   Voyles, *Wastelanding*, xiii.

150   Quoted in Rosier, *Serving Their Country*, 133.

151   Wood, "Navahos," 28.

152 Abrahamian, *Coup*.

153 C. Edward Wells, Public Affairs Officer, American Embassy in
Tehran, Foreign Service Dispatch to the Department of State in
Washington, DC, April 15, 1954; also discussed in Rosier, *Serving
their Country*, 185.

154 Lowell Bennett, Acting Country Public Affairs Officer, USIS
Tehran, "Country Assessment Report for Calendar Year 1965,"
December 29, 1965, 2–3. NA, RG 306: USIA, 1900–2003, Iran,
Folder 2/2, 1960–1967.

155 Winold Reiss, 1886–1953 (n.d.), exhibition brochure, Smithsonian
Institution Archives (hereafter SIA), RU000321, National Museum
of American Art, Office of Program Support, 1965–1981, Box 83.

156 USIS Thessaloniki, program report, March 9, 1964. SIA
RU000321, National Museum of American Art, Office of Program
Support, 1965–1981, Box 83.

157 USIA, memo to USIS Tunis, May 8, 1964, SIA RU000321,
National Museum of American Art, Office of Program Support,
1965–1981, Box 81.

158 USIS Tunis, program report, June 4, 1964, SIA RU000321,
National Museum of American Art, Office of Program Support,
1965–1981, Box 81.

159 USIS Karachi, operations memorandum, July 23, 1965. SIA
RU000321, National Museum of American Art, Office of Program
Support, 1965–1981, Box 81.

160 Dorothy Dunn, letter to Betty J. Abel, February 21, 1968, SIA
RU000321, National Museum of American Art, Office of Program
Support, 1965–1981, Box 81.

161 Dorothy Dunn, letter to Betty J. Abel, February 21, 1967. SIA
RU000321, National Museum of American Art, Office of Program
Support, 1965–1981, Box 81.

162 Allen, "Trans*national* Native American Studies?" 2.

163 Rifkin, *When Did Indians Become Straight?*, 11.

164 Allen, "Trans*national* Native American Studies?," 1, 7. Although
Allen does not overtly discuss diplomacy, his trans-Indigenous
analytic is well suited to that framework.

165 Native students' practice of borrowing themes and motifs, especially from Pueblo peers who pursued an education at the SFIS
comparatively close to home, did at times violate Indigenous protocols limiting the transmission of ceremonial imagery. See Scott,
Strange Mixture.

166 Allen, "Trans*national* Native American Studies?," 2.

167 Dittmer, *Diplomatic Material*, 3. I offer a more sustained analysis
of the diplomatic assemblage as a method for reading exhibitions
in Horton, "Seeing the National Museum of the American Indian
Anew."

168   Allen, "Trans*national* Native American Studies?" 3.

169   See Constantinou and Der Derian, "Introduction"; Wellman, *Sustainable Diplomacy*.

170   Wellman, *Sustainable Diplomacy*, 163.

CHAPTER 2. REBALANCING POWER

An earlier version of this chapter was previously published as "Rebalancing the Cold War: Diné Sandpainting and Earth Diplomacy," *The Art Bulletin* 104, no. 3 (Sept. 2022): 84–116.

1   "Indian Art Gift to Edinburgh," *Scotsman*, September 10, 1966, 7. Institute of American Indian Arts (IAIA) McGrath Papers, MS03, Box 26, F.1.

2   Held annually for three weeks beginning in 1947, the festival contributed to European nations' postwar reconstruction and helped popularize art festivals as a tool of Cold War diplomacy. Miller, *Edinburgh International Festival, 1947–1996*, 5.

3   Wood, "Navahos," 116.

4   Sherry, *Land, Wind, and Hard Words*, 10.

5   "Episode 9: The Navajo, Part I," *The American Indian: Past and Present*, Voice of America, August 14, 1965. NA, RG 306, USIA, Sound Recordings, Voice of America.

6   "Episode 10: The Navajo, Part II," *The American Indian: Past and Present*, Voice of America, August 14, 1965. NA, RG 306, USIA, Sound Recordings, Voice of America.

7   Humalajoki, "'What Is It to Withdraw?,'" 429–30; Wilkins, *Navajo Political Experience*, 100–114.

8   Moorman, "Health of the Navajo-Hopi Indians," 371–72. For more on this relationship, see Ternnert, *White Man's Medicine*.

9   Development accelerated during the Cold War, especially under the leadership of Chairman Raymond Nakai from 1963 to 1970. See Wilkins, *Navajo Political Experience*, 114; Chamberlain, *Under Sacred Ground*.

10   Sherry, *Land, Wind, and Hard Words*, 10. Janet Catherine Berlo discusses Diné sandpainting textiles as a response to uranium mining in "Alberta Thomas, Navajo Pictorial Arts, and Ecocrisis at Dinétah."

11   Rainbow Stevens, in conversation with the author, Chinle, Arizona, June 23, 2018.

12   James McGrath, in conversation with the author, Santa Fe, New Mexico, June 18, 2018.

13   Navajo Nation Heritage and Historic Preservation Department, accessed March 3, 2021, https://www.hpd.navajo-nsn.gov/.

14   On Indigenous research methods, see Mihesuah and Wilson, *Indigenizing the Academy* and Smith, *Decolonizing Methodologies*.

On the significance of Indigenous protocols for art history, see Scott, "Awa Tsireh and the Art of Subtle Resistance."

15   Navajo Nation Cultural Resources Investigation Permit No. Cl8033-E.

16   Tohe, "Grounded in Spiritual Geography," 5.

17   Berlo, "Navajo Cosmoscapes—Up, Down, *Within*," 10.

18   Yazzie, "Navajo Women and Traditions," 11.

19   On the purpose of Diné life, see Lee, *Diné Perspectives*; Witherspoon, *Language and Art in the Navajo Universe*, 13–39.

20   Overviews appear in Parezo, *Navajo Sandpainting*, 1–20; Wyman, *Southwest Indian Drypainting*. Extreme care must be taken when accessing and further disseminating the information cited in my endnotes, given changing Diné protocols concerning the safe circulation of ceremonial knowledge.

21   This history is recounted in Denetdale, *Long Walk*.

22   Voyles, *Wastelanding*, xi.

23   Matthews, "Mythic Dry-Paintings of the Navajos," 221. See also Parezo, "Matthews and the Discovery of Navajo Drypaintings." For consideration of the notion of a "replica" in sandpainting translations, see Berlo, "Navajo Sandpainting in the Age of Crosscultural Replication."

24   Parezo, *Navajo Sandpainting*, 33.

25   On Diné gender multiplicity, see Thomas, "Navajo Cultural Constructions of Gender and Sexuality." "Hastiin" indicates male gender, and Newcomb used masculine pronouns to refer to Tł'a.

26   Parezo, *Navajo Sandpainting*, 27. Newcomb authored the most complete bibliographical account of Tł'a's life in *Klah,* Hosteen; *Navaho Medicine Man and Sand Painter*. On the seventeen sandpainting textiles attributed to Tł'a and Tł'a's nieces in the Wheelwright collections, see McGreevy, "Woven Holy People"; *Woven Holy People*.

27   Parezo, *Navajo Sandpainting*, 29–30.

28   Parezo, *Navajo Sandpainting*, 70; Rainbow Stevens, in conversation with the author.

29   Parezo, *Navajo Sandpainting*, 110; Rainbow Stevens, in conversation with the author.

30   Parezo, *Navajo Sandpainting*, 106–10.

31   "Art and Film Walking Tour of Luther A. Douglas's Navajo Sand Paintings," brochure, 2017. Orma J. Smith Museum of Natural History, The College of Idaho.

32   USIA Circular, "Confirming Itinerary for Project 64–245," April 23, 1964, SIA RU 321, Office of Program Support National Museum of American Art, 1956–1981, with related records from 1947, Box 87, Folder 64–245, Sandpaintings and Hand Craft Indian Exhibit.

33   "Navajo Ceremonial Sandpainting," SIA RU 321, Office of Program Support National Museum of American Art, 1956–1981, with related records from 1947, Box 87, Folder 64–245, Sandpaintings and Hand Craft Indian Exhibit.4

34   Parezo, *Navajo Sandpainting*, 115–17; DuPont sold the product to Devcon Corporation in the late 1960s. "Innovation Starts Here," DuPont, http://www2.dupont.com/Phoenix_Heritage/en _US/1904_b_detail.html (accessed February 7, 2019). See also "Deep Roots," *Elmer's*, accessed February 8, 2019, http://elmers .com/about/deep-roots; "The History of Masonite," accessed March 17, 2021, www.masonite.com/masonite_history.php.

35   Care instructions are found on the back of a small sandpainting by Stevens that I purchased on Ebay in 2018. I examined more than forty durable sandpaintings made by Stevens and members of his family in the collection of Michael Eugene Harris in Albuquerque, New Mexico, on June 6, 2018.

36   Parezo, *Navajo Sandpainting*, 106.

37   Rainbow Stevens, in conversation with the author.

38   Davis, *Healing Ways*, 64. The book was eventually published as Wyman, *Blessingway*.

39   Davis, *Healing Ways*, 62.

40   Davis, *Healing Ways*, 60–62.

41   Davis, *Healing Ways*, 67.

42   Davis, *Healing Ways*, 96. Davis emphasizes that the cooling of Termination fervor during the Kennedy and Johnson administrations paved the way for an expansion of services combined with greater Diné self-determination in medical affairs (73).

43   Parezo, *Navajo Sandpainting*, 73; Trennert, *White Man's Medicine*, 223. The organization persists today; see Diné Hataałii Association, "Guest Column: Our Purpose Is to Continue the Journey Towards Hózhó," *Navajo Times*, July 16, 2020, https:// navajotimes.com/opinion/columns/guest-column-our-purpose-is -to-continue-the-journey-towards-hozho/.

44   Stevens was touring through Latin America when a coalition of psychiatrists, educators, and hataałii founded the Navajo Mental Health Program to train healers at Rough Rock Demonstration School, with financial support from the PHS. Davis, *Healing Ways*, 110–11.

45   For a classic critique of archival "hardening" in relation to colonial power, see Taylor, *Archive and the Repertoire*.

46   McNeley, *Holy Wind in Navajo Philosophy*, 1.

47   Tohe, "Grounded in Spiritual Geography," 3.

48   Rainbow Stevens, in conversation with the author.

49   Rainbow Stevens, in conversation with the author.

50   McGrath, in conversation with the author.

51   Fred Stevens, postcard sent from London to Glenn Harris and family in Chinle, Arizona, dated March 1, 1971. Collection of Michael Eugene Harris.

52   See James McGrath, letter to Ian Gilmour, the English Speaking Union, Edinburgh, Scotland, June 29, 1966; James McGrath, letter to Dr. Carroll, US Information Service, United States Embassy, London, June 23, 1966; James McGrath, letter to James Richardson, Yepi Kopperative, Ankara, Turkey, September 3, 1966, IAIA RG-1, SG-6, 1966, Series 7, Exhibits, Box 3, Folder 3.

53   Ian Gilmour, letter to James McGrath, July 4 1966, IAIA RG-1, SG-6, 1966–Series 7, Exhibits, Box 3, Folder 3.

54   Padmalal and Maya, *Sand Mining*, 3–4.

55   Forty, *Concrete and Culture*, 149.

56   Padmalal and Maya, *Sand Mining*, 57–80.

57   Marco Hernandez, Simon Scarr, and Katy Daigle, "Shifting Sands: The Messy Business of Sand Mining Explained," *Reuters*, February 18, 2021, https://graphics.reuters.com/GLOBAL -ENVIRONMENT/SAND/ygdpzekyavw/; Peduzzi, "Sand, Rarer than One Thinks," 1–2.

58   Vince Beiser and Sim Chi Yin, "The Deadly Global War for Sand," Pulitzer Center Projects, 2016–ongoing, https://pulitzercenter .org/projects/deadly-global-war-sand.

59   Vargas, "On Extraction," 112.

60   Nixon, *Slow Violence and the Environmentalism of the Poor*. Preferred sands, the largest producer of frac sand in the US today, operates one of their two main plants on Navajo Nation land. "Arizona," Preferred Sands, https://preferredsands.com/products /arizona/.

61   Dittmer, *Diplomatic Material*, 3.

62   This number includes seventy-five thousand visitors to the Olympics Popular Arts Exhibit as a whole over the course of fifty-four days. James McGrath, untitled final report, 1969. IAIA McGrath Papers, MS01, Box 1, F. 14.

63   James McGrath, letter to Ernest Colton, Director, Amerika Haus, September 1, 1966, p. 2. IAIA Records RG01, SG–6, 1966, Series 7, Exhibits, Box 3, F.14; Horniman Museum brochure, Autumn 1968, IAIA Records RG03, Box 20, F.4, I.8.

64   "From Handicraft to Art," *Die Welt*, October 11, 1966, English translation. IAIA, McGrath Papers, MS03, Box 20, F. 9, I.2. See also Ruth Faulkner, "We Walk with Beauty in Our Hearts," *Christian Science Monitor*, Saturday, December 31, 1966, 7. IAIA MS03, Box 20, Folder 9, I.9.

65 McGrath, in conversation with the author.

66 Alfred Clah, "Art in the Sand," in *Introductory Notes About Sand-painting*, 1966, p. 1. IAIA, Lloyd H. New Papers, Box 7, Folder 11.

67 McGrath reported 5,000 visitors to Edinburgh; 4,000 in London; and 1,300 in the first three days in Berlin. James McGrath, form letter to exhibiting artists, October 5, 1966, IAIA Records, SG-6, 1966, Series 7, Exhibits, Box 3, Folder 14.

68 See Rushing, "Marketing the Affinity of the Primitive and the Modern"; Steeds et al., *Making Art Global*.

69 Berlo, "Navajo Sandpainting in the Age of Cross-Cultural Replication," 701.

70 Rushing, *Native American Art and the New York Avant-Garde*, 193, 191.

71 Solomon-Godeau, "Going Native," 120.

72 "How, I Asked the Navajo Indian, Do You Find Edinburgh? I Think Your Rain Is Wonderful, Said the Medicine-Man's Son." Publication source missing. IAIA, McGrath Papers, MS03, box 20, F.5.

73 Wauhillau La Hay, "Sand Painter Scores," *Daily News*, October 18, 1966, SIA, Traveling Exhibition Records 1952–1981, box 88, Craft Indian Exhibit, F.1.

74 "Children Flock to Watch Red Indian Fred and His 'Squaw,'" *South London Press*, September 16, 1966, no. 7423. IAIA, McGrath Papers, MS03, Box 20, Folder 1, I.8.

75 Parezo notes that the primary means of sandpainting instruction is "showing" without explanation or generalization in *Navajo Sandpainting*, 122.

76 Berlo, "Navajo Cosmoscapes," 10–11.

77 Gell, *Art and Agency*, 76.

78 Gell, *Art and Agency*, 80, 74.

79 Coates, "Our Far-Flung Correspondents," 105–6.

80 Nisbet, *Ecologies, Environments, and Energy Systems*, 131.

81 Morris, "Anti-Form," 41.

82 For an extensive account of those interpretations, see Guilbaut, *How New York Stole the Idea of Modern Art*.

83 Faris, *Nightway*, 28. Faris reproduced a version of the Nightway that Tł'a related to Wheelwright around 1928 (177–229). There are many versions and it is unclear which one Stevens practiced.

84 Gill, "Whirling Logs and Colored Sands," 49–52.

85 Fred Stevens, untitled document, 1966, Horniman Museum Archives, Americas, Stevens, F. CMA, 1–2.

86 Hatcher, *Visual Metaphors*, 170–71. On controlled dynamism in Diné art and language, see Witherspoon, *Language and Art in the Navajo Universe*, especially 162–72.

87 Austin, "Diné Sovereignty, a Legal and Traditional Analysis," 31. Ethelou Yazzie similarly notes that they "travel on Lightning, Sunbeams, and Rainbows." Yazzie, "Navajo Wisdom and Traditions," 7.

88 Gill, "Whirling Logs and Colored Sands," 52.

89 Fred Stevens, untitled document, 3.

90 "Children Flock to Watch Red Indian Fred and His 'Squaw,'" *South London Press*.

91 Gell, *Art and Agency*, 46.

92 Fred Stevens, untitled document, 3.

93 Kimmerer, "*Mishkos Kenomagwen*, the Lessons of Grass," 27.

94 D. M. Boston, G. E. Williams, and G. W. P. Jarvis, "Conservation of a Navajo Sand-painting," Horniman Museum Archives, 1968, 1.

95 "About Us," Link International Storage Products, http://www.linkint.co.uk/about-us/.

96 Boston, Williams, and Jarvis, "Conservation of a Navajo Sand-Painting," 2.

97 Boston, Williams, and Jarvis, "Conservation of a Navajo Sand-Painting," 3.

98 Wood, "Navahos," 116.

99 Lee, "Introduction," 4.

100 Austin, "Diné Sovereignty," 31, 33.

101 Austin, "Diné Sovereignty," 31.

102 "World Gallery—Displays," Horniman Museum, accessed February 8, 2019, https://www.horniman.ac.uk/visit/displays/world-gallery.

103 Flaherty, *Hotel Mexico*, 205.

104 Flaherty, *Hotel Mexico*, 2.

105 Flaherty, *Hotel Mexico*, 105.

106 Dorotinsky, "Handcraft as Cultural Diplomacy," 4.

107 Joaquín Estefanía, "¡No queremos Olimpiadas, queremos revolución!" *El País*, Madrid, October 2, 2018. https://elpais.com/deportes/2018/10/01/actualidad/1538415487_180518.html.

108 McGrath, in conversation with the author. I have not been able to verify that the rifle shots were part of the massacre.

109 Flaherty, *Hotel Mexico*, 3.

110 See Vergara-Camus, *Land and Freedom*.

111 McGrath in conversation with the author.

112 James McGrath, untitled notes. IAIA, McGrath Papers, IAIA Exhibits–Announcement for 1968 Mexico City Exhibit, 1968, Box 29, Folder 4. Other difficulties with the accompanying exhibition of Native arts are discussed in Dorotinsky, "Handcraft as Cultural Diplomacy," 13–20.

113   McGrath, in conversation with the author; Rainbow Stevens, in conversation with the author.

114   Flaherty, *Hotel Mexico*, 156.

CHAPTER 3. EARTH MOTHERS

1   McLerran, "Textile as Cultural Text," 22–23; For perspectives on *sa'ah naagháii bik' eh hózhǫ́*, see Lee, *Diné Perspectives*; Witherspoon, *Language and Art in the Navajo Universe*, 13–39.

2   Begay, "Weaving Is Life," 48.

3   Begay, "Shi' Sha' Hane' (My Story)," 18. Begay emphasizes that "to be a complete person, a Navajo woman should weave or have some knowledge of weaving" (17). I have chosen to refer to Asdzáá Náádleehé and Na'ashjéii Asdzáá using the English translations of their names, following the lead of Diné commentators cited throughout.

4   Weisiger, *Dreaming of Sheep in Navajo Country*, 80; Thomas, "Shił Yóółt'ool," 36.

5   On the responsibility of Diné women to protect land and home, see Tsosie, "Native Women and Leadership," 33. AnCita Benally insists that "there is nowhere in the sacred history of Diné where women were excluded from leadership or from participation in governance," despite their marginalization from the Navajo Nation government in the twentieth and twenty-first centuries. Benally, "Diné Binahat'á,' a Navajo Government," 36.

6   Gómez-Barris, *Extractive Zone*, 74.

7   Gómez-Barris borrows Giorgio Agamben's phrase, "bare life," to describe the conditions of marginal subjects consigned to death in so far as they are stripped of the means of life through the state legal apparatus. Gómez-Barris, *Extractive Zone*, 75–76; Agamben, *Homo Sacer*.

8   Bacigalupo, *Shamans of the Foye Tree*, 51–52.

9   I thank Helen Molesworth for her playful application of Roland Barthes's theory of the punctum to the photographed purse during our conversations at the Live Panel Discussion for the Wyeth Foundation for American Art Symposium, "Feminism in American Art History," at the National Gallery of Art, December 11, 2020; Barthes, *Camera Lucida*.

10   For example, Hopi artist Alice Kabotie demonstrated basket weaving alongside her husband, painter and silversmith Fred Kabotie, at the World Agricultural Fair in India in 1960. See chapter one and Kabotie, *Fred Kabotie*, 96–104.

11 James McGrath, letter to Ian Gilmour, English Speaking Union, Edinburgh, July 25, 1966. IAIA RG-1, SG-6, 1966, Series 7, Exhibits, box 3, folder 3.

12 Gladstone and Pepion, "Exploring Tradition Indigenous Leadership Concepts," 574; Trafzer, "Introduction," 4.

13 Driskill, "Doubleweaving Two-Spirit Critiques"; Rifkin, *When Did Indians Become Straight?*

14 Cassidy and Althari, "Introduction," 1.

15 Aggestam and Towns, "Introduction," 3.

16 Aggestam and Towns, "Introduction," 4.

17 Warren, "Power and the Promise of Ecological Feminism," 131.

18 Blocker, *Where Is Ana Mendieta?*, 48–49.

19 d'Eaubonne, *Le feminism ou la mort*; Moore, "Eco/Feminist Genealogies," 27.

20 Moore, "Eco/Feminist Genealogies," 24–25; Phillips and Rumens, "Introducing Contemporary Ecofeminism," 3. See also Shiva, *Staying Alive.*

21 Sturgeon, *Ecofeminist Natures*, 129; Spretnak, "Ecofeminism," 5.

22 Sturgeon, *Ecofeminist Natures*, 113–14.

23 Gaard, "Ecofeminism Revisited," 26.

24 Gough and Whitehouse, "Challenging Amnesias," 4. See also Gaard, "Posthumanism, Ecofeminism, and Inter-Species Relations."

25 See, for example, Todd, "Indigenizing the Anthropocene," 4.

26 Allen, *Sacred Hoop*, 215. See also Allen, "Woman I Love Is a Planet," 52–57.

27 Wagner, "Indigenous Roots of United States Feminism," 269.

28 Wagner, "Indigenous Roots of United States Feminism," 269. Wagner quotes Matilda Joslyn Gage, "Onandaga Indians," *New York Evening Post*, November 1, 1875, 3; Gage, *Woman, Church and State*, 5.

29 Jacobs, *Engendered Encounters*. For overviews of changing white and Indigenous representations of Diné women, see Denetdale, "Representing Changing Woman"; Kidwell, "Land Incarnate."

30 Gilio-Whitaker, *As Long as Grass Grows*, 114–16.

31 Gilio-Whitaker, *As Long as Grass Grows*, 117–18.

32 Schor, *Wet*, 66.

33 Blocker, *Where Is Ana Mendieta?*, 47–48.

34 Watts, "Indigenous Place-Thought and Agency," 21.

35 Watts, "Indigenous Place-Thought and Agency," 31–32.

36 Boetzkes, *Ethics of Earth Art*, 146.

37 Gill, *Mother Earth*, 7, 6.

38 Gill, *Mother Earth*, 34–38. Gill quotes Young, "Mother of Us All."

39 Deloria, Jr., "Comfortable Fictions and the Struggle for Turf," 402.

40   Flatley, "Like," 74.

41   Dittmer, *Diplomatic Material*, 12.

42   Berlo, "It's Up to You—," 36–37. See also Wheat, "American Indian Weaving."

43   Mallery, *Picture-Writing of the American Indians*, 287–88, 325.

44   Montano and Yohe, "Blanketing the Plains," 20. See also Mera, *Navajo Textile Arts*, 6.

45   Paper, *Offering Smoke*, 37.

46   For example, the National Museum of the American Indian collection includes a Diné blanket (c. 1840–50) that was in the possession of the Brulé Lakota, decorated with brass, German silver buttons, quill-wrapped cords, horsehair, and other material additions, described by Kathleen Ash-Milby in *Woven by the Grandmothers*, 128–29.

47   Leech, *Reveille in Washington, 1860–1865*, 122, quoted in Pohrt, *American Indian, the American Flag*, 8.

48   Denetdale, "Remembering Our Grandmothers," 87, 79.

49   Denetdale, "Remembering Our Grandmothers," 88.

50   Denetdale, "Remembering Our Grandmothers," 79.

51   M'Closkey, *Swept Under the Rug*, 31.

52   Wheat, "Navajo Blankets," 78; 74.

53   Reichard, *Navajo Religion*, 242, 247, 250; Reichard, *Weaving a Navajo Blanket*, 181. Following her general bias that weaving is a secular art, Reichard acknowledges the spiritual significance of the cross as the foundation of much ceremonial sandpainting but discounts its sacred value in weaving.

54   Herbst and Kopp, "Grandfather's Flag," 24.

55   Herbst and Kopp, "Grandfather's Flag," 24.

56   Denetdale, "Remembering Our Grandmothers," 85–86.

57   Tohe, "There Is No Word for Feminism in My Language," 104.

58   Yazzie, *Navajo Wisdom and Traditions*, 26–27.

59   The recorded account of Tall Chanter, a *hataałii*, from 1884, is discussed in Weisiger, *Dreaming of Sheep in Navajo Country*, 72.

60   Weisiger, *Dreaming of Sheep in Navajo Country*, 75. Weisiger quotes Mr. Yellow Water, Cane Man's Son, and other hataałii who allowed anthropologists to record their accounts of Diné history in the late nineteenth and early twentieth century. "Sheep Is Life" is the name of a sheep camp and gathering for "all those who love sheep, wool, fiber arts, and the diverse cultures that have maintained these lifeways for thousands of years," established by Diné be'iiná, Inc., a nonprofit Diné organization founded in 1991 to promote sustainable livelihood on the Navajo Nation. "About Us," Diné Be' Iiná: The Navajo Lifeway, accessed November 20, 2023, http://navajolifeway.org/navajo-sheep/.

61 Weisiger, *Dreaming of Sheep in Navajo Country*, 77.

62 Denetdale, "Remembering Our Grandmothers," 85. For Diné references to Mother Earth, see Tohe, "Grounded in Spiritual Geography," 5; Roessel, *Women in Navajo Society*, 40; Walters, "Navajo Concept of Art," 31.

63 Yazzie, "Navajo Women and Traditions," 25–26.

64 Yazzie, "Navajo Women and Traditions," 28.

65 Bad Hand, "American Flag in Lakota Tradition," 13.

66 Herbst and Kopp, "Grandfather's Flag," 23.

67 Quoted in Pohrt, *American Indian, the American Flag*, 13.

68 Trafzer, "Introduction," 14.

69 Reichard, *Navaho Religion*, 149.

70 Walters, "Navajo Concept of Art," 30.

71 Denetdale, "*Naal Tsoos Sani*," 127.

72 Walters, "Navajo Concept of Art," 31.

73 Walters, "Navajo Concept of Art," 29.

74 Walters, "Navajo Concept of Art," 31.

75 Rainbow Stevens, in conversation with the author, telephone, October 2, 2020.

76 Gram, *Education at the Edge of Empire*, 118.

77 Gram, *Education at the Edge of Empire*, 121–23.

78 Margaret McKittrick of the EAIA, quoted in Armstrong, *Mary Wheelwright*, 162. See also Mullen, *Culture in the Marketplace*, 117.

79 Rodee, *Old Navajo Rugs*, 83.

80 Rodee, "Oriental Connection," 17.

81 Armstrong, *Mary Wheelwright*, 163, 162.

82 Armstrong, *Mary Wheelwright*, 163.

83 Rodee, *Old Navajo Rugs*, 84–85. Armstrong notes that a new partnership with Wells and Richardson Co. of Burlington, Vermont, was sought to create "more user-friendly dyes" that went by the misleading trade name "Old Navajo Dyes." Armstrong, *Mary Wheelwright*, 166. But Chinle weavers preferred native plants, with yellows and browns foregrounded over reds and blues after 1934.

84 Sarah Boehme, former curator at the Stark Museum of Art, explained that Bertha Stevens was commissioned along with her daughter, Rainbow Stevens, to demonstrate carding, spinning, and weaving May 13–17 and October 21–25, 1981. Email to the author, Friday, April 23, 2021.

85 Rodee, *Old Navajo Rugs*, 84.

86 Rainbow Stevens, in conversation with the author.

87 Dockstader, *Song of the Loom*, 99.

88 Amsden, *Navajo Weaving*; Mera, *Navajo Textile Arts*.

89 M'Closkey, *Swept Under the Rug*, 210.

90   Jacobs stresses the heterogeneity of white women's reasons for participation. Jacobs, *Engendered Encounters*, 150–51.

91   McLerran, "Textile as Cultural Text," 9.

92   Anthropologist Gladys Reichard's detailed studies of Diné women and arts position the commercial rationale as a site of cultural decline, evinced in her historical novel, *Dezba: Woman of the Desert* (1939) about a sheepherder and weaver who provides for her family by selling her art to a local trader while suffering an erosion of customary female power due to federal policies. See Denetdale's critical discussion in "Representing Changing Woman," 3–4.

93   Douglas and D'Harnoncourt, *Indian Art of the United States*, 182–83.

94   Douglas and D'Harnoncourt, *Indian Art of the United States*, 184.

95   Douglas and D'Harnoncourt, *Indian Art of the United States*, 185, 183.

96   Dockstader, *Song of the Loom*, 19.

97   The principle contrasts with the precise repetition of prototypical designs invoked in ceremonial sandpaintings. See Begay, "Shi' Sha' Hane' (My Story)," 25; Berlo, "'It's Up to You—,'"43.

98   M'Closkey, *Swept Under the Rug*, 245–51.

99   Quoted in M'Closkey, *Swept Under the Rug*, 216.

100   Quoted in M'Closkey, *Swept Under the Rug*, 214.

101   Quoted in M'Closkey, *Swept Under the Rug*, 216.

102   Yohe, "Circulation and Silence of Weaving," 110. See also Yohe, "Social Life of Weaving in a Contemporary Navajo Community."

103   M'Closkey, *Swept Under the Rug*, 206.

104   Rainbow Stevens, in conversation with the author.

105   Bertha Stevens and Fred Stevens first taught four-week-long summer workshops at ISOMATA through a National Endowment for the Arts and Humanities grant from 1976 to 1978. Bertha Stevens returned to hold shorter workshops on campus and on site in Chinle from 1983 to 1992. Heather Companiott, email to the author, April 13, 2021; "A Living History of Artistic Excellence," Idyllwild Arts Foundation, https://www.idyllwildarts.org/who-we-are/history/.

106   Rainbow Stevens in conversation with the author. Wilmerine is Rainbow Stevens's legal name.

107   McLerran, "Textile as Cultural Text," 17.

108   Reichard, *Navaho Religion*, 241–247.

109   D. Y. Begay, quoted in McLerran, "Textile as Cultural Text," 10.

110   Ruth Faulkner, "We Walk with Beauty in Our Hearts," *Christian Science Monitor*, Saturday, December 31, 1966, 7. IAIA MS03, Box 20, Folder 9, I.9.

111   Elizabeth Mackay, letter to Lloyd Kiva New, February 18, 1966, 1. IAIA RG-1, SG-6, 1966, Series 7, Exhibits, Box 3, Folder 3.

112   Elizabeth Mackay, letter to James McGrath, February 18, 1966, 1–2. IAIA RG-1, SG-6, 1966, Series 7, Exhibits, Box 3, Folder 3.

113   Elizabeth Mackay, letter to James McGrath, February 18, 1966, 1.

114   Helen Davies, "Navajo Weaving," Museum of Navajo Ceremonial Art, n.d., 1–11. IAIA RG-1, SG-6, 1966, Series 7, Exhibits, Box 3, Folder 7.

115   Elizabeth Mackay, "Exhibition of American Indian Art—Contemporary and Traditional at English Speaking Union Gallery, Edinburgh, 20th August—10 September 1966," n.d., 2–3. IAIA RG-1, SG-6, 1966, Series 7, Exhibits, Box 3, Folder 7.

116   According to Rainbow Stevens, her parents received these names from a Kiowa source at a powwow in Oklahoma in 1954. Rainbow Stevens in conversation with the author, Chinle, Arizona, March 31, 2017.

117   Mackay, "Exhibition of American Indian Art," 3.

118   Parezo and Jones, "What's in a Name?," 376.

119   King, "De/Scribing Squ*w," 4.

120   "Children Flock to Watch Red Indian Fred and His 'Squaw,'" *South London Press*, September 16, 1966, no. 7423. IAIA, McGrath Papers, MS03, Box 20, F.1, I.8.

121   Parezo and Jones, "What's in a Name?," 379.

122   Parezo and Jones, "What's in a Name?," 385.

123   Roessel, *Women in Navajo Society*, 173.

124   Parezo and Jones, "What's in a Name?," 382.

125   Amerian, "The Fashion Gap," 65.

126   Parezo and Jones, "What's in a Name?," 392.

127   Vizenor, "Aesthetics of Survivance" 1.

128   James McGrath, "Lloyd Kiva New and the Early Years of the IAIA," unpublished manuscript (chapter for Lloyd Kiva New Biography c. 2000), 15. IAIA McGrath Papers, Box 29, Folder 8. McGrath received a note of appreciation from Constance Fisher, instructor of the Treaty Organization program at the Turkish-American Association, noting "Our students in the Turkish American participants Intensive Course have been so stimulated by your lectures and exhibits!" October 22, 1966, 1. IAIA MS03, Box 20, Folder 10, I.4.

129   Faulkner, "We Walk with Beauty in Our Hearts."

130   Francaviglia, *Go East, Young Man*, viii.

131   Rainbow Stevens in conversation with the author, Chinle, Arizona, Navajo Nation, June 23, 2018.

132   Becerra et al., "Recreated Practices by Mapuche Women," 1262.

133   Bacigalupo, *Shamans of the Foye Tree*, 58.

134   Luis Inostroza Loebel, "¡Hola niño! Yo soy Aguila Gris," *A La Vuelta* (location and date unknown), 15. IAIA RG-1, SG-8, Series 7, Exhibits, Box 5, Folder 5.

135   "Finalizaron actividades en torno al arte indio en USA," *El Sur* (Concepcion, Chile), July 14, 1968. IAIA RG-1, SG-8, Series 7, Exhibits, Box 5, Folder 5.

136   "Histórico encuentro de navajos y mapuches," *El Diario Austral* (Valdivia, Chile), July 24, 1968. IAIA RG-1, SG-8, Series 7, Exhibits, Box 5, Folder 5.

137   Bacigalupo, "Mapuche Women's Empowerment as Shaman," 61.

138   Rainbow Stevens, in conversation with the author, Chinle, Arizona, Navajo Nation, June 23, 2018.

139   Becerra et al., "Recreated Practices by Mapuche Women," 1267.

140   Hidalgo, "Trariwe de Machi," 2–5.

141   Gómez-Barris, *Extractive Zone*, 78.

142   Bacigalupo, "Mapuche Women's Empowerment as Shaman," 57–60.

143   Francisco Huichaqueo, quoted in Luco, "Hilando en la Memoria," 460.

144   Luco, "Hilando en la Memoria," 470.

145   Luco, "Hilando en la Memoria," 460.

146   Gómez-Barris, *Extractive Zone*, 78.

147   Bacigalupo, "Rethinking Identity and Feminism," 32, 40.

148   Becerra, et al., "Recreated Practices by Mapuche Women that Strengthen Place Identity in New Urban Spaces of Residence in Santiago, Chile," 1268.

149   María Catrileo Chiguailaf, in conversation with the author, Museo Regional de la Araucanía, Temuco, Chile, February 15, 2020; Becerra et al., "Recreated Practices by Mapuche Women," 1268.

150   Chiguailaf, *Diccionario lingüístico etnográfico de la lengua Mapuche*.

151   Chiguailaf, in conversation with the author.

152   "Histórico encuentro de navajos y mapuches."

153   "Muchedumbre en muestra de indios norteamericanos," *Gong* (Temuco, Chile), June 24, 1968, 7. IAIA RG-1, SG-8, Series 7, Exhibits, Box 5, Folder 5.

154   Flatley, "Like," 73.

155   Flatley, "Like," 73. Flatley draws upon Walter Benjamin's theorization of the mimetic faculty in "The Doctrine of the Similar" and "On the Mimetic Faculty," both reproduced in Benjamin, *Walter Benjamin*.

156   Allen, "Trans*national* Native American Studies?," 3.

157   Allen, "Trans*national* Native American Studies?," 3, 5.

| 158 | Allen, "Trans*national* Native American Studies?," 5. |

| 159 | Chiguailaf in conversation with the author. On Mapuche relationships to the Frei government, see Haughney, *Neoliberal Economics*, 42; Hutchison et al., *Chile Reader*, 344. It is not clear who owned the wood-plank building where breakfast was served in Quetrahue. Bertha Stevens and Fred Stevens evidently visited a *ruka*, a customary Mapuche house that typically features wooden walls and a straw roof, while lunch was served in a structure built by members of the Peace Corps. "Histórico encuentro de navajos y mapuches." |

160 Chiguailaf, in conversation with the author.

161 Quoted in "Finalizaron actividades en torno al arte indio en USA."

162 Crow, *Mapuche in Modern Chile*, 117. See also Haughney, *Neoliberal Economics*, 41–44; Mallon, "Mapuche Land Takeover at Rucalán."

CHAPTER 4. TIPIS AND DOMES

1 Interview with Yellow Kidney by Claude Schaeffer, June 11, 1950, Schaeffer Papers, Glenbow Archives, Calgary, Alberta, excerpted in Hungry-Wolf, *Blackfeet Papers Volume Two*, 360.

2 Newspapers reported that it would be put on display at the municipal zoo and entrusted to the new National Museum of Ethnology, a project of Expo 70 that opened in 1974. "Blackfeet Tipi Presented as Nation's Gift Osaka, Japan," *Cut Bank Pioneer*, December 24, 1970, MPIA; "American Indian Tent Given to Osaka City," *Sankei Shimbun*, October 13, 1970. Translation in NA, RG 306, USIA, Office of the Director/Osaka World Exhibition Office Entry #A1 1054-A: Files of the Press Office, 1967–1970, Folder PR 11–2 Press Releases (Presentation of Teepee). Ito Atsunori, associate professor in the Department of Modern Society and Civilization at the museum, helped me search for the whereabouts of the lodge, but we could not locate it by the time this book went to press.

3 Mapping these differences in turn helps to historicize contemporary criticism of Anthropocene, a universalizing paradigm that assigns the culpability for climate change and other ecological disasters to a generic humankind. For a pointed critique informed by Indigenous justice, see Todd and Davis, "On the Importance of a Date."

4 I described my research plan and was informed of protocols for visiting the nation during a phone call to the Blackfeet Nation Tribal Historic Preservation Office in advance of my visits in 2022.

5 Gardner, "1970 Osaka Expo and/as Science Fiction," 26–28.

6   Scott, *Architecture or Techno-utopia*, 1–3. Luca Massidda additionally credits televisual technologies for replacing place-based public spectacles as purveyors of global culture in "Cold War, a Cool Medium, and the Postmodern Death of World Expos," 183–90. As predecessors of art biennials, world fairs remain key sites for understanding ongoing globalization in all its neoliberal and critical forms, as Caroline A. Jones insists in *Global Work of Art*, ix–xvi.

7   Phyllis Montgomery, letter to Jack Masey, August 21, 1969, 1. NA, RG 306, USIA, Office of the Director/Osaka World Exhibition Office Entry #A1 1054-C: Files of the Japan and Washington Liaison Administrative Office, 1967–1972, Folder: Museum of Plains Indian and Crafts Center (Tipi).

8   Montgomery, letter to Jack Masey, 2.

9   Wissler, "Material Culture of Blackfeet Indians," 99.

10   Libhart and Ellison, "Introduction," 11.

11   Tipi, sometimes spelled tepee, is a generic term for the dwelling drawn from the Santee (Dakota) language; the Blackfeet term is niitóyis. See Rosoff, "Tipi," 4; Spang, "Of Tipis and Stereotypes," 108; LaPier, *Invisible Reality*, 31.

12   Noble, "Justice, Transaction, Translation," 342.

13   "Our Lands," Blackfeet Nation, accessed November 20, 2023, blackfeetnation.com/lands/.

14   Spellings for these various groups differ across sources and the US-Canada border; I follow the spellings most common in the United States provided by Ampskapi Pikuni historians Joseph Scott Gladstone and Donald D. Pepion in "Exploring Traditional; Indigenous Leadership Concepts," 571–72.

15   Conaty, "Niitsitapiisinni," 75.

16   Conaty, "Niitsitapiisinni," 95.

17   Libhart and Ellison, "Introduction," 18.

18   Schultz is quoted in Zedeño, "Art as the Road to Perfection," 633.

19   Libhart and Ellison, "Introduction," 18.

20   LaPier, *Invisible Reality*, 25.

21   Accounts of the naming and significance of these three zones differ. I follow LaPier, *Invisible Reality*, 26–27.

22   Pard is quoted in Zedeño, "Art as the Road to Perfection," 637.

23   LaPier, *Invisible Reality*, 32.

24   LaPier, *Invisible Reality*, 31; Conaty, "Niitsitapiisinni," 81.

25   Marr, "Scales of Vision," 97.

26   Gladstone and Pepion, "Exploring Traditional Indigenous Leadership Concepts," 574–76.

27   Rosoff, "Tipi," 4–9.

28   Libhart and Ellison, "Introduction," 7–9

29 Libhart and Ellison, "Introduction," 14.

30 Hungry-Wolf, *Blackfoot Papers Volume Two*, 360.

31 Libhart and Ellison, "Introduction," 34. The Ampskapi Pikuni and Apatosi Pikuni trace their separation to negotiations between Britain and the United States in 1818. Gladstone and Pepion, "Indigenous Leadership Concepts," 573.

32 Noble, "Justice, Transaction, Translation," 343.

33 Ceremonial specialist Awakasinna is quoted on the preference for these terms in Noble, "Justice, Transaction, Translation," 342; Gladstone and Pepion, "Indigenous Leadership Concepts," 579. Kiowa design rights are similarly contrasted with US copyright laws in Greene and Drescher, "The Tipi with Battle Pictures," 429.

34 Zedeño, "Art as the Road to Perfection," 638.

35 Pard is quoted in Zedeño, "Art as the Road to Perfection," 637.

36 Bill Blackman, in conversation with the author, Blackfeet Nation, July 9, 2022.

37 Interview with Yellow Kidney, excerpted in Hungry-Wolf, *Blackfoot Papers Volume Two*, 361.

38 Bastien, *Blackfoot Ways of Knowing*, 17.

39 Interview with Yellow Kidney, excerpted in Hungry-Wolf, *Blackfoot Papers Volume Two*, 362.

40 Gladstone and Pepion, "Indigenous Leadership Concepts," 576.

41 Gladstone and Pepion, "Indigenous Leadership Concepts," 579–81.

42 Bastien, *Blackfoot Ways of Knowing*, 4.

43 Conaty, "Niitsitapiisinni," 84; Noble, "Treaty Ecologies," 315–16.

44 Conaty, "Niitsitapiisinni," 84.

45 Zedeño, "Art as the Road to Perfection," 633, 639.

46 See Hall, "Divergent Wests of Isaac Stevens and Lame Bull," 107–11.

47 Wissler and Kehoe, "Manuscript," 52.

48 Bastien, *Blackfoot Ways of Knowing*, 24.

49 Doris Kicking Woman, in conversation with the author, Blackfeet Nation, July 9, 2022.

50 Old Person, "Amskapi Pikuni from the 1950s to 2010," 177.

51 Rosier, *Rebirth of the Blackfeet Nation*, 3, 269, 274.

52 Kicking Woman, in conversation with the author.

53 Kicking Woman, in conversation with the author.

54 "Blackfeet Tipi Present to Osaka, Japan," 9; Libhart and Ellison, "Introduction," 40.

55 Blackman, in conversation with the author.

56 Howard Rides at the Doore, in conversation with the author, telephone, August 7, 2022.

57 Doore, in conversation with the author.

58 Roger Butterfly, in conversation with the author, Blackfeet Nation, August 10, 2022. Doore, who shared a dorm with Darryl Blackman, told me that Darryl was dismissed one semester prior to graduating. Doore, in conversation with the author.

59 Kicking Woman, in conversation with the author.

60 This account by Jessie Donaldson Shultz is reproduced in Banks, "Jessie Donaldson Shultz and Blackfeet Crafts," 31–32.

61 Verne Dusenberry, letter to Jessie Donaldson Shultz Graham, September 13, 1964, reproduced in Banks, "Jessie Donaldson Shultz and Blackfeet Crafts," 19.

62 Bill Blackman showed me a photograph of Darryl Blackman wearing a beaded buckskin suit and noted that the artist made his own regalia. Blackman, in conversation with the author.

63 Dusenberry, letter to Graham, 19.

64 See essays in Conaty, *We Are Coming Home*.

65 Adolf Hungry-Wolf, in conversation with the author, Blackfeet Nation, July 9, 2022; Kicking Woman, in conversation with the author; Blackman, in conversation with the author, July 9, 2022, and August 10, 2022.

66 Kicking Woman, in conversation with the author.

67 Doore, in conversation with the author.

68 Scriver, *Bronze Inside and Out*, 285.

69 I also learned that a Yellow Crow Tipi—distinguished from the historical Crow Tipi by a yellow-and-blue design and the absence of a medicine bundle—arrived in Kicking Woman's family via a dream sometime in the 1970s. It was transferred to the late Ampskapi Pikuni artist and ceremonial participant Darrell Norman, who included a physical manifestation of the praxis in the Lodgepole Gallery and Tipi Village, a Blackfeet art shop and hotel in Browning that he opened with his German wife, Angelika Harden-Norman, in 1993. Later in the 1990s, the couple sent a version of the tipi to the Museum für Völkerkunde Hamburg, Europe's largest ethnology museum, in Harden-Norman's hometown. Kicking Woman in conversation with the author; Angelika Harden-Norman, in conversation with the author, telephone, June 10, 2022.

70 Libhart and Ellison, "Introduction," 39.

71 The Sioux Indian Museum (formerly the Sioux Indian Museum and Crafts Center) was founded in 1939 and operated the Tipi Shop, Inc., until 1981; the Southern Plains Indian Museum (formerly Southern Plains Indian Museum and Crafts Center), dedicated to the arts of western Oklahoma tribal nations, was founded in 1947–1948.

72 Libhart and Ellison, "Introduction," 40.

73 Libhart and Ellison, "Introduction," 39.

74 "Camps and Retreats Worldwide: Asia," *Nomadics Tipi Makers*, accessed July 15, 2022, tipi.com/campretreats-asia/.

75 Hungry-Wolf, *Blackfoot Papers Volume Two*, 334.

76 Unnamed article, *Glacier Reporter*, November 4, 1971, MPIA.

77 Doore, in conversation with the author.

78 Blackman's payment to design keepers is reported in *Glacier Reporter*, November 4, 1971. Doore could not recall payments made to tipi stewards and noted that the artists were not credited as authors of the museums commissions. Doore, in conversation with the author.

79 Myles Libhart, handwritten notes, 1970, 1. NA, RG 306, USIA, Office of the Director/Osaka World Exhibition Office Entry #A1 1054-A: Files of the Press Office, 1967–1970, Folder: Press Releases (Presentation of Teepee).

80 Eddie Mad Plume is named in Hungry-Wolf, *Blackfoot Papers Volume Two*, 361. Doore, however, remembers Mary Mad Plume as the recipient. Doore, in conversation with the author.

81 Wissler, "Material Culture of the Blackfoot Indians," 109.

82 Lévi-Strauss, *Savage Mind*, 23.

83 Marr, "Scales of Vision," 120.

84 Wharton, "Defining Models," 9–12.

85 Jones, *Global Work of Art*, 38.

86 Marr, "Scales of Vision"; Phillips, *Trading Identities*, 72–102.

87 Burke, "Growing Up on the Plains," 181–83; Santina, "Toys, Models, Collectibles," 12–13.

88 Doore, in conversation with the author.

89 Marr, "Scales of Vision," 121.

90 Brückner and Isenstadt, "Introduction" vii, ix.

91 Brückner and Isenstadt, "Introduction," vii, ix.

92 Ramon Gonyea, letter to Patricia Ewell, January 9, 1970. MPIA.

93 Ramon Gonyea, letter to Myles Libhart, November 18, 1969. MPIA.

94 Montgomery, letter to Jack Masey, 1–2.

95 "Crate—shipping," handwritten notes, Cut Bank Building Service receipt, January 10, 1970, MPIA.

96 Lévi-Strauss, *Savage Mind*, 23; Phillips, *Trading Identities*, 72–102.

97 "US Pavilion: 1970 World Exposition (EXPO '70), Osaka, Japan," *Davis Brody Bond*, accessed November 20, 2023, www.davisbrodybond.com/us-pavilion-1970-world-exposition-expo-70.

98 I cannot determine whether Blackman used earth or commercial paints.

99   "Blackfeet Tipi Presented as Nation's Gift Osaka, Japan."

100   Interview with Yellow Kidney, excerpted in Hungry-Wolf, *Black-foot Papers Volume Two*, 361.

101   Kicking Woman in conversation with the author, Blackfeet Nation, August 10, 2022.

102   Avenell, *Transnational Japan in the Global Environmental Movement*, 35.

103   Dunaway, *Seeing Green*, 87.

104   Smith, *Hippies, Indians, and the Fight for Red Power*, 6–7.

105   Smith, *Everything You Know About Indians Is Wrong*, 26.

106   Richman, "Rediscovery of the Redman," 59; Smith, *Hippies, Indians, and the Fight for Red Power*, 83–84, 126–27; Dunaway, *Seeing Green*, 87–91.

107   Dunaway, *Seeing Green*, 91.

108   Rosier, "Modern America Desperately Needs to Listen," 127.

109   Laubin and Laubin, *Indian Tipi*, 17.

110   Laubin and Laubin, *Indian Tipi*, 18.

111   Kalshoven, "Things in the Making," 61. On the Laubins in particular, see Ellis, "More Real than the Indians Themselves"; Berlo, *Not Native American Art: Fakes, Replicas, and Invented Traditions*, especially chapter 2, "Cultural Cross-Dressers: A Long History of Imitating Indians." See also Deloria, *Playing Indian*, 1998.

112   Brand, *Whole Earth Discipline*, 236.

113   Brand, *Whole Earth Discipline*, 237, 243. Brand quotes Pitt River elder Willard Rhoades in Anderson, *Tending the Wild*, 125.

114   Brand, *Last Whole Earth Catalog*, 100.

115   Brand, *Last Whole Earth Catalog*, 105.

116   Oliver, "Part One," 27–28.

117   See Rapoport, "The Pueblo and the Hogan," 66–79.

118   The photograph is reproduced in Sadler, "Drop City Revisited," 6.

119   Voyd, "Funk Architecture," 156; Scott, *Architecture or Techno-utopia*, 163.

120   Baer is quoted in Scott, *Architecture or Techno-utopia*, 161.

121   Voyd, "Funk Architecture," 157–58.

122   Nisbet, *Ecologies, Environments, and Energy Systems*, 80.

123   Nisbet, *Ecologies, Environments, and Energy Systems*, 85.

124   Massey, "Sumptuary Ecology of Buckminster Fuller's Designs," 191; Nisbet, *Ecologies, Environments, and Energy Systems*, 77.

125   This point is made by Shiva, "Greening of the Global Reach," 60.

126   Turner, "Corporation and the Counterculture," 71.

127   Turner, "Corporation and the Counterculture," 72.

128   Sheinin, "Kookie Thoughts."

129   Kahn, *Domebook 2*, 2.

130   Kahn, *Domebook 2*, 2.

131   Kahn, *Domebook 2*, 4.

132   Kahn, "Interview R. Buckminster Fuller," 90–91.

133   Kahn, "Interview R. Buckminster Fuller," 91.

134   Smith, *Hippies, Indians, and the Fight for Red Power*, 85.

135   Deloria Jr., "This Country Was a Lot Better Off When the Indians Were Running It."

136   "Alcatraz."

137   See the Alcatraz Proclamation reproduced in Smith and Warrior, *Like a Hurricane*, 28–29.

138   Demos, "Means Without End." See also Agamben, *Homo Sacer*.

139   Smith, *Hippies, Indians, and the Fight for Red Power*, 157–65; Smith and Warrior, *Like a Hurricane*, 157.

140   Doore, in conversation with the author.

141   See Smith, *Hippies, Indians, and the Fight for Red Power*, 216; Papastergiadis and Turney, *On Becoming Authentic*, 10.

142   See Avenell, *Transnational Japan in the Global Environmental Movement*; and Broadbent, *Environmental Politics in Japan*.

143   Sakai, "Imperial Nationalism and the Comparative Perspective," 172.

144   See Zaman, "Ainu and Japan's Colonial Legacy."

145   Takayuki, "Full Metal Apache," 29.

146   Takayuki, "Full Metal Apache," 34–45.

147   The first use is traced to an article in *Osaka Nichi-nichi Sinbun* (Osaka Daily News), May 28, 1958.

148   Tatsumi, "Full Metal Apache," 32–33.

149   Komatsu, *Nippon Apacchi-Zoku*, 219–220, translated into English in Tatsumi, "Full Metal Apache," 36.

150   Meadows, "The Cod Talkers' Legacy."

151   Yang, *Yoru wo Kakete*, 152, translated into English in Tatsumi, "Full Metal Apache," 33.

152   Vizenor, *Hiroshima Bugi*; Huang, "Radiation Ecologies in Gerald Vizenor's *Hiroshima Bugi*," 422–23. See also Sokolowski, "Between Dangerous Extremes."

153   Zwigenbeerg, "Coming of a Second Sun," 4–5.

154   Vizenor, *Fugitive Poses*, 21.

155   Vizenor, *Hiroshima Bugi*, 153–54. See also Vizenor, *Manifest Manners*, 42.

156   Gardner, "1970 Osaka Expo and/as Science Fiction," 28.

157   Muir-Harmony, "Limits of U.S. Science Diplomacy in the Space Age," 595, 602.

158   Muir-Harmony, "Limits of U.S. Science Diplomacy in the Space Age," 600.

159   Gardner, "1970 Osaka Expo and/as Science Fiction," 28.

160   Sheinin, "Kookie Thoughts."

161   Masey worked closely with Pavilion Commissioner General Howard L. Chernoff, a former journalist and executive assistant to the director of the USIA. The building was designed by Davis, Brody, Chermayeff, Geismar, deHarak Associates of New York. See "The United States Pavilion," Press Release, January 14, 1970, 1. NA, RG 306, USIA, Office of the Director/Osaka World Exhibition Office Entry #A1 1054-A: Files of the Press Office, 1967–1970, Folder: General Reports, Statistics.

162   Sheinin, "Kookie Thoughts."

163   Quoted in Chernoff, "U.S. Pavilion, Expo 70," Department of State telegram to Loomis, USIA Washington, June 12, 1970. NA, RG 306, USIA, Office of the Director/Osaka World Exhibition Office Entry #A1 1054-A: Files of the Press Office, 1967–1970, Folder: General Reports (Reaction Report).

164   Quoted in Chernoff, "U.S. Pavilion, Expo 70," 4.

165   Turner, "Corporation and the Counterculture," 72–76. See also Beck and Bishop, *Technocrats of the Imagination*, 94–104.

166   Furuhata, "Multimedia Environments and Security Operations," 57, 70, 69, 61. Members of the Self-Defense Forces participated in Japan's Expo 70 Security Team alongside private security companies (70).

167   "United States Pavilion," Press Release, 1.

168   Dan Oleksiw to Frank Shakespeare, June 1969, quoted in Muir-Harmony, "Limits of U.S. Science Diplomacy in the Space Age," 599.

169   Jack Masey, quoted in Muir-Harmony, "Limits of U.S. Science Diplomacy in the Space Age," 616.

170   "United States Pavilion," Press Release, 3.

171   Dockstader, "Folk Arts, Cross-Country," 74–75; Frederick J. Dockstader, letter to H. E. Stingle, May 15, 1970. NA, RG 306, USIA, Office of the Director/Osaka World Exhibition Office Entry #A1 1054-C: Files of the Japan and Washington Liaison Administrative Office, 1967–1972, Folder: Museum of American Indian: Indian, Masks, Pottery, Textiles, Baskets.

172   The cooperative members who created the beadwork included Alice Littleman (Kiowa), Mary Nowlin (Arapaho), Melvin Blackman (Arapaho-Cheyenne), Nettie Standing (Kiowa), and Laverne Capes (Kiowa). "Expo 67," 36–37.

173   Masey and Morgan, *Cold War Confrontations*, 332.

174   This unnamed visitor's reaction is quoted in Masey and Morgan, *Cold War Confrontations*, 344.

175   Quoted in Phillips, "Commemoration/(De)celebration," 103.

176   Phillips, "Commemoration/(De)celebration," 102.

177   Phillips, *Museum Pieces*, 35.

178   On the ambitions of Arthur Erickson and Geoffrey Massey, see
       Bergsma, "Canadian Reject," 30.

179   Keith Crowe, "Eskimos in Japan," 57. See also Geoghegan, "Inuit
       Art and Expo '70," 58–59. On the longer history of exchange
       between Japanese and Inuit artists, see Vorano, *Inuit Prints*; on
       Canada's Cold War export of Inuit arts, see Vorano, "Inuit Art."

180   Atsunori, "Indirect Collection and Attempts Half a Century Later,"
       154–68; Ito Atsunori, email to the author, August 25, 2022.

181   Lockyer, "Logic of Spectacle c. 1970," 571.

182   Yasufumi, "Criticism of Expo 70 in Print," 134.

183   Scott, *Architecture or Techno-utopia*, 3.

184   Banham is quoted in Scott, *Architecture or Techno-utopia*, 1.

185   Komatsu, "Banpaku kara kōgai e," 50, translated and excerpted
       in Gardner, "1970 Osaka Expo and/as Science Fiction," 38.

186   Rifkin, *Beyond Settler Time*, 1.

187   See, for example, Dillon, "Imagining Indigenous Futurisms,"
       Indigenous Futurisms; Medak-Saltzman, "Coming to You from
       the Indigenous Future"; Whyte, "Indigenous Science (Fiction)
       for the Anthropocene."

188   Harjo, *Spiral to the Stars*, 5.

189   See, for example, "Blackfeet Tipi Presented as Nation's Gift
       Osaka, Japan."

190   "Indian Tent Given to Osaka City for Use in Studies of the U.S.A.
       by U.S. Pavilion," *Mainichi Shimbun*, October 13, 1970, transla-
       tion in NA, RG 306, USIA, Office of the Director/Osaka World
       Exhibition Office Entry #A1 1054-A: Files of the Press Office,
       1967–1970, Folder PR 11–2 Press Releases (Presentation of Tee-
       pee); "American Indian Tent Given to Osaka City."

191   Libhart, handwritten notes, 3–12.

192   "Indian Tent Given to Osaka City for Use in Studies of the U.S.A.
       by U.S. Pavilion."

CHAPTER 5. THE TRUTH-LINE

1   Oscar Howe, "A Partial Explanation of Dakota Art," handwrit-
       ten, undated manuscript, 2. OHP, Subgroup 2: Family Papers,
       1903–2011, Series II: Teaching materials, 1965–1976, Box 44,
       Folder 16: Sioux Ceremonies, undated.

2   "Sioux Nation" does not refer to any overarching political
       organization; it has long been composed of "independent and au-
       tonomous nested social groups" who were allied through common
       culture, language, kinship, and diplomatic relations. See Posthu-
       mus, *All My Relatives*, 6; Hämäläinen, *Lakota America*, 16.

3   Galler, "Sustaining the Sioux Confederation," 469.

4   This concept is discussed extensively in Posthumus, *All My Relatives*, 14, 22, 41–42, 56, 62, 80, 204, 208, 215, 219, 223.

5   Deloria, *Speaking of Indians*, 25.

6   Kathleen Ash-Milby notes that he was absent for the 1935–1936 school year in "Origin Story," 69.

7   Howe's biography is detailed in Milton, *Oscar Howe*; Ash-Milby, "Origin Story," 67–87.

8   Berlo and Phillips, *Native North American Art*, 265.

9   Quoted in Anthes, *Native Moderns*, xi.

10   Oscar Howe, letter to Jeanne Snodgrass, April 18, 1958. OHP, Subgroup 1: University Papers, 1915–2016, Series II: Chronology Files, 1915–2010, Box 15, Folder 8: 1958.

11   The most nuanced discussions of this event appear in Anthes, *Native Moderns*, xi–xiii, 142–143; Burke, "Accolades and Acrimony." See also Dockstader, "Revolt of Trader Boy," 47; Meyer, "In Search of Native American Aesthetics," 38–39; Montiel, "American Indian Expressive Arts," 453–455; King, "Oscar Howe," 11; White, "Oscar Howe and the Transformation of Native American Art," 37–38.

12   Front matter, *Panorama* XXIII, no. 10 (1971), 3. OHP Subgroup 1: University Papers, 1915–2016, Series II: Chronology Files, 1915–2010, 1971, Box 17, Folder 3. Note that after the USIA replaced the USIS, the agency retained its former name in overseas locations.

13   "Oscar Howe, Preserving Sioux Art." *Panorama* XXIII, no. 10 (1971), 18. OHP Subgroup 1: University Papers, 1915–2016, Series II: Chronology Files, 1915–2010, 1971, Box 17, Folder 3.

14   Howe's guidelines cautiously specified that "a Short Term American Grantee does not, by virtue of his grant, have diplomatic or other official status during the grant period. He receives his grant as a private citizen and should avoid giving an impression that he is an official spokesman of the United States Government." "General Instructions for the Short Term American Grantee," Bureau of Educational and Cultural Affairs Short Term American Grantees Program, Department of State, 6. OHP, Subgroup 2, Family Papers, Series VI: American Specialist, 1971, Correspondence, 1966–1987, Box 49, Folder 1.

15   Welch, "Bridging Cultures Abroad," 185–208. In addition to a good overview of Howe's tour, this article includes numerous quotations from Welch's revealing email exchange with Arshed in 2006.

16   Oscar Howe interview, Oyate Radio Program, March, 1971, Oscar Howe Oral History Project, American Indian Research Project,

South Dakota Oral History Center, University of South Dakota (hereafter AIRP) #605, 3; Arshed, *Art Scene of Pakistan*, 97.

17 "Oscar Howe, Preserving Sioux Art," 20.

18 Howe, *Oscar Howe*.

19 Oscar Howe, letter to Dorothy Dunn Kramer, April 10, 1959. OHP Subgroup 2: Family Papers, 1903–2011, Series VII: Subject Files, 1935–2011, Box 50, Folder 1: Dorothy Dunn Kramer, 1954–1971 and undated.

20 Amiotte, "Eagles Fly Over," 29.

21 Amiotte and four other Native American students attended the institute, and Howe continued to support the younger artist's career for the remainder of his own. Jon Day, interview with Arthur Amiotte, January 5, 2001, AIRP #1996.

22 Deloria, *God Is Red*, 70, 66–67.

23 Posthumus, *All My Relatives*, 42.

24 Amiotte, "Eagles Fly Over," 29.

25 Amiotte, "Eagles Fly Over," 29.

26 Amiotte, "Road to the Center," 46.

27 Ash-Milby notes that Howe's supervisors dictated the illustrative style of the mural. Ash-Milby, "Origin Story," 71. The murals were restored in 2014. Amy Varland, "Mobridge's Oscar Howe Murals Restored," South Dakota Public Broadcasting, November 11, 2014, https://listen.sdpb.org/post/mobridges-oscar-howe-murals-restored.

28 Galler, "Sustaining the Sioux Confederation," 471.

29 Westerman and White, *Mni Sota Makoce*.

30 Quoted in Walker, *Lakota Belief and Ritual*, 82–83.

31 McLaughlin, *Arts of Diplomacy*, 208.

32 Clemmons, *Dakota in Exile*, 19–20. On the history and significance of the quarry, now managed by the National Park Service, see Hughes, *Perceptions of the Sacred*; Johnson, "George Catlin, Artistic Prospecting, and Dakhóta Agency in the Archive"; TallBear, "Indigenous Reflection on Working Beyond the Human/Not Human."

33 Clemmons, *Dakota in Exile*, 4. Dakota perspectives on the war of 1862 are gathered in Anderson and Woolworth, *Through Dakota Eyes*.

34 Oscar Howe interview, July 12, 1977, AIRP #1044, 4.

35 "Speech of Bone Necklace, Head Chief of the Yanktonnais Trade Before the Northwestern Indian Commission June." Armstrong, *Early Empire Builders of the Great West*, 167–68.

36 On the history and sacred status of this region, see Howe, Soldier, and Lee, *He Sapa Woihanble*.

37 Hämäläinen, *Lakota America*, 372–73.

38   Berlo and Amiotte, "Generosity, Trade, and Reciprocity among the Lakota," 48–50.

39   I am inspired to read the photograph in this manner by Zamir, *Gift of the Face*.

40   Inge Dawn Maresh, in conversation with the author, Zoom, November 4, 2021.

41   "The Art in Embassies Program," brochure, Department of State, n.d. OHP, Subgroup 2: Family Papers, 1903–2011, Series VI: American Specialist, 1971, Correspondence, 1966–1987, Box 48, Folder 16. Dorothy Dunn Kramer, who worked for the AIEP advisory committee under the inaugural Advisor of Fine Arts Nancy Kefauver (see chapter 1), wrote to Howe in 1966, "Oh yes! Mrs. K would like to use any painting of yours you could feel like sending for 2 year loans." Dorothy Dunn Kramer, letter to Oscar Howe, April 2, 1966. OHP Subgroup 2: Family Papers, 1903–2011, Series VII: Subject Files, 1935–2011, Dorothy Dunn Kramer, 1954–1971 and undated, Box 50, Folder 1. In 1969, Howe responded to a program request for additional paintings with a work titled *Li Li Li Li Li Li Li*. Oscar Howe, letter to Stefan P. Munsing, May 7, 1969. OHP, Subgroup 2: Family Papers, 1903–2011, Series VI: American Specialist, 1971, Box 48, Folder 16: (1 of 2).

42   "The Art in Embassies Program Progress Supplement," Department of State, June 1968, 1. OHP, Subgroup 2: Family Papers, 1903–2011, Series VI: American Specialist, 1971, Correspondence, 1966–1987, Box 48, Folder 16.

43   Amiotte, "Lakota Sun Dance," 46.

44   Amiotte, "Lakota Sun Dance," 75–76. See also Crow Dog and Erdoes, *Crow Dog*, 241; Means, *Where White Men Fear to Tread*.

45   Stefan P. Munsing, letter to Oscar Howe, April 8, 1972. OHP, Subgroup 2: Family Papers, 1903–2011, Series VI: American Specialist, 1971, Correspondence, 1966–1987, Box 48, Folder 16.

46   Deloria, *Playing Indian*.

47   Riedel, *Avoiding Armageddon*, 55.

48   Arshed, *Art Scene of Pakistan*, 36.

49   Riedel, *Avoiding Armageddon*, 55–75.

50   Riedel, *Avoiding Armageddon*, 73.

51   Arshed, *Art Scene of Pakistan*, 120.

52   "Islamic Republic of Pakistan: Background Notes," Department of State, July 1969, 2–4. OHP, Subgroup 2: Family Papers, 1903–2011, Series VI: American Specialist, 1971, Itineraries, 1971, Box 48, Folder 13. A second document described the general election in December 1970, anticipating (incorrectly) that the new National Assembly would be called into session by the middle of February, during Howe's tour. "Pakistan—A Brief Background Survey."

OHP, Subgroup 2: Family Papers, 1903–2011, Series VI: American Specialist, 1971, Itineraries, 1971, Box 48, Folder 13.

53 Oscar Howe, "Points of Interest on the Trip," handwritten notes, 1971. OHP, Subgroup 2: Family Papers, 1903–2011, Series VI: American Specialist, 1971, Correspondence, 1966–1987, Box 49, Folder 1.

54 Howe, "Points of Interest on the Trip."

55 Oscar Howe, letter to Dorothy Dunn Kramer, April 10, 1959.

56 Arshed, *Art Scene of Pakistan*, 97.

57 Arshed, *Art Scene of Pakistan*, 97–98.

58 Welch, "Bridging Cultures Abroad," 199.

59 "Introducing His Race's Characteristics to the World: An Indian Came to Izmir," *Yeni ASir*, January 8, 1971. An English translation is archived at OHP, Subgroup 2: Family Papers, 1903–2011, Series VI: American Specialist, 1971, Correspondence, 1966–1987, Box 48, Folder 16.

60 Arshed, *Art Scene of Pakistan*, 97.

61 Oscar Howe, handwritten notes, n.d. OHP, Subgroup 2: Family Papers, 1903–2011, Series VI: American Specialist, 1971, Itineraries, 1971, Box 48, Folder 13.

62 The existence of such a photograph was confirmed by the principal in a subsequent letter to Howe. Rashid Ahmad Arshed, letter to Oscar Howe, August 23, 1971. OHP, Subgroup 2: Family Papers, 1903–2011, Series VI: American Specialist, 1971, Correspondence, 1966–1987, Box 49, Folder 1.

63 Arshed, *Art Scene of Pakistan*, 97.

64 Howe, handwritten notes.

65 Howe, handwritten notes.

66 Quoted in Welch, "Bridging Cultures Abroad," 198–99.

67 Howe, handwritten notes.

68 Howe, "Points of Interest in the Trip."

69 Quoted in Welch, "Bridging Cultures Abroad," 197–99.

70 Oscar Howd to Stefan Munsing, Art in the Embassies Program, March 16, 1971, 871

71 Arshed wrote to Howe in early 1973 that this student, along with several others he taught during the tour, was living in the United States. Rashid Ahmad Arshed, letter to Oscar Howe, January 30, 1973. OHP, Subgroup 2: Family Papers, 1903–2011, Series VI: American Specialist, 1971, Correspondence, 1966–1987, Box 49, Folder 2.

72 Cards and letters are archived in OHP, Subgroup 2: Family Papers, 1903–2011, Series V: Correspondence, 1947–2010, Box 46, Folders 9–10.

73 Riedel, *Avoiding Armageddon*, 73.

74 Maresh in conversation with the author.

75 Milton, *Oscar Howe*, 9–10.

76 Berlo and Amiotte, "Generosity, Trade, and Reciprocity among the Lakota," 48–50.

77 Milton, *Oscar Howe*, 13–15.

78 Oscar Howe, "For Radio," unpublished, undated notes, 1. OHP, Subgroup 2: Family Papers, 1903–2011, Series II: Teaching Materials, 1965–1976, Sioux Ceremonies, undated, Box 44, Folder 16.

79 Milton, *Oscar Howe*, 15.

80 Dunn, *American Indian Painting of the Southwest and Plains Areas*, 283, 287.

81 Horton, "Performing Paint, Claiming Space," 4.

82 On the history of this phenomenon in the United States, see Deloria, *Playing Indian*. Dunn, *American Indian Painting of the Southwest and Plains Areas*, 281.

83 "From Indigenous America to North Africa," 114–17. See also Berlo, "Szwedzicki Portfolios."

84 This was a position that changed throughout Jacobson's career, perhaps in response to students like Howe, who saw that the styles developed at the Santa Fe Indian School and the University of Oklahoma were becoming repetitious and needed to "evolve into something else." Jacobson is quoted in Fur, *Painting Culture*, 240.

85 Oscar Howe, "An Exhibition of Original Painting in Tempera," 1. OHP, Subgroup 2: Family Papers, 1903–2011, Series III: Art career, 1947–2005, "An Exhibition of Original Paintings in Tempera," Oscar Howe's Master's Thesis, University of Oklahoma, 1953, Box 45, Folder 2.

86 Howe, "Exhibition of Original Painting in Tempera," 6.

87 Howe, "Exhibition of Original Painting in Tempera," 1.

88 Howe, "For Radio," 2.

89 Oscar Howe, "Class Art Lecture," May 7, 1963. OHP, Subgroup 1: University Papers, 1915–2016, Series II: Chronology Files, 1915–2010, 1963, Box 16, Folder 4.

90 Howe, "Theories and Beliefs—Dakota," 77.

91 Deloria, *God Is Red*, 66–67.

92 Mary Edman, "Oscar Howe Honors Indians by his Colorful Paintings," *Sioux Falls Argus Leader*, January 1974. OHP, Subgroup 1: University Papers, 1915–2016, Series II: Chronology Files, 1915–2010, 1974, Box 17, Folder 6.

93 Howe, *Oscar Howe, Artist*, n.p.

94 Amiotte, letter to the author, August 15, 2021. While I was unable to locate the term *tahokmu* in any Dakota dictionary, Amiotte

called my attention to similar words in the closely related Lakota dialect that address material culture, including *tawoꞌgmuŋke kaȟya*ꞌ, "made like a spiderweb, it is said . . . [for example] a pattern, say in beadwork"; *tahoꞌgmi*, "the hoop on which a hide or scalp is stretched"; and *tahoꞌgmi kaȟya*ꞌ, "the figure (four curves forming a four-sided figure with the concave sides outward) painted on that part of the robe which covers the back." *Dictionary-Oie Wowapi Wan of Teton Sioux*, 474, 485.

95 Howe, *Oscar Howe, Artist*.

96 TallBear, "Caretaking Relations, Not American Dreaming," 25.

97 Anthes, *Native Moderns*, 148.

98 Will G. Robinson, letter to Mrs. M. Wilmsen, February 21, 1967, OHP, Subgroup 1: University Papers, 1915–2016, Series I: Administrative Files, 1946–2015, Correspondence, 1957–1975, Box 2, Folder 2.

99 Dockstader, "Revolt of Trader Boy," 51.

100 White, "Oscar Howe and the Transformation of Native American Art," 37.

101 Montiel, "Indian American Expressive Arts," 454.

102 Oscar Howe, Art Class Lecture, November 8, 1960, AIRP #1255, 10. Here, Howe's lecture notes quote a description by Lawrence D. Steefel, Jr., of Pablo Picasso's significance in Steefel, "Body Imagery in Picasso's 'Night Fishing at Antibes,'" 360.

103 Howe, letter to Jeanne Snodgrass.

104 Oscar Howe interview, July 12, 1977, AIRP #1044, 11.

105 Gritton, *Institute of American Indian Arts*, 38–39.

106 Howe, "In reference to a statement made by Robert M. Quinn at the South West Indian Art Conference held at the University of Arizona," November 23, 1959. OHP, Subgroup 1: University Papers, 1915–2016, Series II: Chronology Files, 1915–2010, 1959, Box 15, Folder 8.

107 Howe turned down an invitation to teach at the new institute when it opened in 1962, prompting Dunn to write, "I'm glad they had the sense to offer you the Santa Fe job, and I'm glad you had the sense to turn them down . . . the trend seems commercial to me, and this is a pity." Dorothy Dunn Kramer letter to Oscar Howe, October 5, 1962. This and other letters from Dunn are archived OHP Subgroup 2: Family Papers, 1903–2011, Series VII: Subject Files, 1935–2011, Dorothy Dunn Kramer, 1954–1971 and undated, Box 50, Folder 1.

108 Cobb, *Native Activism in Cold War America*, 13.

109 Anthes, *Native Moderns*, 144.

110 Greenberg, "Towards a Newer *Laocoön*," 68.

111 Karmel, "Cubism and the Politics of Form," 124.

112   Oscar Howe, Art Class Lecture, November 10, 1960, AIRP #1250, 15.

113   Howe, Art Class Lecture, 14.

114   Howe, Art Class Lecture, 6.

115   Howe, Art Class Lecture, 10.

116   Kahnweiler, "Preface," quoted in Bois and Streip, "Kahnweiler's Lesson," 40.

117   Karmel, "Cubism and the Politics of Form," 124–25.

118   For a classic account of the hegemonic tendencies at play, see Heidegger, "Age of the World Picture."

119   Oscar Howe, Class Lecture, August 25, 1960. AIRP #1252, 3. In this passage, Howe does identify a form of creativity that is derived from "man's consciousness of his mortality, which is foreign to animals" and "is aimed at nonutilitarian aesthetic purposes." (3–4).

120   Howe, Class Lecture, 4.

121   Here, I am drawing on James Nisbet's notion of "the work of art as an ecological object" in *Ecologies, Environments, and Energy Systems*, 3.

122   Haeckel, *Generelle Morphologie der Organismen*.

123   Ingold, *Being Alive*, 64–65. See also Ingold, *Lines*.

124   Morton, *Ecological Thought*, 11.

125   Albro, *Fabriano*, 59; 91–105.

126   Gaudio, *Engraving the Savage*.

127   Edman, "Oscar Howe Honors Indians by his Colorful Paintings."

128   "Kem-Tone Wall Finish," booklet, American Chemical Society Office of Public Outreach and Sherwin-Williams Company, April 23, 1996, 1.

129   Coll, Keith, and Rosenthal, *United States Army in World War II*, 83–84.

130   Berlo and Phillips, *Native North American Art*, 133.

131   See Anderson, *Creatures of Empire*; Fischer, *Cattle Colonialism*.

132   Berlo and Phillips, *Native North American Art*, 143.

133   Captain Richard H. Pratt, who was in charge of Fort Marion, delivered a speech by that name at George Mason University in 1892 that catalyzed the development of boarding schools across the country. Reprinted in Pratt, "Advantages of Mingling Indians with Whites."

134   Howe, *Oscar Howe, Artist*.

135   Stevens, "Tomahawk," 475.

136   Howe, *Oscar Howe, Artist*.

137   Flatley, "Like," 75.

138   Howe, AIRP #1044, 15.

139   Howe, AIRP #1044, 15. He met his future wife, Adelheid (Heidi) Karla Margarete Hampel, while stationed in Biedelkopf, Germany.

140 Anthes, *Native Moderns*, 158.

141 2nd Annual Invitational Exhibition of American Indian Paintings, United States Department of the Interior, 1965, brochure. OHP, Subgroup 1: University Papers, 1915–2016, Series II: Chronology Files, 1915–2010, 1966, Box 16, Folder 7.

142 Castile, *To Show Heart*, 58.

143 George McGovern, letter to Oscar Howe, January 22, 1957. OHP, Subgroup 2: Family Papers, 1903–2011, Series V: Correspondence, 1947–2010, Correspondence: Incoming, George McGovern, 1955–1997, Box 48, Folder 2.

144 Maresh, in conversation with the author.

145 George McGovern, letter to Oscar Howe, June 17, 1964. OHP, Subgroup 2: Family Papers, 1903–2011, Series V: Correspondence, 1947–2010, Correspondence: Incoming, George McGovern, 1955–1997, Box 48, Folder 2.

146 McGovern, letter to Oscar Howe, April 14, 1973.

147 George McGovern, letter to Hayden Scott, October 3, 1969. OHP, Subgroup 2: Family Papers, 1903–2011, Series VI: American Specialist, 1971, Correspondence, 1966–1987, Box 48, Folder 16.

148 Karl E. Mundt, letter to Virginia Cooper, October 14, 1969. OHP, Subgroup 2: Family Papers, 1903–2011, Series VI: American Specialist, 1971, Correspondence, 1966–1987, Box 48, Folder 16.

149 Philp, *Indian Self Rule*, 309. For more on Reifel's political career, see Flynn, *Without Reservation*.

150 Howe, letter to Dorothy Dunn Kramer, April 10, 1959.

151 Flynn, *Without Reservation*, 161; Montiel, "Dakota Primetime," 115–19; "This Is Your Life, Oscar Howe," *This Is Your Life*, Ralph Edwards Production, NBC April 13, 1960, Television. Price befriended Howe and collected his work alongside other Native American artists as well as Jackson Pollock and Jasper Johns. Price was appointed Chairman of the IACB in 1967. "Indian Arts and Crafts Board has New Chairman and New Member," Bureau of Indian Affairs press release, August 30, 1967, www.bia.gov/as-ia /opa/online-press-release/indian-arts-and-crafts-board-has-new -chairman-and-new-member.

152 Howe, letter to Dorothy Dunn Kramer, April 10, 1959.

153 Will G. Robinson, "Distortion," *Mitchell Daily Republic*, February 29, 1960.

154 Welch, "Oscar Howe's *Wounded Knee Massacre*," 114.

155 Philp, *Termination Revisited*, xxv.

156 Guilbaut, *How New York Stole the Idea of Modern Art*, 25.

157 Welch, "Oscar Howe's *Wounded Knee Massacre*," 112. Welch suggests that this uncharacteristically hard political line may have

been motivated by Howe's personal relationships with descendants
of Wounded Knee survivors, as well as art historical exposure
to other execution scenes by Pablo Picasso and Francisco Goya
(111–12).

158   Howe, letter to Jeanne Snodgrass, April 18, 1958.

159   Hämäläinen, *Lakota America*, 82; Posthumus, *All My Relatives*, 51.

160   Hämäläinen, *Lakota America*, 82.

161   Hämäläinen, *Lakota America*, 84.

162   Hämäläinen, *Lakota America*, 83.

163   Deloria, "Rise of Indian Activism," 397.

164   Treat, *Around the Sacred Fire*, 2, 34.

165   Deloria, *God Is Red*, 36.

166   A formal organization, headquartered in Minneapolis, has been
operative since 1968. See "American Indian Movement Grand
Governing Council," accessed November 20, 2023, http://
aimgrandgoverningcouncil.org/.

167   Bellecourt, *Thunder Before the Storm*, 154.

168   Treat, *Around the Sacred Fire*, 3; Baylor, "Media Framing of
Movement Protest, 245.

169   "Trail of Broken Treaties 20-Point Position Paper," October 1972,
Minneapolis, MN, American Indian Movement Archives, http://
www.aimovement.org/archives/.

170   Arshed discusses the history of the Central Institute for Arts and
Crafts in "Interview with Rashid Arshad."

171   Arshed, letter to Oscar Howe, February 27, 1971, OHP, Sub-
group 2: Family Papers, 1903–2011, Series VI: American
Specialist, 1971, Correspondence, 1966–1987, Box 49,
Folder 2.

172   Oscar Howe, letter to George McGovern, September 9, 1971. OHP,
Subgroup 2: Family Papers, 1903–2011, Series V: Correspon-
dence, 1947–2010, Box 48, Folder 2: Correspondence: Incoming,
George McGovern, 1955–1997, Box 48, Folder 2.

173   McGovern, letter to Oscar Howe, September 24, 1971.

174   Arshed letter to Howe, n.d., mailed on April 9, 1975. OHP,
Subgroup 2: Family Papers, 1903–2011, Series VI: American
Specialist, 1971, Correspondence, 1966–1987, Box 49,
Folder 2.

175   Arshed, *Text and Texture: Contemporary Calligraphic Paintings*, 22.

176   Arshed, letter to Oscar Howe, August 23, 1971. OHP, Sub-
group 2: Family Papers, 1903–2011, Series VI: American
Specialist, 1971, Correspondence, 1966–1987, Box 49,
Folder 2.

1   Karlstrom, "Oral History Interview with Fritz Scholder," 1995, AAA, www.aaa.si.edu/collections/interviews/oral-history -interview-fritz-scholder-11647; Lowe, "Scholder's Legacy," 158; Ramona Scholder, in conversation with the author, Santa Fe, New Mexico, June 5, 2015.

2   Light, "Romania's Problem with Dracula," 63; Arata, "Occidental Tourist," 622–23.

3   Hendershot, *I Was a Cold War Monster*, 48–54.

4   Fisher, *Vampire in the Text*, 11.

5   Light, *Dracula Dilemma*, 61.

6   Karlstrom, "Oral History Interview with Fritz Scholder"; Ramona Scholder, in conversation with the author.

7   Light, *Dracula Dilemma*, 64–65, 87–95; McNally and Florescu, *In Search of Dracula*.

8   Light, "Romania's Problem with Dracula," 64.

9   Karlstrom, "Oral History Interview with Fritz Scholder"; Ramona Scholder, in conversation with the author. It is possible that his destination was Poienari Castle, partial ruins with a long stairway that was rebuilt by Vlad III and later excavated and restored by the Romanian state between 1969 and 1972 to celebrate the ruler's struggle against the Ottomans. It was first promoted as the "true" Dracula's cast in McNally and Florescu, *In Search of Dracula*. See Light, *Dracula Dilemma*, 97–98.

10 Scholder, *Scholder/Indians*, 14. I previously explored the connection between Scholder's experiences with travelers around Santa Fe and his own Cold War journeys abroad in Horton, "Painter, Traveler, Diplomat."

11 Quoted in Smith, *Hippies, Indians, and the Fight for Red Power*, 6.

12 Karlstrom, "Oral History Interview with Fritz Scholder."

13 Karlstrom, "Oral History Interview with Fritz Scholder."

14 Report, American Embassy in Bucharest to USIA, Washington, DC, November 3, 1972. SIA, National Collection of Fine Arts (US), Office of Exhibition and Design, 1970–1974. Box 1, Folder: Scholder/Cannon Traveling; "Scholder-Cannon Exhibition," 1. SIA, National Collection of Fine Arts (US), Department of Twentieth Century Painting and Sculpture, Records, 1965–1975. Box 13, Folder: Scholder exh.—publicity.

15 Smith, "Monster Love," 30. *Indian with Beer Can* is reproduced on Smith, "Monster Love," 31.

16 C. T. Toiu, "The Nostalgic Return," *Luceafărul*, October 7, 1972, 8. SIA, National Collection of Fine Arts (US), Department of Twentieth Century Painting and Sculpture, Records, 1965–1975.

Box 13, Folder: Scholder exh.—publicity. Translation by Alexandra Magearu.

17 Bohlinger, "East Is a Delicate Matter," 390; Lavrentyev, "Red Westerns–A Short History."

18 Cristina Angelescu, "Fritz Scholder and T.C. Cannon . . . Painting." *Saptamina*, October 13, 1971, 12. SIA, National Collection of Fine Arts (US), Department of Twentieth Century Painting and Sculpture, Records, 1965–1975. Box 13, Folder: Scholder exh.—publicity. Translation by Alexandra Magearu.

19 "Scholder-Cannon Exhibition," 2.

20 On international press coverage of AIM, see Kýrová, "Right to Think for Themselves," 76–124.

21 McGrath, "Lloyd Kiva New," 15.

22 Krenn, *Fall-Out Shelters for the Human Spirit*, 238.

23 Burcea, "Policies of Cultural Assimilation in Transylvania," 27–30.

24 Whyte, "Indigenous Science (Fiction) for the Anthropocene," 229.

25 Tóth, *From Wounded Knee to Checkpoint Charlie*, 142–53.

26 Crossen, "Another Wave of Anti-Colonialism," 542–48.

27 "About IITC," International Indian Treaty Council, accessed March 14, 2021, www.iitc.org/about-iitc/; International Indian Treaty Council, "For the Continuing Independence of Native Nations," and Geneva Declaration, "For Human Rights and Fundamental Freedoms," in Cobb, *Say We Are Nations*, 167–71, 172–75, respectively. See also Henderson, *Indigenous Diplomacy and the Rights of Peoples*; Lightfoot, *Global Indigenous Politics*; Tóth, *From Wounded Knee to Checkpoint Charlie*; Lee, "Navajo Nation and the Declaration on the Rights of Indigenous Peoples."

28 Tóth, *From Wounded Knee to Checkpoint Charlie*, 158.

29 T. J. Demos has described earth jurisprudence as "the rights of nature to subsist in a state free from destructive human practices," including "the right to exist and participate in the evolution of life's biodiverse networks of interdependent systems" and notes the recent growth of this discourse in environmental law. Demos, "Rights of Nature," 134.

30 Barreiro, "Geneva, 1977," 62–67.

31 Lightfoot, *Global Indigenous Politics*, 4. Chickasaw and Cheyenne legal scholar James (Sa'ke'j) Youngblood credits "stories, art, and ceremonies" with ensuring that "Indigenous teachings and legal traditions live on [through colonial oppression] . . . so that each people could restore them at the right time and transform them into the Declaration." Henderson, *Indigenous Diplomacy and the Rights of Peoples*, 11.

BIBLIOGRAPHY

::::::::::

ARCHIVES

Archives of American Art, Washington, DC (AAA)

Institute of American Indian Art Archives, Santa Fe, NM (IAIA)

Laboratory of Anthropology Archives, Dorothy Dunn Kramer Papers, Santa Fe, NM (LAB DDK)

Museum of Modern Art Archives, New York, NY (MoMA)

National Anthropological Archives, Solomon McCombs Papers, Washington, DC (NAA SMP)

National Archives, College Park, MD (NACP)

National Archives and Records Administration–Pacific Region, San Francisco, CA (NARA–Pacific Region)

National Gallery of Art Archives, Washington, DC (NGA)

School for Advanced Research Archives, Santa Fe, NM (SAR)

Smithsonian Institution Archives, Washington, DC (SIA)

University of South Dakota Archives and Special Collections, Oscar Howe Papers, Vermillion, SD (OHP)

PUBLISHED SOURCES

Abrahamian, Ervand. *The Coup: 1953, the CIA and the Roots of Modern US–Iranian Relations*. New York: New Press, 2013.

Agamben, Giorgio. *Homo Sacer: Sovereign Power and Bare Life*. 1998. Translated by Daniel Heller-Roazen. Stanford, CA: Stanford University Press.

Aggestam, Karin and Ann E. Towns. "Introduction: The Study of Gender, Diplomacy and Negotiation." In *Gendering Diplomacy and International Negotiation*, edited by Karin Aggestam and Ann E. Towns, 1–22. London: Palgrave Macmillan, 2018.

Akwesasne Notes, ed., "Deskaheh." In *A Basic Call to Consciousness*. 41–55. Summertown, TN: Native Voices, 2005 [1978].

Albro, Sylvia Rodgers. *Fabriano: City of Medieval and Renaissance Papermaking*. New Castle, DE: Oak Knoll Press, 2016.

Allen, Chadwick. "A Trans*national* Native American Studies? Why Not Studies That Are Trans-*Indigenous*?" *Journal of Transnational American Studies* 4, no. 1 (2012): 1–22.

Allen, Paula Gunn. *The Sacred Hoop: Recovering the Feminine in American Indian Traditions*. Boston: Beacon Press, 1986.

Allen, Paula Gunn. "The Woman I Love Is a Planet; The Planet I Love is a Tree." In *Reweaving the World: The Emergence of Ecofeminism*, edited by Irene Diamond and Gloria Feman Orenstein, 52–57. San Francisco: Sierra Club Books, 1990.

Alvin Josephy, Joane Nagel, and Troy R. Johnson. Introduction to "Declaration of Indian Purpose." In *Red Power: The American Indians' Fight for Freedom*, edited by Alvin Josephy, Joane Nagel, and Troy R. Johnson, 13. Lincoln: University of Nebraska Press, 1999.

Amerian, Stephanie M. "The Fashion Gap: The Politics of American and Soviet Fashion, 1945–1959." *Journal of Historical Research in Marketing* 8, no. 1 (2016): 65–82.

Amiotte, Arthur. "Eagles Fly Over." *Parable* 1, no. 3 (Spring 1976): 28–41.

Amiotte, Arthur. "The Lakota Sun Dance: Historical and Contemporary Perspectives." In *Sioux Indian Religion: Tradition and Innovation*, edited by Raymond J. DeMallie and Douglas R. Parks, 74–89. Norman: University of Oklahoma Press, 1987.

Amiotte, Arthur. "The Road to the Center." *Parabola* 9, no. 3 (1984): 46–51.

Amsden, Charles Avery. *Navajo Weaving: It's Technic and History*. Albuquerque: University of New Mexico Press, 1949 [1934].

Anderson, Gary Clayton, and Alan R. Woolworth. *Through Dakota Eyes: Narrative Accounts of the Minnesota Indian War of 1862*. St. Paul: Minnesota Historical Society Press, 1988.

Anderson, Karen. *Changing Woman: A History of Racial Ethnic Women in Modern America*. New York: Oxford University Press, 1996.

Anderson, M. Kat. *Tending the Wild: Native American Knowledge and the Management of California's Natural Resources*. Berkeley: University of California Press, 2005.

Anderson, Virginia DeJohn. *Creatures of Empire: How Domestic Animals Transformed Early America*. Oxford: Oxford University Press, 2004.

Anthes, Bill. *Native Moderns: American Indian Painting, 1940–1960*. Durham, NC: Duke University Press, 2006.

Anthes, Bill. "'Why Injun Artist Me': Acee Blue Eagle's Diasporic Performative." In *Native Diasporas: Indigenous Identities and Settler Colonialism in the Americas*, edited by Gregory D. Smithers and Brooke N. Newman, 411–41. Lincoln: University of Nebraska Press, 2014.

Anthes, Bill, and Kathleen Ash-Milby, eds. *Dakota Modern: The Art of Oscar Howe*. Washington, DC: Smithsonian National Museum of the American Indian, 2022.

Arata, Stephen D. "The Occidental Tourist: 'Dracula' and the Anxiety of Reverse Colonization." *Victorian Studies* 33, no. 4 (Summer 1990): 621–45.

Armstrong, Leatrice A. *Mary Wheelwright: Her Book*. Santa Fe, NM: Wheelwright Museum of the American Indian, 2016.

Armstrong, Moses Kimball. *The Early Empire Builders of the Great West*. White Fish, MT: Kessinger Publishing, 2010.

Arshed, Rashid Ahmad. *Art Scene of Pakistan: The Unwritten Chapter*. Lahore, Pakistan: Sang-e-Meel Publications, 2018.

Arshad, Rashid Ahmad. *Text and Textures: Contemporary Calligraphic Paintings*. Middleton, DE: Self-published booklet, 2018.

Arshad, Rashid. "Interview with Rashid Arshad." Interview by Seher Naveed. *Art Now: Contemporary Art of Pakistan*, February 1, 2014. www.artnowpakistan.com/interview-with-rashid-arshad/.

Ash-Milby, Kathleen. "Origin Story." In *Dakota Modern: The Art of Oscar Howe*, edited by Bill Anthes and Kathleen Ash-Milby, 67–87. Washington, DC: Smithsonian National Museum of the American Indian, 2022.

Ash-Milby, Kathleen. "Woven by the Grandmothers: Twenty-Four Blankets Travel to the Navajo Nation." *Journal of the American Institute for Conservation* (Spring 1988): 1–4.

Atsunori, Ito. "Indirect Collection and Attempts Half a Century Later." In *National Museum of Ethnology 40th Anniversary Special Exhibition: From the Tower of the Sun to Minpaku: Collection Materials of Expo 70*, 154–68. Osaka: National Museum of Ethnology, 2018.

Austin, Justice Raymond D. "Diné Sovereignty, a Legal and Traditional Analysis." In *Navajo Sovereignty: Understandings and Visions of the Diné People*, edited by Lloyd L. Lee, 19–42. Tucson: University of Arizona Press, 2017.

Avenell, Simon Andrew. *Transnational Japan in the Global Environmental Movement*. Honolulu: University of Hawai'i Press, 2017.

Azoulay, Ariella. "The Family of Man: A Visual Universal Declaration of Human Rights." In *The Human Snapshot*, edited by Thomas Keenan and Tirdad Zolgahdr, 19–48. Berlin: Sternberg Press, 2013.

Bacigalupo, Ana Mariella. "Mapuche Women's Empowerment as Shaman—Healers (*Machis*) in Chile." In *The Annual Review of Women in World Religions IV*, edited by Arvind Sharma and Katherine K. Young, 57–129. Albany: State University of New York, 1996.

Bacigalupo, Ana Mariella. "Rethinking Identity and Feminism: Contributions of Mapuche Women and Machi from Southern Chile." *Hypatia* 18, no. 2 (Spring 2003): 32–57.

Bacigalupo, Ana Mariella. *Shamans of the Foye Tree: Gender, Power, and Healing Among Chilean Mapuche*. Austin: University of Texas Press, 2007.

Bad Hand, Howard. "The American Flag in Lakota Tradition." In *The Flag in American Indian Art*, edited by Toby Herbst and Joel Kopp, 11–13. Cooperstown, NY: New York State Historical Association, 1993.

Banerjee, Subhankar. "From the Red Nation to the Red Deal: A Conversation with Melanie K. Yazzie and Nick Estes." In *The Routledge Companion to Contemporary Art, Visual Culture, and Climate Change*, edited by T. J. Demos, Emily Eliza Scott, and Subhankar Banerjee, 446, 439. New York: Routledge, 2021.

Banks, Anne. "Jessie Donaldson Shultz and Blackfeet Crafts." *Montana: The Magazine of Western History* 33, no. 4 (Autumn 1983): 18–35.

Barker, Joanne. "Gender, Sovereignty, Rights: Native Women's Activism against Social Inequality and Violence in Canada." *American Quarterly* 60, no. 2 (June 2008): 259–66.

Barnhisel, Greg. *Cold War Modernists: Art, Literature, and American Cultural Diplomacy*. New York: Columbia University Press, 2015.

Barreiro, José. "Geneva, 1977: A Report on the Hemispheric Movement of Indigenous Peoples." In *A Basic Call to Consciousness*, edited by Akwesasne Notes, 55–78. Summertown, TN: Native Voices, 2005 [1978].

Bartels, Dennis and Alice L. Bartels. "Indigenous Peoples of the Russian North and Cold War Ideology." *Anthropologica* 48, no. 2 (2006): 265–79.

Barthes, Roland. *Camera Lucida: Reflections on Photography*. New York: Hill and Wang, 1981.

Barthes, Roland. "The Great Family of Man." In *Mythologies*, translated by Jonathan Cape and Richard Howard, 196–99. New York: Hill and Wang, 2013.

Bastien, Betty. *Blackfoot Ways of Knowing: The Worldview of the Siksikaitsitapi*. Calgary, ON: University of Calgary Press, 2004.

Baylor, Tim. "Media Framing of Movement Protest: The Case of American Indian Protest." *Social Science Journal* 33, no. 3 (1996): 241–55.

Becerra, Sandra, María Eugenia Merino, Andrew Webb, and Daniela Larrañaga. "Recreated Practices by Mapuche Women that Strengthen Place Identity in New Urban Spaces of Residence in Santiago, Chile." *Ethnic and Racial Studies* 41, no. 7 (2018): 1255–73.

Beck, John, and Ryan Bishop. *Technocrats of the Imagination: Art, Technology, and the Military-Industrial Avant-Garde*. Durham, NC: Duke University Press, 2020.

Begay, D. Y. "Shi' Sha' Hane' (My Story)." In *Woven by the Grandmothers: Nineteenth-Century Navajo Textiles from the National Museum of the American Indian*, edited by Eulalie H. Bonar; translated by Ellavina Perkins and Esther Yazzie, 13–27. Washington, DC: Smithsonian Institution Press and the National Museum of the American Indian, 1996.

Begay, D. Y. "Weaving Is Life: A Navajo Weaver's Perspective." In *Weaving Is Life: Navajo Weavings from the Edwin L. and Ruth E. Kennedy Southwest Native American Collection*, edited by Jennifer McLerran, 48–59. Seattle: University of Washington Press, 2006.

Beiser, Vince, and Sim Chi Yin. "The Deadly Global War for Sand." Pulitzer Center Projects, 2016–ongoing. https://pulitzercenter.org/projects/deadly-global-war-sand.

Bellecourt, Clyde. *The Thunder before the Storm: The Autobiography of Clyde Bellecourt as told to Jon Lurie*. Saint Paul: Minnesota Historical Society Press, 2016.

Benally, AnCita. "Diné Binahat'á,' Navajo Government." PhD diss., University of New Mexico, 2006.

Benjamin, Walter. "On the Mimetic Faculty." In *Walter Benjamin: Selected Writings*. Vol. 2, *1927–1934*, edited by Michael W. Jennings, Howard Eiland, and Gary Smith, translated by Rodney Livingstone et al., 720–22. Cambridge, MA: Harvard University Press, 1999.

Benjamin, Walter. "The Doctrine of the Similar." In *Walter Benjamin: Selected Writings*. Vol. 2, *1927–1934*, edited by Michael W. Jennings, Howard Eiland, and Gary Smith, translated by Rodney Livingstone et al., 694–98. Cambridge, MA: Harvard University Press, 1999.

Bergsma, Emily. "'Canadian Reject': Melvin Charney's Design for the Canadian Pavilion at Expo 70." MA thesis, Concordia University, 2017.

Berlo, Janet Catherine. "Alberta Thomas, Navajo Pictorial Arts, and Ecocrisis at Dinétah." In *A Keener Perception: Ecocritical Studies in American Art History*, edited by Alan C. Braddock and Christoph Irmscher, 237–53. Tuscaloosa: University of Alabama Press, 2009.

Berlo, Janet Catherine. "From Indigenous America to North Africa: The Cosmopolitan World of Oscar Howe Jacobson." In *A World Unconquered: The Art of Oscar Brousse Jacobson*, 103–133. Norman, OK: Fred Jones Jr. Museum of Art, 2015.

Berlo, Janet Catherine. "'It's Up to You—': Individuality, Community and Cosmopolitanism in Navajo Weaving." In *Weaving Is Life: Navajo Weavings from the Edwin L. and Ruth E. Kennedy Southwest Native American Collection*, edited by Jennifer McLerran, 34–47. Seattle: University of Washington Press, 2006.

Berlo, Janet Catherine. "Navajo Cosmoscapes—Up, Down, *Within*." *American Art* 25, no. 1 (Spring 2011): 10–13.

Berlo, Janet Catherine. *Not Native American Art: Fakes, Replicas, and Invented Traditions*. Seattle: University of Washington Press, 2023.

Berlo, Janet Catherine. "Navajo Sandpainting in the Age of Cross-cultural Replication." *Art History* 37, no. 4 (November 2014): 688–707.

Berlo, Janet Catherine. "The Szwedzicki Portfolios of American Indian Art, 1929–1952." *American Indian Art Magazine* 34, no. 2–3 (2009): 36–45; 58–67.

Berlo, Janet Catherine, and Arthur Amiotte. "Generosity, Trade, and Reciprocity among the Lakota: Three Moments in Time." In *Plains Indian Art of the Early Reservation Era: The Donald Danforth Jr. Collection at the Saint Louis Art Museum*, edited by Jill Ahlberg Yohe and Janet Catherine Berlo, 32–73. St. Louis, MO: St. Louis Art Museum, 2016.

Berlo, Janet Catherine, and Ruth B. Phillips. *Native North American Art*. 2nd ed. Oxford: Oxford University Press, 2014.

Bernstein, Bruce, and W. Jackson Rushing. *Modern by Tradition: American Indian Painting in the Studio Style*. Santa Fe: Museum of New Mexico Press, 1995.

Black Boy, Cecil. "Blackfeet Tipi Legends." In *Painted Tipis by Contemporary Plains Artists*, 45–79. Anadarko, OK: Oklahoma Indian Arts and Crafts Cooperative, 1973.

"Blackfeet Tipi Present to Osaka, Japan." *Indian Center News* 9, no. 5. (January 1971), 9.

Blake, Jody. "Cold War Diplomacy and Civil Rights Activism at the First World Festival of Negro Arts." In *Studies in the History of Art Vol. 71, Symposium Papers XLVIII: Romare Bearden, American Modernist*, 43–58. Washington, DC: National Gallery of Art, 2011.

Bleiker, Roland, and Sally Butler. "Radical Dreaming: Indigenous Art and Cultural Diplomacy." *International Political Sociology* 10 (2006): 56–74.

Blocker, Jane. *Where Is Ana Mendieta?: Identity, Performativity, and Exile*. Durham, NC: Duke University Press, 1999.

Boetzkes, Amanda. *The Ethics of Earth Art*. Minneapolis: University of Minnesota Press, 2010.

Bohlinger, Vincent. "'The East Is a Delicate Matter': White Sun of the Desert and the Soviet Western." In *International Westerns: Re-Locating the Frontier*, edited by Cynthia J. Miller and A. Bowdoin Van Riper, 373–93. Lanham, MD: Scarecrow Press, 2014.

Bois, Yve-Alain, and Katharine Streip. "Kahnweiler's Lesson." *Representations* 18 (Spring 1987): 33–68.

Boston, D. M., G. E. Williams, and G. W. P. Jarvis. "Conservation of a Navajo Sand-painting." Horniman Museum and Gardens Archives, 1968, 1.

Brand, Stewart. *Whole Earth Discipline: An Ecopragmatist Manifesto*. New York: Viking Penguin, 2009.

Brand, Stewart, ed. *The Last Whole Earth Catalog: Access to Tools*. New York: Random House, 1971.

Brightman, Marc, Vanessa Grotti, and Olga Ulturgasheva. "Introduction: Rethinking the 'Frontier' in Amazonia and Siberia; Extractive Economies, Indigenous Politics, and Social Transformations." *Cambridge Journal of Anthropology* 26, no. 2 (2006/2007): 1–12.

Broadbent, Jeffrey. *Environmental Politics in Japan: Networks of Power and Protest*. Cambridge: Cambridge University Press, 1998.

Brody, J. J. *Pueblo Indian Painting: Tradition and Modernism in New Mexico, 1900–1930*. Santa Fe, NM: School of American Research Press, 1997.

Brückner, Martin, and Sandy Isenstadt. "Introduction: Modelwork." In *Modelwork: The Material Culture of Making and Knowing*, edited by Martin Brückner, Sandy Isenstadt, and Sarah Wasserman, vii–xx. Minneapolis: University of Minnesota, 2021.

Bunnell, Glenn E. "No Night, No Death, No Winter: A Picture Story of What May Well Be the Last Medicine Lodge Ceremony of the Great Blackfeet Tribe." *Montana: The Magazine of Western History* 8, no. 2 (Spring 1958): 22–25.

Burcea, Horatiu. "Policies of Cultural Assimilation in Transylvania: *Magyarization* and *Romanianization*." MA thesis, Ball State University, 2009.

Bu, Liping. "Educational Exchange and Cultural Diplomacy in the Cold War." *Journal of American Studies* 33, no. 3 (1999): 393–415.

Burke, Christina E., "Accolades and Acrimony: Philbrook's Indian Annual." In *Dakota Modern: The Art of Oscar Howe*, edited by

Bill Anthes and Kathleen Ash-Milby, 125–135. Washington, DC: Smithsonian National Museum of the American Indian, 2022.

Burke, Christina E. "Growing up on the Plains." In *Tipi: Heritage of the Great Plains*, edited by Nancy B. Rosoff and Susan Kennedy Zeller, 169–91. Seattle: University of Washington Press, 2011.

Burns, Emily C. *Transnational Frontiers: The American West in France*. Norman: University of Oklahoma Press, 2018.

Burt, Larry W. *Tribalism in Crisis: Federal Indian Policy, 1953–1961*. Albuquerque: University of New Mexico Press, 1982.

Cajete, Gregory. "Native Science and Sustaining Indigenous Communities." In *Traditional Ecological Knowledge: Learning from Indigenous Practices for Environmental Sustainability*, edited by Melissa K. Nelson and Dan Shilling, 15–26. Cambridge: Cambridge University Press, 2018.

Cassidy, Jennifer A., and Sara Althari. "Introduction: Analysing the Dynamics of Modern Diplomacy through a Gender Lens." In *Gender and Diplomacy*, edited by Jennifer A. Cassidy, 1–12. London: Taylor and Francis, 2017.

Castile, George Pierre. *To Show Heart: Native American Self-Determination and Federal Indian Policy, 1960–1975*. Tucson: University of Arizona Press, 1998.

Caute, David. *The Dancer Defects: The Struggle for Cultural Supremacy during the Cold War*. Oxford: Oxford University Press, 2003.

Chamberlain, Kathleen P. *Under Sacred Ground: A History of Navajo Oil, 1922–1982*. Albuquerque: University of New Mexico, 2000.

Champagne, Duane. "From Full Citizenship to Self-Determination, 1930–1975." In *American Indians, American Presidents: A History*, edited by Clifford E. Trafzer, 145–83. Washington, DC: Smithsonian National Museum of the American Indian, 2009.

Cheryl Suzack, Shari M. Huhndorf, Jeanne Perreault, and Jean Barman, eds. *Indigenous Women and Feminism: Politics, Activism, Culture*. Vancouver: University of British Columbia Press, 2010.

Chiguailaf, María Catrileo. *Diccionario lingüístico etnográfico de la lengua Mapuche*. Valdivia: Universidad Austral de Chile, 2017.

Clemmons, Linda M. *Dakota in Exile: The Untold Stories of Captives in the Aftermath of the U.S.-Dakota War*. Iowa City: University of Iowa Press, 2019.

Clinton, Robert N. "Treaties with Native Nations: Iconic Historical Relics or Modern Necessity?" In *Nation to Nation: Treaties between the United States and American Indian Nations*, edited by Suzan Shown Harjo, 14–33. Washington, DC: National Museum of the American Indian, Smithsonian Institution, 2014.

Coates, Robert M. "Our Far-Flung Correspondents: Indian Affairs, New Style." *New Yorker* 43, no. 17 (1967): 102–12.

Cobb, Daniel M. *Native Activism in Cold War America: The Struggle for Sovereignty*. Lawrence: University Press of Kansas, 2008.

Cobb, Daniel M. "Talking the Language of the Larger World: Politics in Cold War (Native) America." In *Beyond Red Power: American Indian Politics and Activism since 1900*, edited by Daniel M. Cobb and Loretta Fowler, 161–77. Santa Fe, NM: School for Advanced Research, 2007.

Cobb, Daniel M., ed. *Say We are Nations: Documents of Politics and Protest in Indigenous American Since 1887*. Chapel Hill: University of North Carolina Press, 2015.

Coll, Blanche D., Jean E. Keith, and Herbert H. Rosenthal. *United States Army in World War II: The Technical Services: The Corps of Engineers: Troops and Equipment*. Washington, DC: Office of the Chief of Military History, Department of the Army, 1958.

Conastantinou, Costas M., and James Der Derian. "Introduction: Sustaining Global Hope: Sovereignty, Power, and the Transformation of Diplomacy." In *Sustainable Diplomacies*, edited by Costas M. Conastantinou and James Der Derian, 1–22. New York: Palgrave Macmillan, 2010.

Conaty, Gerald T. "Niitsitapiisinni: Our Way of Life." In *We Are Coming Home: Repatriation and the Restoration of Blackfoot Cultural Confidence*, edited by Gerald T. Conaty, 71–118. Edmonton, AB: Athabasca University, 2015.

Conaty, Gerald T., ed. *We Are Coming Home: Repatriation and the Restoration of Blackfoot Cultural Confidence*. Edmonton, AB: Athabasca University, 2015.

Coulthard, Glen Sean. *Red Skin, White Masks: Rejecting the Colonial Politics of Recognition*. Minneapolis: University of Minnesota Press, 2014.

Craig, David R., Laurie Yung, and William T. Borrie. "'Blackfeet Belong to the Mountains': Hope, Loss, and Blackfeet Claims to Glacier National Park, Montana." *Conservation and Society* 10, no. 3 (2012): 232–42.

Crockoft, Eva. "Abstract Expressionism: Weapon of the Cold War." *Artforum* 15, no. 10 (1974): 39–41.

Crossen, Jonathan. "Another Wave of Anti-Colonialism: The Origins of Indigenous Internationalism." *Canadian Journal of History* 52, no. 3 (Winter 2017): 533–59.

Crow Dog, Leonard, and Richard Erdoes. *Crow Dog: Four Generations of Sioux Medicine Men*. New York: Harper Collins, 1995.

Crow, Joanna. *The Mapuche in Modern Chile: A Cultural History*. Gainesville: University Press of Florida, 2013.

Crowe, Keith. "Eskimos in Japan." *Beaver* (Spring 1971): 56–60.

d'Eaubonne, Françoise. *Le feminism ou la mort*. Paris: P. Horay, 1974.

Daily, Charles A. "Major Influences on the Development of Twentieth-Century American Indian Art." (1982). In *Making History: IAIA Museum of Contemporary Native Arts*, edited by Nancy Marie Mithlo, 145–53. Albuquerque: University of New Mexico Press, 2020.

Davenport, Lisa E. *Jazz Diplomacy: Promoting America in the Cold War Era*. Jackson: University Press of Mississippi, 2013.

Davis, Wade. *Healing Ways: Navajo Health Care in the Twentieth Century*. Albuquerque: University of New Mexico Press, 2001.

Deer, Sarah, and Cecilia Knapp. "Muscogee Constitutional Jurisprudence: Vhakv em Pvtakv (The Carpet Under the Law)." *49 Tulsa Law Review* 123 (2013): 123–78.

Deloria, Ella. *Speaking of Indians*. Lincoln: University of Nebraska Press, 1998 [1944].

Deloria, Philip J. *Indians in Unexpected Places*. Lawrence: University Press of Kansas, 2004.

Deloria, Vine, Jr. "Comfortable Fictions and the Struggle for Turf." *American Indian Quarterly* 16, no. 3 (Summer 1992): 397–410.

Deloria, Vine, Jr. *God Is Red: A Native View of Religion*. Boulder, CO: Fulcrum Publishing, 1994 [1972].

Deloria, Vine, Jr. "The Rise of Indian Activism." In *The Red Man in the New World Drama: A Politico-Legal Study with a Pageantry of American Indian History*, edited by Jennings C. Wise, 389–98. New York: Macmillan, 1971.

Deloria, Vine, Jr. "This Country Was a Lot Better Off When the Indians Were Running It." *New York Times Magazine*, March 8, 1970. www.nytimes.com/1970/03/08/archives/this-country-was-a-lot-better-off-when-the-indians-were-running-it.html.

Deloria, Vine, Jr., and Clifford M. Lytle. *The Nations Within: The Past and Future of American Indian Sovereignty*. Austin: University of Texas Press, 1998.

Deloria, Philip J. *Playing Indian*. New Haven, CT: Yale University Press, 1998.

Demos, T. J. *Decolonizing Nature: Contemporary Art and the Politics of Ecology*. Berlin: Sternberg Press, 2016.

Demos, T. J. "Means Without End: Aryreen Anastas and Rene Gabri's *Camp Campaign*." *October* 126 (Fall 2008): 69–90.

Demos, T. J. "Rights of Nature: The Art and Politics of Earth Jurisprudence." In *Elemental: An Arts and Ecology Reader*, 133–51. Manchester, UK: Gaia Project Press, 2016.

Denetdale, Jennifer Nez. "Chairmen, Presidents, and Princesses: The Navajo Nation, Gender, and the Politics of Tradition." *Wicazo Sa Review* 21, no. 1 (Sprint 2006): 9–28.

Denetdale, Jennifer Nez. "*Naal Tsoos Saní*: The Navajo Treaty of 1868, Nation Building, and Self-Determination." In *Nation to Nation: Treaties Between the United States and American Indian Nations*, 117–28. Washington, DC: National Museum of the American Indian, Smithsonian Institution, 2014.

Denetdale, Jennifer Nez. "Remembering Our Grandmothers: Navajo Women and the Power of Oral Tradition." In *Indigenous Peoples' Wisdom and Power: Affirming Our Knowledge through Narratives*, 78–94. London: Routledge, 2006.

Denetdale, Jennifer Nez. "Representing Changing Woman: A Review Essay on Navajo Women." *American Indian Culture and Research Journal* 25, no. 3 (2001): 1–26.

Denetdale, Jennifer Nez. *The Long Walk: The Forced Navajo Exile*. Langhorne, PA: Chelsea House Publications, 2007.

Denson, Andrew. "Native Americans in Cold War Public Diplomacy: Indian Politics, American History and the US Information Agency." *American Indian Culture and Research Journal* 36, no. 2 (2012): 1–22.

Depkat, Volker. "Peace Medal Diplomacy in Indian-White Relations in Nineteenth-Century North America." In *Material Culture in Modern Diplomacy from the 15th to the 20th Century*, edited by Harriet Rudolph and Gregor M. Metzig, 80–99. Berlin: Walter de Gruyter GmbH, 2016.

de Stecher, Annette. "Integrated Practices: Huron-Wendat Traditions of Diplomacy and Museology." *Journal of Curatorial Studies* 3, no. 1 (2014): 50–73.

de Stecher, Annette. "Of Chiefs and Kings: Wendat and British Diplomatic Traditions." *Érudit* 37, no. 2 (2015): 103–30.

de Zegher, Catherine. "Arc Are Ark Arm Art . . . Act!" In *The 18th Biennale of Sydney: All Our Relations*, edited by Catherine de Zegher and Gerald McMaster, 99–143. Sydney: Biennale of Sydney, 2012.

Doyle, Laura, and Laura Winkiel, eds. *Geomodernisms: Race, Modernism, Modernity*. Bloomington: Indian University Press, 2005.

Dictionary-Oie Wowapi Wan of Teton Sioux. Compiled by Rev. Eugene Buechel, S. J., edited by Rev. Paul Manhart, S. J. Pine Ridge: Red Cloud Indian School, South Dakota, 1983.

Dillon, Grace L. "Imagining Indigenous Futurisms." In *Walking the Clouds: An Anthology of Indigenous Science Fiction*, edited by Grace L. Dillon, 1–12. Tucson: University of Arizona Press, 2012.

Dilworth, Leah. *Imagining Indians in the Southwest: Persistent Visions of a Primitive Past*. Washington, DC: Smithsonian Institution Press, 1996.

Dittmer, Jason. *Diplomatic Material: Affect, Assemblage, and Foreign Policy*. Durham, NC: Duke University Press, 2017.

Dockstader, Frederick J. "Folk Arts, Cross-Country." *Art in America* (March–April, 1970): 74–75.

Dockstader, Frederick J. "The Revolt of Trader Boy: Oscar Howe and Indian Art." *American Indian Art Magazine* 8, no. 3 (Summer 1983): 42–51.

Dockstader, Frederick J. *The Song of the Loom: New Traditions in Navajo Weaving*. New York: Hudson Hills Press, 1987.

Dorotinsky, Deborah. "Handcraft as Cultural Diplomacy: The 1968 Mexico Cultural Olympics and U.S. Participation in the International Exhibition of Popular Arts." *Journal of Latin American Cultural Studies* 29, no. 1 (2020): 1–34.

Douglas, Frederic H. and Rene D'Harnoncourt. *Indian Art of the United States*. New York: The Museum of Modern Art, 1941.

Dozier, Edward P. "Factionalism at Santa Clara Pueblo." *Ethnology* 5, no. 2 (April 1966): 172–85.

Dozier, Edward P. *The Pueblo Indians of North America*. Prospect Heights, IL: Waveland Press, 1983 [1970].

Doyle, Laura and Laura Winkiel, eds. *Geomodernisms: Race, Modernism, Modernity*. Bloomington: Indiana University Press, 2005.

Driskill, Qwo-Li. "Doubleweaving Two-Spirit Critiques: Building Alliances between Native and Queer Studies." *GLQ: A Journal of Lesbian and Gay Studies* 16, no. 1–2 (2010): 69–92.

Driskill, Qwo-Li, Chris Finley, Brian Joseph Gilley, and Scott Lauria Morgensen, eds. *Queer Indigenous Studies: Critical Interventions in Theory, Politics, and Literature*. Tucson: University of Arizona Press, 2011.

Dudziak, Mary L. *Cold War Civil Rights: Race and the Image of American Democracy*. Princeton, NJ: Princeton University Press, 2000.

Dunaway, Finis. *Seeing Green: The Uses and Abuses of Environmental Images*. Chicago: University of Chicago Press, 2015.

Dunn, Dorothy. "America's First Painters." *National Geographic* 107, no. 3 (March 1955): 349–77.

Dunn, Dorothy. *American Indian Paintings of the Southwest and Plains Areas*. Albuquerque: University of New Mexico Press, 1968.

Dunn, Dorothy. *Contemporary American Indian Paintings*. Washington, DC: National Gallery of Art, 1953.

Eldridge, Laurie. *Dorothy Dunn and the Art Education of Native Americans*. Bloomington: Indiana University Press, 2001.

Ellis, Clyde. "'More Real than the Indians Themselves': The Early Years of the Indian Lore Movement in the United States." *Montana: The Magazine of Western History* 58, no. 3 (Autumn 2008): 3–22; 92–94.

"Expo 67." *Smoke Signals* 52 (Spring 1967): 36–37.

Faris, James C. *The Nightway: A History and a History of Documentation of a Navajo Ceremonial*. Albuquerque: University of New Mexico Press, 1990.

Farlow, Robert L. "Romania: The Politics of Autonomy." *Current History* 74, no. 436, East Europe (April 1978): 168–71; 185–86.

Feest, Christian F., ed. *Indians and Europe: An Interdisciplinary Collection of Essays*. Lincoln: University of Nebraska Press, 1999.

Fischer, John Ryan. *Cattle Colonialism: An Environmental History of the Conquest of California and Hawaii*. Chapel Hill: University of North Carolina Press, 2015.

Fisher, Jean. *Vampire in the Text: Narratives of Contemporary Art*. London: InIVA, 2003.

Fitzgerald, Michael Ray. "The White Savior and His Junior Partner: The Lone Ranger and Tonto on Cold War Television." *Journal of Popular Culture* 16, no. 1 (2013): 79–108.

Flaherty, George F. *Hotel Mexico: Dwelling on the '68 Movement*. Berkeley: University of California Press, 2016.

Flatley, Jonathan. "Like: Collecting and Collectivity." *October* 132 (Spring 2010): 71–98.

Flynn, Sean J. *Without Reservation: Benjamin Reifel and American Indian Acculturation*. Pierre: South Dakota Historical Society Press, 2018.

Forty, Adrian. *Concrete and Culture: A Material History*. London: Reaktion Books, 2013.

Foster, Hal. *The First Pop Age: Painting and Subjectivity in the Art of Hamilton, Lichtenstein, Warhol, Richter, and Ruscha*. Princeton, NJ: Princeton University Press, 2012.

Fowler, Cynthia. "Gender, Modern Art, and Native Women Painters in the First Half of the Twentieth Century." In *American Women Artists, 1935–1970: Gender, Culture, and Politics*, edited by Helen Langa and Paula Wisotzki, 41–56. New York: Routledge, 2016.

Francaviglia, Richard V. *Go East, Young Man: Imagining the American West as the Orient*. Logan: Utah State University Press, 2011.

Freeman, Elizabeth. *The Wedding Complex: Forms of Belonging in Modern American Culture*. Durham, NC: Duke University Press, 2002.

Friedman, Susan Stanford. "Periodizing Modernism: Postcolonial Modernities and the Space/Time Borders of Modernist Studies." *Modernism/Modernity* 13, no. 3 (September 2006): 425–43.

Fur, Maria Gunlög. *Painting Culture, Painting Nature: Stephen Mopope, Oscar Jacobson, and the Development of Indian Art in Oklahoma*. Norman: University of Oklahoma Press, 2019.

Furuhata, Yuriko. "Multimedia Environments and Security Operations: Expo '70 as a Laboratory of Governance." *Grey Room* 54 (2014): 56–79.

Gaard, Greta. "Ecofeminism Revisited: Rejecting Essentialism and Re-Placing Species in a Material Feminist Environmentalism." *Feminist Formations* 23, no. 2 (Summer 2011): 26–53.

Gaard, Greta. "Posthumanism, Ecofeminism, and Inter-Species Relations." In *Routledge Handbook of Gender and Environment*, edited by Sherilyn MacGregor, 115–29. London: Routledge, 2017.

Gage, Matilda Joslyn. *Woman, Church and State: A Historical Account of the States of Women Through the Christian Ages with Reminiscences of the Matriarchate*. Edited Wally Roesch Wagner. Aberdeen, SD: Sky Carrier Press, 1998.

Galler, Robert W., Jr. "Sustaining the Sioux Confederation: Yanktonai Initiatives and Influence on the Northern Plains, 1680–1880." *Western Historical Quarterly* 39, no. 4 (Winter 2008): 467–90.

Gardner, William O. "The 1970 Osaka Expo and/as Science Fiction." *Review of Japanese Culture and Society* 23 (December 2011): 26–43.

Gaudio, Michael. *Engraving the Savage: The New World and Techniques of Civilization*. Minneapolis: University of Minnesota Press, 2008.

Gell, Alfred. *Art and Agency: An Anthropological Theory*. New York: Clarendon Press, 1998.

Geoghegan, John. "Inuit Art at Expo '70." *Inuit Art Quarterly* 31, no. 4 (2018): 58–59.

Gilio-Whitaker, Dina. *As Long as Grass Grows: The Indigenous Fight for Environmental Justice, From Colonization to Standing Rock*. Boston: Beacon Press, 2020.

Gill, Sam D. *Mother Earth: An American Story*. Chicago: University of Chicago Press, 1987.

Gill, Sam D. "Whirling Logs and Colored Sands." In *Native American Traditions: Sources and Interpretations*, edited by Sam D. Gill, 47–57. Belmont, CA: Wadsworth, 1983.

Gladstone, Joseph Scott, and Donald D. Pepion. "Exploring Traditional Indigenous Leadership Concepts: A Spiritual Foundation for Blackfeet Leadership." *Leadership* 13, no. 5 (2017): 571–89.

Gómez-Barris, Macarena. *The Extractive Zone: Social Ecologies and Decolonial Perspectives*. Durham, NC: Duke University Press, 2017.

Goodyear, Frank H. *Red Cloud: Photographs of a Lakota Chief*. Lincoln: University of Nebraska Press, 2003.

Gough, Annette, and Hilary Whitehouse. "Challenging Amnesias: Re-Collecting Feminist New Materialism/Ecofeminism/Climate/Education." *Environmental Education Research* 25, no. 12 (December, 2019): 1–15.

Gram, John R. *Education at the Edge of Empire: Negotiating Pueblo Identity in New Mexico's Indian Boarding Schools*. Seattle: University of Washington Press, 2015.

Greene, Candace, and Thomas Drescher. "The Tipi with Battle Pictures: The Kiowa Tradition of Intangible Property Rights." *Trademark Reporter* 84, no. 4 (July/August 1994): 418–33.

Greenberg, Clement. "Towards a Newer *Laocoön*." 1940. In *Pollock and After: The Critical Debate*. 2nd ed., edited by Francis Franscina, 61–70. New York: Routledge, 2000.

Grieve, Victoria M. *Little Cold Warriors: American Childhood in the 1950s*. Oxford: Oxford University Press, 2018.

Gritton, Joy L. *The Institute of American Indian Arts: Modernism and US Indian Policy*. Albuquerque: University of New Mexico Press, 2000.

Guilbaut, Serge. *How New York Stole the Idea of Modern Art: Abstract Expressionism, Freedom, and the Cold War*. Chicago: University of Chicago Press, 1983.

Guitérrez, Ramón A. *When Jesus Came, the Corn Mothers Went Away: Marriage, Sexuality, and Power in New Mexico, 1500–1846*. Stanford, CA: Stanford University Press, 1991.

Haas, Ernest. "The Balance of Power: Prescription, Concept, or Propaganda?" *World Politics* 5, no. 4 (July 1953): 442–77.

Haeckel, Ernst. *Generelle Morphologie der Organismen. Allgemeine Grundzüge der organischen Form-Wissenschaft, mechanisch begründet durch die von Charles Darwin reformirte Descendenz-Theorie*. Vol. 2. Berlin: G. Reimer, 1866.

Hall, Mitchell K. *The Vietnam War*. 3rd ed. New York: Routledge, 2018.

Hall, Ryan. "The Divergent Wests of Isaac Stevens and Lame Bull: Finding Motive in the 1855 Treaty." *Pacific Northwest Quarterly* 105, no. 3 (Summer 2014): 107–21.

Hämäläinen, Pekka. *Lakota America: A New History of Indigenous Power*. New Haven, CT: Yale University Press, 2019.

Harjo, Laura. *Spiral to the Stars: Mvskoke Tools of Futurity*. Tucson: University of Arizona Press, 2019.

Harjo, Suzan Shown. Introduction to *Nation to Nation: Treaties between the United States and American Indian Nations*, edited by Suzan Shown Harjo, 1–11. Washington, DC: National Museum of the American Indian, Smithsonian Institution, 2014.

Harney, Elizabeth, and Ruth B. Phillips, eds. *Mapping Modernisms: Art, Indigeneity, Colonialism*. Durham, NC: Duke University Press, 2018.

Harney, Elizabeth, and Ruth B. Phillips. "Introduction: Inside Modernity: Indigeneity, Coloniality, Modernisms." In *Mapping Modernisms: Art, Indigeneity, Colonialism*, edited by Elizabeth Harney and Ruth B. Phillips, 1–32. Durham, NC: Duke University Press, 2018.

Hatcher, Evelyn Payne. *Visual Metaphors: A Formal Analysis of Navajo Art*. American Ethnological Society Monograph, 58. St. Paul, MN: West Publishing Co, 1974.

Haughney, Diane. *Neoliberal Economics, Democratic Transition, and Mapuche Demands for Rights in Chile*. Gainesville: University Press of Florida, 2006.

Hawley, Elizabeth S. "Tonita Peña and the Politics of Pueblo Art." *American Art* 35, no. 1 (Spring 2021): 62–93.

Heidegger, Martin. "The Age of the World Picture." In *The Question Concerning Technology and Other Essays*, translated by Williams Lovitt, 115–54. New York: Harper and Row, 1977.

Hendershot, Cynthia. *I Was a Cold War Monster: Horror Films, Eroticism, and the Cold War Imagination*. Bowling Green, OH: Bowling Green State University Popular Press, 2001.

Henderson, James (Sa'ke'j) Youngblood. *Indigenous Diplomacy and the Rights of Peoples: Achieving UN Recognition*. Saskatoon, SK: Purich Publishing, 2008.

Herbst, Toby, and Joel Kopp, "The Grandfather's Flag." In *The Flag in American Indian Art*, edited by Toby Herbst and Joel Kopp, 15–26. Cooperstown, NY: New York State Historical Association, 1993.

Hidalgo, Susana del Carmen Chacana. "Trariwe de Machi: Investigación y Documentación." Museo Regional de La Araucanía in Temuco, 2017, 2–12. https://www.museoregionalaraucania.gob.cl /sites/www.museoregionalaraucania.gob.cl/files/images/articles -83073_archivo_PDF.pdf.

Hill, W. W. *Ethnography of Santa Clara Pueblo New Mexico*. Albuquerque: University of New Mexico Press, 1982.

Horton, Jessica L. "A Cloudburst in Venice: Fred Kabotie and the U.S. Pavilion of 1932." *American Art* 29, no. 1 (Spring 2015): 54–81.

Horton, Jessica L. "Indigenous Artists Against the Anthropocene." *Art Journal* 76, no. 2 (Summer 2017): 48–69.

Horton, Jessica L. "Painter, Traveler, Diplomat." In *Fritz Scholder: Super Indian, 1967–1980*, by John Lukavic with Jessica Horton, Eric Berkemeyer, and Kent Logan, 41–53. New York: DelMonico Books and Denver Art Museum, 2015.

Horton, Jessica L. "Performing Paint, Claiming Space: Santa Fe Indian School Posters on Paul Coze's Stage in Paris, 1935." *Transatlantica: Revue d'études américaines* 2 (2017). https://journals .openedition.org/transatlantica/11220.

Horton, Jessica L. "Plural Diplomacies between Indian Termination and the Cold War: Contemporary American Indian Paintings in the 'Near East,' 1964–1966." *Journal of Curatorial Studies* 5, no. 3 (October 2016): 340–66.

Horton, Jessica L. "Seeing the National Museum of the American Indian Anew as a Diplomatic Assemblage." *American Art* 36, no. 3 (Fall 2022): 5–9.

Howe, Craig, Lydia Whirlwind Soldier, and Lanniko L. Lee, eds. *He Sapa Woihanble: Black Hills Dream*. St. Paul, MN: Living Justice Press, 2011.

Howe, Oscar. *Oscar Howe, Artist*. Vermillion: University of South Dakota Press, 2004.

Howe, Oscar. "Theories and Beliefs—Dakota." *South Dakota Review* 2, no. 2 (1969): 69–79.

Huang, Hsinya. "Radiation Ecologies in Gerald Vizenor's *Hiroshima Bugi*." *Neohelicon* 44, no. 4: DOI: 0.007/s11059-017-0403-z.

Hughes, David T. *Perceptions of the Sacred: A Review of Selected Native American Groups and Their Relationship with the Catlinite Quarries*. Lincoln, NE: US Department of Interior, National Park Service, 1995.

Humalajoki, Reetta. "'What Is It to Withdraw?': Klamath and Navajo Tribal Councils' Tactics in Negotiating Termination Policy, 1949–1964." *Western Historical Quarterly* 48 (Winter 2017), 429–30.

Humboldt, Alexander Von. *Personal Narrative of a Journey to the Equinoctial Regions of the New Continent*. Translated by Jason Wilson. London: Penguin Books, 1995 [1807].

Hungry-Wolf, Adolf. *Blackfoot Papers Volume One: Pikunni History and Culture*. Skookumchuck, British Columbia: The Good Medicine Cultural Foundation, 2006.

Hungry-Wolf, Adolf. *Blackfoot Papers Volume Two: Pikunni Ceremonial Life*. Skookumchuck, British Columbia: The Good Medicine Cultural Foundation, 2006.

Hutchinson, Elizabeth. "The Dress of His Nation: Romney's Portrait of Joseph Brant." *Winterthur Portfolio* 45, no. 2/3 (Summer/Autumn 2011): 209–28.

Hutchison, Elizabeth Qhay, Thomas Miller Klubock, Nara B. Milanich, and Peter Winn, eds. *The Chile Reader: History, Culture, Politics*. Durham, NC: Duke University Press, 2014.

Hyer, Sally. *One House, One Voice, One Heart: Native American Education at the Santa Fe Indian School*. Santa Fe: Museum of New Mexico Press, 1990.

Igloliorte, Heather. "Arctic Culture/Global Indigeneity." In *Negotiations in a Vacant Lot: Studying the Visual in Canada*, edited by Lynda Jessup, Erin Morton, and Kirsty Robertson, 150–70. Montreal: McGill-Queen's University Press, 2014.

Ingold, Tim. *Being Alive: Essays on Movement, Knowledge and Description*. London: Routledge, 2011.

Ingold, Tim. *Lines: A Brief History*. London: Routledge, 2007.

Institute for American Indian Arts (IAIA). *Indigenous Futurisms: Transcending Past/Present/Future*. Santa Fe, NM: Institute for American Indian Arts Museum of Contemporary Native Arts, 2020.

Isham, Theodore, and Blue Clark. "Creek (Mvsokoke)." *Encyclopedia of Oklahoma History and Culture*. Oklahoma Historical Society, accessed November 23, 2023, www.okhistory.org/publications /enc/entry.php?entry=CR006.

Jacobs, Margaret D. *Engendered Encounters: Feminism and Pueblo Cultures, 1879–1934*. Lincoln: University of Nebraska Press, 1999.

Jantzer-White, Marilee. "Tonita Peña (Quah Ah), Pueblo Painter: Asserting Identity through Continuity and Change." *American Indian Quarterly* 18, no. 3 (Summer 1994): 369–92.

Jean, Dorothy, ed. *Contemporary Indian Artists: Montana/Wyoming/ Idaho*. Washington, DC: Indian Arts and Crafts Board, 1972.

Jones, Caroline A. *The Global Work of Art: World's Fairs, Biennials, and the Aesthetics of Experience*. Chicago: University of Chicago Press, 2016.

Jones, Ruthe Blalock. "Bacone College and the Philbrook Indian Annuals." In *Visions and Voices: Native American Paintings from the Philbrook Museum of Art*, edited by Lydia L. Wyckoff, 51–58. Tulsa, OK: Philbrook Museum of Art, 1996.

Johnson, Annika K. "George Catlin, Artistic Prospecting, and Dakhóta Agency in the Archive." *Archives of American Art Journal* 59, no. 1 (2020): 4–23.

Josephy, Jr., Alvin M., Joane Nagel, and Troy R. Johnson, eds. *Red Power: The American Indians' Fight for Freedom*. Lincoln: University of Nebraska Press, 1999.

Justice, Daniel Heath. "'Go Away Water!': Kinship Criticism and the Decolonization Imperative." In *Reasoning Together: The Native Critics Collective*, edited by Craig S. Womack, Daniel Heath Justice, and Christopher B. Teuton, 147–68. Norman: University of Oklahoma Press, 2008.

Justice, Daniel Heath, Mark Rifkin, and Bethany Schneider, eds. "Sexuality, Nationality, Indigeneity." *GLQ: A Journal of Lesbian and Gay Studies* 16, no. 1–2 (April 2010).

Kabotie, Fred. *Fred Kabotie: Hopi Indian Artist: An Autobiography Told with Bill Belknap*. Flagstaff, AZ: Northland Press, 1977.

Kahn, Lloyd, ed. "Interview with Buckminster Fuller." In *Domebook 2*, 90–91. Bolinas, CA: Pacific Domes, 1971.

Kahnweiler, Daniel-Henry. Preface to *The Sculptures of Picasso*. Translated by A. D. B. Sylvester. London: Rodney Phillips and Company, 1949.

Kalshoven, Petra Tjitske. "Things in the Making: Playing with Imitation." *Etnofoor* 22, no. 1 (2010): 59–74.

Karmel, Pepe. "Cubism and the Politics of Form." In *The Cubism Seminars: CASVA Seminar Papers 3*, edited by Harry Cooper, 123–69. Washington, DC: National Gallery of Art, 2017.

Kidwell, Clara Sue. "The Land Incarnate: Navajo Women and the Dialogue of Colonialism, 1821–1870." In *Negotiators of Change: Historical Perspectives on Native American Women*, edited by Nancy Shoemaker, 135–56. New York: Routledge, 1995.

Kimmerer, Robert Wall. "*Mishkos Kenomagwen*, the Lessons of Grass: Restoring Reciprocity with the Good Green Earth." In *Traditional Ecological Knowledge: Learning from Indigenous Practices for Environmental Sustainability*, edited by Melissa Nelson and Daniel Shilling, 27–56. Cambridge: Cambridge University Press, 2018.

King, C. Richard. "De/Scribing Squ*w: Indigenous Women and Imperial Idioms in the United States." *American Indian Culture and Research Journal* 27, no. 2 (2003): 1–16.

King, Jeanne Snodgrass. "Oscar Howe: Power, Strength, Individualism." *Four Winds* 3, no. 2 (Autumn 1982): 8–15.

Koons, Ryan Abel. "Dancing Breath: Ceremonial Performance Practice, Environment, and Personhood in a Muskogee Creek Community." PhD diss., University of California, Los Angeles, 2016.

Komatsu, Sakyō. "Banpaku kara kōgai e: miraigaku no atarashii dankai" [From Expo to Pollution: The New Stage of Future Studies]. *Jiyū* (December 1970): 43–52.

Komatsu, Sakyō. *Nippon Apacchi-Zoku*. Tokyo: Kadokawa Publishers, 1971 [1964].

Kozloff, Max. "American Painting During the Cold War." *Artforum* (May 1973): 44–54.

Krenn, Michael. *Diplomacy: African Americans and the State Department, 1945–69*. London: Routledge, 1999.

Krenn, Michael. *Fall-Out Shelters for the Human Spirit: American Art and the Cold War*. Chapel Hill: University of North Carolina Press, 2005.

Kýrová, Lucie. "Native Americans, Socialist Propaganda, and the Politics of the Oppressed." Presentation at Native American and Indigenous Studies Conference, May 19–21, 2011, Sacramento, CA.

Kýrová, Lucie. "'The Right to Think for Themselves': Native American Intellectual Sovereignty and Internationalism during the Cold War, 1950–1989." PhD diss., College of William and Mary, 2016.

LaDuke, Winona. *All Our Relations: Native Struggles for Land and Life*. Boston: South End Press, 1999.

Lange, Charles H. "Tablita, or Corn Dances of the Rio Grande Pueblo Indians." *Texas Journal of Science* 9, no. 1 (March 1957): 59–74.

LaPier, Rosalyn R. *Invisible Reality: Storytellers, Storytakers, and the Supernatural World of the Blackfeet*. Lincoln: University of Nebraska Press, 2017.

Latour, Bruno. *An Inquiry into Modes of Existence: An Anthropology of the Moderns*. Translated by Catherine Porter. Cambridge, MA: Harvard University Press, 2013.

Latour, Bruno. *Facing Gaia: Eight Lectures on the New Climatic Regime*. Translated by Catherine Porter. Medford, MA: Polity Press, 2017.

Latour, Bruno. "Diplomacy in the Face of Gaia." In conversation with Heather Davis. In *Art in the Anthropocene: Encounters among Aesthetics, Politics, Environments and Epistemologies*, edited by Heather Davis and Etienne Turpin, 43–56. London: Open Humanities Press, 2015.

Laubin, Reginald, and Gladys Laubin. *The Indian Tipi: Its History, Construction, and Use*. Norman: University of Oklahoma Press, 1977 [1957].

Laurie Eldridge. "Dorothy Dunn and the Art Education of Native Americans." *Studies in Art Education* 42, no. 4 (Summer 2001): 318–32.

Lavrentyev, Sergey. "Red Westerns–A Short History." *Fantom Film Magazine*, September 5, 2011. http://www.fantomfilm.cz/?p=986.

Lee, Lloyd L., ed. *Diné Perspectives: Revitalizing and Reclaiming Navajo Thought*. Tuscon: University of Arizona Press, 2014.

Lee, Lloyd L. Introduction to *Navajo Sovereignty: Understandings and Visions of the Diné People*, edited by Lloyd L. Lee, 3–18. Tucson: University of Arizona Press, 2017.

Lee, Lloyd L. "The Navajo Nation and the Declaration on the Rights of Indigenous Peoples." In *Diné Perspectives: Revitalizing and Reclaiming Navajo Thought*, edited by Lloyd L. Lee, 170–86. Tucson: University of Arizona Press, 2017.

Leech, Margaret. *Reveille in Washington, 1860–1865*. New York: Harper and Brothers, 1941.

LeFree, Betty. *Santa Clara Pottery Today*. Albuquerque: University of New Mexico Press, 1975.

Lévi-Strauss, Claude. *The Savage Mind*. Chicago: University of Chicago Press, 1966.

Libhart, Myles, and Rosemary Ellison. Introduction to *Painted Tipis by Contemporary Plains Artists*, 7–44. Anadarko, OK: Oklahoma Indian Arts and Crafts Cooperative, 1973.

Light, Duncan. *The Dracula Dilemma: Tourism, Identity and the State in Romania*. London: Taylor and Francis, 2017.

Light, Duncan. "Romania's Problem with Dracula." *History Today* (May 2017): 63–65.

Lightfoot, Sheryl. *Global Indigenous Politics: A Subtle Revolution*. London: Routledge, 2016.

Lockyer, Angus. "The Logic of Spectacle c. 1970." *Art History* 30, no. 4 (September 2007): 571–89.

Lowe, Truman. "Scholder's Legacy: A Roundtable Discussion." In *Fritz Scholder: Indian/Not Indian*, edited by Lowery Stokes Sims, 154–75. Washington, DC: Smithsonian National Museum of the American Indian, 2008.

Luco, María Soledad Falabella. "Hilando en la Memoria: Weaving Songs of Resistance in Contemporary Mapuche Political Cultural Activism." In *Women Mobilizing Memory*, edited by Ayşe Gül Altýnay, María José Contreras, Marianne Hirsch, Jean Howard, Banu Karaca, and Alisa Solomon, 459–77. New York: Columbia University Press, 2019.

Lutz, Catherine A., and Jane L. Collins. *Reading National Geographic*. Chicago: University of Chicago Press, 1993.

Mallery, Garrick. *Picture-Writing of the American Indians*. Vol. 1. New York: Dover Publications, 1972.

Mallon, Florencia. "The Mapuche Land Takeover at Rucalán: Interviews with Peasants and Landowners." In *The Chile Reader: History, Culture, Politics*, edited by Elizabeth Qhay Hutchison, Thomas Miller Klubock, Nara B. Milanich, and Peter Winn, 386–92. Durham, NC: Duke University Press, 2014.

Maniaque-Benton, Caroline, ed. *The Whole Earth Field Guide*. Cambridge, MA: MIT Press, 2016.

Marr, Alexander Briar. "Scales of Vision: Kiowa Model Tipis and the Mooney Commission." *Winterthur Portfolio* 49, no. 2/3 (Summer/Autumn 2015): 93–125.

Masco, Joseph. *The Nuclear Borderlands: The Manhattan Project in Post-Cold War New Mexico*. Princeton, NJ: Princeton University Press, 2006.

Masey, Jack, and Conway Lloyd Morgan. *Cold War Confrontations: US Exhibitions and Their Role in the Cultural Cold War*. Baden, Switzerland: Lars Müller Publishers, 2008.

Massey, Jonathan. "The Sumptuary Ecology of Buckminster Fuller's Designs." In *A Keener Perception: Ecocritical Studies in American Art History*, edited by Alan C. Braddock and Christoph Irmscher, 189–212. Tuscaloosa: University of Alabama Press, 2009.

Massidda, Luca. "The Cold War, a Cool Medium, and the Postmodern Death of World Expos." In *World's Fairs in the Cold War: Science, Technology, and the Culture of Progress*, edited by Arhtur P. Molella and Scott Gabriel Knowles, 183–93. Pittsburgh: University of Pittsburgh Press, 2019.

Matthews, Washington. "Mythic Dry-Paintings of the Navajos." In *Washington Matthews: Studies of Navajo Culture, 1880–1894*, edited by Katherine Spencer Halpern and Susan Brown McGreevy, 22–228. Albuquerque: University of New Mexico Press, 1997.

May, Elaine Tyler. *Homeward Bound: American Families in the Cold War*. New York: Basic Books, 1988.

McGeough, Michelle. *Through Their Eyes: Indian Painting in Santa Fe, 1918–1945*. Santa Fe, NM: Wheelwright Museum of the American Indian, 2009.

McGrath, James. "Lloyd Kiva New and the Early Years of the IAIA." In *Lloyd Kiva New Biography*, unpublished manuscript, ca. 2000, 14 (IAIA, McGrath Papers, Box 29, Folder 8.

McGreevy, Susan Brown. "Woven Holy People: Navajo Sandpainting Textiles." *Museum Anthropology* 13, no. 2 (1989): 19–22.

McKee, Yates. "Art and the Ends of Environmentalism: From Biosphere to the Right to Survival." In *Nongovernmental Politics*, edited by Michel Feher with Gaëlle Krikorian and Yates McKee, 539–83. New York: Zone Books, 2007.

McLaughlin, Castle. *Arts of Diplomacy: Lewis and Clark's Indian Collection*. Seattle: University of Washington Press, 2003.

McLerran, Jennifer. *A New Deal for Native Art: Indian Arts and Federal Policy, 1933–1943*. Tucson: University of Arizona Press, 2009.

McLerran, Jennifer. "Textile as Cultural Text: Contemporary Navajo Weaving as Autoethnographic Practice." In *Weaving Is Life: Navajo Weavings from the Edwin L. and Ruth E. Kennedy Southwest Native American Collection*, edited by Jennifer McLerran, 8–33. Seattle: University of Washington Press, 2006.

M'Closkey, Kathy. *Swept Under the Rug: A Hidden History of Navajo Weaving*. Albuquerque: University of New Mexico Press, 2008.

McNally, Raymond T., and Radu Florescu, *In Search of Dracula: A True History of Dracula and Vampire Legends*. New York: Galahad Books, 1972.

McNeley, James Kale. *Holy Wind in Navajo Philosophy*. Tuscon: University of Arizona Press, 1981.

Meadows, William C. "The Cod Talkers' Legacy: Native Languages Helped Turn the Tides in Both World Wars." *American Indian* 21, no. 3 (Fall 2020). www.americanindianmagazine.org/story/code-talkers-legacy-native-languages-helped-turn-tides-both-world-wars.

Means, Russell. *Where White Men Fear to Tread: The Autobiography of Russell Means*. With Marvin J. Wolf. New York: St. Martin's Griffin, 1995.

Medak-Salzman, Danika. "Coming to You from the Indigenous Future: Native Women, Speculative Film Shorts, and the Art of the Possible." *Studies in American Indian Literature* 29, no. 1 (Spring 2017): 139–71.

Mera, H. P. *Navajo Textile Arts*. Santa Barbara, CA: Peregrine Smith, 1975 [1948].

Mercer, Kobena, ed. *Cosmopolitan Modernisms*. Cambridge, MA: MIT Press, 2005.

Meyer, Leroy N. "In Search of Native American Aesthetics." *Journal of Aesthetic Education* 35, no. 4 (Winter 2001): 25–46.

Michelle McGeough. *Through Their Eyes: Indian Painting in Santa Fe, 1918–1945*. Santa Fe, NM: Wheelwright Museum of the American Indian, 2009.

Mihesuah, Devon Abbot, and Angela Cavender Wilson. *Indigenizing the Academy: Transforming Scholarship and Empowering Communities*. Lincoln: University of Nebraska Press, 2004.

Miller, Eileen. *The Edinburgh International Festival, 1947–1996*. Hants, UK: Scholar Press, 1996.

Milton, John R. *Oscar Howe*. Minneapolis, MN: Dillon Press, 1972.

Montano, Roshii, and Jill Ahlberg Yohe, "Blanketing the Plains: *Hanoolchaadi* in Indian Country." *First American Art Magazine* 14 (Spring 2017): 20–25.

Montiel, Anya. "American Indian Expressive Arts." *Oxford Handbook of Native American History*, edited by Frederick E. Hoxie, 453–74. Oxford: Oxford University Press, 2016.

Montiel, Anya. "Dakota Primetime: *This Is Your Life*." In *Dakota Modern: The Art of Oscar Howe*, edited by Bill Anthes and Kathleen Ash-Milby, 115–119. Washington, DC: Smithsonian National Museum of the American Indian, 2022.

Moore, Niamh. "Eco/Feminist Genealogies: Renewing Promises and New Possibilities." In *Contemporary Perspectives on Ecofeminism*, edited by Mary Phillips and Nick Rumens, 19–37. London: Routledge, 2015.

Moorman, Lewis J. "Health of the Navajo-Hopi Indians: General Report of the American Medical Education Association Team." *Journal of American Medical Association* 139, no. 6 (1949): 370–76.

Moreton-Robinson, Aileen, ed. *Sovereign Subjects: Indigenous Sovereignty Matters*. London: Routledge, 2007.

Morgenthau, Hans J. *Politics Among Nations: The Struggle for Power and Peace*. New York: Alfred A. Knopf, 1978.

Morris, Robert. "Anti-Form." In *Continuous Project Altered Daily: The Writings of Robert Morris*, 41–49. Cambridge, MA: MIT Press, 1993.

Morton, Timothy. *The Ecological Thought*. Cambridge, MA: Harvard University Press, 2010.

Muir-Harmony, Teasel. "The Limits of U.S. Science Diplomacy in the Space Age." *Pacific Historical Review* 88, no. 4 (2019): 590–618.

Mullen, Molly H. *Culture in the Marketplace: Gender, Art, and Value in the American Southwest*. Durham, NC: Duke University Press, 2001.

Muller, Kevin R. "From Palace to Longhouse: Portraits of the Four Indian Kings in a Transatlantic Context." *American Art* 22, no. 3 (Fall 2008): 26–49.

Naranjo, Tessie. "Cultural Changes: The Effect of Foreign Systems at Santa Clara Pueblo." In *The Great Southwest of the Fred Harvey Company and the Santa Fe Railway*, edited by Marta Weigle and Barbara A. Babcock, 187–96. Phoenix, AZ: The Heard Museum, 1996.

Nelson, Melissa K. and Dan Shilling, eds. *Traditional Ecological Knowledge: Learning from Indigenous Practices for Environmental Sustainability*. Boston: Cambridge University Press, 2018.

Newcomb, Franc Johnson. *Hosteen Klah, Navaho Medicine Man and Sand Painter*. Norman: University of Oklahoma Press, 1964.

Nisbet, James. *Ecologies, Environments, and Energy Systems in Art of the 1960s and 1970s*. Cambridge, MA: MIT Press, 2014.

Nixon, Rob. *Slow Violence and the Environmentalism of the Poor*. Cambridge, MA: Harvard University Press, 2011.

Noble, Brian. "Justice, Transaction, Translation: Blackfoot Tipi Transfers and WIPO's Search for the Facts of Traditional Knowledge Exchange." *American Anthropologist* 109, no. 2 (2007): 338–49.

Noble, Brian. "Treaty Ecologies: With Persons, Peoples, Animals, and Land." In *Resurgence and Reconciliation: Indigenous-Settler Relations and Earth Teachings*, edited by Michael Asch, John Borrows, and James Tully, 315–42. Toronto: University of Toronto Press, 2018.

Norman, David W. "Land, Technology and the Rise of Experimental Art in Post-Home Rule Greenland." PhD diss., University of Copenhagen, 2021.

Nye, Joseph. *Soft Power: The Means to Success in World Politics*. New York: Public Affairs, 2004.

Oakes, Guy. *The Imaginary War: Civil Defense and American Cold War Culture*. New York: Oxford University Press, 1994.

Old Person, Earl. "The Amskapi Pikuni from the 1950s to 2010." In *Amskapi Pikuni: The Blackfeet People*, 177–81. Albany: State University of New York Press, 2012.

Oliver, Paul. "Part One," 6–29. In *Shelter and Society*, edited by Paul Oliver. New York: Praeger Publishers, 1969.

Olsen, Virginia. "Indian Art, Yesterday and Today." In *Америка: America Illustrated*, 34–38. Washington, DC: United States Information Agency, 1962.

Orenstein, Ronald I. *Ivory, Horn, and Blood: Behind the Elephant and Rhinoceros Poaching Crisis*. Ontario: Firefly Books, 2013.

Ortiz, Alfonso. "Ritual Drama and Pueblo World View," 135–161. In *New Perspectives on the Pueblos*, edited by Alfonso Ortiz. Albuquerque: University of New Mexico Press, 1972.

Ortiz, Alfonso. *The Tewa World: Space, Time, Being, and Becoming in a Pueblo Society*. Chicago: University of Chicago Press, 1969.

Padmalal, D. and K. Maya. *Sand Mining: Environmental Impacts and Selected Case Studies*. New York: Springer, 2014.

Papastergiadis, Nikos and Laura Turney. *On Becoming Authentic: Interview with Jimmie Durham*. Prickly Pear Pamphlet no. 10. Cambridge, UK: Prickly Pear Press, 1996.

Paper, Jordan D. *Dancing for Life: Native North American Religious Traditions*. Westport, CT: Praeger Publishers, 2007.

Paper, Jordan D. *Offering Smoke: The Sacred Pipe and Native American Religion*. Moscow: University of Idaho Press, 1988.

Parezo, Nancy J., and Angelina R. Jones. "What's in a Name?: The 1940s–1950s 'Squaw Dress.'" *American Indian Quarterly* 33, no. 3 (Summer 2009): 373–404.

Parezo, Nancy J. "Matthews and the Discovery of Navajo Drypaintings." In *Washington Matthews: Studies of Navajo Culture, 1880–1894*, edited by Katherine Spencer Halpern and Susan Brown McGreevy, 53–73. Albuquerque: University of New Mexico Press, 1997.

Parezo, Nancy J. *Navajo Sandpainting: From Religious Act to Commercial Art*. Tucson: University of Arizona Press, 1983.

Peduzzi, Pascal. "Sand, Rarer than One Thinks." *UNEP Global Environmental Alert Service* (March 2014): 1–15.

Philipps, Christopher. "The Judgment Seat of Photography." *October* 22 (Fall 1982): 27–63.

Phillips, Mary, and Nick Rumens, "Introducing Contemporary Ecofeminism." In *Contemporary Perspectives on Ecofeminism*, edited by Mary Phillips and Nick Rumens, 1–16. London: Routledge, 2015.

Phillips, Ruth B. "Aesthetic Primitivism Revisited: The Global Diaspora of 'Primitive Art' and the Rise of Indigenous Modernisms." *Journal of Art Historiography*, no. 12 (June 2015): 1–25.

Phillips, Ruth B. "Commemoration/(De)celebration: Super-Shows and the Colonization of Canadian Museums, 1967–92." In *Postmodernism and the Ethical Subject*, edited by Barbara Gabriel and Suzan Ilcan, 99–124. Montreal: McGill-Queen's University Press, 2004.

Phillips, Ruth B. *Museum Pieces: Toward the Indigenization of Canadian Museums*. Montreal: McGill-Queen's University Press, 2011.

Phillips, Ruth B. *Trading Identities: The Souvenir in Native North American Art from the Northeast, 1700–1900*. Seattle: University of Washington Press, 1999.

Philp, Kenneth R. *Indian Self Rule: First-Hand Accounts of Indian-White Relations from Roosevelt to Reagan*. Logan: Utah State University Press, 1995.

Philp, Kenneth R. *Termination Revisited: American Indians on the Trail to Self-Determination, 1933–1953*. Lincoln: University of Nebraska Press, 2002.

Pohrt, Richard A. *The American Indian, the American Flag*. Flint, MI: Flint Institute of Arts, 1975.

Posthumus, David. *All My Relatives: Exploring Lakota Ontology, Belief, and Ritual*. Lincoln: University of Nebraska Press, 2018.

Pratt, Richard H. "The Advantages of Mingling Indians with Whites." In *Americanizing the American Indians: Writings by the "Friends of the Indian," 1880–1900*, edited by Francis Paul Prucha, 260–71. Cambridge, MA: Harvard University Press, 1973.

Prevots, Naima. *Dance for Export: Cultural Diplomacy in the Cold War*. Middletown, CT: Wesleyan University Press, 1998.

Quinney, Anne. "Excess and Identity: The Franco-Romanian Ionesco Combats Rhinoceritis." *South Central Review* 24, no. 3 (2007): 36–52.

Quo-Li Driskill, Chris Finley, Brian Joseph Gilley, and Scott Lauria Morgensen, eds. *Queer Indigenous Studies: Critical Interventions in Theory, Politics, and Literature*. Tucson: University of Arizona Press, 2011.

Rapoport, Amos. "The Pueblo and the Hogan: A Cross-Cultural Comparison of Two Responses to an Environment." In *Shelter and Society*, edited by Paul Oliver, 66–79. New York: Praeger Publishers, 1969.

Rancière, Jacques. *The Politics of Aesthetics*. Translated by Gabriel Rockhill. London: Continuum, 2004.

Reed, Maureen E. *A Woman's Place: Women Writing New Mexico*. Albuquerque: University of New Mexico, 2005.

Reed, Maureen E. "Mixed Messages: Pablita Velarde, Kay Bennett, and the Changing Meaning of Anglo-Indian Intermarriage in Twentieth-Century New Mexico." *Frontiers: A Journal of Women Studies* 26, no. 3 (2005): 101–34.

Reichard, Gladys Amanda. *Navajo Religion: A Study of Symbolism*. Princeton, NJ: Princeton University Press, 1977.

Reichard, Gladys Amanda. *Weaving a Navajo Blanket*. New York: Dover Publications, 1974.

Rickard, Jolene. "Visualizing Sovereignty in the Time of Biometric Sensors." *South Atlantic Quarterly* 110, no. 2 (Spring 2011): 465–86.

Richman, Robin. "Rediscovery of the Redman." *Life* 63, no. 22 (December 1967): 52–71.

Riedel, Bruce. *Avoiding Armageddon: America, India, and Pakistan to the Brink and Back*. Washington, DC: Brookings Institution Press, 2013.

Rifkin, Mark. *Beyond Settler Time: Temporal Sovereignty and Indigenous Self-Determination*. Durham, NC: Duke University Press, 2017.

Rifkin, Mark. *When Did Indians Become Straight? Kinship, the History of Sexuality, and Native Sovereignty*. Oxford: University of Oxford Press, 2011.

Robin Wall Kimmerer, "*Mishkos Kenomagwen*, the Lessons of Grass: Restoring Reciprocity with the Good Green Earth." In *Traditional Ecological Knowledge: Learning from Indigenous Practices for Environmental Sustainability*, edited by Melissa K. Nelson and Dan Shilling, 27–56. Cambridge, UK: Cambridge University Press, 2018.

Robinson, Dylan. *Hungry Listening: Resonant Theory for Indigenous Sound Studies*. Minneapolis: University of Minnesota Press, 2020.

Rodee, Marian E. *Old Navajo Rugs: Their Development from 1900 to 1940*. Albuquerque: University of New Mexico Press, 1981.

Rodee, Marian E. "The Oriental Connection: The Influence of Caucasian Rugs on Navajo Weaving." *Oriental Rug Review* 10, no 2 (December/January 1990): 15–17.

Roediger, Virginia More. *Ceremonial Costumes of the Pueblo Indians: Their Evolution, Fabrication, and Significance in the Prayer Drama*. Berkeley: University of California Press, 1991.

Roessel, Ruth. *Women in Navajo Society*. Rough Rock, AZ: Navajo Resource Center, Rough Rock Demonstration School, 1981.

Rosaldo, Ronato. "Imperialist Nostalgia." *Representations* 26 (Spring 1989): 107–22.

Rosier, Paul C. "'Modern America Desperately Needs to Listen': The Emerging Indian in an Age of Environmental Crisis." *Journal of American History* (December 2013): 711–35.

Rosier, Paul C. *Rebirth of the Blackfeet Nation, 1912–1954*. Lincoln: University of Nebraska Press, 2001.

Rosier, Paul C. *Serving Their Country: American Indian Politics and Patriotism in the Twentieth Century*. Cambridge, MA: Harvard University Press, 2009.

Rosier, Paul C. "They Are Ancestral Homelands: Race, Place and Politics in Cold War Native America." *Journal of American History* 92, no. 4 (2006): 1300–26.

Rosoff, Nancy B. "Tipi: Heritage of the Great Plains." In *Tipi: Heritage of the Great Plains*, edited by Nancy B. Rosoff and Susan Kennedy Zeller, 3–35. Seattle: University of Washington Press, 2011.

Rothman, Tony. *Science a la Mode: Physical Fashions and Fictions*. Princeton, NJ: Princeton University Press, 1989.

Rushing, W. Jackson. "Marketing the Affinity of the Primitive and the Modern: René d'Harnoncourt and 'Indian Art of the United States'" In *The Early Years of Native American Art History: The Politics of Scholarship and Collecting*, edited by Janet Catherine Berlo, 191–236. Seattle: University of Washington Press; Vancouver: University of British Columbia Press, 1992.

Rushing, W. Jackson. *Native American Art and the New York Avant-Garde: A History of Cultural Primitivism*. Austin: University of Texas Press, 1995.

Sachs, Aaron. "The Ultimate 'Other': Post-Colonialism and Alexander Von Humbolt's Ecological Relationship with Nature." *History and Theory* 42, no. 4 (2003): 111–35.

Sadler, Simon. "Drop City Revisited." *Journal of Architectural Education* 59, no. 3 (February 2006): 5–14.

Sakai, Naoki. "Imperial Nationalism and the Comparative Perspective." *Positions: East Asia Cultures Critique* 17, no. 1 (2009): 159–205.

Santina, Adrianne A. "Toys, Models, Collectibles: Miniature Tipis in the Reservation Era." In *Painters, Patrons, and Identity: Essays in Native American Art to Honor J. J. Brody*, edited by Joyce M. Szabo, 9–32. Albuquerque: University of New Mexico Press, 2001.

Saunders, Frances Stonor. *The Cultural Cold War: The CIA and the World of Arts and Letters*. New York: New Press, 2001.

Savelle, Max. *The Origins of American Diplomacy: The International History of Angloamerica, 1492–1763*. New York: Palgrave Macmillan, 1967.

Schaafsma, Polly. *Kachinas in the Pueblo World*. Salt Lake City: University of Utah Press, 2000.

Scholder, Fritz. *Scholder/Indians*. Flagstaff, AZ: Northland Press, 1972.

Schor, Mira. *Wet: On Painting, Feminism, and Art Culture*. Durham, NC: Duke University Press, 1997.

Scott, Felicity D. *Architecture or Techno-utopia: Politics After Modernism*. Cambridge, MA: MIT Press, 2007.

Scott, Sascha T. *A Strange Mixture: The Art and Politics of Painting Pueblo Indians*. Norman: University of Oklahoma Press, 2015.

Scott, Sascha T. "Awa Tsireh and the Art of Subtle Resistance." *Art Bulletin* 95, no. 4 (2013): 597–622.

Scriver, Mary Strachan. *Bronze Inside and Out: A Biographical Memoir of Bob Scriver*. Calgary, Alberta: University of Calgary Press, 2008.

Sekula, Allan. "The Traffic in Photographs." *Art Journal* 41, no. 1 "Photography and the Scholar/Critic" (Spring 1981): 15–25.

Sheehan, Michael. *Balance of Power: History and Theory*. New York: Routledge, 1996.

Sheinin, Daniela. "Kookie Thoughts: Imagining the United States Pavilion at Expo 67; or How I Learned to Stop Worrying and Love the Bubble." *Journal of Transnational American Studies* 5, no. 1 (2013).

Sherry, John. *Land, Wind, and Hard Words: A Story of Navajo Activism*. Albuquerque: University of New Mexico Press, 2002.

Shiva, Vandana. "The Greening of the Global Reach." In *Global Visions: Beyond the New World Order*, edited by Jeremy Brecher,

:::::::::::

John Brown Childs, and Jill Cutler, 53–60. Boston: South End Press, 1993.

Shiva, Vandana. *Staying Alive: Women, Ecology, and Development.* London: Zed Books, 1989.

Shreve, Bradley G. *Red Power Rising: The National Indian Youth Council and the Origins of Native Activism.* Norman: University of Oklahoma Press, 2011.

Siddons, Louise. "Red Power in the Black Panther: Radical Imagination and Intersectional Resistance at Wounded Knee." *American Art* 35, no. 2 (Summer 2021): 2–31.

Slezkine, Yuri. *Arctic Mirrors: Russia and the Small Peoples of the North.* Ithaca, NY: Cornell University Press, 1994.

Smith, Linda Tuhiwai. *Decolonizing Methodologies: Research and Indigenous Peoples.* 2nd ed. London: Zed Books, 2021.

Smith, Paul Chaat. "Monster Love." In *Fritz Scholder: Indian/Not Indian*, edited by Lowery Stokes Sims, 25–35. Washington, DC: Smithsonian National Museum of the American Indian, 2008.

Smith, Paul Chaat. *Everything You Know about Indians Is Wrong.* Minneapolis: University of Minnesota Press, 2009.

Smith, Paul Chaat, and Robert Allen Warrior. *Like a Hurricane: The Indian Movement from Alcatraz to Wounded Knee.* New York: New Press, 1996.

Smith, Sherry L. *Hippies, Indians, and the Fight for Red Power.* Oxford: Oxford University Press, 2012.

Solomon-Godeau, Abigail. "Going Native: Paul Gauguin and the Invention of Primitivist Modernism." *Art in America* 77 (July 1989): 118–29.

"Solomon McCombs." In *Fred Beaver/Solomon McCombs Memorial Exhibition*, 10–14. Tulsa, OK: Thomas Gilcrease Institute of American History and Art, 1981.

Solowoski, Jeanne. "Between Dangerous Extremes: Victimization, Ultranationalism, and Identity Performance in Gerald Vizenor's Hiroshima Bugi: Atomu 57." *American Quarterly* 62, no. 3 (September 2010): 717–38.

Spang, Bently. "Of Tipis and Stereotypes." In *Tipi: Heritage of the Great Plains*, edited by Nancy B. Rosoff and Susan Kennedy Zeller, 107–14. Seattle: University of Washington Press, 2011.

Spencer, Daniel. *Gay and Gaia: Ethics, Ecology, and the Erotic.* Cleveland, OH: Pilgrim Press, 1996.

Spiller, James. *Frontiers for the American Century: Outer Space, Antarctica, and Cold War Nationalism.* New York: Palgrave Macmillan, 2015.

Spragg-Braude, Stacia. *To Walk in Beauty: A Navajo Family's Journey Home.* Santa Fe: Museum of New Mexico Press, 2009.

Spretnak, Charlene. "Ecofeminism: Our Roots and Flowering." In *Reweaving the World: The Emergence of Ecofeminism*, edited by Irene Diamond and Gloria Feman Orenstein, 3–14. San Francisco: Sierra Club Books, 1990.

Steeds, Lucy, et al. *Making Art Global (Part 2): Magiciens de la Terre, 1989*. Cambridge, MA: Afterall Books, 2013.

Steefel, Lawrence D., Jr. "Body Imagery in Picasso's 'Night Fishing at Antibes.'" *Art Journal* 25, no. 4 (Summer 1966): 356–63; 376.

Steichen, Edward. *The Family of Man*. New York: Museum of Modern Art, 1954.

Stengers, Isabelle. *Cosmopolitics II*, translated by Robert Bononno. Minneapolis: University of Minnesota Press, 2010.

Stengers, Isabelle. "We Are Divided." Translated by Kit Schluter. *e-flux* 114 (December 2020).

Stevens, Scott Manning. "Tomahawk: Materiality and Depictions of the Haudenosaunee." *Early American Literature* 53, no. 2 (2018): 475–511.

Sturgeon, Noël. *Ecofeminist Natures: Race, Gender, Feminist Theory, and Political Action*. New York: Routledge, 1997.

Sturgeon, Noël. *Environmentalism in Popular Culture: Gender, Race, Sexuality, and the Politics of the Natural*. Tucson: University of Arizona Press, 2009.

Suzacket, Cheryl, Shari M. Huhndorf, Jeanne Perreault, and Jean Barman, eds. *Indigenous Women and Feminism: Politics, Activism, Culture*. Chicago: University of Chicago Press, 2010.

Swentzell, Rina. "A Feminine World: Pueblo Spaces." In *Making Worlds: Gender, Metaphor, Materiality*, edited by Susan Hardy Aiken, Ann Brigham, Sallie A. Marston, Penny Waterstone, 221–26. Tucson: University of Arizona Press, 1998.

Takayuki Tatsumi. "Full Metal Apache Shinya Tsukamoto's *Tetsuo* Diptych: The Impact of American Narratives upon the Japanese Representation of Cyborgian Identity." *Japanese Journal of American Studies* 7 (1996): 25–47.

TallBear, Kim. "An Indigenous Reflection on Working Beyond the Human/Not Human." *GLQ: A Journal of Lesbian and Gay Studies*, 21, no. 2–3 (June 2015): 230–48.

TallBear, Kim. "Beyond the Life/Not Life Binary: A Feminist-Indigenous Reading of Cryopreservation, Interspecies Thinking and the New Materialisms." In *Cryopolitics: Frozen Life in a Melting World*, edited by Joanna Radin and Emma Kowalm, 179–202. Boston: MIT Press, 2017.

TallBear, Kim. "Caretaking Relations, Not American Dreaming." *Kalfou* 6, no. 1 (Spring 2019): 24–41.

Taylor, Allan Ross. "A Grammar of Blackfoot." PhD diss., University of California, Berkeley, 1969.

Taylor, Alex. "Transnational Transactions: Trade, Diplomacy, and the Circulation of American Art." *American Art* 31, no. 2 (Summer 2017): 89–95.

Taylor, Diane. *The Archive and the Repertoire: Performing Cultural Memory in the Americas*. Durham, NC: Duke University Press, 2003.

Ternnert, Robert A. *White Man's Medicine: Government Doctors and the Navajo, 1863–1955*. Albuquerque: University of New Mexico Press, 1998.

Teves, Stephanie Nohelani, Andrea Smith, and Michelle H. Raheja, eds. *Native Studies Keywords*. Tucson: University of Arizona Press, 2015.

Thomas, Damion L. *Globetrotting: African American Athletes and Cold War Politics*. Urbana: University of Illinois Press, 2012.

Thomas, Nicholas. *Possessions: Indigenous Art/Colonial Culture*. London: Thames and Hudson, 1999.

Thomas, Wesley. "Navajo Cultural Constructions of Gender and Sexuality." In *Two Spirit People: Native American Gender Identity, Sexuality, and Spirituality*, edited by Sue-Ellen Jacobs, Wesley Thomas, and Sabine Lang, 156–73. Urbana: University of Illinois Press, 1997.

Thomas, Wesley. "Shił Yóółt'ooł: Personification of Navajo Weaving." In *Woven by the Grandmothers: Nineteenth-Century Navajo Textiles from the National Museum of the American Indian*, edited by Eulalie H. Bonar, translated by Ellavina Perkins and Esther Yazzie, 33–42. Washington, DC: Smithsonian Institution Press and the National Museum of the American Indian, 1996.

Thrush, Coll. *Indigenous London: Native Travelers at the Heart of Empire*. New Haven, CT: Yale University Press, 2016.

Todd, Zoe. "Indigenizing the Anthropocene." In *Art in the Anthropocene: Encounters Among Aesthetics, Politics, Environments and Epistemologies*, edited by Heather Davis and Etienne Turpin, 241–54. London: Open Humanities Press, 2015.

Tohe, Laura. "Grounded in Spiritual Geography: Restoring *Naabaahii* in *Enemy Slayer, A Navajo Oratorio*." In *Ecocriticism and Indigenous Studies: Conversations from Earth to Cosmos*, edited by Salma Monani and Joni Adamson. New York: Routledge, 2016.

Tohe, Laura. "There Is No Word for Feminism in My Language." *Wicazo Sa Review* (Fall 2000): 103–10.

Tóth, György Ferenc. *From Wounded Knee to Checkpoint Charlie: The Alliance for Sovereignty between American Indians and Central*

Europeans in the Late Cold War. Albany: State University of New York Press, 2016.

Trafzer, Clifford E. Introduction to *American Indians, American Presidents*, edited by Clifford E. Trafzer, 1–31. New York: Harper, 2009.

Treat, James. *Around the Sacred Fire: Native Religious Activism in the Red Power Era*. New York: Palgrave Macmillan, 2003.

Trennert, Robert. *White Man's Medicine: Government Doctors and the Navajo, 1863–1955*. Albuquerque: University of New Mexico Press, 1998.

Trimble, Steven. *Talking with the Clay: The Art of Pueblo Pottery in the 21st Century*. Santa Fe, NM: School for Advanced Research, 2007.

Tsosie, Rebecca. "Native Women and Leadership: An Ethics of Culture and Relationship." In *Indigenous Women and Feminism: Politics, Activism, Culture*, edited by Cheryl Suzack, Shari M. Huhndorf, Jeanne Perreault, and Jean Barman, 29–42. Vancouver: University of British Columbia, 2011.

Turner, Fred. "The Corporation and the Counterculture: Revisiting the Pepsi Pavilion and the Politics of Cold War Multimedia." *Velvet Light Trap* 73 (Spring 2014): 66–78.

Turner, Fred. "*The Family of Man* and the Politics of Attention in Cold War America." *Public Culture* 24, no. 1 (2012): 55–84.

"United Nations Declaration on the Rights of Indigenous Peoples." United Nations, 2007: https://www.un.org/development/desa /indigenouspeoples/wp-content/uploads/sites/19/2018/11 /UNDRIP_E_web.pdf.

Vargas, Elia. "On Extraction: Interview with Art Historian TJ Demos and Artist Lauri Palmer." *State Change 02* (2017): 111–18.

Vasquez, John A., and Colin Elman, eds. *Realism and the Balance of Power: A New Debate*. Upper Saddle River, NJ: Prentice Hall, 2003.

Vergara-Camus, Leandro. *Land and Freedom: The MST, the Zapatistas, and Peasant Alternatives to Neoliberalism*. London: Zed Books, 2014.

Vizenor, Gerald. "Aesthetics of Survivance: Literary Theory and Practice." In *Survivance: Narratives of Presence*, edited by Gerald Vizenor, 1–23. Lincoln: University of Nebraska Press, 2008.

Vizenor, Gerald. *Fugitive Poses*: Native American Indian Scenes of Absence and Presence. Lincoln: University of Nebraska Press, 2000.

Vizenor, Gerald. *Hiroshima Bugi: Atomu 57*. Lincoln: University of Nebraska Press, 2010.

Vizenor, Gerald. *Manifest Manners: Narratives on Postindian Survivance*. Lincoln: University of Nebraska Press, 1999.

Von Eschen, Penny M. *Satchmo Blows up the World: Jazz Ambassadors Play the Cold War*. Cambridge, MA: Harvard University Press, 2006.

Vorano, Norman. "Inuit Art: Canada's Soft Power Resource to Fight Communism." *Journal of Curatorial Studies* 5, no. 3 (2016): 312–37.

Vorano, Norman. *Inuit Prints: Japanese Inspiration*. Ottawa: Canadian Museum of History, 2011.

Voyd, Bill. "Funk Architecture." In *Shelter and Society*, edited by Paul Oliver, 156–64. New York: Praeger Publishers, 1969.

Voyles, Tracy Brynne. *Wastelanding: Legacies of Uranium Mining in Navajo Country*. Minneapolis: University of Minnesota Press, 2015.

Wagner, Sally Roesch. "The Indigenous Roots of United States Feminism." In *Feminist Politics, Activism and Vision: Local and Global Challenges*, edited by Luciana Ricciutelli, Angela Miles, and Margaret McFadden, 267–84. London: Zed Books, 2004.

Walker, James R. *Lakota Belief and Ritual*. Lincoln: University of Nebraska Press, 1980.

Walters, Harry. "The Navajo Concept of Art." In *Woven by the Grand-mothers: Nineteenth-Century Navajo Textiles from the National Museum of the American Indian*, edited by Eulalie H. Bonar, translated by Ellavina Perkins and Esther Yazzie, 29–31. Washington, DC: Smithsonian Institution Press and the National Museum of the American Indian, 1996.

Warren, Karen J. "The Power and the Promise of Ecological Feminism." *Environmental Ethics* 12, no. 2 (Summer 1990): 125–46.

Watkins, Arthur V. "Termination of Federal Supervision: The Removal of Restrictions over Indian Property and Person." *Annals of the American Academy of Political and Social Science* 311 (May 1957): 47–55.

Watson, Mark. "Jimmie Durham's *Building a Nation* and the Ruins of American Exceptionalism." *Art History* 39, no. 5 (November 2016): 984–1013.

Watson, Mark. "Diplomatic Aesthetics: Globalization and Contemporary Native Art." PhD diss., Columbia University, 2012.

Watts, Vanessa. "Indigenous Place-Thought and Agency Amongst Humans and Non-Humans (First Woman and Sky Woman Go on a European World Tour!)." *Decolonization: Indigeneity, Education and Society* 2, no. 1 (2013): 20–34.

Weasel Head, Frank. "Repatriation Experiences of the Kainai." In *We Are Coming Home: Repatriation and the Restoration of Blackfoot Cultural Confidence*, edited by Gerald T. Conaty, 151–82. Edmonton, Alberta: Athabasca University, 2015.

Weaver, Jace. *The Red Atlantic: American Indigenes and the Making of the Modern World, 1000–1927*. Chapel Hill: University of North Carolina Press, 2014.

Weisiger, Marsha. *Dreaming of Sheep in Navajo Country*. Seattle: University of Washington Press, 2009.

Weisiger, Marsha. "Gendered Injustice: Navajo Livestock Reduction in the New Deal Era." *Western Historical Quarterly*, 38, no. 4 (2007): 437–55.

Welch, Eddie. "Bridging Cultures Abroad: Oscar Howe's American Specialist Tour." *South Dakota History* 37, no. 3 (Fall 2007): 185–208.

Welch, Edward. "Oscar Howe's *Wounded Knee Massacre* and the Politics and Popular Culture of an American Masterpiece." *Weber— The Contemporary West* 29, no. 2 (Spring/Summer 2013): 133–40.

Wellman, David Joseph. *Sustainable Diplomacy: Ecology, Religion and Ethics in Muslim-Christian Relations*. New York: Palgrave Macmillan, 2004.

Wellman, David Joseph. "The Promise of Sustainable Diplomacy: Refining the Praxis of Ecological Realism." In *Sustainable Diplomacies*, edited by Costas M. Conastantinou and James Der Derian, 25–45. New York: Palgrave Macmillan, 2010.

Westerman, Gwen, and Bruce White. *Mni Sota Makoce: The Land of the Dakota*. St. Paul: Minnesota Historical Society Press, 2012.

Wharton, Annabel Jane. "Defining Models." In *Modelwork: The Material Culture of Making and Knowing*, edited by Martin Brückner, Sandy Isenstadt, and Sarah Wasserman, 3–20. Minneapolis: University of Minnesota, 2021.

Wheat, Joe Ben. "American Indian Weaving: Early Trade and Commerce Before the Curio Shop." *Oriental Rug Review* 8, nos. 4–5 (1988): 35–40; 11–14.

Wheat, Joe Ben. "Navajo Blankets." In *Woven by the Grandmothers: Nineteenth-Century Navajo Textiles from the National Museum of the American Indian*, edited by Eulalie H. Bonar, translated by Ellavina Perkins and Esther Yazzie, 69–85. Washington, DC: Smithsonian Institution Press and the National Museum of the American Indian, 1996.

White, Mark. "Oscar Howe and the Transformation of Native American Art." *American Indian Art Magazine* 23, no. 1 (Winter 1997): 36–43.

Whyte, Kyle Powys. "Indigenous Science (Fiction) for the Anthropocene: Ancestral Dystopias and Fantasies of Climate Change Crises." *Environment and Planning E: Nature and Space* 1, no. 1–2 (2018): 224–42.

Wickman, Patricia Riles. *The Tree that Bends: Discourse, Power, and the Survival of the Maskókî People*. Tuscaloosa: University of Alabama Press, 1999.

Wilkins, David Eugene. *The Navajo Political Experience*. New York: Rowman and Littlefield, 2003.

William Zartman, ed. *Imbalance of Power: US Hegemony and International Order*. Boulder, CO: Lynne Reinner Publishers, 2009.

Wimmer, Andreas, and Nina Glick Schiller. "Methodological Nationalism, the Social Sciences, and the Study of Migration: An Essay in Historical Epistemology." *International Migration Review* 37, no. 3 (Fall, 2003): 576–610.

Wissler, Clark, and Alice Beck Kehoe. "Manuscript on the History of the Blackfoot Indians in Contact with White Culture, 1933." In *Amskapi Pikuni: The Blackfeet People*, 1–175. Albany: State University of New York Press, 2012.

Wissler, Clark. "Material Culture of Blackfeet Indians." *Anthropological Papers of the American Museum of Natural History* 5 (1910).

Witherspoon, Gary. *Language and Art in the Navajo Universe*. Ann Arbor: University of Michigan Press, 1977.

Witzling, Mara Rose. *Voicing Our Visions: Writings by Women Artists*. New York: Universe, 1991.

Wood, Violet. "The Navajos—A Case History of Progress." In *Америка: America Illustrated*, 28–33. Washington, DC: United States Information Agency, 1962.

Woven Holy People: Navajo Sandpainting Textiles from the Permanent Collection. Santa Fe, NM: Wheelwright Museum of the American Indian, 1982.

Wyckoff, Lydia L. "A Collective History of Native American Painting." In *Visions and Voices: Native American Paintings from the Philbrook Museum of Art*, edited by Lydia L. Wyckoff, 19–49. Tulsa, OK: Philbrook Museum of Art, 1996.

Wyman, Leland C. *Southwest Indian Drypainting*. Albuquerque: University of New Mexico Press, 1983.

Wyman, Leland C. *Blessingway, with Three Versions of the Myth Recorded and Translated from the Navajo by Father Berard Haile*. Tucson: University of Arizona Press, 1970.

Yasufumi Nakamori. "Criticism of Expo '70 in Print: Journals Ken, Bijutsu techō, and Dezain hihyō." *Review of Japanese Culture and Society* 23 (December 2011): 132–44.

Yazzie, Ethelou. "Navajo Wisdom and Traditions." Paper presented at the Fourth International Conference on the Unity of the Sciences, New York City, November 27–30, 1975.

Yazzie, Ethelou. "Navajo Wisdom and Traditions." Paper Presented to the Fourth International Conference on the Unity of the Sciences, New York City, November 17–30, 1975.

Yohe, Jill Ahlberg. "The Circulation and Silence of Weaving Knowledge in Contemporary Navajo Life." *American Indian Culture and Research Journal* 36, no. 4 (2012): 107–26.

Yohe, Jill Ahlberg. "The Social Life of Weaving in a Contemporary Navajo Community." PhD diss., University of New Mexico, 2008.

Young, Philip. "The Mother of Us All: Pocahontas Reconsidered." *Kenyon Review* 24 (Summer 1962): 391–441.

Zaman, Mashiyat. "The Ainu and Japan's Colonial Legacy." *Tokyo Review*, March 23, 2020. www.tokyoreview.net/2020/03/ainu-japan-colonial-legacy/.

Zamir, Shamoon. *The Gift of the Face: Portraiture and Time in Edward S. Curtis's "The North American Indian."* Chapel Hill: University of North Carolina Press, 2014.

Zamir, Shamoon, and Gerd Hurm. Introduction to *The Family of Man Revisited: Photography in a Global Age*, edited by Gerd Hurm, Anke Reitz, and Shamoon Zamir, 1–22. London: I. B. Tauris, 2018.

Zartman, I. William, ed. *Imbalance of Power: US Hegemony and International Order.* Boulder, CO: Lynne Rienner Publishers, 2009.

Zedeño, María Nieves. "Art as the Road to Perfection: The Blackfoot Painted Tipi." *Cambridge Archaeological Journal* 27, no. 4 (2017): 631–42.

Zwigenbeerg, Ran. "'The Coming of a Second Sun': The 1956 Atoms for Peace Exhibit in Hiroshima and Japan's Embrace of Nuclear Power." *Asia-Pacific Journal* 10, no. 6 (2012): 1–15.

INDEX

buffalo (continued)

170, 173, 188–89, 215, 216; Operation Buffalo, 206; in Ben Quintana's *Buffalo Dance*, 75–76; "second" (oil), 176; in Wohaw's drawing, 254–55

Bureau of Educational and Cultural Affairs, 221

Bureau of Indian Affairs (BIA): and American Indian Movement, 4, 199, 265, 272; and Blackfeet Tribal Business Council, 176; and Oscar Howe, 13, 220, 239, 258; Indian Arts and Crafts Board of, 30, 40, 324n151; and Kha-'Po Owingeh, 50, 289n59; and Navajo Nation, 69, 85, 89, 91, 95; 115; Office of Indian Affairs (formerly), 38, 286n9; and the Point Four Program, 54–55; in Fritz Scholder's painting, 4, 13, 271; schools, 38, 39, 91, 239, 258; in Soviet propaganda, 52–53; Termination policy, 4, 42, 176

Burma, 57, 61. *See also* Asia; decolonization; majority world

cabin: and colonial assimilation, 175, 182, 197

Cajete, Gregory, 15

canon: of Euro-American art, 11, 29, 43, 82, 250; and abstract expressionism, 10, 22

capitalism, 28, 37, 38, 167, 173; and American art, 24; and Blackfeet Nation, 176; and climate change, 16; and colonialism, 11, 15, 34, 49, 85, 122, 123, 167, 175; versus communism, 4, 10, 22, 23, 24, 159; "green," 25; and heteronormativity, 124; and Indian assimilation, 4, 12, 17, 36, 39–40, 42, 50, 71, 96, 115, 132, 136, 143; in Mexico, 117; and Pop art, 5; resistance to, 116; in Soviet propaganda, 53; in US propaganda, 56, 82, 84

Carson, Rachel: *Silent Spring*, 190

casein, 253–54

Castillo, Juana María, 121, 122, 152–54, 157–60

Catholic Church, 18

cattle, 175–76, 254–55; "sacred cow" in India, 60–61

Ceaușescu, Nicolae, 270, 275

Central Institute of Arts and Crafts (Karachi), 221, 236–38, 267

Central Intelligence Agency (CIA), 10, 22, 71

ceremony, 13, 37, 61, 75, 240, 248, 266, 275; American Indian Movement revival of, 265; Blackfeet tipi, 163, 173, 174, 176, 177, 178, 182, 183; Dakota "painting of the truth," 237, 243; Diné sandpainting, 32, 80, 86, 87–89, 90, 91, 92, 93, 95–97, 103, 109, 115; in Oscar Howe's biography, 239; Mvskoke, 62; 63–64; pipe, 1, 3, 33, 218, 221, 222, 223, 225, 227, 240, 245, 256, 263, 264, 268, 276–277; Pueblo, 47–49, 51, 271; Sun Dance, 170, 225, 230, 264. *See also* sacred pipe; sandpainting; tipi

Changing Woman (Asdzáá Náádleehé), 32, 71, 121, 132–133, 135, 143, 145–146, 301n10

čhaŋnúŋp-ok'é (Pipestone National Monument), 20–21, 229, 230, 293n134

Cherokee, 40; carpentry, 20; dress, 229

Cheyenne, 3, 72, 130, 178, 315n721, 327n31

Chiguailaf, María Catrileo, x, 157, 160

Chile, x, 82, 102, 276; Biblioteca Nacional in Santiago, 120–22, 152, 154; Chilean North American Institute of Culture in Temuco, 152; government of, 124, 152, 160–61; Museo Regional de La Araucanía in Temuco, 156, 157; Quetrahue, 33, 122, 152–53, 155, 158–60. *See also* Mapuche

Chinle, 91, 101, 135, 136, 140, 143, 144, 151; Chapter Government of the Navajo Nation, 86; weaving, 137, 138, 140, 145, 304n83

Christianity, 49, 51, 171; and gender, 136; in Oscar Howe's painting, 224

Mendieta, Ana, 128; *Silueta Series*, 128–29

methodological nationalism, 23–24

Mexico, 97, 100, 102; City, 32, 82, 117–119, 145, 300n112; International Exhibition of Popular Art, 117–18; *See also* Olympic Games

Middle East, 33, 37, 59, 151, 217. *See also* majority world; "Near East," Pakistan

mining, 4, 83, 122; of sand, 32, 97–101; of uranium, 44, 54, 71, 74, 83, 89, 100, 295n10. *See also* extraction

mitákuye oyás'in, 21, 28, 66, 218, 285n96; in Oscar Howe's art, 223, 227, 231, 252, 254, 264, 266

Mnísota Makhóčhe (Minnesota), 227, 253

Miyamoto Ken'ichi: *Osorubeki Kōgai* (Fearsome Pollution), 190

model: Crow lodge as, 183, 213, 215, 216; Native architectural, 33, 181–82; theory of, 182, 183

modern Native painting movement, 31, 38, 42, 44, 79, 219, 248. *See also Contemporary American Indian Painting*; Dorothy Dunn; Studio School at the Santa Fe Indian School

modernisms: architectural, 193–94, 211; artistic, 14, 24, 58, 237, 218n30; and the art market, 140; canonical, 22, 142, 245, 246–49; in Oscar Howe's art and pedagogy, 33, 218, 219, 222, 230, 235, 238, 242, 249–56, 259, 266, 267; Indigenous, 10, 11, 12, 26, 31, 37, 41, 46, 61, 79, 218, 248; Pakistani, 267, 268

modernity: 10, 11, 26, 34, 36, 93, 203, 211; Indigenous, 14, 42, 60, 67, 127, 130, 219, 230, 245, 258; and the Ecological Indian, 26, 191, 215; and patriarchy, 125

modernization, 62, 270; of American Indians, 10, 12, 14, 42, 46, 61, 73, 84–85, 231; in Chile, 161; in Cold War competition, 4, 5, 7, 10–11, 100, 215; in Japan, 201; in Mexico, 117–18; in Romania, 270

Montiel, Anya, 247, 324n151

Montoya, Gerónima Cruz, 41, 219; *Pueblo Crafts*, 42, plate 3a

Morales, Luisa, 122, 152–61

more-than-humans: in Harrison Begay's *Navajo Woman and Sheep*, 71, 75; in *Contemporary American Indian Paintings*, 38; in Dakota art, 246; and Diné women, 124, 149, 152; gathering 15, 28, 35, 277; and Mapuche machis, 157, 160; in Solomon McCombs's *Creek Woman's Ribbon Dance*, 63; milieus of, 107; in Niitsítapi alliances, 163, 169, 173, 188, 189, 190, 213, 215–16; power of, 6, 14, 118; relationships with, 4, 7, 14, 16, 20, 31, 37, 47, 48, 79, 244, 276; in *The Family of Man*, 65; in sandpainting, 102, 116, 118; vampires as, 275; in Pablita Velarde's *The Betrothal*, 47–49. *See also* earth diplomacy; ecology; kinship; other-than-human, reciprocity

Morris, Robert: *Continuous Project Altered Daily*, 107–9

Morrison, George, 10

Morrisseau, Norval, 210

Morton, Timothy, 253

Mother Earth: essentialized, 32, 123, 126, 128–29, 130; diplomatic potential of, 127, 129, 130, 132, 133, 134, 161; in Indigenous cosmology, 87, 128, 130, 135, 304n62; rights of, 28; and *The Family of Man*, 66. *See also* earth jurisprudence; Earth Mothers; ecofeminism

Muir-Harmony, Teasel, 206

multiculturalism, 126; and art, 11, 24, 41; in US Cold War propaganda, 5, 23, 38, 55, 272

Mundt, Karl E., 259

mural, 40, 69, 210, 225, 242, 258, 318n29

Muscogee (Creek) Nation, 31, 37, 56, 291n98; Creek Indian Council of, 57, 61. *See also* Mvskoke

Steichen, Edward, 65

Stengers, Isabelle, 16, 280n11

Stevens, Bertha (Morning Star), 10, 32, 79, 82, 119, 304n84, plate 4; combinatory approach to weaving, 145–146, plate 8, plate 10; early years, 91, 135–37; at the Idylwild Arts Foundation, 305n105, and Mapuche, 120–23, 152–61; in Mexico, 86; 308n159, plate 9; in Scotland, 146–51; in Turkey, 151. *See also* Diné; weaving

Stevens, Fred (Grey Squirrel), 10, 32, 79, 82, 106; *Big Thunder*, plate 5; early years, 89–95; *Fringed Mouth with Corn*, 80–81; and the medical industry, 95–96; at the Olympics in Mexico, 82, 117–19; and ceremonial protocols, 86, 91, 96; and sand mining, 97; in Scotland, 80–81 103; *The Four Thunders*, plate 4; *Whirling Logs*, 109–16, plate 6. *See also* Diné; sandpainting

Stevens, Scott Manning, 257

Stoker, Bram, 269–70. *See also* Dracula

straight line. *See* truth-line

Studio School at the Santa Fe Indian School (SFIS), x, 31, 38–42, 43, 46, 69, 75, 286n16; Oscar Howe's relationship to, 219, 240, 242, 247–48, 267, 294n165. See also *Contemporary American Indian Painting*; Dorothy Dunn; modern Native painting movement

Sturgeon, Noël, 126, 128

Sun Dance: 225, 229, 230, 264–65; in Oscar Howe's *Sacro-Wi-Dance*, 231–32; Okan as a variant of, 170, 176, 190

Supreme Court, 19, 43

sustainability, 192, 194

sustainable diplomacy, 27–28, 282n48

Swentzell, Rina, 66

Sydney Biennale, 28

tahokmu, 244–46, 247, 263, 266, 321–322n94; in Oscar Howe's *Marpeya Wopazo (A Sign in the Sky)*, 266; in Oscar Howe's *Rider*, 250–52, 255–56

Tailfeathers, Gerald: *Blackfoot Design*, 210

TallBear, Kim, 21, 66, 244–45, 293n134

Taugelchee, Daisy, 140–41

Taylor, Alex, 23

temporality; and global modernisms, 11; and durable sandpainting, 116; and the Indians of All Tribes, 198; Indigenous, 213; and vampires, 275. *See also* Indigenous futurism; progress

Termination, 4, 5, 10, 13, 21, 25, 31, 33, 34, 35, 42, 96, 261, 273, 277, 280n12, 285n2; and anti-communism, 54; and Blackfeet Nation, 175; and the Dawes Act, 50; and kinship (Native), 37, 49–50; Oscar Howe's relationship to, 256, 257, 258–59, 268; and Indian Removal, 19; in international relations, 4–5, 53, 85, 122; and Mscogee (Creek) Nation, 57–58; and Navajo Nation, 85, 95, 297n42; resistance to, 4, 5, 12–13, 36, 43–44, 55, 163, 220, 258, 259, 275; and Romanianization, 275

textile. *See* basket; Bertha Stevens; weaving; *The American Indian: Past and Present*, 54, 84; *The Family of Man*, 37, 52, 124; Indigenous aphorisms in, 31, 64–67, 79; *New Yorker*, 107

Thinking the Expo, 203, 211

tipi (lodge), 12, 311n69; in the American Indian Movement, 198–99; Darryl Blackman's Crow, 33, 162–67, 181–90, 206, 212, 213–16; Paul Coze's, 240; in the counter-culture, 190–98; in Oscar Howe's painting, 240, 255, 257, 264, 265; and the Indians of Canada Pavilion, 208–10; miniature, 181–82; Niitsítapi painted, 169, 170–75; plain, 178, 200; praxis, 162, 169, 170, 174, 175, 178–9, 181, 183, 189, 190, 215; transfer, 177; in Wohaw's drawing, 254–55

Tlatelolco massacre, 117–18, 300n108. *See also* Mexico; Olympic Games